GESTURES

Alan L. Boegehold

GESTURES

ESSAYS IN ANCIENT HISTORY, LITERATURE,
AND PHILOSOPHY PRESENTED TO ALAN L. BOEGEHOLD

On the occasion of his retirement and his seventy-fifth birthday

EDITED BY
GEOFFREY W. BAKEWELL AND JAMES P. SICKINGER

Oxbow Books
3003

Published by
Oxbow Books, Park End Place, Oxford OX1 1HN

© Oxbow Books, Geoffrey W. Bakewell and James P. Sickinger, 2003

ISBN 1 84217 086 4

A CIP record for this book is available from the British Library

This book is available direct from

Oxbow Books, Park End Place Oxford OX1 1HN
(Phone: 01865-241249; Fax: 01865-794449)

and

The David Brown Book Company
PO Box 511, Oakville, CT 06779, USA
(Phone: 860-945-9329; Fax: 860-945-9468)

and

via our website
www.oxbowbooks.com

Printed in Great Britain at
The Short Run Press
Exeter

Table of Contents

PART TWO: HISTORY, LAW, AND EPIGRAPHY

Preface

On March 1 2002 friends, colleagues, and students of Alan L. Boegehold gathered in Providence, Rhode Island to celebrate his retirement after more than forty years of scholarship, teaching, and service. Alan used that occasion to present a sampling of his current work; to his surprise we reciprocated by presenting the following collection of essays – many of them written by those in attendance – as a small token of the respect and of the gratitude felt by so many for the impact that Alan has had on our lives, as teacher, scholar, and friend.

Planning for this volume began in September 1999, when the two of us joined forces and began to gauge interest and solicit contributions; at that initial stage and throughout the entire process we received invaluable support and encouragement from Adele Scafuro. Response to our initial queries was overwhelming and brought the names of many more individuals who wanted to contribute. Quite fortuitously, potential contributions fell neatly into two categories reflecting Alan's diverse interests. The first included essays on literary and philosophical topics, areas in which Alan both taught and published. The second group was representative of Alan's more specialized research in Greek epigraphy, history, and law. This arrangement is reflected in the contents that follow.

We are keenly aware that the present collection includes no contributions on Greek vase painting, a field in which Alan has made significant contributions, and we deeply regret that the demands of time and space made it impossible for us to invite, much less include, contributions from art historians and others who could have contributed or would have liked to participate. In addition, several individuals – including Charlie Bye, William Calder III, Bob Pounder, and John Papademetriou – asked that we acknowledge their debts to Alan, which we gladly do.

Each submission has been read by one or both of us and at least one outside reader. We have generally followed the practices of recent issues the *Transactions of the American Philological Association* in the citation of ancient sources and modern works; slight deviations in individual chapters should be readily recognizable. We have not found a satisfactory solution for the spelling and transliteration of Greek terms, and we have allowed individual authors to follow their own preferences.

Debts are owed to many. We are grateful first of all to the contributors, who offered diverse but fitting papers, and did so in a timely and efficient fashion. Several others lent assistance at various stages, including John Bodel, Christina Clark, Laurel Fulkerson, Martha Habash, John Marincola, Peter Rhodes, Molly Richardson, Loren J. Samons II, William Stephens, Kate Stoddard, W. Jeffery Tatum, and Ian Worthington; to them we express our thanks. Thanks are also due to the departments of Classics at Creighton University and the Florida State University, which assisted with phone and mailing costs. Financial support from the Developing Scholar Award program at the Florida State University helped defray publication costs.

Finally, the two of us owe an immeasurable debt of gratitude to our wives, Rosie Townley Bakewell and Katherine Schwartz Sickinger, who put up with our work on this project, and the absence from family life it brought, with love, patience, and encouragement.

Geoffrey W. Bakewell
James P. Sickinger

Alan L. Boegehold

Alan Lindley Boegehold was born on March 17, 1927, in Detroit, Michigan. His parents, Alfred Lindley Boegehold and Katherine Yager Boegehold, were native New Yorkers who had settled in Michigan where Alan's father worked as an executive for General Motors. Alan attended public schools for most of his youth, but by his own admission was not a stellar student. His youthful adventures included a sojourn to California, where he hoped to earn a living as a cartoonist but ended up working in a movie theatre. He returned to Michigan and finished his last year of high school at the Detroit Country Day School, which he credited with impressing upon him the value of education. In 1944 at age seventeen he entered an engineering program with the U.S. Army at the University of Michigan. On the program's first day Alan met Mortimer Chambers. The two quickly became friends and have remained so ever since. Alan left the engineering program before its completion and finished his army service at Fort Myer, Virginia.

After leaving the army Alan returned to the University of Michigan, where he majored in Latin and graduated in 1950. He spent a few years working in insurance in Albany, New York, before returning to the academic world and beginning graduate study in Classics at Harvard in 1952. Harvard in the 1950s was a lively center for classical studies. Alan's fellow students included not only Mortimer Chambers but also Charlie Bye, William Calder III, James Day, David Pingree, Michael Putnam, and Bill Wyatt. Several of them rejoined Alan as colleagues at Brown in the following decades, and in later years Alan fondly told stories and anecdotes from his graduate school days. (As each generation discovers, one's time in graduate school is indeed formative!) Alan also became a student of Sterling Dow, who proved an able mentor and lifelong friend.

In Cambridge Alan also met Julie Marshall, who had moved to Boston to work as an editor with Houghton Mifflin after graduating from Stanford. Their first meeting took place on a small boat owned by Alan's roommate; when Julie asked what Alan did, he replied that he was pursuing a Ph.D. in Classical Philology at Harvard. And what did he intend to do with that? "Go to Greece." The words would be prophetic. The two were married in 1954, and Greece would form a central part of their relationship over the next half century.

In 1955 Alan was named the Thomas Day Seymour Fellow at the American School of Classical Studies at Athens, and he and Julie spent the next two years at the School, the second with Alan as Harvard's Charles Eliot Norton Fellow. At the American School, the Michigan- and Harvard-trained philologist participated in the famous School trips, traveled in Europe, and dug in the Athenian Agora for two summers.

Although he was not drawn to further excavation, his enthusiasm and respect for archaeology were undiminished. During his tenure at the American School, Alan also completed, under the direction of Sterling Dow, his dissertation on "Aristotle and the Dikasteria," a topic that occupied his energies for much of his career.

Alan and Julie returned to the States and to Alan's first teaching position at the University of Illinois at Champaign-Urbana in 1957. In 1960 the couple returned east, now with daughter Lindley and son David in tow, so that Alan could take up a position in the Department of Classics at Brown University. (Another daughter and son, Allison and Alan, soon followed). Starting the same year at Brown was Michael Putnam. At that time the Brown Classics Department was relatively small and did not offer the Ph.D. As Alan rose through the academic ranks from assistant to full professor over the next decade, he and Michael were joined at Brown by several friends from Harvard – Charles Segal, David Pingree, and Bill Wyatt – and by others from elsewhere, including Charles Fornara. Together they helped build the Brown department into one of the nation's finest.

Alan's early scholarship displayed the traits that have characterized his work throughout his career – an eye for detail and an appreciation of the contributions that visual evidence can make to understanding literary texts. His first article, on Theophrastos' *Characters*, appeared in the *Transactions of the American Philological Association*, but most of his early articles focused on Athenian lawcourts, epigraphy, and vase painting. In 1967 he published a revised edition of Charles A. Robinson Jr.'s *Ancient History*. Arguably his most famous article is his study of the creation of the Athenian state archives, published in the *American Journal of Archaeology* in 1972. In addition to establishing the dates of the archives' foundations, the article explored insightfully differences between ancient and modern conceptions of documents.

At Brown Alan was an inspirational teacher, at both the undergraduate and graduate levels. Among his hallmarks were his patience, his willingness to entertain new ideas, and his approachability. In Greek reading classes he patiently led students through difficult texts; in Greek prose composition he entertained various translations into Greek. Alan's courses also inculcated in students a respect for scholarship and a sense that their work was part of something greater in scope. He himself was a student of Sterling Dow, who had been a student of William Scott Ferguson. And Alan's students became part of that same tradition. In his unassuming way Alan constantly helped us to see our debt to the great scholars in whose footsteps we follow. Moreover, Alan treated students as peers and colleagues whose ideas merited airing and respect. His office door was regularly open, and he was always willing to read authors, both Greek and Latin, even ones outside his primary research interests, with undergraduate and graduate students alike. The range of contributions to this volume best illustrates how freely and widely he gave of his time. Over the years he has supervised some ten doctoral dissertations, on topics ranging from Attic inscriptions and the Gortynian law code to authors such as Aeschylus, Isaeus, and Xenophon.

In addition to his duties as teacher and scholar, Alan also offered considerable services to the disciplines of Classics and Classical Archaeology. He served on the executive board of the Archaeological Institute of America during the 1960s, but most of his energies were devoted to the American School of Classical Studies. For much of the 1960s he served as secretary of both the Executive and Managing Committees. In both 1964 and 1965 he, with Julie's assistance, led the American School's summer sessions. Henry Robinson's report states that "the members of the group were enthusiastic about [Professor Boegehold] and the program arranged for them." All told, Alan led the American School's summer sessions an amazing four times (a tremendous amount of work, as anyone who has led these groups even once knows). In 1968/9 Alan was the School's Annual Professor – a position now known as the Whitehead professor – and taught a course on Athenian documents. His service to the School culminated in the 1990s, when he assumed the burdensome post of Chairman of the American School's Managing Committee. "The School has been very good to me," he said, "and it is time to repay its generosity." His tenure (1990–1998) saw the improvement of the School's holdings and finances; he continues to serve as a member of the board of trustees both of the School itself and of its Gennadius Library.

Alan has also taken his turn as department chair and director of Brown's program in ancient studies. He has been at various times a visiting professor at Harvard, Berkeley, Yale, and Amherst. He co-edited one collection of essays honoring his mentor Sterling Dow (*Studies Presented to Sterling Dow on his Eightieth Birthday, GRBS* Monograph 10) and another, with Adele Scafuro, entitled *Athenian Identity and Civic Ideology*. His publications are diverse: articles and book chapters address such topics as the Amasis Painter, the Athena Nike decree, and the orators. His work on the lawcourts has also continued, culminating in 1995 with the publication of *Agora XXVIII, The Lawcourts at Athens*. The volume fittingly combines literary, epigraphic, and archaeological research – as has so much of Alan's work – and it has rightly won a place as a standard resource in the study of Athenian law.

It would be remiss not to mention one further aspect of Alan's career. Over the years he has proven himself an accomplished translator and poet. His translations of Cavafy first appeared in the *Brown Classical Journal* and have since been published elsewhere, including in *In Simple Clothes*, a collection of ten original translations. Alan is also a poet and author in his own right, and his original works have appeared in the *Brown Classical Journal*, the *Southeastern Review*, and other venues.

Finally, we would like to conclude on a decidedly personal note. Thus far we have praised Alan's academic virtues. But he is also a wonderful human being, and thus we pay tribute to him not only as scholar and teacher, mentor and administrator, but also as a friend. He appreciates many of life's facets, and helps others value them as well. Indeed, he has been without peer in helping his students locate the life of the mind within robust, rich, and fully satisfying lives. He deserves far more than a gesture, for he has helped us celebrate the full range of human milestones; today we are honored to help him celebrate one of his own.

PART ONE

Literature and Philosophy

A Divine Audience for the Celebration of Asopichus' Victory in Pindar's *Fourteenth Olympian Ode**

Lucia Athanassaki

The *Fourteenth Olympian Ode* is a splendid miniature which displays at once formal elements of the hymnic as well as the epinician genre. The occasion for its composition is the celebration of the Olympic victory of the boy Asopichus in the footrace.[1] Throughout the ode, however, Pindar weaves praise of the *laudandus* into far ampler praise and multiple invocations of the Graces collectively and individually in a manner that leaves no doubt that his main interest is to keep in the foreground the Graces and the delights which they bring to men and gods alike.[2] One such delight is the Olympic victory of Asopichus. The boy's victory receives brief description mainly in the form of a message which the personified Echo is asked to deliver to his dead father in the Underworld. Had Pindar composed this ode for a victor sharing the expectations of the notorious Scopas of Thessaly, *mutatis mutandis* he undoubtedly would have been instructed, like Simonides, to apply to the Graces for his fees, for it would appear that their predominance in the ode detracts from the commemoration of the merits of the *laudandus*.[3] In this hypothetical scenario Pindar might have defended

---

* A shorter version of this paper was presented at Brown University and the University of Virginia in the spring of 2001, but its nucleus goes back to a public lecture I gave at Herakleion in the spring of 2000 at a symposium organized by the Herakleion Philological Association. Warmest thanks to all participants in the discussions that followed on all three occasions. I also wish to thank Deborah Boedeker, James Kennelly, and Anastasia-Erasmia Peponi for their valuable comments on the present version.

[1] The date of the ode is most probably 488. For the problem of chronology see Farnell 1932: 102.

[2] Carne-Ross 1975: 187: "Pindar has much to say about the Kharites, plural and singular ... but *Olympian* 14 is the only poem that can be said to belong to them. The victor, who is not mentioned until nearly half the way through the second strophe, seems to give them pride of place and we may do the same."

[3] *Dicunt enim cum cenaret Crannone in Thessalia Simonides apud Scopam fortunatum hominem et nobilem cecinissetque id carmen quod in eum scripsisset, in quo multa ornandi causa poetarum more in Castorem scripta et Pollucem fuissent, nimis illum sordide Simonidi dixisse se dimidium eius ei quod pactus esset pro illo carmine daturum: reliquum a suis Tyndaridis quos aeque laudasset peteret si ei videretur. Paulo post esse ferunt nuntiatum Simonidi ut prodiret: iuvenes stare ad ianuam duos quosdam qui eum magnopere evocarent; surrexisse illum, prodisse, vidisse neminem; hoc interim spatio conclave illud ubi epularetur Scopas concidisse* (Cicero *de orat.* II. 352–53). For a collection of the ancient versions of this story, see Page *PMG ad* 510. There is confusion in the ancient sources concerning the identity of the victor for whom Simonides composed the ode in question. For a discussion of the conflicting ancient views concerning the identiy of the *laudandus*, see Molyneux 1971.

his choice by pointing out that he has given the Graces center-stage in order to maximize the praise of the victor in a minimal composition. Yet in our day the ode is known as a hymn to the Graces among students of Pindar, obviously, on account of the predominance of the hymnic element.[4] In spite of the uneven proportion of hymnic to epinician elements, however, there can be no doubt that the ode is an epinician. A poet could theoretically celebrate mainly gods in an epinician, but the opposite would be unthinkable, an act of *hybris*. Comparison of the *Fourteenth Olympian* with all other epinician odes shows that predominance of the hymnic element is a unique characteristic of this ode.

The following discussion endeavors to explore the purpose and effect of the Pindaric fusion of genres. I suggest that fusion of hymn and epinician is an artistic experiment which aims at testing the limits of the two distinct but related genres in order to maximize the praise of the *laudandus* and enhance the honor of the *laudator* without subjecting either one to the risk of *hybris*.[5] Through comparison of the *Fourteenth Olympian* with other Pindaric epinicians which share a similar narrative pattern, I argue that the effect of fusion of hymnic and epinician elements is the creation of a setting where the Graces and Echo make up a most exclusive audience for poet and victor alike.

The non-triadic form of the ode along with the emphasis on Orchomenos as the dwelling place of the Graces suggests that it is a processional song which a chorus of young men, the light stepping *kōmos* of verses 15–16, sang on their way to the temple of the Graces. Although Pindar does not single out for mention Asopichus' participation in the *kōmos*, the boy must have had an eminent position in the celebration, possibly next to the poet who was leading the chorus playing his lyre.[6] It is impossible to know for sure, of course, if Pindar was present at the celebration. The poet was fairly young at the time and Orchomenos close to Thebes. It is very likely, therefore, that he went to the city of the Graces to lead the chorus. But even if, for any reason, he was not the leader of the chorus, his vicarious presence need not be doubted, for those who had commissioned the ode as well as the singers were conscious that they sang a song which the Theban poet had composed.[7] There has been heated debate in recent years over the nature of epinician performance.[8] The issue is not settled, but the debate

---

[4] Wilamowitz 1922: 151: "Hier ist alles ein Gebet an die Chariten, und das ist nicht nur durch den Ort geboten, sondern kommt ihm von Herzen"; Verdenius 1987: 106: "The poem is a hymn to the Charites combined with a victory ode, but in spite of its beauty the balance of the composition is disturbed by the predominance of the first element"; see also Meyer 1933: 62–63; Carne-Ross 1975; Dönt 1983, who argues that the hymnic structure is sustained throughout the ode; Miller 1977: 225–26.

[5] For the religious risk of epinician poetry see Burnett 1985: 38–60.

[6] For the presence of the poet in the epinicians in general see Mullen 1982: 3–45; for his presence in this ode see Carne-Ross 1985: 64.

[7] For the epinician "I" as the poet's voice see in particular Lefkowitz 1991: 1–71, and D' Alessio 1994; cf. Anzai 1994, who argues in favor of a choral persona.

[8] For the solo hypothesis see Heath 1988; Lefkowitz 1991: 191–201; Heath-Lefkowitz; Lefkowitz 1995. For the choral hypothesis see Burnett 1989; Carey 1989c and 1991; Morgan 1993. Clay 1999 suggests the possibility of the coexistence of both modes of performance depending on the occasion. For the nature and the effect of the choral performance of the epinicians see Mullen 1982; Burnett 1985: 5–14, 38–47; Stehle 1997: 160–69.

has definitely shed light on its complexity. Our evidence allows no certainty, but I find the arguments advanced in favor of choral perfomance more powerful and convincing. In the discussion that follows, depending on whether emphasis is laid on poetry or performance, I use the terms speaker, narrator, *kōmos*, singers, and chorus interchangeably to refer to a chorus of young men who sing in the poet's persona.

The presence of the Graces is stressed right in the opening prayer which begins with reference to the waters of Cephisus as their lot (Καφισίων ὑδάτων / λαχοῖσαι, 1–2) and continues with a restatement of their localization, which qualifies the area as their dwelling place (αἴτε ναίετε καλλίπωλον ἕδραν, 2). The singers immediately proceed to invoke the divinities they are addressing by their most important attributes for the occasion, namely as songful queens of Orchomenos (ἀοίδιμοι βασίλειαι / Χάριτες Ἐρχομενοῦ, 3–4) and guardians of the old race of the Minyans (παλαιγόνων Μινυᾶν ἐπίσκοποι, 4). At the end of their invocation the singers state their request to the Graces. They ask them to listen to their prayer (κλῦτ᾽, ἐπεὶ εὔχομαι, 5) and their request is followed by a brief aretalogy attributing to the favor of the Graces all sweetness and delight in the life of mankind (σὺν γὰρ ὑμῖν τά <τε> τερπνὰ καὶ / τὰ γλυκέ᾽ ἄνεται πάντα βροτοῖς, 5–6), be it wisdom, or beauty, or glory (εἰ σοφός, εἰ καλός, ἔ τις ἀγλαὸς ἀνήρ, 7). Performance on the way or even in front of the temple of the Graces is, of course, a hypothesis. Yet form and diction throughout the ode, which produce the effect of a speaker speaking in the presence of the addressee, argue in favor of this hypothesis.[9] Johannes T. Kakridis, who has stressed that second person narrative indicates that the poet imagines the Graces as being present at Orchomenos, has also suggested that the ode was commissioned for performance during a festival in honor of the Graces.[10] According to Kakridis it was the specific occasion that gave Pindar the idea to compose an epinician in the form of a prayer to the Graces.[11] This is certainly an attractive suggestion which offers adequate explanation for poetic motivation, but in light of our evidence it remains yet another hypothesis.

The aim of prayer is to request divine favor and possibly aid, but divine presence is certainly not a prerequisite for the fulfillment of a wish. Gods hear prayer and may grant its fulfillment without necessarily making an appearance, but on special occasions they may honor an individual with their presence by means of an epiphany. In the *Sixth Olympian Ode*, for instance, Iamus goes alone at night to Alpheus and summons Poseidon and Apollo to request honor for his race.[12] His request is granted by Apollo, who does not appear to him but answers his prayer by asking Iamus to follow his voice. This leads the young hero to the hill of Cronus in a trip shrouded in

---

[9] For the possibility of performance in front of the temple see Schelicha 1968: 97, followed by Verdenius 1987: 119.

[10] Kakridis 1979: 144–146.

[11] Kakridis 1979: 145: "Der Kult der orchomenischen Chariten muss dem böotischen Dichter schon früher vertraut gewesen sein. Diese Vertrautheit gab ihm die Eingebung, das Siegeslied so zu gestalten, dass er die Form eines Gebets an die Chariten annahm." For a discussion of the festival in honor of the Graces in Hellenistic times see Te Riele 1976.

[12] Ἀλφεῷ μέσσῳ καταβαὶς ἐκάλεσσε Ποσειδᾶν᾽ εὐρυβίαν, / ὃν πρόγονον, καὶ τοξοφόρον Δάλου θεοδμάτας σκοπόν, / αἰτέων λαοτρόφον τιμάν τιν᾽ ἑᾷ κεφαλᾷ, / νυκτὸς ὑπαίθριος (58–61).

mystery, where the god grants his wish (61–71). In contrast, in the *First Olympian Ode* Poseidon appears to Pelops upon his summons (πὰρ ποδὶ σχεδὸν φάνη, 74) and promptly grants his wish. In her famous prayer to Aphrodite Sappho summons the goddess to descend from heaven (ἀλλὰ τυίδ᾽ ἔλθ᾽, 5) and describes in pictorial detail the goddess's previous descents in fulfillment of her past prayers.[13] The singers of the *Fourteenth Olympian* do not invite the Graces to come; they only ask them to listen to their song, presumably because they imagine them as dwellers of the *hic* of the performance.[14]

The impression of performance in the presence of the Graces is sustained through-out the ode by a variety of devices. Immediately following the sense of proximity between speaker and addressee, established by their prayer, the chorus shift to third person narrative, regulating thus their distance from the new scene they are in the course of describing. Without the revered Graces not even the gods, say the chorus, arrange dances and feasts (οὐδὲ γὰρ θεοὶ σεμνᾶν Χαρίτων ἄτερ / κοιρανέοντι χοροὺς οὔτε δαῖτας, 8–9).[15] The phrase οὐδὲ γὰρ Χαρίτων ἄτερ, which describes divine lifestyle, echoes the phrase σὺν γὰρ ὑμῖν, which refers to human activities, drawing thus a parallel between the world of gods and the world of men. According to the epinician chorus, in this instance, the common denominator of human and divine world is the indispensable presence of the Graces. Before returning to the *hic et nunc* the singers linger a little longer on their account of life on Olympus in the presence of the Graces. An enhanced restatement of the indispensability of their company (πάντων ταμίαι / ἔργων ἐν οὐρανῷ, 9–10) prefaces the concluding image on Olympus featuring the Graces beside Apollo in eternal worship of Zeus (10–12).

The conclusion of the account of eternal celebration in the company of the Graces on Olympus marks a shift back to second-person narrative, which recaptures the momentarily lost ambiance of immediacy between speaker and addressee. By means of a new invocation of the Graces, this time addressing each one by name, the singers renew and, more important, specify their request. The chorus first ask Aglaia and Euphrosyne to listen to their song (<ὦ> πότνι᾽ Ἀγλαΐα / φιλησίμολπέ τ᾽ Εὐφροσύνα, ... ἐπακοοῖτε νῦν, 13–15) and immediately turn to Thalia, whom they ask to look with favor upon the light stepping *kōmos* (Θαλία τε / ἐρασίμολπε. ἰδοῖσα τόνδε κῶμον ἐπ᾽ εὐμενεῖ τύχᾳ / κοῦφα βιβῶντα, 15–17). The request to the Graces is followed by a self-referential statement which finally reveals the occasion of the performance, the celebration in song of the victory of Asopichus, which the chorus attribute to the favor of Thalia (Λυδῷ γὰρ Ἀσώπιχον ἐν τρόπῳ / ἐν μελέταις τ᾽ ἀείδων ἔμολον, / οὕνεκ᾽ Ὀλυμπιόνικος ἁ Μινύεια / σεῦ ἕκατι, 17–20). This is the last mention of the Graces and, since the singers' only request of the Graces is to look favorably upon the *kōmos*,

---

[13] Sappho fr. 1 Page; for the form of prayer see Page 1955: 16–18.

[14] See Carne-Ross 1985: 65: "... the celebrants first made their way to the temple accompanied by music, and sang the ode there in the immediate presence of the goddesses."

[15] The use of present tenses (κοιρανέοντι, σέβοντι) as well as diction (πάντων ταμίαι, αἰέναον) indicates that it is an iterative narrative describing recurrent activities; see also Verdenius 1987: 113–114.

it is evident that the favor they have been asking of them all along is the successful performance of their song.[16]

Throughout the ode there is an unmistakable emphasis on terms denoting song and dance, hearing, and seeing. Terms of hearing are unquestionably integral elements of prayer, but emphasis on seeing as well as reiteration of the theme of the Graces' love for song and dance suggest that the chorus request not simply their aid for the success of their song in general, but also the favor of their presence at the performance in progress. As in the opening of the strophe where the chorus imagine the Graces as inhabitants and surveyors of the area (ἐπίσκοποι, 4) and ask them to listen, in the opening of the antistrophe they also ask them to listen and Thalia in particular to see (ἰδοῖσα, 16). Likewise in the opening of their prayer the chorus refer collectively to the Graces as ἀοίδιμοι (3). In the antistrophe, where it becomes clear that their request consists in the success of their performance as well as in an invitation to the Graces to attend it, they stress the goddesses' love for song and dance, addressing Euphrosyne as φιλησίμολπε (14) and Thalia as ἐρασίμολπε (16).[17] From a speech-act perspective, their prayer is already fulfilled insofar as their request of the Graces to see and listen is concerned.

In Pindar's epinician world the Graces, like the Muses, have many options to satisfy their love for music. Occasionally, the speaker imagines them as active participants in the epinician performance singing, or participating in the *kōmos*, or standing at the poet's or the victor's side as it were.[18] In the opening of the *Tenth Nemean*, for instance, the epinician speaker asks the Graces to sing of Argos (Δαναοῦ πόλιν … Χάριτες … ὑμνεῖτε, 1–2). Conversely, in the *Fourteenth Olympian* the speaker clearly distinguishes between the role of Graces as performers and spectators. The Graces are represented to fulfill their love for song and dance through their performances on Olympus for a divine audience. On earth, in this particular instance, they are cast in the role of audience. The use of multiple invocations combined with the repeated request to hear and see as well as the absence of any reference to their active participation in the performance indicates that the chorus does not cast them in the role of performers, but of the audience of the epinician performance.

The image of human space populated by immortal figures is enhanced in the immediately following address of the chorus to the personified Echo.[19] As if she were present, they ask her to go to the Underworld to see and announce to the dead father of the *laudandus* the victory of his son (μελαντειχέα νῦν δόμον / Φερσεφόνας ἔλθ᾽, Ἀχοῖ, πατρὶ κλυτὰν φέροισ᾽ ἀγγελίαν, 20–21). The choice of second person combined with the verb of motion ἔλθ᾽ clearly indicates that the chorus imagine Echo, like the

---

[16] See Verdenius 1987: 118.

[17] Dönt 1983: 134: "Die sangesfreudigen Chariten (φιλησίμολπε, ἐρασίμολπε cf. ἀοίδιμοι) werden aufgefordert, τόνδε κῶμον anzusehen und anzuhören, womit zugleich wieder ihre Freude an Festlichkeiten … hervorgehoben wird."

[18] See, for instance, *O*. 3, 4–6; *P*. 4, 1–3; *P*. 9, 1–3; *N*. 9, 1; *O*. 11, 16–19. For the presence of the Muses and the Graces at the epinician performance see Mullen 1982: 21–41; for the Muses and the Graces as sources of inspiration in Pindar's poetry see Duchemin 1955: 21–94.

[19] Carne-Ross 1975: 191 also remarks the absence of human presence up to verse 16.

Graces, present at the performance and ready to go elsewhere to perform an important task. There is good reason indeed for choosing Echo as a member of the audience and a messenger to the Underworld. The most important advantage of Echo as a messenger is that she will repeat verbatim to the dead Cleodamus the message the chorus tell her to convey (vv. 22–24).[20] It is also possible that, like the Graces, she had already local connexions as well, since her beloved Narcissus was the son of Cephisus. Does Pindar imply the same tradition which Ovid tells in the *Metamorphoses*?[21] His choice of Echo as a carrier of the *angelia*, as opposed to the personified Angelia, to whom the poet assigns the same task in the *Eighth Olympian Ode*, argues in favor of an old tradition known to Pindar. But certainty is unattainable. In any event, the poet envisages Echo as a member of the audience and, as Charles Segal has suggested, he may have conceived of her as a local daimon who could descend to the Underwold.[22]

Even if the story connecting Echo with Narcissus and Cephisus is Ovid's invention, comparison of the representation of Echo and Angelia illustrates that the effect of Echo's presence at the epinician celebration is a dististinctive characteristic of the *Fourteenth Olympian Ode*. In the *Eighth Olympian Ode*, in which the epinician speaker also prays to the personified Olympia to receive kindly the *kōmos*, he does not represent Angelia as being present at the celebration, nor does he use second person to address her. At the end of the poem the speaker states that Iphion, the dead father of the *laudandus* Alcimedon, will hear from Angelia the news of Alcimedon's Olympic victory and pass it on to the dead Callimachus, another relative (Ἑρμᾶ δὲ θυγατρὸς ἀκούσαις Ἰφίων / Ἀγγελίας, ἐνέποι κεν Καλλιμάχῳ λιπαρὸν / κόσμον Ὀλυμπίᾳ, 81–83).[23] Even the manner of notification of the dead in the two odes is different. In the *Fourteenth Olympian* the speaker assigns an active role to Echo who must go to the Underworld, see, and tell Cleodamus of his son's victory. In the *Eighth Olympian* the speaker does not assign the active role to Angelia, but to the dead Iphion, who will hear from Angelia about his son's victory under unspecified circumstances and who will be the one to tell Callimachus in turn.[24]

Comparison of the *Fourteenth* with the *Eighth Olympian Ode* is instructive in terms of human and divine presence at the celebration as well. The two odes share a similar scene-setting. In the opening of both odes the speaker prays to personified figures to receive kindly the *kōmos* celebrating the victory, while at the end the good

---

[20] Kurke 1991: 299 suggests that the substance of Echo's message is the father's name which also designates the achievement of his son. See also Verdenius 1987: 124.

[21] A number of scholars have followed Fennel in thinking that Pindar implies this tradition; see Verdenius 1987: 123, who thinks that the personification is Pindar's invention. In addition to scholars cited by Verdenius, see also Osmun 1967, who assumes that Pindar implies a version of the Ovidian myth.

[22] Segal 1985: 204 n. 23.

[23] For a discussion of the variety of ways in which messages reach the Underworld in Pindar's poetry see Segal 1985.

[24] The difference in the notification of the dead in the *Fourteenth* and *Eighth Olympian Ode* respectively is noted by Carey 1989a: 6, who finds it surprising that the victor's father should serve as an intermediary and proposes therefore that Callimachus, not Iphion, must be the dead father.

tidings reach the Underworld through personified figures different from the ones invoked in the beginning. But this is the extent of the common pattern of the two odes, for unlike the *Fourteenth Olympian*, in the *Eighth Olympian Ode* the audience does not consist only in personified figures, but is extended to include the *laudandus* Alcimedon, his brother Timosthenes, and possibly other members of the Blepsiad family.[25] The speaker begins with an invocation of the personified Olympia and a brief description of pyromantic practice in order to probe the will of Zeus before the contests (1–7). There follow an invocation and prayer to the sacred grove of Pisa to receive kindly the *kōmos*, as well as a gnome. Thereupon the speaker proceeds to address Timosthenes and through a swift shift to a plural personal pronoun to include Alcimedon in the immediately following statement in which he traces their ancestry all the way back to Zeus (Τιμόσθενες, ὔμμε δ᾽ ἐκλάρωσεν πότμος / Ζηνὶ γενεθλίῳ, 15–16).[26] The use of the second person is sustained in the mention of Timosthenes' Nemean victory (ὃς σὲ μὲν Νεμέᾳ πρόφατον, 16) thus keeping up the sense of the speaker speaking in the presence of his addressee.[27] In mid-sentence, however, by means of a μέν-δέ structure the speaker shifts his focus to Alcimedon's victory and from this point onward he uses third-person narrative throughout the encomiastic part of the ode. After some gnomes and a praise of Aegina, the present celebration as well as the speaker's human and personified addressees recede into the background in order to yield the floor to mythical time and space. Human space and time is temporarily eclipsed by narration of Telamon's collaboration with the gods for the building of the walls of Troy (30–52).[28] In the mythical scene we hear Apollo addressing Telamon in a dramatized monologue in which he prophesies the glorious deeds of Telamon and his descendants. When the speaker resumes the encomium, he praises the trainer Melesias, Alcimedon, the Blepsiad family, and concludes with the scene in the Underworld, which we have already discussed (53–88).

In spite of the resemblance of the initial scene-setting then, the two odes develop in strikingly different ways. In the *Eighth Olympian* the speaker focuses initially on the scene of the celebration of the victory, but as soon as he has described the setting he veers away from it in a far-and-wide ranging narrative which takes him from the *hic et nunc* of the celebration to Aegina and eventually to Troy. Resumption of Alcimedon's

---

[25] The ancient scholiast identifies Timosthenes as Alcimedon's brother (16), Iphion as the father, and Callimachus as an uncle according to some sources; according to other sources Iphion and Callimachus are mere dead relatives (106a, d, f, k). The identification of Timosthenes as Alcimedon's brother has been challenged by Carey 1989a, who proposes that Timosthenes is Alcimedon's grandfather whom Pindar mentions at verses 70–71. Kurke 1991: 293–98 has raised objections to Carey's identification and has proposed that Alcimedon must have had the same name as the grandfather mentioned at verses 70–72 and that Timosthenes is his brother.

[26] Slater 1969 interprets ὔμμε as "you and your family", but the following *men-de* structure suggests that the reference is to Timosthenes and Alcimedon.

[27] For the variety of Pindar's human addressees see Kambylis 1964: 110–113.

[28] As Mullen 1982: 88 has nicely put it, "if, however, we insist on imagining the ode as a phenomenon in space as well, which is what we do in taking it seriously as dance, then the mythical section as it is being danced will be no less present to us than the beginning or the end, and there will be some sense in which the dancers tranform the narrative from mere fictional representation into a mode of sacred presence that is complete in its own terms."

encomium does not mark a shift to the initial sense of immediacy, for the speaker opts for third-person narrative, adopting thus the status of the observer of the persons whose glorious achievements he celebrates. In contrast, in the *Fourteenth Olympian* the speaker never loses contact with his addressees who remain in sight from beginning to end. Even when he lifts his eye to divine space, his subject of choice involves the activities of precisely the same addressees in their heavenly residence. On the human level the only human presence we are asked to envisage are the participants of the *kōmos*. It is quite remarkable that the speaker does not single out Asopichus' presence in the victory celebration. His praise strategy consists in an epigrammatic mention of the honor his victory conferred upon his homeland (Ὀλυμπιόνικος ἁ Μινύεια, 19) and in the description of the moment when he was crowned with the olive wreath at Pisa (ὅτι οἱ νέαν / κόλποις παρ᾽ εὐδόξοις Πίσας / ἐστεφάνωσε κυδίμων ἀέθλων πτεροῖσι χαίταν, 22–24). The brief mention of Asopichus' victory in the middle of the antistrophe signals at long last the epinician character of the ode, whereas the description of the climactic moment of his victory in the form of a message, which a member of the audience is asked to convey to the Underworld, concludes the poem without removing the epinician performance and its divine audience from focus.

Some of the differences between the *Eighth* and the *Fourteenth Olympian Ode* are, unquestionably, due to their different length, which must have been determined by the specific requirements of each commission. Moreover, the impressive athletic record of Alcimedon and his family compared to the record of Asopichus, undoubtedly, sheds some light on the different function of the *kōmos* scene in the two odes respectively. Description of the *kōmos* in the *Eighth Olympian* is only the foil for the celebration of Aegina and its glorious offspring since time immemorial as well as for the commemoration of the six Panhellenic victories of the *laudandus* and his family (74–76). We do not know of course if Asopichus' Olympic victory was the only one he had ever won, but given his young age it must have been the most impressive. Moreover, the cult of the Graces at Orchomenos was for obvious reasons a source of genial inspiration for the poet. It is no wonder that a poet of Pindar's caliber chose to throw into relief the two themes of paramount importance for epinician poetry and performance, namely Asopichus' Olympic victory and the belief that Orchomenos was the dwelling place of the Graces. Asopichus' youth as well as the cult of the Graces in his homeland explain why Pindar chose to single out for commemoration only his most impressive athletic achievement and his place of origin, but does not account for the predominance of the hymnic element nor for the creation of a fictitious audience consisting only of the Graces and Echo.

Pindar composed the *Fourteenth Olympian Ode* for the young Asopichus early in his career. Comparison of this early piece of work with his later work, which displays integration of hymnic elements in the epinician program, suggests that most probably artistic experimentation lies behind his choice to widen the scope of the hymnic genre so as to subsume epinician praise. In Pindar's later poetry hymn and prayer are fully integrated in the epinician program and, as Bundy has demonstrated, they serve as foils in a series of crescendos for the praise of the *laudandus*.[29] The integration of the opening prayer to the personified Olympia and the grove of Pisa to receive the *kōmos* in the epinician program in the *Eighth Olympian Ode*, which belongs to Pindar's mature poetry, is a representative example of Pindaric practice. We have also seen that, in spite of the similar opening and closure of the *Fourteenth* and *Eighth Olympians*, in the later ode the focus of the speaker is not on the personified figures he initially invokes, but on the *laudandus*, his brother, his trainer, and his family. Naturally, some of the differences are due to the nature of the commission in each case. Unlike the young Asopichus, the Blepsiad family must have requested an elaborate ode which would commemorate their impressive athletic achievements in light of their most glorious ancestral past. Yet the *Fourteenth Olympian* remains unique in its hymnic quality and emphasis on divine presence, even if we compare it with odes of equal length and degree of elaboration.

The *Fourth Olympian*, an ode comparable to the *Fourteenth Olympian* in terms of length and narrative pattern, offers a good example of the subordination of hymnic genre to the epinician program, which characterizes Pindar's later poetry. Like the *Fourteenth Olympian*, the *Fourth Olympian* opens with a hymn to Zeus, which concludes with the prayer to receive kindly the *kōmos*, but the hymnic quality of the ode does not extend far beyond the opening strophe.[30] In the antistrophe the speaker sets off the *laudandus* as the central figure and in the epode he illustrates the truthfulness of his account by means of a short mythological *exemplum*.

The ode begins with an invocation of Zeus (Ἐλατὴρ ὑπέρτατε βροντᾶς ἀκαμαντόποδος Ζεῦ, 1). Immediately, however, address to the god is suspended for the introduction of the purpose of the speaker's arrival. Through the agency of the Seasons, Zeus' daughters, the speaker has come to sing on the lyre of the greatest contests with varied tunes (τεαὶ γὰρ Ὧραι / ὑπὸ ποικιλοφόρμιγγος ἀοιδᾶς ἑλισσόμεναι μ' ἔπεμψαν / ὑψηλοτάτων μάρτυρ' ἀέθλων, 1–3). The immediately following gnome concerning the joy good men should feel at the news of their friends' achievements has special reference to the occasion as well. It designates the relation between the *laudator* and the *laudandus* as *xenia*, but on account of its gnomic quality and of the reiteration of the same idea later in the antistrophe, it also implies the proper attitude of Psaumis' friends to him in general (ξείνων δ' εὖ πρασσόντων / ἔσαναν αὐτίκ' ἀγγελίαν ποτὶ γλυκεῖαν ἐσλοί, 4–5). A second invocation of Zeus follows along with the prayer to receive the *kōmos* celebrating an Olympian victory for the sake of the Graces (Ὀλυμπιονίκαν / δέξαι Χαρίτων θ' ἕκατι τόνδε κῶμον, 8–9). This is the only mention of the Graces in this ode. This minimal reference implies of course the Graces' love for song and dance, but it also illustrates the dramatically different role they play in the *Fourth* and *Fourteenth Olympian Odes* respectively. The roles are completely reversed. Whereas in the *Fourteenth Olympian* the Graces remain the focal point of the ode from beginning to end, in the *Fourth Olympian* the focus shifts onto the *kōmos*, as becomes evident from the statement in the opening of the antistrophe, in

---

[29] See Bundy 1962: 44–47, 76–83.
[30] The prayer ends at v. 13.

which the speaker qualifies the specific *kōmos*, namely the epinician performance in progress, as the most enduring light of mighty deeds (χρονιώτατον φάος εὐρυσθενέων ἀρετᾶν, 10).[31]

Unlike the *Fourteenth Olympian Ode,* which foregrounds the performance of the *kōmos* before the Graces and Echo to the exclusion of any human presence, the *Fourth Olympian* shows a clear tendency not only to give the *laudandus* Psaumis pride of place in the celebration, but to place him in his community at large. Whereas the *Fourteenth Olympian* offers only a glimpse into the climactic moment of Asopichus' wreathing with the olive crown, in the *Fourth Olympian* praise of Psaumis as an Olympian victor and citizen is the single subject of the antistrophe. Immediately following the comment concerning the permanent radiance of epinician praise is a qualification of the purpose of the *kōmos*: they have come to sing of Psaumis' victory (Ψαύμιος γὰρ ἵκει / ὀχέων, 10–11).[32] By means of a relative pronoun the focus shifts from the *kōmos* to the *laudandus* who remains in sight through the end of the antistrophe. First the speaker focuses on Psaumis' Olympic victory. Unlike the *Fourteenth Olympian* in which the Olympic victory is transferred from Asopichus to his homeland, in the case of Psaumis, diction brings out his active role in conferring glory on his homeland (ὃς ἐλαίᾳ στεφανωθεὶς Πισάτιδι κῦδος ὄρσαι / σπεύδει Καμαρίνᾳ, 11–12). After a brief prayer for fulfillment of Psaumis' future wishes, the speaker reiterates Psaumis' praise singling out one athletic and two civic virtues. He praises Psaumis for his eagerness in raising horses (ἐπεί νιν αἰνέω, μάλα μὲν τροφαῖς ἕτοιμον ἵππων, 14), his all-welcoming hospitality (χαίροντά τε ξενίαις πανδόκοις, 15), and his dedication to the city-loving Hesychia (καὶ πρὸς Ἡσυχίαν φιλόπολιν καθαρᾷ γνώμᾳ τετραμμένον, 16). This short list makes clear that the speaker has taken his eyes off the crowning scene at Olympia and focuses instead on Psaumis' everyday life in Camarina among his horses, his guests, and his fellow citizens. The antistrophe closes with the speaker's assertion of the truthfulness of his praise and a gnome on performance as the ultimate proof of human achievement (17–18). In the epode the brief myth concluding with Erginos' speech to Hypsipyle illustrates the importance of achievement as proof of excellence and transfers attention from the present celebration to the mythical past (19–27). Thus human space and time yield to mythical space and time and the ode ends with a mythical athlete singing his own encomium.

With the exception of the *Fourteenth Olympian*, all Pindaric epinicians show a greater or lesser tendency to set off the *laudandus* as the central figure in the epinician celebration.[33] Since the *Fourteenth Olympian* is clearly an epinician, it is legitimate to ask whether the sustained focus on the Graces detracts from Asopichus' merits or enhances them. There can be no single answer to this question, for it depends on the nature of one's expectations. Yet as comparison with the *Fourth Olympian* shows, shift of focus from the Graces to the *laudandus* certainly detracts from the ambiance

---

[31] Farnell 1932 *ad* 10: "the 'light' refers specially to Pindar's poetry sung by the Komos, that will perpetuate the memory of the victory."

[32] Cf. Gerber 1987 *ad* 10–11, who following the ancient scholia (16a and b) understands ὕμνος as the subject of ἵκει.

[33] See also *Ol.* 12 where Ergoteles enjoys a central place in the epinician ode.

of mystique, the uncanny feeling of celebration at a haunted place. In his more elaborate epinician odes Pindar achieves similar effects through mythical narratives which are often partially dramatized. Among his shorter epinicians the *Fourteenth Olympian* has no peer insofar as the surrounding mystique is concerned, in spite of the beauty and power of some of them. The *Eleventh Olympian*, an even shorter ode, best illustrates the point.

After a relatively extended priamel, which occupies the first strophe, and a general statement of his present task (7–10) the speaker turns to the *laudandus* whose Olympic victory he sings in the second person (ἴσθι νῦν, Ἀρχεστράτου / παῖ, τεᾶς, Ἀγησίδαμε, πυγμαχίας ἕνεκεν / κόσμον ἐπὶ στεφάνῳ χρυσέας ἐλαίας / ἁδυμελῆ κελαδήσω, / Ζεφυρίων Λοκρῶν γενεὰν ἀλέγων, 11–15). The effect of second-person narrative is that the speaker sings in the presence of Hagesidamus. The sense of immediacy is retained in the speaker's immediately following request to the Muses to join the *kōmos* (ἔνθα συγκωμάξατ', 16) and in his promise to them that the Epizephyrian Lokrians are hospitable, sophisticated in the arts, and good warriors (ἐγγυάσομαι / ὔμμιν, ὦ Μοῖσαι, φυγόξεινον στρατὸν / μήτ' ἀπείρατον καλῶν / ἀκρόσοφόν τε καὶ αἰχματὰν ἀφίξεσθαι, 16–19).[34] Immediately afterwards the speaker brings the ode swiftly to an end by means of an enigmatic gnome.

There is great resemblance between the *Eleventh Olympian* and the *Fourteenth Olympian* in terms of the nature and the extent of praise of the *laudandus* and his homeland, but the encomiastic strategy is clearly different. Instead of an opening prayer the poet opts for a priamel. Diction makes clear that in this ode, unlike the *Fourteenth Olympian* where the Graces are cast in the role of audience, the speaker envisages the Muses as performers standing by. More important, through balanced use of imperatives and length of address to Hagesidamus and the Muses respectively, the epinician speaker accords the *laudandus* a footing in the celebration equal to that of the Muses. In view of the minimal length of the ode, the presence of Hagesidamus and his townsmen is enormous and ultimately overshadows the presence of the Muses who become less conspicuous by joining the *kōmos* than they would be as its exclusive audience. It is precisely the centrality of the *laudandus* that gives this ode a rather mundane quality compared with the *Fourteenth Olympian*.

In the *Fourteenth Olympian* it is the absence of mention of any human presence other than the *kōmos* that achieves the effect of an ambient mystique. The poet does not draw attention to Asopichus' presence at the celebration, presumably in order to enhance the effect of an exclusive performance before a divine audience. To be sure, the sustained focus on the Graces and Echo does not diminish the achievements of the *laudandus*, simply because they are a major topic of the epinician song. In view of the fact that, with the exception of the multiple invocations of the Graces and Echo to see and listen, the only other subject of the epinician song is the heavenly activities of the Graces it is clear that Asopichus and his homeland receive maximal praise. The

---

[34] For the use of future for the description of the epinician performance in progress see Bundy 1962: 21–22. For such futures Peliccia 1995: 317–34 coins the useful descriptive term "intra-carminal" futures. See also Pfeijffer 1999: 19–43.

parallelism between divine and human activities is implicit, but on account of the presence of the Graces at Orchomenos the Minyans can enjoy on earth delights not very different from those which the gods enjoy on Olympus in the company of the Graces. It would be doubtless hybristic to equate divine with human status. Since in the fictional reality of this ode the Graces perform for the gods, the poet would certainly overstep his bounds if he represented them performing for mortals as well. It is quite remarkable that in the *Fifth Nemean Ode*, where the poet represents the Muses performing for the gods at the wedding of Peleus and Thetis, they are totally absent from the encomiastic part of the ode. If performance of the Graces on earth would draw a dangerously close parallel between the human and the divine world, their worship at Orchomenos pointed to a safe way. In this case all they could be was a most exclusive and charming audience for victor and poet alike. Mention of human presence, other than that of the performers themselves, would undoubtedly dispel the magic of performance before a divine audience.

For all its charming ambiance the *Fourteenth Olympian Ode* remained, as far as our evidence indicates, a single epinician experiment. As the poet's fame grew, his patrons probably claimed a central position in his epinicians. Did Pindar compose the *Fourteenth Olympian Ode* simply to explore the fascinating effects of fusion of the hymnic and epinician genre or in the knowledge that the ode would be performed during a periodic festival in honor of the Graces, as Kakridis has suggested? We will never know. Pindar was about thirty years old when he composed this ode. Under any circumstances performance at the oldest and foremost site of worship of the Graces in Greece must have been an exciting occasion for any young poet; above all for Pindar.[35] And it may have provided the stimulus for experimentation. Yet Kakridis' hypothesis of performance at a time when the Graces were believed to be present, is also attractive especially in view of the resemblance between the ambiance of the *Fourteenth Olympian* ode and the opening of the *Sixth Paean*, composed for the *Theoxenia*, where the chorus pray to Pytho to receive them ἐν ζαθέῳ ... χρόνῳ (1–6).[36]

WORKS CITED

Anzai, M. 1994. "First-Person Forms in Pindar: A Re-examination." *BICS* 39: 141–51.
Alden Smith, R. 1999. "Pindar's Ol. 14: A Literal and Literary Homecoming." *Hermes* 127: 257–62.
Bremer, J.M. 1990. "Pindar's Paradoxical ἐγώ and a Recent Controversy about the Performance of his Epinicia." In S. Slings, ed., *The Poet's "I" in Archaic Greek Lyric*. Amsterdam. 41–58.
Bundy, E.L. 1962. [1986] *Studia Pindarica*. [repr.] Berkeley and Los Angeles.
Burnett, A.P. 1985. *The Art of Bacchylides*. Cambridge, Mass.
———. 1989 "Performing Pindar's Odes." *CPh* 84: 283–93.

---

[35] For the cult of the Graces at Orchomenos and elsewhere, see Farnell 1909: 427–31, 462–63; Hamdorf 1964: 45–46, 103–104.

[36] At the end of the opening triad of the *Sixth Paean*, vv. 52–54, the singers invite the Muses to listen to their song. As Rutherford 2001: 310 suggests, "… the Muses listen to the singer, shifting from the role of bestowers of inspiration to a sort of divine audience." In a very similar manner, in a Pindaric dithyramb for the Athenians a human chorus invite the Olympian gods to attend their performance (fr. 75, 1–13). See Van der Weiden 1991: 190, 193 *ad* 5.

Carey, C. 1989a. "Prosopographica Pindarica." *CQ* n.s. 39: 1–9.

———. 1989b. "Two Transitions in Pindar." *CQ* n.s. 39: 287–95.

———. 1989c. "The Performance of the Victory Ode." *AJPh* 110: 545–65.

———. 1991. "The Victory Ode in Performance. The Case for the Chorus." *CPh* 86: 192–299.

Carne-Ross, D.S. 1975. "Three Preludes for Pindar." *Arion* n.s. 2: 160–93.

———.1985. *Pindar*. New Haven/London.

Clay, J. S. 1999. "Pindar's Sympotic Epinicia." *QUCC* n.s. 62: 25–34.

D' Alessio, G.B. 1994. "First-Person Problems in Pindar." *BICS* 39: 117–39.

Duchemin, J. 1955. *Pindare poète et prophète*. Paris.

Dönt, M. 1983. "Zur 14. olympischen Ode Pindars." *RhM* 126: 126–35.

Farnell, L.R. 1909. *The Cults of the Greek States*. Vol. V. Oxford.

———. 1932. *The Works of Pindar. Vol. II. Critical Commentary*. London.

Gerber, D.E. 1987. "Pindar's Olympian Four: A Commentary." *QUCC* n.s. 25: 7–24.

Hamdorf, F.W. 1964. *Griechische Kultpersonifikationen der vorhellenistischen Zeit*. Mainz.

Heath-Lefkowitz = Heath, M. and M. Lefkowitz. "Epinician Performance." *CPh* 86 (1991): 173–92.

Heath, M. 1988. "Receiving the κῶμος: The Context and Performance of Epinician." *AJPh* 109: 180–95.

Kakridis, J.T. 1979. "Die 14. Olympische Ode. Ein Beitrag zum Problem der Religiosität Pindars." *Serta Philologica Aenipontana* 3: 141–47.

Kambylis, A. 1964. "Anredeformen bei Pindar." *ΧΑΡΙΣ ΚΩΝΣΤΑΝΤΙΝΩΙ ΒΟΥΡΒΕΡΗΙ*, Athens.

Kurke, L. 1991. "Fathers and Sons: A Note on Pindaric Ambiguity." *AJPh* 112: 287–300.

Lefkowitz, M. 1991. *Poetic First Person Fictions. Pindar's "I"*. Oxford.

Meyer, H. 1933. *Hymnische Stilelemente in der frühgriechischen Dichtung*. Würzburg.

Miller, A.M. 1977. "*Thalia Erasimolpos*: Consolation in Pindar's *Fourteenth Olympian*." *TAPhA* 107: 225–34.

Molyneux, H.J. 1971. "Simonides and the Dioscuri." *Phoenix* 25: 197–205.

Morgan, K.A. 1993. "Pindar the Professional and the Rhetoric of the ΚΩΜΟΣ." *CPh* 99: 1–15.

Mullen, W. 1982. *Choreia: Pindar and Dance*. Princeton.

Osmun, G. F. 1967. "Pindar: Olympian XIV.*" *CW* 61: 6–8.

Page, D. 1955. *Sappho and Alcaeus*. Oxford.

Page *PMG* = Page, D. *Poetae melici graeci*. Oxford, 1962.

Pelliccia, H. 1995. *Mind, Body, and Speech in Homer and Pindar*. Hypomnemata 107. Göttingen.

Pfeijffer, I.L. 1999. *First Person Futures in Pindar*. Hermes Einzelschriften 81. Stuttgart.

Rutherford, I. 2001. *Pindar's Paeans. A Reading of the Fragments with a Survey of the Genre*. Oxford.

Schelicha, R.von. 1968. "Interpretation der XIV. Olympischen Ode von Pindar." In *Freiheit und Freundschaft in Hellas*. Amsterdam. 93–105.

Segal, C.P. 1985. "Messages to the Underworld: An Aspect of Poetic Immortalization in Pindar" *AJPh* 106: 199–212.

Stehle, E. 1997. *Performance and Gender in Ancient Greece*. Princeton.

Te Riele, G.J. 1976. "Charitesia." *Miscellanea tragica in honorem J.C. Kamerbeek*. Amsterdam. 285–91.

Van der Weiden, M.J.H. 1991. *The Dithyrambs of Pindar*. Amsterdam.

Wilamowitz-Moellendorff, U. von. 1922. *Pindaros*. Berlin.

2

Ποῖ δὴ καὶ πόθεν; Self-Motion in Plato's *Phaedrus*[*]

Geoffrey W. Bakewell

The proof for the immortality of the soul at *Phaedrus* 245c5–246a2 has attracted scholarly attention out of all proportion to its size. This is partly because of the anomalous nature of the proof. In a dialogue that shimmers with beauty, the proof is dry, technical, and formal. Indeed, the stylistic contrast is so great that Demos sought to isolate the proof as an interpolation.[1] Others have been interested in the proof for the light it sheds on Plato's indebtedness to his philosophical predecessors. Barnes, for instance, attempted to trace the proof's kernel, self-motion, back to Alcmeon.[2] Still others have used the proof as a yardstick to measure Plato not against the pre-Socratics but himself. The fact that several dialogues, most notably *Phaedo*, *Republic*, *Phaedrus*, and *Laws*, contain a variety of proofs for the immortality of the soul suggests the possibility of intellectual development on Plato's part. On this reading, the *Phaedrus* proof represents an important shift from arguments about generation from opposites, learning by anamnesis, the incomposite nature of the soul, and the ability of a form to admit its opposite to arguments about self-motion. In the broader scheme of things this developmental sequence hints that the *Phaedrus* might be ranked among the later dialogues.[3] Still other scholars have looked at the connections between the proof and Plato's successors. In particular, the proof's emphasis on self-motion and sources of motion leads scholars like Hackforth and Guthrie to Aristotle's unmoved mover.[4]

More recently, however, the *Phaedrus* itself has become the primary frame of reference in which to interpret the proof.[5] Griswold, for instance, seeks to connect the proof with the dialogue's emphasis on self-knowledge. For him, one of the *Phaedrus*'s central messages is that an individual's analysis of his own soul leads him to truths about himself and his relations with others.[6] Similarly Ferrari sees in the proof Plato's

---

[*] I dedicate this piece to Alan Boegehold with gratitude and affection; he has taught me much about φιλία.

[1] Demos 1968: 134. This view has generally been rejected, e.g. Blyth 1997: 185 n. 1; Bett 1986: 2 n. 4.

[2] Barnes 1982: 114–120. Blyth 1997: 185 is more skeptical.

[3] Hackforth 1952: 4–5; Bett 1986: 19.

[4] Guthrie 1975: 421; Hackforth 1952: 68.

[5] Pioneering in this regard was Lebeck 1972.

[6] Griswold 1986: 87: "an individual's efforts to understand his own pathe and erga rapidly lead to a level of discourse that articulates truths about himself and other persons."

recognition of the importance of "the contingent aspect of the philosophic life," whose features include "intellectual friendship."[7] While both of these claims seem correct, Griswold and Ferrari do not go far enough in examining the proof's connections with the contingent world of human relations. In fact, the proof is crucial to Socrates' attempts to redefine for Phaedrus the quintessentially interpersonal activities of love and λόγος. For like soul, love and λόγος are also cast as immortal, self-moving causes of motion. Moreover, the emphasis on motion (in proof and dialogue alike) leads us to understand all three – soul, love, and λόγος – as complex entities characterized by internal reciprocity. Indeed, Plato's literary artistry emphasizes this point, using movement to frame and punctuate the afternoon's conversation between Phaedrus and Socrates.

First, a brief analysis of the proof.[8] The statement at 245c5, πᾶσα ψυχὴ ἀθάνατος, constitutes the proposition Socrates is trying to prove. The πᾶσα in this sentence is famously controversial.[9] It is of course an adjective meaning "each, every, all." But what is its meaning here? Is Socrates trying to prove that each and every individual soul is immortal? Or is his point that soul collectively is immortal? And if πᾶσα ψυχή is understood as a collective entity, is it better thought of as a world-soul à la *Timaeus*, or as a substance with universal properties, like water?[10] Ferrari's solution to the difficulty here is elegant and attractive: he views the ambiguity of πᾶσα as intentional.[11] On the one hand, the souls of individuals are central to the *Phaedrus*. It is a dialogue about the affection between two distinct men, Phaedrus and Socrates.[12] The captivating myth of the charioteer and steeds is deployed to illustrate the workings of individual souls. Lovers are classified on the basis of their pyschic differences, one from another. And finally, true rhetoric involves tailoring one's speech to suit the souls of one's individual listeners. In sum, then, the dialogue places a tremendous premium on individual identity and revolves around the intimate familiarity between Socrates and Phaedrus. Towards the start of the dialogue Socrates spots the manuscript hidden in his friend's cloak and states, "I know my Phaedrus; yes indeed, I'm as sure of him as of my own identity."[13] A bit later Phaedrus returns the favor, threatening to withhold any future speeches unless Socrates delivers one of his own. "Don't I know my Socrates?" he says. "If not, I've forgotten my own identity."[14] There are thus a priori grounds for believing that the πᾶσα ψυχή phrase of the proof

---

[7] Ferrari 1987: 125. By the "contingent aspect" he means (128) "those goods which, although external to the philosophic life, nevertheless belong to it more than just accidentally; goods such as intellectual friendship and the thrill of discovery; all those goods, in short, which result from the realisation of the philosophic impulse in our actual lives – and which, of course, are goods that philosophic lovers bring to one another."

[8] The most extensive treatment is that of Blyth 1997.

[9] Frutiger 1976: 131 ff.

[10] Bett 1986: 12 endorses the latter view.

[11] Ferrari 1987: 124.

[12] Nussbaum 1986: 218. She concludes that the dialogue values highly (201) "erotic relationships of long duration between particular individuals (who see each other as such)."

[13] 228a. Unless otherwise noted, all translations are those of Hackforth 1952.

[14] 236c.

has some bearing on the soul of the individual.[15] And yet, as will become clear shortly, the proof also pertains to souls as parts of a larger grouping.

The proof's formal structure is also debated. Some scholars consider it unitary, while others see two interrelated proofs.[16] The latter approach is more straightforward and is followed here.[17] Proof 1 is comprised of the following premises (P1–P6):

P1   Motion is a necessary condition of life, 245c6–8. (τὸ δ᾽ ἄλλο κινοῦν καὶ ὑπ᾽ ἄλλου κινούμενον, παῦλαν ἔχον κινήσεως, παῦλαν ἔχει ζωῆς.)

P2   Unceasing motion is a necessary condition for immortality (derived from P1).

P3   Unceasing motion is a sufficient condition for immortality, 245c5. (τὸ γὰρ ἀεικίνητον ἀθάνατον.)

P4   There are two types of motion: self motion and externally caused motion, 245c5–9. (τὸ δ᾽ ἄλλο κινοῦν καὶ ὑπ᾽ ἄλλου κινούμενον ... τὸ αὐτὸ κινοῦν)

P5   Only self-movers are always in motion, 245c7–8. (μόνον δὴ τὸ αὐτὸ κινοῦν, ἅτε οὐκ ἀπολεῖπον ἑαυτό, οὔποτε λήγει κινούμενον.)

P6   Soul, and only soul, is a self-mover, 245e7–8. (μὴ ἄλλο τι εἶναι τὸ αὐτὸ ἑαυτὸ κινοῦν ἢ ψυχήν)

In premise P1 Socrates seems to imagine motion as broadly defined. For him, κίνησις includes not just locomotion, but any sort of change over time, including growth, thought, generation, and the fulfillment of potentiality. In this regard the passage is akin to *Laws* 893b6–894c8, where the Athenian gives motion a similarly broad scope.[18] For his part Blyth sees Socrates' conflation of κίνησις and γένεσις here in the *Phaedrus* as intentional, a trap set by Plato for the unwary reader.[19] Premise P2 derives from P1. If motion is a necessary condition for life, then unceasing motion forms a condition for unceasing life, i.e. immortality. Premise P3 marks an important expansion of P2. It makes unceasing motion not only a necessary condition for immortality, but a sufficient one. This premise finds explicit mention in the text at 245c5, τὸ γὰρ ἀεικίνητον ἀθάνατον. Oxyrhynchus papyrus 1017 does offer an important textual alternative (τὸ γὰρ <u>αὐτοκίνητον</u> ἀθάνατον), but there is widespread agreement that ἀεικίνητον is the truer reading.[20]

Having established motion as the basis for immortality, Socrates now proceeds to examine it more closely, dividing it into two categories: self-motion and externally caused motion. This premise, P4, is implicit in his statement at 245c5–7: the phrase τὸ δ᾽ ἄλλο κινοῦν καὶ ὑπ᾽ ἄλλου κινούμενον represents a motion transmitter, while τὸ αὐτὸ κινοῦν refers to a self-mover. Socrates' next step, premise P5, is to claim that

---

[15] Cf. Bett 1986: 13–14.

[16] For a survey of the various views see Blyth 1997: 194 n. 18.

[17] E.g. Bett 1986: 3. Blyth 1997: 195 n. 21 attempts to explain away the logical difficulties of the unitarian position by attributing them to a ruse on Plato's part. On his view , Plato attempts to provoke the reader by including in the proof (201) "insinuations to unwarranted conclusions in the manner of a sophistic orator."

[18] Bett 1986: 9; Blyth 1997: 203.

[19] Blyth in fact argues that the entire proof is constructed to spur on the process of dialectic and philosophical inquiry; it forms one way in which Plato compensates for the shortcomings of a written text for putting forward his views.

[20] The definitive treatment is that of Decleva Caizzi 1970: 91–97.

only self-movers are always in motion. This is made explicit at 245c7–8. His reasoning here is that while things moved by others can stop moving, motion is essential to the identity of self-movers. But Socrates elides an important distinction. As Bett notes, motion may be an essential property of self-movers, but they do not necessarily possess this essence eternally.[21] With premise P6, Socrates seeks to establish that soul, and only soul, is a self-mover. He makes this explicit at 245e4–8, πᾶν γὰρ σῶμα, ᾧ μὲν ἔξωθεν τὸ κινεῖσθαι, ἄψυχον, ὡς ταύτης οὔσης φύσεως ψυχῆς· εἰ δ ἔστιν τοῦτο οὕτως ἔχον, μὴ ἄλλο τι εἶναι τὸ αὐτὸ ἑαυτὸ κινοῦν ἢ ψυχήν. Here soul is depicted as the internal animating principle of a living body; it alone is self-moving. Thus the logic of proof 1 runs as follows: only soul is a self-mover, and only self-movers are always in motion. Therefore soul (and only soul) is always in motion. That which is always in motion is immortal; therefore soul (and only soul) is immortal.

The second, interrelated proof for the immortality of soul is comprised of the following premises, P7 to P11:

P7   A self-mover is the source of all motion, 245c9. (μόνον δὴ τὸ αὐτὸ κινοῦν ... τοῖς ἄλλοις ὅσα κινεῖται τοῦτο πηγὴ καὶ ἀρχὴ κινήσεως.)[22]

P8   A source of motion must be without a coming to be, 245d1–2. (ἀρχὴ δὲ ἀγένητον. ἐξ ἀρχῆς γὰρ ἀνάγκη πᾶν τὸ γιγνόμενον γίγνεσθαι, αὐτὴν δὲ μηδ᾽ ἐξ ἑνός.)

P9   That which is without a coming to be must also be indestructible, 245d3–4. (ἐπειδὴ δὲ ἀγένητόν ἐστιν, καὶ ἀδιάφθορον αὐτὸ ἀνάγκη εἶναι.)

P10   That which is ἀγένητον and ἀδιάφθορον is immortal.

P11   Soul, and only soul, is a self-mover, 245e7–8.

This proof is also rooted in self-motion, but takes a different tack. It begins with premise P7 that a self-mover is the source of all motion. Premise P8 is particularly complicated. Socrates wants to claim that an ἀρχή of motion must be without a coming to be, i.e. ἀγένητον. He reasons that everything that comes to be must do so from something. And if a source came to be, it would not be a source: something else would. As he did with premise P2 in the first proof, however, Socrates again blurs the distinction between κίνησις and γένεσις. This conflation now suggests that that which causes κίνησις must be without γένεσις, which is different from saying that that which causes κίνησις must be without κίνησις. According to premise P9, that which is ἀγένητον must also be indestructible, ἀδιάφθορον. Premise P10 is suppressed: that which is ἀγένητον and ἀδιάφθορον is immortal. Finally, premise P11 is identical with premise P6 from the first proof: soul, and only soul, is a self-mover. Thus according to proof 2, soul (and only soul) is a self-mover; therefore soul (and only soul) is the source of all motion. As a source it must be ἀγένητον and ἀδιάφθορον, and is therefore immortal. Socrates supports this line of reasoning with a vivid *per impossibile* claim. If this weren't the case, and a source of motion could be destroyed, the world as we know it would cease to exist, with all heaven and earth collapsing together and standing still.[23]

---

[21] Bett 1986: 5–6; Blyth 1997: 196.
[22] See also 245d6–7: οὕτω δὴ κινήσεως μὲν ἀρχὴ τὸ αὐτὸ αὑτὸ κινοῦν.
[23] 245d8–e2.

Let us now turn to the relationship between the proof and the rest of the *Phaedrus*. The proof's placement demonstrates its connection with the dialogue's emphasis on love. When Socrates begins at 245c5, he has newly embarked on his palinode, an effort to reinstruct Phaedrus as to the nature and value of love. The previous two speeches, those of Lysias and Socrates, had disparaged ἔρως, focusing on the tangible, deleterious effects it often has on the beloved's body, possessions, reputation, and relations with friends and family. Now, however, Socrates changes his tune, and praises love as a form of divine μανία which brings the greatest good fortune to ἐράστης and ἐρώνεος alike. To bolster his claim, he switches his analysis of love from the material plane to the psychic one. Developing a theme of his prior speech, that the proper education of the soul outranks all other concerns, he argues that the primary benefits of love occur in the realm of an individual's soul. Indeed, he says that "our first step towards attaining the truth of the matter [i.e., the nature of ἔρως] is to discern the nature of soul, divine and human, its experiences and its activities."[24] The proof for the immortality of the soul follows immediately afterward, and forms an integral part of Socrates' redefinition of love for Phaedrus.

Like its placement, the proof's content is also connected with love. As we have seen, from Socrates' standpoint the crucial feature of the soul is its self-motion: this is apparent both in the central image of charioteer and horses, and in the language of the proof. Yet in this regard, soul is similar to love, which the dialogue also depicts as a self-mover. At 245b3, for instance, Socrates returns to the basic premise of the first two speeches, that we should give ourselves to those who do not love us rather than those who do. According to him, those earlier speeches constituted an attempt to "scare us into preferring the friendship of the sane to that of the passionate." (ὡς πρὸ τοῦ κεκινημένου τὸν σώφρονα δεῖ προαιρεῖσθαι φίλον). In this formulation he casts the non-lover, ὁ μὴ ἐρῶν, as sane and moderate, σώφρων. He also redefines the lover, ὁ ἐράστης, as κεκινημένος. Although Hackforth translates this last term as "passionate," it is in fact a perfect participle from κινέω.[25] Note particularly the form of the participle. With regard to voice it is not active, but rather middle/passive. Moreover, there are good contextual grounds for treating it as a passive participle rather than a middle.[26] Thus the lover is apparently not self-moving but moved, and the source of this motion is love. Yet thinking back to the terms of the proof for a moment, we will remember that only self-movers can impart motion to others. On this understanding of things, ἔρως appears to be both a self-mover and an ἀρχή of motion. Shortly afterwards Socrates provides a vivid depiction of love acting in this very capacity. At 251a–b he describes the effects of the beloved's beauty on the lover:

---

[24] 245c2–4: δεῖ οὖν πρῶτον ψυχῆς φύσεως πέρι θείας τε καὶ ἀνθρωπίνης ἰδόντα πάθη τε καὶ ἔργα τἀληθὲς νοῆσαι.

[25] Hackforth 1952: 58. On the sexual connotations of the verb κινέω generally see Henderson 1975: 35, 151.

[26] Consider the language of the proof. There self-movers are never described by middle participles alone. Rather, Plato employs either the active participle and a reflexive pronoun in the accusative (e.g., 245c7, τὸ αὐτὸ κινοῦν), or a passive participle with ὑπό and the reflexive pronoun in the genitive (e.g., 245e3, τοῦ ὑφ' ἑαυτοῦ κινουμένου).

First there comes upon him a shuddering and a measure of that awe which the [earlier] vision inspired, and then reverence as at the sight of a god ... Next, with the passing of the shudder, a strange sweating and fever seizes him: for by reason of the stream of beauty entering in through his eyes there comes a warmth, whereby his soul's plumage is fostered; and with that warmth the roots of the wings are melted, which for long had been so hardened and closed up that nothing could grow; then, as the nourishment is poured in, the stump of the wing swells and hastens to grow from the root over the whole substance of the soul.

The vocabulary of this section emphasizes the activity of ἔρως and the passivity of the ἐράστης: shuddering comes upon him (τι τῶν τότε ὑπῆλθεν αὐτὸν δειμάτων, 251a4), sweating and fever seize him (ἱδρὼς καὶ θερμότης ἀήθης λαμβάνει, 251b1), an outflow of beauty enters his eyes (δεξάμενος γὰρ τοῦ κάλλους τὴν ἀπορροὴν διὰ τῶν ὀμμάτων, 251b1–2), he is warmed (ἐθερμάνθη, 251b2), and so forth. The verbs ὑπῆλθεν, λαμβάνει and ἐθερμάνθη in particular emphasize the lover's passivity; he is in the grip of an external force which moves him and causes change within him. Love is thus like the soul of the proof, a self-moving source of motion.[27]

The main thrust of the proof was to establish immortality as a necessary consequence of self-motion: insofar as soul is self-moving, it is immortal. The same holds true for love. A preliminary indication of this appears at 242c2, where Socrates describes love as a god or divine being, θεὸς ἤ τι θεῖον. Gods and divine beings are, of course, immortal by nature. Later, at 256a–e, Socrates dwells at greater length on the immortality of love. According to him, not even death puts an end to it. The ἐράστης and ἐρώμενος who restrain their wanton steeds throughout life afterwards stand together like victors at Olympia.[28] And even those pairs which yielded to temptation during their earthly lives "no more return to the dark pathways beneath the earth, but ... walk together in a life of shining bliss, and [are] furnished in due time with like plumage the one to the other."[29] Thus the ἔρως uniting lovers is imperishable, just like the soul of the proof.

Soul and love are not the only self-moving entities in the *Phaedrus*, however. Just as he redefines love for his companion, Socrates also undertakes to redefine rhetoric. Indeed, Asmis has argued that "the underlying theme that binds the whole dialogue is ... Plato's new definition of rhetoric as a certain *psychagōgia*."[30] More precisely, Socrates describes rhetoric as a ψυχαγωγία τις διὰ λόγων (261a7). This phrase implies that words (λόγοι) have the ability to move (ἄγω) the soul (ψυχή). As such they too constitute a source of motion. And once again, under the terms of the proof, only that which moves itself can impart motion to others. Thus insofar as λόγοι are an ἀρχή of motion, they are self-moving. Phaedrus makes this clear later on at 276a8. Here he describes λόγος as both ζῶν (living) and ἔμψυχος (ensouled), borrowing terminology from the proof. For once, Socrates is quick to agree with his young friend: παντάπασι

---

[27] Griswold 1986: 79, noting this point, asks "might 'soul' and 'eros' be different names for the same entity?" Cf. Blyth 1997: 214.

[28] 256b3–7.

[29] 256d6–e2.

[30] Asmis 1986: 154.

μὲν οὖν, he replies: you bet. At one point, Socrates even jokes about the self-moving nature of λόγος. At 260e–261a he personifies the arguments under discussion, and claims that he hears them approaching and speaking. He goes so far as to address them in the vocative, saying "Come hither, then, you worthy creatures, and impress upon Phaedrus, who is so blessed in his offspring, that unless he gets on with his philosophy he will never get on as a speaker on any subject." (Πάριτε δή, θρέμματα γενναῖα).[31] There is real substance to this conceit of argument as living creature. As Socrates later notes, λόγος proper is able to defend itself, knowing to whom it should speak and to whom it should say nothing.[32] Thus by the standards of the proof λόγος is also a self-moving ἀρχή of motion.

And like soul and love, λόγος is immortal. Indeed, the dialogue is all about the permanence of λόγος. It begins with Phaedrus attempting to prolong the life of Lysias' speech, memorizing the manuscript wholesale.[33] Later on, the very existence of speech in written form becomes an issue. According to Socrates, the Egyptian god Theuth, the inventor of writing, intended it as a permanent repository of human wisdom. King Thamus, however, took a dimmer view of the matter, terming it a spur to forgetfulness.[34] At 275c6 Socrates too takes issue with those who imagine that writing is necessarily something of lasting value, τι σαφὲς καὶ βέβαιον. On the contrary, he claims that written λόγοι can do no more than serve as a reminder to those already knowledgeable about the subject at hand. According to him, written λόγοι are far from immortal. Their longevity is pegged to human longevity; they will survive only as long as knowledgeable people do. In addition to being potentially short-lived, written λόγοι tend to be short-sighted. Among their faults Socrates lists the following: they are unable to answer questions; they repeat the same thing over and over; they are indiscrimate in their approach, addressing themselves to all and sundry. Most importantly, they are unable to defend themselves if abused, but must have recourse to their human parents.[35] Written λόγος thus seems distinctly less than immortal.

Fortunately there is a different sort of λόγος. As Socrates puts it, this is the λόγος that "goes together with knowledge, and is written in the soul of the learner: that can defend itself, and knows to whom it should speak and to whom it should say nothing."[36] Here Phaedrus responds, "You mean no dead discourse, but the living speech." Precisely, says Socrates. And it is this living speech, not written words, which proves immortal. At 276b–277a Socrates proceeds to offer an analogy from the realm of farming: rightly understood, λόγοι are like seeds. If geared to the right sort of soil, and properly planted and raised, they do not remain barren, but multiply. This strain of λόγοι is hearty, able to both fend for itself and reward its sower. And in its production of new seed descended from itself, this varietal is immortal. According to Socrates, each individual, spoken λόγος which is based on knowledge and planted in

---

[31] 261a3.
[32] 276a5–7.
[33] 228b–d.
[34] 274c–275b.
[35] 275d4–e5.
[36] 276a5–7.

an appropriate soul contains the seed of life within it, and will live forever via its off-spring. So in the end, λόγος proper proves to be like love and soul: all three are self-moving, immortal sources of motion.

Viewed as a whole, the *Phaedrus* is a dialogue about many things. Yet philosophically speaking, perhaps its most important feature is the formal introduction of the procedures known as collection (συναγωγή) and division (διαίρεσις). The former allows us to "bring a dispersed plurality under a single form, seeing it all together"[37]; the latter enables us to "divide [something] into forms, following the objective articulation."[38] Taken together, the two activities constitute dialectic, and form the basis of our human ability to speak and think. Moreover, as Socrates notes at 265d, they are extremely useful when it comes to definitions. As we have seen, the *Phaedrus* attempts to redefine both love and λόγος. It also proceeds according to the methods of collection and division. Consider its widely divergent accounts of love. First, there is the cool, bloodless transaction described by Lysias. Next comes the blasphemous version put forward by Socrates, under which love is that "irrational desire pursuing the enjoyment of beauty" and defeating "the judgment that leads to right conduct."[39] Then there is the love of the palinode, that divine μανία sent as a gift from heaven for the advantage of lover and beloved alike.[40] And of course there is, to adapt a phrase from Ferrari, "the background which won't stay background"[41]: the relationship to which attention is drawn time and again, that between Phaedrus and Socrates. Indeed, as Socrates notes somewhat humorously, the redefined ἔρως which emerges proves so unfamiliar that it is practically unrecognizable to someone brought up among sailors![42] The dialogue likewise offers very different sorts of λόγοι.[43] First, there is the sober manuscript of Lysias, recited aloud. Next we get Socrates' forced variation on a theme, shaped according to probability and pitched to popular belief.[44] Finally there is the full palinode, spoken under divine μανία and geared specifically to Phaedrus. This spoken word which knows how to address itself to a particular soul and to answer questions is a far cry from the lifeless, written word proclaiming its ostensible "truths" to all and sundry. Thus in the dialogue Plato uses the procedures of collection and division to refine our understanding of both love and λόγος.

Arguably the most important feature of the resulting redefinitions is reciprocity. In love proper, Socrates claims, the ἔρως of each ἐράστης is matched by the ἀντέρως of the ἐρώμενος. Just as the sight of the beloved stirs new growth in the soul of the lover, so too the beloved's soul grows underneath corresponding emanations from the lover.[45] As Halperin notes, it is only when ἔρως and ἀντέρως meet that "both members

---

[37] 265d3.

[38] 265e1–2. Hackforth's translation of the word ἄρθρα as "forms" seems unnecessarily leading.

[39] 238b8–c4.

[40] 245b5–c1.

[41] Cf. Ferrari 1987: 3, 21.

[42] 243c2–d1.

[43] Cf. Asmis 1986: 154 on the dialogue's redefinition of ψυχαγωγία.

[44] Note the use of the phrase ἐξ εἰκότος at 238e2.

[45] 255b–d. Note especially Socrates' description of the ἐρώμενος as εἴδωλον ἔρωτος ἀντέρωτα ἔχων (255d8).

of the relationship become active, desiring lovers."[46] On this understanding, ἔρως is relational: it is not desire on one person's part, but rather a complex web of love and counterlove requiring the active involvement of both ἐράστης and ἐρώμενος. Similarly, λόγος properly understood involves reciprocity. Λόγος is not really any one word or speech, but rather a complex set of interwoven relationships among various λόγοι. In short, λόγος proper is dialectic, in which each individual λόγος ultimately derives its importance from its relationships with its conflicting, competing, yet ultimately complementary neighbors. Just as ἔρως only makes sense in the context of ἀντέρως, so too the palinode requires the presence of Lysias' manuscript and Socrates' first speech.

The *Phaedrus* seeks to refine our understanding of soul as well as of love and λόγος. Once again, reciprocity is crucial. The proof under discussion here began with the statement ψυχὴ πᾶσα ἀθάνατος. There the phrase πᾶσα ψυχή suggested that the argument had a bearing on individual souls, without however barring the possibility of a collective meaning as well. Love proper is a combination consisting of ἔρως and ἀντέρως, and λόγος proper a set of individual λόγοι which correspond and interact with each other. This suggests that the ψυχὴ πᾶσα of the proof should similarly be understood as a collective term referring to the complex set of relationships among particular souls. Treated as a group, ψυχαί are an immortal, self-moving source of motion. Yet viewed individually, these particular souls can be passive (moved) as well as active (self-moving), and are interdependent rather than self-sufficient.

One of the *Phaedrus'* essential charms is that it does not simply state its views; it represents them, in all their complexity, before our eyes. As Lebeck put it, the dialogue "is what it discusses, exemplifies what it advocates, awakens the reactions which it describes."[47] With regard to love, a tableau of erotic reciprocity emerges from Plato's pages. Socrates is captivated by his companion's shining beauty; Phaedrus in turn is warmed by Socrates' attentions, and begins to rethink his previous preference for the cool, calculating non-lover over the manic, mantic ἐράστης. Indeed, as Socrates embarks on his palinode, he asks Phaedrus: "Where is that boy I was talking to? He must listen to me once more, and not rush off to yield to his non-lover before he hears what I have to say." Phaedrus' response is quite simply electrifying: "Here he is, quite close beside you, whenever you want him."[48]

The dialogue demonstrates its commitment to dialectic reciprocity in like manner. For it is conversation with Socrates that leads Phaedrus to abandon his original devotion to the written word; speeches and counter-speeches, questions and anwers transform him into a disciple of the living λόγος. The dialogue began with Phaedrus praising Lysias' manuscript to the skies. It ends with him taking an implicit rebuke back to the orator. As Socrates says, "if he has done his work with a knowledge of the truth, can defend his statements when challenged, and can demonstrate the inferiority

---

[46] Halperin 1986: 68.
[47] Lebeck 1972: 267.
[48] 243e4–8.

of his writing out of his own mouth,"[49] then he should be called a philosopher. Otherwise he is nothing more than a twister of words, a cutter and paster of phrases.

Finally, the *Phaedrus* presents a picture of psychic reciprocity. Socrates prefaced his proof for the immortality of the soul by citing the need to examine both the πάθη and the ἔργα of the soul, its experiences and doings. And in practice both characters are at once active and passive. Under the influence of Phaedrus, Socrates abandons his customary orbit, the city, and goes for a walk amid the trees and open country that he claims teach him nothing. Indeed, Socrates tells Phaedrus "if you proffer me volumes of speeches I don't doubt you can cart me all around Attica, and anywhere else you please."[50] Phaedrus and his concealed speech have clearly set Socrates in motion, body and soul. Yet Socrates in turn stirs Phaedrus to intellectual movement with respect to love and λόγος. Early on, Phaedrus found both Lysias'speech and its non-lover delightful. But by the end of the dialogue he is a changed man, content to let Socrates' prayer to Pan speak for him as well. "Make it a prayer for me too," he says, "since friends have all things in common."[51] The dramatic interactions of Phaedrus and Socrates thus constitute an example of psychic reciprocity. Individually, each is both mover and moved; taken together, they form a larger self-moving entity.

Motion is clearly an important structuring element for Plato the literary artist. Often he frames his dialogues with remarks about motion, remarks which sometimes take on increased significance as the works wear on. In *Euthyphro*, Euthyphro begins by asking Socrates why he has left the Lyceum for the Royal Stoa.[52] In *Menexenus*, Socrates greets Menexenus by asking him whether he is coming from the agora.[53] In *Protagoras* a companion asks Socrates where he is coming from.[54] In *Lysis* Hippothales asks Socrates not only where he has been, but where he is going.[55] And of course there is the famous beginning to the *Republic*, Socrates' statement "I went down to the Piraeus yesterday ...."[56]

Even amidst this crowd of programmatic, framing remarks about motion, the *Phaedrus* stands out. It begins with Socrates' call for Phaedrus to reexamine the direction he is heading: Ὦ φίλε Φαῖδρε, ποῖ δὴ καὶ πόθεν; he asks. ("Where do you come from, Phaedrus my friend, and where are you going?")[57] The men then take turns leading each other through the landscape, commenting on its features as they pass. Soon they reach the plane tree and sit; physical immobility sets in and is reinforced by Socrates' δαιμόνιον and the noonday heat. But the physical immobility is balanced by continuous mental activity spurred on by the cicadas. Only when erotic, dialectical, and psychic bonds have been formed between Phaedrus and Socrates does

---

[49] 278c5.
[50] 230d7.
[51] 279c6.
[52] 2a1.
[53] 234a1.
[54] 309a1.
[55] 203a7.
[56] 327a1.
[57] 227a1.

the dialogue come to a close. Having chosen a course they agree upon, the two pray to Pan and depart together. What began as a chance meeting between two individuals headed in the (for them) wrong direction ends with joint, self-directed motion back to the polis. Ἴωμεν, says Socrates. ("Let us go.")

WORKS CITED

Asmis, E. 1986. "*Psychagogia* in Plato's *Phaedrus*." *ICS* 11: 153–172.
Barnes, J. 1982. *The Pre-Socratic Philosophers*. London.
Bett, R. 1986. "Immortality and the Nature of the Soul in the *Phaedrus*." *Phronesis* 31: 1–26.
Blyth, D. 1997. "The Ever-Moving Soul in Plato's *Phaedrus*." *AJPh* 118: 185–217.
Decleva Caizzi, F. 1970. "ΑΕΙΚΙΝΗΤΟΝ Ο ΑΥΤΟΚΙΝΗΤΟΝ?" *Acme* 23: 91–97.
Demos, R. 1968. "Plato's Doctrine of the *Psyche* as a Self-Moving Motion." *JHPh* 6: 133–145.
Ferrari, G.R.F. 1987. *Listening to the Cicadas: A Study of Plato's Phaedrus*. Cambridge.
Frutiger, P. 1976. *Les mythes de Platon: Étude philosophique et littéraire*. New York.
Griswold, C.L. 1986. *Self-Knowledge in Plato's Phaedrus*. New Haven.
Guthrie, W.K.C. 1975. *A History of Greek Philosophy*. Vol. IV. Cambridge.
Hackforth, R. 1952. *Plato's Phaedrus*. Cambridge.
Halperin, D. 1986. "Plato and Erotic Reciprocity." *ClAnt* 5: 61–80.
Henderson, J. 1975. *The Maculate Muse: Obscene Language in Attic Comedy*. New Haven.
Lebeck, A. 1972. "The Central Myth of Plato's *Phaedrus*." *GRBS* 13: 267–290.
Nussbaum, M. 1986. *The Fragility of Goodness*. Cambridge.

3

Drinking from the Sources:
John Barton's *Tantalus* and the Epic Cycle

Deborah Boedeker

In the fall of 2000, the Denver Performing Arts Center presented the premiere of *Tantalus*, a new version of the Trojan War story, adapted from the ten-play cycle by British playwright John Barton and directed by Sir Peter Hall and Edward Hall. Following its successful three-month run in Denver, *Tantalus* moved to the U.K., where it played at several regional theaters in early 2001, ending in May with a run at the Barbicon in London. Because of the exceptional length, expense and other demands of the production, it is not likely to be staged again soon.[1] I will focus in this essay on one of *Tantalus'* most striking features (at least for classicists): the relationship of the plays to their ancient sources. The cycle continually reverts to a self-conscious intertextual dialogue, richly learned and playful, with the ancient variants – many of them relatively obscure – that inform it. I offer this contribution in fond tribute to my colleague Alan Boegehold, whose continuing engagement with Greek culture old and new so admirably demonstrates how to join scholarly and creative interests.

Barton's *Tantalus* consists of ten plays – *Apollo, Telephus, Iphigenia, Neoptolemus, Priam, Odysseus, Cassandra, Hermione, Helen, Erigone* – each requiring about an hour and a half to perform, with a briefer Prologue and Epilogue. The cycle covers events relating to the Trojan saga, beginning with the conception of Helen, and ending with the "post-Oresteia" fates of Orestes, Iphigenia, and the offspring of Clytemnestra and Aegisthus. The ancient fabula is framed by a simple plot, set in the present, in which a "Chorus" of nine young women on a barren beach encounter a strange Poet, who promises to tell them unfamiliar versions of the well-known myths (Prologue, p. 15). As his tales are played out, the group becomes increasingly engaged with the stories; at the end of the fourth play (*Neoptolemus*, pp. 220–21) they deliberately enter into the staged actions as the chorus of Trojan Women, and retain this persona through most of the production.

The *Tantalus* performed in Denver and the U.K. was adapted from Barton's work

---

[1] See the account of *Tantalus'* producer Michael Kustow on the challenges of finding funds and venues for the cycle (Kustow 2000: 3–75). Barton's script, *Tantalus: Ten New Plays on Greek Myths*, has been published by Oberon Books (London, 2000). All citations from *Tantalus* refer to this version, unless otherwise noted.

by playwright Colin Teevan in collaboration with Peter Hall.[2] The performance version is shorter than Barton's script by about a third, though it still requires some ten hours to perform,[3] and varies from it in a number of ways, especially, as we shall see, at the end of the production. The changes provoked a well-publicized split between playwright and director in the summer of 2000, after collaborations between the two that had spanned five decades. Barton reportedly was not consulted about Hall's extensive cuts and emendations, withdrew from the undertaking during rehearsals in Denver, and insisted that the production be billed as an "adaptation" of his work.[4]

The nature of the disagreement, as it happens, is ironically appropriate to the subject matter, for *Tantalus* is full of talk about differing versions of the tales told, and the difficulty of deciding among them. In Barton's opening scene, the young women recall conflicting myths about the birth of the world – from Ocean, from fire, from Chaos, from a parthenogenic dance of Eurynome(!)[5] – and reflect:

> But these stories can't all be true
> – Why not? – They are only stories.
> (Prologue, p. 13)

When the Poet comes on the scene, the very first tale he tells is of Leda and the amorous Zeus-swan, who produce the egg from which Helen would be born. The women of the chorus, however, know a different version:

> Wait! That's not how it was.
> Everyone knows that Zeus
> Begot this egg on Nemesis
> And it dropped down from the moon.
> ….
> Both stories cannot be true;
> It must be one or the other.

But the Poet counters:

> Why? With all the best stories
> Each version may well be the true one.
> (Prologue, p. 22)

---

[2] The premiere staging of *Tantalus* in Denver was accompanied by much fanfare, and also by several effective ways of involving audience members who wanted more information and engagement with the production. A website (http://www.dcpa.org/Tantalus/) and printed brochure provided background material, written by Barbara Mackay, on the Trojan War and related myths, as well as on the production itself. The DCPA also sponsored two public events on October 29 and 30, 2000 (in which I was invited to participate by the organizer, John Gibert of the University of Colorado at Boulder): an open discussion of the performance, held on the morning between the first and second days of performance; and a symposium in which short papers were given on topics related to the production. (My symposium paper raised many of the points discussed here.) Hundreds of theater-goers attended each of these events, which were marked by a very high degree of critical discussion. See Gibert 2000–01 for a more detailed summary, and Foley 2001 for general assessment of the performance.

[3] In Denver, some performances took place within the span of a single day, with meals served in the theater during intermissions; others were spread over two or even three days.

[4] See the account in Whitley 2000.

[5] See p. 31 below.

The culmination of *Tantalus'* play with conflicting variants comes in the ninth episode (*Helen*), with a formal trial to determine the truth about Helen and Paris. The Chorus, playing angry Greek women, accuse Helen at a trial held in Delphi with the prophet Calchas presiding. Did she "really" cause the war by going to Troy with Paris (as is assumed in the Homeric epics and most other ancient sources), or was she instead spirited away chastely to Egypt, while only her phantom went to Troy (a variant first attested in Stesichorus frr. 192–193 *PMG*)?[6] Helen defends herself by remembering how, at Hera's behest, Hermes carried her off to Egypt, where she waited all those years for Menelaus to retrieve her (*Helen*, pp. 441–43). Calchas judges that there are indeed two Helens, an explanation that satisfies Helen's loving husband Menelaus even as it baffles the plaintiffs.[7] Helen herself is soon transformed into a star (pp. 448–50) in seeming proof of her innocence – or is it only because of her filiation to Zeus? Again, the "truth" of the matter cannot be fully resolved.

Such uncertainty is very different from the tone of Homeric epic, which strives to give an authoritative version of the heroic past. Plato's little dialogue *Ion* purports to describe the desired effect from the perspective of a professional performer of epic. The rhapsode Ion explains to Socrates how convincingly he performs for his audience: "Whenever I tell a pitiful tale, my eyes fill with tears; and when I tell something frightening or amazing, my hair bristles with fear, and my heart leaps... I see them [my audience] from my platform every time, crying or looking amazed, astounded by what I am saying" (*Ion* 535c–e). There is no questioning of the narrative in such a performance, where dramatic illusion is the key to success, according to the savvy and successful rhapsode. The *Odyssey* itself provides another description of the ideal singer-audience relationship. After Odysseus tells his great tale of wanderings, there is a hushed pause among his Phaeacian hosts: "Thus he spoke, and all grew silent; they were held in rapture through the shadowy halls" (*Odyssey* 13.1–2).

Homeric narrative, then, is typically marked by an omniscient narrative voice, one that represses different versions of the story to establish its own authority with the audience.[8] Athenian tragedies, for all their meta-theatrical references, likewise tend to provide a seamless dramatic illusion that does not overtly raise questions about whether the story "really" happened in some other way. In *Tantalus*, however, so far from suppressing the notion of alternative versions, Barton thematizes the very notion of variance.

Recognizing that a story can be told in different ways, however, is a feature already known in some ancient genres. Stesichorus' "Palinode," for example, in which the

---

[6] Gantz 1993: 574–76 provides a useful discussion of the variants. The version that Helen went instead to Egypt is of course developed at length in Euripides' *Helen*, where it is presented as the "true" version of events, in contrast to the "erroneous" notion of Menelaus and other Greeks that Helen was at Troy. Cf. also Herodotus 2.113–20.

[7] As discussed below, Hall's version diverges quite markedly from Barton's at this point.

[8] In a recent dissertation (Marks 2001), James Marks argues convincingly that the composer/performer of Homeric epic, aware of competing versions of the story he is telling, may devalue alternative versions by casting them as lies (such as the lies Odysseus tells involving his sojourns in Crete and West Greece), or as events that might have happened but did not.

narrator declares that Helen never went to Troy, takes as its starting point the fact that she was *said* to have gone off with Paris. In a passage that raises questions about the reliability of inspired poetic knowledge, the *Theogony* describes Hesiod's encounter with Muses who declare that they can tell both the truth and lies like the truth (*Theog.* 26–8).

Almost too appropriately, one famous example of ancient "source criticism" concerns Tantalus himself. In his most celebrated victory ode, Pindar protests that a particular myth is too brutal and blasphemous to be true. Tantalus was supposed to have fed his own son Pelops to the gods, to see whether they would recognize that they were being served human flesh – and Demeter absentmindedly took a bite. Not so, says Pindar; instead, Poseidon fell in love with Pelops at a banquet hosted by Tantalus, and carried the boy off to Olympus; Tantalus' jealous neighbors made up the story that Pelops' father had served him up to the gods (*Olympian* 1.25–52). In having his narrator openly discuss the accuracy of variant versions, Barton has taken a cue from ancient sources such as Stesichorus, Pindar, and Hesiod, though unlike them (at least the former two), he eschews presenting one version as correct at the expense of another.

Linked with the problem of multiple variants is *Tantalus'* recurrent discussion of the "sources" of story, often represented by springs of water. Two streams, Lethe and Mnemosyne, 'Forgetting' and 'Remembering,' appear in the Prologue (p. 13) and resurface frequently during the work. The Poet encourages the women on the beach to help themselves to both sources, before he begins to perform:

> If you were to drink of the streams
> You'd forget the moment you live in
> And remember all you have lost.
>   (Prologue, p. 16)

Those who drink from these sources become better able to enter into the stories. From time to time in Barton's version, actors hesitant or confused about playing the roles of mythical characters are told to drink from the streams. This happens amusingly in the Prologue when three male actors, rough and unformed, show themselves reluctant to play the role of Paris judging the three goddesses: one declares that Aphrodite makes him nervous, another wants to give the apple to Athena, the third declares that it may be a bad idea to judge among goddesses at all. The Poet and Chorus order the men to drink from the streams, and the story proceeds (Prologue, pp. 33–5).

The published version of *Tantalus* is full of visual and verbal puns about partaking of the sources, some of them along the lines of *in vino veritas*. Though the theme was less conspicuous in Hall's performed version in Denver, it was still suggested in the wine bottles that appeared in many scenes, as well as with a little "Castalian Spring" from which witnesses were made to drink before they addressed the tribunal in Delphi. In that scene, the accusation and judgement of Helen,[9] Apollo's authoritarian prophet Calchas insists on using correct sources in his quest to separate truth from fiction. "It

---

[9] See further below, pp. 35–36.

is true; it is in the sources," he says (p. 426), when Menelaus reminds him that Aethra, Theseus' mother and a witness in the trial, was taken to Troy with Helen. "It too is in the sources," he notes (p. 432), to confirm Aethra's tale of her rape by Poseidon. Later, he warns the Chorus (p. 445), "Never quote unsound sources," when they report that Hermione told them it was not Clytemnestra who killed Agamemnon. The Poet, like the playwright himself, treats the sources more democratically than Calchas at this point. He draws from all kinds without pronouncing on their reliability, and especially enjoys the contradictions and gaps between them.

While *Tantalus* is unquestionably both new and innovative, Barton has derived almost every turn of his plot from ancient Greek literary sources. For example, the tradition (mentioned above) that Helen's mother was Nemesis rather than Leda, known to the women of the Chorus (Prologue, p. 22), is attested in the Cyclic epic *Kypria* (frr. 9–10 *PEG*) and elsewhere. Even the Chorus' bizarre creation myth – that Eurynome danced into being a snake-partner with whom she propagated – seems to be based on a cosmogonic song of Orpheus in the *Argonautica*, where Eurynome and Ophion (whose name suggests *ophis* 'snake') were said to rule on Olympus in the time before Rheia and Kronos.[10]

Some of Barton's sources are more obvious and famous than these lesser-known traditions. Four of his plays, *Iphigenia, Odysseus, Cassandra*, and *Hermione*, are based on Euripidean tragedies that dramatize the fates of women before and after the Trojan War: *Iphigenia at Aulis, Trojan Women, Hecuba,* and *Andromache*. (The Greek sources used here and elsewhere are alluded to literally but rather opaquely, as characters occasionally speak lines of the original.[11]) Even where he is closest to Euripides, however, Barton's adaptations are loose, aimed at a different sensibility as well as different theatrical conventions. For example, in *Tantalus* the horrors of war are dramatized most strikingly by physical violence against the women of Troy, who are stripped by their conquerors and branded as slaves (*Odysseus*, pp. 286–91, a distressingly prolonged and brutal scene in Hall's Denver production[12]). In Euripides' *Trojan Women*, the captives focus much more on the annihilation of their city and loved ones.

Differences in tone and content have led to some invidious comparisons between Barton's work and its Euripidean predecessors.[13] The most sustained negative review I have seen comes from Marianne McDonald, herself an advocate of and expert in modern performances of ancient works. McDonald's pointed criticisms provide insight into *Tantalus'* differences from ancient versions of the myths it explores. She faults Barton's and Hall's lack of an ethical focus, a consistent story, a cathartic

---

[10] Cf. Apollonius, *Argonautica* 1.503–6.

[11] E.g. at *Priam* p. 265, Cassandra speaks in Greek her ironic hymenaeal from *Trojan Women* 308–13, while Neoptolemus as "Pyrrha," preparing his fatal seduction of Priam, gives the speech in English.

[12] See further McDonald 2001: 103 and below, n. 25.

[13] E.g. Nightingale 2000 describes *Odysseus* as "very close but sadly inferior to Euripides' *Trojan Women.*" Billington 2000, too sharply characterizing *Tantalus* as "entirely Barton's own work," in contrast to Barton's 1980 production *The Greeks*, where "seven of the ten plays came from Euripides," concludes, "With all due respect, [Barton] is not a genius on the Euripidean scale."

experience, a sympathetic character (though it should be said that Agamemnon, at least, came across positively to most reviewers).[14] In all these respects, as McDonald points out, *Tantalus* could hardly be more unlike Athenian tragedy, with its strong civic and educational function. McDonald also notes that *Tantalus* lacks the unity of most Athenian tragedies, and that it diverges at many points from ancient accounts, or even makes up new episodes.[15]

Other reviewers, in particular Daniel Mendelsohn, have proposed on the contrary that attending *Tantalus* resembles in some ways the ancient Athenians' participation in the City Dionysia, thanks to the long performance time, inevitable interactions with other audience members during breaks and meals, and not least the fact that the myths are developed in innovative ways.[16] M.D. Usher goes so far as to conclude, "The chief virtue of this massive production is that … it truly succeeds in recreating the dynamics of ancient tragic composition and performance: that is to say, the plays of *Tantalus* are not modern productions of actual tragedies, but stand creatively in relation to their sources as a Greek playwright's did to his."[17]

The innovation and lack of unity that McDonald depreciates are, as she realizes, intentional on Barton's part: his Poet tells the Chorus that he puts together stories made by others, filling in or making up "the bits that are lost and don't fit" (Prologue, p. 15–16). This process develops into an intricate dialogue between Barton's work and its sources, an implied conversation that may delight or bewilder, or in most cases simply escape, the audience.

Like Euripides, Barton relies heavily on the stories included in the Epic Cycle for bits and pieces of his plot material.[18] As the Poet tells the Chorus, his story is named "*Kyklos. Epikou cyclou leipsana*" ('Cycle. Fragments of the Epic Cycle': Prologue, p. 15). *Leipsana* is an important term here, for unlike Euripides, Barton has at hand not the Cyclic epics themselves, but only their paltry remains – and it is precisely their fragmentary state that seems to have attracted the playwright.

The Epic Cycle currently consists of the remains of a dozen or so narrative poems composed in the style of Homeric epic, which at some point in antiquity were collected and arranged to give a long, uneven "chronological" account of events from the marriage of Earth and Sky all the way to the end of the Heroic Age. Attributed to a number of composers, the poems of the Epic Cycle are generally considered later than, and also poetically inferior to, the *Iliad* or *Odyssey*.[19] The former view has been challenged recently by Jonathan Burgess, among others, arguing that the epics which eventually were collected in the Cycle evolved in performance traditions parallel to

---

[14] McDonald 2001: 90–91 and *passim*.

[15] McDonald 2001: 91 (civic ideals), 90–91 and *passim* (unity), 93 and *passim* (divergent and new accounts).

[16] Mendelsohn 2001.

[17] Usher 2000.

[18] See Jouan 1966.

[19] On inferiority to Homeric epic, see especially Griffin 1977, followed closely by Davies 1989. Burgess 1996 provides an interesting and critical overview of scholarship on this issue, to which should be added Chamoux 1973.

(and mutually aware of) those of the *Iliad* or *Odyssey*. The charge of poetic inferiority is revised by James Marks, who finds it preferable to speak of the Cyclic epics as less panhellenic, and thus less widely accepted, than the epics attributed to Homer.[20] Whatever the genesis of the Epic Cycle, however, what remains of it now are short prose summaries of each epic by Proclus (an epitomizer of uncertain date), collected in the *Bibliotheca* of the patriarch Photius (ninth century C.E.).[21] Proclus' summaries are supplemented in modern editions by a number of short passages, especially from the *Cypria*, that happened to be quoted or paraphrased by other ancient authors.[22] Together, these comprise the *leipsana epikou kyklou* that tantalize Barton and his Poet with their wrenchingly condensed and fragmentary state, and perhaps with their inconsistencies as well. Five of the Cyclic Epics focus directly on aspects of the Trojan War, and in them we find most of the myths that are covered in *Tantalus*, including:

> *Cypria.* The wedding of Peleus and Thetis. Theseus abducts Helen. The judgement of Paris. Paris visits Sparta and abducts Helen. The Greek kings are collected to fight at Troy (including the story of the reluctant Odysseus). The abortive Greek landing in Teuthrania results in the wounding and later healing of Telephus by Achilles. Achilles' liaison with Deidamia on Scyros. Agamemnon angers Artemis, who demands the sacrifice of Iphigenia at Aulis.
>
> *Aethiopis.* Heroic combats that took place after the death of Hector, including the death of Achilles and the awarding of his armor to Odysseus rather than Ajax. (In a witty nod to this epic, Barton's Poet is about to recount these tales to the women on the beach as the fourth play begins, but they ask him to move on to the story of the Trojan Horse: *Neoptolemus*, p. 178.)
>
> *Little Iliad.* The arms of Achilles are awarded to Odysseus. Neoptolemus is brought to Troy. Stratagem of the Wooden Horse, and pretended departure of Greeks from Troy. The Trojans bring in the Horse and celebrate. The Greeks take Troy. Neoptolemus chooses Andromache as his prize, but throws her son Astyanax from a tower.
>
> *Sack of Ilium.* The debate at Troy about what to do with the wooden horse, followed by its conveyance into the city. Return of the Greeks from Tenedos, who combine with the warriors inside the Horse to destroy the city. Neoptolemus slaughters Priam. Odysseus throws little Astyanax from the walls. Polyxena is sacrificed at Achilles' tomb. Neoptolemus takes Andromache as his war prize.
>
> *Homecomings.* What happened to the Greek kings on the way back from Troy, or after they got home, including the murders of Agamemnon and Cassandra in Mycenae. Menelaus and Helen's sojourn in Egypt, and their return to Sparta. Not least important for our purposes, this epic also included the story of Tantalus, ancestor of Agamemnon and Menelaus. He greedily obtained from Zeus a life full of pleasures like the gods', but Zeus also placed a stone over his head to prevent him from enjoying them. (The threatening stone is a constant presence in *Tantalus*.)

---

[20] Burgess 1996; Marks 2001, chapter 2.
[21] See Davies 1989: 6–7.
[22] Texts: Allen 1912: 93–144, Bernabé 1987: 1–105, Davies 1988: 13–76; most of the fragments can also be found in the Loeb edition, Evelyn-White 1936: 480–533.

The stories presented in *Tantalus* consciously mirror the inconsistencies of their sources, inconsistencies found even within Proclus' summaries of the Epic Cycle.[23] The fate of little Astyanax provides one example of how Barton expands on choppy and contradictory sources. In the *Little Iliad*, Hector's son is killed by Neoptolemus, but according to the *Sack of Ilium* it was Odysseus who threw Astyanax from the walls of Troy. Barton, evidently aware of these variants, plays it both ways: Odysseus confides to Hecuba that Neoptolemus really did the deed, but that to spare the feelings of Astyanax' mother Andromache – who has been allotted to Neoptolemus as slave and concubine – Odysseus told her that he killed the boy himself (*Odysseus*, p. 299, cf. p. 293). The (surely few) audience members intimately familiar with the fragments of the Epic Cycle may feel as if they are eavesdropping on Barton's mediation between arguing sources, as if finding a way for both of them to be true, or at least understandably mistaken.

Gaps or implausibilities in the sources inspire Barton more than once to make up a motive for an action otherwise deemed inexplicable. Thus he explains how the boy Neoptolemus (also called Pyrrhus) was able to kill Priam and many other Trojans. The Poet discusses the problem with the Chorus:

> POET: But first there is something tricky
> Which we must try to make sense of.
> Achilles' son Pyrrhus
> Was only a boy at the time,
> Yet it's said that he sacked the city
> And slaughtered Priam himself.
>
> CHORUS: But if Pyrrhus killed him
> How can he have been a boy
> – No poet is to be trusted
> On questions involving chronology.
>
> POET: Then I will tell you a story
> No other poet has told.
>
> CHORUS: Then you've made it up? – Confess it.
>
> POET: Not at all, I have made it cohere.
>   (*Neoptolemus,* pp. 178–9 [with punctuation as in the text])

In the tale that ensues, the Poet "explains" Neoptolemus' rage by saying that the young warrior, newly brought to Troy, was with difficulty persuaded by Odysseus to infiltrate the city of Troy by dressing as a girl, pretending to have been left behind as a sacrificial victim by the departing Greeks. When aged Priam takes this attractive "Pyrrha" off for rape or seduction, Neoptolemus kills him (*Priam*, pp. 276). The boy's brutal killing spree is further explained by saying that he was raped by all his fellow Greeks, after he opened the Trojan Horse and joined them inside as they waited for the

---

[23] Chamoux 1973 thinks that Proclus smoothed out the epics for his artificially "continuous" summary of them. See also Davies 1989: 60–62 on inconsistencies that occur even in Proclus' accounts.

right moment to go forth and sack the city. The rage and humiliation from this incident were channeled into his wrath against the Trojans (*Hermione*, pp. 372–4).

Here again, Barton shows himself playfully concerned with the "integrity" of his sources. Neoptolemus, compliant but humiliated, makes Odysseus promise not to reveal the cross-dressing scheme to anyone – including the poets (*Neoptolemus*, p. 206). Hence, Barton cleverly suggests, this part of the story was not known to the sources.

The tension between Barton's sources and his innovations plays out in other ways too. At the end of the *Neoptolemus* play, the nine young women decide that they want to enter the story. (In Hall's Denver production, this was an arresting scene: the Chorus members masked themselves in full view of the audience, and were transformed from outside observers to full participants.) Disgusted with the Greeks' planned deception of the Trojans, the women want to get into the play and create their own version of events. They tell the Poet: "If we went in / we would soon learn the truth of it. / We could change the whole story / Just as you have!" and are optimistic about what they will accomplish: "We are going in! / We shall make our own story" (*Neoptolemus*, p. 220). At the Poet's behest, however, the nine women once again "drink from the sources" before entering the story (*Neoptolemus*, p. 220). When we see them next, they have already adapted to the story as the sources tell it. Instead of warning the Trojans, they now behave like the Trojan women of tradition, and insist on dancing the treacherous Horse into the city (*Priam, passim*).

Along with all its play on variations and surprises, then, Barton's *Tantalus* retains allegiance to the inherited story. As in archaic epic and most tragedies, so here too, the large-scale outline of the saga is accepted: Iphigenia is sacrificed, Troy falls, the women are enslaved, Odysseus wanders, Agamemnon is killed at home. For ancient audiences, the events of the Trojan saga are treated as "facts," known by all to have happened; it would not win an audience's approval to tell the story otherwise.[24] Barton's contemporary version of the saga uses the constraints of tradition somewhat differently. His interest is not in gaining the informed audience's approval of the truth and appropriateness of his version, for many turns of plot (though guaranteed by the Poet to be "in the sources") will be unfamiliar to all but professional mythologists! Rather, the scholarly apparatus forms a frame for *Tantalus'* surprises, like the rules of a game the playwright has constructed for his Poet. No element is "allowed" unless it is preserved in some ancient source – except for material that can fill in gaps between attested events, or provide a "hidden" explanation for stories that are deemed insufficiently motivated by existing versions.

Hall's performance version diverges significantly from this constraint in its final scene. In an episode invented by Barton, but owing something to Hecuba's accusation of Helen in Euripides' *Trojan Women*, the Chorus – now playing Greek women ("Women of the West") – accuse Helen of causing the Trojan War with all its

---

[24] Cf. Marks 2001: 30. Morrison 1992 argues that Homer often comes very close to telling the story otherwise, even in the large scale, with a "reverse expression" in the form, "X would have happened had not Y occurred at just that moment."

sufferings. The plaintiffs, in Hall's version, are decidedly not held in thrall by the sources. When Helen is acquitted by Calchas, the women seek a new solution. Enraged by the verdict, they start to rip apart the oracle and attack the prophet himself.[25] Throughout the production, Calchas has spoken authoritatively about what the gods have decreed and how things must be: Iphigenia must be sacrificed, Neoptolemus must be brought to Troy to end the war, Orestes must marry Hermione. Now, at the point of being toppled from his Delphic seat, Calchas desperately warns the Chorus that they are going too far: what they are doing is "not in the sources." But Hall's Chorus, crying "To Hell with the sources!" attack and destroy Calchas together with his oracular seat (*Helen*, performance version).

In this, the final action of the performed version, the epic cycle of vengeance and destruction expands to a meta-narrative framework. The Women of the West oppose the gods, do violence to the traditional story (the "sources"), and – as the Storyteller puts it – end the Golden Age.[26] At the very end of Hall's version, the Chorus return to being nine girls on the beach. They notice that everything has changed, and want the stories to return. The Storyteller and his little entourage are departing, however, leaving them with the fable of Tantalus, the hero who tried to act like a god (perhaps like the Chorus in overturning the stories?[27]), but was punished with a stone hung over his head and food kept tantalizingly out of reach. Thanks to his abuse of the gods' gifts, Tantalus will never be able to enjoy the blessings he can still perceive.

At the end of Barton's text version of the ninth play (*Helen*), Delphi and Calchas are also destroyed, although by an earthquake rather than the angry women. A tenth play (*Erigone*) follows, however, and a very busy one it is. Soon Apollo is heard rebuilding his oracle, as he has done before (*Erigone*, pp. 464–6); the authority of tradition is being recreated. Now, in Barton's last fling with his disparate sources, narrative twists appear one after another, and are straightened out just as rapidly – always with some basis in the ancient sources.

Iphigenia comes home from the Taurians (as in Euripides' play), to reveal that she was not really Clytemnestra's and Agamemnon's daughter, but Helen's by Theseus (as in Stesichorus 191 *PMG*)[28] – and by the way she was also the mother of Achilles'

---

[25] See McDonald 2001: 103–5 and *passim*, and Foley 2001: 419–22 on the violence and irrationality repeatedly attributed to women in Hall's *Tantalus*. In addition, female characters in *Tantalus* are frequently portrayed as vulnerable to physical brutality, especially rape (a subject of numerous jokes, particularly from the character Peleus). This characteristic, present in Barton's text, was considerably exaggerated in the performance version I saw in Denver, where it attracted a good deal of negative criticism from members of the audience who participated in the public discussions of the production (see n. 2).

[26] This brings full circle the beginning of Hall's production, when the Storyteller says to the girls on the beach that he will tell them a story of how they destroyed the Golden Age.

[27] This interpretation, though I did not find it obvious in the performed version, is supplied in the program notes to Hall's final play: "The storyteller explains that the story is destroyed because they made the same mistake as Tantalus – they imagined themselves to be gods and thought they themselves could dictate the story."

[28] Here again, as with Neoptolemus' rage, Barton supplies a "motive" involving sexual deviance to explain an extreme action: Agamemnon and Iphigenia – not quite father and daughter – had loved each

son Neoptolemus (as in Duris of Samos *FGrHist* 76 F88). Now Orestes, who has just killed Neoptolemus at Delphi, is dismayed to discover that his enemy was really his (supposed) sister's son (*Erigone*, pp. 477–8). Orestes has also just killed his half-brother Aletes (p. 473), the son of Clytemnestra and Aegisthus (as in Hyginus *Fabula* 122). Despondent at the ineluctable cycle of intrafamilial violence, Orestes decides to submit to death at the hands of Aletes' sister Erigone, hoping to end the family curse (according to Apollodorus *Epitome* 6.28, Erigone prosecuted Orestes for the murder of Clytemnestra).

But enough: the old Nurse (an invention of Barton's) who had brought all these characters to birth, comes out to stop "silly" young Erigone from wielding a dangerous axe, as if oblivious to the girl's lethal intent (*Erigone*, pp. 482–3). Against all odds, the Nurse imposes a happy ending on the surviving members of the house of Atreus, by orchestrating the marriage of Orestes and Erigone (as in Apollodorus *Epitome* 6.28).

As this unlikely (but not unattested) wedding is being celebrated, the Chorus, back on the beach again, take on the names and attributes of the nine Muses. For a while they enjoy a burst of Dionysian revelry and freedom with their Poet, confounding the functions of Muses and Maenads. At length the awaited but nearly forgotten boatman, Charon-like, comes to take them back from the island where they had met the Poet and his stories. As Barton's drama closes, the audience hears birdsong and the clanking of metal, noises of nature and culture (especially, alas, warfare). In these sounds, the goddess Mnemosyne tells us, the "mind of Zeus" may sometimes be discerned (p. 510).[29] In Barton's final stage direction, the sources and the singers combine: "the streams bubble and all the Muses sing" (p. 510).

The singing of the Muses has a bittersweet cachet in *Tantalus*. Agamemnon, with Cassandra's encouragement, hears their song as he is about to leave Troy for home, and hopes, "Maybe one day what's lost/ Will be found again" (*Cassandra*, p. 363). Orestes in his misery remembers that he once heard the Muses on Pieria: this was the one thing that made him happy – almost immortal (*Erigone*, p. 476). Yet Barton is interested not only in the effect of the Muses on those who hear their songs, but also on what might inspire (new) Muses to sing. At the beginning of the drama, the Poet had chanted a little rhyme, as the Chorus drank from the streams for the first time:

> If you drink the Pierian Spring
> And close your eyes as you swallow
> You will find even mortals can sing
> As sweet and as brave as Apollo.
>   (Prologue, p. 17)

Apparently the tactic has worked: the beach girls have been transformed into Muses. Having drunk deeply of many sources (as obviously the playwright and his

---

other illicitly, and Iphigenia wanted him to kill her so as to end her love and shame (*Erigone*, pp. 474, 479).

[29] An allusion to the "plan of Zeus" that guides the action of epic. Cf. *Iliad* 1.5. Marks 2001 argues at length that the *Dios boulē* corresponds to the narrative plan in *Iliad*, *Odyssey*, and *Cypria*; a similar idea seems to inform Barton's text here as well.

dramaturge[30] did as well), they will be able to renew the old stories, drawing largely on less familiar, fragmentary versions, such as the cyclic epics.

Is this all? Marianne McDonald misses a moral lesson or uplifting emotion in *Tantalus*. The search for moral meaning is not entirely absent, however, but it too leads to the "epic cycle." When Agamemnon speaks to Cassandra of his belief that Zeus rules justly, she tells him there is no justice. Zeus himself stole power from his father, who stole it from his:

> What has happened already
> Will happen again.
> That is god-law, Agamemnon,
> And it's man-law on earth.
> Epikou Kuklou Leipsana.
>   (*Cassandra*, p. 362)

In this view, history is not a story of development, but a pattern inscribed by unchanging human nature, the ever-repeating "cycle" of wars, vengeance, suffering, betrayal. *Tantalus'* characters talk continually about doing what is "natural" or "only human": raping, looting, destroying cities, making major misjudgments in political, military, or private life. The phrase "epic cycle" comes to suggest that such actions will repeat themselves endlessly.

In Barton's text, then, there is no tragic katharsis, no lesson learned through suffering, let alone a triumph of reason and justice over tradition – no more so than in a play like Euripides' disturbing *Orestes*. Barton's sights here are trained not on moral and political improvement, though the brutality of his drama shows how desirable this might be. The "cycle" metaphor leaves little hope for progress. In place of an uplifting moral, Barton's multi-sourced, open-ended production offers a witty game, demonstrating how to rediscover, question, embellish, select from, and re-imagine the patterns of (hi)story – all while staying almost reverently within a self-imposed creative constraint, the jumbled remains of attested versions.

WORKS CITED

Allen, T.W., ed. 1912. *Homeri Opera*, vol. 5. Oxford.
Barton, J. 2000. *Tantalus: Ten New Plays on Greek Myths*. London.
Bernabé, A., ed. 1987. *Poetarum Epicorum Graecorum. Testimonia et Fragmenta*. Vol. 1. Leipzig.
Billington, M. 2000. Review of *Tantalus*, in *The Guardian*, October 24, 2000.
Burgess, J.S. 1996. "The Non-Homeric *Cypria*." *TAPhA* 126: 77–99.
Chamoux, F. 1973. "La Poésie épique après Homère." *CEA* 2: 5–29.
Davies, M., ed. 1988. *Epicorum Graecorum Fragmenta*. Göttingen.
———. 1989. *The Epic Cycle*. Bristol.
Evelyn-White, H.G., ed. and trans. 1936. *Hesiod, the Homeric Hymns and Homerica*. Rev. ed. (Loeb Classical Library). Cambridge, Mass.
Foley, H.P. 2001. "Tantalus." *AJPh* 122: 415–28.
Gantz, T. 1993. *Early Greek Myths*. 2 vols. Baltimore.

---

[30] Classicist/theater scholar Graham Ley, who consulted with Barton during the writing of *Tantalus*.

Gibert, J. 2000–01. "Tantalus and the Greeks. A World Premiere and an Academic Symposium in Denver." *CJ* 96: 207–210.

Griffin, J. 1977. "The Epic Cycle and the Uniqueness of Homer." *JHS* 97: 39–53.

Jouan, F. 1966. *Euripide et les légendes des chants cypriens, des origines de la guerre de Troie à l' "Iliade."* Paris.

Kustow, M. 2000. *Theatre @ Risk.* London.

Marks, J.R. 2001. "Divine Plan and Narrative Plan in Archaic Greek Epic." Dissertation, University of Texas at Austin.

McDonald, M. 2001. "A Classical Soap Opera for the Cultural Elite: *Tantalus* in Denver." *Arion* 3rd ser. 8: 90–114.

Mendelsohn, D. 2001. "Tragedy in Denver." *The New York Review*, January 11, 2001: 24–7.

Morrison, J.V. 1992. "Alternatives to the Epic Tradition: Homer's Challenges in the *Iliad*." *TAPhA* 122: 61–71.

Nightingale, B. 2000. Review of *Tantalus*, in *The London Times*, October 24, 2000.

Usher, M.D. 2000. "The Barton-Hall Production of *Tantalus*." *BMCR* 2000: 10.28.

Whitley, J. 2000. "Trojan Wars." *The Daily Telegraph*, "Arts and Books" section, September 30, 2000.

4

Mania and Melancholy:
Some Stoic Texts on Insanity

Margaret Graver

The moral psychology of the early Stoa might seem an odd place to look for a sensitive analysis of the phenomena now usually called mental illness. For Stoics are notorious for claiming that "all fools are insane," and notorious, also, for asserting that the vast majority of humans, clever as they might be by ordinary standards, are still, properly speaking, fools. Hence the objection of one Diogenianus, an Epicurean of perhaps the second century C.E.:

> How is this? You say that except for the wise person, there is no human being who is not equally as insane as Orestes and Alcmaeon. And that there have only been one or two wise persons – and all the rest are by reason of their imprudence just as insane as those named![1]

The objection is understandable enough, especially given the disturbing portrayals of Orestes' and Alcmaeon's mental life in Greek drama.[2] If the Stoic language about insanity is taken seriously at all, it asserts far too much, sweeping away the ordinary functional person along with the one for whom moral stricture should be replaced by medication. As a position in ethics, this is worse than useless.

But are the Stoics actually open to the criticism of Diogenianus? They are not open to it if, as I shall argue here, they made a reasonably sharp distinction between two senses of the word "insanity" (*mania*). Part of my claim is that Stoic moral psychology requires such a distinction: to fail to make it amounts to a bowing-out on moral responsibility, one of the central emphases of Stoic ethics. But I will show also that there is a difference of terminology which can serve as evidence that the conceptual distinction was in fact made. This can be traced in the usage in surviving texts of the term *melancholia,* literally "black-biliousness," a term sometimes but not always appended epexegetically to the usual *mania.* "Melancholic" insanity, I will argue, is a disruption of the capacity for rational impression; it is this which is attributed to Orestes and others like him. Significantly, *melancholia* is not attributed to non-wise

---

[1] Quoted by Eusebius, *Praep. evang.* 6.284b = *SVF* 3.668.
[2] Alcmaeon (or Alcmeon) is the son of Eriphyle and Amphiaraus; like Orestes, he kills his mother and sees the Erinyes in his subsequent madness. His experiences were a favorite subject of the tragedians; see Radt *TrGF* 4.149–50, Nauck *TrGF* 379–80.

persons generally: the charge made against them (or, I should say, against *us*) is the less startling charge of susceptibility to the *pathē,* the passions or emotions. As ordinary emotional beings we are only, as it were, "non-melancholically" insane.

The usage-pattern in question does not match either the ordinary-language vocabulary of aberrant mental states (as we find it, for instance, in Athenian comedy) or the usage of the medical writers.[3] It is rather a specialized philosophical usage, meant to reflect a significant conceptual distinction. That distinction corresponds closely to the more familiar distinction between two senses of the word "rational" (*logikos*).[4] To say that a person is insane might be to deny that she is rational in that basic descriptive sense in which rationality characterizes the minds of adult humans, but not those of animals or very young children. Or it might be to deny that she is rational in a stricter, normative sense, in which to be rational is to think and act in accordance with universal right reason. It is the former or descriptive sense of "rational" which carries with it moral accountability. Like Aristotle, the Stoics find it expedient to demarcate a class of behaviors and experiences which fall short of even this minimum standard and for which agents may be absolved of responsibility.[5] The term *melancholia* serves to mark that boundary.

But it is emphatically not part of the Stoic program to offer a blanket excuse for the behavior of humans in general: if anything, this ethics seeks to expand the scope of responsibility by insisting on the rational character of many actions which ordinary intuition tends to excuse as emotion-driven.We might well wonder, then, why Stoics should wish to say that ordinary persons are insane at all. Given the centrality of moral responsibility in their ethics, we might have expected them merely to insist that all those whom ordinary intuition regards as *compos mentis* must remain accountable for every exercise of their (garden-variety) rational nature, even for the most violent of their emotional impulses. Yet what we find is that while these philosophers do maintain this, they also assert that this ordinary susceptibility to emotion is properly described with a term which in ordinary Greek would excuse the agent from accountability. We should seek a motive for this latter assertion.

I suggest here, tentatively, that the Stoics' flamboyantly paradoxical use of *mania* to refer to the condition of humans in general is justified by an identifiable semantic link between the two senses of that term. The connection emerges clearly enough when the concept of loss of rationality is considered in the context of the school's larger theory of emotion. For although Zeno and Chrysippus deny the possibility of *akrasia* as Aristotle understands it, they also admit – and in fact emphasize – that

---

[3] For other uses of the term see Padel 1995: 47–64; Paschall 1939.

[4] Galen at *PHP* 4.2.20 attributes to Chrysippus an explicit statement of the distinction between the two senses of *logikos*, although for reasons of his own he denies that Chrysippus uses the distinction correctly.

[5] Aristotle in *EN* 7.1–6 distinguishes between ordinary vice and *thēriotēs* or brutishness. The latter is associated with a variety of subrational or post-rational states; it may consist in savagery (as of races which habitually practice cannibalism), disease *(nosos),* mental deficiency *(pērōsis),* or insanity *(mania).* Brutishness is "outside the bounds of vice" (1149a) and does far less evil than vice does, though it is also "more to be feared" in oneself (1150a). Aristotle also mentions *melancholia,* but treats it as a form of incontinence (1150b25–30, 1152a18–19, 27–29); he has in mind, apparently, a kind of excitable or peevish temperament in rational persons rather than a loss of rationality.

emotions involve a temporary loss of control by the rational mind.[6] They may believe, also, that repeated or especially intense episodes of certain emotions can actually bring on that complete loss of rationality which is melancholic insanity. The semantic association between *mania* and emotion will in that case serve as a warning to the hearers both of things present and of things to come.

THE MADNESS OF ORESTES

Let us consider first a pair of Greek sources which mention Orestes, with his vision of avenging Furies, as a paradigm of insanity, and which use the term *melancholia* to name his condition. The more informative of these is Aetius, *Placita Philosophorum* 4.12.4–6 *(SVF* 2.54). Aetius is summarizing some earlier account of Chrysippus's distinction among four similar terms concerned with the reception of impressions. *phantasia, phantaston, phantastikon,* and *phantasma.* The *phantasia* is the usual mental impression, and the *phantaston* is related to it as the existent object or state of affairs concerning which the impression is formed. (In this context, what is meant must be a simple perceptual object, e.g., a table, or the fact that the table is flat.) The *phantastikon* and *phantasma* are also related as mental experience and object of experience, but with an important difference:

> The *phantastikon* is an empty attraction, a mental experience which comes about without there being anything to produce the impression, as in the case of one who fights with shadows and punches at emptiness. For a *phantasia* has something underlying it, but the *phantastikon* has nothing. The *phantasma* is that to which we are attracted in the empty attraction which is the *phantastikon.*

The mental experience called *phantastikon* is qualitatively similar to *phantasia*, for here, too, it seems to one that a certain thing is present or is the case (compare D.L. 7.51). But in this case that seeming is not merely false, i.e. not merely inaccurate in its representation of the world, but "empty": the thing that seems present as if with the approximate veridicality of perception is in fact not present at all, not even under some other description.

Such are the mental impressions of the insane. Aetius continues:

> This happens in the case of those who are melancholic and insane. At least, when Orestes in the tragedy says,
>
>> Mother, I beg you, do not set upon me
>> those maidens bloody-faced and snakelike,

---

[6] The nature of the available evidence for Stoic thought frequently precludes mention of specific philosophers: if our sources often speak loosely of "the Stoics" we should be willing to do the same. I do however confess my inclination to believe that the "Stoic" moral psychology discussed in this article is in all essentials the moral psychology of Zeno of Citium, as explicated and in some points developed by Chrysippus in the late third century. Some scholars (most recently Sorabji 2000: 55–65) have argued for a sharp divide between Zeno and Chrysippus on some issues including the possibility of *akrasia;* if this view is accepted, the description of Stoic thought here should be understood to refer to Chrysippus's thought in particular.

for they – they are leaping nearer to me!

he speaks as one who is mad, and sees nothing, but only thinks he sees. Hence Electra tells him,

> Stay calmly in your bed, poor thing;
>> you are not seeing any of those things that seem so clear to you.[7]

So also with Theoklymenos in Homer.

Orestes is "attracted" to his Fury, not of course in the sense of wanting to pursue her, but in that the nature of his mental experience entices him to believe that she is really there, and to pursue a course of action in relation to her. Theoklymenos in *Odyssey* 20.345–70 is similarly given to hallucination: his vision of blood speckling the banquet-hall and ghosts thronging the courtyard is indeed validated by the poet-narrator, but is assumed by others present to be evidence of an altered mental state.

Sextus Empiricus appears to be familiar with the same Stoic discussion. A passage in *Adversus Mathematicos* 7 again invokes Orestes as an instance of hallucination:

> Among persuasive impressions some are true, some false, some both true and false, some neither true nor false. The true ones are those of which one can make a true assertion, as that "it is day" or "it is light," when it is; the false ones are those of which one can make a false assertion, as that the oar is bent underwater or that the colonnade narrows to a point; the ones which are both true and false are such as Orestes in his madness received from Electra. For in that it was as from a real thing, it was true, since Electra was real, but in that it was as from a Fury, it was false, for she was not a Fury. Likewise, if someone in sleep dreams one [i.e. an impression] from Dion (Dion being alive) as from one standing next to him, that is false and an empty attraction.

> ... Among true impressions, some are graspable, others not. The non-graspable ones are those which are received by persons in a diseased condition. For very many of those who have phrenitis and *melancholia* have an impression which is true, but not graspable; rather it comes upon them in this way by chance, so that frequently they are unsure about it and do not assent.[8]

Sextus's account differs in some respects from that of Aetius: in particular, his claim that Orestes's impression is "both true and false" is not easily reconciled with his description of it as an "empty attraction."[9] For present purposes, however, such differences are less significant than is the fact that both sources describe a variety of mental experience which is both highly counter-functional and highly unusual. A person who cannot distinguish between impressions representing existent objects and impressions

---

[7] The quotations are from Euripides, *Orestes* 255–59.

[8] Sextus Empiricus, *AM* 7.243–45, 247.

[9] Pigeaud 1987: 102–106 understands Sextus to be making a distinction between the impression which represents nothing at all (and is therefore "empty," as in Aetius) and the mis-struck impression (*paratupōtikas*) which comes from an existent object but is not in accordance with that object; his example of the latter is Heracles' slaying of his own children for those of Eurystheus (*AM* 7.405, 8.67). But I am not convinced that any Stoic author makes a distinction between Orestes' experience and that of Heracles.

representing nothing at all has lost the characteristic human capacity to receive and process information from the world, and with it the capacity to speak and act appropriately. And one does not meet such people every day. Aetius names just two persons who have been insane; Sextus names only Orestes and, a little further on, Heracles.[10]

Melancholia comes up again in a group of three passages relating what seems to be Chrysippus's position on the loss of virtue. One of these is found in Diogenes Laertius 7.127:

> Chrysippus says that virtue can be lost; Cleanthes that it cannot. The one says that it can be lost through drunkenness and *melancholia,* the other that it cannot be lost because of secure grasps.

A passage in Simplicius gives additional detail on the Chrysippan view:

> Even the Stoics admit that in *melancholiai* and drowsiness and lethargies and in taking medications there is loss of the entire rational condition and along with it virtue itself. [In this case, they say,] vice does not come in to replace it, but the security is relaxed and lapses into what the ancients call the "middle condition."[11]

Diogenes' wording would seem to suggest that there was a clearcut difference of opinion between Cleanthes and Chrysippus on this point. In fact, though, the view reported for Chrysippus could as well be a straightforward development of the existing Stoic view. The school's basic epistemology has it that knowledge has inherent stability. The wise person is not disposed to assent to any impression which is inconsistent with the system of "grasps" he already holds, and so cannot cease to be wise by any of the usual mechanisms of impression and assent. Since virtue consists in knowledge, it, too, is *anapoblēton* or "not such as to be lost." This must be the Cleanthean position, and as far as it goes, Chrysippus would hardly disagree. But Chrysippus does make one relatively minor concession, yielding, no doubt, to dialectical pressure from the skeptical Academy. Virtue, being the perfection of rationality, does depend on the virtuous person's continuing to be a rational creature. If rationality itself can be lost through no fault of one's own, then – and only then – virtue too can be lost. And rationality can in fact be lost, through *melancholia* and also through the effects of disease, lethargy, or certain substances including alcohol. For at one level of description the mind is itself a material substance fully capable of interacting with

---

[10] *AM* 7.249. The Loeb editor (Bury 1935) suspects that Herakles is here confused with Pentheus, who is mentioned at *AM* 7.192 for his impression of a doubled Thebes and doubled sun. Cf. Eur., *Bacchae* 918–19.

[11] Simplicius, *In Aristotelis Categorias* 102a, *CIAG* 402.22–26, *SVF* 3.238. Compare the following from Alexander of Aphrodisias, *De Anima* 161.16 Bruns, *SVF* 3.239. (Alexander's tone is polemical): "Again, if it is possible for the virtuous person to become lethargic or melancholic or 'darkened' or out of his wits, in which states he cannot act in accordance with virtue, then virtue is not self-sufficient as concerns its own activities. For how can they possibly say that one who is out of his wits and needs for that reason to be tied up and to have the assistance of friends, is acting prudently at that time? Unless they merely want to protect their thesis!" Alexander is clearly familiar with the view Diogenes Laertius attributes to Chrysippus, but misunderstands (or deliberately distorts) it to imply that one can be virtuous and melancholically insane at the same time.

other material substances.[12] The stability or systematicity said to obtain among the mind's rational activities, its judgments and decisions, is merely the intentional description of a certain optimal level of tension in the mind's material substrate, the *pneuma*. If alcohol, or high fever, or laudanum, can depress the mental functioning of an ordinary person to the point where the impressions are disordered, decision-making impaired, and speech slurred, there is no reason why the mind of the wise should not be similarly affected.[13]

That *melancholia* or the excess of black bile should be mentioned as one such cause is not in itself surprising. An association between the mysterious dark humor and various more or less disordered mental states appears very early in Greek thought and remains strong in the popular imagination.[14] Hallucinations, also, are a recurring theme.[15] For the purposes of Chrysippus's argument, this is enough. His real interest is in rationality itself, with its characteristic capacity to experience and interpret certain kinds of impressions, and in the possibility that rationality may break down under certain circumstances. *Melancholia* is mentioned merely as one of several generally-recognized physical conditions which may cause such a breakdown. The physiology implied by the term is not at issue here: if it should turn out that the behaviors and experiences he has in mind are in fact caused by something other than black bile, there would be no obstacle to his adopting some other terminology.

Given the context, however, it is important for Chrysippus to insist that all the conditions listed here as examples of loss of rationality are such as can come about without the agent's consent – indeed, without the agent's bearing any responsibility whatever for the onset of the condition. Virtuous persons can get drunk, but only if alcohol is administered to them against their will; they do not voluntarily drink to excess. By the same token, Chrysippus cannot allow for any account of insanity whose etiology depends on the agent's own conscious activities – on a habitual indulgence in terrifying fantasies, for instance. For such causes could not be present in the wise.

---

[12] See Sedley 1993: 313–31.

[13] That relatively early Stoics brought up the example of *melancholia* in the context of discussions about mind-body interactions is further evidenced by ps.-Plutarch, *De libidine et aegritudine* 4–6 (154 Edelstein-Kidd), attributed to Posidonius: "Some things are mental and some corporeal, and some are not mental but are corporeal-in-association-with-the-mind, and some not corporeal but mental-in-association-with-the-body. The ones he calls purely mental are those involved in judgments and suppositions, such as desires, fears, and angers, while the purely corporeal ones are fevers, chills, thickenings, and thinnings; corporeal-in-association-with-the-mind are lethargies, *melancholiai*, "bitings," impressions, and "outpourings"; mental-in-association-with-the-body are tremblings, palenesses, and changes of expression due to fear or grief." Here *melancholia* is classed together with impressions and also with "bitings" and "outpourings," which are usually mentioned as the subjective or "feeling" components of the emotions distress and delight. All of these are perhaps considered to be elements of mental experience which cannot be adequately defined without reference to the material substrate. See further Kidd 1988: 560–562, with Graver 1999: 318–322; Cooper 1998: 81–90; Gill 1998: 124–30.

[14] It appears already in [Hippocrates], *Airs, Waters, Places* 10, and with some frequency from the last third of the fifth century, in Hippocratic texts and in Athenian comedy. See Müri 1953 and, for the subsequent tradition, Radden 2000.

[15] See for instance Cic., *Acad. Pr.* 2.51–52, 2.89–91; Plut., *Adv. Colotem* 1123b.

> They [i.e. wise persons] take wine, but do not get drunk. Neither are they insane
> [viz., in the more general sense of the word; see below]. To be sure, such a person
> is sometimes subject to peculiar impressions because of *melancholia* or delirium,
> not through his own reasoning as to what is choiceworthy, but contrary to [his]
> nature. (D.L. 7.118)

It is still, of course, possible for rationality to break down in more culpable ways in
persons who are capable of error.

THE MADNESS PARADOX

But "melancholic" insanity as we have seen it so far cannot possibly be what is
intended in those Stoic texts which ascribe insanity to the vast majority of humankind.
For to be incapable of receiving rational impressions should mean also that one is
incapable of responsible action – it should reduce one, morally speaking, to the level
of an animal or very young child. And it is not the intention of Stoic ethics to exempt
people in general from accountability for their actions. With this in mind, it is worthy
of note that the term *melancholia* is never used in connection with humankind in
general. Nor (except in the report of Diogenianus) is there any comparison of humans
in general to egregiously insane individuals such as Orestes or Heracles. The generalized *mania* is apparently of a different order. In what, then, does it consist?

The dictum "all the non-wise are mad" has, undeniably, a certain rhetorical flavor.
It is for its rhetorical interest that Cicero includes it among the six theses defended in
his pamphlet *Paradoxes of the Stoics*: here, as in the other so-called paradoxes, he
recognizes an intention to formulate in language which runs contrary to ordinary
opinion *(para doxan)* a doctrine which is otherwise unobjectionable.[16] Once it has
succeeded in arousing the curiosity of the audience, the deliberately provocative
formulation can be cashed out by the expositor in some suitably demystifying way.
The summary of Stoic ethics by Diogenes Laertius unpacks the paradox as follows:

> All the imprudent *(aphronoi)* are mad, for they do not have prudence *(phronēsis),*
> but do everything in accordance with madness, madness being equivalent to
> imprudence. (7.124)

As the opposition between *mania* and *phronēsis* (practical wisdom or, for convenience
of translation, "prudence") was conventional for Greek speakers, this statement has a
reasonable sound.[17] In a Stoic context, however, *phronēsis* cannot be used in any other
way than as the cardinal virtue of prudence; that is, the disposition to act properly in
any and all circumstances.[18] And that like every virtue is restricted to the wise. As the
wise person "does everything well" or in accordance with *phronēsis*, so those of us
who fall short of wisdom "do everything in accordance with madness."

---

[16] The text of the *Paradoxes* is unfortunately truncated just at this point, so that we cannot see how the
discussion played out.

[17] LSJ s.v. φρονέω IV.1.

[18] It is "knowledge of what things are to be done or not to be done or neither"; Stob., *Ecl.* 2.7.5b1 (59.4
Wachsmuth), 5b5 (63.10–11 Wachsmuth).

Yet it is not the case that madness in this Stoic sense is *merely* the same thing as a lack of wisdom. For it is possible also to identify the defining characteristic or sphere of reference within which it is appropriate to describe the flawed condition as one of "insanity," rather than as one of injustice, say, or cowardice – even though in Stoic theory all these conditions are coterminous.[19] Consider the somewhat fuller description of *mania* provided by Stobaeus but derived, very probably, from the Augustan scholar Arius Didymus:

> Again, they say that every inferior person is insane, since such people are ignorant of themselves and of what accords with themselves, and that is just what madness is. Ignorance is the fault opposite to self-control, and when in a certain relational state, [that is,] when rendering the impulses unsettled and fluttery, this is madness. For this reason they also define madness like this: fluttery ignorance.[20]

Here, too, insanity is explained as equivalent to imprudence, since knowledge of self and of what accords with self is just the same thing as *phronēsis*. But in addition to the bare equivalence between insanity and the state of error, we have mention here of the sphere of reference within which the term *mania* is deemed an appropriate label for the non-wise condition. Madness is ignorance "in a certain relational state" *(pros ti pōs echōn)*; that is, it is ignorance considered as rendering the impulses "unsettled and fluttery *(ptoiōdēs)*." A "flutter" *(ptoia)*, we know from later in Arius's summary, is another word for that sort of especially vehement impulse which we ordinarily call an emotion.[21] To be "insane" by this definition is to be susceptible – as the wise are not – to anger, fear, delight, or grief.

In the same vein, several Stoic texts build upon that Greek usage which makes the ambitious person *doxomanēs* or "mad about fame" and the lecherous person *gunaikomanēs* or "mad about women." Athenaeus cites a particularly lively example:

> Chrysippus says in the introduction to his treatise *On Goods and Evils* that it is common usage to attribute "madness" to many people. One sort of madness is called "woman-madness," another "partridge-madness." And some people call ambitious persons "fame-mad," just as they call lovers of women "woman-mad" and lovers of birds "bird-mad," – the words mean the same thing.[22]

---

[19] The doctrine of the unity of the virtues, in which all the knowledge-virtues are coterminous but differentiated by their sphere of reference, applies also to the cardinal faults (D.L. 7.126, Stob., *Ecl.* 2.7.5b5, 5c, 11k (63.6–25, 69.7–8, 106.6–8 Wachsmuth). This is not to say that there are no differences of character among flawed individuals, since there are the "infirmities" and related conditions (below, note 24), and since in any case vices need not be exercised (Sen., *Ben.* 4.27).

[20] Stob., *Ecl.* 2.7.5b13, 68.18–23 Wachsmuth.

[21] Stob., *Ecl.* 2.7.10, 88.11–12 Wachsmuth. The "flutter" terminology is frequently referred to the discussion in Plutarch, *Virt. Mor.* 441c–d, of vacillation between opposing points of view; so, for instance, Long and Sedley 1987, 1: 422. However, the term itself does not appear in that passage, and as vacillation is not always at issue (since emotions do not always, or even usually, involve mental conflict), I am inclined to think that the word *ptoia* is chosen merely to suggest the lightness with which ordinary persons succumb to emotional impulses (*to eukinēton tou pathētikou*; Stob., *Ecl.* 2.7.1, 39.10 Wachsmuth).

[22] Athenaeus, *Deipnosophistae* 11.464d, *SVF* 3.667.

These words belong to ordinary language; they are not invented by Stoics. However the Stoics are more than happy to supply explanations in terms of their own moral psychology for the traits of character so designated. For these various forms of "madness" are identified with the "infirmities" which figure in the theory of personality.[23] The infirmities *(arrōstēmata)*, like the so-called "sicknesses" *(nosēmata)*, are peculiarities in the cognitive processing of ordinary rational individuals, consisting in specific beliefs which predispose those individuals to experience strong emotions in relation to certain objects. The person who is mad about fame, for instance, has "a belief, deeply attached and rooted, that fame is a good thing" and is thus strongly disposed to feel gladness when fame is attained, grief when it is lost, fear when there is risk of losing it, and so on.[24] To be "mad about fame" is thus to have a particularized version of the madness which afflicts all non-wise agents. Every ordinary person is insane in that everyone who has some commitment to the genuine value of externals is liable to experience the wrong sorts of affect. But the emotional lives of some individuals are controlled by particular judgments as to the worth of one external object rather than another. These persons are not more insane than the rest of us, only insane in a more specific way.

THE TERMINOLOGY OF MADNESS

A passage in Cicero brings together both conceptions of insanity and attempts to explain the terminological difference between them. Cicero is defending a bold claim advanced at the beginning of the third *Tusculan Disputation:* that a susceptibility to grief, fear, desire, or anger "is hardly different from insanity" (3.8). In keeping with his usual program of promoting Latin as a vehicle for philosophical expression, he exclaims over the merits of the Latin terminology of mental aberration: since *insania* is literally "non-health," it is an appropriate term for any mental condition which falls short of the ideal of tranquillity, and the Latin speaker still has the word *furor* available for that sort of insanity which requires custodial care. In the course of this discussion he also makes clear what Greek terms correspond to the Latin words he is trying to establish for these concepts.

> Why the Greeks call this state [i.e. the susceptibility to emotion] "madness" *(mania)* I really cannot say. Our language makes clearer distinctions: we discriminate between *insania*, which has a wide application because of its link with folly, and *furor* or "frenzy." The Greeks mean the same thing we do, but they do not have a good word for it. What we call "frenzy," they call *melancholia*, "biliousness," as if the mind were stirred up only by black bile, and not by some more serious form of anger, fear, or grief, as happened with the frenzy (as we say it) of Athamas, Alcmaeon, Ajax, and Orestes.[25] A person in such a condition is

---

[23] Galen, *PHP* 4.5.21–22 (= *SVF* 3.480), quoting Chrysippus, *Peri Pathōn,* book 4.

[24] Stob., *Ecl.* 2.7.10b, c, e (91.3–4, 19–20, 93.1–14 W); Plut., *St. Rep.* 1050c; Cic., *Tusc. Disp.* 4.23–26. A fuller account of this portion of Stoic theory is given in Graver 2002:148–60.

[25] Like Orestes, Alcmaeon, and Pentheus already mentioned, both Athamas and Ajax are examples of that sort of derangement which involves skewed perception. Athamas, the husband of Ino, pursues and

prohibited by the Twelve Tables from managing his own affairs. Hence the law reads not "if he be insane" but "if he be frenzied." For they judged that a person who is foolish and lacking in consistency – that is, in health – was still capable of handling ordinary responsibilities and of managing his life in the usual and customary way, but frenzy, they thought, was a complete darkening of the mind. This would seem to be worse than *insania;* nonetheless, frenzy is the sort of thing that can come upon a wise person, while *insania* cannot. (*Tusc. Disp.* 3.11)

Although Cicero speaks here of "the Greeks" rather than specifically of "the Stoics," there can be no doubt that he has in mind one or more discussions he has encountered in his reading of Stoicism. For not only is his main line of argument here for a specifically Stoic view, but the last sentence quoted expresses the characteristically Chrysippan point about the loss of virtue, an assertion not motivated in Cicero's own account except by his intention to report older views as fully as practicable.

The Cicero passage thus tends to corroborate what we have seen already: that there are in Stoicism two clearly differentiated notions of what it is to be insane. Admittedly, Cicero's report of Greek usage does not match exactly with what we have seen in Greek reports of Stoic views, since in the Aetius and Sextus passages quoted above, *mania* appears together with *melancholia* in reference to the madness of Orestes. Probably what one should say is that *mania* is the unmarked term: it is really the presence or absence of *melancholia* that identifies a case of mental aberration as being of the medicalized and non-culpable variety or conversely as a condition of fault.

The nature of this distinction would appear to be specific to Stoicism. Both *mania* and *melancholia* occur with some frequency in the medical literature, and the two conditions are sometimes sharply distinguished. But in these contexts *mania* is regularly treated as a medical condition with identifiable physical causes. It may appear either as an umbrella term covering several sorts of mental illness, or as a specific diagnostic alternative to *melancholia* on the one hand and phrenitis on the other; for instance, it may be said that *mania* is caused by *yellow* bile, or that it, like phrenitis, is accompanied by fever while *melancholia* is not. In the popular literature – notably in Athenian comedy – *any* of the various terms for insanity may be used loosely to describe conduct which the speaker regards as lacking in good sense.[26] In Stoic texts, by contrast, we find two conceptions of madness which are not only quite different but actually different kinds of conception. On the one hand, we find a moral and epistemological conception which merely redescribes in a particular way the (practically) universal human condition of flawed rationality; on the other, a medicalized notion of insanity applicable to only a small number of persons. This latter, as the conception directly opposed to ordinary rationality, sets the bearer beyond the scope of either responsible action or emotion; in effect, it makes one morally subhuman. The two conceptions thus exclude one another: the ordinary "insane" cannot at the same time be melancholically insane (though they, like the wise, may lapse into that condition), and the melancholically insane cannot be

---

kills his elder son Learchus believing him to be a stag (Apollodorus 1.9.2, 3.4.3); Ajax kills a flock of sheep believing them to be Achaean chieftains.

[26] For examples of usage see Padel 1995: 48; Dover 1968: 201.

"insane" in the paradoxical sense. For to lack rationality is to lack the capacity for assent, and without assent, there is no emotion.

FROM MANIA TO MELANCHOLY

We have seen by now that the surviving reports of Stoic thought do tend to acquit those philosophers of the charge brought against them by Diogenianus. While Stoics have indeed claimed that people in general are insane, no Stoic has said that every human being is "equally as insane as Orestes and Alcmaeon"; rather, the sort of insanity that is handed around to people in general turns out to be a recognizably different condition, a matter of misplaced values only. But it may now seem that the Stoics are open to another charge: that of using language in a misleading way. For Diogenianus's way of understanding the paradox merely presupposes a standard usage of insanity terms, and we have not yet seen that there is anything of substance to be gained by the creation of a specialized usage. If we are not to accuse Chrysippus of obfuscation, we will need to go beyond the conceptual distinction identified thus far to investigate what connection of thought there might be which could justify the association created by the terminology.

I have two suggestions to make here. First, it is possible that the condition of flawed rationality is called *mania* as having some essential similarity with *mania* in its fuller, "melancholic" sense. Since we know that the relevant characteristic of the flawed rational condition is its susceptibility to emotional impulses, we should expect in this case that the terminological link would then be explained by some feature of emotional impulses which makes these impulses in particular resemble the behavior of the insane. It is not unlikely that Chrysippus recognized such a feature in the "pleonastic" or overriding character which, according to one Zenonian definition, distinguishes emotions from other forms of rational impulse.

A series of related discussions in Chrysippus's *Peri Pathōn*, preserved for us by Galen, seeks to explain the pleonastic character of emotions – the way they seem to "carry us away" even against our conscious intention – without conceding that the emotional impulse itself is anything other than a judgment by the rational mind.[27] His explanation is this: just as a runner may not be able to stop running the instant she wishes, so, in the course of an emotional impulse, a subsequent intention to stop having that emotion may not be able to take effect. Neither the impulse to run nor the impulse to (say) grieve could be countermanded by our power of decision, and yet we do not for that reason say that the running-impulse or grieving-impulse is any less a rational impulse than the stopping- or calming-impulse. It is merely that some impulses are of such a vigorous nature that the very performance of them overrides any subsequent impulse to the contrary. It is not necessary, then, to speak of a division of the mind into "reasoning" and "emotional" parts which are at odds with one another. If, however, we consider a person's inner experience at the very moment

---

[27] Galen, *PHP* 4.2.8–18; 4.6.24–46 *(SVF* 3.462, 475, 478), quoting from books 1 and 4 of the *Peri Pathōn.* Particularly helpful discussions of this evidence include Inwood 1997; Price 1995: 145–75; Gill 1998: 113–48.

when she issues to herself the ineffectual command to cease grieving, it does appear that her rational mind has lost the ability to execute its own commands. In this sense only does it make sense for a Stoic to say that emotions are "irrational" or "contrary to reason."

With this discussion in mind, we can see why Chrysippus might insist that all persons who are susceptible to emotions are, in a way, insane. Their insanity is of an episodic nature, to be sure, and it is of a kind which does not absolve anyone of responsibility for actions performed. But it is still the case that during an emotional movement, one is for a time "beside oneself" *(exestēkōs)* or "in an altered state" *(parēllachōs)* or "not oneself" *(ou par' heautōi)*.[28] Cicero catches the thought exactly when, speaking of the effect of anger in social situations, he remarks:

> It is cases like this, surely, that the Stoics are referring to in their claim that all fools are insane. Set aside the emotions, especially anger, and their position will become ridiculous. But they explain that when they say "all fools are insane," it is like "all bogs stink." Not always! But disturb the bog, and you will smell it. Even so the irascible person is not always angry – strike him, though, and you will see him go mad. (*Tusc. Disp.* 4.54)

And if this is one's view as to the nature of emotional movements, then there are valid ethical motivations for making that view widely known. If one's hearers can be persuaded to accept this assessment, they will surely be more receptive to therapeutic arguments intended to eliminate ordinary emotions from our experience.

But there is also a second possibility to be considered. The condition of susceptibility to emotion may be labeled "insanity" on the assumption that episodes of strong emotion not only resemble, but actually have the potential to *cause* mental illness as experienced by Orestes and Ajax. Cicero makes this assumption in *Tusc. Disp.* 3.11, quoted above. There he objects to the Greek term *melancholia* on the grounds that it implies this sort of insanity is caused "only by black bile," when in fact it may be caused "by some more serious form of anger, fear, or grief." Especially as concerns anger, it seems to have been widely believed in antiquity that a particularly powerful episode of emotion could push one over the brink into insanity. We have direct statements to that effect from authors as disparate as Epicurus and Ennius, and the same view is implied in the mythological histories Cicero mentions, notably in that of Ajax, who according to Sophocles was driven to insanity by his anger over the arms of Achilles.[29] If Stoic authors accepted this view, they would again have pressing ethical motivations to stress the connection between emotion and insanity in their psychology. Like parents warning their concert-going children about the effects of loud music on the human ear, they would be concerned both about the intrinsic evils of emotional movements and about their long-term effects on the psyche.[30]

---

[28] Galen, *PHP* 4.6.24–35 = *SVF* 3.475.

[29] *Ajax* 40–41. Cicero quotes an Ennian tag which makes anger the "beginning of insanity" *(initium insaniae; Tusc. Disp.* 4.52). Epicurus's statement is reported by Seneca, *Ep.* 18.14.

[30] Christopher Gill suggests that influence from a Stoic position of this kind can be traced in a pattern of thought typical of some Roman poetry: "akratic surrender to passion generates what the person concerned sees as a kind of madness" (Gill 1997: 218). Gill emphasizes that this etiology is not typically

One question to be asked is whether Cicero's claim about the etiology of madness is compatible with Stoic psychology. Obviously, emotional causes cannot be alleged for the onset of melancholic insanity in the wise, since the wise are completely devoid of ordinary emotion. As concerns the non-wise, though, we have some reason to believe that the Ciceronian account is tenable for a Stoic. An emotion in Chrysippan Stoicism is both a judgment and, simultaneously, an alteration in the *pneuma* of which the mind is composed. Under the latter, psychophysical description, the mental event or "movement" which is an emotion actually alters the size or shape of the mind-material, "contracting" it in the case of grief, "uplifting" it in the case of delight, "stretching it out" in the case of desire, and so on.[31] Since rationality itself consists at this level in a certain level of tension in the *pneuma,* it is entirely possible that such physical changes were thought to be destructive of rationality, especially if the emotions involved are powerful, protracted, or much repeated.

Did any Stoic author, then, speak of anger or other emotions as part of the causal history of insanity, or offer any sort of warning against emotion on that basis? It is arguable that we have just such a statement in Seneca. In a much-discussed passage near the beginning of *De Ira* 2, Seneca distinguishes three "movements" or mental events connected with anger.[32] The first of these is the *propatheia* or pre-emotion, a thought of revenge which crosses the mind without gaining one's assent. The second is just anger itself, as described earlier in the passage: it involves assent and so constitutes a full-fledged desire for revenge, but is still a (descriptively) rational phenomenon. The third movement, which "has overthrown reason," would appear to be a kind of insanity – a particularly dangerous kind, since it has its origin in anger. The passage reads as follows:

> Let me tell you how the emotions begin, how they grow, and how they get carried
> away. The first movement is non-volitional, a kind of preparation for emotion, a
> warning, as it were. The second is volitional but not obstinate, like this, "It is

present in Greek tragedy, where madness is regularly god-induced; see further Padel 1994 with Gill 1996. I suggest, on the contrary, that the pattern is potentially present, in that Ajax and Orestes (at least) are represented as undergoing unusually strong passions prior to their insanity, but that Greek tragedy, through the mechanism of divine intervention, excuses the agent of responsibility for his or her condition in a way that the Stoic-influenced poetry of Seneca and Vergil does not allow.

[31] Galen, *PHP* 4.2.1–5 = *SVF* 3.463.

[32] The interpretation given here should be regarded as provisional: the possibility that 2.4 should be read continuously with 2.5 has never been considered in the secondary literature and will require a fuller defense than I am able to provide in the space available here. For other views on the nature of Seneca's distinction between "second" and "third" movements see Inwood 1993: 180–81; Sorabji 2000: 61–63; Donini 1995: 206–9. Sorabji in particular stresses the similarity between Seneca's verb *efferantur* in 2.4.1 and Gr. *ekpheresthai,* one of the verbs regularly used in Chrysippus's discussions of the excessive element in emotion (Galen *PHP* 4.2.12–18, 4.6.35 = *SVF* 3.462, 478). It should be noted, however, that *efferantur* would be extremely easy for a copyist to confuse with *efferentur,* the corresponding form of *efferari,* "to go feral." As *efferari,* a less-common verb but one Seneca is extremely fond of in such contexts, is cognate with *feritas* in 2.5.2, its acceptance would much strengthen the interpretation offered here. Even with *efferantur,* however, the third movement would seem to be more than anger as understood by Chrysippus. For while Chrysippus has anger as an overriding movement, it is still essentially a judgment that revenge is appropriate (*kathēkei*), while the third movement "wants to take revenge not if it is appropriate, but no matter what."

appropriate for me to take revenge, since I have been injured," or "It is appropriate for this person to be punished, since he has committed a crime." The third movement is already beyond control. It wants to take revenge not if it is appropriate, but no matter what; it has overthrown reason. That first impact on the mind is one we cannot escape by reason, just as we cannot escape those things which I said happen to the body, such as being stimulated by another person's yawn, or blinking when fingers are thrust suddenly toward one's eyes. That second movement, the one that comes about through judgment, is also eliminated by judgment.

And now we must ask concerning those people who rage about at random and delight in human blood, whether they are angry when they kill people from whom they have not received any injury and do not believe that they have – people like Apollodorus or Phalaris. This is not anger, but brutishness *(feritas)*. For it does not do harm because it has received an injury; rather, it is willing even to receive an injury so long as it may do harm. It does not go after whippings and lacerations for punishment, but for pleasure. What then? The origin of this evil is from anger, which, once it has been exercised and satiated so often that it has forgotten about mercy and has cast out every human contract from the mind, passes in the end into cruelty. (Seneca, *De Ira* 2.4–5)

Just as in 2.2–3 Seneca has been careful to distinguish what is properly called anger from the involuntary pre-emotion, so here he sets out to distinguish anger from an irrational state which he calls "brutishness" *(feritas)*. Like Aristotle's *theriotēs* in *Nicomachean Ethics* 7.1–6, this state is heinous but not culpable: persons in this condition need to be controlled, but their behaviors do not have the same meaning as they would if performed by a rational being. To hold them responsible would be like indicting a pit bull for felonious assault. This is not to say, however, that the mental state of such as Phalaris is precisely the same as that of a non-human animal. The dog's impressions are presumably of a simpler kind than those of a human, but they need not be indiscriminate or skewed. The feral human is more dangerous in that he rages about "at random," his behavior lacking even the rudimentary and semi-conceptualized logic of the animal. His impressions are perhaps comparable to those of Orestes, in that they represent to him states of affairs which have no justification *at all*: as Orestes perceives Electra to be a Fury, so Phalaris perceives the imposition of punishments to be somehow intrinsically pleasurable. Hannibal, seeing a trench filled with human blood, exclaims, "What a lovely sight!" This is not rationality merely getting out of hand, carried away in some moment of strong emotion. It is actually the disintegration of rationality.

Yet while these "brutish" behaviors are not generated by a rational process and so cannot count as instances of anger, they, like pre-emotions, are also connected with anger by a specific causal relation.[33] For the disposition to perform them has its origin "from anger" *(ab ira, 2.5.3)*. Repeated episodes of anger have somehow obliterated elements of "mercy" and "human contact" from the mind. The explanation is reminiscent of the etiology of the "sicknesses" and "infirmities" mentioned earlier, for

---

[33] The pre-emotion is a proximate, but not principal, cause of anger (*De Ira* 2.1.3–4; cf. Cic., *De Fato* 41).

those conditions, too, come about through repeated experience of certain emotions.[34] *Feritas* differs from a mere sickness or infirmity, however, in that the latter predispose us to genuine emotions: *doxomania*, for instance, might predispose a person to anger at slights to her reputation. Brutishness goes beyond this. It has "passed over" into a new state, a state in which anger is no longer even possible.

It should be understood that Seneca's motivation in 2.5 is not to understand the psychological disorder for its own sake, but rather to bring out the rational nature of anger by insisting on the relation of logical consequence between injury and revenge. In this, he is very much in accordance with what we have seen throughout these texts relating to melancholic insanity. *Melancholia* is invoked not for its diagnostic or treatment implications, but as a way of defining the boundaries of ordinary human rationality. So important is the concept of rationality to this moral psychology that we should expect Stoics to make every possible move to clarify what in human behavior counts as rational and what does not. Just as they felt it incumbent on them to give some account of pre-rational phenomena in the behaviors of animals and young children and in the pre-emotional movements of adults, so also they sought to distinguish rational states from what we might call the post-rational.

WORKS CITED

Bury, R.G. 1935. *Sextus Empiricus: Against the Logicians*. London and Cambridge, Mass.

Cooper, J. 1998. "Posidonius on Emotions." In J. Sihvola and T. Engberg-Pedersen, eds., *The Emotions in Hellenistic Philosophy*. Dordrecht. 71–112. Also in J. Cooper, *Reason and Emotion*. Princeton, 1999.

Donini, P. 1995. *"Pathos* nello Stoicismo Romano." *Elenchos* 16: 195–216.

Dover, K.J. 1968. *Aristophanes: Clouds*. Oxford.

Gill, C. 1998. "Did Galen Understand Platonic and Stoic Thinking on Emotions?" In J. Sihvola and T. Engberg-Pedersen, eds., *The Emotions in Hellenistic Philosophy*. Dordrecht. 113–48.

Graver, M. 1999. "Philo of Alexandria and the Origins of the Stoic προπάθεια." *Phronesis* 44: 300–325.

———. 2002. *Cicero on the Emotions: Tusculan Disputations 3 and 4*. Chicago.

Inwood, B. 1993. "Seneca and Psychological Dualism." In J. Brunschwig and M. Nussbaum, eds., *Passions and Perceptions: Studies in Hellenistic Philosophy of Mind*. Cambridge. 150–183.

———. 1997. "Why Do Fools Fall in Love?" In R. Sorabji, ed., *Aristotle and After*, *BICS* Supplement 68. London. 55–69.

Kidd, I. 1988. *Posidonius: the Commentary*. Cambridge.

Long, A.A., and D.N. Sedley. 1987. *Hellenistic Philosophers*. 2 vols. Cambridge.

Müri, W. 1953. "Melancholie und schwarze Galle." *Museum Helveticum* 10: 27–38.

Padel, R. 1995. *Whom Gods Destroy: Elements of Greek and Tragic Madness*. Princeton.

Paschall, D.M. 1939. *The Vocabulary of Mental Aberration in Roman Comedy and Petronius*. Baltimore.

Pigeaud, J. 1987. *Folie et cures de la folie chez les médecins de l'antiquité Gréco-Romaine*. Paris.

Price, A. 1995. *Mental Conflict*. London.

Radden, J., ed. 2000. *The Nature of Melancholy: from Aristotle to Kristeva*. Oxford and New York.

Sedley, D. 1993. "Chrysippus on Psychophysical Causality." In J. Brunschwig and M. Nussbaum, eds., *Passions and Perceptions: Studies in Hellenistic Philosophy of Mind*. Cambridge. 313–31.

Sorabji, R. 2000. *Emotion and Peace of Mind*. Oxford.

---

[34] Cic., *Tusc. Disp.* 4.24–25; Epict., *Diss.* 2.18.8–10.

5

A Gesture in Archilochos 118 (West)?[*]

Carolin Hahnemann

Over the last two decades scholars of classical literature have become increasingly attentive to the performative aspects of the texts they are studying. The manifestations of this awareness range from Oliver Taplin's books on ancient stagecraft to Stephen Daitz's recitals of Greek and Latin on audio-cassette. Alan Boegehold's new book adds yet another facet to the prism.[1] Through careful analysis of the transmitted text, Boegehold identifies sentences whose meaning would gain in clarity or vividness if accompanied by a gesture on the part of the performer. (Below I refer to this phenomenon as a "rhetorical gesture."[2]) In order to sharpen our awareness of this particular kind of nonverbal communication, Boegehold cites examples from the works of Homer, Archilochos, Pindar, the tragedians, Aristophanes, the orators, the historians, and Plato. His endeavour is all the more noteworthy for having been pronounced impossible hardly five years earlier.[3] Therefore, I hope to be forgiven for exploring a single piece of the evidence at somewhat disproportionate length.

As Boegehold groups the passages primarily according to their author, he does not assign the various gestures to separate categories. Using Archilochos F 118 (West) as a test case, I here attempt to differentiate between two basic types: complementing and completing gestures. Researchers in various branches of the social sciences, where nonverbal expression has been a subject of investigation much longer than in Classics, have developed a great number of technical terms to describe and distinguish behaviours. That I do not use them is a result of the ghostly nature of the rhetorical gesture. Psychologists and anthropologists study gestures which they can observe

---

[*] I am grateful to Alan Boegehold for having tempted me to an excursion into this field of inquiry, and to Bill McCulloh, Don Lateiner, Peter Bing, and Ralph Rosen for their efforts to lead me back unmuddied.

[1] Boegehold 1999.

[2] Neumann 1965: 10–12 uses the term more specifically for the "geformte und schlagkräftig pointierte Geste" as it emerges on vases of the Classical period. He regards "rhetorische Gesten" as distinct from, though akin to, the less specific "sprechende Handbewegungen" on the one hand and deictic, hortatory, defensive, etc. gestures on the other. I use the term as a collective label for any motion of head and hand that accompanies a speech-act.

[3] By Donald Lateiner in his groundbreaking study of nonverbal behaviours of the characters in the Homeric epics (1995: 20): "Henceforth, the contribution of nonverbal behaviors should be factored in as well, a highly affective and focussed form of human expression allotted to persons in the text and presumably – but for us irretrievably – employed by the performers of the text."

directly in a given environment, while we must rely on a few ancient treatises and the still testimony of the vases. Rarely do we find a scholion that describes the particular movement of head and hand that a performer used to accompany a specific utterance, and even such evidence can be called into doubt. In the case of the fragment which I have chosen for discussion here we have no help from a commentator.

In his discussion of gesture in the archaic poets, Boegehold translates and comments on F 118 (West) as follows: "'I wish I could get to touch Neoboule.' Here Archilochus could touch his own breast."[4] Since nonverbal signals abound in human communication, it seems likely that the sentence was indeed accompanied by some gesture, which the imaginative reader may strive to picture in his mind's eye.[5] But before we can begin to try out various gestures, we must establish that the performative setting for which the poem was intended permitted gesticulation at all. For the claim that the performer of Archilochos F 118 accompanied his recitation by some meaningful wave of the hand presupposes, after all, that he did not have his hands full with an instrument.[6] Fortunately, for the archaic period at least, we have no compelling evidence that he did.[7] Admittedly, legend tells us that Archilochos received a harp from the Muses, but we must not interpret this symbol of his poetic gift as a literal indication that he performed all his various kinds of poems to the accompaniment of this instrument. The same holds true for the poet's depiction with a harp on a vase in Boston.

But ridding the performer of F 118 of the imputed harp meets only the physical prerequisite for a potential gesture. In addition we have to assume that the performer in some way took on the persona of the speaker. Three sources of circumstantial evidence support the probability of such a mimetic element in the delivery of iambic verse. First, there is the comparative testimony of "primitive" song from other cultures, where "miming in character is extremely common."[8] Secondly, the emergence of trochaic tetrameter and iambic trimeter as the spoken verse in drama suggests that they may have served as a vehicle of impersonation already in the preceding century.[9] Third, literary criticism of the fourth century offers a model for a mildly

---

[4] Boegehold 1999: 50. Following Lasserre's numeration, Boegehold cites the fragment as F 89.

[5] I disagree with Lateiner's claim (1995: 15) that we automatically "reimagine interlocutors with all their bodily cues and signals" when reading an ancient work. Modern readers like myself, I fear, are so accustomed to the speedy consumption of dry texts that we must make an "exceptional effort of historical imagination" to restore the "silent ranks of conscientiously edited poetic texts" to a performance in the theatre of our minds (cf. Herington 1984: 4).

[6] Cf. Burnett 1983: 7 n. 11: "But how far can one go with lyre in hand?"

[7] For a list and excellent discussion of the testimonia, cf. Herington 1984, Appendix V, C.

[8] Dover 1964: 215–216. I have placed his formulation "primitive" in quotation marks to avoid its derogatory connotations. For a more detailed formulation of the same observation cf. also Bowra 1962: 28: "[S]inging is often accompanied by some kind of action, such as ... mimetic gestures, which illustrate what the words say and make their references and implications more forceful."

[9] Cf. West 1974: 33 and 1991: 32–34. For a discussion of other, subtler points of influence cf. Rosen 1988.

dramatic kind of recitation which suits the performative parameters of this kind of poetry.[10]

Within the framework of the discussion about the right education for the future guardians of the ideal city in Plato's *Republic*, Socrates divides all stories into three groups according to their method of performance: pure narrative, pure mimesis, and a hybrid of the two (392d6f).[11] As an example of the hybrid he offers the passage from the *Iliad* when Chryses visits the Greek camp to beg for the return of his daughter. When delivering Chryses' plea, Socrates says, the rhapsode assumes the character's personality in voice (φωνή) and gesture (σχῆμα).[12] He strives to make us believe that it is in fact the priest who is speaking, "being an old man."[13] I conclude from this that in impersonating Chryses the rhapsode must at least have changed his vocal inflection from a sober narration to the weeping agitation of an old man. In addition, he may have assumed a stooped posture (perhaps leaning on his trademark staff) and raised tottering hands when praying to Apollo. Though Socrates continually uses epic as his example for the partially mimetic type of delivery, he reminds his interlocutors that other genres belong to this category as well (394c4f.). Since already in Herakleitos (12B 42 DK) and later also in Plato's *Ion* (531a2) Archilochos is mentioned in the same breath with Homer as an author whose works were performed by rhapsodes, we can be sure that some of Archilochos' poems were performed in the partially mimetic mode. It seems most natural to assume that these were poems in a stichic metre like F 118.[14]

In Archilochos' time the setting of the performance would probably have been a symposium, with the number of listeners far smaller than at the rhapsodic contests and the performer not necessarily a professional like Ion.[15] But the difference is one of scale, not of nature. Professionals and amateurs alike will have used impersonation to entertain audiences large or small. As a result, there may well have been a gesture

---

[10] Bartol 1992: 67–70 also seems to regard the performance of iambics as closely related to the performance of epic, while West argues for a strong similarity with comedy. He even supplies artistic evidence that padded dancing predates Archilochos and cites two poems which, in his opinion, indicate that the performer was wearing a leather phallos (1974: 30, 36). I do not believe that either poem requires such costuming. Moreover, I find it hard to imagine that the performer would either change between short poems or deliver all poems in this get-up. (A rhapsodic staff strikes me as a lot more versatile than a comic phallos!) Admittedly, later writers support the theory that archaic poets donned costumes in regard to two poems by Solon (F 1 and F 10). But such yarns seem spun from the same fibre as the detailed accounts of Archilochos' broken engagement to Neoboule: the fallacious quest for a poem's original occasion.

[11] In a recent production of *The Iliad* by the Aquila Theater Company, a handful of artists aided by a few props brilliantly achieved a (different kind of) hybrid between sheer recitation and dramatic enactment.

[12] Plat. *Rep.* 393c5f., but cf. also Aristotle's *Poetics* 1462a. For a definition of σχῆμα in this context, cf. Neumann 1965: 1.

[13] Plat. *Rep.* 393a8–b3: τὰ δὲ μετὰ ταῦτα ὥσπερ αὐτὸς ὢν ὁ Χρύσης λέγει καὶ πειρᾶται ἡμᾶς ὅτι μάλιστα ποιῆσαι μὴ Ὅμηρον δοκεῖν τὸν λέγοντα, ἀλλὰ τὸν ἱερέα, πρεσβύτην ὄντα. (Plato here does not distinguish between poet and performer.)

[14] Thus, e.g., Herington 1984: 39 and 194; but cf. also Bartol's claim to the contrary (1992: 70–71).

[15] Cf. Pellizer 1990: 180.

with F 118. In order to appreciate the various possibilities, let us now consider the verse in the original Greek.

In his first edition of *Iambi et Elegi Graeci*, West prints the fragment as follows: εἰ γὰρ ὣς ἐμοὶ γένοιτο χεῖρα Νεοβούλης θιγεῖν,[16] which in Davenport's translation reads: "O that/ I might but touch/ Neobulé's hand."[17] I suppose that the translator's intention in adding the old-fashioned "but" must have been to strike a note of tender romance, seeing that he regards the verse as "the oldest surviving fragment from a love lyric in Greek." But the imaginary gesture which this translation evokes may be anachronistic in its Victorian modesty. Instead of couples "holding hands," ancient Greek vases frequently show a man grasping the wrist of a woman. The gesture seems to indicate intimacy, while at the same time asserting authority in a variety of contexts, including impending abduction or sex.[18] Surely, nobody would be shocked to find Archilochos' thoughts wandering beyond Neoboule's hand,[19] but a grammatical difficulty bars this interpretation. Nowhere else does χεῖρα θιγγάνω describe the clasp on the wrist. What is worse, there is no authentic instance of θιγγάνω with the accusative in classical Greek at all.[20] Thus we are not surprised to find that for his later selection of fragments West accepted Elmsley's emendation of the unparalleled accusative χεῖρα into the dative χειρὶ, thereby making Νεοβούλης the required genitive object of the verb.[21]

Both the English versions I quoted above leave ὣς untranslated. The omission is justified, if we assume that the word here signals a comparative wish ("would that x were true as surely as y is true"): εἰ/αἰ γὰρ οὕτως/ὣς ... plus the optative, followed by ὣς with the indicative.[22] In the absence of its correlative clause, it is difficult to

---

[16] West 1971: 47.

[17] Davenport 1964: 79 and xvi.

[18] Cf. Sittl 1890: 80–81, 131–33, and passim; Neumann 1965: 59–66, especially n. 218; Lateiner 1995: 57 with n. 48 and 71 with n. 10; Boegehold 1999: 17–18, 19–20, with plates 2–5. For an ancient description of the gesture cf. especially *Od.* 18, 258; *Il.* 24, 671. The phrases θιγγάνω εὐνῆς or γυναικός serve as euphemisms for sexual intercourse in Euripides' *Hippolytos* 885 and 1044, while at *Bacchai* 1183 and *I.A.* 1351 θιγγάνω refers to a brutal killing. Interestingly, in both instances a parent is murdering her/his child, thereby cruelly inverting the touch typical of filial affection (Eur. *Ba.* 1318; Soph. *O.K.* 329).

[19] I doubt that the usage of θιγγάνω would have evoked a specific gesture in the minds of the contemporary listeners. Unfortunately, F 118 constitutes the only instance of the verb among the surviving fragments of Archilochos. The two lyric poems which contain the word are both too badly preserved to shed light on our inquiry (Alkman F 18 and Adesp. 1037 Page). In contrast to Pindar, who does not use θιγγάνω to denote interpersonal contact (cf., e.g., *Pyth.* 9, 122), Bacchylides employs the word to describe Minos' gesture of touching Eriboia's cheeks (17, 11f.). Within this poem's world of heroic decorum such behavior clearly constitutes an outrage, but the same need not be true in the case of Archilochus F 118, depending on the (fictitious) relationship of the speaker to Neoboule and her social status.

[20] Cf. Jebb on Soph. *Ant.* 546. LSJ cites our fragment as the sole instance of that construction with the caveat "si vera lectio". A similar problem occurs in F 115 where, in the absence of the subsequent verse, ἄκουε seems to govern an accusative *personae* instead of a genitive.

[21] West 1989: 47 and 1989: 47. Archilochos uses the instrumental in a comparable phrase at F 146, line 48: μαζῶν τε χερσὶν ἠπίως ἐφηψάμην. While Gerber 1999: 159 avoids taking a stance on the matter by offering two translations of the fragments, Boegehold's rendering suggests that he, too, reads Elmsley's emendation.

[22] Kühner-Gerth, II.2: 494, #7.

capture this function of ὥς in translation.[23] The problem, however, does not encumber West. He "retrieves" the correlative clause by combining fragments 118–120 into a continuous poem:[24]

> I wish I had as sure a chance of fingering Neoboule –
> the workman falling to his flask – and pressing tum to tummy
> and thighs to thighs ...
> as sure as I know how to start the lovely round of singing
> lord Dionysus' dithyramb when the wine has blitzed my brains in.[25]

I am not familar enough with Archilochos' diction to argue that this sequence of clauses does not suit the poet's idiom, but the statistical likelihood of three different fragments, quoted by three different authors, preserving successive verses from the same poem must be very small.[26] Even if we dismiss West's reconstruction as implausible, however, it still aids our inquiry by reminding us that there may have been a verbal explanation of ὥς, now lost with the context of the fragment. In two comparable passages in the *Iliad* the demonstrative links the wish to a previous speech, thus expressing a hope for something to happen in the manner described.[27]

Let us assume for the moment that one of the interpretations of ὥς offered above is correct and, on that basis, consider Boegehold's suggestion that the speaker touched his breast when pronouncing the verse. As a contemporary German I would read this gesture as an indication of the speaker's passionate sincerity or intensity of feeling, but there is no evidence for such a meaning in antiquity.[28] Then (as now) humans instictively placed a hand on the chest in situations that cause the heart to beat faster, such as surprise or terror.[29] If executed intentionally, the same gesture could serve as a sign of submissive pleading which might suit here.[30] Assuming a slightly different timing for a similar gesture, the speaker could point to himself simply for reference, or to give jealous emphasis to the pronoun ἐμοί, seeing that Neoboule is elsewhere

---

[23] Edmonds 1931: 135, translates "I would that so I might be granted to touch Neobulé's hand", adding a footnote on "so."

[24] West 1993: 6. The Greek text of F 119 and F 120 reads:

F 119   καὶ πεσεῖν δρήστην ἐπ' ἀσκόν, κἀπὶ γαστρὶ γαστέρα
                  προσβαλεῖν μηρούς τε μηροῖς.

F 120   ὡς Διωνύσοι' ἄνακτος καλὸν ἐξάρξαι μέλος
                  οἶδα διθύραμβον οἴνωι συγκεραυνωθεὶς φρένας.

[25] As it appears in West's reconstruction, Archilochos' verses furnish an intriguing counterpoint to the Homeric formula at *Iliad* 8.538–41 (cf. 13.825–29): εἰ γὰρ ἐγὼν ὣς/ εἴην ἀθάνατος καὶ ἀγήραος ἤματα πάντα,/ τιοίμην δ', ὡς τίετ' Ἀθηναίη καὶ Ἀπόλλων,/ ὡς νῦν ἡμέρη ἥδε κακὸν φέρει Ἀργείοισιν. While Hektor, true to his heroic nature, wishes for perpetual glory rather than immediate pleasure, he too voices a boast in the correlative clause.

[26] Cf. Burnett 1983: 24 n. 21, to whom the connection seems "needlessly audacious."

[27] *Il.* 4, 189; 7, 157. In *Od.* 3, 218ff. it makes no difference whether we translate ὥς... ὥς "as surely as" or "in this way as", whereas at *Od.* 15, 156–59 I read ὥς as the demonstrative "in this way", with the subsequent ὡς introducing indirect discourse after εἴποιμι (cf. Heubeck-Hoekstra 1989, II: 241–42).

[28] My personal "locus classicus" for this gesture is Fischer-Dieskau singing Schubert. Cf. Sittl 1890: 139 n. 3: "Der Moderne legt gerne die Hand "aufs Herz", wovon der Alte nichts zu wissen scheint".

[29] Sittl 1890: 139 n. 3 and Neumann 1965: 105.

[30] Sittl 1890: 162 n. 4.

accused of welcoming male attention indiscriminately (F 196a, l. 38).[31] Alternatively we may imagine the speaker stretching out his hand toward the absent Neoboule, as lovers on vases do toward their present beloveds. Depending on the execution of the movement, this gesture in turn could convey sweet longing or aggressive urgency.[32]

Though there are still other possibilities, I hope that the sample above suffices to show why I call this type of gesture a "complementing gesture."[33] Individual words as well as the verse as a whole invite the reader to envision different gestures, each of which would make the wish appear in a different colour.[34] In the absence of any context for the fragment, however, we have no basis to determine which colouring the poet himself intended to convey. Considering the multitude of performances the poem must have undergone over several centuries throughout the Greek community, it seems inevitable that there was more than one "authentic" gesture. But the specific shape of the(se) complementing gesture(s) eludes scholarly argument, except in the negative way demonstrated above. Moreover, since the text makes ready sense without the complement of any rhetorical gesture, we cannot even be sure that there was one at all. The best we can do is to collect a farrago of possibilities by analogy to ancient descriptions and depictions.

But matters look less discouraging, if we reverse our basic hypothesis and assume that the context of our fragment did <u>not</u> furnish a verbal explanation for ὥς. Lest we lose ourselves in the vast realms of theory, let us first consider an analogous situation in a text that has survived unfragmented. During the competition between Aischylos and Euripides for the throne of the best poet in Hades, Dionysos recalls his pleasure at the scene from *Persians* when king Dareios is summoned from the dead. Apparently, the chorus in the orchestra greeted the apparition by clapping their hands and shouting:[35] ὁ χορὸς δ' εὐθὺς τὼ χεῖρ' ὡδὶ[36] συγκρούσας εἶπεν "ἰαυοῖ". But how are we, or the original audience for that matter, to picture the chorus clapping their hands "thus"? It seems logical that, instead of explaining it in so many words, Dionysos demonstrated the motion with his own hands.[37] Unless we imagine a gesture on the part of the actor, his utterance remains indefinite: we do understand what he is saying, but we do not understand what he is talking about. To distinguish this type of gesture

---

[31] Sittl 1890: 53–55 adduces a number of instances where a speaker, in referring to himself, touches his own body, while the pictorial evidence is more ambiguous. E.g. Neumann's interpretation of the woman to the left on cup *ARV*[2] 449.4 (1965: 13); differently Boegehold 1999: 33.

[32] In F 146, line 48 (above n. 21), the speaker strokes a girl's breasts; elsewhere physical contact is not so gentle.

[33] Some complementing gestures radically change or even cancel the meaning of a statement, e. g. the crossing of one's fingers while swearing an oath in contemporary America. In this respect I regard the more conventional label "illustrators" as misleading.

[34] Even arrested in a picture a gesture can remain enigmatic. Thus on a famous vase by the Kleophrades painter we see a rhapsode motioning with his staff while from his open mouth pour the words: ὧδέ ποτ' ἐν Τύρινθι. Herington 1984: 15 raises the question whether this "magnificent gesture" served to stress ὧδε. There can be no answer.

[35] Ar. *Frogs* 1029. Neither the corruption in verse 1028 nor the fact that Dionysos does not remember the scene precisely need concern us here.

[36] In texts which employ colloquial Attic idiom deictic "ι" sometimes signals a gesture.

[37] Sittl 1890: 201 n. 1, cites two parallels: Ar. *Wasps* 279 and *Ekkl.* 259f.

from the aforementioned "complementing" kind, I call it a "completing gesture". (A gesture can complete a sentence either semantically, as in the passage above, or syntactically but, since this subdivision has no bearing on our present subject, I will leave it for exploration elsewhere.[38]) Completing gestures furnish interesting matter for comment from the scholar, since knowledge of ancient performative practice can help him make out the point of a semantically incomplete sentence.[39] Even more importantly though, an awareness of the existence of completing gestures can keep the textual critic from doctoring syntactically incomplete sentences unnecessarily.[40]

Having established the distinction between complementing and completing gestures, let us return to our fragment of Archilochos. In his commentary, Moore translates ὥς as the demonstrative "thus", adding that it takes its semantic definition from "a gesture, as often in Greek."[41] Indeed it is attractive to assume that the speaker's hand might have simulated how he would touch Neoboule, just as Herakles demonstrates the size of Charon's ferry (Ar. *Frogs* 139) and Strepsiades shows how tiny his son was when he first gave signs of his remarkable intellect (Ar. *Clouds* 878).[42] Since a semantically incomplete sentence requires determination in one particular respect, the corresponding gestures are less variable than their complementary counterparts. Still, an actor playing Strepsiades may demonstrate the size of his son realistically by holding out one hand above the ground or exaggerate the boy's youth by raising both of his hands some distance apart.

In conclusion, then, we have to admit that no matter how we construct F 118, we cannot retrieve the shape of the gesture that accompanied the verse. But at least we have established that, if we read ὥς one way, there <u>can</u> have been a gesture, and if we read ὥς the other way, there <u>must</u> have been one. This is not nothing.

WORKS CITED

Bartol, K. 1992. "Performance of Iambic Poetry." *CQ* n.s. 42: 65–71.
Boegehold, A.L. 1999. *When a Gesture Was Expected*. Princeton.
Bowra, C.M. 1962. *Primitive Song*. Cleveland.
Burnett, A.P. 1983. *Three Archaic Poets*. Cambridge, Mass.
Davenport, G. 1964. *Carmina Archilochi*. Berkeley and Los Angeles.
Dover, K.J. 1964. "The poetry of Archilochos." In *Archiloque: Entretiens X, Fondation Hardt*, Geneva.

---

[38] The conditional without apodosis comes to mind as the best-known (and most readily accepted) representative of a sentence where a completing gesture seems likely on syntactical grounds (cf. the treatment by Boegehold 1999: 37–39 and passim). Working with a language as elliptical as ancient Greek, however, even the decision about what constitutes a complete sentence can be at times maddeningly difficult.

[39] The scholia on Ar. *Frogs* 308 list no fewer than four possible points of reference for ὁδ', only one of which can be dismissed out of hand. Thanks to his connoisseurship of comic diction and humour, however, Dover (1993: 231) is able to make a persuasive case for yet a different interpretation.

[40] Cf. the many examples given by Boegehold 1999: passim.

[41] Moore 1961: 75.

[42] "Practical" gestures like these are created for the occasion and directly intelligible to the observer regardless of cultural context, while "symbolic" gestures differ from society to society and must be learned like a language. (I have borrowed the refreshingly plain terminology from Monahan 1983.)

————. 1993. *Aristophanes' Frogs*. Oxford.

Edmonds, J.M. 1931. *Elegy and Iambus*. London and New York.

Gerber, D.E. 1999. *Greek Iambic Poetry*. Cambridge, Mass. and London.

Herington, C.J. 1984. *Poetry into Drama*. Berkeley, Los Angeles, and London.

Heubeck-Hoekstra. 1989. *A Commentary on Homer's Odyssey*. Oxford.

Kühner-Gerth=Kühner, R. and B. Gerth. *Ausführliche Grammatik der griechischen Sprache*. 4th ed. 2 vols. Hannover and Leipzig, 1904.

Lateiner, D. 1995. *Sardonic Smile: Nonverbal Behavior in Homeric Epic*. Ann Arbor.

Moore, J.A. 1961. *Selections from the Greek Elegiac, Iambic and Lyric Poets*. Cambridge, Mass.

Monahan, B. 1983. *A Dictionary of Russian Gesture*. Tenafly, N.J.

Neumann, G. 1965. *Gesten und Gebärden in der griechischen Kunst*. Berlin.

Pellizer, E. 1990. "Outlines of a morphology of sympotic entertainment." In O. Murray, ed., *Sympotica*. Oxford. 177–184.

Rosen, R.M. 1988. *Old Comedy and The Iambographic Tradition*. American Classical Studies 19. Atlanta, Ga.

Sittl, C. 1890. *Die Gebärden der Griechen und Römer*. Leipzig.

West, M.L. 1971. *Iambi et Elegi Graeci*. 1st ed. Oxford.

————. 1974. *Studies in Greek Elegy and Iambos*. Berlin/New York.

————. 1980. *Delectus ex Iambis et Elegis Graecis*. Oxford.

————. 1989. *Iambi et Elegi Graeci*. 2nd ed. Oxford.

————. 1991. *Early Greek Music*. Oxford.

————. 1993. *Greek Lyric Poetry*. Oxford and New York.

6

When an Identity Was Expected:
The Slaves in Aristophanes' *Knights*

Jeffrey Henderson

Alan Boegehold has considerably enriched our appreciation of Greek drama by calling attention to its gestural dimensions, and thus reminds us that our texts were but scripts for an enactment in which the appearance, voices, and movements of the performers brought the words to life.[1] In Old Comedy particularly, we can often grasp the meaning of a text only by enlisting what we can imagine of its visual dimensions or discover about its extradramatic context. The ancient question of the identity of the two anonymous slaves who open *Knights* is an interesting case in point.

That these two slaves are never named in the text is consistent with the normal Aristophanic convention whereby "slaves who take an active part in the dialogue ... normally remain anonymous."[2] But it was soon clear to the spectators that these are no ordinary slaves: their nominal identity is political allegory, and they may suggest or even represent particular politicians as well. The manuscripts in fact ignore their nominal status and identify them respectively as Demosthenes and Nikias.

Though these ancient identifications may be correct, they are hardly authoritative: the hypotheses and scholia to the play show that they do not derive from Aristophanes himself but are inferences drawn (probably first in Alexandria) by aligning allusions in the text with historical information external to it. Such inferences are sometimes plausible, sometimes not (no one credits the similar attempts, preserved in Σ 149a, to identify the Sausage Seller with Kleonymos, Hyperbolos or Euboulos), and so must be judged solely on their scholarly merits. This was first pointed out by Dindorf in his edition of 1835, and his skepticism was acted upon editorially by Weise in 1842, who in his text identified the slaves only by their dramatic identifications, Οἰκέτης A and Οἰκέτης B. But the slaves' identification is still controversial: while Weise has been followed by most subsequent editors, Green, Merry, Hall/Geldart, Zacher, Rogers, and Sommerstein follow the manuscripts.[3]

---

[1] Boegehold 1999.
[2] Olson 1992: 310.
[3] For further discussion of the question of the slaves' identity see Richards 1909: 12; Pohlenz 1952: 104–11; Newiger 1957: 11–17; Dover 1972: 93–5 and 1987: 267–78, 307–10; Sommerstein 1980: 46–47; Stone 1980: 31–38; Kraus 1985: 114–19; Tammaro 1991: 143–50; MacDowell 1995: 87–8.

In answering the question, when can a comic character be said to portray an actual person, we may begin by asking what criteria apply when Aristophanes does give a character the name of an actual person, e.g. Sokrates in *Clouds*; Lamachos in *Acharnians*; Euripides in *Acharnians*, *Thesmophoriazusai*, and *Frogs*; Agathon in *Thesmophoriazusai*; and Aischylos in *Frogs*.[4] In these cases we find – even after allowance has been made for elements of comic stereotyping, exaggeration, and fantasy – that (1) much of the humor or point of the character's words, actions, appearance, and relationship to other characters depends on the spectators' knowledge of that person; (2) the character consistently and unambiguously represents that person; and (3) the character has no significant dramatic identity apart from his identification with that person. Thus even if the character identified in the text of *Acharnians* as "Euripides" were instead identified only as ποιητής, our knowledge of the actual Euripides would still entitle us to speak of portraiture, and editors could assign that character's lines to "Euripides" without misrepresenting the dramatic situation. In the case of "Lamachos," whose portrayal seems to us (though it may not have seemed to the original spectators) to contain more of the generic *miles gloriosus* than the individual general, we would be less justified in assigning an actual name if none were given in the text. But given that Aristophanes did name him, the character satisfies the criteria for portraiture no less clearly than does "Euripides."

If we then apply these criteria to a second (and much larger) category of Aristophanic characters – those who are unnamed or who have only a fictitious name or a generic identity – we find that in most cases none of the criteria apply, and in no case do all three criteria apply. In the mock-trial scene in *Wasps* 891–1008, for example, the characters Κύων Κυδαθηναιεύς and Λάβης Αἰξωνεύς satisfy criteria (1) and (2) but not (3), for their characterization includes both resemblance to actual individuals (Kleon and Laches) and a separate, but equally significant, dramatic identity (household dogs). Thus, to identify them as "Kleon" and "Laches" (on a par with e.g. "Euripides" in *Acharnians*) would be to misrepresent Aristophanes' satirical purpose and spoil the joke. Similar are cases where a character with an otherwise autonomous comic identity may occasionally suggest an actual person, as has been alleged of Lysistrata and the Polias priestess Lysimache,[5] or where a mythological character may allegorically represent an actual person, as is alleged of Perikles in Kratinos' *Dionysalexandros* in an ancient hypothesis.[6]

The slaves of *Knights* belong in this second category because, like the dogs of *Wasps*, each has an autonomous dramatic identity that may include, but is not limited by, its resemblance to actual individuals. The question is therefore not, Which

---

[4] For a general survey of Aristophanic naming conventions see Olson 1992: 317, who remarks that in such cases naming was important because "the appearance and behaviour of characters representing real contemporary Athenians onstage was...apparently not normally sufficiently distinctive to make their identity obvious."

[5] See Henderson 1987: xxxviii-xl.

[6] POxyr. 663=70 Austin=*PCG* iv [140], lines 44–48: "Perikles is very clearly ridiculed by innuendo (ἔμφασις) for having brought the war on the Athenians"; cf. Perikles (?) as "king of the satyrs" in Hermippos' *Moirai*, fr. 47.

individuals do these slaves portray? but rather, To what extent (if at all) do the behavior, characterization, and dramatic role of these slaves include references to individuals?

That the character named Paphlagon represents Kleon is made clear in the expository speech in 40–72, where he is identified as a tanner (44) and the winner of the credit for the victory at Pylos (54–57), and where his status in the household of Demos corresponds with Kleon's status in the polis. These points of resemblance are then elaborated in the following dialogue, during which Kleon is even pointed out in the theatre (203), so that by the end of the prologue Aristophanes can say (230–33) that, even though Paphlagon will not be wearing a portrait mask when he appears, the spectators "will recognize him all the same" – a safe promise if the spectators were at all abreast of current affairs, and if only some of what our sources say about Kleon's novel and charismatic style is true. Alongside the actor's evident mimicry of Kleon's voice, rhetorical style, and physical mannerisms – for all of these are repeatedly remarked on during the play – Aristophanes seems to have supplied a characterizing costume: a leather jacket (890–92) and an honorific crown (1225–28).

The tradition underlying the manuscripts' identification of the other two slaves as Demosthenes and Nikias derives from a scholarly desire for symmetry: it was thought that since Paphlagon more or less consistently represents Kleon, and the other two slaves have an analogous position in Demos' household (competitors for the master's favor), they can hardly have remained unidentified, i.e. have remained generic types rather than particular individuals. Since the more prominent slave's first-person reference to Pylos (54–57) seems to point to Demosthenes, it was only natural to suppose that the other slave represents Nikias, the third major figure in the Pylos affair. Thus the slaves would portray two of Kleon's actual "victims": the man from whom Kleon "stole" the credit for victory at Pylos and the man who, by resigning his command, had given Kleon his opportunity for a signal success.

But scholarly notions of dramatic symmetry may not be relevant to Aristophanes' own purposes in this situation, as they seem not to be elsewhere, for example the departure in *Lysistrata* and *Assemblywomen* of the heroine much earlier than a later playwright would consider proper, or the anonymity of the comic hero throughout *Thesmophoriazusai*, or until late in *Acharnians* (406) and *Knights* (1199). Again, as a rule, Aristophanic slaves who take an active part in the dialogue normally remain anonymous, just as named slaves tend to be mutes. During our prologue, and especially in the expository speech (40–72), Demos' slaves are in fact described largely in generic terms: as two among other "servants of Demos" in both a domestic and a political sense. As a result, the dramatic stress tends to fall on the villainous Paphlagon, and that is consonant with the subsequent action, where Demos' slaves will indeed play no significant role. One disappears even before the prologue ends (154); the other serves merely to introduce the Sausage Seller and the Knights (155–246) and thereafter to play the bystander in their contest with the Paphlagon until his own departure just before the parabasis (497).[7] In addition, the two slaves are

---

[7] The interjection at 1254–6, whoever the speaker, is delivered offstage.

characterized in ways inappropriate to civic leaders but true to the slave stereotype: they howl in pain, sing a barbaric dirge, masturbate, steal, and act in a devious and cowardly manner. Thus it would seem that any resemblance our slaves may have to particular individuals is both incidental to their primary generic function and irrelevant to the main action as it develops after the prologue.

Only the first slave says anything that might specifically associate him with a particular individual. In the expository speech, his first-person reference to Pylos (54–57) does suit Demosthenes, though we must note that none of the speaker's other anecdotes, in which he aligns himself with his fellow slaves ("us" in 53, 58, 65, 69), seems suitable as a reference to Demosthenes, and that Paphlagon later speaks of his Pylos "victims" in the plural (355 τοὺς ἐν Πύλῳ στρατηγούς). Later (319–21) this same speaker recalls passing through Pergase en route to his own "fellow-demesmen and friends." Since no slave could speak of fellow-demesmen, and since Pergase lies en route to Demosthenes' own deme, Aphidna, some would identify a (second) reference to him here. But the context clearly shows that here the speaker is identifying himself not with generals but with simple country folk, and so can hardly be prompting the spectators to think of Aphidna. The straightforward implication of his anecdote is that he was going home to Pergase.

More problematic is Paphlagon's accusation of antidemocratic conspiracy in Boiotia (479), where Demosthenes had contributed prominently to Athenian strategic efforts.[8] If this accusation refers to the planning of the campaign for Delion that Demosthenes and his colleague Hippokrates were to undertake later in the year, and if it was meant as a reference to Demosthenes, it is strange that Paphlagon accuses not the slave particularly but his opponents *ensemble*, especially the Knights. It may also be relevant that the campaign strategy was supposed to be a secret. Thus the passage makes better sense as a blanket indictment of oligarchic intrigue, such as Kleon was fond of levelling against his opponents, than as a pointed ad hominem thrust.

Other elements of the first slave's characterization are dislike of Euripidean mannerism (19); skepticism about the existence of the gods (in 30–34, but not in 156, 229, to which we will return); fondness for wine and belief in its power to enhance one's abilities mental, physical and social (85 ff.); and more intelligence, decisiveness, and leadership than his colleague (especially after he has drunk the wine). This combination of traits cannot be associated particularly with Demosthenes or with any other contemporary figure. Indeed we hear of nothing distinctive in Demosthenes' personal traits: our sources portray him as more the soldier than the public personality.[9] The comic poets certainly seem to have found him uninteresting as a subject. If this impression is accurate and not merely due to a gap in our sources, Demosthenes led an unremarkable private life, appeared only infrequently before assemblies or juries, and left no memorable impression when he did.

The second slave says nothing that would explicitly link him with Nikias, so that this identification must rely solely on the criteria of symmetry and characterization.

---

[8] Thuk. 3.96–8, 4.76–7.

[9] *PA* 3585; Davies 1971: 103–4.

For the reasons given above, the criterion of symmetry alone is not compelling, and would be significant only if both slaves consistently represented real individuals, which in the case of the first slave seems unlikely. Dover adds this caution: "If the second slave represents a real person, Nikias is not necessarily the best candidate. We have been influenced by Thucydides' selection, emphasis, and portrayal of the events of 425; so had the Hellenistic scholars; Aristophanes had not."[10] This may be over-cautious. If a candidate is needed, no better one can be suggested: there is no reason to doubt the general reliability of Thukydides' portrayal either of Nikias as Kleon's principal political adversary in 425 or of the importance of Nikias' resignation of the Pylos command to Kleon. Nevertheless, the identification can only be established by finding elements of characterization unmistakably linking the second slave to Nikias.

Sommerstein thinks that we can, for the second slave's "characterization ... (unusually vivid, for a minor personage in Aristophanes) guarantees, in its timidity (16–18), its strong religiosity (30–33), its pessimism (34, 111–2), its dislike of overindulgence (87–88, 97), that it is intended for Nikias."[11] Complaint about slanderous accusations (cf. 6–7) may be added to this list. But in evaluating these potential elements of characterization we must determine (1) whether they especially suit Nikias' public persona in the winter of 424,[12] bearing in mind a second caution of Dover's: "if the slave is Nicias, he is not necessarily invested with the character which the Sicilian Expedition, several years after *Knights*, revealed in Nicias"; and (2) whether our appreciation of their humor or their point requires knowledge of any actual person. After all, the slaves are meant to represent the plight of the entire political establishment in Athens, and vividness can be a property of entirely fictitious characters. For a poet who often prided himself on originality, vividness may have been especially desirable in creating such stock scenes as slave prologues.[13]

Complaint about malicious accusations (6–7 ταῖν διαβολαῖν) would suit Nikias, who was very rich, very prominent as a general and politician, and a particular enemy of Kleon's. Thukydides reports that in 425 Kleon was Nikias' "enemy and detractor" (ἐχθρὸς ὢν καὶ ἐπιτιμῶν), and that in the Pylos debate he had questioned Nikias' manliness (4.27.5); in our play the Sausage-Seller, emulating Kleon, boasts that he will "harass Nikias" (358 Νικίαν ταράξω). Plutarch (*Nik,* 2.6, 4.3) notes Nikias' great fear of accusers (πρὸς τοὺς συκοφάντας εὐθορύβητον) and says that this fear was "a revenue to rogues" (πρόσοδος τοῖς πονηροῖς). As evidence he quotes *Knights* 358,

---

[10] Dover 1987: 310.

[11] Sommerstein 1981: 3.

[12] For our sources about Nikias – principally Thukydides, Plutarch's *Life of Nikias*, and Plato's *Lakhes* – see *PA* 10808, Davies 1971: 403–4. For a review of recent work on Plutarch's *Life* – an important source of anecdotal information about Nikias' character – see Podlecki and Duane 1992: 4103–5.

[13] In the parabasis of *Peace* (742–47) Aristophanes in fact decries rival playwrights' hackneyed treatment of slave-types, including "those who were always running away and practicing deceit and getting beaten, just so that a fellow slave might laugh at his wounds and ask, 'Wretch, what's happened to your skin? It isn't a pig-bristle lash, is it, that's launched a full-scale attack on your sides and clear-cut your back?'" The difference between such slaves and those in *Knights* (aside from the simple fact that in *Knights* both slaves are beaten) may be the assimilation of the slaves' predicament to the predicament of Athenian politicians and the "unusually vivid" characterization of the slaves themselves.

Telekleides 41 (play and date unknown: Nikias pays an accuser for his silence), and Eupolis *Marikas* 193 (produced in 421: Marikas-Hyperbolos twists the testimony of a bystander into a charge of conspiracy against the innocent Nikias). Nevertheless, Kleon did not get his reputation as "a consummate rogue and accuser" (45 πανουργότατον καὶ διαβολώτατόν τινα) by attacking only Nikias, as the expository speech makes very clear (esp. 63–70) and as the whole play bears out. Thus the second slave's complaint does not seem more appropriate to Nikias than to any other victim of Kleon's accusations.

Nikias' record as a commander seems at first glance incompatible with a reputation for timidity and pessimism. He was elected general every year from 427/6 until his death in 413,[14] and Thukydides says that in 422 he "had done better in command than anyone else in his time" (5.16). He had demonstrated his competence shortly before *Knights* in his successful invasion of Korinthia immediately after the victory at Pylos (4.42–5) – an action celebrated in this play (266–68, 595–610) – and in the following summer would again be successful at Kythera (4.53–5). In 415 his strategic resourcefulness in preliminary actions against the Syracusans was noticed favourably even by comic poets.[15] Thereafter, it is true, Nikias displayed a military hesitancy that contributed to Athens' worst defeat of the war. His decision to withdraw to Katane (6.71), delaying further operations until spring (6.97) instead of following up his initial successes, was criticized at the time,[16] and his delay of the withdrawal from Syracuse for twenty-seven days after a lunar eclipse (7.50) proved disastrous. But there is reason to think that such hesitancy had been characteristic of Nikias even before this. Of the Katane withdrawal Plutarch comments, "Everyone blamed Nikias for this, since by his deliberations, delays, and precautions he had let slip the time for action. None would blame the man when he was in action, for when he got going he was vigorous and energetic, but he was slow to get going and lacked assurance to engage" (*Nik.* 16.5).

This impression is confirmed when we move from the battlefield to Athens. According to Thukydides, Nikias had been hesitant about the Sicilian expedition to begin with (in the debates reported in 6.9–25), at one point even offering to resign his command to Alkibiades (6.23.3), and his advocacy of peace in 422 had been motivated by a desire to rest on his laurels and avoid further risk.[17] For Plutarch (esp. *Nik.* 2–5) Nikias' public demeanor – cautious, deferential and timid (ψοφοδεές, as in the title of Menander's play, and ἀθαρσής) – was one of his most distinctive traits; he quotes Phryn. fr. 62 (play and date unknown), "he was an excellent citizen ... and didn't walk in a cowering way (ὑποταγείς), like Nikias." Thukydides plays down Nikias' resignation of his command at Pylos to Kleon, who had accused him of

---

[14] Fornara 1971: 56–65. Plu. *Nik.* 2.2 says that Nikias had been a general with Perikles and had "often" held independent commands, but he may be confusing Nikias with Hagnon, son of Nikias.

[15] *Av.* 362–63, Phryn. fr. 23.

[16] *Av.* 639 μελλονικιᾶν; Thuk. 7.42.5 ὑπερώφθη; Plu., *Nik.* 16.5 (Hermokrates jokes to the Syracusans) "Nikias is ridiculous, since he is a general who will not fight."

[17] For Dover, *HCT* at 4.86.5, Nikias' "one consistent characteristic is his obsessive anxiety to preserve his own reputation as a successful general."

cowardice (4.27.5), and portrays Kleon as the frightened one (28.2). But surely there is some truth in Plutarch's report of the Athenian reaction: "This brought Nikias great disgrace (ἀδοξίαν). It was not to throw away his shield, but something more shameful and ignominious, willingly to throw away his command out of cowardice (δειλίᾳ) and to furnish his enemy with an opportunity for so great a success, voting himself as it were out of office" (*Nik.* 8.2). Plutarch quotes Aristophanes *Farmers* fr. 102 (produced before 421), where a farmer offers his countrymen 2000 drachmas to quit his offices and return home, and they accept, adding the money to what Nikias paid to quit his.

Granted, then, Nikias in 424 could be portrayed as timid and pessimistic. But did Aristophanes so portray him in *Knights*? The second slave does seem more timid and pessimistic than the first: he cannot bring himself openly to suggest desertion (16ff.); his teeth apparently chatter when he suggests prostration before a sacred image (30–32); he is convinced that the gods hate him (34); and he fears that his colleague's luck will turn out to be bad (111–12). On the other hand, the first slave is hardly a paragon of courage and optimism either: he is the first to suggest deserting the master (20); rejects desertion as being too risky (27–9) and unlikely to escape the Paphlagon's notice (74–9); and agrees that suicide may be the best plan (80–1). Conversely, though it is the first slave who persists in finding a positive solution to the predicament, it is the second slave who at great risk steals wine (98–102) and oracles (109–17) from the sleeping Paphlagon, and who keeps watch inside while the first slave recruits the Sausage Seller (154). Thus it is incorrect to imagine the slaves' characterization as being antithetical,[18] so that a courageous Demosthenes may be set against a timid Nikias. Both slaves are demoralized for reasons that are explained in the expository speech (40–72) and that apply also to the other members of Demos' household, of which our slaves are representatives. No portrayal of particular individuals is needed to appreciate this.

"Strong religiosity" seems to have been a notable characteristic of Nikias even before his capitulation in 413 to the soldiers' faith in the army soothsayers, which Thukydides attributes to his being "rather prone to divination (θειασμῷ) and the like" (7.50.4). Plutarch notes Nikias' εὐσέβεια, his terror of τὰ δαιμόνια, his exceptional generosity in public expenditures for the gods,[19] and his maintenance of a private soothsayer, "whom he pretended was for consultation about civic matters but whom for the most part he consulted about his business, particularly his silver mines" (*Nik.* 4.1–2). That such religiosity was unusual in a leader of Aristophanes' day is suggested by the fact that Nikias is the only Athenian leader after Perikles to whom Thukydides attributes religious scruples;[20] and that faith in "divination and the like" was a quality Aristophanes may have found dismaying in a leader is suggested by his contempt for it as a quality in the demos (61 σιβυλλιᾷ, 997–1099).

Nevertheless, one may doubt that the second slave's suggestion about prostration before "some sacred image" (30–34) is aimed at Nikias in particular: the suggestion is

---

[18] As, for example, does Kraus 1985: 119.

[19] Even if there is no evidence for his having masterminded the purification of Delos in 426/5 (Thuk. 3.104), as is often asserted: see Hornblower 1991: 517–8.

[20] See Jordan 1986: 134–7.

adequately motivated by the slaves' apparently hopeless predicament, and it does not exceed conventional (including tragic) notions of slavish and womanish behavior in such a situation. In addition, the second slave's suggestion is made more to set up an incidental joke than to establish his character, so that we may no more call him a religious slave than we may call his colleague an agnostic: the first slave's expression of doubt about the existence of gods (32) is not characterization but simply a feed for the joke, since he will himself soon be advising the Sausage Seller to "make obeisance to the earth and the gods" (156) and invoking the gods as helpers against Paphlagon (229). We may also note that his apparent contempt for Euripidean mannerism (19) is not "in character" for an agnostic, just as the second slave's Euripidean mannerism (16–26) is not "in character" for the pious Nikias. We are entitled to expect that character traits identifying an allegorical figure be consistent.

Our second slave, who twice expresses doubt that drinking is a good idea under the circumstances (87–8, 97), and who does not share the cup with his colleague (107–24), differs in this respect not merely from his colleague and Paphlagon (who has drunk himself to sleep, 104) but also from the typical comic slave, who enjoys wine.[21] For Sommerstein "it is hard to see what the point of all this is – it does not advance the plot, it is not particularly funny, and the first slave's praise of wine as a sharpener of the intellect is hardly consistent with its effect upon Paphlagon – unless it is intended to help the audience identify the second slave with some public figure who had the reputation of a water-drinker and/or, if they have already made the identification, to poke fun at this public figure."[22] Now Plutarch records that Nikias led a remarkably ascetic life, avoiding symposia and all other social activities so as to give the impression of total devotion to his public duties (*Nik.* 5). Thus Sommerstein: "His avoidance of symposia makes it likely in any case that he did not drink much, and besides was so abnormal for an Athenian of his class that it may well have given him the reputation of being a total or almost total abstainer, so that we may take the non-drinking slave as representing Nikias."

But, in purely dramatic terms, is the second slave's cautious attitude so very remarkable? In a situation so grave that suicide is a plausible option (80–84), the first slave's sudden proposal to drink neat wine (85–86) might naturally prompt a response like the second slave's: "Neat wine! Of course *you'd* be thinking of drink. But how can a man plan out anything effective if he's drunk?" (86–87). Note that the second slave does not profess aversion to wine as a general rule[23] but only fears that it might befuddle their wits at this critical moment. By expressing this attitude, which was quite conventional, the second slave enhances the dramatic impact of his colleague's bold inspiration, which turns out to be the beginning of their salvation.

By this time we have been told that the slaves represent Athens' leaders suffering under Kleon's mastery of the demos (40–72), so that, dramatic considerations aside, the non-drinker might still have suggested one leader in particular. But was Nikias'

---

[21] E.g. *Ve.* 9–10, *Lys.* 426–7, *Ek.* 1112–24.

[22] Sommerstein 1980: 46.

[23] The first slave's response, ἄληθες, οὗτος· κρουνοχυτρολήραιον εἶ (89), comments not on the second slave's character but on what he just said, as 90–94 show.

behavior unusual enough to make him the obvious target? Avoidance of symposia and other social distractions need not necessarily lead to a reputation as an abstainer, especially if the point was to cultivate an image of self-sacrifice in the public interest. Plutarch indeed attributes the same strategy not only to Perikles but also to Kleon (*Nik.* 5, *Per.* 7), who is portrayed in *Knights* as a heavy drinker (and as a symposion guest in *Wasps* 1220). And the second slave's belief that drinking is incompatible with important business was hardly atypical in Athens:[24] it was indeed shared, according to Paphlagon, by any number of his opponents (344–50). In fact, Paphlagon's heavy drinking, like his predatory eating, is thematic in the play: it is one secret of his success both in politics (344–62) and at Pylos (1054), and it distinguishes him from all his opponents until the Sausage Seller comes along. It is therefore fitting that the first slave's idea of stealing Paphlagon's wine begins the process that sees Paphlagon being defeated by his own methods. In these ways the wine-routine serves dramatic purposes larger than mere caricature of Nikias or any other individual.[25]

A further difficulty with the identification of the slaves as Demosthenes and Nikias lies in their relationship with one another: why would Aristophanes have cast Nikias, who was Demosthenes' senior in age, military prestige, and political importance, as the less important slave, and why would he have removed him from the action before Paphlagon, who represents Nikias' great enemy, even enters? Surely that confrontation would have made for some delectable humor. Since there is no apparent reason, van Leeuwen suggested switching the assignments of lines 1–9 so that the second slave begins the play and remains onstage after Paphlagon appears; Kraus follows suit, and further explains the second slave's disappearance as corresponding to Nikias' fear of Kleon.[26] But these are solutions to a problem that exists only if we decide in advance that the slaves must represent Demosthenes and Nikias.

Further problems with a particular identity for the slaves emerge when we examine the structure of the prologue and its overall function in the play. A salient feature of the opening dialogue is the paucity of information it reveals about the specifics of the slaves' situation and its connection with the political situation in Athens; these are first revealed and explained in the monologue in 40–72. As in the structurally similar prologues of *Wasps*, *Peace,* and *Birds* (initial dialogue followed by an explanatory monologue), the goal seems to be initial mystification – in *Wasps* 71 ff. and *Peace* 43 ff. the spectators are even invited to guess what the situation is – followed by a formal

---

[24] It gives comic point to the inversions in *Lys.* 1228–30 (where an Athenian ambassador, after a successful diplomatic symposion, decides henceforth to conduct all negotiations drunk) and *Ek.* 137–43 (where a woman surmises that assemblymen must be drunk to reach the decisions they do). Note also the reaction of Philokleon, a typical juror, to his son's suggestion that they go to an upper-class symposion and get drunk: "No way! Drinking is a bad thing. From wine come door-breaking, fights, stone-throwing and then fine-paying while nursing a hangover," *Ve.* 1252–55.

[25] Kratinos, for instance, in *Pytine* (produced the following year), which seems to have stressed the importance of drinking to his own poetic creativity, at least in part to rebut Aristophanes' criticism in the parabasis of *Knights* (526–36), and it is possible that the metaphors in the prologue of *Knights* connecting drinking with creativity echo an earlier play by Kratinos; see now Luppe 2000 and Rosen 2000.

[26] Kraus 1985: 119.

clarification.[27] If the spectators were expected to realize from the beginning that the slaves represent Demosthenes and Nikias – and they would have to, since most of the alleged items of characterization precede the monologue – there seems to be no point to the apparent mystification. Nor is there any apparent reason why Aristophanes, having established his slaves as Demosthenes and Nikias, would make no further use of these identities after the prologue. As we have seen, his decision to keep Demosthenes onstage as the Sausage Seller's helper instead of Nikias would be especially puzzling, in view of the latter's more important political status and (surely) greater potential for caricature.[28]

These dramatic considerations also tell against the hypothesis that the slaves wore portrait-masks[29] or were in some other physical way (gesture, voice, props) identifiable as particular individuals at the very outset, which would explain how the spectators could have appreciated caricature that is not apparent in the dialogue alone. Lines 230–33, which apologize for the Paphlagon's lack of a portrait-mask, certainly prove that portrait-masks were possible and that they might have been expected in this kind of play, but they do not prove that the opening slaves wore such masks and thus created the expectation that Kleon would also be so masked.[30]

Finally, it is possible that the spectators could have known who the slaves would represent by attending or hearing about the proagon, when poets and actors announced the subjects of their plays.[31] But Aristophanes would surely not have omitted from the performance itself any information necessary to the play's intelligibility on the assumption that the spectators could be trusted to know it already.

We may conclude that, although the Paphlagon consistently represents Kleon and the other two slaves *may* at some moments call to mind Demosthenes and Nikias more than other actual individuals, there remains a very substantial lack of coincidence between the dramatic characters (including Paphlagon) and any actual counterparts. Aristophanes' choice of this way to attack Kleon and the politicians generically represented by the opening slaves, rather than by mounting a more direct attack by actually naming them, may have been motivated by fear of retaliation; we can only speculate. But his *dramatic* goals are clear enough. In the unusual allegory of *Knights,* Aristophanes clearly strove to keep constantly and simultaneously in view both the general and the particular, the domestic and the political, the individual and the collective, so that the particulars of the actual world are only ingredients of a more spacious dramatic fantasy. To label any character as, and so equate him fully with, an actual contemporary would therefore be to misrepresent a central aspect of the play's

---

[27] For this technique see Newiger 1957: 11–17.

[28] In the previous year Aristophanes had announced his intention to retaliate against Kleon "next year" by "cutting him into shoeleather for the Knights" (*Ach.* 299–302, cf. 377–82, 630–64). At that time Aristophanes could not have foreseen either Kleon's triumph at Pylos or the roles that Demosthenes and Nikias were to have in it, so that their appearance in his promised play would have been a late addition. But even so, Aristophanes need not have confined their topical roles to the prologue; Pylos and its consequences are otherwise integrated into the play.

[29] For a good discussion of the evidence see Stone 1980: 31–38.

[30] So Sommerstein 1981: 3; Kraus 1985: 117.

[31] Cf. Pl. *Smp.* 194a, Pickard-Cambridge 1968: 67–8.

satirical system. As Richards put it, "As well might Dryden in his great satire have written *Shaftesbury* and *Shadwell* for *Achitophel* and *Og*."[32]

WORKS CITED

Boegehold, A.L. 1999. *When a Gesture Was Expected*. Princeton.

Davies, J.K. 1971. *Athenian Propertied Families 600–300 BC*. Oxford.

Dindorf, W. 1835. *Aristophanis Comoediae*. Oxford.

Dover, K.J. 1972. *Aristophanic Comedy*. California.

———. 1987. *Greek and the Greeks*. Oxford.

Fornara, C.W. 1971. *The Athenian Board of Generals from 501 to 404*. Historia Einzelschrift 16. Wiesbaden.

Green, W.C. 1870. *The Knights and Acharnians of Aristophanes*. London.

Hall, F.W. and Geldart, W.M. 1906². *Aristophanis Comoediae*. Oxford.

Harvey, D. and J. Wilkins, J., eds. 2000. *The Rivals of Aristophanes. Studies in Athenian Old Comedy*. London.

HCT = A.W. Gomme, A. Andrewes and K.J. Dover, *A Historical Commentary on Thucydides*. 5 vols. Oxford 1945–81.

Henderson, J.J. 1987. *Aristophanes Lysistrata*. Oxford.

Hornblower, S. 1991. *A Commentary on Thucydides I*. Oxford.

Jordan, B. 1986. "Religion in Thucydides." *TAPhA* 116: 119–47.

Kraus, W. 1985. *Aristophanes' politische Komödien*. Vienna.

Luppe, W. 2000. "The Rivalry between Aristophanes and Kratinos." In Harvey and Wilkins, 15–21.

MacDowell, D.M. 1995. *Aristophanes and Athens*. Oxford.

Merry, W.W. 1887. *Aristophanes. The Knights*. Oxford.

Newiger, H.-J. 1957. *Metapher und Allegorie. Zetemata* 16. Munich.

Olson, S.D. 1992. "Names and Naming in Aristophanic Comedy." *CQ* n.s. 42: 304–19.

PA = J. Kirchner, *Prosopographia Attica*. Berlin 1901–03.

Pickard-Cambridge, A.W. 1968. *The Dramatic Festivals of Athens*. Rev. ed. by J. Gould and D.M. Lewis. Oxford.

Podlecki, A.J. and S. Duane. 1992. "Work on Plutarch's Greek Lives, 1951–1988." *ANRW* II.33.6: 4053–4127.

Pohlenz, M. 1952. "Aristophanes' Ritter." *NAWG* 5: 95–128.

Richards, H. 1909. *Aristophanes and Others*. London.

Rogers, B.B. 1910. *The Knights of Aristophanes*. London.

Rosen, R. 2000. "Cratinus' *Pytine* and the Construction of the Comic Self." In Harvey and Wilkins, 23–39.

Sommerstein, A. H. 1980. "Notes on Aristophanes' *Knights*." *CQ* n.s. 30: 46–56.

———.1981. *The Comedies of Aristophanes: Vol. 2. Knights*. Warminster.

Stone, L.M. 1980. *Costume in Aristophanic Comedy*. New York.

Tammaro, V. 1991. "Demostene e Nicia nei 'Cavalieri'?" *Eikasmos* 2: 143–52.

van Leeuwen, J. 1900. *Aristophanis Equites*. Leiden.

Weise, C.H. 1842. *Aristophanis Comoediae*. Leipzig.

Zacher, K. 1898. *Aristophanesstudien*. Leipzig.

---

[32] Richards 1909: 12.

7

Nemesis and *Phthonos*

David Konstan

In his treatise on rhetoric, Aristotle defines *to nemesan* – the nominalized infinitive corresponding to the abstract noun *nemesis* – as "feeling pain at someone who appears to be succeeding undeservedly" (2.9, 1837a8–9). So understood, it is, says Aristotle, the opposite of pity, defined in the same treatise as "a kind of pain in the case of an apparent destructive or painful harm in one not deserving to encounter it, which one might expect oneself, or one of one's own, to suffer, and this when it seems near" (2.8, 1835b13–16). Put schematically, *to nemesan* is pain at undeserved good fortune, whereas pity is pain at undeserved misfortune (2.9, 1386b9–12). Both emotions, Aristotle goes on to say, are marks of good character, since people ought neither to prosper nor to suffer undeservingly: for what runs counter to worth is unjust. This is why, Aristotle concludes, we ascribe *to nemesan* to the gods, the point being that it entails an assessment of fairness or lawfulness. On this description, *to nemesan* may reasonably be translated as "being indignant," the emotion we feel when others unfairly acquire what they have done nothing to earn.

Aristotle goes on to note, however, that according to some, not only *to nemesan* but also *phthonos* – the term commonly rendered into English as "envy" – is the opposite of pity, on the grounds that *phthonos* "is related to and is indeed the same thing as *to nemesan*" (2.9, 1386b16–17). But in fact, Aristotle insists, the two are different. For, as he explains, although *phthonos* too is "a disturbing pain arising from the well-being" of another (2.9, 1386b18–19; cf. 2.10, 1387b22–24), it arises not because the other person is undeserving, but simply because he is our equal or similar (2.9, 1386b19–20); and such a person (we feel) ought not to have an advantage over us. In his fuller definition of *phthonos* in the chapter devoted to that emotion (2.10, 1387b23–25), Aristotle states that "*phthonos* is a kind of pain, in respect to one's equals, for their apparent success in things called good, not so as to have the thing oneself but [solely] on their account" – that is, because they have a good that we do not, irrespective of its use to us. It is this indifference both to desert and to one's own need that renders *phthonos* an emotion unsuited to a decent (*epieikēs*) person. As Aristotle conceives it, *phthonos* is motivated by a small-minded concern for image – it is characteristic, he says, of people who are *philodoxoi* and *mikropsukhoi* (2.10, 1387b33–34). So petty a sentiment seems little more than spite or malice (cf. Cairns 1993: 194 n. 51). Indeed, among all the emotions Aristotle discusses in detail in the *Rhetoric*, including anger and calming down, love and hatred, fear, shame, benevolence, pity, *to nemesan* itself, and *zēlos* or emulation, *phthonos* is the only one that he treats as unqualifiedly negative. So too, the psychologists J. Sabini and M. Silver (1986: 169) have remarked that of the seven deadly sins – greed, sloth, wrath, lust, gluttony, pride, and envy – the six "other than envy *involve acts having goals which are not in themselves evil but which have been done inappropriately or to excess....* Envy is out of place on this list, as it does not appear to point to a natural goal. This is the paradox of envy."

Despite the confidence with which Aristotle distinguishes *to nemesan* from *phthonos*, against the view of those who identified them, in the later rhetorical and philosophical tradition it was in fact the contrast between pity and *phthonos* that prevailed – irrespective of the question of desert – rather than that between pity and *to nemesan*.[1] The Stoics, for example, described pity as pain at another's ill fortune, while envy is pain at another's good fortune (e.g., Andronicus *Peri pathōn* 2 p. 12 Kreuttner = *SVF* 3.414). Cicero effectively transposed Aristotle's dictum concerning pity and *to nemesan* when he wrote (*Tusc.* 3.21) that "to pity and to envy [*invidere*] befall the same person, since the same person who is pained at the adverse circumstances of another is pained also at the favorable circumstances of another" (cf. *On the Orator* 1.185, 2.206, 2.216; Ben-Ze'ev 2000: 338–40). Consequently, Cicero concludes in a Stoic vein, a wise man will be subject to neither sentiment.

The Stoics, to be sure, rejected all emotion as incompatible with virtue, and were not interested in defending the value of those emotions based on an assessment of desert, such as pity and *to nemesan*, over ostensibly non-moral passions such as *phthonos* (in any case, the Stoics defined all emotions as judgments). But there was another reason why Aristotle's contrast between pity and *to nemesan* gave way to that between pity and envy: for the term *nemesan* and its associated noun, *nemesis*, were archaic even by Aristotle's time, except in certain contexts, and were no longer central to the Greek emotional lexicon (the more exhaustive Stoic lists, running to a hundred and more *pathē*, do include *nemesis*). *Nemesis* yielded to *phthonos* as pity's opposite by default, as it were. But the replaceability of the one term by the other nevertheless suggests that there is more to be said than Aristotle allows for the similarity between the two in his own time and earlier. In what follows, I trace the evolution of the two terms and defend the view of those who, according to Aristotle, maintained that *phthonos* was "indeed the same thing as *to nemesan*."

I have preferred to speak of *to nemesan* or "being indignant" in connection with Aristotle, rather than use the simple noun *nemesis*, because he himself avoids the latter term in the *Rhetoric*. The reason why is evident from a passage in the *Eudemian Ethics*, where Aristotle avails himself of the word *nemesis* to indicate the virtuous mean between two extremes: the excess is *phthonos*, while the deficiency, according to Aristotle, has no name in ordinary Greek (1220b34–1221a10). Aristotle goes on to explain that *phthonos* – the emotion associated with the *phthonēros* man – consists in being pained at those who are doing well in accord with their deserts, whereas the nameless *pathos*, characteristic of one who delights in the misfortune of others (the

---

[1] There are exceptions, of course; Ps.-Plut. *De Homero* 132 follows Aristotle.

epikhairekakos man), consists in being pleased at those who are faring ill contrary to their deserts. Aristotle labels the man who strikes the mean between these extremes *nemesētikos*, and adds that "what the ancients called *nemesis*" consists in "being pained at [others'] faring ill or faring well contrary to desert, and being pleased at these same states when they are merited." This is why, Aristotle says, people think that Nemesis is a goddess (*EE* 1233b 16–34).

It is clear that Aristotle is self-consciously appropriating an archaic word to designate the emotion associated with the character type he calls *nemesētikos*, so as to have a noun that answers to the vice of *phthonos*. In contemporary diction, Nemesis normally referred to the divinity who for at least two centuries had had a major cult center in the Attic deme of Rhamnous (for a catalogue of all references to the personified deity, see Hornum 1993: 91–152). As defined in the *Eudemian Ethics*, moreover, *nemesis* is a curiously complex emotion, involving both a painful and a pleasurable response to states that may be either good or bad: pleasurable if they are deserved, otherwise painful. So interpreted, *nemesis* encroaches on pity, as Aristotle conceives it, since both entail pain at the undeserved misfortune of another. Aristotle's effort to contrast *nemesis* with *phthonos* in this treatise appears to be something of a dud.

In the *Nicomachean Ethics* (1108b1–10), Aristotle introduces the noun *epikhairekakia*, or "Schadenfreude," to name the opposite pole to *phthonos*, with *nemesis* again serving as the mean. Here, however, *nemesis* is restricted to being a painful response to another's undeserved good fortune, while *phthonos* is extreme in responding painfully to any good fortune, deserved or not. The *epikhairekakos* person, finally, is so far from feeling pain as to take pleasure – at the ill fortune of another, clearly, and irrespective of desert, though Aristotle does not say so explicitly. The reason for this reticence is, I think, that the appropriate opposite to *epikhairekia* should be pleasure taken in another's justified misfortune, and this sense clashes with the more restricted definition of *to nemesan* given in the *Rhetoric*. So much for Aristotle's rather confusing attempt to adapt the opposition between *nemesis* and *phthonos* to his tripartite model of mean and extremes.

Not just the noun *nemesis*, but also the verb *nemesan* and the adjectives derived from it were old-fashioned in Aristotle's time, and where they, or *nemesis*, do occur after the archaic period, it is in a limited set of contexts and formulas that suggest fossilized locutions. Leaving aside cases in which Nemesis refers to the goddess, whether in cult or mythology, it and related terms frequently describe the attitude of a deity or deities (e.g., Thgn. 1.660, 1182; Pind. *Isthm.* 1.3–4; Eur. *Or.* 1361–62; Soph. *Phil.* 518, 602; Hdt. 1.34; Plato *Minos* 319A3–4; Plato Com. *Phaon* fr. 173.13–4 Kassel-Austin; Theoc. *Id.* 27.63; Theophr. *On Piety* fr. 3.1–2; Callim. *Aitia* fr. 96, *Hymn to Delos* 259; Polyb. 27.8.4 [a speech]). Apart from these instances of divine *nemesis*, the most common uses are in the formulas *ou nemesēton* or *anemesēton* (parallel to the expression *ou nemesis*) meaning "there is no blame attaching" to such and such a word or deed. Here again, the reference is often to things said of the gods, in the hope that they will not take offense (e.g., Thgn. 1.280; Plato *Cratylus* 401A5, *Theaetetus* 175E2, *Laws* 684E4, 876C8; Aeschin. *Against Ctesias* 66.1–3; Callim.

Hymn to Artemis 64, *Hymn to Delos* 107). These and similar uses represent a substantial percentage of all occurrences of the root *nemes-* (apart from the proper name Nemesis) in classical and Hellenistic literature down to the first century B.C. There are about 100 such instances in all, of which 33 are to be found in Aristotle alone and another dozen in Plato – amounting together to nearly half the total; outside these two, there are some 10 or 15 occurrences in prose. Later, *nemesis* regains a certain popularity with archaizing or moralizing authors, such as Diodorus Siculus and Dionysius of Halicarnassus (especially in his *Roman Antiquities*), as well as with Plutarch and writers of the Second Sophistic. By way of comparison, the root *phthon-* is found 78 times in Demosthenes alone (a few of these in the morally neutral form *aphthonia* or "abundance").

In Homer, as is well known, *nemesis* is generally aroused at behavior that runs contrary to socially accepted norms ("emotionale Reaktion ... auf Handlungen anderer, die nicht den allg. moralischen Erwartungen entsprechen," Stenger 2000: 818). These norms are not universal in the sense of applying equally to all, but take account of role and status. When Thersites addressed his rude complaint to Agamemnon, the Achaean troops "raged and grew indignant [*koteonto nemessēthen t'*] in their hearts" (*Il.* 2.222–23). Achilles' far harsher rebuke of Agamemnon in Book I evoked no such response in them; here, however, the defiant insubordination of a common soldier excites their pique (cf. Quint. *Inst. Or.* 11.1.37). In a contrary vein, Diomedes silences his henchman Sthenelus' irritation at Agamemnon's reprimand (4.413–17): "I do not *nemesō* at Agamemnon, shepherd of the peoples, for stirring the well-greaved Achaeans to do battle, for just as the glory will be his if the Achaeans should conquer the Trojans and capture holy Troy, so too vast grief is his if the Achaeans should be conquered." Diomedes recognizes that Agamemnon's position of responsibility entitles him to speak in ways that might well have caused offense on the lips of another Greek leader.

Sometimes the bare verb, without an explicit object, leaves the motive for the sentiment vague, as when Apollo feels *nemesis* (*nemesēse*) and shouts encouragement to the Trojans as the Achaeans advance upon the walls of the city (4.507–08). It is reasonable to suppose, however, that, as a god, he is indignant that a mortal army should threaten the city that he favors. When Hera asks Zeus to share her indignation (*Zeu pater, ou nemesizēi;*) at Ares for supporting the Trojan side (5.757–58), she protests that Ares has no sense of what is right (*themista*, 761). Ares, in turn, appeals to Zeus in similar terms after he is wounded by Diomedes at the instigation of Athena (5.872); his point is that it is beyond the province of a mortal to injure a deity (cf. also 8.198; Stenger 2000: 818 observes that the gods respond with *nemesis* "wenn Menschen versuchen, die Grenze zu ihnen zu überschreiten"). Rutherford, who remarks (1992: 146 ad 19.121) that "the sense of divine retribution, common in later Greek and more or less universal in modern usage, is not Homeric," suggests that passages in which a god expresses displeasure at mortal behavior, as Apollo does in *Iliad* 24.53, "perhaps show the germs of the later meaning." But such instances are perfectly in line with the gods' tendency to take offense at mortal audacity or insolence.

Nemesis is sometimes paired in archaic poetry with *aidōs* or shame, and the two emotions are commonly interpreted as the external and internal responses to a violation of customary rules. Walter Leaf observed more than a century ago (1888: 10 ad 13.122): "It is clear that the word [*nemesis*] is 'objective,' expressing the indignation felt by other men. *aidōs*, on the other hand, is subjective, the shame felt by the offender." So too, Stanford (1959: 231 ad 1.350) explains: "Two complementary qualities restrained the fierce self-centred heroes – *aidōs*, which is a feeling of reverence for certain conventions and privileges of gods and men; and the fear of *nemesis*, *i.e.* just indignation against violations of *aidōs*, including public censure and generally punishment as well" (cf. Fisher 1992: 193; Cairns 1993: 51–52). The verb *aideisthai*, however, commonly takes a person as direct object, and both sentiments are best treated as other-regarding, the one indicating respect, the other disapproval. Both, moreover, involve considerations of status. At times the verbs *nemizesthai* (middle) and *aideisthai* seem all but synonymous (e.g., *Odyssey* 1.263; cf. Redfield 1975: 117; Cairns 1993: 85 n. 120). Indeed, one can feel *nemesis* in regard to oneself, by imagining how one would respond if others behaved that way; Achilles cuts short a quarrel between Ajax and Idomeneus by inviting them to do just that (*Iliad* 23.473 ff.; cf. Cairns 1993: 98).[2]

The noun *phthonos*, by contrast, is not found in archaic epic, didactic, or hymnal poetry – that is, the oral hexameter tradition that the Greeks identified collectively under the rubric *epos*. The verb *phthoneō* does indeed occur, but is relatively rare: there are just two instances in the *Iliad*, and these within two lines (4.55–56). In return for the destruction of Troy, Hera surrenders to Zeus two of her favorite cities and declares: "If I *phthoneō* and do not allow [*eaō*] you to demolish them, I shall not succeed, for all that I *phthoneō*, for you are far stronger than I." The meaning of *phthoneō* here would seem to be "refuse," though the stronger sense of "begrudge" is also compatible with the context.

The *Odyssey* offers eight occurrences of *phthoneō* (including the compound *epiphthoneō* at 11.149, again opposed to *eaō*). For example, Alcinous, king of the Phaeacians, says to his daughter Nausicaa, when she asks permission to wash her clothes at the seashore: "I do not *phthoneō* you the mules that you request, nor anything else" (6.68). Here, the sense of *phthoneō* is hardly more than "deny" or "decline to give" (so too at 1.346, 11.381, 17.400, 19.348). In one case, the term seems more charged than the bare idea of "refusal" would suggest. When Odysseus, dressed in rags, seeks entry to his own house and is blocked by the mendicant Irus, who claims sole right to beg inside, Odysseus asserts: "I do you no harm in deed or word, nor do I *phthoneō* what you are given, though you have plenty; this threshold

---

[2] Cairns 1993: 53 observes that "The range of *nemesis* is very wide; it is frequently employed in condemnation of violence or excess, and also in a number of minor social contexts, where it censures infringement of decorum. In some cases it seems to signify little more than anger, although, as Redfield 1975: 117 points out, it always connotes anger in which the subject feels himself justified." This last qualification is doubtless true, but it is equally so of *orgē* or "anger," at least according to Aristotle's definition of *orgē* as "a desire, accompanied by pain, for a perceived revenge, on account of a perceived slight *on the part of those who are not fit to slight one* or one's own" (*Rhet.* 2.2, 1378a31–33).

can hold both of us, and there is no need for you to *phthoneein* others" (18.15–18). Here it would seem that the term assumes the connotation of "begrudge" or "resent," but this sense may be an effect of the context rather than the sign of a true lexical shift (so Herrmann 2003; contra Most 2003; Bulman 1992: 1, 15–16 takes it that Homeric usage is simply loose).

No form of *phthonos* occurs in Hesiod's *Theogony*. The abstraction thus lacks a genealogy and even the minimal degree of personification that this entails, which is the more curious, given the vast array of psychic and other concepts that are so dignified, including *nemesis* itself (223–30): "And baneful Night also bore Nemesis, a misery [*pēma*] for mortals, and after her Deceit and Love and destructive Old Age, and she bore Strife, fierce of temper. Then hateful Strife bore painful Toil and Oblivion and Famine and tearful Aches and Battles and Wars and Slayings and Murders and Feuds and Lies and Equivocal Words and Lawlessness and Madness, all related to one another." This is rather unsavory company for Nemesis, though in keeping with her genesis from Night, and it is plausible to suppose that Nemesis here bears the negative sense of "resentment" or even "hatred" rather than "righteous indignation."

In the *Works and Days*, the verb *phthoneō* occurs once (26), and here it is associated with what Hesiod calls "good Strife," which stirs potters, carpenters, beggars (a reminiscence of the *Odyssey*?), and singers to healthy rivalry with each other. It is more or less synonymous with *speudō*, *zēloō*, and *koteō*, which too are evidently positive terms for competitive effort. The contrast between the benign sense of *phthoneō* here and the unappealing characterization of the personified Nemesis is striking.[3] The verb is occasionally used in the neutral sense of "I don't mind" into the classical period (Aesch. *Seven* 236; Eur. *Medea* 63; Plato *Gorgias* 489A; cf. Xen. *Symp.* 3.5; cf. ibid. 1.12: "it is shameful to begrudge [*phthoneō*] someone the shelter of a roof; let him enter"; Walcot 1978: 26).

The noun *phthonos* makes its first appearance in epinician poetry, and it is prominent, along with its cognates, in the odes of Pindar (25 occurrences, according to Bulman 1992: 1; four times in what remains of Bacchylides; once in Theognis, 1.770; cf. Most 2003). Correspondingly, there is a sharp decline in *nemesis* and its relatives, in comparison with its frequent appearance in archaic poetry (only three times in Pindar, as in Theognis; twice in Aeschylus as contrasted with seventeen times for *phthonos* and related terms, excluding *aphthonos* et sim., in the surviving plays). If there was a transition from *nemesis* to *phthonos*, the moment at which to locate it is at the end of the sixth and beginning of the fifth centuries B.C.

That *nemesis* fell out of favor just as *phthonos* became popular would be nothing more than a coincidence if the two terms were as different in meaning as Aristotle makes them out to be, the former signifying justified indignation and the latter a wholly invidious form of resentment. We have seen, however, that the evidence of

---

[3] There is also a second occurrence of the root *phthon-* in the form *aphthonon*, "abundant" (118), a sense that perhaps points to an original meaning of "deny" or "begrudge" for *phthoneō* (*phthoneō* is the only form that appears in the Homeric Hymns: *To Aphrodite* 4.536; *To Earth Mother of All* 30.8, 16).

Homer and Hesiod speaks against such a sharp contrast. While there is no space here to trace its subsequent history in detail, it is clear that *phthonos* was not regarded as a uniformly negative emotion even in the classical period.

As Aristotle indicates, the contrast between pity and *phthonos* (rather than *to nemesan* and *pthonos*) was a commonplace in his time. As Pindar puts it (*Pyth.* 1.85), "*phthonos* is better than pity [*oiktirmos*]," the point being that success is preferable to failure, despite the envy it may entail (cf. Hdt. 3.52; Thales 108.10δ17 Diels-Kranz). When the Athenian soldiers in Sicily were facing defeat, Nicias attempted to reassure them by observing that they were more deserving of the gods' pity than of their *phthonos* (Thuc. 7.77.4).[4] Lysias, in his funeral oration (2.67), contrasts envy for others' goods with pity for those who have been wronged – the latter clearly considered the more virtuous sentiment (cf. 24.2). Pity, in turn, was associated with unmerited misfortune – as opposed to misfortune *simpliciter* – well before Aristotle, although Aristotle was perhaps the first to make this a formal part of the definition, and the connection between pity and desert underlay appeals to pity in forensic and deliberatory rhetoric (Konstan 2001: 34–43; cf. Euripides' *Suppliant Women* 168 with 186 and 194; 233 with 280; 304, 328 [the words are *oiktos* and *oiktirein*], Ničev 1985). To take one example among many, Isocrates (*On the Chariot* 48.6) asserts that "one must pity those who are unjustly at risk" (cf. *Plataïcus* 52.4; *Against Callimachus* 62; Plato *Protagoras* 323D).

It is not surprising, then, that *phthonos* too – as pity's opposite – should be linked with merit. Isaeus can say of his clients (6.61): "Thus, they do not deserve *phthonos*, but much rather, by Zeus and Apollo, these others do, if they acquire what does not belong to them." *Phthonos* is legitimate when directed at those who do not have title to the goods they possess. Demosthenes, in his speech *Against Meidias* (21.196), assails his opponent: "You would have discovered a great rule, or rather a great art, if in so short a time you could win for yourself two things that are absolutely opposite to each other: *phthonos* for your way of life, and pity for your lies. But pity doesn't fit you in any way, but just the opposite: hatred and *phthonos* and anger. That's what you deserve for what you do." Meidias, according to Demosthenes, has earned *phthonos*, because his arrogance and privilege are not warranted.[5] Toward such an individual, *phthonos* is perfectly appropriate, even required. Clearly the term does not mean "envy" in these contexts, if by envy we understand a gratuitous or improper resentment at another's well-being. So too the verb *phthoneō* may carry the sense, "feel righteous indignation at" (LSJ s.v. I.3, citing Isoc. 8.124, 4.184, Dem. 28.18; cf. Walcot 1978: 3: "even *phthonos* is not wholly bad"; especially Ranulf 1933: 106–11 for the "moral" use of *phthonos* and cognate terms).

---

[4] Nicias hints that the *phthonos* of the gods may have been provoked by the Athenians' overreaching ambition; for the novelty of this concession on the part of an Athenian within Thucydides' history, and its relation to the theme of the other states' envy of Athens, see Tzifopoulos 1995: 100–01; Τζιφόπουλος 1997: 501–04.

[5] The scholia comment unhelpfully: "*phthonos* and pity are two most opposite things" (Dilts 1986: 247).

To be sure, Demosthenes can also affirm to the Athenians (20.140): "*phthonos* is an absolute sign of vice [*kakia*] in human nature, and he who harbors it has no pretext by which to obtain sympathy," in accord with Aristotle's own harsh evaluation of this sentiment (cf. 165; also Plato *Timaeus* 297D: "no *phthonos* concerning anything ever arises in a good man"). We can explain the apparent contradiction in these uses of *phthonos* by observing that it was never a compliment to characterize someone as *phthoneros*, that is, temperamentally given to resenting others' well-being, and manifestations of *phthonos* could be taken as a sign of such a disposition. But this does not mean that *phthonos* is invariably illegitimate. The rich and powerful might attempt to stigmatize all *phthonos* as invidious, but in the world of democratic Athens, the way to avoid *phthonos* was to make proper use of one's advantages in the service of the community at large (cf. Wilson 2000: 172–84 on service to the *dēmos*; Fisher 2003; Saïd 2003). *Phthonos*, then, was not simply a moral flaw, but had a constructive social function as well.[6]

If *phthonos*, so understood, seems to approximate the sense that Aristotle ascribes to *to nemesan*, namely, a response to undeserved prosperity (*eupragein anaxiōs*), Aristotle himself acknowledges that *to nemesan*, in turn, is not simply indignation at the illegitimate acquisitions of another, but is also modulated by what we may call class entitlement. Thus, Aristotle says, "the *nouveaux riches* [*neoploutoi*] who acquire office by means of their wealth offend more than the *anciens riches* [*arkhaioploutoi*]..., the reason being that the latter seem to have what is truly theirs, but the former do not" (*Rhet.* 2.9, 1387a22–25). As Aristotle explains, "what is ancient seems practically natural" (1387a16). The traditional elites are perceived to deserve wealth and office, and hence escape reproach even when they have done nothing to earn them. This connection between *nemesan* and status is not very different from the way the term is used in Homer.

---

[6] Bulman 1992: 1 affirms that "human φθόνος in Pindar is a completely negative emotion" arising from "ignorance of human limitations" and a passion to transcend them (cf. p. 3: "φθόνος is the supreme negative emotion in Pindar"), but that "the φθόνος of the gods is better understood as equivalent to νέμεσις," and should not be translated as "envy" but rather as "retribution," for example at *Isthmian* 7.39–42 (31; survey of examples of human *phthonos* in Pindar on pp. 17–31, and of divine *phthonos* on pp. 31–36). But Bulman offers no explanation for why the word should have such radically different meanings in the two contexts. As Cairns 1996: 20 remarks: "There is no question of a total separation of meaning between human and divine *phthonos*"; when the gods feel *phthonos*, they, like human beings, believe that the emotion is justified (21). Bulman is right, in my view, to reject the attempt of Steinlein 1941: 20 and others to salvage a positive sense for *phthonos* as "a barometer to measure the good fortune possessed by an individual" (Bulman 1992: 5; cf. Milobenski 1964); no self-respecting aristocrat wants to deserve envy in the sense of being perceived to possess good things to which he is not entitled or which he abuses. The *phthonos* that Pindar singles out for blame is that directed against virtue (*Parth.* 1.8–9; cf. *Pythian* 7.19–20 on *phthonos* provoked by *kala*; also *Pythian* 11.29) – that is, the misguided *phthonos* characteristic of the *phthoneroi*, who harbor an illegitimate resentment against their betters. This does not mean that *phthonos* is never deserved, however; and it is just this justified sense of *phthonos* that the gods presumably feel at human excess, and which human beings can feel as well. While Pindar's usage certainly anticipates, as Bulman says (1992: 7), the negative account of *phthonos* in Aristotle, as contrasted for example with *zēlos*, it reveals less a "thoroughly consistent concept of φθόνος" (Bulman 1992: 1) than the social source of the pejorative sense of the term.

All in all, then, *nemesis* appears to overlap considerably with *phthonos* in classical Greek. Both terms represent an emotional response based on the judgment that a person, whether an equal or an inferior, is getting above himself. It is true that, at least in democratic Athens, *phthonos* tended to be associated particularly with what we might call "upward resentment," that is, the anger of the lower classes toward the rich, whereas in Homer, *nemesis* seems more often to express "downward resentment" on the part of superiors – whether gods or mortals – toward inferiors who overstep their station.[7] Aristotle himself points out (*Rhet.* 2.9, 1387b5–8) that those who are worthy of good things and in fact possess them are particularly *nemesētikoi* – prone to feel *nemesis* – because it is unjust that lesser people should be deemed deserving of comparable goods. But Aristotle also notes that the successful tend to be *phthoneroi* (*Rhet.* 2.10, 1387b28–29). The distinction between upward and downward resentment does not seem adequately to differentiate the two concepts.

I shall not speculate on why the term *nemesis* and its congeners fell out favor in the classical period, save to register my view that it is not because they had a significance in archaic epic that had become obsolete in the world of the city-state. Nor shall I attempt to explain the absence of *phthonos* in archaic hexameter poetry, and the morally neutral or, in Hesiod, evidently positive significance of the verb *phthoneō* in contrast to its frequently pejorative sense in the classical era. Glenn Most (2003) has argued that heroic epic self-consciously banished envy as a motive to the margins of the heroic community (e.g., the beggar Irus), preferring to ascribe to the warriors themselves a spirit of noble rivalry. But the absence of the noun in Hesiod, who, as Most notes, did not share the heroic ethos of the Homeric epics, suggests that *phthonos* may not have had the ethically charged meaning that it acquired in the classical period, and may have been something of a late-comer as a central term in the Greek moral vocabulary, displacing, as it came into use, *nemesis* and its relatives.

If *nemesis* came subsequently to be associated more exclusively with divine censure than it had been in archaic poetry, the reason may well be the rise to prominence of the local cult of the goddess Nemesis in the Attic deme of Rhamnous (see especially Stafford 2000). Nemesis' status as a minor deity in myth seems to have been ancient. A tradition perhaps going back to the *Cypria* in the epic cycle makes her the mother of Helen; she sought to avoid Zeus' embrace by changing her shape (like Thetis), but when she assumed the form of a goose, Zeus metamorphosed into a swan and overpowered her. Hence it happened that Helen was hatched from an egg (*Cypria* fr. 9 Bernabé = Athenaeus 8.334B; cf. Apollod. 3.10.7; Hornum 1993: 1–9; Stafford 2000: 78–79; Stenger 2000: 818). But it is plausible that the Athenian victory over the Persians at Marathon, located near the deme of Rhamnous, was perceived as a god-sent curb on the Persians' overweening ambitions, comparable to Apollo's resentment at the Achaeans' attack in the *Iliad*. In her indignation at the Persians, Nemesis

---

[7] Stearns 1989: 12 suggests that envy may be characteristic of the lower orders, since "it involves coveting something or some attribute that someone else has," while jealousy, as the desire to retain what one possesses, is typically "the emotion of the upper classes."

enacted *nemesis*, and this gave a boost, as Stafford argues (2000: 88–89), to her status as emblem of divine retribution.

The importance of the cult of Nemesis insured that *nemesis* would remain a live idea in ancient Greece. As a personified concept, however, Nemesis was no longer just an emotional response to the violation of social limits, but a complexly motivated figure who could feel the very sentiment she stood for. The epigraphical evidence suggests also "a frightful being who can snatch away any success or good fortune a human being has obtained, a sort of *malocchio*" (Hornum 1993: 9), and one epitaph for an 18–year-old boy from the imperial period refers to her as *phthonerēn Nemesin* (Hornum 1993: 174 = no. 35 in his catalogue of inscriptions mentioning Nemesis or *nemesis* on pp. 153–317; also published in G. Mikhailov, *Inscriptiones graecae in Bulgaria repertae* I: 118 n. 220). Unlike Nemesis, *phthonos* seems never to have had a rite or mythology of its own, but it too might be momentarily personified. In Sophocles' *Philoctetes*, the hero, about to suffer a bout of his disease, hands over to Neoptolemus the bow he had received from Heracles with the words (774–78) "Come then, take it, son; and pray [*proskuson*] to Phthonos that this weapon may not bring grief to you, nor be what it was for me and him who owned it before me." As an object of prayer, Phthonos acquires a human character, and one can appeal to it not to exercize the very emotion it names – that is, resentment that a man should possess a weapon greater than that which pertains to mortals (for the personification of Phthonos, cf. also Callim. *H. Apollo* 105–13). The analogy with divine Nemesis is clear, but the positive sense of *phthonos* was not protected in the long run, as *nemesis* was, by official worship.

That the gods were believed to be capable of *phthonos* has scandalized critics both ancient and modern. Plato, for example, declares (*Phaedrus* 247A7) that "envy stands outside the chorus of the gods." Yet Herodotus put into the mouth of Solon the statement that "the divine is wholly *phthoneron*" (1.32.5–6; cf. 8.109), and comparable sentiments are expressed by other contemporary writers (e.g., Pind. *Pyth.* 10.21–22; cf. *Olym.* 13.25–26; Aesch. *Pers.* 362; Eur. *Alcestis* 1137; *Iphigeneia at Aulis* 1097; *Suppl. Women* 348; Dodds 1951: 28–63). Inordinate success or ambition, like that of Croesus in Herodotus' tale, invites the gods' resentment because it threatens to cross the line between mortal and divine. Though described as *phthonos*, this top-down indignation is no different from that expressed by the older term *nemesis*. As Douglas Cairns (1996: 18) observes: "There is in many a passage a strong connexion between 'thinking more than mortal thoughts' and divine *phthonos*" (cf. 18–22 for further examples; Hornum 1993: 9). It is just in relation to the gods that the moral distinction drawn by Aristotle between the *nemesis* and *phthonos* has least salience.[8]

---

[8] In Sophocles' *Electra*, Aegisthus, believing that Orestes lies dead before him, exclaims (1466–67): "O Zeus, I see an apparition that has descended not without *phthonos*; whether *nemesis* too attends on it I cannot say." Aegisthus presumably means that Orestes had offended the gods (hence their *phthonos*), but that perhaps there will be no further vengeance. Ranulf 1933: 90–106 argues that the Greeks of the classical period did not clearly discriminate between cases in which the gods visited misfortune upon human beings because of their guilt (his Type I), randomly (Type II), or out of jealousy (Type III). He

We have seen that, in the *Eudemian Ethics*, Aristotle explains the worship of Nemesis by her connection with justice, and that, in the *Rhetoric*, he says that *to nemesan* is ascribed to the gods for much the same reason. Aristotle himself conceives of the divine as wholly contemplative in nature (*NE* 10.8,1178b8–23), and hence devoid of emotion. His association of *nemesis* with divinity serves to underscore the distinction he draws between *to nemesan* as a virtuous sentiment and the vice of *phthonos*, once he had resuscitated the archaic expression *to nemesan* as a technical term to denote a morally acceptable opposite to pity as he defined it. But if religious personification helped to enhance the moral aspect of *nemesis*, it is equally true that *phthonos* suffered the opposite process of pejoration from its neutral or even positive sense in archaic poetry to its status as a moral failing in philosophy and rhetorical topoi of the classical period, where it is censured for being directed indiscriminately at all excellence or superiority (e.g., Aeschin. 2.22, 51, 54, 129; 3.81; Isoc. 12.15–16; 14.4, 8, 13, 163–64, 244–46; Lys. 3.9). Even in these cases, it is usually implicit that *phthonos* is not so much wrong in principle as unjustified in the particular instance, since the individual in question is in truth both exceptional and a benefit to the community. Aristotle himself notes that people feel *phthonos* only at the success of those who are or seem their equals (*Rhet.* 2.10, 1387b25–26) and are near themselves in station (1388a6–9), the logic being that equals *deserve* to prosper equally.

It is beyond the scope of this paper to speculate on why *phthonos* acquired so negative a reputation in the classical period. A proper analysis would require situating *phthonos* in the ideological struggles between the elites and the masses in the Greek world, and especially in Athens, from the sixth to the fourth centuries. It seems particularly to have been a charge leveled at the poorer classes by the rich – hence its "bottom-up" character in forensic and philosophical discourse, as well as in aristocratic lyric poetry.[9] But the term no doubt circulated in all levels of society and had a certain semantic homogeneity across the culture.[10]

---

allows, however, that "the expression 'jealousy of the gods' may stand for 'moral disapproval on the part of the gods' in Euripides" (110). Ranulf's erroneous assumption that the "original sense" of *phthonos* was jealousy (111) leads him to assume that this meaning was progressively "toned down," thus acquiring a moral significance it did not originally possess; but the analogy between divine *phthonos* and divine *nemesis* undermines his theory.

[9] For Pindar's role, see n. 6 above. There is perhaps a hint of a wider contention over the class character of *phthonos* in the view expressed by the chorus of sailors in Sophocles' *Ajax*. Aware that Odysseus is accusing Ajax of having slaughtered the army's cattle, they remark: "About you he is very persuasive, and everyone who hears him speak rejoices the more insolently over your troubles, since one never misses when casting at great spirits. If someone were to say such things against me, he would persuade no one, for *phthonos* stalks the one who has" (150–57). The object of envy here is not so much one who exceeds his station (the older view) as one whose station or character is above the ordinary: Odysseus is cast as a demagogue (often his role in tragedy, although not in this one) who is stirring up resentment among the masses. The chorus members themselves defend a hierarchical order based on a mutually beneficial relationship between a great or noble individual and lesser men (158–61), a point that senseless people – an allusion to the rabble – are incapable of grasping (162–63).

[10] There is an interesting analogy to the differentiation between the archaic *nemesis* and more recent *phthonos* in the pair, *homilos* (Homeric) and *okhlos*, meaning "crowd." As Karpyuk 2000: 81 observes, *okhlos* "surfaces for the first time" in the "first half of the fifth century B.C.," when there was considerable activity in the coining of new terms. "Aeschylus, Sophocles, and Thucydides used the two

There is an analogy, indeed, in the complex senses of the term "envy" in modern English. We have cited Sabini and Silver's observation that envy stands out as perverse even in the company of the six other capital sins, and it gives rise to some of the harshest judgments in the whole range of the emotions. The popular writer Nancy Friday (1997: 9) reports: "Envy, I would learn, is that one emotion in all human life about which nothing good can be said"; according to the philosopher Richard Wohlheim (1999: 91), envy is an example of an emotion that is "invariably malformed"; and the social theorist and psychologist Robert Solomon observes (1993: 207): "Envy is an essentially vicious emotion, bitter and vindictive" (cf. Walcot 1978: 165; Fuentes 2001: 54, "envy is a powerless poison"; Farrell 1989: 254 on envy as "something objectionable and, in its extreme forms, even sinful").

Yet some investigators argue that envy is not a wholly negative sentiment, but may – as in ancient Greek usage – have a socially constructive function. The socio-linguist Anna Wierzbicka (1999: 234) judges that "*Envy*, which used to be regarded as one of the seven deadly sins..., appears to be now seen as a less grave offense; after all, it can be said to imply only a desire for equality, which is one of the key modern ideals." So too, the economist Robert Frank (1988: 15) affirms that "it may pay people to feel envious, because feeling that way makes them better bargainers.... Feelings of envy are also closely linked to feelings about fairness." And the sociologist J.M. Barbalet (1998: 106), after citing Adam Smith's (1982: 243) characterization of envy as the "odious and detestable passion," comments that "Envy is not thought of today as a shameful thing .... Envy is simply the emotional form of a desire for benefits which others are believed to possess."[11] Indeed, nearly four centuries ago Descartes (1988: 262 art. 182) had already written: "What one commonly calls envy is a vice that consists in a perversity of nature, which makes certain people angry at the good that they see coming into the possession other men. But I use the word here to mean a passion that is not always vicious. Envy, then, insofar as it is a passion, is a kind of sadness mixed with hatred that occurs when one sees a good coming into the possession of those who, one thinks, are unworthy of it" – a sense very like Aristotle's definition of *to nemesan*.

Why should envy have such different, and apparently contrary or incompatible, meanings in Anglo-American culture? It may be that the term is changing valences as modern society becomes more egalitarian in its ideology, as Wierzbicka and others suggest. Perhaps, too, the idea of envy both reflects and confirms polarized social roles within the modern, politically democratic state. Thus, Arlie Hochschild (1975: 291) observes: "While the moral injunction against envy applies to winners and losers alike, envy is unequally distributed among winners and losers. In other words, the socially induced feeling and the rule against it are systematically discrepant." Envy is both a natural response to systemic inequality and a stigmatized feeling at the level of

---

words interchangeably," but in the course of the fifth century *okhlos* assumed the pejorative connotation of "mob."

[11] Cf. Ben-Ze'ev 2000: 262, 283; Farrell 1989: 262: "envy does not, in our culture, come in for anything like the abuse that jealousy tends to receive." Farrell 1989: 253, 263 questions whether "friendly envy" or admiration counts as envy at all.

individual morality. To seem anything other than petty, envy must, according to Hochschild, find expression in a social movement (292).[12]

An analogous social dynamic may have contributed to the complex sense of *phthonos* in classical Athens. That is a question that awaits further research. In this paper, I have attempted to show that the opposition between *nemesis* and *phthonos* to which Aristotle testifies, and which many modern scholars accept as the full story, masks a complementary similarity between the two sentiments, insofar as both denote a resentment at people who "get above themselves" and violate the status rules of a highly class-conscious society. This is why *phthonos* in classical prose and poetry could substitute for *nemesis* in archaic epic as the term for divine displeasure at human immoderation. The further evolution of the two words, and their polarization as moral concepts, was not due to an original difference in meaning but was shaped by cultural and historical factors, such as the rise of the cult of Nemesis and the politically charged use of *phthonos* in the ideological discourse of the polis. Even so, the affinity between the two concepts was never wholly eclipsed in classical Greek.

WORKS CITED

Barbalet, J.M. 1998. *Emotion, Social Theory, and Social Structure: A Macrosociological Approach.* Cambridge.

Ben-Ze'ev, A. 2000. *The Subtlety of Emotions.* Cambridge, Mass.

Bulman, P. 1992. *Phthonos in Pindar.* University of California Publications: Classical Studies 35. Berkeley.

Cairns, D.L. 1993. *Aidōs: The Psychology and Ethics of Honour and Shame in Ancient Greek Literature.* Oxford.

Cairns, D.L. 1996. "Hybris, Dishonour, and Thinking Big." *JHS* 116: 1–32.

Descartes, R. 1988. *Les Passions de l'âme: Précédé de La Pathéthique cartésienne par Jean-Maurice Monnoyer.* Paris.

Dilts, M.R., ed. 1986. *Scholia in Demosthenem.* Vol. 2. Leipzig.

Dodds, E.R. 1951. *The Greeks and the Irrational.* Berkeley.

Farrell, D.M. 1989. "Of Jealousy and Envy." In G. Graham and H. LaFollette, eds., *Person to Person.* Philadelphia. 245–68.

Fisher, N.R.E. 1992. *Hybris: A Study in the Values of Honour and Shame in Ancient Greece.* Warminster.

———. 2003. "Let Envy be Absent: Envy, Liturgies and Reciprocity in Athens." In Konstan and Rutter, eds.

Frank, R.H. 1988. *Passions within Reason: The Strategic Role of the Emotions.* New York.

Friday, N. 1997. *Jealousy.* 2nd. ed. New York.

Fuentes, C. 2001. *Instinto de Inez.* Madrid.

Herrmann, F.-G. 2003. "Phthonos in the World of Plato's Timaeus." In Konstan and Rutter, eds.

Hochschild, A.R. 1975. "The Sociology of Feeling and Emotion: Selected Possibilities." In M. Millman and R.M. Kanter, eds., *Another Voice: Feminist Perspectives on Social Life and Social Science.* Garden City, N.Y. 280–307.

Hornum, M.B. 1993. *Nemesis, The Roman State, and the Games.* Religions in the Graeco-Roman World 117. Leiden.

Karpyuk, S. 2000. "Crowd in Archaic and Classical Greece." *Hyperboreus* 6: 79–102.

Konstan, D. 2001. *Pity Transformed.* London.

---

[12] Emanuel Swedenborg wrote in 1768 that "there is a just and an unjust jealousy" (English translation in Swedenborg 1928; cited by Stearns 1989: 15).

Konstan, D. and N. Rutter, eds. 2003. *Envy, Spite, and Jealousy: The Rivalrous Emotions in Ancient Greece*. Edinburgh.

Leaf, W., ed. 1888. *The Iliad. Vol. 2: Books XIII–XXIV*. London.

Milobenski, E. 1964. *Der Neid in der griechischen Philosophie*. Wiesbaden.

Most, G. 2003. "Epinician Envies." In Konstan and Rutter, eds.

Ničev, A. 1985. "La notion de pitié chez Sophocle." In J. Brunschwig, C. Imbert, and A. Roger, eds., *Histoire et structure: A la mémoire de Victor Goldschmidt*. Paris.

Ranulf, S. 1933. *The Jealousy of the Gods and Criminal Law at Athens: A Contribution to the Sociology of Moral Indignation*. 2 vols. London and Copenhagen.

Redfield, J.M. 1975. *Nature and Culture in the Iliad*. Chicago.

Rutherford, R.B., ed. 1992. *Homer: Odyssey Books XIX and XX*. Cambridge.

Sabini, J. and M. Silver. 1986. "Envy." In R. Harré, ed., *The Social Construction of the Emotions*. Oxford. 167–83.

Saïd, S. 2003. "Envy and Emulation in Isocrates." In Konstan and Rutter, eds.

Solomon, R.C. 1993. *The Passions: Emotions and the Meaning of Life*. Rev. ed. Indianapolis.

Stafford, E. 2000. *Worshipping Virtues: Personification and the Divine in Ancient Greece*. London.

Stanford, W.B., ed. 1959. *Homer: Odyssey Books I–XII*. 2nd ed. London.

Stearns, P.N. 1989. *Jealousy: The Evolution of an Emotion in American History*. New York.

Steinlein, W. 1941. *Φθόνος und verwandte Begriffe in der älteren griechischen Literatur*. Diss. Erlangen.

Stenger, J. 2000. "Nemesis." In H. Cancik and H. Schneider, eds., *Der neue Pauly: Enzyklopädie der Antike*, vol. 8. Stuttgart. Cols. 818–19.

Swedenborg, E. 1928 [orig. 1768]. *The Delights of Wisdom Pertaining to Conjugal Love, after which Follow the Pleasures of Insanity Pertaining to Scortatory Love*. Trans. S.M. Warren; rev. by L.H. Tafel. New York.

Tzifopoulos, Y.Z. 1995. "Thucydidean Rhetoric and the Propaganda of the Persian Wars Topos." *PP* 50: 91–115.

Τζιφόπουλος, Γιάννης. 1997. "Ἡ ρητορική τῶν Περσικῶν πολέμων: ἡ ἑρμενεία τῆς Ἱστορίας στίς Ἱστορίες τοῦ Θουκυδίδη." *Πράκκτικα: Πρωτο Πανελληνιο και Διεθνες Συνεδριο Αρχαιας Ελληνικης Φιλολογιας (23–26 Μαϊου 1994)*. Ed. J-Th. A. Papademetriou. Athens: Hellenic Society for Humanistic Studies and International Centre for Humanistic Research, 38.

Walcot, P. 1978. *Envy and the Greeks: A Study of Human Behavior*. Warminster.

Wierzbicka, A. 1999. *Emotions across Languages and Cultures: Diversity and Universals*. Cambridge.

Wilson, P. 2000. *The Athenian Institution of the Khoregia: The Chorus, the City, and the Stage*. Cambridge.

Wollheim, R. 1999. *On the Emotions*. New Haven.

8

A Reading of Ausonius, *Professores* I

Joseph Pucci

As a group, and individually, the *Professores* of Ausonius remain unevenly examined. Much attention has been paid to the larger historical, social, and political aspects of the collection, especially to the ways in which the poems can be mined for prosopographical and cultural data.[1] Yet, with respect to the literary qualities of the collection, the prevailing sentiment is best summed up by Green's cryptic comment that "[i]n terms of general content and religious assumptions the *Professores* are broadly similar to the *Parentalia*, and like the earlier series they should not be analysed in rhetorical terms."[2] Insofar as this unhelpful comment can be understood, I aim to disprove it. Taking my cue from the literary evidence commended in the initial poem of the collection, I offer in what follows a literary reading of *Professores* 1, written to commemorate Tiberius Victor Minervius. My claim is that this poem in fact can be read with some profit in "rhetorical terms," that is, as a literary work carefully produced and meant for attentive reading.[3]

Among other points, I hope to argue in what follows that Ausonius carefully balances his ostensible praise for his oldest teacher by framing his renown against a backdrop that counsels caution in the world and wariness of fame and glory. Thus, while Ausonius praises these very qualities in Minervius, lauding his international repute, his innate talents, and his importance in training the powerful men of the early fourth century, he also seems to offer a portrait of Minervius caught in repose, who understood how to live for himself, apart from the world, a knowledge that is his greatest claim to fame. As this reading of the poem is owed to an analysis of allusions to the poetry of Martial, Horace, Lucan, and Ovid, I work through the poem line by line, attending both to surface narrative as well as to the deeper layers of meaning elicited through allusion.[4] So far as I know, the analysis ventured below is the first

---

[1] Among other studies of this sort are Favez 1948; Hopkins 1961; Booth 1978; Booth 1982; Green 1985; and, most recently, Sivan 1993.

[2] Green 1991: 329.

[3] The few "literary" readings published on the *Professores* are really little more than lists of verbal borrowings, usually with little or no interpretive guidance ventured. These would include Colton 1973: 41–51; Szelest 1975a: 75–87; Szelest 1975b: 156–163; Colton 1976: 40–42; and Hall 1979: 227–228.

[4] Studies of allusion (sometimes unhappily called "intertextuality") in Latin literature have appeared with great frequency in the last decade or so, though no study analyzes the ways in which Ausonius made

attempt to make sense of Ausonius' obvious verbal borrowings in this poem, which have been much noted but little analyzed.

Green sees in this poem a tripartite structure, with vv. 1–12 comprising an introduction, vv. 13–30 forming a "centrepiece ... describ[ing Minervius'] eloquence and memory," and vv. 31–42 reviewing his character.[5] The structure I would commend is bipartite, with the midpoint at vv. 20–21, the first half of the poem treating external issues bearing on the life of Minervius, his fame in the world, his *patria*, his talents and fame in relation to Isocrates, Demosthenes, etc; and the second half describing Minervius' personal qualities, his memory, speech patterns, character, etc.

The concern with Minervius in the world is established in no uncertain, and in quite specific, terms in vv. 1–10:

> Primus, Burdigalae columen, dicere, Minervi,[6]
>   Alter rhetoricae Quintiliane togae,
> Illustres quondam quo praeceptore fuerunt
>   Constantinopolis, Roma, dehinc patria,
> Non equidem certans cum maiestate duarum,   5
>   Solo sed potior nomine, quod patria.
> Asserat usque licet Fabium Calagurris alumnum,
>   Non sit Burdigalae dum cathedra inferior.
> Mille foro dedit hic iuvenes, bis mille senatus
>   Adiecit numero purpureisque togis,   10

> You shall be named first, Minervius, chief ornament of Bordeaux, a second Quintilian to adorn the rhetorician's gown. Your teaching in its day made glorious Constantinople, Rome, and lastly our native town; which, though it cannot vie with that pair in dignity, yet for its name alone is sweeter, because it is our native place: let Calagurra make every claim to Fabius as her son, if the chair of Bordeaux receive no less degree. A thousand pupils has Minervius given to the courts, and twice a thousand to the Senate's rank and to the purple robes.[7]

Not content to qualify the life of Minervius in local and individual terms, Ausonius instead identifies him in vv. 1–10 in culturally specific terms, as a second Quintilian, thus linking this local boy made good to the most illustrious rhetor of Latin antiquity. Yet, this *alter Quintilian[us]*, *Burdigalae columen* is also more than a local figure whose reputation spread beyond Gaul, for he taught not only in Bordeaux, but also in Constantinople and Rome. Impressively, his teaching was such that it made these great imperial cities *illustres*, though even Minervius' incomparable teaching could not lift Bordeaux's fame to their heights. Yet Bordeaux's fame, though not equal to Rome's or to Constantinople's, to be sure, is nonetheless a sweeter name to hear (*potior nomine*) because it is, precisely, Bordeaux, that is to say, the *patria* of Minervius (and of Ausonius).

---

use of his classical inheritance in a systematic way. Pucci 1998 sets forth a historical sketch – ancient and modern – of allusion as a literary category, with full bibliography.

   [5] Green 1991: 330.

   [6] My text is Green 1999: 46–47.

   [7] All translations of *Professores* 1 are from Evelyn White 1919: 97, 99, 101, with some modifications. Translations otherwise unascribed are my own.

In saying all of this, of course, it is hard not to hear versions of Ausonius' own life informing his treatment of Minervius. As he often does in renditions of his own life – in the *Prefaces*[8] to the *Parentalia*, for example – Ausonius focuses on social space, here stressing the regional associations of Minervius while holding his fame up for flattering comparison to Quintilian. Thus, Minervius remains in Ausonius' version of his life first and foremost a local figure who happened to have played on an international stage, but who is still closely associated with his *patria* in terms of memory and of repute. As the poet goes on to say, the chair of rhetoric at Bordeaux can stand the comparison with Calagurra, the birthplace of Quintilian, so strong are the talents of Minervius, so firm the traditions of rhetorical training in Bordeaux.

If Ausonius has commended Minervius in geographic and professional terms, he also complicates the picture of his illustrious teacher, inscribing an allusion to Martial in v. 2 that offers up a specific depiction of Quintilian. Ausonius' phrase, *alter rhetoricae Quintiliane togae*, yokes his poem's opening to Martial's comparable phrase, *gloria Romanae, Quintiliane, togae* (2.90.2). But this is not an unproblematic linkage, for there, in an epigram written to Quintilian, Martial praises the famous rhetor by expressing, in counterpoise to Quintilian's illustrious renown, his own desires to be free of the constraints represented by rhetorical study.

In fact, far from being a praise piece, Martial's poem is laced with sarcasm:

> Quintiliane, vagae moderator summe iuventae,[9]
> Gloria Romanae, Quintiliane, togae,
> Vivere quod propero pauper nec inutilis annis,
> Da veniam: properat vivere nemo satis.

> Quintilian, supreme guide of wayward youth, glory of the Roman toga, forgive me that I, a poor man and not crippled with years, am in haste to live. No man is enough in haste to live.[10]

The poem establishes a dichotomy between two kinds of lives. On the one hand, there is the glorious path that Quintilian commends to the youths of Rome as *vagae moderator summe iuventae*, whose guidance corrects erring boys by training them for rhetorical togae – thus making delinquents into props of the establishment.

Martial, however, holds himself up precisely as a kind of delinquent, as a *vaga iuventa* who in fact prefers living to the kind of supreme guidance offered by Quintilian. Others may prefer to live their lives in bondage to the establishment (*Differat hoc patrios optat qui vincere census / Atriaque immodicis artat imaginibus*, vv. 5–6) and those who want to be richer than their fathers can put off living, can crowd their halls with statues of dead ancestors, acquiring all the material possessions they desire while refusing to understand or to know life's attractions. And, of course, rhetorical training is a prerequisite to making one's way in the world that offers up wealth, possessions, grand preferment. But Martial wants something much simpler:

---

[8] On this see Pucci 2000: 121–130.
[9] My text of Martial is Lindsay 1929.
[10] The translation, with slight modification, is from Ker 1929, 1: 197.

> Me focus et nigros non indignantia fumos
>   Tecta iuvant et fons vivus et herba rudis.
> Sit mihi verna satur, sit non doctissima coniunx,
>   Sit nox cum somno, sit sine lite dies.   10

My pleasure is a hearth, and a roof that does not resent black smoke, and a running stream, and fresh grass. Let me have a well-fed, home-bred slave, a wife not over educated, the night with sleep, the day without a quarrel.

It is enough, he says, and more than enough, to have these things. In other words, there is, in Martial's poem, a specific rejection of the worlds Quintilian represents, not simply the worlds of wealth and accomplishment, but that of rhetoric as well.

Because Ausonius links Minervius at every turn in *Prof.* 1 with Quintilian, it is necessary to see in Martial's rejection of Quintilian's world an explicit rejection of the same world on Ausonius' part. This rejection is furthered along in vv. 9–10, where Ausonius depicts Minervius as a teacher of establishment figures – precisely the role Quintilian assumes when he is called by Martial *vagae moderator summe iuventae.* Minervius is the figure, after all, who trained for the courts "one thousand youths" (*mille iuvenes),* and who added to the senate and to the purple robes two thousand others. But in problematizing his depiction of Minervius, Ausonius also begins to articulate an alternate version of his teacher that stresses different themes, motivations, aims.

After offering up a depiction of Minervius that places into doubt the poet's praise of his famous teacher, Ausonius goes on at vv. 11 ff. to insinuate himself into his poem in relation to Minervius:

> Mille foro dedit hic iuvenes, bis mille senatus
>   Adiecit numero purpureisque togis,   10
> Me quoque: sed quoniam multa est praetexta, silebo
>   Teque canam de te, non ab honore meo.

A thousand pupils has Minervius given to the courts, and twice a thousand to the Senate's ranks and to the purple robes. I, too, was of that number; but since the toga is a manifold thing, I will refrain, and will sing of you through your own accomplishments and not through my own honor.

This insinuation accomplishes several goals. First, it affirms the fact that Ausonius studied with Minervius, thus linking the two figures historically. Second, it links Ausonius with those figures – the *iuvenes* of v. 9 and the others – who gained preferment by having been at one time or another taught by Minervius. This important influence is made clearer still in in v. 11, where the poet affirms his own Minervian pedigree, claiming that this important early teacher added him to the number of those who wore the purple toga.

But as quickly as he says this, Ausonius shifts the poem's emphasis. Since "the toga is a manifold thing," the poet prefers to pass over any further discussion of it or of himself (*sed quoniam multa est praetexta, silebo*).[11]   Instead, Ausonius says that he will "sing of you [Minervius], through your own accomplishments" (*teque canam de te*) rather than refer to "my own honor" (*non ab honore meo*). There follow a series of lines in which the talents of Minervius are exposed for readers against the backdrop of both Latin and Greek forebears:

> Sive panegyricos placeat contendere libros
>   In Panathenaicis tu numerandus eris:
> Seu libeat fictas ludorum evolvere lites,   15
>   Ancipitem palmam Quintilianus habet.
> Dicendi torrens tibi copia, quae tamen aurum,
>   Non etiam luteam volveret illuviem;
> Et Demosthenicum, quod ter primum ille vocavit,
>   In te sic viguit, cedat ut ipse tibi.   20

> Should panegyric be the field of rivalry, then must you be classed with the orator of the *Panathenaicus*; or if the test be to develop the mock law-suits of our schools, Quintilian must look to his laurels. Your speech was like a torrent in full spate, yet one which whirled down pure gold without muddy sediment. As for that art in Demosthenes which that great man thrice over called the orator's chief virtue, it was so strong in you that the master himself gives place to you.

Three figures – and talents – are held up here for praise. First, Minervius' talent for panegyric compares favorably to Isocrates, who exhibits a similar talent in the *Panathenaicus*. Then, Quintilian reappears in Ausonius' praise of Minervius' penchant for developing the mock law suits (*controversiae*) which formed an important part of rhetorical training in the schools. Then, finally, Minervius' delivery is held to favorable comparison with Demosthenes' ability to deliver a speech, so much so that Demosthenes himself, according to Ausonius, is willing to yield to Minervius on this score.

The fresh mention of Quintilian again raises an interpretive connundrum, revealed in the phrase, *dicendi torrens tibi copia* (v. 17), which links to Juvenal's similar phrase, *torrens dicendi copia* (10.9). The tone in Juvenal is hardly positive:

> Omnibus in terris, quae sunt a Gadibus usque[12]
> Auroram et Gangen, pauci dinoscere possunt
> Vera bona atque illis multum diversa, remota
> Erroris nebula. Quid enim ratione timemus
> Aut cupimus? Quid tam dextro pede concipis, ut te   5
> Conatus non paeniteat votique peracti?
> Evertere domos totas optantibus ipsis
> Di faciles. Nocitura toga, nocitura petuntur

---

[11] The phrase has been variously interpreted, but the most straightforward reading must take pride of place. Ausonius has just mentioned *purpureisque togis* in the previous line; *praetexta* is another name for *purpurea toga*. There is a pun here on "multa," meaning "layered" as applied to the layers of the toga, I think, which I attempt to pick up in the phrase "manifold." On the problems attending to the interpretation of these lines, see Green 1991: 331, v. 11.

[12] My text of Juvenal is Willis 1997.

Militia; torrens dicendi copia multis
Et sua mortifera est facundia, viribus ille   10
Confisus periit admirandisque lacertis, ...

> In all the lands that stretch from Gades to the Ganges and the Morn, there are but
> few who can distinguish true blessings from their opposites, putting aside the mists
> of error. For when does reason direct our desires or our fears? What project do we
> form so auspiciously that we do not repent us of our effort and of the granted wish?
> Whole households have been destroyed by the compliant Gods in answer to the
> masters' prayers; in camp and city alike we ask for things that will be our ruin.
> Many a man has met death from the flowing abundance of speech; others from the
> strength and wondrous thews in which they have trusted.[13]

Against the backdrop of human desires, Juvenal depicts human wants as the sources of
decline and death. True goods are difficult to discern, he says, because we are
creatures of emotion rather than reason. Thus, since we often fail to think things
through thoroughly, we often ask for things that lead to our own demise. Among
these, Juvenal lists "the flowing abundance of speech" (*torrens dicendi copia*), making
the wickedness of spoken language a prime example of the chasm between human
desires and their abilities to be sated.

 Nor, as Ausonius knows, is it any kind of speech that Juvenal has in mind here, but
that kind commended by Quintilian and practiced and taught by Minervius. Moreover,
Satire 10 is a whirlwind of criticism of all manner of social and political convention,
against which Juvenal commends his readers to gather spiritual resources, to live
soundly in a sound body and soul, to look deep within in order to live the tranquil life.
Against the tendency, therefore, to practice those arts of speaking that allow one to
enter into the mainstream of Roman social and political life, Juvenal's satire holds up
those specific rhetorical talents as an initial danger in a litany of dozens of noxious
habits. The antidote, much as was commended by Martial's epigram to Quintilian, is
to reject such habits for a life based on self-knowledge, on tranquillity of soul and
soundness of mind.

 By the mid-point of his poem, Ausonius has made two broad claims for Minervius'
talents in the context of Quintilian's grand model. In both instances, the linkages to
this most famous of orators[14] undercut the ostensible praise his lines otherwise would
seem to ply – and in both instances, the undercurrent of criticism involves rejecting
the world that rhetorical training best prepares one for in order to pursue a more
private, spiritual, sequestered life.

 The emphasis on finding one's spiritual way apart from the madding crowd is
developed more fully in the poem's second half, where Minervius' accomplishments
in the world become the backdrop for a more committed treatment of his *bona
naturalia*, his innate talents:

Anne et divini bona naturalia doni
  Adiciam, memori quam fueris animo,

---

[13] The translation is from Ramsay 1918: 193.
[14] On the specific fame of Quintilian in late antiquity, see Green 1991: 330–331 n. 2.

Audita ut vel lecta semel ceu fixa teneres,
    Auribus et libris esset ut una fides?
Vidimus et quondam tabulae certamine longo   25
    Omnes qui fuerant te enumerasse bolos,
Alternis vicibus quos praecipitante rotatu
    Fundunt excisi per cava buxa gradus,
Narrantem fido per singula puncta recursu
    Quae data, per longas quae revocata moras.   30
Nullo felle tibi mens livida, tum sale multo
    Lingua dicax blandis et sine lite iocis.
Mensa nitens, quam non censoria regula culpet
    Nec nolit Frugi Piso vocare suam;
Nonnumquam pollens natalibus et dape festa,   35
    Non tamen angustas ut tenuaret opes.
Quamquam heredis egens, bis sex quinquennia functus,
    Fletus es a nobis ut pater et iuvenis.
Et nunc, sive aliquid post fata extrema superfit,
    Vivis adhuc aevi, quod periit, meminens;   40
Sive nihil superest nec habent longa otia sensus,
    Tu tibi vixisti; nos tua fama iuvat.

> Shall I speak also of your natural gifts and that divine blessing, your memory, which was so prodigious that you retained what you had heard or read over once as though it were engraven on your mind, and that your ear was as retentive as a book? Once, after a long contested game, I have seen you repeat all the throws made by either side when the dice were tipped out with a sharp spin over the fillets cut out in the hollowed boxwood of the dicebox; and recount move by move, without mistake, which pieces had been lost, which won back, through long stretches of the game. No malice ever blackened your heart: your tongue, though free and full of wit, indulged only in kindly jests that held no sting. Your table showed that refinement with which a censor's code could find no fault: Piso the Frugal would not blush to call it his. Sometimes, as on birthdays or some other feast, it was furnished with greater luxury, but never so lavishly as to diminish your slender means. And when you died after six decades, although you left no heir, you were mourned by me as a father and a youth. And now, if anything survives after Fate has struck her final blow, you are living yet and not unmindful of your days gone by; or, if nothing at all remains, and death's long repose knows no feeling, you have lived for yourself: we take pleasure in your fame.

Of the several characteristics mentioned by Ausonius, Minervius' memory is praised first, in vv. 22–30, as a kind of text, for, so Ausonius tells us, whatever Minervius heard or read was engraved on his mind, never to be forgotten. In fact, so prodigious was his memory that, according to Ausonius, Minervius was able, after a long contested dice game, to repeat the throws of the dice made by both sides, from beginning to end without error.

Minervius' wit also comes in for praise, especially since the orator possessed it in spades but never used it maliciously. Of equal importance in this description are Horace's words from *Sat.* 1.10.1–4, which linger in the background of Ausonius' praise:

Nempe incomposito dixi pede currere versus[15]
Lucili. Quis tam Lucili fautor inepte est
Ut non hoc fateatur? At idem, quod sale multo
Urbem defricuit, charta laudatur eadem.

> To be sure I did say that the verses of Lucilius run on with halting foot. Who is a
> partisan of Lucilius so in-and-out of season as not to confess this? And yet on the
> self-same page the self-same poet is praised because he rubbed the city down with
> much salt.[16]

These lines offer up an initial defense of Horace's prior criticisms of Lucilius in *Sat.*
1.4. There, the poet had claimed that satire was not in a real sense poetry, but, deriving
from comedy, simply replicated the normal discourse of conversation. These
comments had led, in turn, and more severely, to Horace's likening of Lucilius to a
muddy river or a prolix speaker, who did not really know how to practice his craft
properly (*Sat.* 1.4.6–13).

Here, in *Sat.* 1.10, Horace softens his criticism of Lucilius, but now condemns his
predecessor with faint praise. In particular, he draws attention to Lucilius' wit, but in
the same breath notes that Lucilius' other faults are many. Wit, *sale multo*, is thus held
up by Horace as the strongest link in an otherwise dissolving chain of poetic faults,
and it is this image that Ausonius uses to frame his description of Minervius' wit.

Ausonius also relies on Horace's language to speak of Minervius' simplicity,
which, according to the poet, was so exemplary that it would have earned the praises
of Piso the Frugal (vv. 33–34). Minervius was not stingy, nor was he extravagant and
no matter the occasion always managed to balance the needs of the moment with his
own sense of decorum. He possessed a *mensa nitens*, a phrase owed to the opening
lines of *Sat.* 2.2:

Quae virtus et quanta, boni, sit vivere parvo
(nec meus hic sermo est, sed quae praecepit Ofellus
rusticus, abnormis sapiens crassaque Minerva)
discite, non inter lances mensasque nitentis, ...

> What and how great, my friends, is the virtue of frugal living – now this is no talk
> of mine, but is the teaching of Ofellus, a peasant, a philosopher unschooled and of
> rough mother-wit – learn I say not amid the tables' shining dishes ... [17]

These words introduce a lengthy treatment of plain living and frugality. In particular,
Horace focuses on the need, so far as human appetites are concerned, for taking what
is necessary, rather than cultivating more refined tastes through indulging beyond
one's needs. Among several examples offered, gluttony looms as perhaps the most
important here. According to Horace, no one will refuse plain food if hungry, and any
who do are not truly hungry, only gluttonous. Thus gluttony and the other sorts of
excesses recalled eventually by him allow Horace to affirm a philosophical position

---

[15] My text of Horace is Wickham and Garrod 1901.
[16] The translation is from Fairclough 1929: 115.
[17] The translation is from Fairclough 1929: 137.

not obviously connected to his ostensible discussion, viz., that to be truly healthy, one must find pleasure in oneself.

Perhaps more important for Ausonius' purposes, Horace goes on in *Sat*. 2.2 further to refine this opening variation on the typical satirical theme of excess by concluding in an untypical way. At vv. 129 ff., through the words of his speaker Ofellus, Horace affirms not the efficacy of his prior points, but the inevitability of human mortality and transiency and the dominance of death over all things. For this reason, Ofellus declares, we must put forth a brave heart (*fortiaque ... pectora*, v. 136) against the tough odds of death's dominion. Moreover, the Horatian images of death and human transiency that swirl beneath the surface praises of Minervius point to the concluding verses of Ausonius' poem, where Minervius' death is straightforwardly mourned by the poet, but where phrasing from Lucan's *De bello civili* forms their backdrop.

Ausonius' concluding verses (vv. 37 ff.) are, in fact, somewhat jarring both in what they report and how they report it. It is not unexpected to find Minervius' death mentioned at the conclusion of a poem devoted to his fame. But less expected, perhaps, is the way the poet quickly shifts to this important topic almost off-handedly, following on the heels of his treatment, in vv. 33 ff., of the poet's frugality.

If nothing else, this shift allows Ausonius the chance to insinuate himself into the emotional texture of the poem again, for he notes that he mourned Minervius as a father and a youth (v. 38), that is, as his teacher and as a man who died before his time. So, too, the transience of life and the finality of death are dramatized in the suddenness with which this narrative shift occurs. But something else is at work in these lines, for what Ausonius goes on to say of Minervius' death has more the markings of philosophic speculation than one expects in laudatory pieces of this kind. This speculative sense is supported by the shared phrasing that links Ausonius' lines to two moments from the *De bello civili*:

> ... te fata extrema petente
> vita digna fui? ...   (8.652–53)
> Am I worthy to live, now that you are seeking your final rewards?

> ... si quid sensus post fata relictum est,[18]   (8.749)
> ... if any feeling after death remains ...

Both lines recall the dizzying activities of Lucan's eighth book, where the death of Pompey holds center stage, but in particular they focus on the transience of human life, the inevitability of death, the importance of valuing life by measures that truly matter – issues already adumbrated in the earlier allusions to Horace's *Satires*. Vv. 652 ff. come from Cornelia's lengthy speech after the spirit of Pompey, muttering "*si mirantur, amant*," flitters off into the ether. Her words are bitter, emotional, laden with the ironies and regrets of the lives she and Pompey lived alone and together. She wants to die, she says, and calls Pompey *perfide* for leaving her in the lurch to become a victim of Caesar's whims. "Am I worthy to live," she asks in the lines Ausonius has remembered, "now that you are seeking your final rewards?" (*te fata extrema petente /*

---

[18] My text is Shackleton Bailey 1988.

vita digna fui?). She is kept from suicide by her attendants and is whisked away in her ship after she falls into the cool oblivion of a faint.

By distinction, vv. 749 ff. recall the words of Cordus, who, having decided to pay proper obeisance to Pompey's corpse, steals the pyre from an unnamed body and submits Pompey's flesh to the flames. The specific words recalled here are those of a prayer Cordus speaks by way of seeking pardon for having disturbed another man's pyre. If any feeling exists after death, he says in the words recalled by Ausonius, then the unnamed man willingly gives up his pyre for Pompey, losing the guilt he otherwise would feel in the knowledge that he was being burnt while Pompey's corpse lay unburied.

While Ausonius concludes his verses on Minervius ostensibly by presenting two options of afterlife (either the dead are aware of their fate or not), either of which allow for the celebration of his illustrious life, he has in fact framed his concluding gambit in a loaded way. In the first instance, he laces his seemingly nonchalant attitude toward death in the emotionally charged language of Lucan's eighth book, recalling two powerful scenes that, though involving two disparate figures, articulate comparable views of death. Those views, in turn, center on the importance of making correct, considered, choices in one's life, and in being prepared to suffer the consequences whatever those choices bring. Cornelia laments the fall of her husband and her own situation in the lurch, but her words in the scene recalled by Ausonius stand for the raw feeling she experiences at this moment and the clarity of purpose it makes possible. Her regrets are for herself only as she understands herself in relation to Pompey. At the same time, Pompey's death, with its makeshift burial, purloined pyre, and lone and frightened mourner, stands in stark contrast to his illustrious life, whose course eventually led from the heights to this fateful, sad night of stolen obeisance.

Ausonius would thus seem to frame the conclusion to his celebration of Minervius' life in a way that offers a warning, but he also brings his poem round again to the themes suggested at the start. Recall that there, the poet celebrated Minervius' worldly fame by comparing it to Quintilian's renown, but leavened that praise with allusions to Martial and to Horace that drew sharp distinctions between Minervius' public role as teacher and lawyer and the private life he might have (may well have) led apart from the crowd. When Ausonius offers up the two options of after-life as a frame in which we might celebrate Minevius' life by not worrying too much about his death, his words take on added dimension given the care with which he has prepared his readers for them. That preparation, exploiting as it does the situations imagined for us by Martial and by Horace, also includes, as we have just seen, the dissolving, inordinately clear, worlds of Lucan's Cornelia and Pompey.

It also includes a specific world imagined for us by Ovid, whose words are recalled in Ausonius' important final phrase, *tu tibi vixisti,* "you have lived for yourself," which would seem to link Minervius to the figure of exiled Ovid at *Tristia* 3.4.5:

O mihi care quidem semper, sed tempore duro[19]
  Cognite, res postquam procubuere meae,
Usibus edocto si quicquam credis amico,
  Vive tibi et longe nomina magna fuge.
Vive tibi ...   5

> O, you were were ever dear to me, but whom I really came to know in the cruel hour when my fortune fell in ruins, if you believe a friend who has been taught by experience, live for yourself, flee afar from great names! Live for yourself ...[20]

Here the poet warns an unnamed friend not to be covetous of fame in any form, but rather, "to live for yourself" and avoid "great names." But more than this, Ovid's poem witnesses a deep friendship unmovable in bad times as in good, for which the poet offers up thanks.

More than affirming this friendship, however, Ovid's poem ratifies those things that have fostered this friendship, functioning at a deeper level as a celebration of the spiritual awareness, the mental posture, involved in both cultivating and recognizing love of a kind imagined here. It is an affect that stands in flattering comparison to the emotion that swirls around Pompey's final moments; and Ovid's friend is one who presumably has lived the sort of life commended by Ausonius already. Born a part of the world of the establishment, rubbing elbows with "great names," yet he has also moved in a closer, quieter circle apart from the important crowds, has considered his needs in distinction to his wants, has drawn back from grand accomplishment enough to regret personal loss, even though in the case of Ovid's friendship, it involves public, political risk to show it.

And it is precisely the display of emotion, of devotion, that Ovid recalls most vividly in his own poem: the look on his friend's face when he learned, presumably from Ovid, that the poet had been banished to the East (vv. 37–38). That look, with its tears and sad complaints, is emotionally laden, to be sure, but it bears little resemblance to the emotion elicited by Cornelia, or by Cordus, whose words swirl around this moment in Ausonius' poem also. When Ausonius declares, then, that Minervius lived for himself, his language leads us to think of him in terms of Ovid or of Ovid's friend, both of whom, living in the competitive and oftentimes superficial world of the establishment, came in their own ways to appreciate longer, deeper realities than the world of *negotium* could offer. This would seem to be the world Minervius knew also. It is clearly a world known to Ausonius. How much his old teacher taught him of its prized habitats and quiet revelations is hard to say, but it means something, I think, to remember that Ausonius always opts in his verses, whenever the choice is to be made, for the life of the heart and of the mind over and against the world of *negotium*. If this poem is any indication, so, ultimately, did Minervius.

---

[19] My text is Hall 1995.
[20] My translation is Wheeler 1924: 115.

WORKS CITED

Booth, A.D. 1978. "Notes on Ausonius' *Professores.*" *Phoenix* 32: 235–249.

———. 1982. "The Academic Career of Ausonius." *Phoenix* 36: 329–343.

Colton, R.E. 1973. "Ausonius and Juvenal." *CJ* 69: 41–51.

———. 1976. "Horace in Ausonius' *Parentalia* and *Professores.*" *CB* 51: 40–42.

Evelyn-White, H.G. 1919. *Ausonius.* Cambridge, Mass. and London.

Fairclough, H. Rushton 1929. *Horace, Satires, Epistles, and Ars Poetica.* Cambridge, Mass. and London.

Favez, C. 1948. "Une école gallo-romaine au ive siècle." *Latomus* 7: 223–233.

Green, R.P.H. 1985. "Still Waters Run Deep: A New Study of the *Professores* of Bordeaux." *CQ* n.s. 35: 491–506.

———. 1991. *The Works of Ausonius.* Oxford.

———. 1999. *Decimi Magni Ausonii Opera.* Oxford.

Hall, J.B. 1979. "Notes on Ausonius, *Prof. Burd.* 16.9 ff. (Peiper), Publilius Syrus 341, and Martial XI.50 (49)." *CQ* n.s. 24: 227–228.

———. 1995. *P. Ovidi Nasonis Tristia.* Stuttgart.

Hopkins, M.K. 1961. "Social Mobility in the Later Roman Empire: The Evidence of Ausonius." *CQ* n.s. 11: 239–249.

Ker, W.C.A. 1929. *Martial.* 2 vols. Cambridge, Mass. and London.

Lindsay, W.M. 1929. *Marci Valerii Martialis Epigrammata.* Oxford.

Pucci, J. 1998. *The Full-Knowing Reader: Allusion and the Power of the Reader in the Western Literary Tradition.* New Haven and London.

———. 2000. "Ausonius the Centaur: A Reading of the First *Preface.*" *NECJ* 27.3: 121–130.

Ramsay, G.G. 1918. *Juvenal and Persius,* Cambridge, Mass. and London.

Shackleton Bailey, D.R. 1988. *M. Annaei Lucani De Bello Civili Libri X.* Stuttgart.

Sivan, H. 1993. *Ausonius of Bordeaux: Genesis of a Gallic Aristocracy.* London and New York.

Szelest, H. 1975a. "*Valete manes inclitorum rhetorum* (Ausonius' "Commemoratio professorum Burdigalensium")." *Eos* 63: 75–87.

———. 1975b. "Lyrische Motive in Ausonius' Sammlung *Commemoratio professorum Burdigalensium.*" *Ziva antika* 25: 156–163.

Wheeler, A.L. 1924. *Ovid, Tristia, Ex Ponto.* Cambridge, Mass. and London.

Wickham E.C. and H.W. Garrod. 1901. *Q. Horati Flacci Opera.* Oxford.

Willis, J. 1997. *D. Iunii Iuvenalis Saturae sedecim.* Stuttgart.

9

Horace *epi*. 1. 13: Compliments to Augustus[*]

Michael C. J. Putnam

Ut proficiscentem docui te saepe diuque,
Augusto reddes signata volumina, Vinni,
si validus, si laetus erit, si denique poscet;
ne studio nostri pecces odiumque libellis
sedulus importes opera vehemente minister.   5
si te forte meae gravis uret sarcina chartae,
abicito potius, quam quo perferre iuberis
clitellas ferus impingas Asinaeque paternum
cognomen vertas in risum et fabula fias.
viribus uteris per clivos flumina lamas.   10
victor propositi simul ac perveneris illuc,
sic positum servabis onus, ne forte sub ala
fasciculum portes librorum, ut rusticus agnum,
ut vinosa glomus furtivae Pirria lanae,
ut cum pilleolo soleas conviva tribulis   15
ne volgo narres te sudavisse ferendo
carmina quae possint oculos aurisque morari
Caesaris. oratus multa prece nitere porro;
vade, vale; cave ne titubes mandataque frangas.

As I taught you, Vinnius, often and at length, as you were setting out, you will deliver the rolls, sealed, to Augustus, if he is in good health, if in good spirits, if, in short, he asks for them – lest out of eagerness on our behalf you trip and with officious service bring resentment to the little books from excess of effort. If by chance the heaviness of my manuscript's pack is searing you, hurl it from you rather than wildly dash the saddle-bag down where you are ordered to deliver it and turn your father's *cognomen* Asina into a laughing stock and become the subject of story.

Put your strength to use through hills, streams, bogs. As soon as you have arrived there, mission accomplished, you will guard your burden, so placed that you do not chance to carry the little bundle of books under your arm, as a rustic would a lamb, as drunken Pirria a ball of stolen wool, as a tribesman invited for dinner his slippers along with his cap. Don't bruit abroad that you have sweated while carrying verses that may keep the attention of Caesar's eyes and ears. Though entreated by many a plea, press on, further. On your way! Fare well! Take care not to totter and break your charges.

Those engaged by the careful symmetry with which Horace situates poems addressed to Maecenas may at first find *epi.* 1. 13 anomalous.[1] The invocations to the poet's patron that delimit the first collection of *Carmina*, *c.* 1. 1 and 3. 29, gain their clear analogy in *epi.* 1. 1 and 1. 19. Since the placement of other apostrophes to Maecenas in *c.* 1–3 is also highlighted – *c.* 1. 20, for instance, at the initiation of the second half of book 1, *c.* 2. 20, as he concludes the second gathering – we expect nothing less also of his subsequent work, the first collection of *epistulae*. Instead we find only one further poem addressed to the poet's patron, the aberrant *epi.* 1. 7. I would like to suggest that the anomaly is only in appearance. If we move forward six poems from *epi.* 1. 7, which itself follows a sextet of offerings initiated with the first poem, and backward the same number from the book's penultimate piece, we find ourselves in each instance at poem 13. But instead of an expected, balance-fulfilling bow to Maecenas, in league with poems 1, 7 and 19, we find an exhortation to Vinnius Asina to take all precautions in the arduous enterprise of carrying some poetry by the speaker to none other than Caesar Augustus.[2]

Such a double invocation, on the surface to Vinnius yet with secondary, but overriding, reference to the emperor, is, I will argue, exactly Horace's point. The displacement of patron by address to a go-between, executing an errand from poet to the lord of the land, shows Horace at his most tactful. Since the oblique dedicatee, the final receiver of the poetry within the poem, is none other than the emperor himself, the poet is not being insulting to Maecenas, whose calculating eye might have expected a further offering to himself. Nor does he open himself to the charge of forwardness by addressing Augustus forthrightly, which is to say, by appearing to deliver his poetry and make his presentation in person. And likewise his emissary, who will approach the emperor directly, is advised to behave with the utmost discretion.[3] Nevertheless, since numerological balance primes the reader to await a poem to Maecenas, his substitution by Caesar can't help but suggest that the latter, while not the poem's actual recipient, is in some unstated sense, the writer's patron, at the least on a level with Maecenas.

---

[*] I offer the following glance at Plautine Horace to the recipient of these essays in the hope that it will engage his Aristophanic sense of fun. It is dedicated to him in thanks for two score years and one of colleagueship both wise and warm.

[1] I have found the following critiques of *epi.* 1. 13 of special importance: Fraenkel 1957: 350–56; McGann 1969; Clarke 1972; Ahleid 1974; Connor 1982; Kilpatrick 1986; Johnson 1993; Ferri 1993; Peratelli 1993, especially 215–16, who views Horace's anxiety over the public's reception of his odes as a major theme of the poem.

Commentaries of value are: Préaux 1968; Mayer 1994; Fedeli 1997.

I follow the text of Klingner 1959, with minor orthographic changes.

I am grateful to Adele Scafuro, for casting a keen eye on a draft of this essay, and to Michael Fontaine for Plautine advice.

[2] For conjecture on the reality of Vinnius, based largely on Pliny the Elder's reference to Vinnius Valens, centurion under Augustus known for his strength (*HN* 7. 82), see Nisbet 1959: 75–76, and McGann 1963: 258–59.

[3] On the dignified conduct expected of a Roman is such situations, see McGann 1969: 66 and Ahleid 1974: 54 and 59 n. 37, quoting Plautus *Poenulus* (522–25), a play much cited in the pages that follow.

In one overt respect the emperor does in fact control the poem. Horace's very act of naming, however indirect, is a structuring device, guiding us from the epistle's second to its penultimate verse. *Augusto* receives the first three syllables of line 2 while *Caesaris* claims the same position in line 18. The latter designation gains particular stress. Not only does it demarcate a strong caesura in the second foot while indicating a sense pause in enjambment, it also works alliteratively with the trisyllabic *carmina* which opens the preceding line. The collocation hints, through a figure of sound, that there is a close linkage between Caesar and song, to be further effected by the ministrations of Vinnius Asina, should he pay heed to the speaker's advice. It is an intimacy to which we will return in a moment.

But it is the energized humor of the poem itself which obviates any potential seriousness that might arise if poet and poetry confronted the emperor directly.[4] That humor is focused non-stop on the figure of Vinnius Asina, on whom the poet can appropriately and immediately center anxieties for the reception of his poetic efforts which he cannot appear to betray directly to Augustus. Because the speaker must yet again importune him, now by letter, during the progress of his journey as he presumably had *viva voce* at its outset – often and over time – to treat both his burden and its recipient with requisite caution, we have a sense that, though Vinnius may not be too adept a student, the intense feelings of his educator about both journey and outcome are beyond a doubt. The very fact of a missive, imagined or otherwise, sent in pursuit of the already traveling Vinnius both continues the latter's training and adds to the hyperbolic presentation of the whole adventure. He must, urges our speaker (let's call him Horace), zealously attend to his mission, withstand what trials might come his way, use all his powers to surmount *clivos, flumina, lamas* (the asyndeton secures both quickness and fervor), press on in the struggle to reach his destination. This is all to occur while he is carrying his galling charge of *libelli*, this "tiny packet" (*fasciculum*) of *libri*, this weight (*onus*), the "heavy burden of my paper" (*meae gravis ... sarcina chartae*) that forms a chiasmus around the verb *uret*, to emphasize the burning with which such a bulk of odic verse (*carmina*) can brand the conveyor!

But the essence of Horace's humor centers on the figure of Vinnius Asina who, already from his apostrophe in the poem's second line, is juxtaposed to, and by assonance and alliteration meshed with, the speaker's *volumina* while the address to him, at line's end, forms a challenging counterpoint with the naming of the august *Princeps* at the start of the verse. There is no clearer or more amusing example in ancient literature of *nomina* illustrated in the *omina* that accompany its bearer's career. In the case of our poem's addressee this connection is born out in both parts of his nomenclature. Even before he is told not to behave like *vinosa Pirria* (14) and not to carry his precious cargo like her stolen wool, we realize that he may have a propensity to do exactly that, to endanger his charge and his mission by behaving in a tipsy manner. The last line of the poem, given its position of prominence, grants emphatic

---

[4] The humor of the poem is touched upon, among others, by McGann 1969: 65–66; Ahleid 1974: 48; Connor 1982: 148–51, who also finds a serious side to it in Horace's neurotic worries about Vinnius' clumsiness; and Ferri 1993: 69–70 (with n. 11 for further bibliography), who rightly compares Vinnius to the *servus currens* of New Comedy.

play to Vinnius' emblematic potential. In his final directive the speaker cautions Vinnius not to totter, presumably under the influence of alcohol, so as to fall and "break" what has been entrusted to him. The metaphor inherent in the poem's last word, *frangas*, confirms the complementarity we have seen from the poem's start between the bearer and his *mandata*. Vinous Vinnius is imagined as carrying fragile "jars" of the poet's lyric "wine" which, if ill-treated, could easily be smashed.[5] And this marked word-play licenses us to pursue the poet's early hints of such a parallelism. The *volumina* are sealed, but so regularly are wine-jars. We know now the make-up of the "merchandise" which Vinnius is carrying from one destination to another (*importes*), and it is appropriate that his role as the speaker's go-between be designated *minister* (5), agent maneuvering from expéditeur to destinataire.[6] He is also, as another Horatian context, to which we will shortly return, reminds us, both servant and potential server of the wine that he carries (to present the "wine" is presumably to pour it as well). Its seal he must refrain from breaking (no sipping from this precious vintage before delivery to its illustrious connoisseur!) and its container must not be in danger of shattering.[7]

The second part of the addressee's name, his father's *cognomen* Asina (8–9), likewise comes in for a share of Horace's wit.[8] Though he is not to behave like a donkey,

---

[5] Of the many instances in Horace where wine and poetry are interassociated, perhaps the most intricate is *c.* 1. 20. The classic study of the topic is by Commager 1957.

[6] The first of such rare uses in poetry of *importo* is by Plautus (*Epi.* 343).

[7] *Minister*, as the 'servant' (purveyor) of wine, has its precedent at Cat. 27. 1 and its refined Horatian imitation at *c.* 1. 38. 6, to be discussed shortly.

For *frango* (19) in relation to a wine jar, see Hor. *sat.* 2. 8. 81 (*fracta lagoena*), and for *signum* and *signare* and the sealing of wine, *epi.* 2. 2. 134 (*signo laeso ... lagoenae*). For detailed commentary cf. Brink 1982: 353–54 and Courtney 1980 on Juv. *sat.* 14. 131. Cicero (*Fam.* 16. 26. 2) tells of how his mother sealed even empty containers!

[8] The play on Asina is found as early as Scipio Africanus Minor's punning on the name of Ti. Claudius Asellus (see Cic. *de ora.* 2. 258; Macr. *Sat.* 1. 6. 29). His jibe rests on a proverb which, in Cicero's quote, begins *agas asellum* and apparently ended *cursum non docebitur* (see Otto 1890: 42, s. v. *asinus, asellus.*) The prominence, therefore, of *docui* at the exact syllabic center of the opening line of *epi.* 1. 13 has special point. Vinnius, the Asina, is coming close to living up to his name and becoming a living instance of an indocile beast of burden. The drollery in Horace's importunate "teaching" of this intractable creature is that it had already begun intensely before Vinnius had first set out. It must now continue by means of our pursuing *epistula*, with instructor, in the form of a letter, catching up with student, to continue with his education as his journey progresses.

Though the context lacks the epistle's aptness of nomenclature, Horace had already referred to the proverb at *sat.* 1. 1. 90–91:

> ...infelix operam perdas, ut si quis asellum
> in campo doceat parentem currere frenis?

> ... would you waste your time fruitlessly, as if someone were to teach a donkey to run on a racecourse in obedience to the reins?

Pseudo-Acro's comment (on *sat.* 1. 1. 88) is *à propos*: "For who wishes to teach a donkey to race" (*...qui vult docere asinum currere*). "For he," the commentator continues, "who trains a donkey to race wastes his time because it is the horse that must be trained" (*Nam qui in cursum exercet asinum, perdit operam, quia exercendus est equus*). An allied proverb, quoted by Cicero (*in Pis.* 73), is equally to the point: *Quid nunc te, asine, litteras doceam? non opus est verbis sed fustibus* ("For what now, you donkey? Am I to teach you letters? [For that] I don't need words but a cudgel.") (For further details see

which is to say like an uncultured creature (*ferus*) and not a civilized human, Horace has prepared us, again metaphorically, for just such a prospect. As we have seen, Horace designates the poetic burden that Vinnius carries as a *sarcina*, which can refer to the pack of either man or beast. But the poet soon particularizes this load by also calling what Vinnius carries *clitellae*, an object Festus (52M) defines as follows: *clitellae dicuntur ... eae quibus sarcinae conligatae mulis* (*clitellae* are called those *sarcinae* which [are carried along] bound to [the backs of] mules). Not only does Horace's use of *clitellae* animalize Vinnius, it specifically unites him with a member of the *equus asinus* family and thereby intimates that he is prone to incorporating in fact what his name might only superficially adumbrate. Once again, as in the case of the word Vinnius, Horace has earlier suggested such a metaphorical possibility through the word *pecces* (4) which, in the ninth line of the book's first epistle, he had applied to himself, poet past his lyric prime, figured as an aging horse who should be let out to pasture lest he falter before the public. Both characters are in danger of being laughed at should they stumble or fall – the Horatian steed, lest he be *ridendus* (*epi*. 1. 1. 9), Vinnius, lest he turn his father's name *in risum*. And for Vinnius in particular, his two *nomina* come together, as they unify the epistle, in the metaphorical journey from *pecces* to *titubes*, from the animal who must beware of tripping to the drunken carrier whose bibulous teetering threatens the integrity of his oenerous freight.[9]

Horace enriches and corroborates the force of his humor by a series of diverse elements that take us generically from the world of the verse epistle into the realm of comedy. Any Roman, pondering the possibility of Vinnius Asina acting out his name so that he might become the "you" subject of a comic performance (*fabula fias*), would think of the title, if not the content, of Plautus' *Asinaria*.[10] Moreover, Pseudo-

---

Otto 1890: 40–41, and Tosi 1997: 226, #484.) Nisbet 1961, *ad loc.*, refers to Housman 1930: 11–13, who notes that *asinus* was a term of abuse since the correct Latin name for donkey was *asellus*. The potential insult, whether appreciated by Vinnius or not, adds another fillip to the possibility that he is unteachable. And where in our thinking does that leave the impatient didactic epistolographer?

Horace uses *asellus* on three other occasions and never *asinus* (*sat*. 1. 9. 20, *epi*. 1. 29. 15 and 2. 1. 199). Each has a proverbial ring to it. Augustus himself (*Epi*. fr. XXII [*Imperatoris Caesaris Augusti Operum Fragmenta*, ed. H. Malcovati [Turin, 1967]) addresses his grandson Caius as *meus asellus iucundissimus*.

[9] Given the context, Horace may wish us to remember that the Latin idiom for "produce a play" is *fabulam docere* (see *OLD* s.v. *docere*, #5, for examples). Vinnius Asina, his "student" and protagonist, is in fact in danger of becoming a *fabula*, whose plot-line Horace is in the process of wittily concocting.

[10] The first exampled use of *fabula* as "play" is by Naevius (*com. fr.* 1 in *CRF* ed. Ribbeck [Leipzig, 1873]). Plautus employs the word on five occasions in *Pseudolus* alone (2, 388 [in the phrase *fabulae fiunt*], 564, 720, and 1334).

The phrase *in risum* (9) is apparently used here for the first time. But in conjunction with *fabula* as both story or legend and (comic) play or plot, we may remember that in Plautus' epitaph (as quoted by Gellius [*NA* 1. 24. 3], from Varro's *de Poetis*), where *Risus, Ludus Iocusque / et Numeri* are all said to weep at the poet's passing, the word *Risus* stands for something like comic stage performance. Likewise, when Propertius begins the final poem of his third book (3. 25. 1–2):

> Risus eram positis inter convivia mensis,
> et de me poterat quilibet esse loquax…,

> (I was a laughing-stock, when places were set in the midst of drinking bouts, and anyone whosoever was in a position to chatter about me…),

Acro (on *epi.* 1. 13. 14) informs us that in one of the comedies of Titinius, writing also in the second century BCE, there is the character of a serving woman who steals a ball of wool and is apprehended.[11] When we turn to specific vocabulary, we find that the adjective *vinosus* appears, before Horace's *epistulae*, only at Plautus *Curc.* 79 where it is appropriately applied to an old servant (*anus*) named Leaena who is *vinosissima* .[12] Likewise the word *clitellae*, the burden mules bear, has a comedic reference, since it is first used in Plautus *Mos.* 778. It is adopted by Horace, first, in *sat.* 1. 5. 47, where the *muli* are momentarily relieved of their saddlebags at Capua on the way to Brundisium, and then in our verse letter.[13]

But it is the phrase *cave ne titubes*, centered in the poem's last line, that carries special emphasis in this context. "Horace's" command to his addressee is an echo of the words which the titular hero-slave in Plautus' *Pseudolus* uses, at line 942, to confront a fellow-slave.[14] The resonance with comedy is confirmed on several levels. One concerns a technical detail – the length of the final "e" in the singular imperative of the verb *caveo*. Its "iambic shortening" is a feature of comedy, and *cave* is so treated in Horace's *Satires* (2. 3. 38 and 177; 2. 5. 75) whose lexicon and prosody often overlap with those of comedy.[15] In the intervening *Epodes* (6. 11), *Odes* (1. 14. 16; 3. 7. 24) and, most prominent for our purposes, *Epistles* 1 (1. 6. 32), however, the final

---

he means not only that he has become a butt of ridicule but that the story of his relationship with Cynthia has, in the view of some, the ingredients of a comic plot, however macabre. As so often for *epi.* 1. 13, there is an apt parallel in Plautus, this time with the parasite Gelasimus (and with a bilingual pun on his name) in *Stichus* (174–77):

> Gelasimo nomen indidit parvo pater,
> (propter pauperiem hoc adeo nomen repperi)
> quia inde iam a pusillo ridiculus fui,
> eo quia paupertas fecit ridiculus forem;…

(My father bestowed on me the name Gelasimus when I was little – I took this name on account of our poverty – since even then, from the time when I was the littlest boy, I was an object of laughter, since poverty saw to it that I be ridiculous.)

As far as the title *Asinaria* is concerned, we know also that around 90 BCE Pomponius wrote an Atellan farce called *Asina* and Novius one entitled *Asinius* (*CRF* 226 and 255, respectively). See also Horsfall 1982: 293.

[11] *Apud Titinium in quadam fabula inducitur ancilla, quae lanae glomus furatur et deprehenditur* (In a certain play of Titinius a servant woman is brought on, who steals a ball and is caught).

The exclusively prosaic quality of *glomus* is noted by Fedeli 1997, commenting on lines 11–15.

[12] Horace's only other uses of *vinosus* are at *epi* 1. 1. 38 and 1. 19. 6 (*vinosus Homerus*). The latter is one of several connections between *epi.* 1. 13 and the final two epistles of Horace's first book. In *epi.* 1. 19, Vinnius is replaced by Maecenas, the person to be taught (*docui*, 1. 13. 1) by the person already tutored (*docte*, 1. 19. 1), the vinous addressee by the patron who already knows about Horatian "wine" and is soon to learn more. And in the "seal" poem (*epi.* 1. 20), Vinnius Asina and his *signata volumina* are replaced by the *sigilla* (3), hated by the truant prostitute *liber* which itself is reformulated as a disobedient *asellus* (15), shoved against a rock by its disapproving master.

[13] The cognate adjective *clitellarius*, applied to mules carrying pack-saddles, occurs first at Pl. *Mos.* 780, and to *asini*, first at Cato *Agr.* 10. 1. See Otto 1890: 57 for proverbial uses of *clitellae*. We find the same nexus of *sarcina*, *clitellae* and *onus* at Livy 25. 36. 7 and 10.

[14] Cf. also *Ps.* 44 and 765 for further uses of *titubo*, and 1296 for another example of *cave ne* (now of Pseudolus himself). Plautus' only other uses of *titubo* are at *Men.* 142 and *M. G.* 248 and 946.

[15] See, for example, Muecke 1993 on *sat.* 2. 3. 38.

"e" is treated as long. To have recourse to iambic shortening of *cave* at the conclusion of *epi.* 1. 13, especially when its final syllable is exemplified as lengthened seven poems earlier in the collection, is, therefore, a distinct bow toward comic procedure.

There are more expansive reasons why both plot and language of Plautine comedy, but especially of *Pseudolus*, would have appealed to Horace as he constructed his witty epistle.[16] Two letters, for instance, figure prominently in its story-line – those of Phoenicium to Calidorus and of Polymachaeroplagides to Ballio. A variety of words for letter (*epistula, sumbolon/symbolon, signum, imago, libellus*) in fact pervades the play.[17] In context they are often accompanied by the caution that epistolary correspondence remain sealed (Plautus uses the verb *obsigno* four times during the play). Moreover the punning relationship between *nomen* and *omen,* upon which Horace builds so much of his word-play at the expense of Vinnius Asina, is at Plautus' service in *Pseudolus* with a regularity rarely paralleled elsewhere in his comedies.[18] The title figure himself sets the tone: Is he to be believed and trusted? What is true, what fabricated, about his doings? Phoenicium should be prepared to have a *poeniceo corio* (228), if she doesn't behave, and Ballio to have his defenses battered down (*exballistabo,* 585). On three occasions Harpax is true to his name, whether the playwright's paronomasia is in Latin or Greek (655–56, 1010), and the pun is reasserted through two appearances of the verb *harpago* (139, 957). Charinus is more than once associated with χάρις (712; and cf. 736) and Simia spends a hundred lines "aping" Harpax.

One other conceit, around which Horace builds much of the last half of his poem, may also find its source in Plautus' *Pseudolus.* The epistle-writer asks his messenger not to carry his precious burden under his armpit (*ala*), and not to say that he had sweated (*sudavisse*) in the course of his journey. (Horace's piling up of analogies, which stay with us not least because of the vivid use of asyndeton, for what Vinnius ought not to be – a country bumpkin with a lamb under his arm, Pirra with her wool, an invitee to dinner lugging slippers and cap with him – is part of the fun.) Put in a circumspect but still graphic manner, his conduct is to be such that his merchandise will attract the eyes and ears (*oculos aurisque*) of the emperor, but not the nose![19] This implicit bit of ribaldry, founded on negative olfactory sensation stemming from underarm redolence, has a vivid history in Latin letters that takes us from Catullus 69, and its sequel, 71, to Horace's twelfth *epode* (especially line 5) to our present

---

[16] For a discussion of Horace's mentions of Plautus and what they tell us of the playwright's reception in the age of Augustus, see Jocelyn 1995.

[17] There are more than thirty such usages.

[18] The *locus classicus* in Plautus on the relation of *nomen* and *omen,* where the words are in fact employed, is *Persa* 625, where Saturio's nameless daughter christens herself Lucris in a context where "profit" is a key notion. For a list of further examples in Plautus see Petersmann 1973 on *St.* 174, with reference to Kiessling and Heinze 1957 on *sat.* 1. 7. 32.

The phrase *nomen omen* is used by Mayer 1994 in discussing Vinnius' *cognomen* and its "agricultural origin."

[19] The inclusion of all three senses in Lucretius' lists at *DRN* 2. 511 and 4. 486 may help point up Horace's careful omission (cf. also Ovid *M.* 12.435 and Sen. *Oed.* 187–89).

collection of *epistulae* where the speaker, inviting Torquatus to a dinner whose ambiance is impeccable, can pronounce (*epi.* 1. 5. 29):

> sed nimis arta premunt olidae convivia caprae.
> But smelly goats afflict banquets that are too close.

The genealogy of this fancy leads back again to *Pseudolus* (738) where Charinus speaks of his slave, Simia, as having "a goat under his armpits" (*hircum ab alis*)![20]

Such is Horace's roundabout but splendidly witty means of taking his reader along with Vinnius and the *volumina*, that in different ways belong to poet, to bearer and to both present and future receivers, quasi directly into the presence of Augustus at the end of the poem, which is also to say at the termination of Vinnius' itinerary. But this is not the finale of Horace's *dramma giocoso,* for we are fortunate to have preserved an excerpt of the epistle which the emperor sent in reply. It is the recipient of Horace's verses who creates the concluding scene in this on-going skit, countering the poet's *facetiae* with drollery of his own. Here are his words, as quoted in Horace's abridged *vita*, drawn ultimately from Suetonius' *De Poetis*:

> pertulit ad me Onysius libellum tuum, quem ego ut excusantem quantuluscumque est boni consulo. vereri autem mihi videris ne maiores libelli tui sint quam ipse es. sed tibi statura deest, corpusculum non deest. itaque licebit in sextariolo scribas, quo circuitus voluminis tui sit ὀγκωδέστατος, sicut est ventriculi.[21]

> (Onysius has delivered me your little book which, tiny as it is, I accept in good part, as an apology. But you seem to me to be frightened that your little books may be larger than you are yourself. But it is only height that you lack, not a small body's substance. So you may write on a tiny pint-pot so that the circumference of your volume may be quite rounded out, like your little paunch.)

The connection between verse epistle and prose response is clear enough.[22] The first sentence extends Horace's own nomenclatural play on Vinnius' paternal *cognomen* by

---

[20] *Pseudolus* 136 also deserves mention in tracing parallels between Plautus and Horace. Ballio enters whipping a troop of slaves:
  neque ego homines magis asinos numquam vidi, ita plagis costae callent: ...
I never saw men more like donkeys, their ribs are so callous from blows of the whip.
  The fact that some men are like donkeys, and need cudgeling in order to get them to behave, has appropriate resonance in a poem as concerned with donkeys, and the proverbs attached to them, as it is indebted to Plautus, and especially to *Pseudolus*.

[21] The text is that of Klingner 1959, though I accept Reifferscheidt's emendation *excusantem* for the manuscripts' *accusantem*. (Fraenkel 1957: 20 obelizes the phrase *ut accusantem*.) There is no reason to doubt the historicity of the letter. Suetonius, as secretary *a studiis*, *a bibliothecis* and *ab epistulis* to the emperor Hadrian until his apparently summary dismissal in 122, would have had full access to the imperial archives, including the correspondence of Augustus. In his life of Augustus (87–8) he exhibits detailed knowledge of his subject's vocabulary and habits of writing. In the *vita Augusti* alone he quotes from, or refers to, the letters of the emperor some sixteen times, and twice mentions a letter or letters written in his own hand (*autographa quadam epistula* [71. 2]; *litterae autographae* [87. 1]).
  Augustus apparently invents the word *sextariolus*. The superlative of ὀγκώδης appears already at Aris. *Po.* 1459b35.

[22] The connection is rejected by Fraenkel 1957: 20 n. 2 as follows: "J. Bernays, *Rh. Mus.* xvii, 1862, 313f (*Ges. Abh.* [Berlin, 1885] 11. 305f.) identified the Onysius of the letter with Vinnius Asina, the

entitling him Onysius. Augustus thus at once does him the verbal honor of turning his name into Greek (ὄνος) while drawing to the surface Horace's tacit word-play on *onus* (12), the burden that the human donkey carries on its way.[23] Augustus amuses himself with, and for, his poet friend, with metonymical appropriateness accompanied by sonic figuration, by turning *onus* into ὄνος, the weight into the animal that bears it, just as the animal himself suffers parallel lexical metamorphosis from Latin to Greek.

Though the comedy may continue, masks are off. The graceful, brilliantly facetious indirection of the poet's presentation of his lyric verse to the emperor yields to the immediacy of Augustus' response, a response which doesn't eschew twitting Horace on the size of his belly in language which a poet, with adherence to Callimachean refinement, might take amiss, if applied by someone involved in a serious act of disapproval.[24] But the poet, too, must keep his humor in this exchange, and accept the emperor's foolery. Horace's corpulescence may offer ready analogy for what he writes on and even for the volume of his *volumen*. His slim spirit and its raffiné enterprise are quite different, as the teasing emperor well knew.

A series of interrelated questions remains, when *vita* and *epistula* are juxtaposed: What were the book or books in question which Vinnius is said to be carrying? When were they written and what are we to imagine was Augustus' whereabouts at the time *epi.* 1. 13 was "dispatched"? (We would be well within our rights as readers to interpret the scenario of the epistle as totally imagined except for the undeniable "historical

---

messenger who was to carry a copy of Horace's *carmina* to Augustus (*Epist.* i. 13); this wild guess ought not to have been revived by Rostagni, loc. cit. [= A. Rostagni, ed., *Suetonio: De Poetis* (Turin, 1944), 118]. The Greek of the Princeps was proof against any temptation to combine Onysius and ὄνος." Perhaps Fraenkel is thinking of Suetonius' statement (*Aug.* 89) about the limitations of the emperor's abilities to express himself in Greek: *non tamen ut aut loqueretur expedite aut componere aliquid auderet; nam et si quid res exigeret, Latine formabat vertendumque alii dabat* (nevertheless, he didn't dare either to speak or to compose anything extempore [in Greek]; for should the situation demand it, he shaped [his thoughts] in Latin and gave [them] to someone else to translate). Whatever hesitancy Suetonius' words may imply about the emperor's part, his word-play on ὀγκώδης (see below n. 23) and his incorporation of Greek in his letter to Virgil (see below n. 28) are among the several challenges to Fraenkel's assumption. The most recent discussion of the interchange is by Ferri 1993: 68 n. 10.

[23] The pun ("calembour") is noted by Préaux 1968 on line 13.

[24] The word ὀγκώδης, when applied to poetry, means bombastic (Philodemus περὶ ποιημάτων 5. 5) or, to rhetoric, turgid (Dion. Hal. *Din.* 7).

There may be a still further play to ὀγκωδέστατος which would not be overindulgent for someone who moves easily from Asina and *onus* to Onysius and ὄνος. There is a secondary meaning to ὀγκώδης, namely "making a donkey's braying noise." This adjective is attested only in Aelian (*NA* 12. 34), but the verb from which it is derived, ὀγκάομαι, has a history going back to Theopompus and Aristotle. For those concerned with Horace's literary background its most interesting appearance is Call. *Aet.* fr. 1. 31Pf., where it is associated with the non-Callimachean braying of the long-eared donkey in contradistinction to the clear voice of the cicada which the speaker takes to himself. To move from one meaning of ὀγκώδης to another, from grandiloquence of expression to raucousness of sound, would be an easy progress for someone steeped in Callimachean poetics, especially in a context where punning on the name of Asina has on several occasions been the order of the day. (The double sense of ὀγκώδης is also noted by Johnson 1993: 36–37.) If my supposition is correct, then we have further reason to applaud the virtuosity of the emperor's Greek.

reality" of the emperor's reply to his artist.)[25] But the two *epistulae* between them suggest other possibilities, once we reach beyond the apparent contradiction the two letters pose between what "Horace" sent and what Augustus received. The Horatian epistle, in order, tells of *signata volumina, libellis, chartae, fasciculum librorum, carmina*, not to speak of metaphors such as *sarcina, clitellas* and *onus*, or calls attention to details of the plot, such as the sheer energy required to carry out the *propositum* and the combat of nature demanded of Vinnius to succeed in such a mission (*victor*). But the very exaggeration that permeates so much of the poem, not to speak of the non-stop humor which it supports, tends by its conclusion to undermine both the specific details and the general tone of its hyperbole. Augustus completes the subversion. We hear now of only one *libellus*, one which its recipient accepts with goodwill, however small it may be (*quantuluscumque*). And to bring the point home, Augustus seems to be at pains to provoke a contrast between the one book of inconsequential size and the poet's corpulence, about which he makes his multivalent joke.

But Horace's *epistula* may, ironically, offer us a clue that corroborates the truth of Augustus' response, with its deflection of his poet's comic overstatement. The bounding words of line 5, *sedulus* and *minister*, happen also to be the same words that begin and end line 6 of *c. 1. 38* whose second, and last, stanza I quote in its entirety:

> simplici myrto nihil adlabores
> sedulus curo: neque te ministrum
> dedecet myrtus, neque me sub arta
>   vite bibentem.

> It is my unceasing concern that you add nothing to the myrtle's simplicity: the myrtle fails to befit neither you, [wine's] pourer, nor me, as I drink underneath the tight-knit vine.

It is by means of an exactly similar pattern of allusion that, earlier in the first book of epistles, at 1. 3. 36 –

> ... pascitur in vestrum reditum votiva iuvenca.

> ... a cow is being fed as votive offering for your return. –

Horace constructs an intentional bow to Virgil's third *georgic* (219):

> pascitur in magna Sila formosa iuvenca

> a beautiful cow is feeding on mighty Sila.[26]

But Horace's self-reference has special force in this context where consequential indirection often carries the day. The creator of the epistle is looking to the sphragis, the seal poem, which concludes the first book of his masterful trilogy of *Carmina*, in

---

[25] The general consensus of scholars is that the *onus* which Vinnius carries is the first three books of *Carmina* (see Fraenkel 1957: 352, with reference to Lachmann 1876, 2: 155). The several difficulties involved with such a presentation of the odes after their publication are outlined by Wickham 1891: 275–76 in an "Additional Note" to his commentary on *epi.* 1. 13. Clarke 1972 argues for *Epistles* I as the poetry in question.

[26] Mayer 1994 notes the allusion ("a bold intertext") which he interprets in his addenda (p. 275).

other words to an ode which, unlike any other in a gathering of poems with the possible exception of the first, stands for the collection as a whole.[27] If this suggestion is correct, then the *carmina* of *epi.* 1. 13. 17 – the contents, as the poetic epistle would have it, of *libelli* (4) and a bundle of *libri* (13), but limited, in Augustus' more pragmatic appraisal, to a single *libellus* – look to exactly that, the brilliant assemblage of odes known to us as the first book of *Carmina*. The intimacy which we earlier saw in the linking of *carmina* and *Caesaris* at the initiation of lines 17 and 18, through allusion takes a different though no less significant turn. In a poem where we expect Maecenas we find Vinnius, but the latter, palpable addressee though he be, remains in fact only an intermediary between the poet and the grandest of patrons – in the distance, literally and figuratively. What Horace is offering the emperor, through his allusion to the seal poem of book 1 and with the help of Augustus' own limitation of *libelli* and *libri* to *libellus*, is nothing less than the first book of the odes itself. This presentation is oblique, disguised by means of the apostrophe to Vinnius (he is the recipient of the letter, after all, not Augustus) and by the abundance of comic display that shrouds what might seem too serious or, in fact, too forward a gesture if performed overtly. But the compliment to the Princeps is as enormous as it is wittily back-handed.

This suggestion may solve another practical problem. The three initial volumes of *Carmina* were published in 23 BCE and the first book of *Epistulae* in 20 or shortly thereafter. The assumption has been that *epi.* 1. 13 was written after 23 and therefore after the first *Carmina* were issued as a trilogy. But this supposition raises a question which critics have duly noted: Are we to reason that Augustus, who was in Rome from the middle of 24 to that of 22, had not approved, not to say known, of the *Odes* before his departure from the city at the latter date for Sicily and the East?[28] Are we meant to imagine *epi.* 1. 13 as somehow speeding Vinnius on his way south and east in 22 or later (Augustus did not return until 19), carrying a copy of a poetic gathering already issued, which all the cognoscenti of Rome would have read except its Princeps, especially given the fact that the emperor was in Rome during the year of its publication?

A more likely scenario for the "plot" of *epi.* 1. 13 is that we are in fact dealing with the *Carmina*, specifically their first book, but at a time before, not after, they were presented to the public. This proposal gains support from the fact that Augustus was in Gaul and Spain from the middle of 27 to that of 24. A "dramatic date" for *epi.* 1. 13 during that period makes sense of all the evidence. Neither Augustus nor the Roman literary world in general would have yet known of the collection as a whole. Therefore the emperor would receive a poetic gift as fresh for him as it would be for the Roman literati in 23. Moreover if Augustus is in fact considered to be in Spain, campaigning against the Cantabri or recovering from the near mortal illness that struck him there (he is, we remember, to be *validus*, before Vinnius makes his presentation), then there

---

[27] In the context of "sealing," the phrase *signata volumina* takes on still further significance (see above n. 7). For detailed discussion of final poems see Kranz 1961.

[28] For discussion of Augustus' whereabouts during these years, see Syme 1939: 331–33 (for 27–24 BCE), 371–72 and 388 (for 22–19).

may be an element of truth lurking in the hyperbolic description of the journey Vinnius must undertake, if he is in fact to be imagined transporting his precious cargo from Rome to Hispania Citerior and not on some less plausible route, from a Sabine retreat, say, to the royal dwelling on the Palatine.

But, should the poem's immediacy claim our belief in the reality of its story line, such a response gains some corroboration from evidence elsewhere. It may not be completely coincidental that one of the two excerpts from letters of Augustus addressed to Virgil was written from Spain during the Cantabrian campaign. In it he inquires about the *Aeneid*, craving a draft, or at least an excerpt, of the epic in the process of evolution.[29] If the emperor's interest in the masterpieces being produced under his regime was such that an outline or snippet from Virgil might bring satisfaction, he would no doubt have been gratified by the arrival of the first completed segment of another contemporary chef d'oeuvre. The *epistula* accompanying its deliverer would have added, however indirectly, to Augustus' pleasure, grounded not a little in amusement at his poet's deft charm.

Works Cited

Ahleid, F. 1974. "Horatius Epistula 1, 13." *Lampas* 7: 43–59.

Brink. C.O. 1982. *Horace on Poetry: Epistles Book II*. Cambridge.

Clarke, M.L. 1972. "Horace, *Epistles* i. 13." *CR* 22: 157–59.

Commager, S. 1957. "The Function of Wine in Horace's Odes." *TAPhA* 88: 68–80.

Connor, P.J. 1982. "Book despatch: Horace epistles 1.20 and 1.13." *Ramus* 11: 145–52.

Courtney, E. 1980. *A Commentary on the Satires of Juvenal*. London.

Fedeli, P. 1997. *Q. Orazio Flacco: Le Opere: II*. Vol. 4. Rome.

Ferri, R. 1993. *I dispiaceri di un epicureo*. Biblioteca di materiali e discussioni per l'analisi dei testi classici 11. Pisa. 67–71.

Fraenkel, E. 1957. *Horace*. Oxford.

Heinze, R. and A. Kiessling, eds. 1957. *Q. Horatius Flaccus: Satiren*. Berlin.

Horsfall, N. 1982. *Cambridge History of Classical Literature: II: Latin Literature*. Cambridge.

Housman, A.E. 1930. "The Latin for *Ass*." *CQ* 24: 11–13.

Jocelyn, H.D. 1995. "Horace and the Reputation of Plautus in the Late First Century BC." In S. J. Harrison, ed., *Homage to Horace: A Bimillenary Celebration*. Oxford. 228–47.

Johnson, W.R. 1993. *Horace and the dialectic of freedom: readings in epistles* 1. Cornell Studies in Classical Philology 53. Ithaca.

Kilpatrick, R.S. 1986. *The Poetry of Friendship: Horace, Epistles* 1. Edmonton.

Klingner, F., ed. *Q. Horati Flacci: Opera*. Leipzig 1959.

Kranz, W. 1961, "Sphragis. Ichformen und Namensiegel als Eingangs- und Schlussmotiv antiker Dichtung." *RhM* 104: 3–46, 97–124.

Lachmann, K. 1876. *Kleine Schriften zur classischen Philologie*. Vol. 2. Berlin.

Mayer, R., ed. 1994. *Horace: Epistles: Book 1*. Cambridge.

McGann, M. J. 1963. "Vinnius Valens, son of Vinnius Asina?." *CQ* n.s. 13: 258–59.

———. 1969. *Studies in Horace's first book of Epistles. Collection Latomus* 100. Brussels.

Muecke, F. ed., 1993. *Horace: Satires II*. Warminster.

Nisbet, R.G.M. 1959. "Notes on Horace, Epistles 1." *CQ* n.s. 9: 75–76

———., ed. 1961. *M. Tulli Ciceronis: in L. Calpurnium Pisonem Oratio*. Oxford.

---

[29] The quotation is from Donatus' *Vita* 30–31 (*Epi.* fr. XXXVI). Augustus employs Greek for "outline" (ὑπογραφή) and "segment" (κῶλον). See further White 1993: 115–16 with 301–2 n. 10–11.

Otto, A. 1890. *Die Sprichwörter der Römer*. Leipzig.

Peratelli, A. 1993. "Destinazioni delle Epistole." In R. Uglione, ed., *Atti del convegno nazionale di studi su Orazio: Torino, 13–14–15 Aprile 1992*. Turin. 205–18.

Petersmann, H., ed. 1973. *T. Maccius Plautus*: *Stichus*. Heidelberg.

Préaux, J., ed. 1968. *Horatius*: *Epîtres, livre 1*. Paris.

Syme R. 1939. *The Roman Revolution*. Oxford.

Tosi, R., ed. 1997. *Dizionario delle Sentenze Latine e Greche*. Milan.

White, P. 1993. *Promised Verse*. Cambridge.

Wickham, E.C., ed. 1891. *Quinti Horatii Flacci*: *Opera Omnia*: *II*. Oxford.

10

When A Gesture Was Misinterpreted: *didonai titthion* in Menander's *Samia*[*]

Adele C. Scafuro

No one would deny that proofs play an important role in New Comedy. Consider, for example, comedies set in Athens, and consider, in particular, the popular and conventional scene of recognition (*anagnōrisis*). Sometimes such scenes take the shape of the identification of a "displaced person" – that is, of someone who was kidnapped or shipwrecked as a child, raised in a foreign city and brought up as person X but who, upon return to Athens as a young adult, is *identified* as person Y.[1] Identification is likely to have important consequences – conferral of citizenship and bestowal in marriage.[2] So it is in Terence's *Andria*, based on a Menandrian Greek original: little

---

[*] I presented an early version of this essay to a Brown Classics Faculty Colloquium, and later versions to the University of Crete in Rethymno and the Oxford Philological Society. I am grateful to L. Athanassaki and P.G.McC. Brown for constructive comments. Still later drafts have been read by M. L. Gill, T. Tuozzo, and W. F. Wyatt; I am grateful to these readers as well but I remain responsible for wayward thinking. Unless otherwise indicated, translations are my own.
    It is a pleasure to offer this essay to Alan L. Boegehold, colleague and friend for nearly twenty years, and friend, I hope, for many more to come!

[1] In his important discussions of recognition (*anagnōrisis*) in *Poetics* cc. 11 and 16, Aristotle does not distinguish between recognition and "identification." In my view, identification is a sub-division of recognition: while identification might be considered a "change from ignorance to knowledge" (1452a30–31) and hence a "recognition" of a general kind, it is *specifically* a change that creates a new identity for a particular person. Whereas Orestes in the *I.T.* after a separation of many years recognizes Iphigeneia, he does not cause a change in her identity – she is still Iphigeneia, daughter of Agamemnon and Klytemnestra; on the other hand, after the messenger in *O.T.* gives information to Oidipous about his true parentage, he not only comes to recognize who he is, he also has a new identity: he is no longer the son of the Korinthian Polybos and Merope, he is now the son of the Theban Laios and Iokaste. Although in the corpus of extant Greek tragedies recognitions of the "Iphigeneia type" are more numerous (*e.g.*, the recognitions of Orestes by Elektra in the plays of Sophokles and Euripides, of Helen by Menelaos in Euripides' *Helen*), identifications of the "Oidipous type" must have been common. The *Ion*, of course, stands out, together with the *O.T.*, as the only extant examples, but "identifications" were featured in lost plays such as the *Tyro* of Sophokles, Astyadamos, and Karkinos – and in many more. In "tragedies of identification," the character who acquires a new identity was separated from his parents at birth, exposed, and then "adopted" by substitute parents; recognition of the character's real parents thus entails the acquisition of a new identity.

[2] When Philoumene in Menander's *Sikyonios* has her true identity confirmed, she no longer is an appendage of questionable status in Stratophanes' household, she is the daughter of Kichesias of

Glycerium, shipwrecked with her uncle off the coast of Andros and then raised on that island, subsequently returns to Athens to the house of her Andrian "sister," the courtesan Chrysis; in the penultimate scene of the play, Chremes with the aid of an Andrian man who was kinsman to Glycerium's Andrian rescuer and acquainted with her uncle before his death, puts together the clues: the deceased uncle was Chremes' brother; "Glycerium" is his long-lost daughter Pasibula; now, with birthright proven, she may marry her Athenian fiancé. The identification presented in the play has become almost a legal proof; though not presented before magistrates, it is presented before witnesses who, if comedy were real life, might be called upon in the future for testimony about the girl's identity. While we do not have to understand the play as explicitly anticipating that the identification be used in this way, nevertheless, the configuration of identification as a "proof" belongs to this legal context.

Because "scenes of identification" use arguments that prove the case for identity – or, at least, arguments that make a persuasive case – there is a conscious and conscientious highlighting of the means of acquiring and presenting persuasive proof for identification in some of these comedies.[3] The proofs are not, of course, limited to demonstrations of personal or civic identity.[4] Sometimes "proofs" are given that a particular event has taken place (e.g., Onesimos' masterful deduction in *Epitrepontes* that his master raped a girl at the Tauropolia)[5] or that an event is not likely to take place in the future (e.g., Davos' proof in the *Andria* that Chremes has *not* promised his daughter in marriage to Pamphilus).[6] Attentiveness to proving is apparent in a number of plays of Menander and in several Menandrian-based plays of Plautus and Terence: *Aspis, Epitrepontes, Samia, Sikyonios, Cistellaria, Adelphoe, Andria, Eunuchus, Heauton Timorumenos*. Possibly other writers of New Comedy also shared this attentiveness and it may not be peculiar to Menander – but I have found in the Menandrian plays a striking preoccupation with "proving" that justifies setting them apart from others. "Proving" is used in various ways: sometimes proofs appear as the dynamic that moves the play along – often they are carefully deduced arguments that are overthrown in a subsequent parallel scene and replaced by a more compelling proof – as happens, as we shall see, in Acts 3 and 4 of the *Samia*; occasionally, proving becomes a thematic concern of the drama itself – as it does in *Epitrepontes, Sikyonios* and *Andria*, and probably in the *Aspis* as well.[7] It is the purpose of this essay to focus on one Menandrian comedy and to suggest that Menander's preoccupation with "proving" has both a philosophical basis and a foundation in the tradition of rhetoric. While it cannot be proven with certainty that Menander is reproducing Peripatetic ideas, it can be shown that his intellectual framework for proving and

---

Skambonidai and the soon-to-be-wedded wife of Stratophanes. When Glykera discovers her true father in *Perikeiromene*, she no longer will be Polemon's *pallakē*, but his *gametē gunē*.

[3] This is especially so in the "explicit citizen comedies" – *Sikyonios, Andria, Eunuchus* – that is, comedies which involve an identification of a character as an Athenian.

[4] Cf. *Poetics*, 1452a33–36.

[5] Men. *Epit.* 445–54.

[6] Ter. *An.* 346–69.

[7] See Scafuro 1997: 347–349.

argumentation shares common ground with that school.[8] That, of course, may be a result of the Peripatetic habit of drawing upon what is common knowledge – especially, in analyses of rhetoric, by drawing upon the lawcourts and tragedy for the presentation of its ideas. Menander's rhetorical strategies illustrate, at the very least, specific intellectual habits that are the web not only of his art, but of his culture.

Before setting out on the main course of my argument and examining Menander's preoccupation with proof, it will be useful to consider Aristotle's discussion of *dianoia* in *Poetics* 6 and 19. In the earlier chapter, he joins together *ēthos* (basically, "character") and *dianoia* (basically, "intelligence") as qualities belonging to the *personae* of tragedy:

> Since tragedy is a *mimēsis* of an action and since it is acted out by certain actors who by necessity have certain qualities that are in accordance with their *ēthos* and *dianoia* (for it is through these that we say that actions are of a certain quality and there are by nature two causes of actions, *dianoia* and *ēthos*, and it is in accordance with these that all succeed or fail), plot is therefore a *mimēsis* of action. For I mean by plot an arrangement of incidents; by *ēthē*, that in accordance with which we say the actors have particular qualities; and by *dianoia*, whatever is said to prove something or to articulate a maxim. (1449b36–50a7).

In c.19, he adds this to his account of *dianoia*:

> As for *dianoia*, let what is set down in the books about rhetoric hold good, since it more properly belongs to that study. To *dianoia* belong as many subjects as must be fashioned by speech. Its parts are: proving and refutation and producing emotions such as pity or fear or anger and the like, and even greatness and smallness. (1456a34–56b2)

Too little attention has been paid to the *dianoia* of Menandrian characters. And yet it is not difficult to see how integral *dianoia* is to *ēthos* although the latter has, paradoxically, overshadowed it and become a stock theme in modern interpretations of Menander. As healthy restorative, one might point to *NE* 1103e5 as Lucas does in his commentary on *Poetics* 6, where Aristotle "divides ἀρετή into ἠθική and διανοητική ... On a man's διάνοια depends his power to assess a situation, on his ἦθος his reaction to it."[9] One's assessment of a situation is closely related to his reaction to it. Menander is by no means concerned with *ēthos* by itself, but rather with the way his characters think, the way they make assessments and deductions, the way that *ēthos* is sometimes a function of *dianoia*. From this perspective, it comes as no surprise that some of Menander's best creations are the intellectually superior and often vain characters such as Demeas in *Samia* or Simo in Terence's adaptation of Menander's *Andria*, or those clever marginal characters – Onesimos and Habrotonon in *Epitrepontes*, Davos and Thais in the Terentian adaptions of *Andria* and *Eunuchus* respectively.

---

[8] It is said that Menander was a student of Theophrastos (Diog. Laet. 5.36). For discussion of the difficulty of demonstrating a real connection between Menander and the Lyceum, see Sandbach 1967: 239; Webster 1974: 68–70 has a brief discussion of "Aristotle and Probability" in his chapter on "the professional code."

[9] Lucas 1968: 99–100 on 6.1449b38.

I now begin the main course of this essay with a brief consideration of rhetorical *tekmēria*; in the midst of that discussion I sidetrack into the medical tradition; after that, I turn to proofs in the *Samia*.

I. RHETORICAL *TEKMĒRIA*

Aristotle in the second chapter of the *Rhetoric* (1.1355b35–39) speaks of two types of proof (*pistis*), the non-artificial or artless (*atekhnoi*) and the artificial or artful (*entekhnoi*). The *atekhnoi* are those not furnished "by ourselves," but "already in existence" – for example, witnesses, reports of tortures, contracts, and laws; the *entekhnoi* are all those that can be constructed "methodically" and by ourselves. Whereas the *atekhnoi* are at hand for our use, the *entekhnoi* must be discovered or invented by us. Aristotle expends much care in explaining the *entekhnoi*, which effect persuasion through the *ēthos* of the speaker or by arousing the *pathē* of his listeners or through the *logos* itself (1.1356a1–4). This third type of artful proof may be an argument that uses example, i.e., "rhetorical induction," or one that applies an enthymeme, i.e., "rhetorical *sullogismos*."[10]

Aristotle tells us how *sullogismos* operates in numerous passages in his corpus.[11] In *Topics* 1.1.100a25–27, for example, we read: "A *sullogismos* ("deduction," "inference") is an argument in which, certain things being posited, something different from the things laid down necessarily results through the things laid down."[12] A recent commentator writes of this passage:

---

[10] *Rhet.* 1356b4–6: καλῶ δ᾽ ἐνθύμημα μὲν ῥητορικὸν συλλογισμόν, παράδειγμα δὲ ἐπαγωγὴν ῥητορικήν. Ross 1965: 499 comments about the "rhetorical syllogism": "... inasmuch as the object of oratory is not knowledge but the producing of conviction, to say that enthymeme is a rhetorical syllogism is to tell us that it lacks something that a scientific demonstration has." A rhetorical syllogism, Ross suggests, "may be inferior to demonstration by being "syllogistically invalid," or it may proceed from a premise that states ... a probability;" or "it may be syllogistically correct and start from premises that are strictly true, but these may not give the reason stated in the conclusion, but only a symptom from which it can be inferred." Burnyeat offers a detailed examination of this issue in a number of articles (1982, 1994, and 1996); see n. 12 below. Modern bibliography on the Aristotelian syllogism and enthymeme is enormous; consult Burnyeat 1994: 51–55 and most recently, Allen 2001: 15–86.

[11] For Aristotelian citations, see the following note. The meaning of *sullogismos* vacillates in Aristotle; sometimes it means an argument; at other times, it means a subset of the class of arguments that are valid inferences or deductions; *sullogismos*, moreover, might be further modified by "rhetorical," "dialectical," or "apodeiktic"; see Lloyd 1996: 10–11; Frede 1974: 1–32, esp. 16–23; Patzig 1968: 1–15. Scholars have argued whether all such discussions represent the fully matured view of syllogistic that is manifest in *Posterior Analytics* (the "unitarian view") or whether discussions of *sullogismoi* (sometimes within the same work) represent different stages in Aristotle's thought (the "developmental view"); for references, see Burnyeat 1994: 31–34 and Allen 2001: 22 and n. 14. Luckily we need not be involved in this debate.

[12] *Topics* 1.1. 100a25–27: ἔστι δὴ συλλογισμὸς λόγος ἐν ὧι τεθέντων τινῶν ἕτερόν τι τῶν κειμένων ἐξ ἀνάγκης συμβαίνει διὰ τῶν κειμένων. Similarly, *A.Pr.* 1. 24b18–22. Cf. *Rhet.* 1356b16–18: τὸ δὲ τινῶν ὄντων ἕτερόν τι [διὰ ταῦτα?] συμβαίνειν παρὰ ταῦτα τῶι ταῦτα εἶναι ἢ καθόλου ἢ ὡς ἐπὶ τὸ πολὺ ἐκεῖ μὲν συλλογισμὸς ἐνταῦθα δὲ ἐνθύμημα καλεῖται ("when, certain things being the case, something different results [because of them] in addition to them by virtue of their being the case, either universally or for the most part, there [i.e., in dialectic] it is called *sullogismos*, here [i.e., in rhetoric] enthymeme"). It is possible, as Burnyeat (1994: 18) and others have argued, that Aristotle deliberately omitted the

This is a broad definition of logical consequence, applicable to a very wide range of arguments. We find virtually the same definition at the beginning of the *Prior Analytics*, a treatise more closely associated with demonstrative argument. In each place, Aristotle makes it clear that the general notion of deduction transcends the venue in which a deduction takes place: the same deduction can be presented through question and answer, thus making it dialectical, or through the assertion of its premises in monologue, after the manner of demonstration. What *is* essential to a deduction, however, is that it contain premises and a conclusion which necessarily follows from them: deductions are, by definition, *valid arguments*.[13]

One kind of *sullogismos* or deduction is an argument consisting of three propositions; the first two are premises that contain a common or middle term; the third is a conclusion that is drawn from the premises. An example of such a syllogism is as follows:

> All human infants born with two X chromosomes are female at birth,
> Human Baby Ryan was born with two X chromosomes,
> Therefore human Baby Ryan is female at birth.[14]

To assert the validity of this syllogism means that the premises are true and therefore the conclusion must also be true.[15]

Aristotle in the *Rhetoric* gives different names to the materials out of which premises (*protaseis*) are made on the basis of their capacity to provide absolute or contingent proof – for premises might consist of *eikota* (probabilities), *sēmeia* (signs), or *tekmēria* (necessary signs).[16] Furthermore, "some signs (*sēmeia*)" he says, "are

---

requirement in the *Rhetoric* that the conclusion should result "necessarily;" if so, Aristotle may have meant "to relax the requirement that the premises must provide a logically sufficient justification for the conclusion ... It is a question whether ... it would be a reasonable inference that the apparent relaxation in the definition of *syllogismos* is a deliberate attempt by Aristotle to fashion a concept of degenerate deduction that can be applied to contexts where conclusive proof is not to be had."

[13] Smith 1997: xxii.

[14] Sometimes a line drawn beneath the two premises is used to represent the "therefore" of the last proposition; that convention is occasionally followed in this essay. The same syllogism offered above might also be represented in the form of an "if ... then" inference; thus: "*If* all human infants born with two X chromosomes are female at birth *and* human baby Ryan was born with two X chromosomes, *then* human Baby Ryan is female at birth." A syllogism might also be represented with variables (Frede, 1974: 19 suggests rather that the letters be considered "constants," comparing the use of letters in geometry); thus:

> All M is P,
> S is M,
> S is P.

Patzig 1968: 3: "to assert that the syllogism is valid means that, if terms are substituted for M, P, and S such as to make both premises into true propositions, then the conclusion, "S is P," must also be recognised as true." Frede 1974: 8 comments that arguments of this sort (in which singular terms are used) "will hardly qualify as a syllogism in Aristotle's system in *An. Pr.* A 4–6. But later in the *Analytics* (cf. 47b15ff; 70a16ff) Aristotle does not seem to object to singular terms as such in syllogisms, and S.E. (*P.H.* II, 196–197) uses arguments of that form as standard examples for Peripatetic syllogisms."

[15] That my "exemplary" syllogism happens to be controversial in contemporary science (see, e.g., Fausto-Sterling 2000: 48–56) is in keeping with Aristotle's exemplary *tekmēria*.

[16] Ross 1965: 499 brings this list of components from *Rhet.* 2.1402b13–14 into conformity with that in *A.Pr.* 70a10 which contains only the first and fourth (*eikos* and *sēmeion*) by pointing out that elsewhere

related as the particular to the universal – e.g., if someone were to say it is a *sēmeion* that all wise men are just because Sokrates was both wise and just" (i.e., *"if Sokrates is wise and just, then all wise men are also just"*). And other signs, he continues a little later, are related "as the universal to the particular – e.g., if one were to say that it is a *sēmeion* that one has a fever because he has difficulty breathing" (i.e., *"if all men who have difficulty breathing have a fever and if X has difficulty breathing, then X has a fever"*).[17] While the particularizing premise about Socrates in the first example is arguably true, the conclusion is not valid; and while the second argument is valid, its purportedly universalizing premise obviously admits of exceptions and so is not true. But Aristotle in the same passage provides two examples of a "necessary sign" (*tekmērion*), that is, a sign that provides the "evidence" necessitating the conclusion: "if one were to say that it is a sign that [a particular person] was ill because he had a fever; or that it is a sign that [a particular woman] has given birth, because she has milk. Of signs, this kind only is necessary; for only this kind of sign, if true, is irrefutable" (*Rhet.* 1357b14–17: τὸ δέ, οἷον εἴ τις εἴπειεν σημεῖον ὅτι νοσεῖ, πυρέττει γάρ, ἢ τέτοκεν, ὅτι γάλα ἔχει, ἀναγκαῖον. ὅπερ τῶν σημείων τεκμήριον μόνον ἐστίν· μόνον γάρ, ἂν ἀληθὲς ἦι, ἄλυτόν ἐστιν).

Aristotle uses the same example of "the woman with milk" in the *Prior Analytics* while discussing the three forms (or "figures") which syllogisms may take; there he adds the example of another woman, "the pale-faced one," to illustrate a refutable sign – that a woman is pregnant because she is pale. Thus:

> <An enthymeme, then, is a *sullogismos* composed out of probabilities or signs, ... >... and a sign is understood in three ways ... 13–14: E.g., the proof that a woman is pregnant because she has milk (τὸ μὲν δεῖξαι κύουσαν διὰ τὸ γάλα ἔχειν) is by the first figure; ... 16–17: The proof that the wise are good because Pittakos was good is by the third figure ... 20–23: And the proof that a woman is pregnant because she is pale (τὸ δὲ κύειν, ὅτι ὠχρά) is intended to be by the middle figure; for since paleness is a characteristic of women in pregnancy and is associated with this particular woman,[18] they suppose that she is proved to be pregnant .. (ἐπεὶ γὰρ ἕπεται ταῖς κυούσαις τὸ ὠχρόν, ἀκολουθεῖ δὲ καὶ ταύτηι, δεδεῖχθαι οἴονται ὅτι κύει..) 28–37: In this way *sullogismoi* are effected; but whereas a *sullogismos* in the first figure cannot be refuted if it is true, since it is universal, a *sullogismos* in the last figure can be refuted even if the conclusion is true because the *sullogismos* is neither universal nor relevant. For if Pittakos is good, it is not necessary for this reason that all other wise men are good. A *sullogismos* in the middle figure is always and in every way refutable, since we never find a *sullogismos* with the terms in this relation; for if a pregnant woman is pale and this woman is pale, it is not necessary that she is pregnant.[19]

---

paradeigma is coordinate with *enthumēma* (as induction, *Rhet.* 1356b 4–6) and that *tekmērion* is really one species of *sēmeion* (70b 1–6).

[17] *Rhet.* 1357b11–13 and 17–19. Aristotle does not formulate the syllogism or enthememe in this passage (the parenthetical transformations are mine); the first is certainly *asullogiston*.

[18] Literally: "Paleness follows pregnant women and paleness follows this woman."

[19] *A. Pr.* 70a10, 11 (text of Ross, who has transferred the clause in angular brackets from 70a10 to 70a2); trans. of Tredennick (Loeb), modified.

Aristotle in the *Rhetoric* and in his logical works did not invent deductive reasoning; rather, he worked out the first classification of formal logic. His examples, drawn from everyday domestic experiences, possibly – as we shall see – from the medical tradition – or, especially in the case of the *topoi*, from speeches delivered in the courts or even at times in tragedies, are within the reach of every male Athenian. Aristotle did not suppose that people ordinarily presented their arguments in strict syllogistic form; indeed, he expressly says in the *Rhetoric* that a fully syllogistic argument is too long and hence too incomprehensible for a *kritēs* who is imagined as being a "simple fellow" (1357a7–10). An obvious or well-known premise might be omitted since the listener can supply it for himself: "For example," says Aristotle, "to prove that Dorieus won a contest for which the prize was a crown, it is enough to say "Dorieus won at the Olympic Games"; to add, "the prize of a crown there" is unnecessary – for everyone knows that" (1357a17–21). Aristotle himself leaves his students the task of working out the contours of particular deductions when he provides examples of *tekmēria* in the *Rhetoric*; thus, from his statement "it is a sign that [a particular woman] has given birth, because she has milk," we construct the following argument:

> All women with milk have given birth,
> <u>Maria has milk,</u>
> Maria has given birth.

It may be part of pedagogical method to leave the formulation of the particular argument or syllogism to students; they are the ones, after all, who must juggle multiple *tekmēria* in their heads and select the best for the purpose of proving their arguments whether in court or in the Assembly or in debate with logicians.

In fact, Aristotle's disposition to work with particular cases, to cite example after example, betrays the same kind of pedagogical instinct that is more explicit in the dialogues of Plato (because they are in fact dialogues) where one can witness the interlocutor leading his students on with one question after another, "how would such and such function in this case? Would it be the same in this case? And in this?" We can probably assume similar interrogation in the lost dialogues of Aristotle – a student trying to think up counter examples, or better examples of *sēmeia* to be used in rhetorical syllogisms, more obvious or more subtle, more valid or more respectable (*endoxotera*), possibly, even, deceptive ones or simply more numerous – in the process of education with teacher and fellow students. Some examples might become well known or even celebrated. Such, I would argue, is the example of the necessary sign (*tekmērion*) that a woman with milk is pregnant. We have seen that Aristotle used the example both in the *Rhetoric* and in the *Prior Analytics*. The author of the *Menexenus* had used the same *tekmērion* even earlier – not as a premise in a syllogism, but rather as an analogue to support a larger argument of the autochthonous birth of Attica's early inhabitants. Thus at *Men.* 237E:

> And there is a great proof (*tekmērion*) of this statement that this land has given birth to the forefathers of these men and ourselves. For every creature has nourishment sufficient for whatever it brings forth – by means of which it is evident that a woman is truly a mother or not [and instead pretends that someone

else's infant is her own] – that is, if she has founts of nourishment for her offspring.[20]

For the author of this text, the milk of a woman is proof of her maternity.

The "woman with milk" remained a stock example of a necessary sign in philosophical circles; it was later so used by the Stoics – as Sextus Empiricus reports:

> *P.H.* 2.104: ... [The Stoics] say, "A sign is an antecedent judgment in a valid hypothetical premise, which serves to reveal the consequent ..."

> 106: And "Antecedent," they say, "is the precedent clause in a hypothetical premise which begins with truth and ends in truth. And it serves to reveal the consequent, since the clause, 'this woman has milk' (γάλα ἔχει αὕτη) seems to be evidential of the clause, 'she has conceived' (κεκύηκεν αὕτη) in the proposition, 'if this woman has milk, she has conceived (εἰ γάλα ἔχει αὕτη, κεκύηκεν αὕτη).'"[21]

No doubt that women – possibly forever – had known, even more precisely, of what their milk "was a sign" – but the point I hope to make here is that in the fourth century the proposition (that if a woman has milk she has conceived or borne a child) became celebrated and valued as an exemplary *tekmērion* in philosophical circles.

Before proceeding further in the later rhetorical tradition, it will be worthwhile to pause here, digress a bit, and not gloss over the different appearances of the necessary sign in our syllogism. The sign, that a woman has milk, is indicative of a pregnant woman (κύουσαν) in the *Prior Analytics*, of a woman who has borne a child in the *Rhetoric* (τέτοκεν), and of a woman who has done – well, what exactly has she done (κεκύηκεν), according to the Stoics via Sextus? "Has conceived and so is pregnant?" Or "Has been pregnant and so has given birth?" It is disheartening to see the stock example of a sign which purports to be infallible appearing so variegated, ambiguously, and indecisively in the philosophic/rhetorical tradition: for if milk is a sign of a woman who is pregnant, it cannot at the same time be a sign that she has given birth.[22] But Aristotle has it one way in the *Prior Analytics* and another way in

---

[20] *Men.* 237E: μέγα δὲ τεκμήριον τούτωι τῶι λόγωι, ὅτι ἥδε ἔτεκεν ἡ γῆ τοὺς τῶνδέ τε καὶ ἡμετέρους προγόνους. πᾶν γὰρ τὸ τεκὸν τροφὴν ἔχει ἐπιτηδείαν ᾧ ἂν τέκῃ, ᾧ καὶ γυνὴ δήλη τεκοῦσά τε ἀληθῶς καὶ μή, [ἀλλ᾽ ὑποβαλλομένη: del. Hartman] ἐὰν μὴ ἔχῃ πηγὰς τροφῆς τῶι γεννωμένωι. The meaning of ὑποβαλλομένη in the phrase bracketed by Hartman is clear from Eur. *Alc.* 637–39: οὐδ᾽ ἡ τεκεῖν φάσκουσα καὶ κεκλημένη/ μήτηρ μ᾽ ἔτικτε, δουλίου δ᾽ ἀφ᾽ αἵματος/ μαστῶι γυναικὸς σῆς ὑπεβλήθην λάθραι. The acquisition of "supposititious children" becomes a well-known comic motif, e.g., Aristoph. *Thesm.* 339–40, 502–16 and Plautus *Truc.* II.4, where the supposititious children are respectively associated with adulterous wives and prostitutes, attempting to retain, respectively, husbands and clients. The aptness of the motif for a person of the status of the speaker (Aspasia) of *Men.* 237E may have prompted a glossing copyist to insert the explanation that would have been unnecessary for a contemporary audience.

[21] *P.H.* 2.104; trans. of Bury (Loeb), modified.

[22] While the depiction of what the Stoics call the consequent (τὸ λῆγον) varies in all our examples, the antecedent clause (προκαθηγούμενον) remains the same, "the woman with milk"; that phrase, however, is itself ambiguous: does it refer to milk that is stored away inside a woman, to milk that is apparent to the eye, gustible, and so knowable as milk and not some substance that might be mistaken for milk, or does it refer to milk whether stored away or apparent to the eye? Probably it can mean any of these things. Comparison with phraseology in the Hippocratic corpus is corroborative: while there is a more precise

the *Rhetoric*. And it seems as though the Stoics may have had it both ways – by virtue of ambiguity rather than by virtue of precision.[23]

Some explanations for the different formulations may be offered. In Aristotle's biological works, we find two different versions of the relationship between *pregnancy* and milk production: thus at *HA* 522a4, Aristotle says that milk starts to be formed as soon as the animal becomes pregnant,[24] and at *GA* 776a15–16, he says that milk does not appear until the mother is about to give birth.[25] The medical truth of the matter, as we know it today, is not entirely different from a combination of these testimonies – namely, that from early pregnancy, a form of milk called colostrum is produced and this might be secreted during pregnancy; in the first three days following birth, it is colustrum that is passed on to the infant; but this substance is thereafter replaced by milk.[26] Probably one could only have known a version of that truth in antiquity by having questioned many women; observation of one's own wife or women within one's acquaintance may not have produced varying results. Of relevance, then, is the fact that the Hippocratic Corpus offers the view that milk is present in women both before giving birth and afterwards; while the view of the origin and evolution of pre-partum milk arises from non-empirical theory,[27] yet many statements about women's milk do seem to derive from the direct observation of women by medical practitioners.

Of course, the predominant explanation of the origin of milk, both in that corpus and in Aristotle, is scientifically bizarre (see n. 27) and we need not digress that far afield – our interest here is in the appearance of the "woman with milk" in *tekmēria*. And in this respect, too, the Hippocratic Corpus is relevant. In the first place, the "practical medical tradition" (i.e., the oral or literary preservation of the empirical observation of patients and of argument based on observation) that forms the basis of

---

formulation for "milk outside the body" (cf. Hipp. *Aph.* 5.52, quoted below), ἔχειν γάλα appears to be a standard phrase.

[23] There are further problems as well. As Burnyeat 1982: 204 n. 30 has pointed out, "concerning animals in general Aristotle believes that it is only a for the most part truth that pregnancy is a necessary condition for lactation; some animals have been known to produce milk without getting pregnant (*HA* 522a2ff). That means we must at least have "All humans who have milk are pregnant" rather than "All who have milk are pregnant," ... and we had better waive modern reports that in certain parts of the world human grandmothers are induced by suckling to give milk." We had also better specify "all *human women* ..." since Aristotle at *HA* 522a12–20 includes men in his discussion of male animals who (exceptionally) have milk.

[24] *HA* 522a4: οὐ γίνεται δὲ γάλα, πρὶν ἢ ἔγκυον γένηται, οὐδενὶ τῶν ζῴων ὡς ἐπὶ τὸ πολύ. ὅταν δ' ἔγκυον ἦι, γίνεται μέν, ἄχρηστον δὲ τὸ πρῶτον καὶ ὕστερον. For discussion of ancient Greek views on the timing of milk's appearance in women, see Dean-Jones 1994: 219–222.

[25] *GA* 776a15–16: τὸ δὲ γάλα γίνεται τοῖς θήλεσιν ὅσα ζωιτοκεῖ ἐν αὑτοῖς χρήσιμον μὲν εἰς τὸν χρόνον τὸν τοῦ τόκου. Dean-Jones 1994: 221 reasonably suggests that Aristotle speaks of two periods of milk production (at the beginning of pregnancy and at the time of birth) not because he has changed his view but because he is thinking of two different grades of milk, of which the earlier, wheyish sort would not be suitable for an infant.

[26] Stoppard 1998: 94–95, 221.

[27] The predominant explanation of the origin of milk is pithily summarized in an interesting "Aeschylean formula" (cf. *Agam.* 494–5: κάσις/ πηλοῦ ξύνουρος διψία κόνις), where milk is called ἀδελφὰ τῶν ἐπιμηνίων (*Epid.* 2.3.17); see Dean-Jones 1994: 215–217 (conversion of menstrual blood into milk) and 218–19 (alternative view).

many of the medical treatises found in the Corpus may have been an inspiration for the syllogistic formulations of philosophers. The material is apt for expropriation, for in statements such as "if x, y, and z symptoms are present, the patient is likely to die," we have the premise for a syllogism.[28] But it is not simply the formulation of sign inferences that is so easily derivative from the medical tradition; it is also, on occasion, the subject matter – note, for example, the collocation of the necessary *tekmēria* of fever and having milk in the passage from the *Rhetoric* and the sign of the pale complected woman at *A.Pr.* 2.27. 70a 9–12.[29] Comparison of our examples from Aristotle with particular examples, especially from *Aphorisms*, are suggestive not of a direct literary source but of a tradition perhaps freely drawn upon both for the logical formulation of arguments and occasionally for the substance of premises. Thus:

Example 1, *Aph.* 5.52 (signs of a healthy and unhealthy embryo): Ἢν γυναικὶ ἐν γαστρὶ ἐχούσηι γάλα πολὺ ἐκ τῶν μαζῶν ῥυῆι, ἀσθενὲς τὸ ἔμβρυον σημαίνει· ἢν δὲ στερεοὶ οἱ μαστοὶ ἔωσιν, ὑγιεινότερον τὸ ἔμβρυον σημαίνει.

Example 1: If milk flows abundantly from the breasts of a pregnant woman, it indicates that the foetus is sickly; but if the breasts be hard, it indicates that the foetus is healthier.

Example 2, *Aph.* 5.39 (signs of the cessation of *menses*): Ἢν γυνὴ μὴ κύουσα, μηδὲ τετοκυῖα, γάλα ἔχηι, ταύτης τὰ καταμήνια ἐκλέλοιπεν.

Example 2: If a woman has milk who is neither pregnant nor has given birth, then her *menses* are suppressed.

Example 3, *de mulierum affectionibus* i–iii 27 (signs of dead or nearly dead foetuses): Ἧισιν ἐν γαστρὶ ἐχούσηι περὶ τὸν ἕβδομον ἢ ὄγδοον μῆνα ἐξαπίνης τὸ πλήρωμα τῶν μαζῶν καὶ τῆς γαστρὸς ξυμπίπτει, καὶ οἱ μαζοὶ ξυνισχναίνονται, καὶ τὸ γάλα οὐ φαίνεται, φάναι τὸ παιδίον ἢ τεθνηκὸς εἶναι ἢ ζώειν τε καὶ εἶναι ἠπεδανόν.

Example 3: Women in the seventh or eighth month of pregnancy suffer a sudden fullness of their breasts and abdomen and their breasts shrivel up and no milk appears: they say the child is dead – or lives but is weak.

In the instances cited here, it always happens that the "patients" belong to perceptible categories of women distinguishable by the measure of pregnancy (e.g.,

---

[28] *Aphorisms*, upon which ancient testimony confers Hippocratic authorship, is particularly rich in sign inferences, esp. bks. 4–7; *Aph.* 5.30–45 contains an interesting run of such formulations pertaining to pregnant women.

[29] Cf. M. Burnyeat 1994: 38, speaking of "relaxed" forms of reasoning such as ""inference to the best explanation" (in older parlance, inference from effect to cause) without which not only rhetoric and public deliberation, but medicine too, would be severely curtailed" explains in his n. 98: "medicine deserves mention not only because two of the examples in *A.Pr.* 2.27 and three in S₁ [= *Rhet.* 1357a22–58a2] have a medical slant, but also because much of the subsequent history of sign inferences is the history of medicine." It may also be true, and perhaps of great interest and certainly worth further investigation, that much of the *prior* history of sign inference was devised by early medical practitioners.

pregnant, non-pregnant, post-pregnant); practitioners know in advance, when they calculate what her symptoms are symptoms of, whether the patient is pregnant or has given birth – or neither the one nor the other. In example 1, the apparently mutually exclusive symptoms of an abundant flow of milk on the one hand and "hard breasts" on the other are considered for women who are pregnant. In example 2, the symptom of having milk is considered for women who are neither pregnant nor have given birth. In example 3, the symptom of experiencing a change from a sudden fullness of breasts and abdomen to a shriveling up of breasts is considered explicitly for those women who are in the seventh or eighth month of pregnancy. The practitioner's knowledge of a particular woman's "(non-)pregnancy status" thus becomes part of the premise of the diagnostic argument – that is, the formulations of the three examples cited here allow us to infer their derivation from medical *practice*. Herein we might find the explanation for the vacillation in the sign involving the "woman with milk." If the sign emerged from the medical tradition, then it will have emerged from the observations of practitioners of the women standing (or sitting or lying) before them who are individually known to them as being pregnant *or* as having given birth *or* as neither; the syllogism, purportedly of universal application, is tailored by practitioners for the particular cases before them. They will say of a "woman with milk" that "she is pregnant" when she is self-evidently pregnant or otherwise known as pregnant; and they will say "she has given birth" when a woman known to have been pregnant recently now comes before them, no longer pregnant but nursing an infant. The vacillating sign involving the "woman with milk" thus may derive from medical practice.[30]

Now to tie up this digression before it goes too far afield: I have called attention to the fluctuating appearance of premises concerning the "woman with milk" in Aristotle and the Stoics and I have suggested an origin for them in the practical medical tradition, where the premise, if actually stated, would be: "A woman with milk is either pregnant or has just given birth – or she is not pregnant and her *menses* are suppressed."[31] Regardless of the vacillation, we can conclude that when the presence of milk is used as part of a premise to demonstrate a necessary sign, the speaker or author believes that the necessary sign is true and infallible; moreover, his belief in the infallibility of the sign is traceable to contemporary medical views. Conversely, when Aristotle demonstrates a fallible sign, as he does in the *Prior Analytics* with the premise, "a woman's pale complexion is a sign that she is pregnant," he may have been using a symptom that was characteristic of many pregnant women; but since the symptom was not peculiar to that group, it could not be considered infallible or necessary.

Similar fallible proofs appear in the *Rhetorica ad Herennium* (2.25. 39), where they are used as an example of a *vitiosa confirmatio rationis* :

---

[30] I am indebted to Dean-Jones *per ep.* for inspiring this interpretation: "the sign in the *Rhet.* that woman with milk has borne an infant "is "needed" to connect a woman with recent child-bearing. That is, it is to be differentiated as a sign from that of a woman who has milk AND a hugely swollen belly."

[31] Cf. *Aph.* 5.39: Ἢν γυνὴ μὴ κύουσα, μηδὲ τετοκυῖα, γάλα ἔχῃ, ταύτης τὰ καταμήνια ἐκλέλοιπεν.

> Item vitiosa confirmatio est rationis cum ea re quae plures res significat abutimur pro certo unius rei signo, hoc modo: "Necesse est, quoniam pallet, aegrotasse;" aut "Necesse est peperisse, quoniam sustinet puerum infantem." Nam haec sua sponte certa signa non habent; sin cetera quoque similia concurrunt, nonnihil illiusmodi signa adaugent suspicionem.

> Likewise is the proof of an argument faulty when we apply something which signifies many things as if it were a sure sign of one thing, in this way: "Since she is pale, she must have been ill;" or, "Since she *sustinet* an infant boy, she must have given birth." For these do not of themselves involve sure signs; but if other similar indications also occur, signs of such sort increase the suspicion [of motherhood] a great deal.

The Rhetor (probably indirectly) has altered the two *exempla* used by Aristotle to demonstrate a necessary sign at *Rhet.* 1357b14–17 (that one is ill because he has a fever, and that a woman has given birth because she has milk). For the Rhetor, it is not a necessary sign that one is ill because she is pale or that a woman has given birth because she *sustinet* a boy infant. Here we have evidence of a live rhetorical/philosophic tradition: the Rhetor's variations belong to an on-going discussion concerning what constitutes necessary proof or probable proof or invalid proof. Of interest is the particular type of fallibility in his second exemplum – a fallibility of ambiguous language rather than of ambiguous or non-exclusive symptom. This sort of fallibility was not evident in the exemplum of Aristotle – that if a woman is pale she is pregnant. But as the Rhetor *ad Herennium* so well demonstrates: a mother who *sustinet* an infant has not necessarily given birth. For what does *sustinet* mean here? – sustain? lift up? give sustenance? We might imagine that the Aristotelian and Stoic stock example of the necessary sign had encouraged (and not quenched) such distortions in the service of pedagogy: e.g., how can the necessary sign be made unnecessary? Answer: Add ambiguity! Make as your premise that a woman gives sustenance – but don't specify what that sustenance is. Or change the conclusion – that she must be the mother of the infant she nourishes; then she might be a nurse, and not necessarily the mother, of the particular infant she *sustinet*. Or use a non-universalizing statement for your premise – that a pale complected woman is pregnant. Although we may consign to imagination my picture of Athenian young men intent on discovering new necessary signs and trying to find ways to refute particular formulations, nevertheless, we have the Rhetor's treatise as evidence that some such discussions must have taken place in the centuries between Aristotle and himself.

It is within this broad rhetorical/philosophic context that Menander's preoccupation with proving should be set: while we need not understand Menander's preoccupation as deeply bound up with the philosophical issues of a particular school,[32] yet he was nurtured in an age in which types of proof had undergone philosophical and systematic analysis, in which related propositions based on everyday-life experiences had been sought after, evaluated and characterized as necessary – or probable, or only

---

[32] See n. 8 above.

so in particular instances. Menander himself explores evidentiary and epistemological problems with great gusto; he delights in the creation of deductive proofs based on the most ordinary facts and vulgar propositions, in the creation of their refutations when the case would have seemed impossible of such dissolution, in a persistent, ever badgering questioning of the epistemological basis of a given thing's ontological status.

II. PROOF IN THE *SAMIA*

In the opening scenes of the play, Moskhion, the young lover of the comedy, provides the background for the dramatic situation. His adoptive father Demeas is away on a long business trip with Nikeratos – Nikeratos is a poor neighbor and the father of Plangon; during the fathers' absence, Moskhion got the girl pregnant and she has recently given birth; he has promised to marry her upon his father's return but is fearful of approaching him; Khrysis, Demeas' Samian concubine, has agreed to pretend the infant is the offspring of her union with Demeas. At the end of Act 1, Demeas and Nikeratos have returned from Byzantium and appear together onstage; they have agreed to a marriage between Moskhion and Plangon without as yet having consulted the two young people. In Act 2, Demeas learns of the birth of "his child"; in dialogue with Moskhion, he expresses a disinclination to raise the *nothos* but is apparently persuaded by Moskhion's argument; he then tells Moskhion of the marriage he has arranged for him; Moskhion eagerly accepts. At the beginning of Act 3, trouble erupts when Demeas draws the false conclusion that the infant is not *his* child but Moskhion's and Khrysis'; in Act 4, Nikeratos will discover that the infant was in fact borne by his daughter. It is the discovery of the infant's parentage in Acts 3 and 4 that will be our major concern.

Demeas enters the stage at the beginning of Act 3 and delivers a long monologue (206–82). He confides to the audience that an unexpected calamity has beset him right at the moment when he was preparing his son's wedding. He is so overwrought that he does not know for certain whether he sees straight anymore (213–15). He asks the audience to be the judges of his assessment of the situation:

> ἦ 'στ[ὶ] πιθανόν; σκέψασθε πότερο[ν εὖ φρονῶ
> ἢ μαίνομ', οὐδέν τ' εἰς ἀκρίβειαν [τότε
> λαβὼν ἐπάγομαι μέγ' ἀτύχημα [(216–18)

The reading of the opening words of 216 is not certain; the text as printed in the OCT can be translated: "Is it plausible? Consider whether I'm sane or mad and by interpreting nothing with accuracy I bring great misfortune upon myself."[33]

Demeas proceeds to give a straightforward account of what he has recently seen and heard.[34] He begins by describing the preparations for the wedding, the disarray

---

[33] Gomme and Sandbach 1973 on v. 216 suggest that Menander may have written εἰς τὸ πιθανὸν σκέψασθε, "just look at the probability of it."

caused by the haste in which they had to be carried out – the infant crying, supplies peremptorily solicited. He himself had gone down to the storeroom, selecting more items and examining them, tarrying, not hurrying. From there he overheard Moskhion's old nurse; she had come downstairs to the weaving room – which was contiguous with the storeroom in which he was standing – to quiet the baby. As she offered comfort, she recalled aloud how she had lovingly nursed Moskhion himself not long ago – and then added casually, "and now, ever since this child of Moskhion has been born." (246). After a gap of a few verses in the text, Demeas reports that a servant came running into the weaving room, reproaching the nurse for her loud talk, telling her, "the master was close by" – and sending her upstairs. Demeas then left the storeroom calmly, as if having heard nothing, having perceived nothing. Next, he reports seeing Khrysis at vv. 265–66:

> αὐτὴν δ' ἔχουσαν αὐτὸ τὴν Σαμίαν ὁρῶ
> ἔξω καθ' αὑτὴν <καὶ> διδοῦσαν τιτθίον· (265–66)

He saw her holding the infant outside the door, all by herself, and *didousan titthion*; he draws an inference in the next two verses:

> ὥσθ' ὅτι μὲν αὐτῆς ἐστι τοῦτο γνώριμον
> εἶναι ...   (267–68)

That the infant belongs to Khrysis is a clearly knowable fact.

Until now, Demeas has had no reason to doubt Khrysis' motherhood – he had been informed immediately upon his return from overseas that she had given birth; that she *didousan titthion* can come as no surprise. But Demeas' belief in his paternity of the infant has now been shaken; and if he should not be the father, then is Khrysis still, of necessity, the mother? Hence the formulation of his secret observation of Khrysis as a "proof" – and a "proof" moreover, that has become inextricably bound up, via those telling particles, μέν/δέ, with the circumstantial case against his son:

> αὐτὴν δ' ἔχουσαν αὐτὸ τὴν Σαμίαν ὁρῶ
> ἔξω καθ' αὑτὴν <καὶ> διδοῦσαν τιτθίον·
> ὥσθ' ὅτι μὲν αὐτῆς ἐστι τοῦτο γνώριμον
> εἶναι, πατρὸς δ' ὅτου ποτ' ἐστίν, εἴτ' ἐμὸν
> εἴτ' – οὐ λέγω δ', ἄνδρες, πρὸς ὑμᾶς τοῦτ' ἐγώ,
> οὐχ ὑπονοῶ....   (265–70)

> I see her, my Samian, holding the infant,
> outside the door, by herself <and> *didousan titthion*;
> therefore, *while* it is a clearly knowable fact that the infant is hers,
> *yet* who in the world the father is – whether the infant is mine
> or – but I keep silence before you, gentlemen,
> I'm not suspicious.

---

[34] Bain 1985 on v. 219 points out the similarity of Demeas' speech (219ff.) to the "messenger scene" of tragedy: "Bad news is broken in a general way before an extended narrative explaining and justifying the speaker's gloom. Such narratives often begin like this with a phrase like "When we ..." . cf. Eur. *Med*. 1136."

Demeas will not be angry – yet (271); his son's conduct in the past has always been exemplary (272–74). Still, he cannot refrain from recapitulating the evidence: it was Moskhion's nurse speaking when she thought he was not present (275–77), Khrysis loves the infant and she has compelled Demeas against his will to bring it up (277–79). Demeas' assessment of the situation has become an implicit indictment of son and concubine. Recall the opening of the monologue, where Demeas had asked the members of the audience whether his presentation of the case was plausible and accurate. In retrospect, he has asked them to judge whether the case against the two alleged lovers is correct. The audience, however, is aware of Demeas' mistake, of the inaccuracy of his reasoning, of its unpersuasiveness: although Demeas will seek further validation for the nurse's clear statement of Moskhion's new status as father (268–74) – and he does so in the very next scene – he seeks no further validation for his inference of Khrysis' motherhood. Blinded by anger against Khrysis and by his vision of Moskhion's *kosmiotēs* (273 and 344), Demeas' striving for accuracy suffers a severe lapse precisely when he applies the logical proof to the argument for Khrysis' motherhood. His reasoning betrays his character.

In the following scene, in dialogue with his slave Parmenon, Demeas seeks confirmation of Moskhion's fatherhood, first, obliquely – he knows, he says, that Parmenon has joined in concealing something from him – he speaks as one "not making a conjecture" (οὐ γὰρ εἰκάζων λέγω 311); he then asks for the identity of the parent (313: τό παιδίον τίνος ἐστιν;), and, upon Parmenon's reply that the infant is Khrysis', he asks straight out for the identity of the father (314). When Parmenon responds that Khrysis says it is he, Demeas bluffs the slave into making a confession of the truth: "I know everthing accurately," he says, "and I have learned that the father is Moskhion, that you know this too, and that Khrysis is now bringing up the infant on his account" (316–18). Parmenon acknowledges that it is so – without, of course, clarifying that Khrysis is not the mother. In Demeas' following monologue (325–56), he determines his course of action based on the false inference of Khrysis' maternity: he will endure his son's deed in silence and continue preparations for his marriage; but Khrysis he will expel from the house.

In Act 4 of the play, after Demeas confronts Moskhion with his "knowledge" (466, 477–79), Moskhion clears up the error at last by confessing that Plangon, not Khrysis, is the mother of the infant (528–29). Demeas is sceptical at first, but Moskhion asserts that "proof is at hand" and that he has "nothing to gain" by the admission (οὗ λαβεῖν ἔλεγχόν ἐστι; καὶ τί κερδανῶ πλέον; 531). The "proof" comes with the arrival of an explosively angry Nikeratos on stage; indeed, so angry is he that in the course of the scene he threatens to burn the infant (553–54), to kill his wife (561, 580), to strike Demeas (575), and to beat Khrysis with a stick (577). The immediate cause of anger is the sight he has beheld at home; his eyewitness testimony closely resembles Demeas' earlier report about Khrysis:

> τὴν θυγατέρ' < ἄρτι > τὴν ἐμὴν τῶι παιδίωι
> τιτθίον διδοῦσαν ἔνδον κατέλαβον. (535–36)

Demeas immediately acknowledges to Moskhion his acceptance of the proof (537–38); nevertheless, he at first tries to dissuade Nikeratos from believing what he thinks he has witnessed (542,543); later, he even tries to cajole him with stories of divine impregnation (589–609); finally, he calms the irate father with assurances that Moskhion will indeed marry Plangon (610). The scene ends with Demeas' thanks to the gods that he has discovered nothing to be true of what he had once thought to have happened (οὐθὲν εὑρηκὼς ἀληθὲς ὧν τότ᾽ ᾤμην γεγονέναι, 615).

The complication of the comedy derives from Demeas' false inference that Khrysis is the mother of Moskhion's baby. Recall once again vv. 265–70 (cited above). The articulation of the "proof" should hold our attention: it is an inferential proof (note especially ὥσθ᾽) with an unexpressed premise. Put in traditional form, it runs:

> [Women *didousai titthion* have given birth to the infant
> to whom they *didoasi titthion*.]
> <u>Khrysis *didōsi titthion*.</u>
> Khrysis has given birth to the infant to whom she *didōsi titthion*.

Earlier a reason was suggested for Demeas' formulation of Khrysis' maternity as a "proof": since he may no longer be the infant's father, he now considers whether Khrysis may not really be the mother. The proof is, of course, faulty – it is a *vitiosa confirmatio rationis*, preserving a distortion of that celebrated exemplum of a necessary sign, that a woman with milk has borne an infant. The faultiness of the proof allows the comic plot to thicken. So the dramatic function of the proof is clear; but why Menander should have chosen the particular words he uses deserves reflection.

Let us begin by examining further what Demeas means when he describes Khrysis' action as *didousan titthion*. Some interpreters have argued that Khrysis was represented in the missing parts of the play as having recently given birth to an infant who either died or was exposed; some have adduced additional arguments from the preserved text.[35] For our larger purposes here (i.e., the exploration of the formulation

---

[35] Sandbach 1986: 158–160 and Dedoussi 1988: 39–42 cite recent bibliography. Moskhion's use of τρέφειν at v. 78 is not decisive (he is asking whether they are to permit Khrysis τρέφειν the infant; τρέφειν is ambiguous (see Hofmann 1975: 168–169). Dedoussi, who rejects the argument that Khrysis had recently given birth, presents the most persuasive case. Supplements for vv. 54–56 have played a significant role in the controversy; text of 54–56 with modest supplement and no punctuation:

> τὸ π]αιδίον γενόμενον εἴληφ᾽ οὐ πάλαι
> ἀπὸ]ταὐτομάτου δὲ συμβέβηκε καὶ μάλα
>]ν ἡ Χρυσίς καλοῦμεν τοῦτο γὰρ

Vv. 54–56 with more interpretive supplements and punctuation (observe that the subject of εἴληφ᾽ may be first or third person – thus Moskhion or Khrysis – and that it is crucial to understand what "has happened" in v. 55 as something that could have happened ἀπὸ] ταὐτομάτου):

> (i)   τὸ π]αιδίον γενόμενον εἴληφ᾽ οὐ πάλαι·
>   ἀπὸ]ταὐτομάτου δὲ συμβέβηκε καὶ μάλ᾽ <εὖ·>
>   ἔτικτε]ν ἡ Χρυσίς· καλοῦμεν τοῦτο γὰρ

55 μάλα **B**: μάλ᾽ <εὖ·> Austin post Jacques 56 ἔτικτε]ν: Sandbach 1972 ὥστ᾽ <ἔτ᾽>εκεν Arnott post Austin

> (ii)   τὸ π]αιδίον γενόμενον εἴληφ᾽ οὐ πάλαι –
>   ἀπὸ]ταὐτομάτου δὲ συμβέβηκε καὶ μάλα
>   εἰς καιρό]ν – ἡ Χρυσίς· καλοῦμεν τοῦτο γὰρ

56 εἰς καιρό]ν Gaiser post Blume εὔκαιρο]ν Sandbach 1990

of the proof), it is immaterial whether or not Khrysis in fact had recently given birth. In either case, Demeas will have made the same false inference: both the hidden major premise (women *didousai titthion* have given birth to the infant to whom they *didoasi titthion*) and necessarily the conclusion (Khrysis is the mother of this particular infant) are incorrect.

Only the recovery of additional text of the *Samia* will solve, positively and conclusively, the mystery surrounding Khrysis' child-bearing and nursing activities; nevertheless, the phrase *didousan titthion* still beckons for attention, not necessarily to support the position of those who hold that Khrysis had *not* given birth recently (which is the view I favor) but principally to suggest what the phrase conveys – its meaning, its flavor, its fit. Thus far we have only briefly considered what it may have meant to Demeas in v. 266 and we shall return to these reflections shortly; but now we may ask: what did it mean to the members of his audience, here and elsewhere in the play? Interpretation of the verbal activity will have been colored by what had been reported of Khrysis' maternal status. If audience members had been told that she had borne a child of her own, then the phrase may have conveyed, by context, "nursing" or "feeding"; but if they had not been informed of so important a detail, then the phrase may have conveyed no more than it literally says: "giving tittie." Indeed, in the next act, when Nikeratos announces that he has seen his daughter *didousan titthion* (536 and 540), Demeas responds with, "Perhaps she was playing" (τυχὸν ἔπαιζεν 542). Clearly, on Demeas' own evidence, the phrase *didousan titthion* does not necessarily imply "actual feeding."[36] If we grant this point, then we must also grant that Menander has formulated the eyewitness testimony of both Demeas and Nikeratos with ambiguous phraseology: both report they have witnessed a woman *didousan titthion* to the infant (Demeas at 266: διδοῦσαν τιτθίον, and Nikeratos at 536 τιτθίον διδοῦσαν and again at 540 διδοῦσαν τιτθίον) – but neither man precisely says the infant actually received nourishment thereby. At these three crucial points in the play, then, Menander has chosen to use identical and ambiguous wording, whereas he might have used language that would have specified the nursing activity of woman and infant – Greek, after all, does not lack these words.

(iii) τὸ παιδίον γενόμενον εἴληφ' οὐ πάλαι –
   ἀπὸ ταὐτομάτου δὲ συμβέβηκε – καὶ μάλα
   σέσωκε]ν – ἡ Χρυσίς· καλοῦμεν τοῦτο γὰρ
56 σέσωκε]ν Dedoussi (*ZPE* [99] 1993:19).

[36] *Titthion didousan* may not imply anything specific at all. *Didōmi* not infrequently appears in comedy with an infinitive, meaning 'giving to eat or drink' (LSJ[9] I.4); thus, e.g., Aristoph. F 208 K-A; Crat. F 132 K-A; Diph. F 17.7–9 K-A; Eup. F 271 K-A; Heg. F 1 K-A. While no example of an infinitive (e.g., παίζειν or θῆσθαι) appears with *didonai titthion* or *titthon* (but note *Od.* 4.89: παρέχουσιν [sc. sheep] ἐπηετανὸν γάλα θῆσθαι), it is perhaps relevant that in the two passages in which Lysias uses the phrase *didonai titthon*, he adds an explanatory purpose clause. Thus at 1.10, the speaker reports that his wife would often go downstairs to sleep with the child "in order to give her breast to him and to keep it from crying" (ἵνα τὸν τιτθὸν αὐτῶι διδῶι καὶ μὴ βοᾶι); and at 1.12, he says, "And I kept telling my wife to go away and give the child her breast so that he would stop crying" (δοῦναι τῶι παιδίωι τὸν τιτθόν, ἵνα παύσηται κλᾶον).

Let us consider, then, the words Menander chose not to use. He did not use the aoristic θῆσθαι, a highly poetic word that is used of mothers suckling offspring.[37] Nor did he use θηλάζω, another verb that signifies the suckling activity of women and other mammals – but the verb appears to be confined to prose works, occurring most frequently, though not exclusively, in biological and medical treatises. Finally, he did not use τιτθεύω (a verb cognate with the nouns τίτθη, τιτθός, τιτθίον) meaning "to serve as nurse" or "to nurse" or "to suckle"; the verb is not frequently used, though it makes occasional appearances in biological and medical treatises and appears, as well, in an oration of Demosthenes (Dem. 57.35 [*ter*], 40, 42, 44) in passages where the speaker is arguing for the respectability of his mother who had hired herself out as a wetnurse. Menander has Demeas use the verb in the *Samia*, in the very speech which we have focussed upon, when he quotes the words spoken by Moskhion's old nurse at vv. 245ff.: "Alas! Why it was just yesterday that I was lovingly nursing Moskhion himself." On the basis of the possible verbs that were at Menander's disposal as a comic poet, it would seem that he had hardly any alternative among verbs that unambiguously connoted "suckling" – unless he were to repeat a verb used just 20 lines earlier – which would *not* be at all extraordinary for our playwright (consider, for example, vv. 536 and 540)!

So, what exactly did the two men see and what did their words convey to the audience? I submit that the respective gazes of Demeas and Nikeratos were rivetted upon *titthia* and that neither man paused long enough to reflect whether any nutriment was delivered. Both men, in addition, mentally computed – one falsely, one correctly – maternity, nevertheless, their phrase conveys only what they beheld, a woman *didousa titthion* – that is: first Demeas and Nikeratos saw a woman "giving her tittie"; then, probably no longer than a fraction of a second later, each of them, in a separate mental process, equated the action he beheld with an action characteristic of a mother, "giving her breast." Whether the phrase *didousa titthion, of itself,* was additionally meant to convey, to the audience, a specific function for the breast-giving, "to comfort the infant with play" or "to comfort the infant with milk," I do not think we can discern and I do not think it matters – either might have produced an inference of maternity.[38]

Now, let us be still more attentive to the phrase Menander used, and especially to the diminutive object, *titthion*. Comparison with the non-diminutive form is instructive. *Titthos* is anatomical in color; it frequently appears in medical works (though not in Aristotle's biological works); it is also the word used to designate

---

[37] E.g., *Od.* 4.89 (of sheep); *h. Apollo* 123.

[38] The author who has never borne a child reports this experience: Ten years ago, she and her sister, together with a newly born daughter, were making a weekend visit to their parents who lived outside New York City. The sister was summoned back to the city for urgent business on Saturday morning, leaving Infant Mandy in her maiden aunt's care. All went reasonably well until the middle of the night when Infant Mandy began to cry without cease and the author lifted her from the crib and set her in bed beside her – at which point, and with no invitation – Infant Mandy discovered her aunt's *titthos*, made her attack, and would not let go. This was not a giving but a taking. She ceased crying; aunt in great surprise and not a little pain finally unfastened the little girl. Now, what would an observer have thought?

certain dedicatory offerings at the shrine of Asklepias.[39] The exceptional appearances of that noun in non-anatomical prose-writers are of interest. Diodoros Siculus uses it in a gruesome passage (20.71) depicting some of the atrocities of Agathokles; the word *titthos* has probably been chosen for anatomical objectivity; that sensational writer, Duris of Samos, is likely to be the source.[40] The speaker of Lysias I ("On the murder of Eratosthenes") had used the term in the very collocation that we find in Menander, *didonai titthon*, to depict the past conduct of his adulterous wife in carefully sculpted and calm narrative – indeed, it was on his own orders *dounai titthon* to a crying infant that the woman allegedly skipped out to visit her lover.[41] The noun retains anatomical, objective, even loveless color.[42] The diminutive *titthion*, on the other hand, is found exclusively in comedy.[43] J. Henderson depicts its usage in Old Comedy this way: "it is always used as a symbol of female beauty and male sexual pleasure, rather than, say, to express any kind of female biological function apart from sexuality."[44]

In New Comedy, the diminutive appears only in Menander's *Samia*.[45] Should we assume that its use is restricted here, as it is in Old Comedy, to expressing a "symbol of female beauty and male sexual pleasure" – and that it does not express a "biological function"? And should we assume that *titthion* in the *Samia* conveys the same meaning each of the three times it appears? These questions suggest possibilities for exploration rather than hard and fast rules for application. *Titthion* is used first by Demeas of his mistress' attribute and secondly by Nikeratos of his daughter's; the object in each instance is, in itself, appealingly affective – so the diminutive seems appropriate. Yet both men infer maternity – which suggests that *titthion* signals a biological function and so has shifted away from its Aristophanic usage. Acceptance of dissonance may be the best solution for the interpretive dilemma: emotion and language are out of harmony; *titthion* is softly and comically jarring – an endearing word oxymoronically spoken by an aging lover (21–26) pretending he is at one with

---

[39] *IG* II² 1534.223, 281.

[40] Diod. Sic. 20.71: τῶν δὲ γυναικῶν τῶν εὐπόρων τινῶν μὲν καρκίνοις σιδηροῖς τὰ σφυρὰ πιέζων συνέτεινε, τινῶν δὲ τοὺς τιτθοὺς ἀπέτεμνεν, ταῖς δ' ἐγκύοις πλίνθους ἐπὶ τὴν ὀσφῦν ἐπιτιθεὶς τὶ ἔμβρυον ἀπὸ τοῦ βάρους ἐξέθλιβεν.

[41] Lysias 1.10 and 12; see n. 36.

[42] Similarly, the surprising *titthoi* at *Thesm.* 640; see the following note.

[43] E.g., Aristoph. *Ach.* 1199; *Pax* 863; *Lys.* 83; *Thesm.* 143, 691; *Ranae* 415; *Plutus* 1067. Exceptionally, *titthos* rather than *titthion* occurs at *Thesm.* 640 – perhaps pointedly; Γυνὴ A says of Mnesilokhos, the male intruder and female impersonator: καὶ νὴ Δία τιτθούς γ' ὥσπερ ἡμεῖς οὐκ ἔχει.

[44] Henderson 1991: 148. Usage of *titthion* at *Thesm.* 691 might be considered the exception that proves the rule. There Γυνὴ A complains that Mnesilokhos has seized τὸ παιδίον clean away ἀπὸ τοῦ τιτθίου; the attacker taunts her with the reply that she will never again feed a morsel (ψωμιεῖς) to the infant – he will make a bloody sacrifice of it unless he is released. Of course, the infant turns out to be a flask (and the woman "nursing a drink"?).

[45] *Titthia* occurs in Antiphanes F 105.4 K-A, a passage which describes the different oils, perfumes, and herbs with which a courtesan (?) anoints the different parts of her body – so, an erotic passage. Antiphanes' career seems to have extended well into the fourth century.

the world[46] and by a father with no pretence of concealing anger at all – in an idiom that properly calls for anatomical *titthos*.[47] The spectacle beheld by each man was somehow out of place – the *titthion* of the concubine ought not to be shared with anyone and that of the daughter ought not to be shared prematurely – the thoughts, respectively, of hurt and jealous lover and of enraged and loving father. So, a meaningful conflation of anatomical *titthos* and familiar or hypochoristic *titthion*, with different evocations for the one man and the other. And for the members of the audience: while the softly jarring joy of *titthia* thrice recollected might hold their attention, the verbal action of which it is the object becomes blurred in the background: non-specific, drab *didousan* recedes before the prominence of surprising and playful perhaps even show-stopping *titthia*. This is masterful writing: both Khrysis and Plangon, in parallel scenes, have been caught committing their act of – of what? – of *didousan titthion*. And for what end? – As a game (cf. v. 542)? To provide comfort? – Or milk?

I have focussed on Menander's simple words here in order to demonstrate how rich they are – how emotionally charged – how comical – how carefully chosen – and to suggest the reason for their selection, namely to enable the members of the audience to perceive Demeas' mistake: they know literally what he saw and they know immediately that his inference is incorrect. Perhaps they know this because they have been informed early on in the play that Khrysis is only pretending to be a mother (as Habrotonon pretends in *Epitrepontes*); but some members of the audience will additionally recognize that the inference is formulated faultily; its unstated premise is not universally true: not all women who *didoasi* their *titthia* to infants are mothers.[48]

The rich oddity and wit of *Samia* Acts 3 and 4 in part stem from a fundamental subversion of social and biological expectation, that whereas paternity is usually an inference, maternity is an infallibly knowable thing. Of relevance, perhaps, is a statement in book 2 of the *Rhetoric* where Aristotle offers examples of *topoi* and now is giving attention to the *topos* of induction (*epagōgē*): "e.g., on the basis of the case of the woman of Peparethos, it is argued that, where children are concerned (περὶ τῶν τέκνων), women everywhere discern the truth. For at Athens when Mantias the politician was in dispute with his son, the mother made this her assertion [sc.?, "women know the fathers of their children"]..." (1398a33–1398b3). In this instance, we know the mother "who made the assertion" from Dem. 39 and [Dem.] 40, and we know she swore an oath when challenged by Mantias in the course of an arbitration after her son (Boiotos, *aka* Mantitheos) had sued him for paternal recognition. And she swore, allegedly contrary to Mantias' expectation and private agreement, that he

---

[46] The jarring effect of Demeas' usage is all the more noticeable since he uses *titthion*, an essentially *domestic* word, as he *publicly* addresses the audience as *andres* (269).

[47] Cf. Lys. 1.10 and 12, n. 36 above.

[48] It is the faultiness of Aristotle's middle figure argument (see text at n. 19) combined with that of the ambiguous *sustinet* in the Rhetor *ad Herennium* (2.25. 39).

was the father of her son. The arbitrator accepted her word and decided the case in the son's favor; Mantias abided by the verdict.[49]

The case was apparently renowned in Athens; the woman's family was both distinguished and notorious, and she herself respectable enough to remain unnamed in the *Rhetoric*.[50] Granted the conventionality of names for unmarried maidens in comedy (Pamphile, Philoumene, Plangon) – nonetheless, is it possible that in Menander's choice of name for the infant's mother in *Samia* – the very same name as the mother who swears the oath of paternity in Dem. 39 and [Dem.] 40, Plangon – we have a clue to the inspiration for Menander's comic exploration of the problem of maternity – i.e., that it is a comic subversion of the cultural norm? While we cannot conjecture the frequency of paternity disputes in Athens, the numerous occasions for a father's acknowledgement of a son (e.g., *amphidromia*, *hebdomē*, *dekatē*, phratry and deme enrolment) and our occasional knowledge of procedural arrangements for dispute (such as that depicted in Dem. 39 and [Dem.] 40) suggest that formal and informal paternity suits may not have been a rarity. [51] But a "maternity dispute"? Against mothers who exposed their children – or acquired them in secret from their husbands? Brought by children who survived the ordeal? Sheer fantasy! And while a woman's word may have been decisive in asserting the paternity of her child (*Rhet.* 1398a33–1398b3, Dem. 39.2–4, [Dem.] 40.6–11), how would the question of maternity be decided? By the oath of a man? By trinkets of identification (Kreousa vs. Ion)? By the milk of a woman? The comic fantasy may well have originated in such ratiocinations as these pitted against a cultural norm of paternity dispute; the solution of Boiotos' case resting on Plangon's word, memorialized by Aristotle in the *Rhetoric*, may have been a catalyst for such whimsy. In any event, it interested Menander enormously; witness not only the plot of *Samia*, but that of *Epitrepontes* as well.

It remains now to offer some concluding remarks on Menander's decision to formulate Demeas' discovery as a faulty deduction. The overriding reason for his doing so appears to be this: the logical formulation of the case for motherhood is part of the rhetorical strategies of a speech that is attentive on the whole to the epistemological basis of its evidentiary procedure. We recall that Demeas had begun the assessment of his situation by inviting the audience to examine its persuasiveness – i.e., from the beginning he reveals a self-consciousness about the evidentiary nature of his account:

---

[49] Dem. 39.2–4 and [Dem.] 40.6–11. The official arbitration that preceded the trial was completed by the time of the return of Athenian forces from Euboea (cf. Dem. 39.17; Dem. 5.5; Aeschin. 3.86–88; Plut. *Phok.* 12), probably in late 348 (the date of the Athenian expedition is uncertain, and historians have assigned it to different years: 350, 349, and 348). The trial may certainly have taken place by the end of the year.

[50] Plangon was the daughter of Pamphilos of Keiriadai who was a Hipparch in the Korinthian War (Lys. 15.5) and a General in Aigina in 389/8 (Xen. *Hell.* v.1.2); for failure of achievement there, he seems to have been prosecuted for embezzlement and his estate confiscated and sold. For sources, see Davies 1971: 365.

[51] For the occasions of acknowledgement, see Scafuro 1994: 156–198.

ἢ ’στ[ὶ] πιθανόν; σκέψασθε πότερο[ν εὖ φρονῶ
ἢ μαίνομ᾽, οὐδέν τ᾽ εἰς ἀκρίβειαν [τότε
λαβὼν ἐπάγομαι μέγ᾽ ἀτύχημα [(216–18)

"Is it persuasive?" he asks and then continues, "Consider whether I am sane or mad and by interpreting nothing with accuracy I am bringing a great misfortune upon myself." The testimony about Khrysis' activity with the infant was part of the case against Moskhion; the conclusion (ὥσθ᾽ ὅτι μὲν αὐτῆς ἐστι τοῦτο γνώριμον / εἶναι...267–68) was drawn from that testimony as if it were the conclusion of a syllogism – "that being the case, then this." The conclusion is marked "philosophically" by the adjective *gnōrimon* "knowable" – which Sandbach observes is the way Aristotle occasionally uses the word – and, we might add, the way he uses it in the context of inferential arguments.[52] *Gnōrimon* belongs to Demeas' "cognitive terminology." Having deduced the "knowable," he himself becomes knowledgable. To Parmenon in the following dialogue, he (mis-)represents himself as οὐ...εἰκάζων (311) and as εἰδότα γ᾽ ἀκριβῶς πάντα (316). He is only dissuaded from his own false deductions when Moskhion admits that Plangon is the infant's mother and assures him that proof (ἔλεγχον, 531) is at hand.

Demeas' character as a "philosophical type" is in fact clinched by his adverting to the logical formulation as the proof of Khrysis' motherhood. Nikeratos, on the other hand, quick to fly off the handle without thinking through the consequences of his action, nevertheless interprets the "sign" of Plangon's activity correctly: to Demeas' attempt ("perhaps she was just playing") to dissuade Nikeratos from his interpretation, the latter was ready with *corroborative evidence* – the girl had fainted upon seeing her father approach (542–43). To Demeas' "disbelief" (545) and derision (546), Nikeratos had objected: οὗτος οὐκ ἔστιν λόγος, "This is not a *logos*" (546). Not what? – "Not a story?" "Not a logician's argument?" The philosophic type is thus met by the non-philosophic; all is clear-cut for the latter – no need for fancy rationalizations. The cultural script is the text for both; but whereas for Demeas, it is inscribed with the aid of epistemology (and no matter that he is inept with its flourishes), for Nikeratos, it is common knowledge, the writing on the wall, plain for all to see.

If we do not see Demeas' proof of Khrysis' motherhood as the (mis-)application of the stock example of a necessary sign in philosophical circles, we miss an important element in the drama. Indeed, so important to the plotting of the play is Demeas' misconstrual of a necessary sign, that we might pose an alternative to a traditional summary of the play's action: rather than seeing the comedy as Menander's exploration of the relationship between father and (adopted) son, we might see it as Menander's exploration of the question: when is a necessary sign not a necessary sign? And to answer that question, we will see Menander appropriating a celebrated example of a necessary sign and exploring the comic possibilities for its misconstrual. The "man of reason" will be shown up, the rough-neck *authekastos* (550) will see things correctly. And Menander with great vigor and energy will portray the

---

[52] Gomme and Sandbach 1973 on *Samia* 267, citing *Po.An.* 83b36: εἰ δὲ τόδε διὰ τῶνδε γνώριμον, and 100b9: αἱ ἀρχαὶ τῶν ἀποδείξεων γνωριμώτεραι; we may add 68b25; 76b21; 83b3, 27, 29; *Pr.An.* 68b35.

consequences of their modes of reasoning. Such an interpretation of the play reveals itself once we heed the *dianoia* of its characters.

The interpretation offered here of the *Samia* is meant as a corrective to the modern disposition to view Menander's philosophic interests exclusively in the realm of ethics. The text of Menander's *Samia* is replete with joy and mischievousness in the presentation of argument, in establishing and destroying the epistemological basis of evidentiary proof. To sum this up as "comic error and its dissolution" and to move on quickly to dissections of *ēthos* is to miss the rich detail of comic reason.

WORKS CITED

Allen, J. 2001. *Inference from Signs. Ancient Debates about the Nature of Evidence*. Oxford.

Bain, D.M. 1985. *Menander Samia*. Warminster.

Burnyeat, M. 1982. "The Origins of Non-deductive Inference." In J. Barnes et al., eds., *Science and Speculation: Studies in Hellenistic Theory and Practice*. Cambridge. 193–238.

———. 1994. "Enthymeme: Aristotle on the Logic of Persuasion." In D.J. Furley and A. Nehamas, eds., *Aristotle's Rhetoric: Philosophic Essays*. Princeton. 3–55.

———. 1996. "Enthymeme: Aristotle on the Rationality of Rhetoric." In A.O. Rorty, ed., *Essays on Aristotle's Rhetoric*. Berkeley. 88–115.

Davies, J.K. 1971. *Athenian Propertied Families*. Oxford.

Dean-Jones, L. 1994. *Women's Bodies in Classical Greek Science*. Oxford.

Dedoussi, C. 1988. "The Future of Plangon's Child in Menander's Samia." *LCM* 13.3: 39–42.

Fausto-Sterling, A. 2000. *Sexing the Body: Gender Politics and the Construction of Sexuality*. New York.

Frede, M. 1974. "Stoic vs. Aristotelian Syllogistic." *Archiv für Geschichte der Philosophie* 56: 1–32 (Reprinted in *Essays in Ancient Philosophy* [Minnesota 1987]: 99–124).

Gomme, A.W., and F.H. Sandbach. 1973. *Menander. A Commentary*. Oxford.

Henderson, J. 1991. *The Maculate Muse*. Oxford.

Hofmann, H. 1975. "A New Interpretation of Certain Aspects in Menander's Samia." *Proceedings of the XIV International Congress of Papyrologists*. London. 168–75.

Lloyd, G.E.R. 1996. *Aristotelian Explorations*. Cambridge.

Lucas, D.W. 1968. *Aristotle Poetics*. Oxford.

Patzig, G. 1968. *Aristotle's Theory of the Syllogism*. Trans. J. Barnes. Dordrecht.

Ross, W.D. 1965. *Aristotle's Prior and Posterior Analytics*. Rev. ed. Oxford.

Sandbach, F.H. 1967. Review of A. Barigazzi, *La formazione spirituale di Menandro* in *Gnomon* 39: 238–242.

———. 1986. "Two notes on Menander (Epitrepontes and Samia)." *LCM* 11.9: 156–60.

Scafuro, A.C. 1994. "Witnessing and False Witnessing: Proving Citizenship and Kin Identity in Fourth-Century Athens." In A.L. Boegehold and A.C. Scafuro, eds., *Athenian Identity and Civic Ideology*. Baltimore. 156–198.

———. 1997. *The Forensic Stage: Settling Disputes in Graeco-Roman New Comedy*. Cambridge.

Smith, R. 1997 *Aristotle Topics, Books I and VIII with excerpts from related texts*. Oxford.

Stoppard, M., MD. 1998. *Pregnancy and Birth*. Rev. ed. London.

Webster, T.B.L. 1974. *An Introduction to Menander*. Manchester.

11

Optical Illusions in Ancient Greece[*]

Philip Thibodeau

"If you toss a golden ring into a cup or other vessel, and the vessel is empty, from a suitable distance what is placed inside it will become invisible ... However, if you fill it with water up to the brim, then from the same distance the ring lying in the vessel will be seen; the reason is that the visual current is no longer running straight over the brim but touches the water which is filled to the brim, and so bends and goes to the depth of the vessel, where it meets the ring."
  – Cleomedes, *Caelestia*, fourth century A.D. (2.6 Todd)

"Perform a Magic Coin Trick with Light Waves."
"Here's what you need: a coin, a bowl, a pitcher of water, a helper."
"Here's what you do: 1. Place the coin in the bottom of the bowl. 2. Step back from the bowl until you cannot see the coin. 3. Have your helper slowly pour water from the pitcher into the bowl. Soon the coin will come into view again."
"The coin seems to move because the light waves changed direction in the water. Show this trick to your friends. If they doubt you, you can have one of them hold the coin down with a finger. As you pour in the water, both the coin and the fingertip will come into view, as if by magic."
  – Margaret Kend and Phyllis S. Williams, 1992, *Barron's Science Wizardry for Kids*, New York, p. 60.

The coin trick described above, which remains a staple of children's books on science and magic, can be traced all the way back to Euclid and Archimedes.[1] Perhaps it will not come as a surprise that one or two optical illusions from antiquity should have survived to the present day more or less unaltered in form. Yet there are more than a few survivals of this sort. By about 300 B.C., Greek philosophers had developed a set of optical illusions which, save for a few additions, would persist as standard examples for more than a thousand years. Even today, interest in many of

---

[*] The original inspiration for this essay was a conversation with Alan Boegehold concerning one of his forthcoming projects, on species of 'verbal illusions' in Greek literature. This essay is in effect an extended response to a question about the nature of ancient optical illusions which came up in course of the discussion. I dedicate it with gratitude and respect to someone who has been a wise teacher, mentor, and friend.
[1] Euclid *Catop., praef.*; Archimedes *ap.* Olympiodorus *in Meteor.* 211.18–23; Sen. *QN* 1.6.5.

them is far from exhausted. Take the case of the motion aftereffect – or, as it is sometimes called, the waterfall illusion: if one stares for a while at a rock in the middle of a waterfall or fast-moving stream, then turns quickly to face the adjacent scenery, the scenery will appear to drift for some time in a direction opposite the motion of the running water. This illusion, which was first described by Aristotle and was mentioned by Lucretius, has in the past two decades been the subject of approximately five hundred research articles by investigators in the field of cognitive science![2] So it is not just the writers of children's books who have benefited from the insight of the ancients.

The aim of this essay is to trace the history of visual illusions back to its beginnings in Greece, to determine when and for what reason illusions were first discussed. I have provided in the footnotes a running catalogue of references in ancient authors to the major examples. The bulk of the paper, however, is devoted to a series of hypotheses concerning origins: the origin of the concept of an optical illusion; the origins of the different general classes of illusions; and the origins of the particular examples used to illustrate them.[3]

THE HISTORY OF AN ILLUSION

Although it is tempting to speak of certain Greek thinkers "discovering" optical illusions, it is important to understand rightly from the start what could have been discovered. It was certainly not misleading visual phenomena *per se*: the impression, for example, that the shoreline appears to retreat when seen from a moving boat could hardly have been strange to people as reliant on sea-travel as were the Greeks. Accordingly, the first notice of the illusion on record (which is in Aristotle) is nothing more than that, a first written record.[4] Another illusion involving false motion, vertigo, was first investigated at length by Theophrastus, who talks of people being affected by dizziness when they run in small circles or look down from cliffs.[5] But of course humans are naturally prone to dizziness and loss of balance; when Odysseus reaches the beach of Phaeacia at the end of *Odyssey* book 6, he is so weary that he staggers about, barely able to stand up straight.[6] Other illusions first mentioned during the classical period – the afterimage that lingers in the eye after one looks at the sun,[7] the

---

[2] Waterfall illusion: Arist. *de Somn.* 459b18–21; Lucr. 4.420–425. Discussion of these passages can be found in Verstraten 1996. Forty papers per year: see the chart in Mather, Verstraten, and Anstis 1998: viii. The neurological basis of the waterfall illusion is fairly well understood; current research is focused mainly on the ways in which the illusion interacts with other features of human vision.

[3] There is no systematic or analytic treatment, but see Wade 1998. There are useful notes also in Smith 1996. Hankinson 1995 is a good introduction to the philosophical issues involved. For a fascinating look at how modern cognitive science accounts for visual illusions, see Hoffman 1998.

[4] Arist. *de Somn.* 460b25–27; Eucl. *Opt.* props. 50–55, discussed in Theisen 1984; Lucr. 4.387–390; Cic. *Acad.* 2.25.81; Ptol. *Opt.* 2.132.; Sextus, *PH* 1.107.

[5] Theophr. *de Vert.*; cf. ps.-Arist. *Prob.* 872a18–872b4; Lucr. 4.400–403; Ptol. *Opt.* 2.121.

[6] *Od.* 6.453–63.

[7] Arist. *de Somn.* 459b12–18; Ptol. *Opt.* 2.107.

doubling of visible objects which occurs when you touch your eyeball[8] – must likewise have had long if unremarked natural histories. Thus it is in general misleading to speak of the visual phenomena themselves being first discovered at some point.

What did get discovered was the *concept* of optical illusions. The concept can be expressed by saying that there are certain natural and persistently occurring visual phenomena which represent some true state of affairs as its opposite.[9] Such a concept drew philosophers to take an interest in the visual phenomena, because the phenomena could be deployed as evidence in arguments against the reliability of the senses. The first thinker who seems to have discussed sensory illusions as such is Anaxagoras. An account has been preserved of a demonstration of his designed to show the limitations of the eye.[10] Suppose that a black liquid is mixed with a white liquid one drop at a time. The mixture will gradually turn dark, yet the change made by each individual drop will go unseen. A considerable amount of black must be added before the accumulated small changes can become visible. How then does one know that the mixture darkens with the addition of each drop? Because one extrapolates from the final result to the intermediate steps, which are real but too subtle to be seen at the moment they occur. Anaxagoras concluded from this experiment that vision is in some sense "weak," and that what does detect the change is not the senses but reason. Later authors use different examples – usually the invisibly slow motion of the sun across the sky – to draw attention to the same kind of illusory phenomenon: that something which is truly changing appears to the eye *not* to change.[11]

Plato drew a similar lesson from the existence of illusions in the *Republic*.

> *Socrates*: The same magnitude does not appear equal when seen from nearby and from afar. – *Glaucon*: It does not. – And the same things appear curved and straight when seen in water and out of it, and both concave and convex, due to the visual deception associated with colors, all of this confusion obviously existing in our souls. And it is by exploiting this affection in our natures that shadow painting (σκιαγραφία) reaches the level of magic, just as wonder-working and many other related frauds do. – True – So haven't measuring, counting, and weighing turned out to be most welcome assistants in this, preventing what merely appears greater, lesser, more or heavier from ruling in us, rather than what has been calculated, measured, or weighed? – But of course. – Yet this is obviously the task of the calculating part in the soul. – Of the calculating part, yes. – And often, when this measures and indicates that certain things are bigger or smaller or equal to other things, contrary appearances will be associated with the same object simultaneously – Yes. – Didn't we say that it is impossible for the same thing to

---

[8] Arist. *de Somn.* 462a1–3; Lucr. 4.447–452; Cic. *Acad.* 2.25.80; double-vision is discussed in connection with drunkenness at ps.-Arist. *Prob.* 872b5–14.

[9] I have adopted this broad definition from one given by Richard Gregory; as Gregory points out, although we know a great deal about the physical and physiological causes of optical illusions, consensus about a formal definition remains as elusive as ever: Gregory 1996.

[10] Anaxagoras, fr. 21 DK (= Sext. Emp. *adv. M.* 7.90).

[11] The slow sun: Lucr. 4.391–396; Philod. *de Sign.* 15 De Lacy; Cic. *Acad.* 2.26.82; Sen. *QN* 1.3.10; Ptol. *Opt.* 2.82; Cleomedes *Cael.* 2.111–113 Todd.

suppose contraries about the same objects simultaneously? – And we said so rightly. – Therefore the part of the soul whose opinion is at variance with the measurements could not be the same as the part whose opinion is in accordance with the measurements. – No, it could not.[12]

Plato begins by invoking several optical illusions, and goes on to use our natural response to them as evidence that sensation and reason constitute different parts of the soul. His purpose is to make a point about the structure of the soul, but we can turn his argument around to examine the logical underpinnings of illusions. When presented with two or more sensations that are at variance with each other, an observer who wants to determine which one is true must have recourse to a part of her soul that operates independent of the senses. This part then establishes the truth by taking measurements; whichever of the sensations (if any) turns out to match the result of the measurement is accepted as true. But if one sensation is true, then the other or others are false, as a result of some "visual deception" (πλάνην τῆς ὄψεως). An illusion, therefore, is a sense perception which can be shown to be false, given some concrete notion of truth.[13]

Since these passages from Plato and Anaxagoras are the earliest to treat of the subject, we can safely say that the concept of an optical illusion was first articulated and exploited during the second half of the fifth-century B.C. Once recognized, the concept came to serve as a kind of net for gathering together particular examples, such as the bent-oar illusion and the others which Plato describes. It should be noted that there is no single, agreed-upon word for "optical illusion" in Greek – the nearest terms include πλάνη, ἀπάτη, and τὸ πάθος τῆς ὄψεως, to name just a few. Nevertheless, illusions can be readily identified because they tend to cluster together in texts, often being cited in lists.[14] In this study, I take the occurrence of a visual phenomenon in one of these ancient lists to be sufficient grounds for calling it an optical illusion.

As noted earlier, many illusions are familiar phenomena, ready to be observed and classified as such. Yet the philosophers who first explored illusions exhibit a persistent and rather striking tendency to draw their examples from the realm of the visual arts.

ILLUSIONS AND PAINTING

Before dealing with fifth-century arts, we need to consider some earlier anticipations of illusionism. At first glance the discourse surrounding works of art in the archaic period does seem to entail a concept of visual illusions *in nuce*. In the pseudo-Hesiodic *Scutum*, for example, various figures on Hercules' shield are said to bear a striking resemblance to living beings: centaurs on it are "as if alive," Ares is red with

---

[12] *Resp.* 10, 602c7–603a3.

[13] It is generally accepted by modern philosophers that a concept of optical illusions cannot be upheld without assuming some fairly coherent notion of truth: see Hankinson 1995: 22.

[14] In addition to the passage from the *Republic* previously cited, there are lists at Arist. *de Somn.* 459b7–21; Lucr. 4.379–468; Sen. *QN* 1.3.9–10; Ptol. *Opt.* bk. 2; Sext. Emp. *PH* 118–120, Diog. Laer. 9.85–86; Calcid. *in Tim.* 237 (= *SVF* 2.863); Tert. *de An.* 17.2.

blood "as if he were murdering living people," and the Muses are "similar to women singing shrill."[15] Yet to qualify as illusions in terms of the definition given above, the figures must be accompanied by some indications that they are "in truth" not alive, not moving, not *actually* ζῷα – indications which are entirely missing from the ecphrasis. Even the repeated references it makes to the metals from which the figures are cast, rather than serving to undercut the impression of lifelikeness, only strengthen the aura of magic which surrounds the shield.[16] When informed that Perseus is engraved in gold, and that he is "neither touching the shield with his feet, yet is not far from it – a great wonder to describe, since he was completed unattached," we do not stop to reflect on the fallibility of our senses, but are struck instead by the magic of Hephaestus' art: it is a characteristic aim of magic to make the inanimate (gold) seem animate (flying Perseus).[17] So the point that must be emphasized is this: the premise that art somehow resembles life – what we might call the principle of verisimilitude – although shared by almost all artists and audiences of art in pagan antiquity, does not necessarily imply that works of painting or sculpture are illusionistic, according to the formal definition of illusion just elaborated. This is confirmed by the fact that the principle of verisimilitude itself never makes an appearance on any of the ancient lists of optical illusions, even though it could easily be rewritten as an illusion, e.g. by saying that in art what is truly dead appears alive.[18]

The principle of verisimilitude did however have a key role to play in leading certain painterly *techniques* to be regarded as illusionistic: for although painting in general is left out of consideration, particular painterly techniques exert a strong influence on the contents of the ancient lists, in a manner I shall now describe. The following thumbnail sketch of the growth of naturalism in Greek art is intended to do no more than show the logic behind the development of illusionistic techniques. For most of the archaic period, the principle of verisimilitude applied mainly to painted figures and to their parts, that is, to bodies, limbs, and material pieces. It made – and still makes – sense for viewers of archaic vase paintings to scrutinize, say, the legs or heads of the human figures, or the wheels of chariots, or horses' equipage, and to comment on how lifelike or energetic the parts as well as their wholes look. One can see this older conception of the art reflected in the *Encomium of Helen*, where Gorgias describes the task of painting by saying that "whenever painters bring to perfection one body and figure out of many colors and many bodies, they delight the eye."[19] In other words: as an artist working in a medium, the painter's job is to use many different colors to create a single shape; as an artist making images, his job is to make

---

[15] Hes. *Scut.* 189, 194, 206.

[16] Metals: cf. ll. 141–2, 208, 225–6, etc.

[17] ll. 217–218.

[18] And why is painting generally not cited as an illusion? Aristotle observes (*de Mem.* 450b21–451a13) that one can think of a painting as one of two different things: as a "representation" (εἰκών) of an object, with features that remind us of the object, or as a "living being" (ζῷον), meant to be contemplated for its own sake. Although they differ in their essences (450b23), these two descriptive entities do not fall into a true/false dichotomy, i.e. accepting that the painting is one thing does not entail that it is not the other thing. So, under neither description is painting illusory.

[19] *Hel.* 18.

"one body" out of "many bodies." At both levels of description, medium as well as representation, the contrast is simply one between parts and the whole. There is no sense that representation involves working with anything more abstract than parts, whether colors or bodies.

But around the beginning of the fifth century, the principle of verisimilitude gets extended in a fascinating new direction. It no longer applies just to bodily parts, but encompasses parts in a much more general sense of the word, covering what we might call abstractions, like aspect, size, outline, form, and depth. One might look at the arm of a figure on a black-figure vase from the mid sixth-century and comment on how alive it looks. But characters on red-figure vases from the beginning of the fifth-century onward invite one to attend to other features as well: to look at the form or outline of the arm, and see how closely it matches, as a matter of geometrical congruence, the visible form of a real arm; to attend to the relative dimensions of parts, and to see how well the dimensions in the painting reflect the relative dimensions in reality; or, in the case of some of the fragmentary survivals from fourth-century wall-painting, to study the blending of hues, and to consider how closely these mimic the blend of hues in nature.[20]

The reason why this new focus on forms rather than parts encourages the recognition of optical illusions is simply that it changes the logic of the discourse associated with painting. Among the Greeks, visual forms are typically placed in categories articulated by contrary terms, such as: rectangular and square, bright and shaded, bent and straight, curved and flat.[21] An illustration of the new way of talking about art can be seen in Xenophon's *Memorabilia,* where Socrates is shown asking a famous painter of his day, "Parrhasius, is painting the representation of visible things? Certainly by making likenesses with colors you imitate forms that are high and hollow, dark and light, hard and soft, rough and smooth, and young and old."[22] There is a noticeable shift here from what Gorgias said about painting. First, painters are said to reproduce forms not bodies; secondly, those forms are arranged into various abstract categories; finally, those categories are defined by contraries.

Now it was noted earlier that optical illusions occur whenever there is a polar opposition between real and apparent visual forms. Thus, once painting begins to aim at the reproduction of general forms, and once its audience begins to talk about it in such a way, it can be readily mined for optical illusions. To take a simple example: in archaic times, someone might have felt that a painting of a chariot wheel was illusory – yet he would have been hard pressed to say what made it an illusion, since there is no concrete thing or body which could be called the opposite of a wheel.[23] On the other hand, if the form of a wheel, which is a circle, is represented in a painting as an ellipse – something done for the first time around the start of the fifth century – then the illusion almost cries out to be noticed: what is truly a circle appears to be non-

---

[20] For illustrations, see the photos in Bruno 1977.

[21] For a fascinating discussion of this cultural habit, see Lloyd 1966, part one.

[22] *Mem.* 3.10.1.

[23] Compare Aristotle's observation that particular ordinary objects, which he calls "primary substances," do not possess opposites (*Categ.* 3b24–26).

circular, looks like an ellipse.[24] A similar line of reasoning will apply to any object depicted by painted representations with a form unlike or contrary to something called its true form. Thus, the extension of painterly verisimilitude from parts to forms invites the kind of logical analysis which allows one to name a painted form an illusion.

Among the many innovations in technique which extended the reach of the principle of verisimilitude, new methods for portraying depth attracted special attention. This is because depth in a painting creates an obvious illusion: what is truly flat – the picture plane – appears curved. A number of different methods were used to promote this illusion, two of which, perspective and shading, will be discussed here. The first, linear perspective with a central vanishing point, has unfortunately resisted the best efforts of scholars trying to piece together its early history.[25] A major problem is that there are many ways to approximate perspective in painting which do not count as linear perspective proper because, for instance, they employ no common vanishing point. In addition, there is little in the way of pictorial evidence for such techniques before the mid fourth century, at which point a number of Apulian vase paintings appear displaying *roughly* convergent parallel lines in their depictions of temples and other fixed structures.[26] As a result, the following passage from Vitruvius has had to bear most of the weight of claims for whether Greeks did or did not devise some system of linear perspective before the fourth century:

> To begin with, Agatharchus, during a production of a play by Aeschylus at Athens, created a stage-set and left behind a commentary on it. Inspired by this, Democritus and Anaxagoras wrote on the same topic, namely, how lines ought to correspond in a natural fashion to the eyesight and the extension of the visual rays, once a definite place has been established as the center, in order that well-defined images from an ill-defined object may create the appearance of buildings in paintings of stage-sets, and shapes produced on vertical flat surfaces may appear to be retreating in some places and projecting in others.[27]

If this testimony is accurate, then the names Agatharchus, Democritus, and Anaxagoras would date the development of this technique, which is known as σκηνογραφία, to the second half of the fifth century.[28] Although the meaning of the various claims made in this passage need not concern us here, there are two items in it relating to illusions which are important to note. The first is the clear statement of the purpose behind perspective representations: "in order that ... shapes produced on

---

[24] Circle seen as an ellipse: Eucl. *Opt.* 36; ps.-Arist. *Probl.* 911b27–912a28; Geminus *Auszüge*, Schoene 30.3–4. For developments in the representation of chariot wheels and shields during the fifth century, see Richter 1970: 24, 25.

[25] The bibliography on this topic is extensive; art-historical studies include Christensen 1999; Pollitt 1974; White 1956; articles with a more technical/geometrical focus include Knorr 1991; Tobin 1990; Andersen 1987; Brownson 1981. Despite some conceptual flaws, the most well-known attempt to join the two approaches is still the best general account: Panofsky 1991, sects. 1–2.

[26] Christensen 1999 focuses on the evidence from these vases.

[27] Vitruvius 7. pr. 11.

[28] Vitruvius 1.2.2: "*Skenographia* is the sketching of a facade and retreating sides, with a correspondence of all lines to the center of a compass." See also the discussion in Pollitt 1974: 236–247.

vertical flat surfaces may appear to be retreating in some places and projecting in others." In other words, the method is designed to create an illusion of *depth* in an object (the picture plane) which in reality has no depth. Second, the injunction to orient "all lines" with respect to a fixed center suggests that the illusion of the tapering portico – "the same porch seen from either end appears tapered, but from its middle appears everywhere symmetrical" – has its origin in various treatises on σκηνογραφία.[29]

A second technique for creating illusions of depth did more to capture the attention of ancient writers, is much better represented in extant artifacts, and accordingly is better understood by modern commentators. This is the illusion that regions on a painted surface rendered in bright colors appear to jut forward, while areas with darker hues appear recessed. The systematic exploitation of this illusion was called σκιαγραφία; according to Pliny, the technique was invented by Apollodorus (who was nicknamed ὁ σκιαγράφος, "the Shadow Painter") around the time of the Peloponnesian Wars, and was perfected by his student Zeuxis. The technique specifically involved juxtaposing bright and dark colors, and carefully blending them together in such a way that solid objects, such as human limbs, produce a strong impression of three-dimensional contour and bulk. The large collection of testimonia assembled by Pollitt demonstrates just how familiar this method was in antiquity.[30] An account by the Peripatetic commentator Alexander of Aphrodisias (late second century A.D.) describes both the natural illusion and its exploitation by artists:

> More vivid objects appear to be closer to the eye, and the less vivid, further away. Painters, who have observed this optical illusion (πάθος τῆς ὄψεως), construct figures in the picture plane so that some appear to be closer to the eye and some more distant. They create this illusion for vision by juxtaposing colors that have stronger and weaker stimuli.[31]

We have already seen this illusion referred to briefly in the passage from the *Republic* quoted above. Plato characterizes it by saying that figures, which are in truth flat, appear "concave and convex" to the eye. Plato was a younger contemporary of Zeuxis, and it seems quite certain that his various allusions to σκιαγραφία constitute responses to the painter's work.[32]

Another well-known illusion, the so-called tower illusion, is one I would suggest also has its roots in painting.[33] The typical formula for describing it was to say that a

---

[29] Quotation from Sext. Emp. *ad M.* 7.108; see also Lucr. 4.426–431; Sen. *De Ben.* 7.1.5; Sen. *NQ* 1.3.9; Tert. *De An.* 17.2; Calc. *in Tim.* 237.

[30] See Pollitt 1974: 247–254; additional references can be found at ps.-Aristot. *de Aud.* 801a32–7; Longinus 17.3; Ptol. *Opt.* 2.127; Schol. ad Arat. *Phaen.* 828.

[31] Alexander of Aphrodisias *de An.* 2.1.50.24–51.4.

[32] Cf. Pollitt 1974: 247–249.

[33] References to the tower illusion: Diog. Laer. 9.85, 10.34; Lucr. 4.353–63, 501–2; Sext. Emp. *adv. M* 7.208, *PH* 1.118; Plut. *Adv. Col.* 1121a.; Diog. Oen. fr. 69 Smith; Calc. *in Tim.* 272 Waszink (= *SVF* 2.863); Petron., *Anth. Lat.* 650, ll.3–4; Macr. *Sat.* 7.14.20; Nemesius 7.188 Morani; Isidore 15.2.19; Alexander *Probl. Phys.* 1.37 (Ideler *Phys. et Med. Graeci Min.* pp.13–14); Sen. *QN* 1.3.9; Tert. *De An.* 17.2, 17.6; Olymp. *in Meteor.* 2.5.96; Ptol. *Opt.* 2.97; Philop. *in De An.* p.511.6 Hayduck; Geminus *Auszüge*, Schoene 22.11–12, and 116.13 Aujac.

square tower when viewed from a distance appears round. Proposition 9 of Euclid's *Optics*, although it omits to name the tower, demonstrates clearly how the illusion works:[34]

> When seen from a distance rectangular magnitudes will appear rounded. For let there be rectangle BC standing high and seen from a distance. Therefore, since every visible object possesses a certain measure of distance where it is no longer seen once it gets there, angle C is not seen, and only points D and E appear. The same thing will happen to each of the remaining angles, with the result that the whole will appear rounded.

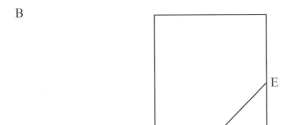

Notice that it is the profile of the tower in elevation ("standing high"), not plan, that looks round – the distant tower will resemble an upright playing card, square but with blunted corners.

Without a doubt the strangest thing about the round tower illusion is that it does not exist. I myself have never seen a distant building whose corners I would describe as round in appearance, and this has been the experience of other, independent observers as well.[35] It is true that from a certain distance a square tower becomes indistinguishable from one with a circular profile.[36] Still, that is not how the ancient illusion is

---

[34] This reference may be the earliest (late fourth century), although texts from Epicurus (Diog. Laer. 10.34) and the ps.-Aristotelian *Problemata* (15.6) which describe it date from roughly the same age. The illusion may even go back to Democritus, as Berryman 1998 suggests, but the suggestion hinges on how much of the material cited in Philoponus *in Gen. et Corr.* 23.1–16 goes back to Democritus.

[35] Cf. Berryman 1998: 183 n. 13, where she reports her informal investigations of the effect, conducted with the help of several other observers.

[36] Cf. Berryman 1998: 183 n. 13: "Alexis, Elizabeth, Nicholas, and Sheila Asher tested this claim on the UT-Austin clock tower and tell me that in fact it isn't that the square tower looks round, but that it's impossible to tell whether it's round or square."
Ruskin makes the same point with an interesting demonstration:
> Draw on a piece of white paper, a square and a circle, each about a twelfth or a eighth of an inch in diameter, and blacken them so that their forms may be very distinct; place your paper against the wall at the end of the room, and retire from it a greater or less distance according as you have drawn the figures larger or smaller. You will come to a point where, thought you can see both the spots with perfect plainness, you cannot tell which is the square and which the circle. (Ruskin 1903–1912, 3: 329).

supposed to operate: whenever it is described with sufficient detail, one can clearly see that it should occur even with an isolated tower. Thus it is very hard to imagine how the illusion might have sprung from first-hand observation.

One clue to its provenance can be found in Roman wall-painting. Several paintings of landscapes from Pompeii depict distant buildings with profiles which are unmistakably round or blurry; the famous frieze from the Vatican Library which illustrates scenes from the *Odyssey* actually portrays, in the panel where the Laestrygonians attack Odysseus' men, distant towers that are blurry and rounded.[37] The artist apparently produced the effect using a combination of devices. First, in order to imitate the effects of aerial perspective, or atmospheric haze, washes are applied to areas of the paintings with remote vistas; such washes typically have the effect of blurring lines and corners which might otherwise be sharp, and reduce the contrast between adjacent patches of color. Secondly, in the frieze the contours of distant objects are rendered with quasi-impressionistic, painterly strokes in a way that creates a noticeable contrast with the crisply delineated objects in the near ground.

The techniques used in the *Odyssey* frieze were already well-known in the mid fourth century, if not earlier. A passage from Aristotle clearly states that washes were used by painters to depict objects seen through water or through "air," which is to say, with aerial perspective.[38] The treatment of such atmospheric effects presupposes that the objects being represented were located in the far background.[39] As for the visibly sketch-like, painterly brushstrokes in the images, different reconstructions of *skiagraphia* have shown that painters like Zeuxis developed it into an almost impressionistic style.[40] Thus, the same methods used to render the towers in the *Odyssey* frieze blurry first came into use around the time of the earliest notices of the tower illusion in the fourth century.

It is easier now to see how the tower illusion might have come to be accepted as genuine by philosophical and other technical writers. When the practice of using washes and brushstrokes to make objects seem distant was developed, objects like towers that might be placed in the background would begin to acquire "rounded" corners. Word of this new painterly convention could then have reached our philosophical sources by any of a number of different routes. It may be that philosophers themselves noticed how towers look in paintings and interpreted the images as faithful reproductions of what painters saw. Or, it may be that painters discussed this convention among themselves or in their writings, formulating a rule of thumb to the effect that "square towers in the distance *ought to be sketched with* rounded corners."

---

[37] That the round distant towers in the *Odyssey* frieze illustrate the tower illusion was first noted by Leach 1988: 51, 52. Reproductions of the relevant frieze can be seen in Leach, and in Ling 1991: 108.

[38] Aristotle, *de Sens.* 440a8–10: "One way [sc. to produce colors] is to have them appear through one another, just as painters sometimes do when they apply one tint over a second, brighter tint, whenever they want to make something appear to be in water or air."

[39] Cf. *de Col.* 794a12–13: "Air seen from close up appears to have no color ... while when viewed in depth, its close up parts seem to be of a dark blue color."

[40] See the excellent discussion, with bibliography, in Bruno 1977, ch. 1, 3, 9.

This might then have been misread by philosophers as an indication of how objects really look: "square towers in the distance *appear to have* rounded corners."

That word of the illusion came to philosophy from painting can also be inferred from Lucretius' description, which likely goes directly back to Epicurus:

> When we observe a city's square towers from a distance, it often happens that they appear round, because from a distance each angle seems dull – or more accurately, is not seen: its impact is lost, its blow does not slip into our eyes. Because when *simulacra* [sc. Epicurean visual films] pass through a great quantity of air, the air forces that impact to become weak through many collisions. When for this reason each and every angle escapes our notice, the result is as if stone structures had been ground down on a lathe – although not like things that are truly round right in front of us; instead they appear somewhat reproduced, as if in a shadow-painting (*sed quasi adumbratim paulum simulata videntur*).[41]

If my account of the illusion's origins is correct, then this last qualification amounts to an admission that remote towers do not *really* appear round to the naked eye. In fact, on the interpretation I am suggesting, its argument is circular: to see how towers actually look, one is referred to paintings of towers; but it was by examining paintings of towers that the actual appearance of towers was determined in the first place. We can detect here an assumption which other sources make more explicit: the idea that artistic depictions offer the most reliable record of appearances, since they reveal how experts on the visual world – artists – actually see things. The Stoic speaker in Cicero's *Academica* comments on the superior abilities of artists in this respect by saying, "how many things there are that painters can see in shadows and highlights which we fail to see!" [42]

To this point I have dealt with painted illusions involving *depth* and *shape*. Yet another illusion connected to painting involves *size*; it is what I will call the diminution illusion. This too is a natural illusion, since all sighted people are quite aware of the fact that large objects appear small or diminished when observed from a distance. Nevertheless, size diminution leaves no clear impression on Greek literature or art until some time in the fifth century, when the first representations and references to it appear.[43]

What makes the diminution illusion unusual is that it prompted artists to develop two, almost diametrically opposed responses to it. The first is described in Plato's *Sophist*:

> *Stranger*: The perfect case of this (sc. of making likenesses) is when someone produces an imitation by rendering the proportions of a model in height, width, and

---

[41] Lucr. 4.353–363.

[42] *Acad.* 2.7.20.

[43] For later references to diminution, see Eucl. *Opt.* 4–5, Sext. Emp. *adv. M.* 7.208–9 (Epicurus); Calc. *in Tim.* 237 (= *SVF* 2.863), etc.

Note that diminution and linear perspective are not the same thing: linear perspective presupposes diminution, while diminution does not imply the use of linear perspective. Pompeian wall-paintings, for example, typically display consistent diminution, without showing anything like consistent central point perspective.

depth, along with the colors appropriate to each particular. – *Theatetus*: What? Don't all imitators try to do something like this? – Well, perhaps not those who sculpt or paint large works. For if they were to render the limbs in their true proportions, then, as you know, the upper parts would look smaller than they need to be, and the lower parts bigger, since we see the former from a distance, and the latter from close up. – That is so. – So aren't artists now saying farewell to the truth when they produce in their images not the real proportions but those which will look good? – Absolutely.[44]

The diminution illusion presents makers of monumental paintings and statues with a problem, because it prevents spectators from seeing their works in their true forms. The passage implies, and other sources confirm, that artists deal with the problem by exaggerating the size of the upper limbs and upper figures, so that the effects of diminution would be cancelled out.[45] In other words, their artistic response to the illusion was to find a way of *compensating* for it.

The second approach, which for obvious reasons could only be adopted by painters, was not to eliminate the illusion but to *represent* it – to make certain figures smaller as a way of indicating their position in the background. A *terminus post quem* for the invention of this technique can be found in the early fifth century, based on what we know of the paintings of the early master Polygnotus. The style of his works' spatial and figural composition can be inferred from the detailed description in Pausanias of his mural-paintings of the underworld at Delphi, and from the famous "Niobid Krater" in the Louvre, which is widely believed to reflect Polygnotan style.[46] In the scenes on the krater, figures that are supposed to lie behind the foreground characters are actually represented higher up in the picture plane – but without suffering any diminution in size. Thus, diminution seems not to have been represented in painting in Polygnotus' day, c. 470–450 B.C.

After Polygnotus, a *terminus ante quem* for the new technique comes from an Apulian vase from the early fourth century, which shows a temple on a distant hill with roughly the same dimensions as an altar in the foreground (which is small enough for someone to sit on).[47] Our literary evidence then falls nicely into the middle of the range (early fifth/ early fourth century) established by the artifacts. Plato makes reference to diminution in the *Sophist* and the *Republic* passages previously quoted, and elsewhere.[48] In addition, a passing comment in Lucian's dialogue *Zeuxis* praises the painter, who was a contemporary of Socrates, for employing a "magnitude system" (τοῦ μεγέθους τὸν λόγον) in his work.[49] Provided that this is not a reference to linear perspective, Lucian would seem to be alluding to size diminution.

---

[44] *Soph.* 235d6–236a7.

[45] Other references to refinements in colossal art: Philo Byz. *Mech.* 4.4; Vitr. 3.3.11–13, Geminus *Auszüge* 30.6–11 Schoene, Tzetzes *Chil.* 8.333 ff. and *Epist.* 77. For discussion, see Rykwert 1996: 220–229.

[46] See Pollitt 1990: 126–141 for testimonia relating to Polygnotus. The representation of background figures in the "Niobid Krater" is discussed and illustrated in Richter 1970: 36.

[47] Illustrated in Richter 1970, no. 197.

[48] Pl. *Prt.* 356c5, *Philb.* 41e9.

[49] Luc. *Zeux.* 3.

How do these different approaches relate to each other? The sculptors and painters Plato mentions in the *Sophist* are looking at their art and trying to find ways to eliminate an unwelcome distortion created by diminution. The painter or painters who first represented diminution in their pictures were looking at the world at large, seeking to extend the principle of verisimilitude by accounting for diminution, and thus do something no one had done before. Plato himself was trying to highlight the scandalous fact that artists were in his day choosing to imitate visual appearances rather than physical realities. Now it may be that Plato had an independent interest in this illusion, which the work of the artists merely helped to confirm. Yet I suspect that the shock of the new – the experience of a viewer first wondering why the figures in Zeuxis' paintings are so small, and then, after being told that figures in the distance really do look that way, realizing that it is so – is what drove the interest Plato and his contemporaries had in the illusion. We should keep in mind that Plato lists diminution together with σκιαγραφία, "wonder-working," and "other frauds," in a category he labels "magic." Moreover, painting highlights the effect of the illusion by juxtaposing its figures in a picture plane, where their closeness allows them to measure one other; measurement being, of course, the one thing that gets at the truth, and isolates false appearances.

MIRRORS

The earliest mirrors found in Greece date to the mid sixth century, and, to judge from their popularity throughout the Mediterranean in earlier times, they were probably being used long before that.[50] Apart from their obvious value as tools to assist grooming, mirrors have long been regarded as powerful instruments of magic and divination. There is a very old superstition that reflections in mirrors and related objects, such as water-filled vessels, are really spirits, or visions of the future.[51] But strictly speaking, the belief that the image in a mirror is a soul does not count as an optical illusion, because there is no firm dichotomy between reality/unreality. It is just not part of the superstition that one thinks of the image as unreal, or "just an image."

Once more we must turn to Plato to find mirrors described as venues for illusions. His works offer the first record of the observation that objects in mirrors appear reversed.[52] The *Timaeus* states that when things are viewed in plane mirrors, "what is on the right appears to be on the left."[53] Later writers follow Plato's way of putting the matter when they report how things look in plane mirrors.[54] The meaning of this statement is not immediately obvious, however. If you look at your reflection in a

---

[50] On mirrors in ancient culture, see Melchior-Bonnet 1994: 102–108 and Goldberg 1985: 95–119.

[51] For bibliography on the practice of scrying with mirrors, see Nelson 2000.

[52] Of course Plato may not be have been the first person to note the illusion; yet a comment of Aristotle's seems telling: at the time Democritus was writing on vision, "nothing had yet been made clear even at a general level concerning images and reflection" (*de Sens.* 438a9).

[53] *Tim.* 46b3–6; a similar description of "opposite sensation" coming from mirrors occurs at *Soph.* 266c1–4.

[54] Right and left in mirrors: Euclid, *Cat.* 19; Lucr. 4.292–301, Ptol. *Opt.* 2.138; Apul. *Apol.* 16; Macr. *Sat.* 7.14.7.

plane mirror and raise your right hand, the reflection of that hand will appear on your right, just as your left hand's reflection is on your left. Therefore it might seem equally or even more natural to say that what is on your right appears to be on your right, and *vice versa*. But clearly if the phenomenon was described this way the appearances would no longer be in conflict with reality, and there would be no illusion.

One way to make sense of Plato's formulation is to think about how a person looking into a mirror conceives of the experience. Instead of regarding a mirror as a box in which ghosts are at work, one might also think of it as an automatic painting, a machine for creating flawless, instantaneous reproductions of visible forms. This second way is precisely how Plato did think of mirrors, as his repeated (and unfair) comparison between the work of painters and the action of mirrors shows.[55] Now, because a mirror shares with painting the ability to represent the forms of objects, then, if you are Plato, you may well incline to compare the mirror's "portrait" with its original – just as Plato famously does with painted portraits in book 10 of the *Republic*. It is at this point that the discrepancy becomes evident: the right side of a person's body appears on the right in the mirror but on the left in the portrait, and vice versa. Here, then, is one way in which Plato may have come to notice the mirror-reversal illusion. It seems to follow from a certain concept of what a mirror is, and what it does. Putting mirrors and paintings in the same category highlights their most noticeable formal difference, that what is on the left in the one is on the right in the other. This difference becomes yet another item on the list of optical illusions.[56]

CONCLUSION

Where do optical illusions come from? As we have seen, there are a number of answers to this question, depending on what one means by the term. The *concept* of illusions, as we have seen, was a by-product of the concern philosophers in the late fifth century had to draw a line between reason and the senses; it was then that optical illusions, even if they had previously been known, began to attract serious attention.

Together with the concept came the different *categories* of illusions. Many of the examples we have been considering can be arranged into elementary categories, like so:

> Straight/Curved (the oar which is truly straight appears bent)
> Flat/Curved (the painting which is truly flat appears to have contour)
> Square/Round (the tower which is truly square appears round)
> Round/Oblong (the shield which is truly round appears elliptical)
> Right/Left (the hand which is truly on the right appears on the left)
> Large/Small (the figure which is truly large appears small)
> Resting/Moving (the coastline which is truly stationary appears to move)
> One/Many (the object which is truly single appears double, sc. when the eye is pressed)

---

[55] In *Resp.* 10, 596c2–596e8, and *Soph.* 233d9–234c1, read with 239d1–240a2.

[56] Closely related to this question concerning the historical origins of the mirror-reversal illusion is the following conundrum: why should left and right appear to be reversed in a mirror-image while top and down appear unreversed? This curious problem does not derive from the physical optics but is instead largely an artifact of the criteria we use to designate left and right as such. A number of different solutions can be given to it: for one set, see Block 1974.

If some general concept of illusion prompts one to go searching for particular cases, then these various categories are like slots which will need to be filled. In fact, any list of primary opposites that one could draw up should be able to predict the kinds of illusions that will appear. It is interesting to see that several of the pairs listed above are either identical or very similar to items on a list of Pythagorean first principles which Aristotle cites:

> Limit/Unlimited
> Odd/Even
> One/Many
> Right/Left
> Male/Female
> Resting/Moving
> Straight/Curved
> Light/Darkness
> Good/Bad
> Square/Oblong[57]

Nothing of immediate historical interest follows from the affiliation between the charts: I do not mean to imply, say, Pythagorean influence. Yet the overlap confirms that to a very large degree illusions were conceptually defined. This focus on categories is not even restricted to the fifth and fourth centuries, when the illusions were first discovered. It is quite common for later writers to name illusions not by giving an example but by citing a category, so that to refer to the tower illusion, for instance, it is enough to say that "square things appear round."[58]

Finally, there are the specific *examples*. As mentioned at the beginning of the paper, a number of these seem simply to derive from natural observation (vertigo, the retreating coastline, etc.); I have so far omitted to include one of the most famous natural illusions of all, the straight oar which appears bent when placed in the water.[59] Yet we have also seen that quite a few illusions were first officially recognized through the mediation of art. In such cases, philosophy seems to have used art as a kind of tool for investigating the character of the visual realm. There is some historical irony in the fact that ancient philosophy, which often maintained a fairly patronizing attitude towards art due to art's affinity with fiction, should have mined artistic representations for "raw data" about the sensory world – and in some cases, borrowed and accepted as real illusions which are non-existent!

---

[57] *Metaph.* 986a24–34.
[58] Cf. Geminus *Auszüge* 28.7–9 Schoene, Sext. Emp. *PH* 118–120, Diog. Laer. 9.85–86.
[59] Plato *Resp.* 602c10; Lucr. 4.438–442; Sext. Emp. *adv M.* 7.242–246 (= *SVF* 2.65), *PH* 1.119–120, Cicero *Acad.* 2.19, 2.79; Geminus *Auszüge* 28.9 Schoene; Macr. 7.14.20; Tertul. *De An.* 17; ps.-Galen *Hist. Phil.* 78.290; Vitruvius 6.2.2.

WORKS CITED

Andersen, K. 1987. "Ancient Roots of Linear Perspective." In J.L. Berggren and B.R. Goldstein, eds., *From Ancient Omens to Statistical Mechanics.* Copenhagen. 75–89.

Berryman, S. 1998. "Euclid and the Skeptic: A Paper on Vision, Doubt, Geometry, Light, and Drunkenness." *Phronesis* 43.2: 176–196.

Block, N.J. 1974. "Why do Mirrors Reverse Right/Left but not Up/Down?" *JPh* 71.9: 259–277.

Brownson, C.D. 1981. "Euclid's *Optics* and its Compatibility with Linear Perspective." *Archive for History of Exact Sciences* 24: 165–194.

Bruno, V. 1977. *Form and Color in Greek Painting.* New York.

Christensen, J. 1999. "Vindicating Vitruvius on the Subject of Perspective." *JHS* 119: 161–166.

Goldberg, B. 1985. *The Mirror and Man.* Charlottesville, Va.

Gregory, R. 1996. "What are Illusions?" *Perception* 25: 503–504.

Hankinson, R.J. 1995. *The Skeptics.* New York.

Hoffman, D.D. 1998. *Visual Intelligence: How We Create What We See.* New York.

Knorr, W.R. 1991. "On the Principle of Linear Perspective in Euclid's *Optics*." *Centaurus* 34: 193–210.

Leach, E.W. 1988. *The Rhetoric of Space: Literary and Artistic Representations of Landscape in Republican and Augustan Rome.* Princeton.

Ling, R. 1991. *Roman Painting.* London.

Lloyd, G.E.R. 1966. *Polarity and Analogy.* London.

Mather, G., F. Verstraten, and S. Anstis. 1998. *The Motion Aftereffect.* Cambridge, Mass.

Melchior-Bonnet, S. 1994. *The Mirrors: A History.* Trans. K. H. Jewett. New York.

Nelson, M. 2000. "Narcissus: Myth and Magic." *CJ* 95: 363–389.

Panofsky, E. 1991. *Perspective as Symbolic Form.* Trans. C.S. Wood. New York.

Pollitt, J. J. 1974. *The Ancient View of Greek Art.* New Haven.

———. 1990. *The Art of Ancient Greece.* New York.

Richter, G. M. A. 1970. *Perspective in Greek and Roman Art.* New York.

Ruskin, J., 1903–1912. *Works.* Ed. by E.T. Cook and A. Wedderburn. 31 vols. London.

Rykwert, J. 1996. *The Dancing Column.* Cambridge, Mass.

Smith, A. Mark. 1996. *Ptolemy's Theory of Visual Perception: An English Translation of the Optics with Introduction and Commentary.* Transactions of the American Philosophical Society, vol. 86 no. 2. Philadelphia.

Theisen, W. 1984. "Euclid, Relativity, and Sailing." *HM* 11: 81–85.

Tobin, R. 1990. "Ancient Perspective and Euclid's *Optics*." *JWI* 53: 14–41.

Verstraten, F. A. J. 1996. "On the Ancient History of the Direction of the Motion Aftereffect." *Perception* 25: 1177–88.

Wade, N. 1998. *A Natural History of Vision.* Cambridge, Mass.

White, J. 1956. *Perspective in Ancient Drawing and Painting.* London.

12

Gesture

W. F. Wyatt, Jr.

Alan Boegehold has long been interested in gestures,[1] and I hope he will accept this brief offering as a gesture of respect both to his scholarly work and to him as a person. His interest has been in physical gestures, gestures indeed that in many instances can be held to replace speech. My own interest is in verbal gestures that indicate mood or attitude and serve to explicate or clarify the spoken word.

We are all aware that we use such gestures and are adept in using them, but we do not often consider the semiotics of verbal gestures. A few examples. One often says – or is alleged to say – something like [ummm], a verbal gesture that is interpreted to mean "I'm not listening" or "I'm not interested;" or in a more benign interpretation "I'm thinking about it." "I'm not interested," though, is perhaps better conveyed by a non-committal "Oh?" with rising intonation. These sounds are not words, to be sure, but some utterances composed of words are used as gestures or indicators of attitude rather than as conveyors of literal meaning. I provide an imaginary conversation between imaginary spouses whom I'll call A and B:

> A – I've something to tell you.
> B – What's that?
> A – I bought a new car today.
> B – You what?
> A – I bought a new car today
> *or* (more provocatively): You heard me, I said…

Clearly the words are not to be interpreted literally, for B obviously heard what A had said and did not need to have the sentence repeated. A by the same token did not need to repeat what he/she had said previously. A semiotic interpretation:

> A – hesitation (?)
> B – apprehension
> A – [statement] forthrightness with (possibly feigned) contrition
> B – outrage
> A – defiance

I leave this little dialogue at this point and to the reader's imagination to complete. Suffice it to say that the words in the dialogue – save those reporting the purchase –

---

[1] Boegehold 1999.

are all affective utterances, indicators of mood rather than meaning. It would be misleading or a mistake to render them in a foreign tongue literally as if they were regular lexical items.[2]

Ancient Greek had a number of such mood indicators, chief perhaps among them being the Greek particles. English equivalents are words like *hopefully, actually, frankly* all of which are intended to convey to the hearer the speaker's attitude towards what he/she is saying. Otherwise we lack particles pretty much, save in the colloquial *you know* and the perplexing *like*. In addition there was the category of interjections which are more clearly emotive terms.

I was confronted with these words and related issues when revising A.T. Murray's Loeb translation of *The Iliad*.[3] There I had to devise a "translation" for the word δαιμονίη / δαιμόνιε. Murray varied his translation, using now one solution, now another. I, however, endeavoring to remain true to the formulaic nature of Homeric diction, wanted one translation, on the principle that one word in the original should (usually and ideally) be represented by a single word in the translation. I failed in this, and had to go with pretty much what Murray chose and leave it at that.[4]

Other perplexities were caused by ὦ πέπον and ὦ πόποι, terms and expressions I dealt with both in my translation, whether satisfactorily or not, and in my article on "Interjections."[5] There is no need to develop my thoughts on those subjects here. I want instead to approach the word τέττα, hapax in *Iliad* 4.412. Diomedes' comrade Sthenelos has just upbraided Agamemnon for a slighting comparison of the *Epigonoi* with their fathers. They – Diomedes and Sthenelos among them – had actually taken Thebes, while their fathers perished through their own foolhardiness. Diomedes tells him to be silent, Agamemnon is justified in doing/saying what he said:

> τέττα, σιωπῇ ἧσο, ἐμῷ δ' ἐπιπείθεο μύθῳ.
> οὐ γὰρ ἐγὼ νεμεσῶ Ἀγαμέμνονος ποιμένι λαῶν
> ὀτρύνοντι μάχεσθαι ἐυκνήμιδας Ἀχαιούς·

But what is τέττα? Is it an exclamation? Or a term of affectionate address, as LSJ would have it ? Given that the word is a hapax, any speculation is hazardous. Murray has "good friend," thus more or less following LSJ, and I cravenly follow him. The

---

[2] In Russian the phrase *bozhe moi,* literally "My God," was translated in the notes to an elementary text as "my goodness." I was struck by this atheistic rendering of an (originally) religious phrase. The translator was correct, however, for the deity was not being invoked, any more than in our language do we call upon the deity when expressing surprise or shock by saying "My God!"

[3] Murray-Wyatt 1999.

[4] A number of options occurred to me, most excluded for cultural reasons. "For heaven's sake!" or "Good heavens" might do, but the (latent) Christian theology stood in the way; as did the fact that gods can use the word. "Good gracious" might do for women, or "good god!" followed by the person's name, as in 6.407 = "good god, Hector." I replaced Murray's "Good sir" at 13.448 with "you're mad," which I think is about right. One could try here and there: "Are you crazy?" or simply "you're crazy;" or "what's got into you?" Cf. Kirk 1985: 111 *ad Il.* 1.561; Janko 1992: 104 *ad Il.* 13.448-9 has "possessed by a *daimon*" which must be right, even when, as in 1.561, used of a goddess. Richardson 1993: 294 *ad Il.* 24.194 (Murray-Wyatt "lady") suggests something like "my dear," and refers back to *Il.* 1.561 and a dissertation by Brunius-Nilsson (1955: 12ff.).

[5] Wyatt 1998.

line preceding the line in question, however, rather argues against any sort of friendly address:

Τὸν δ᾽ ἄρ᾽ ὑπόδρα ἰδὼν προσέφη κρατερὸς Διομήδης

"Good friend" will not do.[6]

Because an imperative follows, the word is clearly either a vocative – to a noun *τέττης, otherwise unattested (save in scholia to this line) – or it is an interjection like ὦ πέπον and ὦ πόποι and unlike ἄττα, the parallel adduced by Leaf ad loc. The unattested noun would be a very strange looking one if it did exist; and one might expect such a noun to be of wider use and application. Rather I shall assume it to be an interjection, an interjection meaning (roughly) "shut up."[7]

One knows that the phonology of interjections differs or can differ from the regular phonology of a language.[8] Thus in English we lack a bilabial voiceless fricative in our phonological system, and yet have the interjection pronounced with that sound but spelled *whew,* an interjection that can mean roughly: "there, that's done" or "wow." The Greeks had their φεῦ which may have been pronounced in the same way, and the Romans their *heu(s).* In English as well we have the sound spelled something like <shhhhhhhh>, a prolonged sibilant. We possess the sound normally, to be sure, but do not ordinarily lengthen it to the degree we do in this case. We lack nasalized vowels in English, but the query, spelled *hunh,* contains such a vowel. Though dictionaries may spell it <huh>, there is nasalization.[9]

Most relevant for our purposes, however, is the alveolar click we possess, a sound like that made when calling a cat, and which is spelled either <tsk> or <tut>. This latter spelling has given rise in fact to a verb "to tut," the participle of which – with reduplication – is *tuttutting.* To cut the argument short, I suspect that τέττα is the Greek representation of the alveolar click, and that as in English, the click had been partially lexicalized by containing both reduplication and a final [a], like the final [a] of letters of the alphabet like ἄλφα, βῆτα.

---

[6] Chantraine 1968: 1096, s. v. τατᾶ, compares Lithuanian and Slavic forms meaning "father," as does Frisk 1972, 2: 860. Comparisons of this sort represent the phonological fallacy which holds that phonological correspondence, both unexamined and unmotivated, is sufficient to establish an "etymology." Before this comparison can even be considered we should have to establish that the word in fact means "father." Ancient testimony, where not embarrassed, does indeed provide the meaning "father" and compares, as does modern, the nursery word ἄττα, but without authority. Eustathius 490.35ff. discusses the form, and holds that it is untranslatable. Elsewhere (659.52) he regards it as προσφώνησις ἔχουσά τινα σεβασμόν, and provides analogies: τὸ μὲν τέττα φίλου, τὸ δὲ ἄττα τροφέως, τὸ δὲ πάππα πατρός, τὸ δὲ ἠθεῖε ἀδελφοῦ. This testimony is both schematic and essentially worthless.

[7] The two possibilities – noun and interjection – are mentioned by the scholia ad loc. Cf. Erbse 1969 ad loc. I.518. I assume with the ancient scholiast that τέττα is an ἐπίρρημα σχετλιαστικόν.

[8] On interjections in Greek cf. Kühner-Blass 1.2.252-3; and for English, Quirk, Greenbaum, and Svartvik 1972: 44-5, 413-4.

[9] I do not know how to represent the taunt [nyæ nyæ], but assume a palatalized <n> plus [æ]. It means – usually in the mouth of children – something like "naughty, naughty;" or "that's what you get." I cannot be more precise on this one. The verbal gesture is often accompanied by the physical gesture of rubbing the index finger of one hand on the extended index finger of the other.

Modern Greek possesses this alveolar click, and is used to signify "no," usually accompanied by an upward thrust of the head or simply a raising of the eyebrows. I do not propose a connection with Modern Greek here, but do not exclude it either. What can the alveolar click have meant to Homeric man? It could have meant either "no, don't," or perhaps more likely "shhh, shut up."[10] Because I cannot specify with certainty the exact intent, I leave the semantics loose, and hold only that the form signifies disapproval of an interlocutor's words or actions.

Phonologically I posit that Homeric Greeks used the alveolar click to signify disapproval, and they (may have) pronounced it double, as in English <tut tut>: [click click]. In order, though, to integrate the interjection into verse, vowels were required, and the closest approximations were <e> for the first syllable, and the <a> that was added to prepositions and letters of the alphabet in order to make them conform to the regular rules of Greek phonology. Furthermore they represented the click itself with the letter *tau,* single initially and doubled internally. This letter came as close as Greek spelling could to the actual sound, since *tau,* a dental, is close to the alveolar location of the click. One knows that in Attic the same phonological relation of single and double *tau* occurs with τήμερον (beside Ionic σήμερον) "today;" and Attic θάλαττα beside Ionic θάλασσα "sea."[11]

This line of speculation brings us back to our honorand, who some years ago speculated that the *tau* of the Nessos amphora was in fact the same sign as that seen in Ionic inscriptions representing the (later) cluster of Ionic <ss>, Attic <tt>.[12] It is at least conceivable that in the first writing down of the *Iliad* this Ionic symbol was used in order to represent the sequence [ts] (that in turn replaced the click sound). Whether or not this is the case, I hold that τέττα is a verbal gesture meaning something like "don't" or "quiet," and was pronounced originally at least as an alveolar click. It subsequently was realized as [ts] and was represented in writing as *tau* when all such clusters lost their sibilant element.

---

[10] The etymology of σιγή σιωπή is unknown. Chantraine 1968: 1001 speaks (correctly) of "une syllabe expressif comme dans σίττα;" Frisk 1954, 2: 701-2 speaks of "lautmalender Ursprung," but then goes on to compare some Old High German forms. Comparison with σίττα is apt and provides a direct parallel with the formation of τέττα. Σίττα, I assume, since used to call or guide animals, might be an alveolar lateral click, a sound that appears as <x> in Xhosa writing, something I would represent in English writing by <tschuk>. Yet it could also represent a sound like [ssst] or perhaps even [fssst], a sound I think I recall having heard made by shepherds in Greece – the <f> formed with the upper teeth drawn back across the lower lip, almost a whistle. I feel that σῖγα – the immediate origin of the words for "silence" – contains not a click but a fricative, either [s] or (perhaps more likely) [sh]. Ψῆττα, ταχέως, εὐθέως clearly represents [pst], like the English *psst.*

[11] If I am correct in positing an alveolar click in τέττα and onomatopoeic intent (and origin) in σῖγα, κτλ., then the beginning of the line in its entirety with its assibilation and sibilants enjoins silence, not only in meaning, but also in sound. For I assume that τέττα, originally a click, was replaced by an assibilated [ts] that was represented by τ (ττ). For the history of assibilated and affricate sounds, cf. my article on palatalization in Greek, Wyatt 1968: 6-14 and, more fully, Lejeune 1972:100–111.

[12] Boegehold 1962: 405-6 with pl. 20. On the sign (*sampi*) and the supposed sound, cf. Jeffery 1961: 70–1 and index s.v. *sampi.*

WORKS CITED

Boegehold, A.L. 1962. "The Nessos Amphora – A Note on the Inscription." *AJA* 66: 405–6.

Boegehold, A.L. 1999. *When a Gesture Was Expected*. Princeton.

Brunius-Nilsson, E. 1955. *ΔAIMONIE, an inquiry into a mode of apostrophe in old Greek literature*. Upsala.

Chantraine, P. 1968. *Dictionnaire étymologique de la langue grecque, histoire des mots*. Paris.

Erbse, H. 1969. *Scholia Graeca in Homeri Iliadem*. Berlin.

Frisk, H. 1954. *Griechisches etymologische Wörterbuch*. 2 Vols. Heidelberg.

Janko, R. 1992. *The Iliad: A Commentary. Volume IV: books 13–16*. Cambridge.

Jeffery, L.H. 1961. *The Local Scripts of Archaic Greece*. Oxford.

Kirk, G.S. 1985. *The Iliad: A Commentary. Volume I: books 1–4*. Cambridge.

Kühner, R. 1892. *Ausführliche grammatik der griechischen sprache*. 3rd ed. Volume 1. Rev. by F. Blass. Hannover.

Lejeune, M. 1972. *Phonétique historique du mycénien et du grec ancien*. Paris.

Murray-Wyatt 1999= Murray, A.T. *The Iliad*. Rev. by W.F. Wyatt, Jr. Cambridge, Mass.

Quirk, R., S. Greenbaum, and J. Svartvik. 1972. *A Grammar of Contemporary English*. New York.

Richardson, N. 1993. *The Iliad: A Commentary. Volume 6: Books 21–24*. Cambridge.

Wyatt, W.F. 1968. "Greek Names in -σσος/-ττος." *Glotta* 46: 6–14.

Wyatt, W.F. 1998. "Interjections." *NECJ* 26: 35–36.

PART TWO

History, Law, and Epigraphy

13

Some Observations on the Appianos Sarcophagus (*IGUR* 1700)*

Gregory Bucher

Ῥώ[μη]ς πανχρυσέοιο Τύχης ἱερατίδα τειμὴν
    παρ βασιλῆος ἔχων Αὐσονίοιο κράτους,
Ἀππιανὸς βιότοιο πανηγύρεως ἀπολαύων
    λάρνακα λαϊνέην τῷδ᾿ ἀνέθηκα τόπῳ,
5   κηδείαν ἐς ἐμὴν καὶ κουριδίης ἀλόχοιο
    ἐσθλῆς Εὐτυχίας ᾗ συνέζησα βίον.

Ζώσῃ ἅπαντα παρέσχεν ἐμοι πάρος ἐσθλὰ βίοιο
    Ἀππιανὸς γαμέτης ἔξοχα τειόμενος·
καὶ μετὰ φῶς βιότοιο γέρας τόδε με‹ί›ζον ἔτευξε
10   ἄμφω κηδεύσας, τοὐμον ἐόν τε δέμας·
οὐ γὰρ ὁ τεθνῶτας¹ καταθεὶς κεῖνο[ς] τόδ᾿ ἔρεξεν,
    ἀλλ᾿ ὁ πρὸ τοῦ θανάτου τοῦτο νόῳ θέμενος.

13   δωδεχέτην ἔλαβον, ἔζησεν ἔτη σὺν ἐμοὶ λαʹ

---

* I gratefully acknowledge the invaluable assistance of the following colleagues: Ernst Badian, Laura Hyatt Booth, Glen Bowersock, Christina Clark, Bjorn Ewald, Ted Lendon, Christian Mileta, Kurt Raaflaub, Alex Sens, Alan Shapiro, Sarolta Takács, Ralf von den Hoff, and an anonymous referee.
¹ Moretti 1984–85, followed by *SEG* 35.1045, prints τεθνῶτας. All other editions have τεθνῶτας. I add here a translation into English as an aid to interpretation. I have attempted to balance a literal translation of the text with the retention of its trademark idiosyncrasies (such as short-order repetition of words). I reserve commentary for the body of this essay.

> While possessing the priestly honor of Tyche of all-golden Rome,
>   an honor granted by the Emperor of Ausonian might,
> I, Appianos, enjoying a pleasurable life,
>   set up a stone sarcophagus in this place
> 5   for my burial and that of my wedded wife,
>   the good Eutychia, with whom I lived my life.
>
> While I was alive, my husband Appianos provided me
>   with all the good things of life, honoring me exceptionally.
> After the light of life, he created this greater honor,
> 10   having seen to the burial of both our bodies, mine and his;
> For he who laid our dead bodies to rest did not make this,
>   but he who conceived it before death.
>
> 13   I married her when she was 12, she lived 31 years with me.

I. INTRODUCTION. DESCRIPTION OF THE SARCOPHAGUS

In 1987 Luigi Moretti published this epitaph inscribed upon a sarcophagus which had mysteriously "come to light" in the Camposanto teutonico del Vaticano sometime after his visit to the site in 1978–79.[2] Moretti complemented his publication of the text with a brief, cautious argument that the poet might have been the Antonine historian Appian of Alexandria, and his arguments were accepted and corroborated by Étienne Famerie in a biographical introduction to his 1998 study of Appian's language. The identification is based chiefly on 1) Moretti's Hadrianic or Antonine date for the letter forms, 2) the great rarity of the name Appianos, especially at Rome, and 3) the implied prominence of a man imperially appointed (παρ βασιλῆος ἔχων) to a priesthood.[3] Paul Goukowsky has now added an ingenious argument that the priesthood mentioned in the epigram's first verse was that of the newly-formed Hadrianic cult of Venus and Rome.[4] These arguments take the case about as far as the factual content of the epigram permits, and persuasive as they may be, they fall far short of certainty. Credible objections to the identification can be raised on several counts, and my chief objective in this essay is to explore them and demonstrate that they do not exclude an identification of Appianos with Appian. The most serious objections revolve around a fundamental problem: do epigram and sarcophagus fall within the limits of what we would expect in self-commemoration from Appian, a well educated *lettré* of high Alexandrian birth and ultimately an equestrian of procuratorial rank who lived a large portion of his life in Rome? I hope that the range of topics covered in the pursuit of my goal will – however faintly – evoke the many talents of Alan Boegehold, to whom, as a teacher and a friend, I am deeply indebted.

The little-known Camposanto, nestled between the Basilica of S. Pietro and the papal audience hall, has been a burial ground for (predominantly) German Catholic pilgrims and inhabitants of Rome since the middle ages; though not a site of scientific excavation, it has seen active creation of memorials and monuments in this century, and our sarcophagus, currently (2000) mortared atop a garden wall containing memorials, provides a monumental cap to the wall; only about half of the sides and rear are free of earth, and the interior is being used to hold gardening equipment.[5]

---

[2] The publication history of this inscription explains its late appearance in Appian scholarship: Moretti 1984–85 (appearing in 1987), the *editio princeps*; *SEG* 35 (1985): 1045 (appearing in 1988); Bousquet 1988, no. 69 (313–14); *IGUR* 1700 (ed. by Moretti, 1990); *APh* 64 (1993), number 1340 (appearing in 1996); Famerie 1998: 11–12; Goukowsky 1998.

All dates are A.D. "Appian" = the Antonine historian, "Appianos" = the poet of *IGUR* 1700.

That Appianos composed his own epitaph is a working hypothesis which the picture of the poet's competence drawn in this essay supports, as well as the content and tone of the epigram, which I discuss only briefly in anticipation of a fuller discussion in another forum. As to the mysterious apparition of the sarcophagus, Moretti diplomatically states that the sarcophagus "è venuto . . . alla luce," continuing in an apposite footnote (1984–85: 241 n. 18): "Quanto al sarcophago di cui qui si tratta, non si trovava certamente nel Camposanto teutonico quando ebbi a visitarlo l'ultima volta nel 1978–1979."

[3] For the arguments, Moretti 1984–85: 243–46; Famerie 1998: 12; Goukowsky 1998: 840–42.

[4] Goukowsky 1998: 843–47 and *passim*.

[5] I have not seen the sarcophagus. All physical and textual data offered here are based entirely upon Moretti's autoptic data and materials generously provided by Dr. Ewald and Ms. Booth.

The plain white limestone sarcophagus holds a large *tabula ansata* nearly spanning its face; the *tabula* is in turn framed by two engaged Corinthian columns, both in low relief. The stonecarver left three thin raised lines on the face of the sarcophagus in order to articulate the space, namely framing lines at top and bottom of the vertical part of the face, and a "ground line" which runs under the columns and the *tabula*, notionally supporting all three. A thin register is thus formed by the space between the "ground" and lower framing lines, and interestingly, below that lowest framing line, stone which might have formed another register of about equal height has been carved away to form an unusual beveled edge along the entire lower edge of the face, a fact not apparent in Moretti's photographs. The lower bevel is picked up by two small bevels on the vertical edges of the face, running between the "ground line" and the top framing line. My informants tell me that the remnants of seats for lid clamps are still visible in the face, most obviously at the top of the fracture which mars the left side of the *tabula ansata*. There are no visible traces of decoration on those parts of the sides and rear which can be inspected. In photographs generously furnished to me by colleagues there appears to be rough finishing of at least the left exterior with a claw chisel. This seems to agree with the rough working of (*i.a.*) the *ansae* on the face of the *tabula*, easily visible in Moretti's photographs taken in raking sunlight. My informants also confirm Moretti's measurements of the sarcophagus (L X H X D = 196 X 45 X 93 centimeters), and reaffirm that the sarcophagus is of a size to have held two bodies.

The epigram, carved in letters 2 to 2.2 cm high, consists of six well preserved elegiac distichs. In the *editio princeps* Moretti dated the letter forms to the reign of Hadrian or Antoninus Pius. The epitaph is a speaking inscription with the first three distichs left-justified within a space notionally comprising the left half of the *tabula ansata,* in the voice of Appianos. The latter three, left-justified within the space comprising the right half of the *tabula*, are in the voice of Appianos' wife Eutychia. There is a thirteenth line of text in the bottom register below Eutychia's verses. It is in Appianos' voice and records Eutychia's death. My informants tell me it is not carved as deeply as the six distichs, and that the letter forms – N and O particularly – betray a different hand.[6]

II. THE EPIGRAM

Under the influence of Simonides, early epigrammatists conventionally sought to employ elegiac distichs and Homeric diction.[7] Hellenistic practice saw the development of interesting, heterogeneous variations in meter and idiom, but just in our period the better practitioners were beginning to revive tighter Homeric standards. While

---

[6] Moretti 1984–85: 244 calls the line a "*dettaglio anagrafico.*" Famerie 1998: 11 n. 43 appears to misread Moretti's photographs, stating that Appianos' distichs are "gravés sur une face," Eutychia's "gravés sur l'autre face."

[7] Homeric diction in Greek poetry generally: Dihle 1994: 44–45; Homeric diction in Simonides: Segal 1985: 224, Poltera 1997: 541; Simonides' later influence: Bowra 1961: 322; popularity of epigrams into the Roman period: Bowie 1996: 53–54.

micromeasurement of metric or linguistic purism is beyond our ability given our limited data, we should see politically interested cultural competition as one factor pushing poets away from the heterogeneous Hellenistic idiom in a manner analogous to that which Simon Swain has advocated in his recent study of the move to Attic purism in imperial Greek. Swain explains this move as a strategy to retain dignity through opposing past cultural superiority to current Roman political domination.[8] In technical respects and as a reflection of a good education our epigram points to an Appianos who fits into the pattern of Greeks exploiting their native language to establish a claim to status, but the points where Appianos appears to fall short might prompt us to envision him as emanating from a social class below the historian's, and this is the first issue I propose to address.

In forming an estimation of Appianos we must remember that the poets who composed subliterary epigrams for practical, *ad hoc* purposes such as epitaphs did not automatically and mechanically follow the rules prescribed by ancient theorists and obeyed by the best practitioners, as Adolf Wilhelm masterfully showed long ago.[9] A poet who exploits metrical license to the limit or grapples in an unorthodox way with numbers or awkward proper names may fly in the face of the rules, but is not necessarily to be dismissed as ill-educated or inept; on the other hand, I think we might reasonably question the education and abilities of a poet who produces a dactylic heptameter or randomly inserts pentameters into a series of hexameters. While elegance is the mark of an artist and flows from a gift greater than mere education, firm, basic control over one's product seems to be a good starting point in distinguishing a *pepaideumenos* from lesser practitioners. How does Appianos' use of the epigrammatic form stack up against contemporary practice? On the basis of Kaibel's collection of Greek epitaphs in Rome (*IG* XIV 1314–2238), Kajanto established a useful benchmark, finding 17% (or 135 of 806 epitaphs, after excluding unhelpful fragments) to be epigrams. In Attica, by contrast, he found only about 3% of imperial epitaphs to be epigrams (60 out of 2050). As he noted, the frequency of Greek epigrams at Rome is unparalleled elsewhere in the ancient world, a state of affairs corroborated by the recent compilation of the Greek inscriptions of Rome by Moretti, who found 350, or about 30% of all epitaphs to be epigrams.[10] The lively social competition this reveals is also tellingly illustrated by the 22 Latin epitaphs from Rome supplemented by Greek epigrams; Kajanto pointed to this as strong evidence of the power of Greek to confer status quite apart from the tactics normally available to native speakers within the framework of Latin inscriptions, concluding that "the

---

[8] The "politics of purism": Swain 1995: 33–42; Wifstrand 1933: 155–77. See also Bowie 1989: 53–66.

[9] Wilhelm 1938 made a good case that they sometimes broke the rules by design, e.g., in accommodating a proper name to a verse in defiance of metrical niceties. See Wagner 1883 for much comparative evidence.

[10] Kajanto 1963: 5–6. Moretti 1979: iii: "nam epigrammata graeca circiter 30% sunt inter omnes titulos funerarios graecos urbanos, quod nusquam in aliis aevi antiqui civitatibus occurrit." Moretti's selection criteria (counting fragments) invalidate a direct comparison with Kajanto's numbers, but there is no doubt as to the anomalously high number of epigrams among the Greek epitaphs of Rome, surely due in some measure to invidious competition for status in the capital city.

persons recorded in Rome's Greek epitaphs were, in general, of a higher social status than the population represented on the Latin gravestones of the city."[11] Perhaps we might more accurately say that the people deploying the most sophisticated Greek epitaphs were using them strategically to assert a claim to superiority which we are disposed to accept even today. To highlight the special status of our inscription further, consider that of Moretti's 350 epigrams, only a dozen or so are as long as ours, and only a very few longer: our lengthy inscription has few peers.[12] If a man putting a lengthy Greek epigram on his tomb at Rome *ipso facto* stakes a claim to élite status, this does not help us locate him within a continuum potentially running from gauche freedmen of the sort parodied by Petronius to consulars like Arrian.[13] If we want to estimate Appianos' education, which (with a few exceptions such as the *familia Caesaris*) ought to track his social status, we will have to subject his style and techniques to closer scrutiny.[14] His flaws are easily exposed, but at the same time it is clear that he operates at a much higher level than those practitioners we can easily find who had only a shaky control over their poetry, or indeed the vast ranks for whom even a simple prose epitaph was a struggle. Moretti immediately spotted γέρας, δέμας, κουριδίη, and ἄλοχος as shopworn examples of what he disparaged as a "trite vocabulary,"[15] and it is certainly difficult to imagine composing an epitaph without them or their prosaic cousins. Banal they are, but not vulgar. In my opinion, Moretti overlooked the epigrammatist's traditional obligation to aim for Homeric diction, and indeed, the majority of the words in the poem are Homeric. For example, Moretti searched hard for epigraphic attestation of λάρναξ used with the meaning "sarcophagus" rather than the usual "cinerary urn," but the word was available to any ancient poet familiar with Homer (*Il.* 24.795), and the effortless extension of the word's semantic range from 'cinerary urn' to 'sarcophagus' is amply justified by metrical convenience.[16] Our poet is well enough educated to feel the pull of Homeric diction, and enough of a *Kenner* to be able to pull out a rarer specimen alongside the "trite" ones. Some figures: the six distichs contain 71 words, which reduce to 64 when we throw out repetitions. Of these, 51 are found in Homer, and 40 match Homeric examples in accidence and elision. The presence of unremarkable Homeric words such as τε and καί means nothing, but looking past these, our poet appears to have self-

---

[11] Kajanto 1963: 5–6.

[12] Number of long epigrams: Moretti 1984–85: 243, though his inclusion of fragmentary epitaphs may skew the statistical picture.

[13] Arrian: see *SEG* 26: 1215 (dedicatory, not funerary). For the sake of comparison consider the first verse of Arrian's epigram: κρεσσονά σοι χρυσοῖο καὶ ἀργύρου ἄμβροτα δῶρα, which succeds as a hexameter thanks to two successive instances of correption. For a recent collection of the bibliography on the Arrian epigram see Fein 1994: 177–78.

[14] See Goukowsky 1998: 837 nn. 15–16 and 838 for argumentation that Appianos and Eutychia were of high rank, some of it weakened (for our purposes) by the presupposition that Appianos was in fact Appian.

[15] Moretti 1984–85: 244.

[16] On λάρναξ, Moretti 1984–85: 243 n. 19. A century later it will be a natural choice for an Antiochene *vir egregius* of ducenarius rank to employ in a Roman prose epitaph (*IGUR* 306): see further below.

consciously sought to conform to Homeric diction.[17] The picture offered by our poet's diction is supported by his sowing his epigram with Homeric forms begging the reader to recognize their origins: genitives singular in -οιο, βασιλῆος for βασιλέως (admittedly forced on the poet *metri gratia*), the compound adjective πανχρύσεος, and the possessive ἑόν.

The non-Homeric words mostly have decent pedigrees except for a few interesting cases: πανήγυρις occurs in classical Attic, but the meaning "pleasure" or "happiness" is late,[18] and the very rare *koine* adjective ἱερατίς is only attested otherwise in the Christian *Narratio Iosephi* (3).[19] Though technically Homeric, κράτος demands a second look, because near-contemporary authors such as Cassius Dio use it in prose without apology for "empire," a decidedly unhomeric cast to the word. The two inflated periphrases ἱερατίδα τειμήν for "priesthood" and Αὐσονίοιο κράτους for "Roman Empire" are deliberately parallel in their stylistic attempt to elevate the tone of the epigram and ought to be respected as attempts to avoid the banal. Accordingly I translate Αὐσονίοιο κράτους as "Ausonian might," just as I translate ἱερατίδα τειμήν as "priestly honor," avoiding the simpler and more prosaic terms they stand for.[20] I therefore cautiously count κράτος as further evidence for a conscious adherence to Homeric diction in our epigram.

The benchmarks assembled by West in *Greek Metre* reveal that our poet's versification is reasonably strict. The pentameters avoid short vowels before the caesura and accented syllables at the end of the verse; only a single harmless instance of correption (v. 7, ζώσῃ ἄπαντα) attracts our attention.[21] The poet's orthography likewise does not mark him out as notably inferior to contemporary practitioners. The parallel pair τειμή/τείω suggests that Appianos has the postclassical habit of regularly using the grapheme <ΕΙ> for the phoneme /i:/. πανχρύσεος, with its nonassimilation of

---

[17] The non-Homeric words: Ῥώμης, Τύχης, ἱερατίδα, Αὐσονίοιο, Ἀππιανός, πανηγύρεως, τόπῳ, κηδείαν, Εὐτυχίας, συνέζησα, γαμέτης, κηδεύσας, and τοὐμόν. Αὐσόνιος occurs in Apollonius (4.553, 590, 660) and under the Empire became a standard way to refer to Romans while maintaining poetic diction and meter. Moretti (245 n. 28) cites *IGR* I.682, *IGUR* 1156, 1163, 1176, 1260, 1294, 1319, and 1334. τόπος occurs in Aeschylus (see LSJ⁹ s.v.); κηδεία in Apollonius (2.836); συζῶ in Aristophanes (*Frag.* 580); γαμέτης in Aeschylus (*Prom.* 897); κηδεύω in Sophocles (*El.* 1141); and though τοὐμόν is not Homeric, it is a crasis of two words that are, of course.

[18] See Moretti 1984–85: 245 n. 26.

[19] Lampe 1961: s.v. ἱερατίς. The *Narratio* induced Lampe to take ἱερατίς as a feminine noun, "priestess." Our inscription shows this is impossible, because ἱερατίδα would be in apposition to τειμήν, which makes no sense. The word is clearly an adjective, used as such here (ἱερατίδα τειμήν "priestly honor") and used substantivally in the *Narratio*. I am grateful to Prof. Bowersock for pointing this out to me.

[20] Moretti 1984–85: 245 n. 28 and Goukowsky 1998: 836 offer the direct translation Αὐσονίοιο κράτους = 'Impero Romano'/'l'empire Ausonien' and Moretti suggests that this might be the first appearance of κράτος with that meaning. Famerie 1998: 11 is more conservative: 'pouvoir de l'empereur ausonien.' Aelius Aristides uses the word with a meaning close to "control" (*Rom.* 66: κράτος ἀρχῆς); Appian uses it for "strength" or "intensity" (*BC* 2.35.141: κατὰ κράτος); For Dio: Freyburger-Galland 1997: 33 (cf. 58–59); *P. Oxy.* 41 I, 2 (late 3ʳᵈ or early 4ᵗʰ century) exhibits the meaning "Empire" (εἰς αἰῶνα τὸ κράτος τῶν Ῥωμαίων). More examples can be found in Bauer-Arndt-Gingrich-Danker 449 s.v. κράτος.

[21] West 1982: 157–59, 181–82.

ν + velar stop (e.g., <NX> for <ΓΧ>) is also nonclassical, but frankly both practices were so widespread in postclassical Greek and *koine* as not to offer any counter-evidence to the proposition that Appianos was well educated.[22]

Though technically rather fastidious, our poet does not exhibit a professional polish. He ranges between the orotund-pompous (ὁ τεθνῶτας καταθεὶς κεῖνος: v. 11) and cliché-prosaic (ἦ συνέζησα βίον: v. 6), though without being enslaved to either style. In my view, the poet's combination of good and mediocre habits is amateurish, evoking a smart, well-read *pepaideumenos* who knows the rules and the ideal he should strive for but lacks the reflexes conferred by long practice.

The thirteenth line, which Moretti described as *extra metrum,* is interesting and merits consideration on its own, quite apart from what it may tell us about Appianos. The differences in the hand that carved it, its open acknowledgement of Eutychia's death, and its segregation in the register running under the *tabula ansata* all suggest that the thirteenth verse was occasioned by Eutychia's death and postdates the distichs above, which do not confront death directly.[23] Given its content, its placement under Eutychia's distichs is natural. Prose codas giving the age of the deceased (usually with some variant of the formula ἐτῶν + number) are so common that it was natural for Moretti and the other commentators to assume this is one of them, especially since the prosaic numeral λα′ (31) brings up the rear.[24]

The thirteenth line is almost certainly a hexameter, however, employing a device which makes assessment of the poet's skill more difficult because despite a certain awkwardness, it betrays genuine ingenuity. For the verse to scan properly, the number at the end must be vocalized as a syllable, a Hellenistic technique stemming from witty poets' attempts to surprise their readers. The flagship example is a sundial inscription from the *Palatine Anthology* reportedly also found inscribed on a sundial in Herculaneum (Kaibel 1122 = *IG* XIV 713 = Page *FGE* 91 = *A. P.* 10.43):

ἓξ ὧραι μόχθοις ἱκανώταται· αἱ δὲ μετ᾽ αὐτάς
γράμμασι δεικνύμεναι ΖΗΘΙ λέγουσι βροτοῖς.

The leisure hours after midday, hours 7, 8, 9, and 10, or ζ′, η′, θ′, and ι′, can be sounded to form the imperative ζῆθι, "enjoy life!" The word γράμμασι prompts us to read the letters individually, as numbers, but the following λέγουσι instantly engineers a perceptual shift, offering a *frisson* of recognition as we see that the clock is actually speaking a word and urging us to enjoy the afternoon.[25] We cannot date this epigram beyond the obvious *terminus ante quem* of AD 79, but it most probably reflects an early, inventive stage in the exploitation of numbers in meter, just as the following

---

[22] <EI> for /i:/ in Attica: Teodorsson 1974: 78, 294–95 and Threatte 1980: 196–99; in Hellenistic Attic, Teodorsson 1978: 21–24; in *koine* translations of Latin documents, García Domingo 1979: 102–103; in papyri of the Roman and Byzantine periods, Gignac 1976: 190. For nonassimilation of NX see Threatte 1980: 588–90 for Attica; Gignac 1976: 168–69 for papyri.

[23] Goukowsky 1998: 835–38 reaches the same conclusion.

[24] Unmetrical: Moretti 1984–85: 243; Famerie 1998: 11; and Goukowsky 1998: 835. Bousquet 1988: 313–314 sees a "heptamètre maladroit," reading the number as τρίακονθ᾽ ἕν.

[25] See Page 1981: 393–94.

examples reflect a later stage, where the impulse to wit has been superseded by a simpler desire to escape a metrical crux.[26]

1)   τέκνα τέκνων ἐσιδὼν Ἑρμῆς Ἑσπέρου ἐτῶν ξ′ (Kaibel 279: "*lege* ξῑ′"), a hexameter which barely limps along by letting the mute plosive κ + liquid ν fail to make position in the first syllable of τέκνων and a defiant thesis lengthening of the penultima of Ἑσπέρου with immediately following correption.

2)   ἡ παναρίστη Σπούδη ἐνθάδε κεῖμαι ἐτῶν κα′ (Wagner 88: "*lege* κα"; = Kaibel 283). This is a functional hexameter once we read the numeral as a syllable and a close parallel to our verse, though here the poet has produced a finer one, preparing the way for the final monosyllable with a bucolic caesura and avoiding breakage of Hermann's rule.[27]

3)   μνησθείης, ἀγαθὴ ψυχή, Γερμανικέ·
      ἡλικίας τριέτης καὶ μηνῶν δ′ ἐνθάδε κεῖται.

In this Roman epitaph (*IG* XIV 1518 = *IGUR* 1182 = Kaibel 701), the number 4, δ′, functions as a simple monosyllable.

If our poet's final verse does not match his earlier efforts, nor stand out against contemporary subliterary production, we might seek an adequate explanation in the content of the verse, his wife's death. Even at that, the forced versification can be balanced against the cleverness of incorporating the number into the meter, the use of the (conveniently dactylic) adjective form δωδεχέτην, which smacks of poetic diction, and the use of the metrically suboptimal ἔλαβον to avoid a form of the prosaically legalistic παραλαμβάνω.[28] The thirteenth verse also sidesteps the tired cliché of giving age at death, making us calculate Eutychia's from the rarer combination of her age at marriage and the duration of her life with Appianos, a type of periphrasis reminiscent of the use of the phrases ἱερατίδα τειμήν and Αὐσονίοιο κράτους discussed above.[29]

We can sharpen our picture of Appianos' epigram even further by contrasting it with a contemporary Alexandrian cenotaph. The Alexandrian jeweller Kanobos died while on a sojourn in Rome and was buried there; his grieving widow caused a cenotaph to be raised in Alexandria. In a 14–verse epigram Kanobos' epigraphic *persona* tells us of his homeland, his profession, the circumstances of his death and the creation of his cenotaph, and concludes with an exhortation to shed a tear over his brief life. Kanobos can be excluded as the poet, and, given what we can deduce of Kanobos' station from his trade, his widow is also an unlikely candidate, despite "his"

---

[26] American personalized license plates offer an apt modern analogy ("GR8 MOM"). We ought not to forget that the entire spectrum of literate Romans exhibited a fascination with letters and games and that this, too, puts Appianos' choice of this device in a more favorable light. See Purcell 1995, esp. 34–37.

[27] West 1982: 37–38, 155, 178; Hermann's bridge in our period: Maas 1962: 62 ("invariably respected"). Hexameters ending with monosyllables: Maas 1962: 64.

[28] See Kajanto 1963: 15 on adjectival forms for numbers and avoidance of legalisms.

[29] In Rome, Kajanto 1963: 13–16 finds duration of marriage in only 25 out of 498 (5%) Greek epitaphs recording marriage, and only 21 out of 1191 Latin ones (1.7%). Our poet uses this tactic to sidestep a cliché statement of age at death, occuring in 42% of the Greek epitaphs of Rome.

telling us that the monument was raised φροντίδι ἐμῆς ἀλόχου.[30] We should bear in mind, therefore, that this is probably the product of a poet-for-hire.

1   Πατρὶς Ἀλεξάνδρεια Μακηδονὶς Αἰγύπτοιο,
      κοσμοτρόφον δάπεδον μεγάλου Πλουτῆος ἄνακτος,
      ἡ δὲ τέχνη χρυσοῖο καὶ ἀργύρου ἠδὲ μετάλλων.
4   Δὶς δέκα ἕξ ζήσας ἔτεσιν καὶ μηνὶ δὲ πέμπτῳ
      λαμπρὸν ἀπ᾽ ὀφθαλμῶν ἔλιπον φάος ἠελίοιο·
      κεῖμαι δ᾽ Εἰταλίδος γαίης νέκυς, ἐν δέκα μησὶν
        ξείνῃ ἐν ἀλλοδαπῇ χειρσὶ ποριζόμενος.
8   Οὔνομα δὴ γενετῆρες ἐμοὶ θήκαντο Κάνωβον.
      Ἐνθάδ᾽ ἐμοῦ φάσεως καθαρὸν τόδε σῆμα πρόκειται,
      φροντίδι ἐμῆς ἀλόχου, παραμυθία συνζοίης,
        στοργῆς μοι τριετοὺς εὐσεβίην θεμένης.
12   Στῆσον ἴχνος, παροδεῖτα, καὶ ἄφθονον ἐνθάδε δάκρυ
      σπείσας ἐκ βλεφάρων κλαῖε τὸν ἐν φθιμένοις
      Αὐσονίων χώρῃ κείμενον ὠκύμορον.

The stichic hexameters are interrupted by pentameters in a pattern that seems random, probably motivated by metrical necessity, and verse 10 cannot be made to function as it stands. Like Appianos, this poet knows elegiac verse is natural to epigram, but is unable to control his product sufficiently to create the canonical alternating verse pattern. Like Appianos, this poet feels the pull of Homeric diction. His epigram has 87 words, of which 78 are not repetitions; 18 words are not to be found in the extant works of Homer, which makes his approach to the ideal nearly as good as Appianos'. As in Appianos' epigram, the exceptions are often compromises to accommodate proper names and matters peculiar to this situation. Ἀλεξάνδρεια, Μακεδονίς, κοσμοτρόφον, μετάλλων, Εἰταλίδος, and similar words occasion no surprise; Πλουτῆος, a form of Pluto's name, has been used for Plutus *metri gratia*; φάσεως has been brought in from astronomical language, it seems; and συνζοίης is best explained as a genitive form of an otherwise unattested συνζοίη.[31] Though this poet recognizably works with many of the same tools and methods as Appianos he is markedly inferior, failing to meet the minimal demands of elegiac verse despite his use as building blocks of the standard tropes of death and lamentation so ably catalogued by Richmond Lattimore. Unlike Appianos, who veers into self-complimentary and complacent description of his success and happiness at the moment he composes his epigram and trumpets his foresight in preparing a burial for himself and Eutychia, our poet has been commissioned to produce an epitaph and has done so in workmanlike

---

[30] Bars to women's self-expression in our period: Swain 1996: 412–13. For text and commentary on the inscription, see Bernand 1969: 102–107 and plate I. The letter forms date the inscription to the first two centuries of our era with editors inclining to the second: Bernand 1969: 103 n. 1.

[31] Πλουτῆος is a (metrically convenient) collateral form of Πλούτωνος, not Πλούτου, the personified god of wealth who is meant here. Εἰταλίδος, like variants of Αὐσόνιος, is not Homeric, and φάσεως has been most convincingly interpreted as being derived from non-Homeric astronomical language. See Bernand 1969: 104–107.

fashion. He registers the bitter complaint of a man who regrets being dead and thinks he was cheated by fate; he acknowledges the grief of the survivors; and he seeks consolatory acknowledgement for the deceased from the world of the living – ideas which in most cases can be traced as far back as the eleventh book of the *Odyssey*.[32] Appianos is not free of the pull of cliché; it is a matter of degree, with Appianos imposing his own self-serving program on his epitaph rather than shaking clichés out of his sleeve and arranging them into a familiar product.

III. THE SARCOPHAGUS

Does the cheap, unpretentious limestone sarcophagus under consideration militate against Appianos' identification with an Alexandrian ἐς τὰ πρῶτα ἥκων ἐν τῇ πατρίδι and ultimately successful enough at Rome to have become an *eques* and reached procuratorial rank?[33] Anyone familiar with the impressive imperial relief sarcophagi produced in earnest in Rome beginning in the second century cannot but initially see ours as shabby.

It is clear from the absence of sophisticated ornamentation that the inscription is the sarcophagus' focal point; what little decoration there is works by symmetry and articulation of space to set the inscription off. This unusual type has few parallels. Koch-Sichtermann publish a few first-century *tabula ansata* types from the vicinity of Rome, but they bear only short Latin inscriptions and lack framing columns.[34] A rapid search turns up a northern Italian type characterized by a squarish *tabula ansata* sometimes surmounted by a tondo portrait of the deceased and other decorative elements between framing columns, human figures, or erotes (clearly another type with at least modest artistic pretentions); a number of sarcophagi from Roman Greece give prominence to the texts they bear, but none are quite like ours.[35] In themselves, *tabulae ansatae* are common enough on sarcophagi that we are not faced with an inexplicable *unicum* here, but with a type which consciously exploits this common element to seek a simultaneous minimum of artistic and maximum of literary pretension. An important and misunderstood *comparandum* demonstrates that our type was suitable for élites and points to the reason why.

A broken tablet which Moretti states once formed part of a sarcophagus was found reused in the steps of the apse of S. Clemente in Rome. It bears a Greek prose inscription (*IGUR* 306; *IG* XIV 1347) in a poorly drafted *tabula ansata* recording that

---

[32] So, for example, loss of the sun's light (v. 5, already implicit at *Iliad* 1.88: Lattimore 1962: 161–165; open acknowledgement of death (κεῖμαι νέκυς, v. 6), references to grieving and concern (φροντίδι ἀλόχου, παραμυθία συνζοίης, v. 10), and the inevitable call to the wayfarer to shed a tear for a man who has died too soon in a foreign land (vv. 12–14): Lattimore 184–87, 234–37.

[33] I thank Prof. Lendon for raising this perceptive question. For what is known of Appian's life see Gabba 1968: vii-xi; Gowing 1992: 9–18; Brodersen 1993: 352–55. The quotation is from Appian's autobiographical notice in the *Roman History* (*Pr.* 14.62).

[34] Koch-Sichtermann 1982: 36–41.

[35] See, for example, Koch-Sichtermann 1982, figures 318–324; 326, 329–330; 332; 345–7; 358–361; 376, 382, 383, 386, 394.

the Antiochene *eques* of procuratorial rank Cocceius Iulianus Synesius (*PLRE* "Synesius" s.v. 2), *vir egregius* and *ducenarius*, set up the memorial (μνήμην) for his wife and child; the sarcophagus is styled τὴν μουσόπλαστον λάρνακα:[36]

Αἰλίᾳ Ματρώνῃ τῇ ἀμειμήτῳ συμβίῳ τὴν μουσόπλαστον λάρνακα |
καὶ Κοκκηίῳ Βεννιανῷ κρατίστῳ τῷ ποθεινοτάτῳ υἱῷ Κοκκήιος |
Ἰουλιανὸς Συνέσιος, κράτιστος δουκηνάριος, Ἀντιοχεὺς τῶν |
πρὸς Δάφνην, τὴν διὰ παντὸς μνήμην ἐποιήσατο.

The editors of *PLRE* understand the titulature κράτιστος δουκηνάριος to reproduce the Latin *vir egregius ducenarius*, a form which dates to the second half of the third century, perhaps a little more than a century after Appianos.[37]

Unfortunately, breakage and reuse of the tablet prompted misinterpretation of the adjective μουσόπλαστον. LSJ[9] offer the definition "ornamented" on the sole basis of this inscription, and they must have consulted only *IG* XIV, which has no illustration. Moretti's interpretation of μουσόπλαστον ("id est sarcophagum Musarum imaginibus condecoratum") appears to follow LSJ[9] but ignores his own published photograph of the barren tablet, which has no hint of any decoration beside the rough *tabula ansata*.[38] The difficulty in considering this inscription is compounded by the poor photograph published by Moretti.

The top and right edges of the face are intact, and the *tabula ansata*, if originally centered on the face horizontally, would have spanned nearly 87% of the face of the sarcophagus. Not only are there no visible framing elements in the small right-hand extremity of the face surrounding the *tabula*'s surviving *ansa*, but the area in and around the *ansa* appears to retain its antique finish. This would serve as a guarantee that decorative elements (such as columns or muses) were not simply chiselled off when the stone was adapted for reuse among the spolia of S. Clemente. Mottling and roughness in the strip above the *tabula ansata* (a register about 21 cm tall) are hard to interpret, but since these marks extend into the area bounded by the *tabula ansata* (which remains intact despite being shallowly drafted), they, too, appear to be excluded as marks caused by stripping away earlier decoration. On top of everything else, a relief band running above a giant *tabula ansata* is typologically unattested in the huge corpus of muse sarcophagi.[39] However, in itself the crudeness of the drafting of the *tabula ansata* is sufficient to show that this sarcophagus never bore the work of an artist.

What this means is that μουσόπλαστος is unattested as a reference to artistic decoration, and we are free to reconsider the word in its context, which is on a barren sarcophagus sporting a longish Greek epitaph composed by a high-ranking *eques* from Antioch. If the allusion to the muses does not refer to plastic decoration the best interpretation appears to be that it is an indirect form of the traditional invocation of

---

[36] Moretti's text (*IGUR* 306).
[37] Date: *SEG* 30.1193; Eck 1980: 275.
[38] LSJ[9] in full: μουσόπλαστος, "ornamented, λάρναξ *IG* 14.1347." Moretti saw the stone in person (1972: 23: "contuli").
[39] Koch-Sichtermann 1982: 197–203.

them in the composition of a text important to the author (cf. Hom. *Od.* 1.1). The inscription adequately attests the concern Cocceius felt to honor his dead wife and son, and like Appianos, he clearly perceived the power of a Greek text. Like Appianos, he made a bold statement by eliminating the artistic embellishment from his sarcophagus in order to make the operative element – the text – stand out the more. If I am right in my interpretation of this tablet, not only can we amend an incorrect entry in LSJ[9], but we can see that Appianos' sarcophagus contrasts very favorably with a similar one commissioned by an equestrian of ducenarius rank.[40] Finally, it appears that Cocceius' sarcophagus reveals a deliberate pretension in its minimalist presentation of a text which may help us understand why such an apparently barren format was appealing to élites. This type of sarcophagus requires further thought, but Cocceius' monument to his wife and son shows us that Appianos' sarcophagus is perfectly suitable for a bureaucrat of Appian's rank.

If we can deduce the (perhaps prospective) existence of a formal space to hold the λάρνακα λαϊνέην from the phrase τῷδ' ... τόπῳ (v. 4), then the date of the inscription, its probable provenience on or near Mons Vaticanus, and the clues to Appianos' high status from the sarcophagus and epigram argue that this space was in all probability a typical contemporary tomb of *opus latericium* lying along one of the roads leading out of Rome along the foot of the Vatican. Indeed, the sarcophagus' suspicious, recent appearance in the immediate vicinity of the Vatican *scavi* (the Camposanto teutonico is about 100 meters from the entrance to the excavations); the secrecy attending the first campaign of excavation under S. Pietro from 1940–1949; the flawed handling of the recovered material (including the temporary misplacing of the alleged bones of St. Peter!); the coincidence of the date attributed to Appianos' sarcophagus and the period during which the necropolis was active (2nd and 3rd centuries AD); and the dismemberment of the cemetery in antiquity to build Constantine's basilica all make the idea that the sarcophagus was found recently somewhere in the ancient fill around S. Pietro attractive.[41] In the absence of an attested provenience, certainty is impossible, of course.

I would like to close with a brief speculation on the significance of the Homeric παγχρυσέοιο in Appianos' epigram. For Moretti and Famerie it is an unremarkable panegyric of the city, and Goukowsky arrives at the same conclusion after explicitly making the argument that it modifies not Τύχης but Ῥώμης, as shown by the place-ment of the caesuras.[42] Our poet, seemingly familiar with the common Latin tradition of styling Rome *aurea* (*prima urbes inter, divum domus, aurea Roma*: Aus. *Ordo* 1;

---

[40] I am dependent upon Moretti's characterization of the tablet as part of a sarcophagus. I would suggest "fashioned by the muses" or "fashioned with the aid of the muses" as suitable replacements for the current entry in LSJ[9].

[41] On the Vatican excavations see Guarducci 1992 (with bibliography).

[42] Moretti 1984–84: 243: "Io, Appiano, che dal sovrano dell' Impero degli Ausoni ho l'onore del sacerdozio di Tyche di Roma tutta d'oro;" Famerie 1998: 11: "La Fortune de Rome qui brille de ses ors, j'en ai le sacerdoce, don du pouvoir de l'empereur ausonien;" Goukowsky 1998: 836: "Moi qui tiens du souverain de l'empire Ausonien le prêtrise de la Fortune de Rome toute d'or." On l'épithet de Rome, Goukowsky 1998: 836 nn. 12–13.

cf. also Juvenc. *Pr.* 2; Ov. *Ars* 3.113; Mart. 9.59.2), dresses up the epithet a bit and domesticates it for Greek poetry by using a Homeric compound form. Why "golden"? If not simply because the epithet was ready to hand, we might think of gold's moral implication (as early as Hesiod *Op.* 109–126). Would it be too much to suggest that a priest of the cult of Venus and Rome, perhaps, as Goukowsky argues, composing his epitaph during Hadrian's reign, might have had the physically dazzling gilt-bronze roofs of such recent contemporary Trajanic and Hadrianic architectural wonders as the Basilica Ulpia and the Pantheon in mind?[43] We might in fact unite both interpretations, seeing a reference to the outward strength of Rome, symbolized by the wealth of the city, reflecting a perceived moral strength within.

IV. CONCLUSION

Was Appianos the historian Appian? Even if we are persuaded by the epigram's contents, we must admit frankly that the case falls short of being established. Goukowsky's identification of the priesthood helps but does not advance us too far, because we know so little about the composition of the college and its functions. Appianos' occasional sinking diction, his odd final verse, and his seemingly non-descript limestone sarcophagus do require careful consideration, but when duly considered cannot be used to pose material objections to the identification of the poet with the equestrian procurator Appian. The next stage in the study of this inscription, to which I have attempted to point the way in this essay, ought to be an analysis of the rhetorical strategies and stylistic devices employed by the poet, and a comparison of the poem with other contemporary epitaphs with the goal of understanding the poet's purposes in placing this epigram on this odd sarcophagus in a Roman context.

WORKS CITED

Bauer-Arndt-Gingrich-Danker = Arndt, W., Gingrich, F.W. 1979. *A Greek-English Lexicon of the New Testament and other Early Christian Literature*², revised and augmented by F.W. Gingrich and F.W. Danker. Chicago.

Bernand, É. 1969. *Inscriptions métriques de l'Égypte gréco-romaine. Recherches sur la poésie épigrammatique des grecs en Égypte. Annales Littéraires de l'université de Besançon*, vol. 98. Paris.

Bousquet, J. 1988. *Bulletin Épigraphique* 69: 313–314.

Bowie, E.L. 1989. "Greek Sophists and Greek Poetry in the Second Sophistic." *ANRW* II 33.1: 209–258.

———. 1990. "Greek Poetry in the Antonine Age." In D.A. Russell, ed., *Antonine Literature*. Oxford. 53–90.

Bowra, C.M. 1961. *Greek Lyric Poetry from Alcman to Simonides*². Oxford.

Brodersen, K. 1993. "Appian und sein Werk." *ANRW* II 34.1: 339–363.

Dihle, A. 1994. *A History of Greek Literature from Homer to the Hellenistic Period*. Trans. C. Krojzl. London.

Eck, W. 1980. Rev. of *IGUR* II.1 and II.2. *Gnomon* 52: 273–276.

---

[43] On the gilt roofing of the Basilica Ulpia and Pantheon (and possibly the rest of the Forum of Trajan and the Capitolium), see Packer 1997, I: 241, 442, based upon Paus. 5.12.6, 10.5.11.

Famerie, É. 1998. *Le latin et le grec d'Appien. Contribution à l'étude du lexique d'un historien grec de Rome*. Geneva.

Fein, S. 1994. *Die Beziehungen der Kaiser Trajan und Hadrian zu den Litterati*. Stuttgart.

Freyburger-Galland, M.-L. 1997. *Aspects du vocabulaire politique et institutionnel de Dion Cassius*. Paris.

Gabba, E. 1967. *Appiani Bellorum civilium liber primus*[2]. Florence.

García Domingo, E. 1979. *Latinismos en la koiné (en los documentos epigráficos desde el 212 a. J. C. hasta el 14 d. J. C.). Grammática y léxico griego-latino, latino-griego*. Burgos.

Gignac, F.T. 1976. *A Grammar of the Greek Papyri of the Roman and Byzantine Periods*. Vol. I, *Phonology*. Milan.

Goukowsky, P. 1998. "Appien d'Alexandrie, prêtre de Rome sous Hadrien?" *Comptes rendus des séances – Académie des inscriptions & belles lettres* fascicle III, Jul.-Oct. 1998: 835–856.

Gowing, A.M. 1992. *The Triumviral Narratives of Appian and Cassius Dio*. Ann Arbor.

Guarducci, M. 1992. "Vatican: Investigations under St. Peter's Basilica." In *The Encyclopedia of the Early Church* II.862. Oxford.

Kaibel, G. 1878. *Epigrammata Graeca ex lapidibus conlecta*. Berlin.

Kajanto, I. 1963. *A Study of the Greek Epitaphs of Rome. Acta Instituti Romani Finlandiae* II:3. Helsinki.

Koch, G. and H. Sichtermann. 1982. *Römische Sarkophage*. Munich.

Lampe, G.W.H. 1961. *A Patristic Greek Lexicon*. Oxford.

Lattimore, R. 1962. *Themes in Greek and Roman Epitaphs*. Urbana.

Maas, P. 1962. *Greek Metre*. Oxford.

Moretti, L. 1972–1990. *Inscriptiones Graecae Urbis Romae* I-IV. Rome.

———. 1984–1985. "Due epigrammi greci inediti di Roma." *RPAA* 57: 233–246.

Packer, J.E. 1997. *The Forum of Trajan in Rome*. 2 vols. Berkeley.

Page, D.L. 1981. *Further Greek Epigrams*. Rev. by R.D. Dawe and J. Diggle. Cambridge.

Peek, W. 1955. *Griechische Vers-Inschriften. I. Grab-Epigramme*. Berlin.

Poltera, O. 1997. *Le langage de Simonide*. Bern.

Purcell, N. 1995. "Literate Games: Roman Urban Society and the Game of *Alea*." *P&P* 147: 3–37.

Segal, C. 1985. "Choral Lyric of the Fifth Century." In P.E. Easterling and B.W. Knox, eds., *The Cambridge History of Classical Literature*. Cambridge. 222–244

Swain, S. 1996. *Hellenism and Empire. Language, Classicism, and Power in the Greek World AD 50–250*. Oxford.

Teodorsson, S.-T. 1974. *The Phonemic System of the Attic Dialect 400—340 B.C.* Lund.

———. 1977. *The Phonology of Ptolemaic Koine*. Lund.

———. 1978. *The Phonology of Attic in the Hellenistic Period*. Lund.

Threatte, L. 1980. *The Grammar of Attic Inscriptions. Vol. 1 Phonology*. Berlin.

Wagner, R. 1883. *Quaestiones de epigrammatis graecis ex lapidibus collectis grammaticae*. Leipzig.

West, M.L. 1982. *Greek Metre*. Oxford.

Wifstrand, A. 1933. *Von Kallimachos zu Nonnos. Metrische-stilistische Untersuchungen zur späteren griechischen epik und zu verwandten Gedichtgattungen*. Publications of the New Society at Lund 16. Lund.

Wilhelm, A. 1938. "Das Epithalmion in Lukianos' Συμπόσιον ἢ Λαπίθαι." *WS* 56: 54–89.

14

The First Tragic Contest: Revision Revised[*]

Anne P. Burnett

It has been customary in recent years to refer to the tragic performances at the Greater Dionysia as beginning possibly in the time of the Pisistratids but more probably under Cleisthenes. The later date, however, disrupts the antique view of the initial development of the tragic genre, for if the first City contests are postponed until ca. 501 B.C., the early victories attributed to Thespis, Choerilus and Phrynichus must either be discounted as ancient fictions,[1] or explained away as rural performances.[2] Worse, the evolving generic characteristics noted by ancient scholars – extended length, a second actor, replacement of make-up with masks, chorus members with female personae, more elaborate metres and hundreds of new dance-patterns[3] – must all have appeared in a single dazzling decade. These difficulties seem serious enough to suggest a review of the case for Cleisthenic foundation.

The trend towards the later dating owes much to an article by W.R. Connor entitled, "City Dionysia and Athenian Democracy,"[4] where there is a double line of argument. A positive assertion of the appropriateness of a god called Eleuthereus to the new democracy is followed by a debunking of the epigraphical evidence for foundation under the tyrants. It comes in second place, but the discrediting of the accepted Pisistratid date is essential to the case, and the attack upon the late, dubious, and now illegible witness of item no. 43 of the Marmor Parium has an initial air of success. In that third-century chronicle a dramatic victory is reported for Thespis as falling in one of the years between 538 and 528 B.C.[5] Or more generally as coming after Pisistratus' final assumption of power, item 40, and before the deed of

---

[*] For A.L.B. after almost fifty years of friendship.

[1] Aristoxenus accused Heraclides Ponticus of attributing works of his own to Thespis (Diog. Laert. 5.92).

[2] The Suda lists four titles for Thespis; also a victory for Phrynichus in 511 B.C., while it records Choerilus' first tragic contest in 523/0; see Sickinger 1999: 44.

[3] The inventions of Phrynichus alone were reputed countless as the waves of the sea in a winter storm: Plut. *Quaest. conv.* 8.732f.

[4] Connor 1990.

[5] The year-count number is not complete and the gap could contain from three to five unit-signs; see West 1989: 253 n. 13.

Harmodius and Aristogeiton, item 45. Jacoby reviewed reports from men who had seen the stone in better condition, considered earlier scholarly conjectures, and produced the following text (*FGrHist* 239 A 43):

ἀφ' οὗ Θέσπις ὁ ποιητὴς [ὑπεκρίνα]το πρῶτος, ὃς ἐδίδαξε δρᾶμ[α ἐν
ἄ]στει, [καὶ ἆθλον ἐ]τέθη ὁ [τ]ράγος, ἔτη ΗΗΓ[ΔΔ], ἄρχοντος
Ἀθ[ήνη|σι] ... ναιου τοῦ προτέρου.

Nothing to do with the Greater Dionysia, says Connor, noting that the phrase ἐν ἄστει is a conjecture which stands in a space where some early observers thought they saw the letters ΝΑΛΣΤΙΝ. From which he concludes that this entry actually records a victory won by Thespis somewhere in the country.[6]

To this there are serious objections. The Parian who composed this list knew a universal history and a collection of Heuremata but he also used one or more of the Atthidographers,[7] and when his chronicle records an Attic epoch-event, that event always belongs to the City of Athens. Connor does not note the one case in which an extra-City event *is* mentioned, but it is most instructive. Item no. 39 reports an innovation in the festival calendar of Athens, the establishment of the City's first comic chorus, with prize, archon year, and year-count from the present all noted. Extra information about the rural beginnings of the genre is also included, but in a dangling phrase that interrupts the formula for a City event:

ἀφ' οὗ ἐν Ἀθ[ήν]αις κωμω[ιδῶν χο]ρ[ὸς ἐτ]έθη, [στη]σάν[των
πρώ]των Ἰκαριέων, εὑρόντος Σουσαρίωνος, καὶ ἆθλον ἐτέθη κτλ.

Following Connor's suppositions, this model might have produced an item placed after no. 46 (first men's dithyrambic chorus) in which the city's first tragic contest was noted with a victor's name, while an aside gave credit to Thespis as inventor of the performance-type. The comic model would not, however, have found imitation in the item no. 43 that Connor would restore, one that took as its major event a small-time victory won in some out-of-town contest. And in fact there is no evidence for the existence of rural choral contests anywhere in 6th century Attica, much less of one important enough to boast a list of victors and a fixed date of foundation.[8]

As for the witness of the so-called Fasti (*IG* II² 2318), ostensibly a record of victories starting at the beginning of the Dionysia, Connor simply quotes from Pickard-Cambridge: "It certainly would not have gone back as far as 534 B.C. ... perhaps the most probable view places the beginning of the record in or about 501 B.C."[9] It is notable, however, that the same authority ended his more detailed investigation in a much more open position: "there can be no certainty as to the date when the record began."[10] Difficulties abound, since the number of columns missing

---

[6] Connor 1990: 32 suggests no alternative to Jacoby's formulaic ἐν ἄστει; he favors Ikaria as the site of Thespis' first victory but does not attempt to find this name on the stone.

[7] Jacoby 1904: 88–93; 1949: 227 n. 5.

[8] Earliest evidence is from an Ikarian decree, *IG* I³ 254 (2nd half of fifth c.); see Whitehead 1986: 212.

[9] Connor 1990: 12, citing Pickard-Cambridge 1968: 72.

[10] Pickard-Cambridge 1968: 103.

at the beginning of this list is not known, while the preserved columns vary between 140 and 141 lines.[11] Furthermore, no one can be sure exactly when the dithyrambic contests were first included in the Dionysia or what form the record might have taken before that year.[12] Consequently calculations about the number of lost entries, and therefore the number of festivals reported, cannot be definitive. Martin West, for example, concluded that if the dithyrambic victories began in 509/8, if the choregic system went back before the time of Cleisthenes, if the heading τραγωιδῶν was not repeated in the pre-dithyrambic section (and why should it be?), and if one column was lost at the beginning, then the Fasti could have begun as early as 528 B.C.,[13] which is also the latest possible reading of the year set by the Marmor Parium for the victory of Thespis. Nothing is proved, but it is obvious that the Fasti cannot be cited as destroying the tradition of a Pisistratid foundation for the tragic contest.

Finally, there is another inscription with a missing first column or columns that is relevant. This is the record of tragic victors at *IG* II² 2325. Assuming that a single initial column has been lost, Cavaignac asserted that this list could not have begun earlier than 510 B.C. because the lost lines could have listed only eight poets for the years before the first Aeschylean victory in 484 B.C.[14] With two lost columns, however, there would be space for twenty-three names, as Snell pointed out,[15] and this total could easily stretch back into the 520's or 530's, since favorites like Choerilus were reputed to have had multiple victories.[16] The number of poets ready to work in the new genre must have been extremely limited in the beginning; there might even have been years when fresh rivals could not be found and old pieces had to be replayed.[17] Later antiquity believed that, though he was trained by Thespis, Phrynichus took the prize only in 511/08,[18] before which time the master-poet presumably won repeatedly (though later scholars remembered only four of his titles). The names of a small group of early multiple victors would have demanded a minimum number of lines.

In sum, the epigraphical evidence does not support the notion of a Cleisthenic inauguration of tragic performances at the City Dionysia, nor does it destroy the traditional connection with the tyranny. Instead it seems to indicate a date round about 528 B.C. for a first tragic victory won in Athens in a dramatic contest established in

---

[11] Capps 1943: 9.

[12] Cavaignac 1947: 3–4 concluded that the men's dithyrambic contest was not introduced until ca. 502 B.C. with the boys' coming after, perhaps in 498; West on the other hand assumes that both came in 509/8 (1989: 251 n. 1).

[13] West 1989: 251 n. 1.

[14] Cavaignac: 1947: 2–3.

[15] Snell 1966: 37.

[16] The thirteen recorded for Choerilus by the Suda (s.v.) would seriously crowd the decades just after 500 B.C. (=*TGrF* i 2 T1).

[17] " Hier wage ich keine Entscheidung, zumal nicht einmal feststeht, wann die Eintragungen begannen, ob in dieser frühen Zeit die Wettkämpfe immer regelmässig stattfanden und on (sic) man sorgfältig über sie Buch führte" (Snell 1966: 37).

[18] In all, he had seven victorious dramas whose titles were duly remembered; Suda s.v. Φρύνιχος =*TGrF* i. 3 T1.

the later years of Pisistratus.[19] But what about the positive arguments urged to prove that the City Dionysia, and consequently tragedy, are innately Cleisthenic and democratic? These center on the cult title, Eleuthereus, which is proposed as proof, first, that the festival was introduced at the time of the annexation of Eleutherae, and second, that it proclaimed itself an expression of a new freedom experienced by Attic citizens. Since it is not necessary to annex territory in order to take in a cult from abroad, since it is not known when this particular cult entered Attica,[20] and finally since the incorporation of the border township of Eleutherae cannot itself be dated, the first assertion dwindles to nothing. Connor can only claim that "it would not be surprising" if a "likely" annexation, made "probably" in 506 B.C., "were marked by some addition to Athenian cults" (1990: 10, 11, 12). And even this is too strong, because the *aition* of the Eleuthereus cult depends upon the essential *foreignness* of the god who is introduced. He comes from the time when kings ruled (Paus. 1.2.4), and he is called Eleuthereus because his statue was brought from the realm of King Eleuther, whose daughters had been driven mad, then healed.[21] His exotic celebrations seemed ridiculous and repugnant to Athenians who finally received him only after they had been fearfully stricken in their private parts (schol. Ar. *Acharn.* 243a). The story, in other words, has everything to do with Dionysus, but nothing to do with any change in the political status of Eleutherae.[22]

It is also held that, because it celebrates a god called Eleuthereus, the City Dionysia must have been the invention of a city newly freed from tyranny and conscious of its democratic *eleutheria*.[23] The cult title was admittedly traditional, but by this argument the City discovered in the name a kind of political pun that made the Dionysus of this name a god who *liberated* men from tyrants.[24] As they make this argument, advocates of a Cleisthenic festival must dismiss recent discussions of the term *eleutheria*, wherein the sense of internal political freedom is shown to develop only after the

---

[19] There is, however, no sure indication that the performance of the first "tragedies" coincided with the inauguration of the City Dionysia. "It is not implausible that Pisistratus should have assisted the process" (an expansion of the Dionysia) "by some particular initiative of his own. But it should be remembered that this is mere assumption" (West 1989: 254).

[20] Without comment Connor 1990: 9 n. 9 notes, "Ernst Badian has pointed out that the text of Pausanias" (1.2.5) "admits the possibility that the *xoanon* had been conveyed to Athens before the incorporation of Eleutherae into Attica."

[21] Suda s.v. Μελαναιγίς Διονυσός 451. For association with the phallic procession of the Dionysia, see Burkert 1985: 122 n. 3.

[22] Nilsson (1951: 129) said categorically: "Die Kultübertragung ist natürlich nicht an den politischen Zusammenschluss gebunden." Compare Sourvinou-Inwood 1994: 275, "it is clear that the festival of the City Dionysia must not be interpreted as an annexation ritual and its origins must not be tied with the history of Eleutherai."

[23] As if the popularity of Liberace in America in the 1950's were to be seen as proof of libertarian beliefs among the oldsters of that time.

[24] Connor 1990: 8. In support of this idea Connor describes the reception of Demetrius Poliorcetes in 307 B.C. and suggests that "behind both the honors paid to Demetrius and the establishment of the City Dionysia may have been a common ritual pattern used to celebrate the end of an oppressive rule" (18–19). In contradiction, Sourvinou-Inwood 1994: 277 argues that the ritual pattern in both cases has nothing to do with liberation, but is one of *xenismos* offered to a god on his arrival.

Persian War.[25] Their one seeming support comes from Herodotus' mention (3.142) of a new cult of Zeus Eleutherios, founded on Samos on the occasion of Polykrates' fall. This detail, however, occurs in a chapter clearly meant to flatter an immediate Athenian audience by producing a negative foil.[26] Unlike the Athenians, says the historian, the Samians when their tyrant fell had neither the sense nor the courage to create a city of equality (*isonomia*): they were a people who did not wish to be free (οὐ γὰρ δή ... ἐβούλοντο εἶναι ἐλεύθεροι). [27] Their Eleutherios cult was founded, not by the demos but by a weak ex-tyrant, Maeandrius, who was in fact only looking for a priesthood.[28] All of which is tailor-made for Herodotus' explanation of why Samos was the first Hellenic city to fall to the Persians (3.139), but not a strong witness to an early anti-tyrannical cult of Zeus Eleutherios on Samos. Nor would such a cult, were it well-documented, indicate that the Dionysus Eleuthereus of Athens was a god inimical to tyrants and associated with their overthrow. He was a divinity who punished his enemies with sickness or blight, then removed these physical sufferings when he was accepted.[29] Through drunkenness and ecstatic possession his power released people from slavery to the mundane, momentarily making equals of all, but nothing in his legends or his rites suggests a particular political sense.[30]

II.

In largest outline the Greater Dionysia was shaped as a rite of *xenismos*, as the City welcomed an incoming god. There was a defining procession in which the cult statue and the divinity's special insignia, borne by the *phallophoroi,* were brought in from outside and carried from place to place. Minor celebrations at the shrines of other gods expressed the reception of Eleuthereus into the civic religion,[31] and Xenophon (*Hipparch.* 3.2) mentions in particular choruses that rejoiced at the altar of the Twelve Gods (dedicated by Hippias, probably in 522/1). These lesser performances, however, were capped by choral dancing for Dionysus himself, probably held in the Agora until the early 5th century, when there was a catastrophic collapse of bleachers (Photius s.v. ἴκρια). [32] This ultimate dancing for Dionysus, however, was in two ways unlike the

---

[25] See, e.g., Raaflaub 1981 and 1985.

[26] On the fictive quality of the "Samian logoi," see Immerwahr 1956–7: 320.

[27] Ostwald 1969: 165 is ready to suppose that Maeandrius was the "source" of Cleisthenes' notion of *isonomia*, but it seems far more likely that Herodotus reversed the direction of influence, making his Samians fail in their fictive prevision of later Athenian concepts.

[28] This would be, by half a century, the earliest political cult foundation, and it would celebrate liberation, not from a foreign enemy (as in the case of the mainland Zeus Eleutherios cult after Plataea) but from a tyrant. Raaflaub 1985: 139 notes, however, that Maeandrius' foundation would also represent (according to Herodotus) a private manoevre for power on the part of the tyrant's successor, not a public act of thanks for liberation. He asks why such a cult would have survived, since according to the tale the manoevre failed and the newly appointed priest left the country.

[29] Schol. Ar. *Ach.* 243.

[30] Cf. Berve 1967: 60, who calls it an "unpolitischen Kult."

[31] Sourvinou-Inwood 1994: 283.

[32] But see Webster's dissent, Pickard-Cambridge 1962: 145 n. 1.

celebrations of the other gods: first, because it was set up in contest form, and second, because it was (in the 5th century at any rate) reduplicated. Groups of singing dancers rivalled one another in a pair of competitions, and though the two performance-modes were closely similar, these two tests were organized and administered in two very different ways. In the tragic competition, two or three poets from Attica or elsewhere were chosen by the archon; each found an unspecified number of dancers, taught them to sing, dressed them, perhaps gave them masks, and in the beginning themselves took spoken parts that interrupted the choral song. (Even after the choregic system was introduced, the poet was paramount.) In the dithyrambic competition, by contrast, ten choral-leaders appointed by the ten tribes each chose a poet and saw to the training and dressing of 50 boys or men who would perform in unmasked unison. The one contest produced, as victor, a single artist who might hail from anywhere, and so it proclaimed the City as a pan-Hellenic centre of artistic activity and innovation.[33] The other made two of the City's tribes victorious, thus strengthening tribal loyalties and glorifying the inner order of post-Cleisthenic Athens.[34]

In the revised chronological scheme, Cleisthenes at some time between 509 and 501 B.C. founds a Dionysia which features just one choral contest, that of the dithyramb, organized through and for the newly defined tribes.[35] Then, after a few years, he adds a second contest[36] held among poets who specialize in the mixed genre in which speaker and chorus both impersonate fictive creatures. This "rural" performance has supposedly been polished through decades of country competition, so that it is ready to accommodate an Aeschylus, but this cannot have been the case because the double choral contests of the Greater Dionysia (whenever established) represent a new phenomenon[37] to which the City's comic competitions[38] offer the single parallel. Early choral rites did not take a competitive form,[39] either in Attica or anywhere else. Singing dancers were of central importance in the great Spartan festivals but no ancient description pits one band against another in pre-classical

---

[33] After the reorganization of Cleisthenes the list of potential judges came from the ten tribes; it was reduced by Council selection, and by the archon's draw; finally the votes of five of the ten, selected by the archon's draw, were actually counted.

[34] The choregos actually accepted the prize, but as representative of his tribe.

[35] One wonders why he would have put his new festival under the control of the eponymous archon and a group of *epimeletai* chosen by the Assembly with no reference to tribal representation (Pickard-Cambridge 1968: 58).

[36] Connor 1990: 13 puts this event in close association with the addition of comedy.

[37] As at Delos and Delphi, there were at the Panathenaia earlier contests for individual rhapsodes and instrumentalists which some associated with Solon (Diog. Laert. 1.57), others with Hipparchus (ps.-Plat. *Hipp.* 228b); see Davison 1958. Herodotus (5.67.1) reported seventh-century rhapsodic contests in Sikyon.

[38] Marmor Parium, item 39. See Pickard-Cambridge 1962: 18; Parke 1977: 104. Kolb 1977: 125, 132 argued that this was part of an aristocratic enlargement of the Lenaia festival, the new performances taking place in the orchestra of a Lenaion in the Agora.

[39] No one of the 17 items in Appendix I of Herington (1985: 161–66) bears witness to choruses *in competition*. The women's races at the Temple of Hera at Olympia seem not to have been choral, and the race referred to in Alcman's Parthenaion is most probably metaphorical.

times.[40] Herodotus, speaking of the "tragic" choruses of Sikyon (5.67.5), does not use any phrase that suggests competition, and Thucydides, when describing the old-time Delian festival, cleanly separates the dances produced by various cities from the contests of athletes and musicians (3.104.3–6).[41] In Attica, country festivals were evidently becoming more elaborate in the 6th century, as witness the new comic choruses in Ikaria (Marmor Parium, item 39), but the earliest indication of a choral competition held outside Athens comes only in the second half of the 5th century.[42] In the pre-Cleisthenic townships, cult activities were in the hands of traditional priestly organizations, expenses coming from their treasuries, or from specified kinship groups, while choruses were drawn traditionally from particular age-groups or families.[43] From time to time the authorities might have decided that a certain festival should be celebrated more lavishly than last year, perhaps with additional sacrifices, finer costumes, or even a commissioned song to replace the traditional chant. They would not, however, have had either motive or means for setting up multiple bands of dancers to compete with one another.[44] (In a strictly cultic setting, what would become of a defeated group?) Custom-bound rural festivals without money or competitive pressure would not have disguised locals proud of their right to appear in an annual chorus, nor would they have encouraged longer and more complicated speeches from an impersonating leader who might even represent a woman.[45]

This being the case, anyone subscribing to the later foundation of the Dionysia must explain why Cleisthenes would set up a rough and puny country dance-mode as a worthy partner for his tribal dithyrambs, and why he would organize his second choral contest so differently from the first.[46] Why admit foreign poets as potential victors, and why let choruses be drawn from any place and any age-group, so that even non-citizens might dance? Why, furthermore, would a leader who was expanding a new-made festival in the first decade of the fifth century establish the *proagōn* as preliminary to his tragic contest? This curious institution demanded that each competing poet should, on the day of the opening procession, appear with his uncostumed chorus[47] at

---

[40] Plutarch, at *Ages.* 29, speaks of ἀγωνιζομένων χορῶν in 4th c. Sparta, placing them "in the theatre."

[41] Speaking of the time after the Pisistratid purification, Thucydides says that there were individual contests of athletes and musicians, and cities sent choruses; then the *agones* fell into disuse, but choruses were still sent by Athenians and islanders. For Hellenistic choregic monuments on Delos, see *BCH* 7 (1883): 103–25. Bacchylides 17 is sometimes cited as proof of Delian contests of paians or dithyrambs, but the closing prayer need not be a prayer for victory; see bibliography cited by Schröder 2000 passim.

[42] *IG* I³ 254, an Ikarian decree where the appointment of two choregoi suggests, though it does not prove, a contest; see Whitehead 1986: 215–18. The dramatic contests of the 4th c. demes seem to have been imitations of the City's festivals; see Pickard-Cambridge 1968: 51.

[43] At Arist. *Ath. Pol.* 21.6 Cleisthenes respects old priesthoods belonging to particular families and phratries; see Whitehead 1986: 177 n. 3; Frost 1990: 5.

[44] Burkert 1966: 95 speaks of "the general inflexibility of Greek cults."

[45] Suda s.v. Φρύνιχος 762 .

[46] Why, moreover, would he put the festival as a whole under the direction of *epimeletai* elected by the people at large? This, according to Arist. *Ath. Pol.* 56.4, was the original arrangement, only later changed so as to represent the tribes.

[47] This heightened the effect of Sophocles' gesture, in honor of Euripides' death, when he robed his chorus in black for its appearance at this preliminary test; *Vita Eurip.* 3.11 Schwartz.

a certain place (the Odeion, once it was built),[48] there to describe (ἀπαγγέλλειν, Schol. Ar.*Vesp.* 1109) and demonstrate (ἐπιδείξεσθαι Pl. *Symp.* 194b) to the people (Plato makes Agathon call them *aphronoi*) the dramas he means to enter in the upcoming competition.[49] The structure of the test implies that a poet might fail, yet as soon as the machinery for granting choruses and naming choregoi was in place the required appearance, on the eve of the contest, of poets long since hired by the city (*demoteleis*)[50] represented the height of futility. Which is the point of Socrates' ironic praise of Agathon's "courage" as he faced the public at his *proagōn*.[51] In sum, then, since this institution was just as redundant among the dramatic preliminaries of the first decade of the 5th century as it was in the times of Sophocles and Agathon, we can only conclude that it was put in place before, not in conjunction with, the contest arrangements that are reflected in the Fasti. Among practices that rendered it obsolete it will have been observed as an honored remnant from an older festival program.[52]

Since the Greater Dionysia's contests in tragedy and dithyramb describe the celebrating City in two different ways, the easiest assumption is that they came into being in two different phases of the City's history. [53] The Marmor Parium notes the existence of tragic contests in the City before the death of Pisistratus, then places the inauguration of the men's contest in the dithyramb after the exploit of the tyrannicides, and this sequence – unquestioned in antiquity – is by far the easiest to accept. The Pisistratid festival will have come into being when the eponymous archon was given supervision of an annual procession for Eleuthereus, a holiday which was evidently not in the control of a rigid college of priests. And the choral contest that nurtured tragedy will have been introduced if not immediately then soon after, for prizes were reputedly being won at least as early as the '20's of the sixth century. Then, as the dramatic competition gained in notoriety, the festival's original organization was evidently expanded to give civic aid to the poet-trainers who were to take part.[54] The City thus provided rivalry, money, and fame as spurs to innovation, while the dramatists supplied a new mode in which tales were not told but enacted. There was, after all, a rightness in the combination of drama with this festival, since taking in a new and slightly unruly performance from the country was analogous to taking in the

---

[48] The Odeion became also the locale of official post-performance scrutiny; see Melchinger 1974: 14.

[49] Aeschin. 3. 66–7 (*Against Ctesiphon*) and schol.; also *Vita Eurip.* (Dindorf *P. Scen.* 17.47). See Rohde 1883: 251–68; Pickard-Cambridge 1968: 63–4, 67–8; Melchinger 1974: 14, 42, 129, 251 n. 39.

[50] See Rohde 1883: 261, who could explain the practice only as a kind of enacted *pronunciatio tituli* (268); Melchinger 1974: 42 calls it simply the "fierliche Eröffnung des Festes"; Parke 1977: 133 suggests that it provided necessary "publicity."

[51] Pl. *Symp.* 194b.

[52] After 420 the *proagōn* became entangled in the sacrifices for Asclepius (Aeschin. loc.cit.) There was a *proagōn* also at the Lenaia, but it is notable that this preliminary was not imitated in the dramatic festivals that other cities copied from the Athenian; see Rohde 1883: 259, 264.

[53] Or, as Sourvinou-Inwood 1994: 276 would have it: "the articulation into Cleisthenic tribes of the agonistic segment was superimposed onto an earlier nexus that was otherwise articulated."

[54] "The great innovation … was the assumption by the Demos of the responsibility for the maintenance of the contests ... by the system of choregi ... who were appointed by the archon for the tragedies"(Capps 1943: 10); this flexibility allowed the later absorption of purely civic actions like the reception of ambassadors, display of tribute, etc. See Pickard-Cambridge 1968: 59; Goldhill 1994: 368.

god, and also to taking in outsiders who arrived with the beginning of the sailing season.

Viewed as a whole this carnival-like celebration of the openness of a City that welcomes strangers suits the last decades of the tyrants much better than it would the time of Cleisthenes. And consider the one detail already mentioned. The *proagōn* is finally explicable if it was designed as a preliminary process necessary to the newly devised contest in its original form. Accompanied by their dancers, self-selected poets,[55] both known and unknown, good and bad, would gather on the eve of a contest, attracted by its prize. All were required to make an initial uncostumed appearance, but only a few groups would be allowed to compete, while the others would be refused as unprepossessing or badly trained, or because their announced material was offensive. (If, for example, this simpler system of selection had still been effective in 494 B.C., Phrynichus' play about Miletus might never have been staged.) The entire festival was officially under the direction of the archon but he did not yet choose the contenders for the dramatic *agon*, nor were *choregoi* yet appointed to support the chosen. Instead, an accidental sample from tomorrow's audience – whoever happened to be gathered at a specified public place – was allowed to decide which poets might and which might not lead out their choruses.[56]

WORKS CITED

Berve, H. 1967. *Die Tyrannis bei den Griechen*. Munich.

Burkert, W. 1966. "Greek Tragedy and Sacrificial Ritual." *GRBS* 7:87–121.

———. 1985. "Herodot über die Namen der Götter." *MH* 42: 121–32.

Capps, E. 1943. "A New Fragment of the List of Victors." *Hesperia* 12: 1–11.

Cavaignac, E. 1947. "Les Fastes du Théatre Attique au Ve siècle." *Publication de la Faculté des Lettres de l'Université de Strasbourg*, fasc.106, vol. III. 1–31.

Connor, W.R. 1990. "City Dionysia and Athenian Democracy." *In Aspects of Athenian Democracy. Classica et Mediaevalia* XL. Copenhagen. 7–32.

Davison, J.A. 1958. "Notes on the Panathenaia." *JHS* 78: 23–42.

Frost, F.J. 1990. "Peisistratus, the Cults and the Unification of Attica." *AW* 21: 3–9.

Goldhill, S. 1994. "Representing Democracy." In R. Osborne, S. Hornblower, eds., *Ritual, Finance, Politics*. Oxford. 360–69.

Herington, C.J. 1985. *Poetry into Drama*. Berkeley.

Immerwahr, H. 1956–7. "Samian Stories." *CR* 52: 312–22.

Jacoby, F. 1904. "Ueber das Marmor Parium." *RhM* 59: 61–107.

———. 1949. *Atthis*. Oxford.

Kinzl, K.H. 1980. "Zur Vor- und Frühgeschichte der attischen Tragödie." *Klio* 62: 177–90.

Kolb, F. 1977. "Die Bau- Religions- und Kulturpolitik der Pisistratiden." *JdI* 92: 99–138.

de Libero, L. 1996. *Die archaische Tyrannis*. Stuttgart.

Melchinger, E. 1974. *Das Theater der Tragödie*. Munich.

Nilsson, M. 1951. "Der Ursprung der Tragödie." *Opuscula Selecta* I. Lund. 61–145.

Ostwald, M. 1969. *Beginnings of the Athenian Democracy*. Oxford.

---

[55] What Capps 1943: 10 called ἐθελονταί.

[56] Plato obviously had the *proagōn* in mind at *Laws* 7. 817 b-d, when he imagined tragic poets from abroad who approached the city asking, "May we pay your city and its territory a visit or may we not? May we bring our poetry with us, or what decision have you reached ?" Note in particular ἐπιδείξαντες in the recommended revised procedure which will ideally bring such visitors before magistrates.

Parke, H.W. 1977. *Festivals of the Athenians*. Ithaca, N.Y.

Pickard-Cambridge, A.W. 1968. *The Dramatic Festivals of Athens*. Rev. ed. by J. Gould and D.M. Lewis. Oxford.

———. 1962. *Dithyramb, Tragedy and Comedy*. Rev. ed. by T.B.L. Webster. Oxford.

Raaflaub, K. 1981. *Zum Freiheitsbegriff der Griechen*. Berlin.

———. 1985. *Die Entdeckung der Freiheit*. Munich.

Rohde, E. 1883. "Scenica." *RhM* 38: 251–92.

Schröder, S. 2000. "Das Lied des Bakchylides von der Fahrt des Theseus." *RhM* 143: 128–60.

Sickinger, J.P. 1999. *Public Records and Archives in Classical Athens*. Chapel Hill.

Snell, B. 1966. "Zu den Urkunden dramatischer Aufführungen." *Nachrichten der Akademie der Wissenschaften in Göttingen* 2. Phil.-hist. Kl. (Göttingen). 1–7.

Sourvinou-Inwood, C. 1994. "Something to do with Athens." In R. Osborne and S. Hornblower, eds., *Ritual, Finance, Politics*. Oxford. 271–90.

Stahl, M. 1987. *Aristokraten und Tyrannen*. Stuttgart.

West, M. 1989. "The Early Chronology of Attic Tragedy." *CQ* n.s. 39: 251 254.

Whitehead, D. 1986. *The Demes of Attica*. Princeton.

15

Notes for a Philologist

John McK. Camp, II

Few people I know come as close as Alan Boegehold to the true definition of a philologist: one who loves language, learning, and words. His love of Greek has been a constant in his life and career. Whether deciphering the meaning of a dipinto on a Corinthian vase, puzzling over the reading of an Attic inscription, interpreting the meaning of a literary text, translating a poem of Cavafy, or searching for the right combination of words for his own poetic expression, Alan has devoted himself to the fine points and nuances of the Greek language at all periods. Most recently, he has even explored the world of missing words, filling in ellipses with the appropriate gestures.

It seems an appropriate gesture, then, for his non-philological admirers to try to follow his lead, however uncertainly or inexpertly, and consider anomalies or interesting aspects of the Greek language as it has changed over time. The following instances have come to my attention during years spent wandering through Greece and Ionia, most of them in Alan's company. I am not equipped to fully discuss their significance; that is left for Alan and those who follow in his footsteps. These observations on oddities of spelling or pronunciation are offered here as little more than reminders of happy times together. Proceeding chronologically, we start with the sublime and end with the ridiculous.

THE THEMISTHOKLES OSTRAKA

Alan has always worked equally as comfortably with inscriptions, dipinti, and grafitti as with the literary texts, and it is interesting to note the gap which occurs occasionally between the words on an object and the version which has come down to us in the manuscript tradition. A classic example derives from the ostraka, the informal ballots used to determine which Athenian statesman was to take an extended vacation from public life. A popular candidate, on more than one occasion, was Themistokles, architect of Athenian naval supremacy. In all literary texts, his name is spelled "Themistokles," with a *tau* in the third syllable, as the etymology of his name would require.[1] On the ostraka, however, the spelling of the name is Themisthokles, with

---

[1] Vanderpool 1970: 13 and Lang 1990: 14.

theta in the third syllable. This is the case for more than 90% of the examples found in the Agora excavations. The 190 ostraka from the North slope also have the same preponderance of *theta*; only two examples have been found with *tau* in the third syllable.[2] Presumably these hundreds of examples are a reliable guide to how the name was pronounced on the streets of Athens in the early 5th century. Since the appearance of Vanderpool (1970) and Lang (1990), another large deposit with Themisthokles ostraka has appeared, a group of about 150, divided between Themistokles and Xanthippos, son of Arriphron and father of Perikles.[3] These, too, confirm the preference for *theta* over *tau*; all 34 examples preserving the third syllable have the theta. This latest deposit will by published by J. Sickinger, a student of Alan's, and it remains to be seen if this information will be refined in any way.

THE LABYADAI INSCRIPTION

A second example of alternate spellings in a text has only recently come to light. A long inscription from Delphi, found in 1894, preserves the rules and regulations of a phratry, the Labyadai. These regulations, written down around the end of the 5th century B.C., were drawn from a variety of earlier sources, one of which is cited as: "The following is written on the rock in Phanoteos."[4] Phanoteos/Panopeus is a small Phocian town on the border with Boiotia, so insignificant by Roman times that Pausanias (10.4.1) was reluctant to call it a polis. In 1993 a group of American School students visited the site, soon after a fire had cleared the hill of brush. Within minutes, the original version of the regulations preserved in the Delphi copy was found, inscribed, as promised, on the rock. The letters are large, retrograde, and generally well preserved, and it is clear that the text in Delphi is a close copy, with only minor variations. A date somewhere in the late 6th or early 5th century seems likely, and the two texts are therefore about a century apart in date.

The section copied at Delphi concerns certain parts of sacrifices assigned by Phanotos, the eponymous hero of Phanoteos/Panopeus, to his daughter, Boupyga, presumably the origin of certain priestly or phratry rights. (Various readings have been proposed in the Delphi copy for both the name of Phanotos and his daughter Boupyga; these can now be laid to rest by the secure readings on the text of the original.) The Delphi copy is a faithful one, though a number of differences in spelling or orthography may be noted, such as several instances of *omicron* in the original, changed to *omega* in the copy, and the ἡεμιριν[ία (half-grown sheep) of the original changed to ἡεμιρρηνία in the copy, with double rather than single *rho*, and *eta* rather than *iota*.[5] Finally, the two instances of δέρματα in the original both appear as

---

[2] Lang 1990: 142–59, esp. 159; see also Threatte 1980: 463–4.

[3] Camp 1999: 268–74.

[4] Rougemont 1977: 69–81 with bibliography on pp. 26–27.

[5] See Buck 1955, no. 55a on p. 51. For double *rho* in Athenian texts, see Threatte 1980: 519–21; also in the ostraka, Lang 1990: 14–15. For the confusion of *eta* and *iota* in Athens, mostly very late, see Threatte 1980: 165–70.

δάρματα in the copy. There is something unusual here, as the expected sequence of development at Delphi is from αρ in early texts to ερ later.[6]

MAUSSOLLOS AND MITHRADATES

Few people have a last name so open to mispronunciation and misspelling as Alan Boegehold; I have seen or heard an amazing array of possibilities over the years. It may come as slight comfort that, along with Themistokles, some of the other big names of antiquity had a similar problem, in particular the dynasts of Caria and Pontus. Maussollos is perhaps the best known, his magnificent tomb lavishly adorned with sculpture becoming known as one of the Seven Wonders of the world, causing his name to be memorialized thereafter in the naming of any elaborate funerary monument as a mausoleum. It is for others to determine how and why the spelling was altered as it passed into modern usage through Latin, but the correct Greek form of the name in Maussollos' lifetime is preserved at Labraunda, the sanctuary of Zeus outside Mylasa, former capital of Caria. There, on the architrave of Andron B, we read in letters over 10 centimeters high: ΜΑΥΣΣΩΛΛΟΣ ΕΚΑΤΟΜΝΩ [ΑΝΕΘΗΚΕ ΤΟΝ Α]ΝΔΡΩΝΑ [ΚΑ]Ι ΤΑ ΕΝΕΟΝΤΑ ΔΙΙ ΛΑΜΒΡΑΥΝΔΩΙ.[7]

King Mithradates of Pontus also presumably knew how he preferred his name to be spelled – Mithradates rather than the form Mithridates commonly found in texts – when he minted coins in his name.[8]

B FOR V

Any classicist who has spent as much time as Alan in Greece has to wonder about the development of modern Greek pronunciation, so different from that of ancient Greek. Or is it?

Iotacism is one example, the confusion of iota for ει, η, or υ, something common in modern Greek usage which in fact turns up as early as the 5th century B.C. on a few ostraka.[9]

Another is the use of *beta* in modern Greek, pronounced as the sound made by the letter V. In dozens of Greek inscriptions the name of the emperor Nerva is transliterated in Greek as ΝΕΡΟΥΑ, the ΟΥ apparently approximating the V sound of Latin. In at least two instances in Athens, however, the Greek B (*beta*) is used, ΝΕΡΒΑ: on the dedicatory inscription of the Library of Pantainos in Athens, and on an inscribed statue base of the Emperor Trajan which almost certainly originally stood in the Library, both dated to the years around A.D. 100. A third occurrence of *beta* for V concerns the Roman consul of A.D. 157, M. Ceionius Civica Barbaros, rendered on an inscribed statue base in Athens as ΚΕΙΒΙΚΑ ΒΑΡΒΑΡΟΝ. In at least three instances, then, the Greek *beta* served as the sound represented by the Latin V as early

---

[6] See Buck 1955: 23 for examples from Phokis.
[7] Crampa 1972: 9–11.
[8] Davis and Kraay 1973: 264–69, with plates 204–209.
[9] Lang 1990: 113–14.

as the 2nd century A.D.[10] The possible association of the three Athenian examples is tantalizing: the two instances of NEPBA both probably stood in the same building, though they were commissioned by different people: the dedicatory inscription by Titius Flavius Pantainos and/or his children, the statue base by Tiberius Claudius Atticus Herodes, the son of Tiberius Claudius Atticus Herodes, who dedicated the statue of Trajan. The Civica base was found built into the late Roman fortification wall, some 120 meters south of the Library of Pantainos along the Panathenaic Way; there is no certain way of knowing where it stood originally. The proximity of the three examples, together with the familial connection of two of them, is worth noting, whatever its significance, if any.

Though rare, examples are not limited to Athens: NEPBA appears also on the imperial nomenclature of Hadrian in the dedication on the architrave of the temple of Apollo at Claros, in Ionia.

Another way of rendering Latin V in Greek was the *digamma*. In most Greek alphabets, and especially at Athens, the *digamma* disappears early on, usually by the Classical period. Occupying the sixth position in the alphabet, it serves rather like a rough breathing, changing the pronunciation of vowels, especially *alpha*. It is often transliterated in English as a double-u (w), as in the Mycenaean official preserved in Linear B texts: *wanax*. Despite its lapse elsewhere, in Boiotia it continued in use until well into the Hellenistic period. At Chaironeia it shows up on several Hellenistic inscriptions, often, appropriately enough, in the name Fanaxidamos. Perhaps the latest example can be dated to the first century B.C., where it appears on the inscribed base for the trophy set up by Sulla after the battle of 86 B.C. honoring the two local heroes, Fanaxidamos and Homoloichos.[11]

A Good Road

Many of our walks in Greece have taken Alan, Julie, and me along the handsome cobbled roads which were the main lines of communication throughout Greece in the period of the Tourkokratia, The name for such a well-built Turkish road in Greece is "*kalderimi.*" I had never considered the etymology until one day as Mustapha Duran Uz and I were walking along a stretch of similar cobbled road near Lagina in western Turkey and he turned to me and said "*kalos dromos.*" Here, linguistically, is the ebb and flow of history in the Eastern Mediterranean, the Turkish corruption of the Greek "good road" coming back to Greece as the term for a Turkish road. Such linguistic cross-fertilization between uneasy neighbors is reminiscent of the signs one sees occasionally on the cross-Channel ferry at the other end of Europe: THIS WAY TO THE BUFFET/PAR ICI POUR LE SNACK BAR.

---

[10] Library dedication: Meritt 1946: 233, no. 64; statue base for Trajan: Shear 1973: 175–76; statue base for Civica Barbaros: Meritt 1957: 220, no. 78. Cf. also Threatte 1980: 444–47; also Allen 1965: 40–42 for the ou-w-v in Latin, and the confusion of the u-consonant with b.

[11] For the Chaironeia trophy and the name Fanaxidamos, see Camp et al. 1992; for other Hellenistic uses of *digamma* at Chaironeia see Fossey and Roesch 1978.

THE END

Talk of snacks leads us to that last great bastion of linguistic oddities, translations on Greek menus. We have all encountered them, but my personal favorites seem always to involve difficulties in defining parts of animals many of us would prefer not to eat. The Santaroza ouzeri near the Arsakeion lawcourts used to serve "bulls' balls," rendered in Greek as ἀμελήτητα βοδινού ("unmentionables"), which in English came out as "innominates of veal" and in French as "inoubliables de veau." The Aktaion restaurant in Corfu served breaded brains (μυαλά πανέ) as "bread-crumbled brain balls." And closer to home, the Epirus restaurant just outside the Agora excavations serves patsas (tripe) translated for tourists a little too truthfully as "abdomen-bowel soup."

This is perhaps enough; as Alan's old friend Charlie Beye might say, "This party is going right downhill." And a Greek taverna such as the Epirus is a good place to stop, where we may raise our glasses and salute a valued friend and honored philologist on the occasion of his 75th birthday.

WORKS CITED

Allen, W.S. 1965. *Vox Latina*. Cambridge.

Buck, C.D. 1955. *The Greek Dialects*. Chicago.

Camp, J. 1999. "Excavations in the Athenian Agora, 1996 and 1997." *Hesperia* 68: 268–74.

Camp, J. et al. 1992. "A Trophy from the Battle of Chaironeia of 86 B.C." *AJA* 96: 443–55.

Camp, J. et al. 1997. "An Athenian Dedication to Herakles at Panopeus." *Hesperia* 66: 261–69.

Crampa, J. 1972. *Labraunda*. Vol. III, part 2. *The Greek Inscriptions*. Stockholm.

Davis, N. and C.M. Kraay. 1973. *The Hellenistic Kingdoms: Portrait Coins and History*. London.

Fossey, J. and P. Roesch. 1978. "Neufs actes d'affranchissement de Cheronee." *ZPE* 29: 123–37.

Lang, M. 1990. *Ostraka*. Volume XXV, *The Athenian Agora*. Princeton.

Meritt, B.D. 1946. "Greek Inscriptions." *Hesperia* 15: 169–253.

———. 1957. "Greek Inscriptions." *Hesperia* 26: 198–221.

Rougement, G. 1977. *Corpus des inscriptions de Delphes*. Vol. I, *Lois sacrées et règlements religieux*. Paris.

Shear, T.L. Jr. 1973. "The Athenian Agora: Excavations of 1971." *Hesperia* 42: 121–79.

Threatte, L. 1980. *The Grammar of Attic Inscriptions*. Vol. 1. Berlin.

Vanderpool., E. 1970. *Ostracism at Athens*. Lectures in Memory of Louise Taft Semple: second series, 1966–70. Cincinnati.

16

Two Passages in Thucydides

Mortimer Chambers

The scholarship of Alan Boegehold, with whom I have shared for more than fifty years an interest in *hellenika*, has often focused on small, even overlooked, pieces of evidence from which he has drawn permanently convincing conclusions. Nowhere has he done this more felicitously than in his book, *When a Gesture Was Expected*, in which he exploits apparent gaps in syntax to discover when a gesture was made in reading a work orally. In effect, he has shown us how to read and understand Greek and other texts. In this modest tribute to him, I offer comments on two passages in the author whom we have often discussed together, the greatest historian of antiquity.

BOOK 1, CHAPTER 9

Thucydides, in Book 1, argues that Agamemnon raised his armada against Troy through his power, rather than through reliance on the oaths taken by other Greek princes to recapture Helen, the wife of Menelaus. He then pauses to give a brief summary of the genealogy of Agamemnon and his house.[1] He reviews some of the history of the house of Atreus thus:

> To come to Agamemnon, it seems to me that it was because he was the most powerful man of his time, and not so much because the suitors of Helen were already bound by the oaths of Tyndareos, that he could summon them together and assemble his fleet. Moreover, those who have received the clearest accounts of Peloponnesian affairs from ancestral tradition say that first of all Pelops arrived, with his wealth from Asia, among poor people and through his riches both attained power for himself and got the territory named after him, even though he was an immigrant. Even greater possessions, they say, fell to the lot of his descendants when Eurystheus died in Attica at the hands of the Heraclids. Atreus was this man's maternal uncle, and because of their family ties Eurystheus had entrusted to him Mycenae and the sovereignty over it when he set out with his force; Atreus himself had been exiled by his father on account of the death of Chrysippus.
>
> When Eurystheus failed to return, Atreus took over the kingdom of Mycenae and all that Eurystheus had ruled; the Mycenaeans also wanted this change because

---

[1] 1.9.1–3.

they feared the Heraclids, and Atreus was also reputed to be a man of power and had made himself popular with the ordinary people.

And so the descendants of Pelops gained the upper hand over those of Perseus. Agamemnon received this heritage and, since he had come to dominate the rest in naval power as well, assembled his force and led the expedition in my opinion not so much through good will as through fear.

There is, however, an issue of translation concerning the words "those who have received the clearest accounts of Peloponnesian affairs from ancestral tradition." This interpretation was offered by Lorenzo Valla, the first translator of Thucydides, who gave us "qui exploratissime Peloponnensium gesta, a maioribus natu sibi per manus tradita, cognoverunt," etc. That is, *gesta* is governed by *Peloponnensium*, "deeds of the Peloponnesians." This translation was followed by Renaissance translators (French, Spanish, Latin, et al.), in the wake of Valla; then by Hobbes (1629), William Smith (1753), Gail (1807), Poppo (ed. minor, 1843, 1866), Classen (1872), Stahl (1886, in his revision of Poppo), Morris (1887, in his English edition based on Classen), and Hornblower (*Commentary*: "those who preserve…say").

But another interpretation makes *Peloponnensium* a partitive genitive: "Those of the Peloponnesians who have received the clearest accounts," etc. This version is found in, e.g., Haacke (1823), Bloomfield (1829), Dale (1856), Crawley (1876), Steup (1897, 1919, in his revision of Classen), Marchant (1905), C. Forster Smith (Loeb, 1919), Gomme (1945), de Romilly (1953), Warner (1954), and Lattimore (1998). Krüger (ed. 3, 1860) allows both versions as possible.

There is, however, evidence about how the passage was understood in antiquity. Poppo (ed. maxima, 1823–1851, commentary on book 1, 1831) pointed to Dionysius of Halicarnassus, *Ant. Rom.* 5.18.1, ὡς οἱ τὰ Ῥωμαίων σαφέστατα γράφουσι. Then, in his ed. minor of 1843,[2] he added a phrase from Cassius Dio, Fr. 6.5, φασὶ δὲ οἱ τὰ σαφέστατα Σαβίνων εἰδότες. These imitations of Thucydides' words suggest that ancient Greeks would have agreed with Valla's interpretation, "those who have received the clearest accounts of Peloponnesian affairs say," etc. I therefore believe that this is the right translation.

We have other information about the house of Atreus from Homer. At *Iliad* 2.105 he describes Agamemnon's scepter and explains how it was passed down through the family. The passage in book 2 thus gives us Homer's version of the stemma of this house.

Homer's stemma, and the transmission of the scepter, is: Hephaestus made it and gave it to Zeus son of Kronos. Zeus gave it to Hermes (also known as "Argeiphontes"), Hermes gave it to Pelops, son of Zeus's son Tantalus, who gave it to his son Atreus. Atreus, on the point of death, gave it to his brother Thyestes; Thyestes gave it to Agamemnon, son of Atreus.

The scholiast to this passage in Homer, commenting on the history of the family, says:

---

[2] Gotha 1843–1856.

Pelops had a son, Chrysippus, from an earlier wife; he then married Hippodameia, daughter of Oinomaos, and had several children with her. Because Chrysippus was greatly loved by Pelops, his stepmother and the other children bore a grudge against him and plotted his death lest Pelops should bequeath the scepter to him; they also brought Atreus and Thyestes, the oldest of the children, into this enterprise. Now when Chrysippus had been killed, Pelops learned of it and exiled the children, because they had been his murderers; and he laid a solemn curse on them and their progeny to the effect that they should be killed. So they all went into exile, some to one place in Pisa, some to another; but when Pelops died, Atreus, by virtue of being the elder, invaded with a large army and conquered the several places. Hellanicus gives this account.

Thus we gain a fragment of the fifth-century historian Hellanicus, which Felix Jacoby edited as *FGrHist* 4 F 157. Since both Thucydides and Hellanicus have discussed some of the same legendary figures, one might ask immediately whether there is any relationship between their accounts.

Let us look at Thucydides' attitude to Hellanicus, who is the only historian whom Thucydides cites by name. At 1.97.2 he says of him that he treated the period between the Persian and Peloponnesian wars, but did so "both briefly and inaccurately with respect to chronology, τοῖς χρόνοις οὐκ ἀκριβῶς."

Strange to say, these last four words are perhaps not perfectly explained in the great commentary of Gomme and his successors.[3] Gomme thought that οὐκ ἀκριβῶς in respect of time meant that Hellanicus "got his events in the wrong order," and referred to Thucydides' frequent pointers to chronology in the Pentekontaetia (πρῶτον μέν, ἔπειτα, and so on).[4] Dover decided that the criticism of Hellanicus "relates to some specific chronological errors in his work."[5]

These theories could be right, but they should be supplemented with the view of Jacoby,[6] namely that the criticism of 1.97.2, οὐκ ἀκριβῶς, is echoed precisely at 5.20.2, where Thucydides says that it is οὐκ ἀκριβές to arrange events by magistrates' years, and we know that Hellanicus did this.[7] This is Thucydides' decisive criticism and gives the key to understanding the criticism at 1.97.2.[8] Thucydides considered it better to work with τοὺς χρόνους (5.20.2), that is, "'by the natural divisions of time,' that is, in effect, the seasons" (Gomme). He does not say so, but surely he thought that the organic narrative of a campaign season, roughly April to October, should not be divided between two years with a break at midsummer, when a new archon took office and a new official year began. Such an interruption would spoil, for example, the narrative of a continuing

---

[3] Gomme, Andrewes, and Dover, *HCT*; Hornblower, *Commentary*.

[4] Gomme, *HCT*, 1: 361. He refers (363 n. 1), to the article of E. Harrison, *Cambr. Univ. Reporter*, March 12, 1912 (also in *PCPS* 1912), which suggests that some measurements of time in Thucydides may be corrections of Hellanicus, such as the statement that the battle of Oinophyta followed that of Tanagra by exactly 62 days, 1.108.2.

[5] Dover, *HCT*, 5: 381.

[6] *FGrHist* IIIb, Supplement, 1.19.

[7] *FGrHist* 323a F 25–26, where Hellanicus cites the archon of 407/6.

[8] Hornblower, *Commentary*, on 2.2.1, comes close to this interpretation, but without calling attention to the correspondence of ἀκριβῶς . . . ἀκριβές, which above all reveals Thucydides' meaning.

military campaign. Thus at 1.97.2 he may well mean that Hellanicus was inaccurate with respect to the seasons of the year: it was impossible to tell from his narrative at what season – spring, summer, fall – a given event took place, because he was locked into his arbitrary and misleading divisions of the natural year.

We further know that Thucydides had read and used Hellanicus' chronicle about the priestesses at Argos (*FGrHist* 4 F 74–84). He uses it to date the beginning of the war (2.2.1) and also draws information from it at 4.133.2–3.

To return to Hellanicus and the house of Atreus, did Thucydides depend on Hellanicus for his information? Classen was the first, to my knowledge, to suggest this: "Th. wird vorzugsweise den Hellanikos vor Augen haben" (on 1.9). Stahl, in his revision of Poppo, agreed, and Ulrich Koehler suggested that Hellanicus told this story in his *Aiolika*.[9] Gomme, on 1.9.2, took note of the fragment of Hellanicus, *FGrHist* 4 F 157 in Jacoby, but was cautious: "Thucydides may be thinking especially of him, but he doubtless had other writers in mind as well, and the dates of Hellanikos' publications are uncertain." Hornblower (on 1.9.2) follows the same path as Gomme: "Hellanikos […] gave some of the material also found in this ch. of Th., see *FGrHist* 4 F 157, but Th. need not have had him in mind in particular. There were surely other writers who could be said to 'preserve Peloponnesian tradition clearly.'"

Jacoby was less doubtful than Gomme or Hornblower about Thucydides' dependence on Hellanicus:[10] "auch die weitere geschichte der Pelopiden, wie H[ellanikos] sie gab, rekapituliert kurz und auf den hauptstamm sich beschränkend Thuk." Jacoby had also earlier identified Hellanicus as Thucydides' source in his great study of Hecataeus.[11]

But perhaps a closer comparison of the two passages permits a different view.

1. Thucydides: Pelops arrived from Asia with wealth and became influential.

   Hellanicus: Pelops was already the father of Chrysippus. He married Hippodameia and had several other children.[12]

2. Thucydides: Eurystheus was killed in Attica by the Heraclids.

   Hellanicus: Eurystheus and the Heraclids are not mentioned.

3. Thucydides: Pelops banished Atreus because of his part in Chrysippus' death.

   Hellanicus: Hippodameia and Chrysippus' siblings plotted Chrysippus' death. Atreus and Thyestes accomplished it. Pelops banished his children. He laid a curse on them. Some of the children went to Pisa.

4. Thucydides: Eurystheus turned Mycenae over to Atreus before setting out for Attica. When Eurystheus failed to return, the people of Mycenae wanted Atreus to become or remain their ruler; they feared the Heraclids, and Atreus was reputed to be powerful and had won their favor.

   Hellanicus: Atreus took over places in the area (Mycenae is not mentioned by name) by means of a large force after the death of his father Pelops.

---

[9] Koehler 1877: 375. For our one fragment of the *Aiolika*: *FGrHist* 4 F 32.

[10] In his commentary to *FGrHist* 4 F 157.

[11] *RE* VII (1912) s.v. "Hekataios," 2677: "Er [Thucydides] tadelt ihn [Hellanicus] I 97, 2 mit Namen und übernimmt I 9, 2 die Geschichte des Atridenhauses."

[12] One of these children was Atreus.

The general lines of the story of the house of Atreus are similar in both versions, as they had to be within the traditions of Greek legend. But Thucydides and Hellanicus diverge, indeed disagree, in several respects, above all in the way Atreus became ruler of Mycenae. For Hellanicus, he did so by superior force, while Thucydides sees this as the result of his popularity with the people. The only real agreement between the two sources is at point 3, over the murder of Chrysippus and the banishment of Atreus by his father Pelops. Note that Thucydides omits to mention the curse laid by Pelops on his children, a matter brushed aside by Jacoby.[13]

In other respects, too, there are elements in the two versions that do not suggest that Thucydides depended on Hellanicus. The historian's narrative is longer than the summary of the scholiast, yet he omits to mention the marriage between Pelops and Hippodameia, the name of Thyestes, and Pisa as the place of the children's exile. I admit that, if we had Hellanicus' own full text, the two versions might look more similar than they now do. But, judging from the evidence that we have, I suggest that Hellanicus, in whatever work of his we care to suggest, was not the source for Thucydides in 1.9.

But if not Hellanicus, who has the support of the master, Jacoby, who then? Merely to show that there are other possibilities, one should note that Charon of Lampsacus is said by the Suda, s.v. Χάρων, to have written Πρυτάνεις τοὺς τῶν Λακεδαιμονίων (ἔστι δὲ χρονικά).[14] We have no certain fragments from this work, but perhaps its author, or some other authority, may have seemed to Thucydides the man who "had received the clearest accounts of Peloponnesian affairs from ancestral tradition."

BOOK 6, CHAPTER 6

I turn now to an argument about a single letter, the Greek sigma. In 6.1–5 Thucydides surveys early Sicily and the peoples inhabiting it. In 6.6.1 he looks back at this survey, as he narrates the story of an embassy sent by the Sicilian town of Egesta to Athens in 416 B.C. The embassy was sent to ask for military help from Athens. The Athenians agreed, a fact leading to the Sicilian expedition that set out in 415. The historian comments, "And such was the magnitude (τοσήνδε) of the island that the Athenians were now bent upon invading; being ambitious in real truth of conquering the whole, although they had also the specious design of succouring their kindred and other allies in the island" (tr. Crawley).

The Greek for "their kindred, etc.," is τοῖς ἑαυτῶν ξυγγενέσι καὶ τοῖς προσγεγενημένοις (ABCF; προγεγ- EGM) ξυμμάχοις. Again our first translator, Lorenzo Valla, is instructive. The scholiast glosses ξυγγενέσι with τοῖς Χαλκιδεῦσιν, doubtless on the grounds that the city of Leontini, with which Athens was allied, was a colony from Chalcis in Euboea. Valla adopted the gloss and translated, "Chalcidensibus, suis cognatis ac pristinis sociis." The several Latin translations that follow Valla

---

[13] "dass Thuk. ihn [sc. the curse] nicht erwähnt, ist bedeutungslos": commentary to *FGrHist* 4 F 157, p. 470.

[14] *FGrHist* 262 T 1.

(Stephanus, 1564; Portus, 1594; Hudson, 1696, and others) retain "Chalcidensibus" but print it in italics or parentheses to mark it as a gloss.

Valla's "pristinis" suggests that he may have had προγεγενημένοις in whatever manuscript he chose to follow. Dover, *ad loc.*, in a typically instructive note, points out that the two readings in our MSS "exhibit a universal uncertainty in the transmission of these prefixes [sc. προ-, προσ-] in prose texts." Editors vary between προγεγενημένοις (Classen and Classen-Steup, Stahl, in his revision of Poppo, Alberti 2000) and προσ- (Aldus, Camerarius, Stephanus, Portus, Hudson, Duker, Gail, Bekker, Haacke, Krüger, Poppo[1–2], Arnold, Stuart Jones, Hude, ed. maxima, 1901, Boehme-Widmann, de Romilly-Bodin, to look no farther). Hobbes (1629) gives "their kindred and new confederates," which suggests that his Greek text also had προσ-.

Can we choose, then, between προ- and προσ-? Some towns in Sicily were, at least in theory and tradition, related to the Athenians as Ionians (Leontini, Catana, Zancle, and others), and these are the ξυγγενεῖς whom the Athenians professedly wanted to support. In addition, in 427 the Athenians had acquired the Dorian town of Camarina as an ally,[15] and in 426 they had gained some allies among Sicels.[16] These allies might all be included among the "pre-existing" allies, who were on the Athenian side before 415, and προγεγενημένοις might stand.

But, as Dover points out, if προ- is right, the preposition seems to look forward to the immediately following sentence: "But they [the Athenians] were especially incited by envoys from Egesta, who had come to Athens and urgently asked for their help." Indeed, the preposition προσ-, if it is accepted, does the very same thing, for the narrative goes on at once with the appeal of the envoys from Egesta. So the position of Egesta within Athenian foreign policy is relevant to our choice of preposition in the Greek word.

When Dover wrote, it was still widely believed that Egesta had made an alliance with Athens in 458/7. The evidence for this date was thought to be found in the inscription *IG* I[3] 11, which records the making of the alliance. Many had dated the inscription to that year; that is, to the archonship of Habron, the last two letters of which name are clear on the stone where the archon of the year is named. If the alliance was formed in 458/7, the reference in Thucydides to Egesta could be to an ally of long standing, the people of Egesta could be reckoned among the "pre-existing" allies of Athens, and προγεγενημένοις could be defended.

However, it has been shown, I believe, that the archon's name on the inscription recording the alliance was Antiphon and that the alliance is therefore to be dated to 418/7.[17] This dating removes the evidence for an Athens-Egesta alliance in the middle of the fifth century. Therefore Egesta was not one of Athens' "pre-existing" allies. Rather, Egesta was one of the προσγεγενημένοι ξύμμαχοι, that is, states which, in Dover's words, " 'had *also* become [Athens'] allies,' sc. in addition to those whose

---

[15] Thuc. 3.86.1–2.
[16] Thuc. 3.103.1–2.
[17] Chambers, Gallucci, and Spanos 1990.

claim rested on kinship." I therefore submit that the right preposition in our passage is προσ- rather than προ-, as most editors have in fact printed.

There is still an unsatisfying detail, which continues to puzzle me. No matter when Egesta became an ally of Athens, in 458/7 or, better, in 418/7, the envoys from Egesta ought to refer to this alliance as they appear before the Athenians in 416 and ask for help (Thuc. 6.6.2). No argument could possibly be more natural or more persuasive than to say, "You Athenians have made an alliance with us, and we now ask you to act on it." But, in Thucydides' narrative, they do not. Rather, they point to an alliance that the Athenians made, not with them but apparently with Leontini (though the Greek is rather ambiguous)[18] in the time of Laches, the Athenian general who was active in Sicily in 427 (Thuc. 3.86). It is on the basis of that alliance – the one between Athens and Leontini – that they ask for military aid, not on the basis of the alliance that Athens had made with them.

I can see only two explanations of this strange omission in the speech of Egesta's envoys as Thucydides reports it. (1) The Athenians knew that Egesta was their ally and did not need to be reminded of it. (2) We suggested in 1990 that Thucydides, in exile from about 423 until 404,[19] perhaps had not heard that a formal alliance had been made in 418/7, as is shown by the much-discussed inscription *IG* I[3] 11. If so, he had no knowledge that would allow him to make the Egestan envoys appeal to an already existing alliance. I admit that I find neither of these explanations ideal.

WORKS CITED

Busolt, G. 1904. *Griechische Geschichte*. III.2. 2nd ed. Gotha.

Chambers, M. 2000. "Wilamowitz on Thucydides." In W.M. Calder III et al., eds., *Wilamowitz in Greifswald*. Hildesheim. 504–23.

Chambers, M., R. Gallucci, and P. Spanos. 1990. "Athens' Alliance with Egesta in the Year of Antiphon." *ZPE* 83: 38–63.

HCT = A.W. Gomme, A. Andrewes, and K.J. Dover. *A Historical Commentary on Thucydides*. 5 vols. Oxford, 1945–1981.

Hornblower, *Commentary* = S. Hornblower, *A Commentary on Thucydides*. 2 vols. Oxford, 1991–1996.

Koehler, U. 1877. *Commentationes philologae in honorem Theodori Mommseni*. Berlin.

---

[18] In favor of Leontini as the city with whom Athens had made the alliance to which the Egestan envoys refer: Chambers, Gallucci, and Spanos 1990: 58–60.

[19] "It befell me to be away from my country for twenty years after my command at Amphipolis," 5.26.5. It is credible that Thucydides was recalled by a decree proposed by Oenobius, who had been an Athenian general in 410/09, as Pausanias states (1.23.11). This decree recalling the historian was probably proposed in 405/4, exactly the 20th year after 424/3, when the historian went into exile. For this chronology see Busolt 1904: 628 n. 2. In defense of Pausanias' report, see Chambers 2000: 514–18.

17

Livy's Narrative Habit[*]

Jane D. Chaplin

I. INTRODUCTION

Despite the emergence of increasingly nuanced and sophisticated work on the Roman historians towards the end of the twentieth century,[1] as a group they still tend to suffer from being regarded as moralistic, didactic, and patriotic, rather than as possessing the analytical and self-critical characteristics attributed to the better of their Greek counterparts.[2] Far from being an exception to this rule, Livy is arguably the most frequently cited example. Something of a paradox encourages the view that he lacks sufficient capacity to offer critical insight into the events he relates: on the one hand, he chose to write history on an enormous scale, and his breadth of historical vision was demonstrated conclusively by T.J. Luce;[3] on the other hand, as has long been recognized, Livy composed by episodes.[4] Correspondingly, it is hardly surprising that secondary literature tends to address individual episodes within books or themes across books. Either approach, however, obscures the connections the historian forges from one episode to another, and in amongst his carefully constructed and appropriately appreciated trees, Livy's forest vanishes, taking with it a large part of his approach to writing history. Both the size and the style of the *Ab Urbe Condita*

[*] Work on this paper was supported by a grant from the Middlebury College Faculty Professional Development Fund. Clemence Schultz commented on its most embryonic form and increased my appreciation of Dionysius for Halicarnassus. A very early version was delivered at the CAAS meeting in October 1994. Chris Pelling was kind enough to read a later version and introduce me to bibliography on Plutarch and Shakespeare. Further bibliography and suggestions for improvement came from an anonymous referee. Anne Alwis, Robert Parker, and Marc Witkin provided invaluable assistance on individual points. I am also once again guilty of abusing the goodwill of Chris Kraus, David Levene, and most especially Tony Woodman, all of whom read it early and late. Alan was naturally unaware of the paper's intended destination when, at Kurt Raaflaub's generous invitation, I had the pleasure of giving a version to a helpful and receptive audience at Brown in November 2000. The greatest debt to be acknowledged here, however, was incurred not in the composition of the essay, but over the course of nearly two decades: as teacher, mentor, and above all friend, Alan has made so great a difference in my life that this contribution is nothing more than a nod to reciprocity.

[1] See Kraus and Woodman 1997 for a sample of the results of this work.

[2] See e. g. Mellor 1999: 4 and 10–11.

[3] Luce 1977: 230–297.

[4] The view was most fully laid out by Witte 1910 and was recently endorsed in Oakley's magisterial commentary (1997: 125–128).

discourage sustained sequential reading of it, and yet of all the major historians, Livy was, on anecdotal evidence at least, the most inclined to sustained sequential composition. The value of reading his text as he wrote is perhaps most evident in Christina Kraus' commentary on Book 6. A concise discussion in the introduction lays out Livy's persistent reliance on chiasmus and interweaving, from the level of individual syllables and sounds to the arrangement of material,[5] and the commentary notes the use of this stylistic tendency throughout. The result is a reading of Livy that uncovers the microscopic and macroscopic alike.

This paper is intended as a small contribution in the latter direction. By laying out interconnections between two episodes in Book 2 – Menenius Agrippa's fable of the 'Belly and the Limbs' and Gnaeus Marcius Coriolanus' career – I will show that the tendency to extract episodes from their setting steers readers away from recognizing how Livy prefers to let his interpretation of the past emerge from narrative exposition; and that without that recognition, any appreciation of his historiographic achievement is bound to be limited. The first part of the paper is largely descriptive, comprising an overview of the events in which Menenius and Coriolanus figure and a brief consideration of scholarly discussions of their histories, which examine these events in isolation from the surrounding context and thus without reference to each other. The second part of the paper deals with the structural and thematic connections between the two episodes. In the conclusion I will consider why Livy decided to include the fable of the Belly and the Limbs; my argument is that he saw how the Greek folk tale could be used as a distillation of Roman political history and so incorporated the traditional fable in such a way as to foreshadow the famine of 492. This position leads to some general implications for his historiography: specifically, that we can appreciate it more fully if we do not extract episodes from their context, that Livy tends to enact ideas instead of expounding on them, and that his status as a historian has suffered accordingly.

II. MENENIUS AGRIPPA AND GNAEUS MARCIUS CORIOLANUS IN BOOK 2

Book 2 starts with the beginning of the republic, in 509, and goes down to 468. It includes many well-known episodes: Brutus' execution of his sons for treason; the heroic exploits of Horatius Cocles, Mucius Scaevola, and Cloelia in the face of the Etruscan offensive under Lars Porsenna; the first secession of the plebs and the establishment of the tribunate; the military brilliance of Coriolanus, his defection to the Volsci, the embassy of women who halt his march on Rome; and the formation of the Fabian army against Veii and its defeat at the Cremera. The backdrop to these events is the evolving relationship between the plebeians and the patricians, which alternates between hostility and conflict on the one hand and an ability to unite in the face of an external threat on the other.

The tension between the orders reaches a particularly high peak with the plebs' secession to the Sacred Mount, a step they take when the Senate does not reward their

---

[5] Kraus 1994: 21–24.

military service by alleviating a pervasive problem with debt-bondage. Although the civil disobedience in 494 has a long build-up, stretching over some nine chapters of internal and external strife (2.23.1–32.1), the secession itself, from the plebeians' departure to their return and the establishment of the tribunate, occupies not even two full chapters (2.32.2–33.3). The plebeians are persuaded to return to the city by one Menenius Agrippa; a man of plebeian origins, he makes his entry into Livy's narrative here as the patricians' ambassador. Livy allots Menenius' speech about a quarter of his compressed narrative of the secession. The core of the speech is the fable of the belly and the limbs,[6] which consequently dominates the episode. It runs as follows:

> Sic placuit igitur oratorem ad plebem mitti Menenium Agrippam, facundum uirum et quod inde oriundus erat plebi carum. Is intromissus in castra prisco illo dicendi et horrido modo nihil aliud quam hoc narrasse fertur: tempore quo in homine non ut nunc omnia in unum consentiant, sed singulis membris suum cuique consilium, suus sermo fuerit, indignatas reliquas partes sua cura, suo labore ac ministerio uentri omnia quaeri, uentrem in medio quietum nihil aliud quam datis uoluptatibus frui; conspirasse inde ne manus ad os cibum ferrent, nec os acciperet datum, nec dentes conficerent. Hac ira, dum uentrem fame domare uellent, ipsa una membra totumque corpus ad extremam tabem uenisse. Inde apparuisse uentris quoque haud segne ministerium esse, nec magis ali quam alere eum, reddentem in omnes corporis partes hunc quo uiuimus uigemusque, diuisum pariter in uenas maturum confecto cibo sanguinem. Comparando hinc quam intestina corporis seditio similis esset irae plebis in patres, flexisse mentes hominum (2.32.8–12).[7]

Menenius' fable engenders good feeling, and the secession ends with the creation of the first tribunes, men invested with the privilege of sacrosanctity and the responsibility of intervening with the consuls on behalf of the plebeians.

The fable's most striking feature is its singularity,[8] and no one has believed the story to be original to its speaker or its setting. Scholars have theorized about how the

---

[6] For recent, extensive discussions of fables in ancient literature, see Adrados 1999 and van Dijk 1997.

[7] Accordingly they agreed that Menenius Agrippa should be sent to speak to the plebs; he was an articulate man who was dear to the plebs because he had come from their ranks. When he was admitted to the camp, he is said to have narrated, in that old and rough way of speaking, nothing other than this: once upon a time, everything in man did not work together as is the case nowadays, but each individual limb had its own power of intellect and its own capacity to speak; the other parts were insulted and complained that everything was supplied to the belly by their responsibility, by their labor and service, and that the belly, passively in the middle, lived off of nothing other than the pleasures supplied to it; consequently, the limbs conspired that the hands would not bring food to the mouth, and the mouth would not accept anything given to it, nor would the teeth do any masticating. Because of this anger, while they wished to curb the belly with hunger, each limb on its own and the entire body reached the outer limit of starvation. And so it became apparent that the belly also performed a vigorous service, that it nourished as much as it was nourished, returning to each part of the body that vital fluid by which we live and flourish, processed from digested food and spread equally through the veins. At this point, by comparing how the internal revolt of the body was similar to the anger of the plebeians against the *patres*, Menenius is said to have changed the men's minds.

[8] The closest parallels are two anecdotes told by Titus Quinctius Flamininus and recounted by Livy in the middle of the fourth decade: Flamininus compares Philip's supposedly vast and varied army to a dinner he was served by a host who openly admitted that spices had transformed the flesh of swine into apparently exotic game (35.49.6–7); and he later tells the Achaeans that they resemble a tortoise: fine as

fable was incorporated into the annalistic tradition, the case being made for every century between Menenius and Livy.[9] It is not necessary to go into detail about the various arguments involved: the point is simply that there is no historical relationship between the fable and either plebeian unrest in the early years of the republic or Menenius Agrippa. One commentator on the passage begins his discussion by going so far as to say that Menenius Agrippa's parable sticks out like a sore thumb in early Roman history.[10]

Part of the improbability of any direct association between the fable and Menenius or the first secession is its content. Although Menenius' tale is the oldest attested version, the body-state analogy on which the fable is based belongs to the tradition of Greek political thought. While the analogy had appeared in Latin literature well before Livy – according to Plutarch, Cato the Elder compared the people to a belly without ears (*Mor.* 198 D) – its history in Greek literature goes back much farther, almost certainly originating in the αἶνος tradition of early Greek literature.[11] Livy accentuates the fact that the story is alien to its setting by drawing attention to a gap between the sophisticated substance and Menenius' rough and ready delivery with the words *prisco illo dicendi et horrido modo*.[12] Not surprisingly then, scholars have treated the fable as an isolated piece of Greek political theory interpolated into Roman historiography.

Directly after the plebs' return to the city and the institution of the tribunate, Livy embarks on the story of Coriolanus. Livy devotes considerably more space to Coriolanus' career and the events in which he figures than he does to Menenius and his fable. Cn. Marcius first distinguishes himself at Corioli, where his bravery earns him his *cognomen* (2.33.5). Next he features in the grain shortage of 492, where his opposition to selling emergency supplies at a reduced price leads to his exile (2.34.1–35.6). He defects to the Volsci and plots Rome's downfall with Attius Tullius (2.35.6–8). They decide to capitalize on the situation at Rome, where the celebration of some games provides the Volsci with an excuse to show up in the city in large numbers. Attius manipulates the Senate into expelling the Volsci from Rome (2.37.1–9);

---

long as they stay within the shell of the Peloponnese, they are vulnerable the moment they stick their neck out (36.32.5–8). The two anecdotes also surface in Plutarch's 'Life of Flamininus' (*Flam.* 17.2 and 4), and Briscoe (1981: 213 and 269) thinks Polybius is the source for both of the later authors (although the relevant section of his narrative is no longer extant). It seems likely that Flamininus actually told such stories and thus, although they bear a superficial resemblance to Menenius' fable, they are qualitatively different in that they almost certainly go back to the person credited with relating them.

[9] For example, Momigliano 1942: 117–118 wants to associate its insertion with the achievement of political harmony in Rome at the beginning of the fourth century; Drummond 1989: 214 takes the position that the story could not have become part of Roman history before the third century; Hillgruber 1996: 55–56 suggests a Gracchan date; and in his seminal article on the fable, Nestle 1927: 350 argues for as late as the middle of the first century.

[10] Nestle 1927: 350 uses the term "geologic erratic" (*ein erratischer Block*), meaning a rock which does not fit geologically with its find-spot.

[11] Nestle 1927: 350–356 and Gombel 1934: 27–44. Adrados 1999: 329–330, however, discusses Menenius' tale in the context of Egyptian fables revolving around disputes.

[12] See Ogilvie [1965] 1970: 313 and Gabba 1991: 84 for some discussion of Livy's choice of words here. Laird 1999: 116–152 discusses the presentation of speeches in historiographic texts.

invoking their ill-treatment, Attius thereupon incites his countrymen to declare war, with none other than Marcius Coriolanus and himself as their generals (2.38.1–6). Coriolanus devastates town after town and rejects the appeals of the Senate to halt his march on Rome (2.39.1–12). The narrative culminates in the most famous episode associated with Coriolanus: the embassy of the women of Rome and the crucial intervention of his mother Veturia (2.40.1–10). Livy concludes by noting various traditions about Coriolanus' eventual demise (2.40.10–12). So, whereas the secession begins and comes to its peaceful conclusion in under two chapters, Coriolanus' history is spread over eight (2.33–40).

The early republic is a notoriously tough historical nut, and both the first secession and the career of Coriolanus have come in for their share of skepticism. Just as with Menenius and his fable, one challenge presented by Coriolanus' biography is the influence of Greek models. Cicero, for example, noted the similarity between Coriolanus and Themistocles (*Brut.* 41–3), and modern commentators have seen aspects of the Iliadic Achilles and Phoenix's Meleager in Livy's Coriolanus.[13] Also featured in Livy's account is Coriolanus' decision not to destroy fields belonging to patricians (2.39.5), a topos going back to Thucydides and Pericles' stated concern about Archidamus' protection of Pericles' property (Thuc. 2.13.1) and recycled by Livy for Hannibal and Fabius (22.23.4).

The foreign elements highlight the improbability that Livy's narrative has an intrinsic and necessary connection to its chronological setting. As with Menenius, there is a long-standing scholarly acknowledgment of the mismatch between the story and its setting.[14] Consequently, scholars have instead addressed different internal aspects of the narrative, such as its historicity, the lessons derived in antiquity from Coriolanus' reversal of fortune, the sources, and the prominent role of women.[15] The consensus of such work is that the Livian narrative is more 'legendary' than historical and at best, must be treated with caution.[16]

In short, Menenius' fable and Coriolanus the troubled war hero are back-to-back stories that do not fit the historical circumstances in which they figure and that bear traces of Greek origins or influence. Further, they have both been read as disembodied units, partly for those reasons and partly because the fable of the belly and the limbs has attracted predominantly literary interest while Coriolanus has fallen mostly to

---

[13] The comparison of Coriolanus and Achilles is in Aly 1936: 44. Schönberger 1955: 246–248 makes the case for Meleager as Livy's model for the Roman. Bonjour 1975: 171–175 argues against both (also rejecting the suggestion of Ogilvie [1965] 1970: 334 that Euripides' Jocasta influenced Livy's Veturia).

[14] Mommsen 1870 made a thorough case against any essential relationship between early republican history and the story as represented in extant sources.

[15] For historical aspects, see e.g. Salmon 1930 and *RE* suppl. V, 1931, s. v. *Marcius* (W. Schur). Lehman 1952 looks at the different lessons classical authors extracted from Coriolanus. Russell 1963 elaborates on the point, made by Mommsen among others, that Plutarch derived his version solely from that of Dionysius. Bonjour 1975 discusses the role of women in the episode (another aspect noted by Mommsen). The secondary literature on Coriolanus, of which this is just a sample, is substantial and wide-ranging, but there is no in-depth exploration of the connections with Menenius in Livy Book 2.

[16] Cornell acknowledges Coriolanus' legendary qualities (1995: 10, 13, and 307), but uses him as an example of broader patterns (1995: 144, 255 with note, and 306); cf. Cornell 1989: 287–288.

students of early republican history. While all this is understandable, it has the unfortunate consequence of sequestering the stories from each other. Even the secondary literature that might have treated them together does not do so. For example, in his superb commentary on the first pentad, R. M. Ogilvie uses headings – 'The Final Act: The First Secession of the Plebs' for 2.31.7–33.3 and 'Coriolanus' for 2.33.3–40 – that establish boundaries between the two.[17] Since this arrangement leads readers away from seeing interconnections between Menenius and Coriolanus, the authoritative position Ogilvie's work has in Livian scholarship is unfortunate here. Erich Burck, whose study of Livy's narrative style in the first pentad also occupies a prominent position, treats Book 2 in a more continuous fashion, and his transition from the first secession to the Corioli campaign implicitly acknowledges the absence of a sharp division in this section of the text.[18] Nevertheless, he presents Book 2 as comprising four, almost entirely self-contained units: the consolidation of the republic up to the death of Tarquin (chapters 1–21), the struggle of the orders up to the settlement of 493 and the establishment of the tribunate (chapters 22–33.5), Coriolanus (33.6–40), and the rest (41–65).[19] Furthermore, when he discusses the second of these four, he argues that Livy relates the plebeians' return and the establishment of the tribunate only briefly in order to give his account its necessary ending. Burck then turns directly to the story of Coriolanus as the second book's third discrete narrative unit.[20]

III. STRUCTURAL AND THEMATIC CONNECTIONS

The treatments of Ogilvie and Burck point to a central question in the composition and reception of historical texts: how do authors demarcate and audiences perceive beginnings and endings within any narration of past events? Recent discussion of closure in classical literature offers possible ways to think about these issues. For example, Don Fowler noted the problem of closure within books.[21] That is, even with texts where we know that book divisions are original, the author may very well also include breaks and transitions within those larger units. Fowler gave the conclusion of the destruction of Alba Longa as an example of this practice in Livy (1.29.6).[22] One could point to others; they are particularly common after battles, and in Book 1 the reign of each king ends with a summary.

   Yet, in the kind of sequential narrative Livy writes, firm divisions are rare. In the two stories under consideration here, there is nothing especially emphatic. The movement from Menenius' speech to the attack on Corioli runs as follows:

---

[17] Ogilvie [1965] 1970: 309 and 318.

[18] Burck [1934] 1964: 70.

[19] *Ibid.*: 51–52.

[20] *Ibid.*: 70.

[21] The first treatment is in Fowler 1989: 82–96 (2000: 246–259), with follow-up in Fowler 1997: 13–15 (2000: 296–299). Fusillo 1997: 224–226 and Rutherford 1997: 55–58 also discuss intratextual closure, for the ancient novel and Greek lyric, respectively.

[22] Fowler [1989: 90] 2000: 253.

Agi deinde de concordia coeptum, concessumque in condiciones ut plebi sui magistratus essent sacrosancti quibus auxilii latio aduersus consules esset, neue cui patrum capere eum magistratum liceret. Ita tribuni plebei creati duo, C. Licinius et L. Albinius; hi tres collegas sibi creauerunt. In his Sicinium fuisse, seditionis auctorem; de duobus, qui fuerint, minus conuenit. Sunt qui duos tantum in Sacro monte creatos tribunos esse dicant, ibique sacratam legem latam. Per secessionem plebis Sp. Cassius et Postumus Cominius consulatum inierunt. Iis consulibus cum Latinis populis ictum foedus. Ad id feriendum consul alter Romae mansit: alter ad Volscum bellum missus Antiates Volscos fundit fugatque; compulsos in oppidum Longulam persecutus moenibus potitur. Inde protinus Poluscam, item Volscorum, cepit; tum magna ui adortus est Coriolos (2.33.1–5).[23]

The creation of the tribunate – with which the year 494 and the secession officially end – is given complete with alternative traditions concerning how many tribunes were named and where the oath guaranteeing their sanctity took place. The consuls of 493, the year of Coriolanus' meteoric rise to prominence, enter office during the secession: *per secessionem plebis Sp. Cassius et Postumus Cominius consulatum inierunt* (2.33.3). The latter is fighting the Volsci three clauses later; two clauses after that the struggle over Corioli is introduced. In other words, instead of using the inauguration of the consuls, the standard signal of a new year in annalistic historiography, to create a break between the secession and the next episode, Livy chooses to run them together. While the first secession undoubtedly can and does stand on its own and while the discussion of variant traditions can be a closural element in historical texts,[24] nothing in this passage suggests an absolute segregation of the events of 494 from those of the following year.[25] On the contrary, the overlap between the secession and the next consular year invites us to read on.

The structural fusion of the secession and Coriolanus' career becomes clearer when we do so. The warrior makes a dramatic entry, repelling a surprise attack and then penetrating the walls of Corioli. His success and the consequent tumult inspire the rest of the Roman forces, making the young man the hero of the battle and giving him his

---

[23] Discussion of their harmonious relations then began, and among the terms was the agreement that the plebeians should have their own, sacrosanct magistrates who would have the right of bringing help to the plebeians against the consuls, and none of the *patres* would be permitted to hold this magistracy. So it was that two plebeian tribunes were chosen, Gaius Licinius and Lucius Albinius; they chose three colleagues for themselves. Among these last was Sicinius, the author of the revolt; there is less agreement about the other two. Some people say that just two tribunes were chosen on the Sacred Mount, and that the law of sacrosanctity was passed there. During the secession of the plebs Spurius Cassius and Postumius Cominius entered upon their consulship. A treaty was concluded with the Latins while they were in office. One consul stayed at Rome to oversee the making of the treaty; the other was sent to the Volscian war where he overwhelmed and put to flight the Volsci of Antium. In his pursuit, he drove them into the town of Longula and took control of the city walls. His next conquest, immediately after that, was Polusca, also a Volscian city; then he attacked Corioli with maximum force.

[24] Luce 1965: 216–217 notes that Livy tends to discuss conflicting information about magistrates' identity when they enter office and discrepancies about their activities at the end of the year. This particular passage is a hybrid of the two categories.

[25] Oakley 1997: 122–124 discusses places in Books 2–10 where episodes do not coincide with the end of a consular year.

cognomen. Livy presents this victory as the Romans' major accomplishment of the year, only briefly appending a notice about the conclusion of the *foedus Cassianum*, overseen by the other consul.

At this point it might seem that Livy has his audience well into the story of Coriolanus, but the final entry for the year is the obituary for Menenius Agrippa:

> Eodem anno Agrippa Menenius moritur, uir omni uita pariter patribus ac plebi carus, post secessionem carior plebi factus. Huic interpreti arbitroque concordiae ciuium, legato patrum ad plebem, reductori plebis Romanae in urbem sumptus funeri defuit; extulit eum plebs sextantibus conlatis in capita (2.33.10–11).[26]

Though the obituary states that throughout Menenius' life he was on good terms with plebeians and patricians alike, Livy says virtually nothing about his consulship a decade earlier in 503.[27] His role in the narrative is confined to the secession, and the death notice centers around the goodwill he inspired on that occasion. Key words link Menenius' two moments of prominence: the phrase *plebi carus* in the obituary echoes the introduction to the secession (2.32.8); *concordia* too appears here and at the conclusion of the secession (2.33.1).

There is more to this passage than its contents and the way they direct the reader's attention backwards; the positioning too is significant. Since the siege of Corioli, the signing of the treaty, and Menenius' death all occurred in the same year, Livy could have put the obituary first and used it as a formal closing device for the secession.[28] Although in annalistic historiography death notices are generally placed at the end of the textual year, Livy sometimes includes them in the course of events.[29] Here he has eschewed what might appear to be a simple and satisfying order: the secession in 494; then, with the beginning of 493, the death of Menenius, followed by the consular activities, first what we – modern students of the ancient world, that is – consider the historically important *foedus Cassianum*, and second the siege of Corioli and Coriolanus' emergence as a focal character for the events that will dominate the following years, especially the famine and his march on Rome. Livy offers a rather

---

[26] That same year Menenius Agrippa died, a man dear to the *patres* and the plebs alike throughout his entire life, who became dearer still to the plebs after the secession. This mediator and overseer of harmonious relations among the citizens, the ambassador of the *patres* to the plebs, the man who led the Roman plebs back to the city, this man could not afford the expenses of a funeral. The plebs made individual contributions of pennies and laid him to rest.

[27] His name is mentioned as a dating device only, and the events of the year are related impersonally; the fighting against the Aurunci includes no names, not even for the triumph celebrated afterwards (2.16.7–9).

[28] This point has been made, though unfortunately not in print, by Chris Pelling. In his article on Coriolanus as shaped by Dionysius, Plutarch, and Shakespeare, he does note (Pelling 1997: 5) the emphatic position Dionysius gives Menenius' obituary by placing it last in Book 6.

[29] Examples include L. Iunius Brutus, whose life is summed up twice, once on the field of battle and then in an oration (2.7.4 and 8), Valerius Publicola (2.16.7), the deaths of the Scipios in Spain (25.36.14–16), and M. Claudius Marcellus (27.27.11–14). The obituaries for Attalus (33.21.1–5) and Scipio Africanus (38.53.9–11) are also not postponed to the end of the year, but one might object that Attalus, a foreign king, does not belong in Roman annalistic material, and that Scipio Africanus' death is shrouded in complexity. For a discussion of Livy's death notices, see Pomeroy 1988.

different arrangement and emphases. The consuls for 493 are introduced as having entered office during the secession; Livy then briefly mentions the striking of the treaty only to pass on to a much more expansive account of the Volscian war and Coriolanus' heroism at Corioli, which, he claims, so eclipsed the other consul's reputation that, had the latter's name not been enshrined in the treaty, Cassius' role as consul would have been forgotten altogether. This is the only other reference to the treaty; from it Livy moves directly to the obituary notice for Menenius.

In short, of the three topics for 493 – Sp. Cassius and the treaty, Cominius and the Volscian war, and the death of Menenius Agrippa – Livy minimizes the first, plays up the second, and lingers over the third. This kind of manipulation of his material is something that he does readily and purposefully. As different studies have shown, Livy orders formal annalistic elements to a variety of ends.[30] In this particular case, to appreciate why Livy chose not to segregate Menenius and the secession from Coriolanus and his rebellion and why he foregrounds the Volscian campaign at the expense of the treaty, we have to read on into the narrative of Coriolanus.

Almost immediately after Menenius' obituary, Livy makes an explicit causal connection between the secession and Coriolanus' career. Having named the consuls for 492, Livy explains that the food shortage that turned into famine arose because the fields had not been cultivated during the plebs' absence: *caritas primum annonae ex incultis per secessionem plebis agris, fames deinde, qualis clausis solet* (2.34.2). The repetition of *per secessionem plebis,* just used to usher in the consuls of 493, hints at a meaningful overlap among these events. The consuls send out embassies to buy food both from neighboring territories and from Sicily. The first food to arrive is immediately distributed to the plebs and prevents starvation (2.34.5). When supplies arrive the following year from Sicily, however, the Senate meets to discuss the price at which the imported grain should be made available to the plebeians. At this point Livy exposes Coriolanus as an enemy of tribunician power, and his speech again links the current situation to the secession:

> In primis Marcius Coriolanus, hostis tribuniciae potestatis, 'Si annonam' inquit 'ueterem uolunt, ius pristinum reddant patribus ... Secedat (sc. Sicinius) nunc; auocet plebem; patet uia in Sacrum montem aliosque colles; rapiant frumenta ex agris nostris, quemadmodum tertio anno <ante> rapuere. Vtantur annona quam furore suo fecere. Audeo dicere hoc malo domitos ipsos potius cultores agrorum fore quam ut armati per secessionem coli prohibeant' (2.34.8–11).[31]

---

[30] Levene 1993 analyzes the placement of the prodigy lists to show how Livy manipulates so-called annalistic material (such as death notices) for artistic purposes; see, e. g., 1993: 77, 102–103, and 124–125. Rich 1997 demonstrates the freedom with which Livy arranges *res internae* and *externae* from year to year in Books 2–10.

[31] Chief among them, Marcius Coriolanus, an enemy of tribunician power, said, "If they want their old grain supply, let them restore the original law to the *patres* ... Let Sicinius secede now; let him call out the plebs; the way lies open, to the Sacred Mount and the other hills; let them snatch grain from our fields just as they did three years ago. Let them use the grain supply they sowed with their own madness. I venture to say that overcome by this evil they will sooner be tillers of fields than arm themselves and use a secession to prevent cultivation."

Whereas Menenius' famous fable is reported indirectly, Coriolanus gets to speak for himself. By appearing to give the audience unfiltered access to the speaker, *oratio recta* elevates Coriolanus and gives his view a special weight,[32] which Livy uses to stress the causal connection between the secession and the famine: according to Coriolanus, plebeian conduct during the secession triggered the food crisis. Coriolanus' claim contradicts the earlier narrative where Livy describes the secession as lasting several days only and emphasizes its pacific nature: *ibi sine ullo duce uallo fossaque communitis castris quieti, rem nullam nisi necessariam ad uictum sumendo, per aliquot dies neque lacessiti neque lacessentes sese tenuere* (2.32.4).[33] According to this description, the plebeians neither destroyed fields and property nor were absent long enough to interfere irreparably with agricultural tasks.

Coriolanus' allegation is not consistent with this account. Curiously, although scholars accept the historicity of the food shortage, neither the time-lag (with the secession preceding the famine by more than one agricultural cycle) nor the brevity of the secession, as reported by Livy, seems to have aroused comment. The version of Dionysius of Halicarnassus is more plausible on this point. He reports that the secession lasted from the autumnal equinox to the winter solstice, the period during which plowing and planting should have been done (7.1.1–2). This time-table makes more sense from an agricultural perspective; the loss of an entire crop could trigger a shortage later on.[34] The comparison with Dionysius suggests that Livy wanted the events linked (hence the compression of time and the repeated phrase *per secessionem plebis* at 2.33.3 and 34.2) and used Coriolanus to tie the narrative together. His punitive attitude in the debate over the price of the grain arises from his resentment of *tribunicia potestas*, the direct outcome of the secession; his hostility to the plebs results in his exile; the rest of his story follows from there.

The plebeians' reaction to Coriolanus' speech also highlights the intertwining of the events. While even the Senate finds Coriolanus' opinion harsh, the plebeians are infuriated and accuse Coriolanus of trying to starve them to death:

> Et senatui nimis atrox uisa sententia est, et plebem ira prope armauit. Fame se iam sicut hostes peti, cibo uictuque fraudari; peregrinum frumentum, quae sola alimenta ex insperato fortuna dederit, ab ore rapi. Nisi Cn. Marcio uincti dedantur tribuni, nisi de tergo plebis Romanae satisfiat (2.35.1).[35]

---

[32] Laird 1999: xiii and 135–136.

[33] What we should understand by *aliquot dies* is unclear. According to Packard 1968, the phrase occurs twenty-six times; *per dies aliquot* appears ten times. Since Livy also uses *per aliquot decem dies* and *per aliquot horas, menses, annos,* and *noctes,* the phrase seems to mean something between more than just two or three days, but probably not anything close to a month.

[34] On the food crisis of 492 see Frederiksen 1984: 166 and Garnsey 1988: 167–181 *passim.* Virlouvet 1985 occasionally has pertinent remarks in her study of the relationship between food shortages and riots.

[35] Where Coriolanus' view seemed excessively harsh to the Senate, the plebeians were practically up in arms with rage: they said that they were being attacked with starvation as if they were public enemies, and that they were being cheated of food and sustenance; imported grain – the sole source of nourishment unexpectedly conferred on them by chance – would be ripped from their mouths, unless they bound the tribunes and delivered them to Gnaeus Marcius, unless he was appeased by the flesh off their backs.

Here Coriolanus is snatching food from plebeian mouths, denying the Roman people nourishment, and forcing them to starvation because of the tribunes, the product of the secession. By having the interested parties refer explicitly and implicitly to the secession, Livy makes the debate over the distribution of supplies a bridge back to the circumstances and content of Menenius' fable.

Coriolanus and Menenius are linked yet again at the latter's final appearance in the text. Discussing the occasion when Menenius' son Titus was on trial, Livy says that the Senate supported him as much as it had Coriolanus during his trial; because of his failure during his consulship to bring aid at the battle of the Cremera, Titus incurred ill-will that neither his powerful backers nor his father's popularity could combat: *inuidiae erat amissum Cremerae praesidium, cum haud procul inde statiua consul habuisset; ea oppressit, cum et patres haud minus quam pro Coriolano adnisi essent et patris Agrippae fauor hauddum exoleuisset* (2.52.3–4). The comparison with Coriolanus reprises the earlier connection between the words of Menenius and the behavior of Coriolanus.

In addition to the structural and causal strands running through the episodes involving Menenius and Coriolanus, their sections of the text share nourishment as a central motif. First, even in his abbreviated account of the first secession, Livy takes space to mention how the plebeians fed themselves on the Sacred Mount: the key phrase is *rem nullam nisi necessariam ad uictum sumendo* (2.32.4). And Menenius Agrippa's fable obviously focuses on food; the explicit lesson is that the belly's processing and re-distribution of it are commensurate with the limbs' initial collection and delivery of it. But the significance of food goes beyond this surface level. As I noted before, while the analogy between the human body and the body politic is familiar from Greek literature, Menenius' particular version has no direct precedent in earlier extant texts.[36]

Comparison with other uses of the analogy, however, brings out the special features of Livy's. Ogilvie identifies passages in Xenophon and Isocrates (as cited by Polyaenus) which draw on analogies between bodily functions and a functional community. Neither, however, resembles Menenius' fable very much. The passage from Xenophon is about cooperation between pairs, specifically pairs of feet and pairs of hands; and the comparison in Isocrates is between parts of the army and parts of the body, with no reference to the stomach.[37] In his extensive study of the fable of the belly and the limbs in world literature, Gombel notes as a possible precursor the fable of the head and tail of the serpent, found in Babrius' Aesopic collection. The serpent's two ends fight over which of them should lead the way; when the tail has a turn at it, they both end up dead.[38] While the story again involves body parts and cooperation, digestion and the belly are absent. As Lincoln points out, the fable in Livy is distinctive precisely because it makes the belly, rather than the head, the most

---

[36] See Nestle 1927: 354–355 on the Greek origins of the body-state analogy and Gombel 1934: 39 on Livy as the oldest surviving version of the fable of the belly and the limbs.

[37] Ogilvie [1965] 1970: 312, with references to Xenophon *Mem.* 2.3.18 and Polyaenus *Strat.* 3.9.22.

[38] Gombel 1934: 28–39 discusses the history of this fable in both ancient and later texts. See n. 11 above for Adrados' view that Menenius' fable should be classified with Egyptian dispute narratives.

important part of the human body. In Lincoln's reading, while this departure from a more traditional hierarchy initially lowers (literally) the patricians, as dispensers of food they end up being the key component anyway.[39] Thus, considered among various other parables based on the body and communal cooperation, Menenius Agrippa's places unusual importance on the stomach and its functions.

The same conclusion emerges from comparisons with the other main sources for the first secession: Dionysius of Halicarnassus' account of early Rome and Plutarch's life of Coriolanus.[40] Of the three writers, Dionysius crafted the longest speech for Menenius; the most relevant passage is as follows:

Ἔοικέ πως ἀνθρωπείῳ σώματι πόλις. σύνθετον γὰρ καὶ ἐκ πολλῶν μερῶν ἐστιν
ἑκάτερον· καὶ οὔτε δύναμιν ἔχει ἕκαστον τὴν αὐτὴν τῶν ἐν αὐτοῖς μερῶν οὔτε
χρείας παρέχεται τὰς ἴσας. εἰ δὴ λάβοι τὰ μέρη τοῦ ἀνθρωπείου σώματος ἰδίαν
αἴσθησιν καθ' αὑτὰ καὶ φωνήν, ἔπειτα στάσις ἐν αὐτοῖς ἐμπέσοι καθ' ἓν γενομένοις
τοῖς ἄλλοις ἅπασι πρὸς τὴν γαστέρα μόνην, καὶ λέγοιεν οἱ μὲν πόδες, ὅτι πᾶν ἐπ'
αὐτοῖς ἐπίκειται τὸ σῶμα· αἱ δὲ χεῖρες, ὅτι τὰς τέχνας ἐργάζονται καὶ τἀπιτήδεια
ἐκπορίζουσι καὶ μάχονται πολεμίοις καὶ ἄλλα πολλὰ ὠφελήματα παρέχουσιν εἰς τὸ
κοινόν· οἱ δὲ ὦμοι, ὅτι τὰ ἄχθη πάντα ἐπ' αὐτοῖς κομίζεται· τὸ δὲ στόμα, ὅτι
φθέγγεται· ἡ δὲ κεφαλή, ὅτι ὁρᾷ καὶ ἀκούει καὶ τὰς ἄλλας αἰσθήσεις περιλαβοῦσα
πάσας ἔχει, δι' ὧν σῴζεται τὸ πρᾶγμα· εἶτα φαῖεν πρὸς τὴν γαστέρα· "Σὺ δ', ὦ
χρηστή, τί τούτων ποιεῖς ἢ τίς ἐστιν ἡ σὴ χάρις ἡμῖν καὶ ὠφέλεια; ἀλλὰ σύ γε
τοσοῦτον ἀπέχεις τοῦ πράττειν καὶ συγκατορθοῦν ἡμῖν <τι> τῶν κοινῇ χρησίμων,
ὥστε καὶ ἀντιπράττεις καὶ ἐνοχλεῖς καί, πρᾶγμα ἀφόρητον, ὑπηρετεῖν ἀναγκάζεις
καὶ φέρειν ἁπανταχόθεν εἰς τὴν ἐκπλήρωσιν τῶν σεαυτῆς ἐπιθυμιῶν. φέρε, τί οὐ
μεταποιούμεθα τῆς ἐλευθερίας, καὶ τῶν πολλῶν ἀφιέμεθα πραγματειῶν ἃς ἕνεκα
ταύτης ὑπομένομεν;" εἰ δὴ ταῦτα δόξειεν αὐτοῖς καὶ μηδὲν ἔτι δρῴη τὸ ἑαυτοῦ
ἔργον, ἔσθ' ὅπως ἂν ἐπὶ τὸ πολὺ διαρκέσαι δυνηθείη τὸ σῶμα, ἀλλ' οὐκ ἂν ἐντὸς
ὀλίγων ἡμερῶν τῷ κακίστῳ τῶν μόρων ἀναλωθείη, λιμῷ; οὐκ ἂν ἔχοι ἄλλως τις
εἰπεῖν. τὸν αὐτὸν δὴ τρόπον ὑπολάβετε καὶ περὶ πόλεως. (*Rom. Ant.* 6.86.1–3).[41]

---

[39] Lincoln 1989: 147.

[40] The Greek versions are quoted solely to highlight the distinctive character of Livy's rendition. Both come from texts that repay closer reading than is possible here. Although there is general agreement that Plutarch worked from Dionysius (see e.g. Russell 1963), the argument has been made that he also knew Livy's version; see Pelling 1997: 5–6 n. 6, who also discusses Plutarch's decision to include Menenius and his speech in the biography of Coriolanus.

[41] A state seems in some way comparable to the human body. For each is a composite, and of multiple parts; nor does any of the parts have the same capacity as any of the others, nor do they perform interchangeable functions. Indeed if the parts of the human body should take individual sense-perception and speech for themselves, and then sedition should fall upon them, as all the others joined in opposing the stomach by itself, and the feet should say that the whole body rests on them; and the hands, that they do the skilled labor and procure the provisions and fight against enemies and provide many other benefits to the common good; and the shoulders, that they carry all the burdens upon themselves; and the mouth, that it does the talking; and the head, that it sees and hears and that combining the other senses it holds together everything through which the entire operation is preserved; and then they should say to the stomach: "But you, my good madam, which of these do you do, or what is your benefit or contribution to us? You instead refrain to such an extent from acting and from helping us in accomplishing anything beneficial to the common good that you work against us and hinder us, and – an intolerable thing – you force us to serve you and to bring things from all over for the fulfillment of your own desires. Come, why

In comparison with this version, Livy's is much more narrowly focused on the body as a consumer of food. Although Menenius begins with the term *membrum* (limb), he refers specifically only to body parts that have to do with eating: *manus, os, dentes*. Dionysius, conversely, describes the activities of more prominent body parts: the feet support the body; the hands do most of the physical labor; the shoulders do the carrying; the mouth does the talking; and the head takes care of sense perception. The difference between the two authors is especially clear for the two organs they both include: Livy's hands simply carry food to the mouth; Dionysius' hands perform skilled labor, provide life's necessities, fight wars, and do many other things for the common good. Even more pointedly, Livy's *os* eats; Dionysius' στόμα talks. This contrast underscores the unconventionality of Livy's version. His Menenius assigns the rational powers of thinking and speaking to the individual parts while in Dionysius these rest with the head and mouth. Dionysius' perspective is the expected one. The effect in Livy's is to de-emphasize *consilium* and *sermo*, which are common to all, and to exaggerate the task of the stomach, which is also described in much greater detail.[42] In sum, faced with a fable that uses the body to illustrate the importance of reciprocity in intra-state relations, Livy chose to make it revolve around the consumption and absorption of food in an apparently unprecedented way.

The significance of Livy's shaping will become clear when the fable is considered in its context, but it is worth looking at the other main version extant as a contrast to Livy's since Plutarch's Menenius gives more attention to the political aspects of the analogy:

> Ταῦτ' ἔδεισεν ἡ βουλή, καὶ τοὺς ἐπιεικεῖς μάλιστα καὶ δημοτικοὺς τῶν πρεσβυτέρων ἐξαπέστειλε. προηγόρει δὲ Μενήνιος Ἀγρίππας, καὶ πολλὰ μὲν τοῦ δήμου δεόμενος, πολλὰ δ' ὑπὲρ τῆς βουλῆς παρρησιαζόμενος, τελευτῶντι τῷ λόγῳ περιῆλθεν εἰς σχῆμα μύθου διαμνημονευόμενον. ἔφη γὰρ ἀνθρώπου τὰ μέλη πάντα πρὸς τὴν γαστέρα στασιάσαι, καὶ κατηγορεῖν αὐτῆς, ὡς μόνης ἀργοῦ καὶ ἀσυμβόλου καθεζομένης ἐν τῷ σώματι, τῶν δ' ἄλλων εἰς τὰς ἐκείνης ὀρέξεις πόνους τε μεγάλους καὶ λειτουργίας ὑπομενόντων· τὴν δὲ γαστέρα τῆς εὐηθείας αὐτῶν καταγελᾶν, ἀγνοούντων ὅτι τὴν τροφὴν ὑπολαμβάνει μὲν εἰς αὐτὴν ἅπασαν, ἀναπέμπει δ' αὖθις ἐξ αὑτῆς καὶ διανέμει τοῖς ἄλλοις. "Οὗτος οὖν," ἔφη, "καὶ τῆς συγκλήτου λόγος ἐστίν, ὦ πολῖται, πρὸς ὑμᾶς· τὰ γὰρ ἐκεῖ τυγχάνοντα τῆς προσηκούσης οἰκονομίας βουλεύματα καὶ πράγματα πᾶσιν ὑμῖν ἐπιφέρει καὶ διανέμει τὸ χρήσιμον καὶ ὠφέλιμον" (*Cor.* 6.2–4).[43]

---

do we not make a bid for freedom and cast off the duties which we endure for its sake?" If they should thus indeed come to agreement and should no longer do their proper tasks, is it not the case that the body would not be able to last for long, but would it not within a few days be ruined by the worst of all fates, famine? No one could deny it. Now consider the same condition in a state. (Translation with acknowledgment to the Loeb.)

[42] Cf. Lincoln's point above about Livy's inversion of head and stomach within the traditional hierarchy of the body-state analogy.

[43] These matters frightened the Senate, and it dispatched those of the elders who were particularly suitable and close to the plebs in nature. Menenius Agrippa was the leader, and he, having beseeched the plebs at great length and having spoken freely at great length on behalf of the Senate, at the end of his speech came round to a famous fable. He said that all of a man's limbs revolted from the stomach, and accused it of being the only one to sit idly and unproductively in the body, while the others endured great

Probably the most noticeable feature of this version is how little it touches on the body and how much the emphasis has shifted to politics. The limbs (τὰ μέλη) are mentioned once, the γαστήρ twice; digestive action is summed up by τροφή, in strong contrast to Livy's longer and far more graphic account. Political vocabulary is the dominant language here: for example, the βουλή and the δῆμος, παρρησιαζόμενος and στασιάσαι, λειτουργίας and the tell-tale address to the limbs in the vocative ὦ πολῖται.

These comparisons might be developed further: Dionysius chooses to lead off with the parable's message while Livy and Plutarch reserve it for the end; where Livy opts for indirect discourse throughout, Dionysius gives Menenius a full-blown oration, of which this is only a fraction, and Plutarch mixes summary with direct speech. But the crucial distinction is that where Dionysius deals with multiple bodily functions and where Plutarch emphasizes the political part of the analogy over the digestive, Livy dwells on the latter.

While not as concentrated as in the brief rendition of the first secession, food and the body are also recurring elements in Livy's account of Coriolanus. As we saw, and as scholars have long recognized, the story of Coriolanus does not have a necessary connection to its historical setting; instead, as we also noted, Livy involves Coriolanus in this part of the narrative by having him participate in the senatorial debate on the distribution of grain (2.34.7–11). His hostile views there precipitate his exile and eventual downfall. Thus the very subject of Menenius' analogy, now actualized with real food, real hunger, and a real center of distribution, also weaves Coriolanus into the course of events. Food and the body resurface at the end of Coriolanus' career too. One of the questions his mother poses to him is '*Potuisti populari hanc terram quae te genuit atque aluit?*' (2.40.6).[44] The last word has particular significance: not just a general term for a mother's nurturing of a child and hence appropriate for Veturia's challenge to her son, *alo* is the verb used for the activity of the stomach as described by Menenius.[45] Coriolanus is here a disobedient limb, attacking the source of his nourishment.

A story framed within Coriolanus' shows the same preoccupation with bodily and civic well-being. After Coriolanus aligns himself with the Volsci and Attius Tullius, Livy embarks on what appears to be a digression (2.36.1–8) revolving around the celebration of sacred games. The original celebration was polluted, and Jupiter communicates his displeasure in a dream which comes to a plebeian named Titus Latinius. The latter disobeys the order to report the matter because he fears the patrician consuls more than Jupiter's message that, unless the games are repeated, danger will befall the city. Latinius' son dies; the dream reappears; Latinius grows weak as he delays.

---

labors and public services to serve the stomach's appetites; but the belly laughed at their simple-mindedness in not recognizing that it received into itself all the nourishment only to send it back out again and to distribute it to the others. "This then," he said, "is the relation of the Senate, my fellow citizens, to you. The business and affairs which meet there with the necessary management bring and distribute to you one and all what is useful and beneficial". (Translation with acknowledgement to the Loeb.)

[44] See Bonjour 1975 for the significance of *hanc terram* and an interpretation of Coriolanus' story as a didactic and patriotic tale about love for one's homeland, a pressingly topical question for Livy's Italy.

[45] *OLD* and *TLL* s.v. *alo*.

Finally, having consulted his family, he informs the Senate and walks away instantly cured (2.36.1–8).

The story initially appears to bear no relationship to its context and, as readers at least since Mommsen have noted, it is not intrinsic to the narrative of Coriolanus.[46] Burck, however, notes an important distinction between Livy's placement of the episode and that of Dionysius. As Burck points out, the Greek historian sets it at the end of 490, before he announces the consuls of 489 and embarks on the story of Coriolanus' exile. This arrangement isolates the story completely. Livy, by contrast, places it after Coriolanus' arrival among the Volsci and before Attius Tullius' appearance at the second celebration of the games. Latinius' dream is thus thoroughly integrated into the narrative, and the effect of the arrangement is to encourage the reader to seek connections between Latinius and the surrounding material.[47] Of course there is a connection in the plot-line: Attius Tullius cunningly tells the consuls in secret that his countrymen might take advantage of the distraction caused by the games to spring a surprise attack on the Romans. The consuls share the information with the Senate, and the decision is made to ban the Volsci from Rome (2.37.1–8). The inhospitable treatment renders them willing to renew the war with the Romans.

Beyond playing a structural part in the larger story, Latinius' dream is connected to it thematically. Here too a human body and the body politic share the same state of health. As Latinius shrinks from exposing the imminent danger to Rome, he becomes physically weak: *cunctantem tamen ac prolatantem ingens uis morbi adorta est debilitate subita* (2.36.5).[48] His recovery is thorough and remarkable: *inde in curiam iussu consulum delatus, eadem illa cum patribus ingenti omnium admiratione enarrasset, ecce aliud miraculum: qui captus omnibus membris delatus in curiam esset, eum functum officio pedibus suis domum redisse traditum memoriae est* (2.36.7– 8).[49] There is a strong emphasis on Latinius' physical powers: before he tells his dream to the senators he is hampered in every limb; having performed his duty he walks home on his own two feet. Latinius recognizes his civic obligation in time and, once the city can recover its religious well-being, he regains his physical health.

Livy's placement of Latinius' story within that of Coriolanus encourages a comparison of the two men. They might be considered opposites: Latinius is an ordinary plebeian at Rome, Coriolanus a military hero conspiring with the enemy; they are further differentiated by the ways they endanger Rome, with Latinius passively failing to report the dream and Coriolanus actively leading an army against the city. And yet both men put Rome at risk, and only consultation with family members re-directs their behavior. The critical difference is that, while Latinius solicits advice, Coriolanus must have it forced upon him (2.36.6 and 2.40.1–9). Appropriately enough, having

---

[46] Mommsen 1870: 7; see also the discussion in Ogilvie [1965] 1970 : 327.

[47] Burck [1934] 1964: 73.

[48] Nevertheless an extremely powerful illness overcame him as he delayed and procrastinated.

[49] He was then carried into the *curia* by order of the consuls. In the presence of the *patres* Latinius recounted the exact same story, to the amazement of all and, behold, there was another miracle! The tradition is that the very man who was carried into the *curia* paralyzed in every limb returned home on his own two feet once he had performed his duty.

fulfilled his patriotic duty, Latinius returns home (*domum redisse*, 2.36.8) while Coriolanus, at least in the version Livy prefers, lives out a miserable old age in exile (2.40.11). Livy's decision to insert Latinius into Coriolanus' career and to make him essential to the narrative, as well as thematically consistent, suggests that he valued the relevance of Latinius for Coriolanus. By interweaving the two, Livy makes the ordinary plebeian a foil for Coriolanus, one who can model the reciprocally beneficial relationship between the good citizen and his political community.

Latinius' story also recalls Menenius' fable. The civil disobedience of the limbs led to their enfeeblement; only cooperation with the belly saved them. The loss and restoration of major motor functions, as they relate to the commonwealth, occupy a central place in both.[50] Taken as a trio, Menenius, Coriolanus, and Latinius present a consistent message about the links among food, physical vigor, proper civic conduct, and the thriving of the body politic. In short, both structural and thematic concerns suggest that Livy composed his versions of the first secession and Coriolanus' career not as distinct units, but as complements to one another.

IV. CONCLUSION: ANALOGY AND ENACTMENT

These interconnections appear to be original to Livy. Of course his is the earliest extant version of the fable of the belly and the limbs, and although there are earlier sources for Coriolanus, without narrative context we cannot judge what connections others saw or developed between the two stories. The conventional method of evaluating the narrative of Livy's early books is to use Dionysius as a comparison, as has been done for the episodes here.[51] Most obviously, Livy chooses to compress where Dionysius expands, but this difference is significant in itself. As Gabba has shown, Dionysius exploits the first stage of the conflict of the orders, including Coriolanus' actions, to trace out in detail issues facing a contemporary audience. These questions are mostly political, and Dionysius' version of Menenius' speech is an essay on leadership; Dionysius chose to develop this part of the Roman past for its instructive qualities, especially as an exploration of successful government. In other words, though drawing on the same tradition as Livy, Dionysius sees different themes in it.[52]

The Roman historian has his own reasons for relating the chief accomplishments of Menenius and Coriolanus in complementary fashion. Menenius tells a story about what happens when the other parts of the body stop providing sustenance to the stomach. Denied food, the belly cannot supply nutrients to the limbs. Menenius presents the story as an analogy for the plebeians' refusal to participate in the life of

---

[50] The same word, *membrum*, occurs in both passages (2.32.9 and 36.8), but that is not overly surprising.

[51] The most extensive comparative treatment of the first secession and Coriolanus is Burck [1934] 1964: 61–76; Reichenberger [1931] 1964: 383–391 compares the two authors' accounts of Coriolanus in an attempt to reconstruct what lay in the annalistic record.

[52] Gabba 1991: 84–85 and 201–203.

the city; they accept the analogy and rejoin the community. Two years later, there is a food shortage, the Senate sends out embassies to buy supplies, and it then must determine how to distribute the imports to the starving plebeians. So what Livy apparently found in his sources was first a fable about a central organ processing and dispensing food and then a famine where the Senate provides for the feeding of the citizenry. Without independent access to his sources, we can never be certain, but it seems that Livy saw the essential compatibility of Menenius' fable with the received view of the course of events and wrote about both in such a way that the food crisis of the late 490s became an actualization of the Greek parable. This is the reason that he emphasizes the digestive aspects of the fable, interweaves Menenius and the resolution of the secession with Coriolanus' career, and dwells on food as a theme throughout these chapters. This kind of exposition through narrative is not as obvious as the explicit commentary found in some other historians, particularly the major Greek historians. Nonetheless, it has a sophisticated subtlety of its own, and Livy's preference for enacting his perception of events rather than spelling it out should not be mistaken for historical insensitivity. It is simply a different approach to writing history.

This discussion of how Livy placed Menenius' fable into the narrative of the opening decades of the republic points to three conclusions. First, while the habit of extracting portions of Livy's narrative to analyze them as isolated episodes is understandable, valid, and productive, this case is a salutary reminder that Livy saw Roman history as a coherent whole and set his careful miniatures in a broad canvas. If we choose to focus on individual episodes, we should keep in mind that we might be missing a larger picture. Second, again as this case shows, just because a historian does not state his ideas directly, we should not assume that he is not offering an interpretation of the events he is recording. Interestingly, this point was made in passing by H.H. Scullard in his biography of Scipio Africanus. Commenting on the relative merits of Polybius and Livy as sources, he noted, "Livy in epic form works his judgment into his historical narrative so that it partly becomes the narrative, while Polybius appears in his own person as critic and shows us how he forms his judgments."[53] John Marincola puts forward the same general idea more prominently when summing up the question of how the ancient historians position themselves with regard to 'inquiry':

> As a rule, Roman historians are more reluctant to give details of themselves and to discourse on methodological problems within the text of their works, but this is not to say that they do not have the same concerns as the Greek historians. Rather, they reveal them in a different way, at occasional points in the narrative and often without calling attention to them. Our discussion of inquiry, for example, can use numerous explicit remarks by the Greek historians about the investigatory aspect of history. For the Romans, however, we must look at what they say impersonally throughout the text of their work, when they are looking at individual incidents or problems. Not surprisingly, this has led some to think that the Romans had no

---

[53] Scullard 1970: 27.

concern with inquiry, but it is rather the case that the Roman tradition, for whatever reason, did not parade the author's inquiry as an explicit element for winning credibility. The manner of conveying one's knowledge of the problems inherent in inquiry was to indicate it gradually throughout the work, in ways that would then be picked up by the audience.[54]

Since Scullard wrote nearly thirty years before Marincola, it seems that this perception of how the Roman historians worked still has not become scholarly orthodoxy. The point thus bears repeating. While the commentary of a Thucydides or a Polybius draws the reader's attention to the author's analysis of his material, a historian need not editorialize to articulate an interpretation of the past. If we read Livy's narrative sensitive to the various ways he constructed it, we are more likely to appreciate his perception of the Romans' history.

WORKS CITED

Adrados, F.R. 1999. *History of the Graeco-Roman Fable. Volume One. Introduction and from the Origins to the Hellenistic Age*. Rev. and updated by the author and G.-J. van Dijk and translated by L.A. Ray. Leiden, Boston, and Köln.

Aly, W. 1936. *Livius und Ennius. Von Römischer Art. Neue Wege zur Antike*, Heft 5. Leipzig and Berlin.

Bonjour, M. 1975. "Les personnages féminins et la terre natale dans l'épisode de Coriolan (Liv., 2, 40)." *REL* 53: 157–181.

Briscoe, J. 1981. *A Commentary on Livy Books XXXIV–XXXVII*. Oxford.

Burck, E. [1934] 1964. *Die Erzählungskunst des T. Livius*. Repr. with new introduction. Berlin and Zurich.

Cornell, T.J. 1989. "Rome and Latium to 390 B. C." In F.W. Walbank et. al, eds., *The Cambridge Ancient History*. Vol. 7.2. 2nd ed. Cambridge. 243–308.

———. 1995. *The Beginnings of Rome. Italy and Rome from the Bronze Age to the Punic Wars (c. 1000–264 BC)*. New York and London.

van Dijk, J.G.M. 1997. *Αἶνοι, Λόγοι, Μῦθοι. Fables in Archaic, Classical and Hellenistic Greek Literature. With a Study of the Theory and Terminology of the Genre*. Leiden, New York, and Köln.

Drummond, A. 1989. "The Plebeian Movement." In F.W. Walbank et. al, eds., *The Cambridge Ancient History*. Vol. 7.2. 2nd ed. Cambridge. 212–227.

Fowler, D. [1989] 2000. "First Thoughts on Closure: Problems and Prospects." In *Roman Constructions. Readings in Postmodern Latin*. Oxford. 239–283 [repr. from *Materiali e discussioni per l'analisi dei testi classici* 22: 75–122].

———. [1997] 2000. "Second Thoughts on Closure." In *Roman Constructions. Readings in Postmodern Latin*. Oxford. 284–307 [repr. from D.H. Roberts, F.M. Dunn, and D. Fowler, eds., *Classical Closure: Reading the End in Greek and Latin Literature*. Princeton. 3–22].

Frederiksen, M. 1984. *Campania*. Ed. with additions by N. Purcell. Hertford, England.

Fusillo, M. 1997. "How Novels End: Some Patterns of Closure in Ancient Narrative." In D.H. Roberts, F.M. Dunn, and D. Fowler, eds., *Classical Closure: Reading the End in Greek and Latin Literature*. Princeton. 209–227.

Gabba, E. 1991. *Dionysius and the History of Archaic Rome*, Berkeley, Los Angeles, and Oxford.

Garnsey, P. 1988. *Famine and Food Supply in the Graeco-Roman World. Responses to Risk and Crisis*. Cambridge.

Gombel, H. 1934. *Die Fabel 'Vom Magen und den Gliedern' in der Weltliteratur*. Beihefte zur *Zeitschrift für romanische Philologie* 80. Halle.

---

[54] Marincola 1997: 264–265.

Hillgruber, M. 1996. "Die Erzählung des Menenius Agrippa. Eine griechische Fabel in der römischen Geschichtsschreibung." *A&A* 42: 42–56.

Kraus, C.S. 1994. *Livy. Ab Vrbe Condita. Book VI.* Cambridge.

Kraus, C.S. and A.J. Woodman. 1997. *Latin Historians. Greece and Rome* New Surveys in the Classics No. 27. Oxford.

Laird, A. 1999. *Powers of Expression, Expressions of Power: Speech Presentation and Latin Literature.* Oxford.

Lehman, A.D. 1952. "The Coriolanus Story in Antiquity." *CJ* 47: 329–336.

Levene, D.S. 1993. *Religion in Livy.* Leiden, New York and Köln.

Lincoln, B. 1989. *Discourse and the Construction of Society: Comparative Studies of Myth, Ritual, and Classification.* Oxford and New York.

Luce, T.J. 1965. "The Dating of Livy's First Decade." *TAPhA* 96: 209–240.

———. 1977. *Livy. The Composition of his History.* Princeton.

Marincola, J. 1997. *Authority and Tradition in Ancient Historiography.* Cambridge.

Mellor, R. 1999. *The Roman Historians.* New York and London.

Momigliano, A. 1942. "Camillus and Concord." *CQ* 36: 111–120.

Mommsen, Th. 1870. "Die Erzählung von Cn. Marcius Coriolanus." *Hermes* 4: 1–26.

Nestle, W. 1927. "Die Fabel des Menenius Agrippa." *Klio* 21: 350–360.

Oakley, S.P. 1997. *A Commentary on Livy Books VI-X.* Vol. I. Oxford.

Ogilvie, R.M. [1965] 1970. *A Commentary on Livy, Books 1–5.* Repr. with addenda. Oxford.

Packard, D.W. 1968. *A Concordance to Livy.* 4 Vols. Cambridge, Mass.

Pelling, C. 1997. "The Shaping of Coriolanus: Dionysius, Plutarch, and Shakespeare." In M.A. McGrail, ed., *Shakespeare's Plutarch. Poetica* 48. 3–32.

Pomeroy, A.J. 1988. "Livy's Death Notices." *G&R* 35: 172–83.

Reichenberger, A. [1931] 1964. "Die Coriolan-Erzählung." In E. Burck ed., *Wege zu Livius.* Darmstadt. 383–391 [repr. from "Studien zum Erzählungsstil des Titus Livius." Diss., Heidelberg. 23–29].

Rich, J. 1997. "Structuring Roman History: the Consular Year and the Roman Historical Tradition." *Histos* 1 (http://www.dur.ac.uk/Classics/histos/1997/rich1.html).

Russell, D.A. 1963. "Plutarch's Life of Coriolanus." *JRS* 53: 21–28.

Rutherford, I. 1997. "Odes and Ends: Closure in Greek Lyric." In D.H. Roberts, F.M. Dunn, and D. Fowler, eds., *Classical Closure: Reading the End in Greek and Latin Literature.* Princeton. 43–61.

Salmon, E.T. 1930. "Historical Elements in the Story of Coriolanus." *CQ* 24: 96–101.

Schönberger, O. 1955. "Zur Coriolan-Episode bei Livius." *Hermes* 83: 245–248.

Schur, W. *RE* suppl. V. 1931, coll. 653–660 (*Marcius* 51).

Scullard, H.H. 1970. *Scipio Africanus: Soldier and Politician.* Bristol, England.

Virlouvet, C. 1985. *Famines et émeutes à Rome des origines de la République à la mort de Néron.* Collection de l'école française de Rome 87. Rome.

Witte, K. 1910. "Über die Form der Darstellung in Livius Geschichtswerk." *RhM* 65: 270–305, 359–419.

18

Athenian Prostitution as a Liberal Profession[*]

Edward. E. Cohen

I deal here with Athenian prostitution as a business – and specifically as a "liberal profession" (in Greek terms, an *eleutherios tekhnē*[1]) – an aspect that has been largely ignored in the cascade of recent studies directed toward cultural, political, or gender aspects of the purchase of sex. My thesis is that certain baffling historical phenomena (such as the predilection of wool workers to "moonlight" as prostitutes, the disclosure by the *phialai exeleutherikai* inscriptions that at Athens "women seem just as likely to have jobs as do men" (Todd 1997: 122), and the insistence of male and female *hetairoi,-ai* on working pursuant to written contract) reflect an obsessive Athenian concern not with the inherent morality of an occupation like prostitution, but with the extent of a worker's freedom from another person's control or supervision – in Greek terms, the relative degree to which a working individual appears to be *eleutheros* or *doulos* (*-ē*). At Athens a prostitute might enjoy esteem as a practitioner of a trade involving service for limited periods of time in individually-negotiated arrangements – provided that the sex worker (like any other worker) did not fall under the control or supervision of another person. Of the two principal clusters of ancient Greek words relating to prostitution, those terms cognate to *pernanai* ("sell") connote a dependent status repellent to free persons, while those cognate to *hetairein* ("be a companion") denote an acceptable independence of occupation.[2]

---

[*] I am delighted to dedicate this article to Alan Boegehold, from whom I have learned much in many discussions over many years.

[1] ἐλευθέριος (-α) τέχνη: Plu. *Mor.* 122D. Although the English use of "liberal" as "suitable for free persons" ("liberal profession," "liberal education") is derived from the Latin *liberalis,* the Athenians employed *eleutherios* (and its cognates) in the same sense. See, for example, Xen. *Apom.* 2.7.4 (ἐλευθερίως πεπαιδευμένους). Cf. Xen. *Apom.* 2.84; Pl. *Nomoi* 823e; Aristot. *Pol.* 1338a32. In contrast, "prostitution appropriate to slaves" was ἡ τῶν πορνῶν ἐργασία (Dem. 59.113).

[2] In actual usage, however, the Greeks did not consistently differentiate *pernanai* (and related terms) from *hetairein* (and related terms). Since *pornos* and its cognates tended to be derogatory, and *hetairos* euphemistic (cf. Aiskh. 1.51–52), an author's choice between one or the other of these two groupings would not necessarily reflect an objective and consistent distinction between the two clusters, but might correspond merely to the speaker's desired characterization of a person in immediate context. In a single speech an individual is sometimes referred to indiscriminately by both terms. See Dem. 48.53, 56; Aiskhin. 1 passim. Cf. the variant denomination of Sinope in Dem. 22.56, 59.116. Comic writers are similarly inconsistent: see Anaxilas (Fr. 22 [K.-A.], lines 1, 22, 31)(a passage describing the same women as *hetairai* at the beginning and end, but in the middle as *pornai*). Aristoph. *Plout.* 149–55 describes Corinthian *hetairai* and *pornoi* as acting in exactly the same fashion (καὶ τάς γ᾽ ἑταίρας φασὶ τὰς

A. ATHENIAN WORK ETHICS

In the modern world, prostitution is, of course, not "just another job": contemporary societies in general condemn commercial sex as morally degenerate and humanly exploitative.[3] Labor laws deny sexual workers rights available to others. Prostitutional arrangements are denied recognition as legitimate contracts of employment.[4] Prostitutes are even branded as criminals in most countries.[5] Historians of ancient Greece often assert that prostitution likewise evoked Athenian antipathy[6] – sometimes citing as evidence remarks by unrepresentative theorists opposed to all forms of commercial endeavor or erotic expression.[7] In fact, prostitution was lawful and pervasive in Attika.[8] Lauded by comic poets as a democratic and ethically desirable alternative to other forms of non-marital sex,[9] prostitution gained social legitimacy from its association with the goddess Aphrodite,[10] who was believed to aid *hetairai* in securing wealthy clients and whose cult sites (outside Attika) sometimes offered

---

Κορινθίας ... καὶ τούς γε παῖδάς φασι ταὐτὸ τοῦτο δρᾶν ... τοὺς πόρνους). For ancient and modern treatments of the terms, and various (usually incompatible) efforts to distinguish them, see E. Cohen (forthcoming).

[3] Traditional values, however, are now being increasingly contested by prostitutional rights organizations: see, for example, the web sites of the Prostitutes' Education Network (http://bayswan.org/penet.htm) and of the National Task Force on Prostitution (http://bayswan.org/biblio.html). Cf. Bindman 1997; McClintock 1993; Jenness 1993. In the Netherlands, organizations like the Red Thread have succeeded in legalizing brothels, but public antipathy and official harassment continue (N.Y. Times, August 12, 2001).

[4] Pateman 1988: 191; Richards 1982: 115, 121; Ericcson 1980: 335–66; McIntosh 1978: 54.

[5] Ironically, emerging challenges in Western countries to demonization of commercial sex (n. 3 above) have been paralleled by the continuing encroachment in other societies of Western antagonism to erotic trade. In Japan, prostitution was a licensed profession from at least the fourteenth century until it was proscribed, as a result of the American occupation – although many Japanese still defend its compatibility with Eastern, rather than Christian, social and sexual morals. See Garon 1997: 89–90; cf. Fowler 1998.

[6] Kapparis 1999: 5 ("disreputable"); Henry 1986; D. Cohen 1991: 179; Brock 1994: 338, 341; Seltman 1953: 115. Cf. Davidson 1997: 89: "a large group of women in ancient Athens ... were forced (or chose)" to work first in wool, then in sex, "tainting the reputation of the textile industry."

[7] For philosophers' proposed constraints on sex, see Plato *Rep.* 458d–461b, *Nomoi* 840d–841e; Aristot. *Pol.* 1334b29–1335b37, 1335b38–1336a2. For traditional abhorrence of "money-making" activities, see E. Cohen 2000: 187–90.

[8] Cf. Xen. *Apom.* 2.2.4 (prostitutes available everywhere: τῶν γε ἀφροδισίων ἕνεκα ... τούτου γε τῶν ἀπολυσόντων μεσταὶ μὲν αἱ ὁδοί, μεστὰ δὲ τὰ οἰκήματα). Harrison 1968: 37 infers from the charges set forth in Aiskhin. 1 the existence of a γραφὴ ἑταιρήσεως, effectively prohibiting prostitution by male citizens. But there is no allusion in the speech to any such statute (despite Aiskhines' invocation of a host of other proscriptions). Lipsius [1905–15] 1966: 436 correctly dismisses the possibility of even an unenforced legal ban on prostitution.

[9] See Philemon Fr. 3 (K-A); Euboulos Fr. 67 and Fr. 82 (K-A).

[10] "Hetairai in ancient Athens prayed and made offerings to their patron deity Aphrodite, just as wives and pregnant women worshipped Hera and Artemis respectively" (Neils 2000: 216). Cf. Thornton 1997: 152. At Korinth supplicants to Aphrodite actively sought prostitutes' help: Athen. 13.573c. On the perceived power of Aphrodite in human affairs ("les puissances de l'amour en Grèce antique"), see Calame 1996: 11–20.

"sacred prostitutes."[11] Within Attika, the shrine of Aphrodite Pandemos, near the Akropolis,[12] was said to have been built from the proceeds of one of Solon's innovations, the state's purchase and employment of female slaves as prostitutes. Despite the doubtful historicity of this tale,[13] the laudatory connection of democracy's founder with the foundation of brothels does provide startling insight into a fourth-century Athens that treated prostitution as a " 'democratic' reform" (Kurke 1999: 199), "as an intrinsic element of the democracy" (Halperin 1990: 100). And through its "tax on prostitution" (*pornikon telos*), Athens – which never did restrict "victimless sexual conduct"[14] – was an active accessory to the sexual labors of its residents.[15] Even the city's Goddess, Athena, titular deity of crafts, listed prostitutes among her benefactors (Harris 1995: 144–49), and a monument honoring a famed *hetaira* stood on the Athenian Akropolis next to a statue of Aphrodite (Pausanias 1.23.2).

Another form of labor, however, did evoke moral outrage. Athenians uniformly disapproved of free persons engaging in work that required regular and repetitive service for a single employer on an ongoing basis over a continuing period – what we would term a "job." For free Athenians, a pervasive moral tenet was "the obligation to maintain an independence of occupation ... and at all costs to avoid seeming to work in a 'slavish' way for another."[16] In Aristotle's words, "the nature of the free man prevents his living under the control of another."[17] Isokrates equates hired employment (*thēteia*) with slavery.[18] Isaios laments the free men, and Demosthenes the free women, compelled by a "lack of necessities" to labor for pay: free people "should be pitied" if economic necessity forces them into "slavish" (*doulika*) employment.[19]

---

[11] Aid in obtaining customers: Athen. 13.588c. On sacred prostitution: see Wake 1932; Legras 1997: 250–58, who (at p. 250 n. 5) provides references to earlier literature; Beard and Henderson 1997; Lentakis 1998: 321–44; Kurke 1999: 220–46.

[12] For the temple of Athena Pandemos (located immediately below that of Athena Nike at the Propylaia), see Paus. 1.22.3; Beschi 1967–68; for Aphrodite's temple on the Sacred Way, see Travlos 1937; *IG* II² 4570, 4574–85.

[13] Athen. 13.569d-f= Philemon Fr. 3 (K-A), Nikandros of Kolophon *FGrHist* 271/2 F 9. *Pace* Herter 1960 [1985]: 73, most scholars dismiss the report as unfounded: see Halperin 1990: 100–101.

[14] Wallace 1997: 151–52 and ff. Attic law mandated the recognition of "whatever arrangements either party willingly agreed upon with the other": τοῖς νόμοις τοῖς ὑμετέροις (scil. Ἀθηναίοις) οἳ κελεύουσι, ὅσα ἄν τις ἑκὼν ἕτερος ἑτέρῳ ὁμολογήσῃ κύρια εἶναι (Dem. 56.2). Similarly: Dem. 42.12, 47.77; Hyper. 5.13; Dein. 3.4; Plato, *Symp.* 196c. For occasional limitations on other personal freedoms, cf., however, Wallace 1993, 1994a, 1994b and 1996.

[15] Andreades [1928] 1992: 358 terms Athens' fiscal involvement "scandalous" (σκανδαλώδη). But Aiskhines reports matter-of-factly: καθ᾽ ἕκαστον ἐνιαυτὸν ἡ βουλὴ πωλεῖ τὸ πορνικὸν τέλος· καὶ τοὺς πριαμένους τὸ τέλος οὐκ εἰκάζειν, ἀλλ᾽ ἀκριβῶς εἰδέναι τοὺς ταύτῃ χρωμένους τῇ ἐργασίᾳ (1.119). Cf. Pollux 7.202, 9.29; Lentakis 1998: 130–54; Pirenne-Delfore 1994: 117. Similar tax at Cos: Reinach 1892; Khatzibasileiou 1981: 8.55–56.

[16] Fisher 1998a: 70. Similarly: Cartledge 1993: 148–49; Fisher 1993.

[17] Aristot. *Rhet.* 1367a33: ἐλευθέρου γὰρ τὸ μὴ πρὸς ἄλλον ζῆν. Jameson 1997: 100 notes free persons' "reluctance to admit to the need of working for someone else." Cf. Humphreys [1983] 1993:10; Finley 1981: 122.

[18] 14.48. Cf. Aristot. *Rhet.* 1367a30–32: ἐλευθέρου γὰρ σημεῖον· οὐδὲν ποιεῖν ἔργον θητικόν.

[19] Isaios 5.39: δι᾽ ἔνδειαν τῶν ἐπιτηδείων. Dem. 57.45: πολλὰ δουλικὰ καὶ ταπεινὰ πράγματα τοὺς ἐλευθέρους ἡ πενία βιάζεται ποιεῖν, ἐφ᾽ οἷς ἐλεοῖντ᾽ ἂν ... πολλαὶ καὶ τιτθαὶ καὶ ἔριθοι καὶ τρυγήτριαι

Receipt of a salary (*misthophoria*) was the hallmark of a slave. When the Athenian state required coin-testers and mint-workers for continuing service, legislation explicitly provided for the payment of *misthophoriai* to the skilled public slaves (*dēmosioi*) who provided these services on a regular basis (and for their punishment in the event of absenteeism).[20] Even lucrative managerial positions were disdained by free persons: most supervisors accordingly were slaves,[21] even on large estates where high compensation had to be offered to motivate unfree but highly-skilled individuals.[22] Thus, in Xenophon's *Memorabilia* (§2.8), Sokrates proposes permanent employment as an estate supervisor to Eutheros, an impoverished free man. Such *epitropoi*, Sokrates notes, were well compensated (§6) for even routine services (§3). But Eutheros curtly rejects the suggestion: managing an employer's property was only appropriate for a slave (§4).

Athenian morality thus tended to focus on the structure of work relationships, and not on the actual nature of the labor undertaken. Confounding modern expectations, the same labor functions might be performed indiscriminately by slave workers or by free "foreign residents" [*metics*] or by "citizens" [*politai*].[23] (In fact, the shoes for the public slaves working at Eleusis were made by a cobbler who was a *politēs*![24]) In the Athenian navy, *politai*, metics and slaves served as crew members without differentiation of status or work assignment: a master and his slave even appear often to have been rowers on the same trireme.[25] Within Athenian households, free women worked alongside domestic slaves at many tasks.[26] Yet the willingness of Athenian "citizens" to do the same work as foreigners or slaves was accompanied by a scrupulous effort to avoid even the appearance of being "employed" at a job. Service outside the Athenian household by free persons was usually for a single specific task or for a limited period of time and seldom exclusive to a single employer: we typically encounter Athenian businessmen working on their own for a variety of customers, or agents undertaking a limited task for an individual client.[27] Even slaves attempted to

---

γεγόνασιν ὑπὸ τῶν τῆς πόλεως κατ᾽ ἐκείνους τοὺς χρόνους συμφορῶν ἀσταὶ γυναῖκες. On *misthōtoi*, see Martini 1997: 49.

[20] *SEG* 26.72, lines 49–55. See Figueira 1998: 536–47; Alessandri 1984; Stumpf 1986. Cf. *IG* II² 1492.137; *IG* II² 1388.61–62.

[21] As employees, unfree labor fell into two categories: "management slaves" (*epitropoi*) and workers (*ergatai*): δούλων δὲ εἴδη δύο, ἐπίτροπος καὶ ἐργάτης. *Oikonomikos* A.5.1 (attributed to Aristotle).

[22] See Xen. *Oik.* 12.3; 1.16–17.

[23] R. Osborne 1995: 30; Hopper 1979: 140; Finley 1981: 99; Ehrenberg 1962: 162, 183, 185; Loomis 1998: 236–39. This concurrence is especially well-attested in the construction trades: Randall 1953; Burford 1972; E. Cohen 2000: 134–35, 187.

[24] *IG* II² 1672.190. Cf. *IG* II² 1672.70–71.

[25] See *IG* I³ 1032, Thouk. 7.13.2 which together confirm that "slaves regularly formed a substantial proportion of the rowers on Athenian triremes, and their masters included fellow oarsmen" (Graham 1998: 110). Cf. Graham 1992; Welwei 1974. See the discussion of Isokrates 8.48 at Burke 1992: 218.

[26] See, for example, Iskhomakhos' wife at Xen. *Oik.* 7.6. The wife's role, however, was often essentially managerial: see E. Cohen 2000: 37–38.

[27] Cf. the maritime entrepreneur who introduces a client to the bank of Herakleides in Dem. 33.7; Agyrrhios who serves Pasion as a representative in litigational matters (Isok. 17.31–32.; cf. Stroud 1998: 22, Strauss 1987: 142); Arkhestratos who provided the bond for Pasion (Isok. 17.43); Stephanos' relationship with the banker Aristolokhos at Dem. 45.64.

avoid the appearance of "slavish employment": the Athenian institution of "servants living independently" (*douloi khōris oikountes*) permitted unfree persons to conduct their own businesses, establish their own households, and sometimes even to own their own slaves[28] – with little contact, and most importantly, virtually without supervision from their owners.[29] The presence, or absence, of supervision and control was a critical, perhaps the central, factor in Athenian evaluation of work situations.

B. SEX AND TEXTILES: WEAVING A WEB OF EROTIC DEPENDENCE

Athenian aversion to the dependence inherent in salaried employment meant that providing sex in brothels was appropriate only for slaves. In actual practice, numerous opportunities for self-employment of free persons in craft or trade,[30] and the wide availability of paid public positions,[31] left only slaves (and family members) as potential employees for the many Athenian businesses (workshops, stores, brothels, banks, and numerous other *ergasiai*) that needed the labor of individuals over a continuing period of time.[32] "Nowhere in the sources do we hear of private establishments employing a staff of hired workers as their normal operation" (Finley 1981: 262–63 n. 6). Athenians assumed, correctly, that persons performing repetitive functions in a commercial context – whether bank staff[33] or sexual workers – were likely to be slaves.[34] At Kolonos Agoraios, the site of Athens' incipient version of a labor market,[35] *douloi* constituted virtually all of those standing for hire.[36]

---

[28] See E. Cohen 2000: 145–54; Hervagault and Mactoux 1974; Perotti 1974. For the banking *oikoi* of slaves and former slaves, see E. Cohen 1992: Chapter 4.

[29] The *douloi* Xenon, Euphron, Euphraios and Kallistratos – while still enslaved – as principals operated the largest bank in Athens, that of Pasion. Their only involvement with their owners appears to have been annual payment of lease obligations. Dem. 36.14, 43, 46, 48. Cf. Meidas, a slave who ran a substantial perfume business but provided his owner with reports only monthly and again subject only to a fixed payment (Hyper. *Ath.* 9).

[30] See below, p. 228.

[31] The Athenian state offered paid service in the armed forces, and compensation for frequent jury duty and assembly meetings; for "incapacitated" *politai* of limited means, there were outright public grants (Aristot. *Ath. Pol.* 49.4). Cf. Lysias 24 in which an Athenian unable to work easily at his own business but too poor to buy a slave doesn't even consider the possibility of hiring a free man to work for him: instead he seeks public assistance (§6).

[32] For the complex commercialization of the fourth-century Athenian economy, see Shipton 1997. Cf. Theokhares 1983: 100–14; Gophas 1994; Kanellopoulos 1987: 19–22.

[33] For example: in questioning whether collateral security had actually been delivered, a creditor assumes that a bank's workers would have been exclusively servile (Dem. 49.51: τίς ὁ παραλαβὼν τῶν οἰκετῶν τῶν ἡμετέρων;).

[34] A few free persons – motivated by abject circumstance or financial incentives – might occasionally have accepted paid employment (see above n. 19 and accompanying text).

[35] Marx believed that the formation of a labor market necessarily meant the introduction of "wage slavery," a precursor to classical capitalism (1970–72: I.170; cf. Lane 1991: 310–11). But this proposition is not confirmed by the continued dominance of the Athenian economy by household-based businesses primarily utilizing household members.

[36] Pherekrates Fr. 142 (K-A). See Fuks 1951: 171–73; Garlan 1980: 8–9. The prime ancient Greek term for "slave" was *doulos* (masc. plur. *douloi*, fem. sing. *doulē*, fem. plur. *doulai*). On the multiplicity of unfree statuses in ancient Greece, and the corresponding multitude of descriptive terms, see Gschnitzer

Most slaves, however, worked "at home," that is, within the household (*oikos*) with which virtually all persons at Athens, both free and unfree, were affiliated.[37] It was the *oikos* (and not the individual[38] or family[39]) that occupied central position in Athenian society.[40] As an entity encompassing the physical attributes of a residence, the complement of members now (or in some cases previously) living in that residence, and the assets relating to those members,[41] the *oikos* was "the basic economic unit of the polis" (Sourvinou-Inwood 1995: 113). "Since economic enterprises largely existed and were managed within the structure of households," the *oikos* dominated "the economy of Greek city-states" (Foxhall 1994: 139). As a result, " 'firm' and private household" were, in Moses Finley's words, "one and the same,"[42] and so, for those slaves working in brothels, their *oikos* was likely to be both their place of work and their residence.[43]

1964: 1283–1310; Carrière-Hervagault 1973: 45–79; Mactoux 1980: 21–124. Cf. Faraguna 1999: 58–59; E. Cohen 1992: 74 n. 63.

[37] Aristot. *Pol.* 1253b6–7: πρῶτα δὲ καὶ ἐλάχιστα μέρη οἰκίας δεσπότης καὶ δοῦλος, καὶ πόσις καὶ ἄλοχος, καὶ πατὴρ καὶ τέκνα. Cf. *Pol.* 1253b4–7: οἰκία δὲ τέλειος ἐκ δούλων καὶ ἐλευθέρων. In a ceremony analogous to that which greeted the entry of a bride, a newly-purchased slave was welcomed into the *oikos* with an outpouring of figs, dates and other delicacies intended to portend a "sweet and pleasant" future. See Lex. Seguer. (Bekker) 269.9. Cf. Aristoph. *Plout.* 768 and schol.; Dem. 45.74; Pollux 3.77; Harpokration and Suidas, s.v. καταχύσματα. (Acceptance of slaves as inferior members of a family has been characteristic of many societies [cf., for example, pre-colonial slavery in West Africa: Miers and Kopytoff 1977: 11]).

[38] Communitarians, critical of the contemporary orientation toward individual rights, often insist that the Hellenic "notion of the political community as a common project is alien to the modern liberal individualistic world" (MacIntyre 1981: 146–47). Cf. Sandel 1984: 87; Yack 1993: 30. For the differing ancient and modern approaches to individual status and rights, see Ostwald 1996 and the essays in H. Jones 1998. Morris 1987: 3 notes that in ancient Greece "there were no natural rights of the individual" (but for a more nuanced view, see Miller 1974, 1995, passim).

[39] The ancient Greeks did not even have a word for *family*, in the modern sense of a nuclear or extended grouping of people living together (ἀνώνυμον γὰρ ἡ γυναικὸς καὶ ἀνδρὸς σύζευξις: Aristot. *Pol.* 1253b9–10). Finley notes: "the necessity never made itself felt to provide a specific name for the restricted concept evoked by our word 'family' " ([1973] 1999: 18–19).

[40] Juridically, "the polis was an aggregation of *oikoi*" (Wolff 1944: 93) with a legal system based on "the rights of families as corporate groups" (Todd 1993: 206). See Aristot. *Pol.* 1252; Xen. *Oik.* esp. 1.5, 6.4; Lys. 1 and 32. Cf. Cox 1998: 13; Ogden 1996: 42; Strauss 1993: 35, 43; Patterson 1990: 43–44, 51, 55–57, 59, 1981: 9–10; Jameson 1990: 179; Foxhall 1989, 1994, and 1996: 140–52; Sissa 1986; Hallett 1984: 72–76; Sealey 1984: 112; Hunter 1981: 15; Lotze 1981: 169; Fisher 1976: 2, 5 ff.; Lacey 1968: 88–90; Ledl 1907–8.

[41] Although "the different senses of the word" can be studied separately (as MacDowell 1989 does) – and in context a particular aspect may be emphasized (as with the physical premises in Antiph. 2d.8) – the unique signification of the term lies in its denotation of an *entity*. For each of the separate notations of physical place, the human beings associated with that place and assets of value belonging to those persons, Greek offers a plenitude of alternative terms, most particularly *oikia* for the physical house, *klēros* for the assets and *agkhisteia* for a circle of related persons.

[42] [1953] 1984: 69. Cf. Plácido 1997. Even "slaves living independently" (δοῦλοι χωρὶς οἰκοῦντες) and "public slaves" (δημόσιοι) tended to create their own quasi-*oikoi*: see E. Cohen 2000: 136–37, 148–52. Identity of firm and household appears to have been widespread in antiquity: for the ancient Near East, see Silver 1995: 50–54; for Rome, Kirschenbaum 1987: 122–23.

[43] Kapparis 1999: 228 ("prostitutes working in brothels lived on the premises"). Cf. Herodas 2.36 (Cunningham 1971: 88). Many professions and crafts (*tekhnai*) are known to have been conducted at

In fact, substantial ancient evidence shows that "the prostitution of slaves was paradigmatically based in brothels" (porneia)[44] and that pornai – in contrast to the predominantly free hetairoi and hetairai chronicled in the literary tradition[45] – were predominantly slaves (doulai). Aiskhines makes explicit the contrast between free hetairoi and slave pornoi when he urges Timarkhos, charged with prostitution, to respond to the accusations not as a pornos, but as a prostitute who is a free man.[46] Demosthenes warns that if Athenian juries do not uphold laws relating to citizenship, the work of pornai will fall to the daughters of "citizens," but that hetairai will be indistinguishable from (other) free women.[47] Herodas assumes that pornai are slaves: to protect his pornai, Battaros invokes a law dealing with doulai.[48] In fact, the words pornē and doulē occur together so commonly that a study by the Italian scholar Citti has concluded that mention of the term pornē in ancient Greek necessarily evokes the mental image of a doulē: the two words form "una coppia nominale," "a verbal coupling."[49] Thus the defendant in Lysias 4, seeking to have a woman give evidence under torture, refers to her not merely as a "slave"[50] but as a "slave pornē" (in Greek doulē pornē).[51] In fact, her characterization as a "doulē" is based only on the defendant's characterization of her as a pornē: the plaintiff insists that she is free,[52] and no evidence (other than her characterization as a doulē) suggests that she is enslaved. Theopompos, the fourth-century historian, emphasizes the linkage between the two terms in describing a certain Pythionike, a slave who had belonged to three

---

home. See Aeschin. 1.124 (single house used in turn as a business-place and home by a doctor, smith, fuller, carpenter and as a brothel); Dem. 47.56; Men. Sam. 234–36; Pollux 1.80. Even the permanent physical premises of an Athenian bank were usually coextensive with the personal residence of the trapeza's proprietor: see Dem. 49.22; 52.8; 52.14. Cf. Bettali 1985; Jameson 1990: 185; Pesando 1987: 47–55.

[44] Flemming 1999: 43. Cf. Davidson 1997: 90–99; Kapparis 1999: 228–29.

[45] "Ces hétaïres étaient en fait les seules femmes vraiment libres de l'Athènes classique" (Mossé 1983: 63). Cf. Klees 1998: 147 n. 16.

[46] ἃ δὲ πείθει σε Δημοσθένης λέγειν, οὐκ ἀνδρός ἐστιν ἐλευθέρου, ἀλλὰ πόρνου περὶ τῶν τόπων διαφερομένου (1.123).

[47] Dem. 59.113: ... προπηλακισθέντος δὲ τοῦ νόμου ... ἡ μὲν τῶν πορνῶν ἐργασία ἥξει εἰς τὰς τῶν πολιτῶν θυγατέρας ... τὸ δὲ τῶν ἐλευθέρων γυναικῶν ἀξίωμα εἰς τὰς ἑταίρας, ἂν ἄδειαν λάβωσι τοῦ ἐξεῖναι αὐταῖς παιδοποιεῖσθαι ὡς ἂν βούλωνται καὶ τελετῶν καὶ ἱερῶν καὶ τιμῶν μετέχειν τῶν ἐν τῇ πόλει.

[48] Mime 2: 30, 36–37, 46–48: ἐγὼ δ]ὲ πό[ρ]νας ἐκ Τύρου ... οὐδὲ τῶν πορνέων βίηι λαβὼν οἴχωκεν· ... ἐπὴν δ' ἐλεύθερός τις αἰκίσηι δούλην ... τῆς δίκης τὸ τίμημα διπλοῦν τελείτω.

[49] 1997: 92. Citti sees the two terms as virtually synonymous: "uno dei due termini comportasse l'altro" (1997: 95). Cf. Marzi 1979: 29.

[50] Only unfree persons were putatively subject to examination under torture in private disputes. But – despite much surviving rhetorical posturing – no slave is known to have actually given testimony under torture in private disputes. Todd 1990: 33–34 summarizes: "on forty-two occasions in the orators we find the challenge, either 'torture my slaves for evidence' or 'let me torture yours'. Forty times this challenge was flatly rejected; twice (Isoc. 17.15–16, Dem. 37.42) it was accepted but not carried through." Various explanations have been proffered for this pattern: see Thür 1977; Gagarin 1996, 2001; Mirhady 1996, 2000; Allen 2000: 365–66 n. 14.

[51] Lys. 4.19: ἀγανακτῶ δ', ὦ βουλή, εἰ διὰ πόρνην καὶ δούλην ἄνθρωπον περὶ τῶν μεγίστων εἰς κίνδυνον καθέστηκα.

[52] §12: φησὶν αὐτὴν ἐλευθέραν εἶναι. §14: αὐτὴν ἐλευθέραν ἐσκήπτετο εἶναι.

separate owners, and was therefore "thrice a *doulē* and thrice a *pornē*" (*tri-doulon kai tri-pornon*).[53] A scholiast explains a passage in Demosthenes by offering the example of "*douloi* and sons of *pornai*."[54] Libanios, in a rhetorical critique, brands Aiskhines as an individual born of a father who was a *doulos* and a mother who was a *pornē*.[55] And, as one might expect, the fullest examples of this verbal combination are to be found in patristic works.[56]

Within their brothels, Athenian prostitutes – like other slaves – would have received considerable instruction in the provision of sexual services. Athenian society functioned through an enormous network of hundreds of distinct occupations, most unrelated to agriculture.[57] To maintain this diverse specialization, in the many fields requiring knowledge and skill (*tekhnai*)[58] – handicraft, catering and medicine, for example – *douloi* and *doulai* normally received substantial training,[59] vocational education that free persons often lacked.[60] Slaves working in *trapezai* were taught the intricacies of finance and accounting,[61] and slaves working as prostitutes are known to have received specialized training, sometimes starting in childhood.[62] Yet even the best educated and most highly skilled *douloi* generally also performed domestic labors within the household.[63] Thus slaves working as doctors or doctors' assistants are known to have devoted part of their time to household duties.[64] (Aiskhines, charging

---

[53] μὴ μόνον τρίδουλον, ἀλλὰ καὶ τρίπορνον αὐτήν (Athen. 13.595a= *FGrHist* 115 F 253).

[54] Εἴη ἂν ἐκεῖνα λέγων, ἅπερ ἀπαιτῶν τὰς εἰσφορὰς ὁ Ἀνδροτίων ἐλοιδορεῖτο, δούλους καλῶν καὶ ἐκ πορνῶν. Y L (Dilts 1986: 274, Scholion 69).

[55] Libanios 8.301–302 (Foerster): θαυμαστὸν οὐδὲν εἰ γεγονὼς ἐκ δούλου πατρὸς καὶ τούτου πονηροῦ καὶ πόρνης μητρὸς κ. τ. λ.

[56] Cf. John Chrysostom, *Epist. Ad Romanos*, PG 63.554.12, *In Joannem* PG 59.165.23; *De Mansuetudine* PG 63.554.12.

[57] For a survey of "the extensive horizontal specialization in the Athenian economy," and the resultant profusion of discrete labor functions, see Harris 2002.

[58] Cf. Xen. *Oik.* 1.1: ἆρα γε ἡ οἰκονομία ἐπιστήμης τινὸς ὄνομα ἐστιν, ὥσπερ ἡ ἰατρικὴ καὶ ἡ χαλκευτικὴ καὶ ἡ τεκτονικὴ ... Ἦ καὶ ὥσπερ τούτων τῶν τεχνῶν κ.τ.λ. Cf. Pollux 4.7, 22. On prostitution as a *tekhnē*, see Dem. 59.18.

[59] Cf. Xen. *Oik.* 7.41, 12.4; Aristot. *Oik.* 1344a27–29 and passim. Training of artisans and caterers: see, for example, Dem. 45.71 (τοῦτον εἰ συνέβη μάγειρον ἤ τινος ἄλλης τέχνης δημιουργὸν πρίασθαι, τὴν τοῦ δεσπότου τέχνην ἂν μαθὼν κ.τ.λ.). Medicine: Klees 1998: 96–100; Sigerist 1970: 74.

[60] Aristarkhos contrasts the vocationally useless "liberal education" of free persons with slaves' training in *tekhnai* (crafts or trades requiring knowledge and skill: Xen. *Oik.* 1.1; Pollux 4.7.22): his female relatives lack the knowledge and skills of slaves (ὁ μὲν γὰρ τεχνίτας τρέφει, ἐγὼ δ' ἐλευθερίως πεπαιδευμένους: *Apom.* 2.7.4).

[61] Dem. 45.72 (with regard to the great *trapezitēs* Phormion who entered banking as a slave): ἐπειδὴ δ' ὁ πατὴρ ὁ ἡμέτερος τραπεζίτης ὢν ἐκτήσατ' αὐτὸν καὶ γράμματ' ἐπαίδευσεν καὶ τὴν τέχνην ἐδίδαξεν. ... The *douloi* Xenon, Euphron, Euphraios and Kallistratos – while still enslaved – as principals operated the largest bank in Athens, that of Pasion (see Dem. 36.43, 46, 48; E. Cohen 1992: 76).

[62] See, for example, Dem. 59.18: Νικαρέτη ... δεινὴ δὲ καὶ δυναμένη φύσιν μικρῶν παιδίων συνιδεῖν εὐπρεπῆ, καὶ ταῦτα ἐπισταμένη θρέψαι καὶ παιδεῦσαι ἐμπείρως, τέχνην ταύτην κατεσκευασμένη. Kapparis comments: "she knew how to educate them to become commercially successful courtesans" (1999: 207). See Alkiphron 4 passim; Louk. Ἑταιρ. Διαλ. 4.3, 10.4. Cf. Vonoyeke 1990: 33–35.

[63] Garlan 1988: 62: "domestic slaves devoted part of their time" to "strictly productive work," although "slaves were, in most cases, simply general 'dogsbodies'" (*ibid.*).

[64] Garlan 1988: 68. Cf. Kudlien 1968; Joly 1969.

Timarkhos with betraying his free status by acting in a slavish fashion, specifically accuses him of combining work as a prostitute with a purported pursuit of training in medicine.[65])

This pattern of multiple tasking provides the context for a division of labor in which some female slaves worked as both prostitutes and wool-workers. Brothel prostitution and wool-working, even at supervisory levels, were major Athenian industries in which women's services were dominant. Female *pornai*, believed to be far more numerous than male *pornoi*,[66] typically worked under a senior woman who "knew how to run her business ... and how to keep the women under strict control."[67] Similarly wool-working – "the characteristic area of feminine expertise normally cited by ancient authors"[68] – was entirely dependent on female labor.[69] Although many free women were skilled in this craft, and often supervised or even worked along with their slaves,[70] the actual production and servicing of textiles were almost entirely the work of unfree women.[71] Aristotle, in defending slavery as natural and necessary, focuses on this *tekhnē* and its slave workers: so long as shuttles could not spin by themselves, owners would have need for slaves.[72] Even under the sting of unwonted poverty, the Athenian Aristarkhos only reluctantly put his free female dependents to work producing wool, and even then he himself refused personally to be involved in the labor.[73] With good reason: because wool-working was identified as a strictly female activity, a man so engaged was *ipso facto* marked as effeminate.[74]

Reflecting such factors as slaves' personal characteristics, owners' economic situation, and numerous other elements of chance and opportunity, the actual work assignments of unfree persons would have varied greatly. Many *pornai* would likely

---

[65] Aiskhin. 1.40: ἐκάθητο ἐν Πειραιεῖ ἐπὶ τοῦ Εὐθυδίκου ἰατρείου, προφάσει μὲν τῆς τέχνης μαθητής, τῇ δ᾽ ἀληθείᾳ πωλεῖν αὑτὸν προῃρημένος.

[66] Davidson 1997: 77. *Pornoi* generally provided sex in smallish individual rooms (οἰκήματα) accessible from the street (see Isai. 6.19, Aiskhin. 1.74, Athen. 220d), not in the imposing domestic establishments where *pornai* are known to have gathered in large central halls for presentation to customers (Xenarkhos Fr. 4 [K-A]; Euboulos Frs. 67, 82 [K-A]).

[67] Kapparis 1999: 207. Cf. Carey 1992: 94. For female *mastropoi*, see E. Cohen, forthcoming.

[68] Brock 1994; 338. Cf. Plato *Alk.* 126e, *Lysis* 208d-e, *Nomoi* 805e-806a; Xen. *Mem.* 3.9.11, *Lak. Pol.* 1.3.

[69] "una delle attività di competenza esclusiva delle donne" (Faraguna 1999: 70). Market trade seems to have been centered in the ἱματιόπωλις ἀγορά (Pollux 7.78): see Wycherley 1957: 200, no. 663 and 187–88, no. 614. Clothing for slaves was an important part of this trade: Bettalli 1982: 264, 271–72.

[70] Aristoph. *Batr.* 1349–51, *Lys.* 519–20, 536–37, 728–30, *Neph.* 53–55; Plato *Rep.* 455c; Xen. *Oik.* 7.6, 21, 36; Plut. *Mor.* 830c (citing Krates the Cynic).

[71] *Dyeing*: Eup. Fr. 434, Aristoph. *Ekkl.* 215; *Weaving*: SEG 18.36 B2; *Linen-working*: Aiskhin. 1.97, Alexis Fr. 36; *Sewing*: *IG* II² 1556.28, Antiph. *Alestria* Frs. 21–24, Jordan 1985: n. 72. *Wool-working*: Scenes on Attic vases: Webster 1972: Chapters 16 and 17. The best treatment of "l'importanza della mandopera servile nella manifattura tessile" is Faraguna 1999: 72–79. Cf. Jameson 1977/78: 134 n. 63; Tod 1950: 10–11.

[72] εἰ γὰρ ἠδύνατο ἕκαστον τῶν ὀργάνων κελευσθὲν ἢ προαισθανόμενον ἀποτελεῖν τὸ αὑτοῦ ἔργον ... οὕτως αἱ κερκίδες ἐκέρκιζον αὐταὶ ... οὐδὲν ἂν ἔδει ... οὔτε τοῖς δεσπόταις δούλων (*Pol.* 1253b33–1254a1).

[73] Xen. *Apom.* 2.7.12: αἰτιῶνται αὐτὸν μόνον τῶν ἐν τῇ οἰκίᾳ ἀργὸν ἐσθίειν.

[74] Cf. Midas (Athen. 516b), Sardanapalos (Diod. Sik. 2.23), Kallon (Diod. Sik. 32.11).

have had no involvement in textile work, and many wool workers, no involvement in commercial sex – but substantial evidence suggests that numerous female slaves were used both as wool workers and brothel prostitutes.[75] Athena (as goddess of female crafts) joined Aphrodite in receiving the real-life offerings of Athenian prostitutes[76] – and was portrayed in literature as the recipient of dedications by wool-workers who were also working or hoped to work as prostitutes. Surviving Athenian vases offer a number of scenes linking female erotic and textile labor, including depictions of young men bringing gifts or money-bags to women working with wool[77] and scenes of women with names appropriate to prostitutes (Aphrodisia and Obole) putting aside their wool while male customers approach or wait.[78] A water-jar depicts a naked woman spinning wool before a clothed seated woman, "clearly the madam who forces her *pornai* to work during the off hours."[79] Material culture provides the evidence of more than 100 loom-weights found (along with hundreds of drinking vessels) in virtually every room in the classical levels of a labyrinthine building that has been identified as a *porneion*.[80]

This involvement of individual women in both erotic and wool-working commerce explains a series of dedications that have baffled scholars. The *phialai exeleutherikai* tablets – our prime source of information on the manumission of Athenian slaves – document the freeing (in the 320's) of approximately 375 slaves,[81] each of whom offers a 100–drachma silver bowl (*phialē*) after his or her acquittal in formalistic, i.e. fictitious actions (*dikai apostasiou*) brought by ex-owners.[82] In these inscriptions, occupations are recorded for 52 of 86 ex-slaves who are probably or certainly female, but for only 62 of 110 probable or certain males.[83] For scholars accustomed to

---

[75] Rodenwaldt 1932; Keuls 1983; Neils 2000. Davidson summarizes: "a large group of women ... were forced (or chose)" to work at both pursuits (1997: 89).

[76] Parthenon dedications to Athena from *hetairai*: Harris 1995: 244–49. Aphrodite as patron goddess of prostitutes, above pp. 215–216.

[77] See, for example, *ARV²* 101.3 (Robert 1919: 125–29); *ARV²* 557.123; *ARV²* 795.100; Heidelberg 64/5 (kalpis by the Nausikaa Painter). Cf. *ARV²* 276.70 (discussed in Meyer 1988). Other examples: von Reden 1995: 206–209.

[78] Munich, Zanker: Münzen und Medaillen AG, *Auktion* 51 (Basel 1975), discussed at Williams 1983: 96–97. Cf. *ARV²* 189.72.1632; *ARV²* 275.50.

[79] Neils 2000: 209. The vase is in Copenhagen (Nat. Mus. 153= *ARV²* 1131, 161 and Williams 1983: 96, fig. 7.4). Cf. *ARV²* 795.10294–7.

[80] So-called Building Z located by the city wall at the Sacred Gate, in an area long identified as one of the red-light districts of ancient Athens. Among the remains was an amulet depicting Aphrodite Ourania riding a goat across the night sky. For the site, structure, excavation and contents of this building, see Lind 1988; Knigge 1988: esp. 88–94.

[81] These documents have been published in *IG* II² (1553–78) and re-published (in part) by Lewis in 1959 and 1968 (to incorporate additional finds from the Athenian Agora excavations). See Kränzlein 1975 for a survey of scholarly work on these texts; for early treatments of the original 19th-century fragments (starting with Pittakis in Ἐφ. ἀρχ. 1830), see Calderini [1908] 1965: 424–34.

[82] On the *dikē apostasiou*, see Klees 1998: 348–54; Todd 1993: 190–92.

[83] For this discussion, I follow calculations made by Todd, who produced, as he notes, "deliberately conservative figures" (1997: 121). For example, he disregards 12 *talasiourgoi* as being of "uncertain sex," even though 5 of the 12 have names that are typically feminine, and wool-working seems to have been an exclusively female pursuit (see above). As apparent confirmation of the undercounting by Todd of female

thinking of Athenian women, and especially slave women, as hapless objects of male domination locked away in the interior of society, consigned to ignorance and reserved for exploitation,[84] this information – showing manumitted slave women as more likely than slave men to have had an occupation – is "most surprising" and "too straightforward an inference" (Todd 1997: 122). As a result, scholars have resorted to a "corrective approach" in an effort to make the ancient evidence conform to modern expectation.[85] Todd dismisses the testimony of the *phialai exeleutherikai* as an "illusion" (1997: 122). Rosivach (1989), noting that a majority (29) of the 52 working women are designated as *talasiourgoi* ("wool-workers"), finds a simple solution: the standard Liddell-Scott Greek/English Lexicon must be corrected. He insists that the word *"talasiourgos"* does not mean "wool-worker" as the Lexicon (1996 Supplement) claims: with a "diagnostic reading," *"talasiourgos"* actually means "housewife."[86] So "corrected," the inscriptions would report just the opposite of the actual texts: relatively few Athenian freedwomen would have had occupations. With this alteration, however, the inscriptions would now present what even Todd sees as "a curious omission from the texts" – the absence of "female household slaves" (Todd 1997: 23).

But scholars need not manufacture such a "curious omission" through "corrective" mutilation of the actual texts. In my opinion, the "plain meaning" of the inscriptions – interpreted in the context of the linkage between prostitution and wool-working – makes good sense without "corrective" interpretation.

Scholars have long conjectured that slaves obtaining manumission at Athens were likely to be disproportionately those who had special access to a free person's support and/or possessed skills that produced relatively high compensation – a portion of

---

talasiourgoi, there is not a single *talasiourgos* among the 110 slaves who (by Todd's reckoning) are "probably" or "certainly" male (1997: 121–22). Of the total of 375, Todd found 179 to be of "uncertain sex" (meaning that without regard to other possible indicia of sex, their names were not followed by the formulaic language οἰκῶν [male] οἰκοῦσα [female] or ἀποφυγών [male]/ ἀποφυγοῦσα [female]. Many of these omissions, however, reflect the fragmentary nature of the surviving inscribed materials.)

[84] According to Schaps 1979: 96, Athenian society was "an extremely patriarchal one in theory, not only legal theory but the generally accepted social understanding of the people." In practice, Athenian patriarchy was supposedly yet more "severe and crass" than that of modern "patriarchal industrial societies" (Keuls 1985: 12). Cf. Joshel and Murnaghan 1998: 3; Wright [1923] 1969: 1; Vidal-Naquet 1986: 206–207; Cantarella 1987: 38; Schuller 1985, passim. Recently, such views have been yielding to more nuanced interpretations: see Sourvinou-Inwood 1995; E. Cohen 2000: 30–48.

[85] In French terms, "documentation 'surdéterminée'" requires "une lecture 'symptomale'" (Garlan 1982: 31). "Diagnostic reading," a popular tool of francophone methodology, is viewed as merely a defensive response to the inevitable subjectivity of those espousing objective pretensions: "very few of the apparently purely scholarly debates on [Greek slavery] avoid, in one way or another, consciously or unconsciously, adopting a particular ideological perspective" (Garlan 1988: 23). For decades, scholars dismissed the evidence that Building Z was a brothel, and denied that the sale of sex had some coherent relationship to the many scenes on vases showing young men bringing gifts or money-bags to women working with wool (see Davidson 1997: 85–90).

[86] Although Rosivach sometimes substitutes "home-maker" for "housewife," he generally uses "wife" in its literal sense, even trying to identify *de facto* husbands. But this interpretation is impossible: on Lewis's "Great Inscription," two *talasiourgoi* are grouped with a single man (Side B, Col. I, lines 253–66).

which (termed *apophora*) slaves often retained[87] – thus providing funds for the purchase of a slave's freedom or, at the least, offering a source of repayment of monies advanced by others.[88] But enslaved wool-workers would have had virtually no opportunity to earn or accumulate personal funds, or to gain access to possible benefactors: they generally toiled in anonymity at repetitive chores in a supervised production process requiring the joint labor of a number of workers,[89] often producing goods intended not for the market (and the generation of cash) but for the *oikos* itself.[90] Elegiac literature records the plaintive complaints of women relegated to the famished poverty of wool-work.[91] Prostitutes by contrast might earn enormous fees, and were (obviously) in a position to establish a "personal relationship" with the payers of those fees. Loomis, in an exhaustive survey of prices charged for the services of ancient Greek prostitutes,[92] has shown that "a high-class and socially acceptable" prostitute might earn as much as 1,000 *drachmas* (perhaps US$50,000–$100,000 in purchasing power equivalence),[93] and not less than 2 *drachmas* per individual servicing, "depending on her age, attractions, mood at the moment, and the resources and urgency of the customer" (1998: 185). Typical fees for an "average prostitute" were not less than one-half *drachma* per act (ibid.). Surviving material even explains in detail how Neaira, an alleged slave prostitute, bought her freedom through a combination of her own earnings and assistance from several of her "lovers," who had developed an emotional relationship with her.[94] This contrast between the impoverished wool-worker and the potentially high-earning prostitute (and the linkage between the two pursuits) is confirmed by a number of Hellenistic epigrams that describe dedications to Athena or to Aphrodite offered by women aspiring to abandon the impoverishment of wool-working in order to devote

---

[87] See, for example, Andok. 1.38; Aiskhin. 1.97; Men. *Epitrep.* 380; Xen. *Ath. Pol.* 1.10–11. *Apophora* in construction trade: Randall 1953; Burford 1963. In workshops: Francotte 1900: 12; Bolkestein 1958: 63. Pottery: Webster 1973. For slaves operating retail establishments and banks, see n. 29 above.

[88] See Faraguna 1999: 72, Finley [1951] 1985: 104–105. Lenders (operating as groups of *eranistai*) appear with frequency on the *phialai exeleutherikai* inscriptions. See *IG* II² 1553.7–10, 20–23; 1556 B27–29; 1557 B105–107; 1558 A37–43; 1559 A II 26–31; 1566 A27–29; 1568 B18–23; 1569 A III 18–21; 1570.24–26, 57–62, 82–84; 1571.8–13; and 1572.8–11; Lewis 1959: Face A, lines 141–42 and 566–67, Face B, lines 2 and 153; Lewis 1968: 368, line 8. The silver bowls themselves are generally believed to have been paid for by the freed persons. This again would have required considerable funds. (We have no reliable information on prices paid to owners at Athens in connection with manumissions.)

[89] See Xen. *Oik.* 2.7; Timokles Fr. 33 (K-A: comm.), Σὺνέριθοι: συνέριθοι Ἀττικοί, συνυφαίνουσαι Ἕλληνες.

[90] Rosivach 1989. But there were some workers of high skill producing specialized product for sale in the market, such as the craftswoman expert in lace-making described at Aiskhin. 1.97 (ἀμόργινα ἐπισταμένην ἐργάζεσθαι καὶ εἰς τὴν ἀγορὰν ἐκφεροῦσαν). An otherwise ordinary female slave skilled at wool-working might be worth twice the price of an untrained *doulē* (Xen. *Oik.* 7.41).

[91] See *Anth. Pal.* 6.285 (κακῶν λιμηρὰ γυναικῶν ἔργα); 6.283 (μίσθια νῦν σπαθίοις πενιχροῖς πηνίσματα κρούει); 6.48 (λιμηρῆς ἄρμενον ἐργασίης); 6.284 (εὔκλωστον δὲ γυναικῶν νῆμα καὶ ἠλακάτην ἀργὸς ἔχοι τάλαρος).

[92] 1998: 166–85, 309–12, 334–35, and passim. Cf. Halperin 1990: 107–12, Schneider 1913: 1343–44. Loomis disregards reports of prices that are "pretty clearly an exaggeration" (1998: 185).

[93] On comparative monetary values, see E. Cohen 1992: xiv, 22 (n. 92); Gallo 1987: esp. 57–63.

[94] See Dem. 59.29–32 (and the discussion in Kapparis 1999: 227–35).

themselves entirely to sexual commerce.[95] In a clever ditty by Nikarkhos, a woman has placed on a raging fire spindles and other equipment connected with Athena. For this woman, wool-working is an impoverished ("famished") occupation appropriate only for "base females" (*kakōn gynaikōn*).[96] In contrast, prostitution offers a "pleasured life" (*terpnon bioton*) of festivals, revelry, and music in which Aphrodite, freeing her from wool-working, and "sharing in the (new) labor," will be her 10% partner.[97] In another epigram, a woman named Bitto dedicates to Athena the textile apparatus of the work she hates, "the tools of impoverished enterprise": emulating Paris, she's casting her vote for Aphrodite's labor instead.[98] Yet another woman – whose sexual labors have reaped finery through lucrative assignations – would choose now entirely to abandon wool-working,[99] an option not available to the subject of a further elegy, an aging female who in contrast has had to abandon lucrative prostitution and is now left only with the impoverished yields of wool-working.[100]

The unexpurgated texts of the *phialai exeleutherikai* – showing that "women seem just as likely to have jobs as do men" (Todd 1997: 122) – thus make perfectly good sense: slaves working in wool can be properly described as *talasiourgoi* ("wool-workers"). They need not be denominated by modern scholars as "housewives." Earnings from prostitution – and useful relationships developed from this *métier* – would have provided a financial and/or personal mechanism for obtaining freedom, and slaves who commanded earnings from prostitution would likely have figured prominently among those gaining manumission. Not surprisingly, therefore, some of the freed slaves carry names that are typical Athenian designations for sex workers – Glykera ("Sweetie') and Malthake ("Softie"). Others – like the musicians (a flute-girl, a harpist) who "entertained" at male social functions – are recorded under callings that

---

[95] For a survey of these poems and similar material, see Davidson 1997: 87–88.

[96] *Anth. Pal.* 6.285: κακῶν λιμηρὰ γυναικῶν ἔργα (5–6).

[97] Ibid.: εἵλετο δὲ στεφάνους καὶ πηκτίδα καὶ μετὰ κώμων (7)

ἡ παῖς τερπνὸν ἔχειν ἐν θαλίαις βίοτον·
εἶπε δέ, "παντός σοι δεκάτην ἀπὸ λήμματος οἴσω
Κύπρι· σὺ δ' ἐργασίην καὶ λαβὲ καὶ μετάδος."

For the mechanisms through which slaves might share their revenues (or profits) with their owners, and otherwise maintain an independent existence, see E. Cohen 1998: 114–23.

[98] *Anth. Pal.* 6.48: κερκίδα τὴν φιλοεργὸν Ἀθηναίῃ θέτο Βιττώ

ἄνθεμα, λιμηρῆς ἄρμενον ἐργασίης,
πάντας ἀποστύξασα γυνὴ τότε τοὺς ἐν ἐρίθοις
μόχθους καὶ στυγερὰς φροντίδας ἱστοπόνων·
εἶπε δ' Ἀθηναίη "τῶν Κύπριδος ἅψομαι ἔργων,
τὴν Πάριδος κατὰ σοῦ ψῆφον ἐνεγκαμένη."

[99] *Anth. Pal.* 6.284: λάθρη κοιμηθεῖσα Φιλαίνιον εἰς Ἀγαμήδους

κόλπους τὴν φαιὴν εἰργάσατο χλανίδα.
Αὐτὴ Κύπρις ἔριθος, εὔκλωστον δὲ γυναικῶν
Νῆμα καὶ ἠλακάτην ἀργὸς ἔχοι τάλαρος.

[100] *Anth. Pal.* 6.283: ἡ τὸ πρὶν αὐχήσασα πολυχρύσοις ἐπ' ἐρασταῖς ...

μίσθια νῦν σπαθίοις πενιχροῖς πηνίσματα κρούει.

are known frequently to have been coupled with the provision of sexual services.[101] But, most explicitly, the *phialai exeleutherikai* inscriptions record a relatively large number of freed persons (both male and female) who are denominated *"pais"* (or *"paidion,"* diminutive of *pais*). (Of the 185 persons for whom occupations are recorded, 16 are denominated *"pais"* or *"paidion,"* of whom 3 are definitely female, 2 certainly male, and the others of uncertain sex.) This term – although often carrying the meaning of "servant" or "child" – frequently refers to persons engaging in sexual activity at the behest of an importuning male who offers something of value.[102] Appearing in a formulaic list of occupations, "prostitute" (as Todd notes [1997: 123]) is an appropriate possible translation.[103] In contrast, neither *pornai (-oi)* or *hetairai (-oi)* would be suitable designations for these newly-liberated persons: *pornē (-os)* – as we have seen (above p. 220) – was a virtual synonym for "slave," an incongruous appellation for a dedication attesting to free status; *hetaira (-os)* – as we shall see (below p. 228) – was a term scrupulously trumpeted as the calling of a free person, an honorific perhaps overly ostentatious for a formerly enslaved worker. Of course, many females are recorded in these inscriptions as *talasiourgoi*. Were they women whose identity was primarily as wool-workers but whose freedom was owed to the wages of sex, or were they persons now retired from compensated sexual activity? Or were some of these *talasiourgoi* part of the small minority of highly-skilled (and possibly highly-compensated) specialist producers of exquisite textile products crafted to meet market demand?[104] We will never know. The extraordinarily elliptical language of the inscriptions, the highly fragmentary state in which they have survived, and our ignorance of their social and legal context leave us unable to determine even whether the choice of occupation attributed to each worker was made by the newly-freed persons, by their former owners, by some *polis* official – or perhaps even by the stone cutter(s).[105] Yet these lists of *paides* and *talasiourgoi* and other freed persons, evidence for a process of manumission otherwise unknown, do offer a context for the situations portrayed in epigrammatic literature. They help explain a paradox otherwise inexplicable, a mystery raised by the anonymous poet of the Palatine Anthology and, I think, answered by our discussion – of how Philainion, the wool-worker, made herself a gray coat sleeping in the embrace of Agamedes.[106]

---

[101] These musicians "might also be called on to provide sexual entertainment" (Rhodes 1981: 574). See Metagenes 4 (K-A); Adespota 1025.1 (K-A); Aristoph. *Akh.* 551; Theopompos *FGrHist* 115 F 290. Cf. Krenkel 1988: 1294; Herter 1960 (1985): 86 n. 290.

[102] According to Dover, in (homo)sexual relationships, "…the passive partner is called 'pais,' ('boy'), a word also used for 'child,' 'girl,' 'son,' 'daughter,' and 'slave' " (1978 [1989]: 16). "Pais" frequently appears on vases as a denomination for attractive young men or women. For male and female *paides* identified as objects of sexual desire, see Plato, *Nomoi* 836a7 (ἐρώτων παίδων τε ἀρρένων καὶ θηλειῶν).

[103] Cf. Rosivach 1989: 368–69.

[104] See above n. 90.

[105] "The truth of the matter is that our evidence is inadequate." Lewis 1959: 238.

[106] *Anth. Pal.* 6.284: λάθρη κοιμηθεῖσα Φιλαίνιον εἰς Ἀγαμήδους
κόλπους τὴν φαιὴν εἰργάσατο χλανίδα.

C. Never on Sunday: "Free" Labor and Sexual Contracts

Antagonism to work under a master should not be confused with antipathy to labor itself.[107] Numerous Athenians were self-employed in a great variety of pursuits. According to Xenophon, in addition to farmers, the Athenian Assembly was full of clothes cleaners, leather workers, metal workers, craftsmen, traders and merchants.[108] Many free residents followed entrepreneurial pursuits,[109] and many others pursued numerous specialized callings,[110] including prostitution.[111] Harris (2002) has estimated that perhaps half of all *politai* (perhaps 10,000 citizens) pursued non-agricultural work in hundreds of individuals *métiers*. For extended relationships in all these areas, Athenian morality mandated clear manifestations of egalitarian independence of occupation. And so, not surprisingly, among the Athenian *hetairoi* and *hetairai* who became notorious for accomplishment and/or wealth, there is virtually no indication of personal enslavement, or of slave-like brothel dependence.[112]

To the contrary, for the *hetairoi* of Athens, contractual arrangements for sexual services – whether directly explicit, as in Lysias 3, or constructed with greater complexity, as in Hypereides 5 – were the norm. References to such contractual arrangements were so commonplace that the phrase "whoring under contract" (*syngraphē*) – a usage popularized by a prominent *politēs* who had worked as a prostitute – had become idiomatic in local discourse.[113] Requests were routinely anticipated in court proceedings for written confirmation of commercial sexual acts.[114] As with written agreements for other commercial undertakings, contracts for sexual services appear on occasion even to have been deposited for safeguarding with third persons,[115] and prostitutional obligations, as was the case with other contractual

---

[107] For the distinction, and an analysis of its historical basis, see Wood 1988: 126–45, esp. 139. Some Athenians, however, did tend to view work as essentially the obligation of unfree persons: ἐστὶ γὰρ τὸ μὲν ἥδεσθαι καὶ τὸ τρυφᾶν ἐλευθέρων ... τὸ δὲ πονεῖν δούλων καὶ ταπεινῶν. *Peri Hēdonēs* (quoted in Athen. 512b4–6). See Wehrli 1969: fr. 55.

[108] Τοὺς γναφέας αὐτῶν ἢ τοὺς σκυτέας ἢ τοὺς τέκτονας ἢ τοὺς χαλκέας ἢ τοὺς γεωργοὺς ἢ τοὺς ἐμπόρους ἢ τοὺς ἐν τῇ ἀγορᾷ μεταβαλλομένους ... ἐκ γὰρ τούτων ἁπάντων ἡ ἐκκλησία συνίσταται (*Apom.* 3.7.6). Similarly: Plat. *Prōtag.* 319d. Cf. Humphreys 1978: 148.

[109] See Thompson 1983; Garnsey 1980. For the significance of such activities in the ancient world, see Goody 1986: 177–84.

[110] For a survey of "the extensive horizontal specialization in the Athenian economy," and the resultant profusion of discrete labor functions, see Harris 2002.

[111] For the male and female "citizens" known to have been prostitutes, see E. Cohen 2000: 167–77.

[112] "Unter der Gruppe der renommierten Hetären, die als Spitzenverdienerinnen galten (μεγαλόμισθοι) (Athen. 570b; 558a-e), waren Sklavinnen kaum anzutreffen" (Klees 1998: 147 n. 16). Cf. n. 45 above.

[113] Aiskhin. 1.165: πόθεν οὖν ἴσχυκε καὶ σύνηθες γεγένηται λέγειν, ὡς κατὰ γραμματεῖον ἤδη τινὲς ἡταίρησαν, ἐρῶ. ἀνὴρ εἷς τῶν πολιτῶν ... λέγεται κατὰ συνθήκας ἡταιρηκέναι τὰς παρ' Ἀντικλεῖ κειμένας· οὐκ ὢν < δ'> ἰδιώτης, ἀλλὰ πρὸς τὰ κοινὰ προσιὼν καὶ λοιδορίαις περιπίπτων, εἰς συνήθειαν ἐποίησε τοῦ λόγου τούτου τὴν πόλιν καταστῆναι, καὶ διὰ τοῦτο ἐρωτῶσί τινες, εἰ κατὰ γραμματεῖον ἡ πρᾶξις γεγένηται.

[114] Aiskhin. 1.160: Ἐὰν δ' ἐπιχειρῶσι λέγειν ὡς οὐχ ἡταίρηκεν ὅστις μὴ κατὰ συγγραφὰς ἐμισθώθη, καὶ γραμματεῖον καὶ μάρτυρας ἀξιῶσί με τούτων παρασχέσθαι.... Cf. § 165: ἐρωτῶσί τινες εἰ κατὰ γραμματεῖον ἡ πρᾶξις γεγένηται.

[115] Aiskhin. 1.165: λέγεται κατὰ συνθήκας ἡταιρηκέναι τὰς παρ' Ἀντικλεῖ κειμένας. For safekeeping of maritime loan agreements, for example, see Dem. 34.6; Dem. 56.15.

arrangements, were undertaken with a panoply of witnesses to confirm the agreements.[116]

Even female prostitutes are known to have entered into elaborate contractual commitments. In Plautus' *Asinaria,* an adaptation of a Hellenic original,[117] there is presented, in comic version but at considerable length, a contract in writing (termed *syngraphus,* the Latin rendering of the Greek *syngraphē*), providing for Philaenium, daughter of Cleareta, to spend her time exclusively with the Athenian Diabolus for a period of one year at a price of 2,000 drachmas, a "gift" paid in advance.[118] The contract contains extended provisions of humorous paranoia – for example, Philaenium is not even to gaze upon another man and must swear only by female deities. Similar Greek contractual arrangements with courtesans are alluded to in a number of other Plautine comedies and in a work of Turpilius (who seems often to have adapted plays from Menander).[119] From Athenian sources, we know directly of the complex financial arrangements made by a *hetaira* in Korinth with the Athenian Phrynion – and with Timanoridas the Korinthian, Eukrates of Leukas and other of her "lovers."[120] The same woman later, acting on her own behalf in a private arbitration proceeding at Athens,[121] reached agreement with two Athenian patrons requiring mutual consent for any alteration in the terms governing allocations of property and obligations of maintenance undertaken in exchange for her provision of sexual services to both men.[122]

These formal contracts, however, were not the sole indicia of a labor relationship compatible with Athenian work ethics. Other manifestations included control over one's physical and familial surroundings (the antithesis of servile confinement in a brothel), the freedom to choose the clients with whom one associates (the antithesis of compulsory sexual submission to any would-be purchaser), the appearance of leisurely dedication to cultural and social activities,[123] and the pursuit of work not only as an

---

[116] Aiskhin. 1.125: ἀγοραῖα τεκμήρια. Without witnesses, even written agreements were unrecognized and unenforceable until very late in the fourth-century. See Thomas 1989: 41–45; Pringsheim 1955.

[117] For the validity of the use of Roman comic material as evidence for Athenian legal and social practices, see Scafuro 1997: 16–19; Paoli 1976: 76–77.

[118] Lines 751–54: Diabolus Glauci filius Clearetae | lenae dedit dono argenti viginti minas, | Philaenium ut secum esset noctes et dies | hunc annum totum.

[119] See Plaut. *Merc.* 536 ff., *Bach.* Fr. 10 and 896 ff.; Turpilius Com. Fr. 112 Ribbeck *Leuc.* Cf. Schonbeck 1981: 150–51 and 203 n. 73; Herter 1960: 81, nn. 193 and 194.

[120] See n. 94 above.

[121] Dem. 59. 45–46: συνῆγον αὐτοὺς οἱ ἐπιτήδειοι καὶ ἔπεισαν δίαιταν ἐπιτρέψαι αὐτοῖς ... ἀκούσαντες ἀμφοτέρων καὶ αὐτῆς τῆς ἀνθρώπου τὰ πεπραγμένα, γνώμην ἀπεφήναντο ... τὴν μὲν ἄνθρωπον ἐλευθέραν εἶναι καὶ αὐτὴν αὑτῆς κυρίαν.

[122] Dem. 59.46: ἃ δ᾽ ἐξῆλθεν ἔχουσα Νέαιρα παρὰ Φρυνίωνος χωρὶς ἱματίων καὶ χρυσίων καὶ θεραπαινῶν, ἃ αὐτῇ τῇ ἀνθρώπῳ ἠγοράσθη, ἀποδοῦναι Φρυνίωνι πάντα· συνεῖναι δ᾽ ἑκατέρῳ ἡμέραν παρ᾽ ἡμέραν· ἐὰν δὲ καὶ ἄλλως πως ἀλλήλους πείθωσι, ταῦτα κύρια εἶναι· τὰ δ᾽ ἐπιτήδεια τῇ ἀνθρώπῳ τὸν ἔχοντα ἀεὶ παρέχειν.

[123] For the Athenian elite idealization of such pursuits, see Fisher 1998b: 84–86; Stocks 1936; de Ste. Croix 1981: 114–117.

economic necessity but as a mechanism of self-definition.[124] All of these attributes are emphasized in Xenophon's description of Sokrates' meeting with the *hetaira* Theodote, ("a woman of the sort who sleeps with men who are persuasive") – emphasizing her freedom of selection – whose livelihood comes from the benefactions of men who have become "friends" – an elevation of her relationships from master/servant or customer/commodity into the independence inherent in personalized reciprocity.[125] Sokrates is awed by the domestic world she controls: Theodote lives in luxurious surroundings, apparently with her mother, in a home furnished sumptuously in every way; she dresses and adorns herself consummately, and is accompanied by a retinue of finely-outfitted and attractive maid servants.[126] Exploring the sources of her prosperity, Sokrates' queries ("do you own land? rental property? craftsmen?"[127]) assume that she herself might be a citizen (*politis*) whose possessions include real-estate and slaves. When Theodote asserts total indifference to Sokrates' efforts to help her increase her income from her "friends" through systematic pursuit of "fine and wealthy" benefactors (§9), they each are playing appropriate roles. Xenophon, seeking to refute the charge that Sokrates was a deleterious "destroyer" of the young,[128] offers in these *Memoirs* examples of how the sage was in fact a practical dispenser of sound ideas,[129] including business advice (such as the suggestions that brought prosperity to Aristarkhos and his female relatives in the wool business (above, p. 222). But Theodote in her turn is careful to manifest the values of "free" Athenian labor. She herself has no desire or capacity to implement Sokrates' schemes to maximize profit,[130] but she is willing to let him work for her.[131] She spends her time posing for

---

[124] On the Athenians' tendency to idealize labor not as a form of production but as "cultural self-definition" ("kulturellen Selbstdefinition") see von Reden 1992; Loraux 1995: 44–58; Vernant 1971: 2.17. Cf. Schwimmer 1979.

[125] *Apom.* 3.11: §1· Γυναικὸς ... καλῆς ... καὶ οἵας συνεῖναι τῷ πείθοντι ... §4: Πόθεν οὖν, ἔφη, τὰ ἐπιτήδεια ἔχεις; Ἐάν τις, ἔφη, φίλος μοι γενόμενος εὖ ποιεῖν ἐθέλῃ, οὗτός μοι βίος ἐστί. Athenians generally felt an obligation to help their friends, and an expectation of resultant gratitude (and an entitlement to future reciprocity). See Millett 1991: 24–52. For the "fundamental difference between the social consequences of exchange based on coinage on the one hand and on gift exchange on the other" (von Reden 1997: 154) and similar paradigmatic economic alterations, see Kurke 1994: 42; Seaford 1994: 199. Cf. Seaford 1998; von Reden 1998; Steiner 1994; Kurke 1989.

[126] ὁ Σωκράτης ὁρῶν αὐτήν τε πολυτελῶς κεκοσμημένην καὶ μητέρα παροῦσαν αὐτῇ ἐν ἐσθῆτί τε καὶ θεραπείᾳ οὐ τῇ τυχούσῃ, καὶ θεραπαίνας πολλὰς καὶ εὐειδεῖς καὶ οὐδὲ ταύτας ἠμελημένως ἐχούσας, καὶ τοῖς ἄλλοις τὴν οἰκίαν ἀφθόνως κατεσκευασμένην. ... νὴ τὴν Ἥραν, ἔφη, ὦ Θεοδότη, καλόν γε τὸ κτῆμα. ... (§§4,5).

[127] ἔστι σοι ἀγρός; ... Ἀλλ' ἆρα οἰκία προσόδους ἔχουσα; ... Ἀλλὰ μὴ χειροτέχναι τινές; (§4).

[128] Cf. 1.1.1 (πολλάκις ἐθαύμασα τίσι ποτὲ λόγοις Ἀθηναίους ἔπεισαν οἱ γραψάμενοι Σωκράτην ὡς ... ἀδικεῖ δὲ καὶ τοὺς νέους διαφθείρων) and 2.7.1 (καὶ μὴν τὰς ἀπορίας γε τῶν φίλων τὰς μὲν δι' ἄγνοιαν ἐπειρᾶτο γνώμῃ ἀκεῖσθαι, τὰς δὲ δι' ἔνδειαν διδάσκων κατὰ δύναμιν ἀλλήλοις ἐπαρκεῖν).

[129] Sokrates explains how she might acquire clients and maximize their contributions to her (§9: ὅπως ἐμβάλῃ αὐτοὺς εἰς τὰ σὰ δίκτυα; §12: οὕτω γὰρ ἂν μάλιστα φίλοι γίγνοιντο καὶ πλεῖστον χρόνον φιλοῖεν καὶ μέγιστα εὐεργετοῖεν; §14: τηνικαῦτα γὰρ πολὺ διαφέρει τὰ αὐτὰ δῶρα ἢ πρὶν ἐπιθυμῆσαι διδόναι).

[130] §10: Μὰ τὸν Δί', ἐγὼ τούτων οὐδὲν μηχανῶμαι.

[131] § 15: Τί οὖν οὐ σύ μοι, ὦ Σώκρατες, ἐγένου συνθηρατὴς τῶν φίλων;

artists, leaving potential customers like Sokrates and his friends waiting.[132] Whatever the reality of her situation – and here Xenophon, as so often, presents a portrait of shimmering but unconfirmable verisimilitude and of incredible but not impossible idealization – Theodote is the reification of the Athenian working *imaginaire* ("self-image"): she is the wealthy and independent "happy hooker" highly acceptable to, and therefore ever-present, in Athenian society, totally unacceptable and therefore ever-suppressed by a large portion of modern scholarship.[133]

WORKS CITED

Alessandri, S. 1984. "Il significato storico della legge di Nicofonte sul dokimastes monetario." *ASNP* 3rd Ser. 14: 369–93.

Allen, D. 2000. *The World of Prometheus: The Politics of Punishing in Democratic Athens*. Princeton.

Andreades, A. (1928) 1992. Ιστορία της ελληνικής δημοσίας οικονομίας. Vol. 1. Rev. ed. Athens.

Beard, M. and J. Henderson. 1997. "With This Body I Thee Worship: Sacred Prostitution in Antiquity." *Gender and History* 9: 480–523.

Benveniste, E. 1973. *Indo-European Language and Society*. London.

Beschi, L. 1967–68. "Contributi di topografia ateniese." *ASAA* 45/46: 520–26.

Bettalli, M. 1982. "Note sulla produzione tessile ad Atene in età classica." *Opus* 1: 261–78.

———. 1985. "Case, Botteghe, Ergasteria: Note sui luoghi di produzione et di vendita nell' Atene classica." *Opus* 4: 29–41.

Bindman, J. 1997. Redefining Prostitution as Sex Work. Website: http://www.walnet.org/csis/papers/redefining/htm.

Brock, R. 1994. "The Labour of Women in Classical Athens." *CQ* n.s. 44: 336–46.

Burford, A. 1972. *Craftsmen in Greek and Roman Society*. London.

Burke, E. 1992. "The Economy of Athens in the Classical Era." *TAPhA* 122: 199–226.

Calame, C. 1996. L' Éros dans la Grèce antique. Paris. (English translation: Princeton 1999.)

Calderini, A. [1908] 1965. *La manomissione e la condizione dei liberti in Grecia*. Rome.

Carey, C. ed. 1992. *Apollodoros Against Neaira [Demosthenes] 59*. Warminster.

Carrière-Hervagault, M.-P. 1973. "Esclaves et affranchis chez les orateurs attiques: documents et étude." In *Actes du colloque 1971 sur l'esclavage. Annales Littéraires de l'Université de Besançon*. Paris. 45–79.

Cartledge, P. 1993. *The Greeks: A Portrait of Self and Others*. Oxford.

Chantraine, P. 1968–70. *Dictionnaire étymologique de la Langue grecque*. 2 vols. Paris.

Citti, V. 1997. "Una coppia nominale in Lisia." In M. Moggi and G. Cordiano, eds., *Schiavi e dipendenti nell'ambito dell' "oikos" e della "familia."* Pisa. 91–96.

Cohen, D. 1991. *Law, Sexuality and Society: The Enforcement of Morals in Classical Athens*. Cambridge.

Cohen, E. 1992. *Athenian Economy and Society: A Banking Perspective*. Princeton.

———. 1998. "The Wealthy Slaves of Athens: Legal Rights, Economic Obligations." In H. Jones, ed., *Le monde antique et les droits de l'homme. Actes de la 50ᵉ session de la société Fernand de Visscher pour l'histoire des droits de l'antiquité*. Brussels, September 16–19, 1996. Brussels 1998. 105–29.

———. 2000. *The Athenian Nation*. Princeton.

———. (forthcoming). *Athenian Prostitution: The Business of Sex*.

Cox, C.A. 1998. *Household Interests: Property, Marriage Strategies and Family Dynamics in Ancient Athens*. Princeton.

---

[132] § 2: οὕτω μὲν δὴ πορευθέντες πρὸς τὴν Θεοδότην καὶ καταλαβόντες ζωγράφῳ τινὶ παρεστηκυῖαν ἐθεάσαντο. Παυσαμένου δὲ τοῦ ζωγράφου ... § 3: ἡμεῖς δὲ ἤδη τε ὧν ἐθεασάμεθα ἐπιθυμοῦμεν ἅψασθαι καὶ ἄπιμεν ὑποκνιζόμενοι καὶ ἀπελθόντες ποθήσομεν.

[133] *L'imaginaire*, for Sartre and Lacan, and for French ancient historians, carries a considerable element of idealization: see Loraux 1993: 3–22.

Cunningham, I. 1971. *Herodas Mimiambi*. Oxford.

Davidson, J. 1997. *Courtesans and Fishcakes: The Consuming Passions of Classical Athens*. London.

Dilts, M. 1986. *Scholia Demosthenica*. Vol. 2. Leipzig.

Dover, K. 1978 [1989]. *Greek Homosexuality*. London.

Ehrenberg, V. 1962. *The People of Aristophanes: A Sociology of Old Attic Comedy*. New York.

Ericcson, L. 1980. "Charges against Prostitution: An Attempt at a Philosophical Assessment." *Ethics* 90: 335–66.

Faraguna, M. 1999. "Aspetti della schiavitù domestica femminile in Attica tra oratoria ed epigrafia." In F. Merola and A. Storchi Marino, eds., *Femmes-esclaves: modèles d'interprétation anthropologique, économique, juridique*. Atti del XXI Colloquio internazionale del G.I.R.E.A. Naples. 57–79.

Figueira, T. 1998. *The Power of Money: Coinage and Politics in the Athenian Empire*. Philadelphia.

Finley, M. [1951] 1985. *Studies in Land and Credit in Ancient Athens*. With new introduction by P. Millett. New Brunswick, N. J.

———. [1953] 1984. "Land, Debt and the Man of Property in Classical Athens." *Political Science Quarterly* 68: 249–68. (Reprinted as and quoted here from Chapter 4 in Finley 1981, pp. 62–76.)

———. [1973] 1999. *The Ancient Economy*. 3rd ed. Updated with a new foreword by I. Morris. Berkeley.

———. 1981. *Economy and Society in Ancient Greece*. Ed. by B. Shaw and R. Saller. London.

Fisher, N. 1976. *Social Values in Classical Athens*. London.

———. 1993. *Slavery in Classical Greece*. London.

———. 1998a. "Violence, Masculinity and the Law in Athens." In L. Foxhall and J. Salmon, eds., *When Men Were Men: Masculinity, Power and Identity in Classical Antiquity*. London. 68–97.

———. 1998b. "Gymnasia and the Democratic Values of Leisure." In P. Cartledge, P. Millett, and S. von Reden, eds., *Kosmos: Essays in Order, Conflict and Community in Classical Athens*. Cambridge. 84–104.

Flemming, R. 1999. "Quae corpore quaestum facit: The Sexual Economy of Female Prostitution in the Roman Empire." *JRS* 89: 38–61.

Fowler, E. 1998. *San'ya Blues: Laboring Life in Contemporary Tokyo*. Ithaca, N.Y.

Foxhall, L. 1989. "Household, Gender and Property in Classical Athens." *CQ* n.s. 39: 22–44.

———. 1994. "Pandora Unbound: A Feminist Critique of Foucault's History of Sexuality." In A. Cornwall and N. Lindisturre, eds., *Dislocating Masculinity: Comparative Ethnographies*. London. 133–46.

———. 1996. "The Law and the Lady." In L. Foxhall and A.D.E. Lewis, eds., *Greek Law in its Political Setting*. Oxford. 133–152.

Fuks, A. 1951. "Kolonos misthios: Labour Exchange in Classical Athens." Eranos 49: 171–73.

Gagarin, M. 1996. "The Torture of Slaves in Athenian Law." CPh 91: 1–18.

———. 2001. Review of *Law and Social Status in Classical Athens*, edited by V. Hunter and J. Edmonson, pp. 53–74. Oxford University Press 2000. In *Bryn Mawr Classical Review* (e-journal at *owner-bmcr-l@brynmawr.edu)* (2001.10.3).

Gallo, L. 1987. "Salari e inflazione: Atene tra V e IV sec. A. C." *ASNP* 3rd ser. 17.1: 19–63.

Garlan, Y. 1980. "Le Travail libre en Grèce ancienne." In P. Garnsey, ed., *Non-Slave Labour in the Greco-Roman World*. Cambridge. 6–22.

———. 1988. *Slavery in Ancient Greece*. Ithaca, N.Y. (Originally published as Les esclaves en Grèce ancienne. Paris 1982.)

Garnsey, P., ed. 1980. *Non-Slave Labour in the Greco-Roman* World. Cambridge.

Garon, S. 1998. *Molding Japanese Minds: The State in Everyday Life*. Princeton.

Geertz, C. 1973. *The Interpretation of Cultures*. New York.

Gill, C., N. Postlethwaite and R. Seaford, eds. 1998. *Reciprocity in Ancient Greece*. Oxford.

Goody, J. 1986. *The Logic of Writing and the Organization of Society*. Cambridge.

Gophas, D. 1994. Θάλασσα και Συναλλαγές στην αρχαία Ελλάδα. Athens.

Graham, A. 1992. "Thucydides 7.13.2 and the Crews of Athenian Triremes." *TAPhA* 122: 257–70.

———. 1998. "Thucydides 7.13.2 and the Crews of Athenian Triremes: An Addendum." *TAPhA* 128: 89–114.

Gschnitzer, F. 1964. Studien zur griechischen Terminologie der Sklaverei. 1. *Grundzüge des vorhellenistischen Sprachgebrauchs* (Abhandlung der Akademie d. Wiss. u. d. Lit. Mainz. Geistes- und sozialwissenschaftliche klasse). Wiesbaden.

Hallett, J. 1984. *Fathers and Daughters in Roman Society: Women and the Elite Family*. Princeton.

Halperin, D. M. 1990. *One Hundred Years of Homosexuality and Other Essays on Greek Love*. New York.

Harris, D. 1995. *The Treasures of the Parthenon and Erechtheion*. Oxford.

Harris E. 1992. "Women and Lending in Athenian Society: A Horos Re-Examined." *Phoenix* 46: 309–21.

———. 2002. "Workshop, Marketplace and Household: The Nature of Technical Specialization in Classical Athens and its Influence on Economy and Society." In P. Cartledge, E. Cohen, and L. Foxhall, eds. *Money, Labour and Land: Approaches to the Economies of Ancient Greece*. London. 67–99.

Harrison, A. 1968, 1971. *The Law of Athens*. 2 Vols. Oxford.

Hasebroek, J. 1923. "Die betriebsformen der griechischen Handels im IV. Jahrhundert." *Hermes* 58: 393–425.

Henry, M. 1986. "Ethos, Mythos, Praxis: Women in Menander's Comedy." *Helios* n.s. 13.2: 141–50.

Herter, H. 1960 [1985]. "Il mondo delle cortigiane e delle prostitute." In G. Arrigoni, ed., *Le donne in Grecia*. Rome. 363–97. (Abridged Italian translation of "Die Soziologie der antiken Prostitution im Lichte der heidnischen und christlichen Schriftum." *JbAC* 3 [1960]: 70–111.)

Hervagault, M.-P. and M.-M. Mactoux. 1974. "Esclaves et société d'après Démosthène." In *Actes du colloque 1972 sur l'esclavage. Annales Littéraires de l'Université de Besançon*. Paris.

Hillgruber, M. 1988. *Die zehnte Rede des Lysias*. Berlin.

Hirzel, R. [1918] 1962. *Der Name. Ein Beitrag zu seiner Geschichte im Altertum und Besonders bei den Griechen*. Abhandlungen der Philologische-Historischen Klasse der Sächsischen Akademie der Wissenschaften 36.2. Amsterdam.

Hopper, R. 1979. *Trade and Industry in Classical Greece*. London.

Humphreys S. 1978. *Anthropology and the Greeks*. London.

———. [1983] 1993. *The Family, Women and Death*. 2nd ed. Ann Arbor.

Hunter, V. 1981. "Classics and Anthropology." *Phoenix* 35: 144–55.

Jameson, M. 1977–78. "Agriculture and Slavery in Classical Athens." *CJ* 73: 122–45.

———. 1990. "Private Space and the Greek City." In O. Murray and S. Price, eds., *The Greek City from Homer to Alexander*. Oxford. 171–95.

———. 1997. "Women and Democracy in Fourth-Century Athens." In P. Brulé and J. Oulhen, eds., *Esclavage, guerre, économie en Grèce ancienne: Hommages à Yvon Garlan*. Rennes. 95–107.

Jeness, V. 1998. *Making It Work: The Prostitutes' Right Movement in Perspective*. New York.

Joly, R. 1969. "Esclaves et médecins dans la Grèce antique." *Sudhoffs Archiv* 53: 1–14.

Jones, H., ed. 1998. *Le monde antique et les droits de l'homme. Actes de la 50ᵉ session de la société Fernand de Visscher pour l'histoire des droits de l'antiquité*. Brussels, September 16–19,1996. Brussels.

Jordan, D. 1985. "A Survey of Greek Defixiones not Included in the Special Corpora." *GRBS* 26: 151–97.

Joshel S., and S. Murnaghan. 1998. "Introduction: Differential Equations." In S. Murnaghan and S. Joshel, eds., *Women and Slaves in Greco-Roman Culture*. London. 1–21.

Kanellopoulos, A. 1987. Ἀρχαιοελληνικὰ πρότυπα τῆς Κοινῆς Ἀγορᾶς. Athens.

Kapparis, K. 1999. *Apollodoros "Against Neaira" [D.59]*. Berlin.

Karras, R. 1996. *Common Women: Prostitution and Sexuality in Medieval England*. New York.

Keuls, E. 1983. " 'The Hetaera and the Housewife': The Splitting of the Female Psyche in Greek Art." *Mededelingen van het Nederlands Historisch Instituut te Rome* 44–45: 23–40.

———. 1985. *The Reign of the Phallus: Sexual Politics in Ancient Athens*. New York.

Khatzibasileiou, B. 1981. Τα δημοσιονομικά της Κω από μαρτυρίες αρχαίων επιγραφών = Vol. 8 of Κωακά.

Kirschenbaum, A. 1987. *Sons, Slaves, and Freedmen in Roman Commerce*. Jerusalem.

Klees, H. 1998. *Sklavenleben im klassischen Griechenland*=(Vol. 30 of *Forschungen zur antiken Sklaverei*, edited by H. Bellen). Stuttgart.

Knigge, U. 1988. *Der Kerameikos von Athens*. Athens.

Kränzlein, A. 1975. "Die attischen Aufzeichnungen über die Einlieferung von phialai exeleutherikai." In H. J. Wolff, ed., *Symposion 1971*. Cologne. 255–64.

Krenkel, W. 1988. "Prostitution." In M. Grant and R. Kitzinger, eds., *Civilization of the Ancient Mediterranean: Greece and Rome*. New York. 1291–97.

Kudlien, F. 1998. *Die Sklaven in der griechischen Medezin der klassischen und hellenistischen Zeit* (=Vol. 2 of *Forschungen zur antiken Sklaverei*, edited by J. Vogt). Stuttgart.

Kurke, L. 1989. "Kapēlia and deceit." *AJPh* 110: 535–44.

———. 1994. "Herodotus and the Language of Metals." *Helios* 22: 36–64.

———. 1999. *Coins, Bodies, Games, and Gold: The Politics of Meaning in Archaic Greece*. Princeton.

Lacey, W. C. 1968. *The Family in Classical Greece*. London.

Lane, R. E. 1991. *The Market Experience*. Cambridge.

Ledl, A. 1907. "Das attische Bürgerrecht und die Frauen. I." *WS* 29: 173–227.

Legras, B. 1997. "La prostitution féminine dans l'Égypte ptolémaîque." In G. Thür and J. Vélissaropoulos-Karakostas, eds., *Symposion 1995*. Köln. 249–64.

Lentakis, A. 1998. Ἡ πορνεία. Vol. 3 of Ο έρωτας στην αρχαία Ελλάδα. Athens.

Lewis, D. 1959. "Attic Manumissions." *Hesperia* 28: 208–38.

———. 1968. "Dedications of Phialai at Athens." *Hesperia* 37: 368–80.

Lind, H. 1988. "Ein Hetärentum am Heiligen Tor?" *MH* 45: 158–69.

Lipsius, J. [1905–15] 1966. *Das attische Recht und Rechtsverfahren*. 3 vols. Hildesheim.

Loomis, W. 1998. *Wages, Welfare Costs and Inflation in Classical Athens*. Ann Arbor.

Loraux, N. [1984] 1993. *The Children of Athena: Athenian Ideas about Citizenship and the Division between the Sexes*. Trans. C. Levine. Princeton. (Published originally as *Les enfants d'Athéna: Idées athéniennes sur la citoyenneté et la division des sexes*. Paris.)

———. 1995. *The Experiences of Tiresias: The Feminine and the Greek Man*. Princeton. (Published originally as *Les Expériences de Tirésias. Le féminin et l'homme grec*. Paris 1990.)

Lotze, D. 1981. "Zwischen Politen und Metöken: Pasivbürger im klassischen Athen?" *Klio* 63: 159–78.

Mactoux, M.-M. 1980. "Douleia." *Esclavage et pratiques discursives dans l'Athènes classique*. Paris.

MacDowell, D. 1989. "The Oikos in Athenian Law." *CQ* n.s. 39: 10–21.

MacIntyre, A. 1981. *After Virtue: A Study in Moral Theory*. South Bend.

Martini, R. 1997. "Sul contratto d'opera nell'Atene classica." In G. Thür and J. Vélissaropoulos-Karakostas, eds., *Symposion 1995*. Köln. 49–55.

Marx, K. 1970–72. *Capital*. 3 Vols. London. (English translation of Das Kapital.)

Marzi, M. ed. 1979. *Lisia. Per ferimento premeditato*. Città di Castello.

McClintock, A., ed. 1993. "Sex Work Issues." *Social Text 37* (special edition devoted to sexual workers' issues).

McIntosh, M. 1978. "Who Needs Prostitutes? The Ideology of Male Sexual Needs." In C. Smart and B. Smart, eds., *Women, Sexuality and Social Control*. 53–64. London.

Meyer, M. 1988. "Männer mit Geld. Zu einer rotfigurigen Vase mit 'Alltagsszene'." *JdAI* 103: 87–125.

Miers, S. and I. Kopytoff, eds. 1977. *Slavery in Africa*. Madison, Wisc.

Miller, F. D., Jr. 1974. "The State and the Community in Aristotle's Politics." *Reason Papers* 1: 61–69.

———. 1995. *Nature, Justice, and Rights in Aristotle's "Politics."* Oxford.

Millett P. 1991. *Lending and Borrowing in Ancient Athens*. Cambridge.

Mirhady, D. 1996. "Torture and Rhetoric in Athens." *JHS* 116: 119–31.

———. 2000. "The Athenian Rationale for Torture." In V. Hunter and J. Edmonson, eds., *Law and Social Status in Classical Athens*. Oxford. 53–74.

Morris, I. 1987. *Burial and Ancient Society: The Rise of the Greek City-State*. Cambridge.

———.1994. "The Athenian Economy Twenty Years after the Ancient Economy." *CPh* 89: 351–66.

Mossé, C. 1983. La Femme dans la Grèce antique. Paris.

Neils, J. 2000. "Others within the Other: An Intimate Look at Hetairai and Maenads." In B. Cohen, ed., *Not the Classical Ideal: Athens and the Construction of the Other in Greek Art*. Leiden. 203–26.

Ogden, D. 1996. *Greek Bastardy in the Classical and the Hellenistic Periods*. Oxford.

Osborne, R. 1995. "The Economics and Politics of Slavery at Athens." In A. Powell, ed., *The Greek World*. London. 27–43.

Ostwald, M. 1996. "Shares and Rights: 'Citizenship' Greek Style and American Style." In J. Ober and C. Hedrick, eds., *Dēmokratia: A Conversation on Democracies, Ancient and Modern*. Princeton. 49–61.

Paoli, U. 1976. *Altri Studi di Diritto Greco e Romano*. Milan.

Pateman, C. 1988. *The Sexual Contract*. Cambridge.

Patterson, C. 1990. "Those Athenian Bastards." *CA* 9: 40–73.

Perotti, E. 1974. "Esclaves ΧΩΡΙΣ ΟΙΚΟΥΝΤΕΣ." In *Actes du colloque 1972 sur l'esclavage. Annales Littéraires de l'Université de Besançon*. Paris. 47–56. (Translation of "Una categoria particolare di schiavi attici, i χωρὶς οἰκοῦντες." *Rendiconti del'reale Istituto Lombardo di Scienze e Lettere* 106 [1972]: 375–88.)

Pesando, F. 1987. *Oikos e ktesis. La casa greca in età classica*. Perugia.

Pirenne-Delforge, V. 1994. *L'Aphrodite grecque. Kernos Supp*. 4. Liège-Athens.

Placido, D. 1997. "Los 'oikétai,' entre la dependencia personal y la producción para el mercado." In M. Moggi and G. Cordianno, eds., *Schiavi e dipendenti nell'ambito dell' "oikos" e della "familia."* Pisa. 105–16.

Pringsheim, F. 1955. "The Transition from Witnessed to Written Transactions in Athens." In *Aequitas und Bona Fides: Festgabe für A. Simonius*. Basel. 287–97.

Randall, R. 1953. "The Erechtheum Workmen." *AJA* 57: 199–210.

Reden, S. von. 1992. "Arbeit und Zivilisation. Kriterien der Selbstdefinition im antiken Athen." *Münstersche Beiträge z. antiken Handelsgeschichte* 11: 1–31.

———. 1995. *Exchange in Ancient Greece*. London.

———. 1997. "Money, Law and Exchange: Coinage in the Greek Polis." *JHS* 117: 154–76.

———. 1998. "The Commodification of Symbols: Reciprocity and its Perversions in Menander." In Gill, Postlethwaite and Seaford, eds. *Reprocity in Ancient Greece*. 255–78.

Reinach, T. 1892. "L'impôt sur les courtisanes à Cos." *REG* 5: 99–102.

Rhodes, P. 1981. *A Commentary on the Aristotelian Athenaion Politeia*. Oxford.

Richards, D. 1982. *Sex, Drugs, Death and the Law: An Essay on Human Rights and Decriminalization*. Totowa, N.J.

Robert, C. 1919. *Archaeologische Hermeneutik*. Berlin.

Rodenwaldt, G. 1932. "Spinnene Hetären." *AA*: 7–22.

Rosivach, V. 1989. "Talasiourgoi and Paidia in IG ii^2 1553–78: a Note on Athenian Social History." *Historia* 38: 365–70.

Ruschenbusch, E. 1966. *Solōnos Nomoi*. Wiesbaden.

Ste. Croix, G.E.M. de. 1981. *The Class Struggle in the Ancient Greek World*. London.

Sandel, M. 1984. "The Procedural Republic and the Unencumbered Self." *Political Theory* 12: 81–96.

Scafuro, A. 1997. *The Forensic Stage: Settling Disputes in Graeco-Roman New Comedy*. Cambridge.

Schaps, D. 1979. *Economic Rights of Women in Ancient Greece*. Edinburgh.

Schneider, K. 1913. "Hetairai." In *Real-Encyclopädie der klassischen Altertumswissenschaft*, rev. G. Wissowa et al. Stuttgart, 1894–1972, 8: 1331–1372.

Schonbeck, H.-P. 1981. *Beiträge zur Interpretation der plautinischen "Bacchides."* Düsseldorf.

Schwimmer, E. 1979. "The Self and the Product: Concepts of Work in Comparative Perspective." In S. Wallmann, ed., Social Anthropology of Work. London. 287–315.

Seaford, R. 1994. *Reciprocity and Ritual*. Oxford.

———. 1998. "Introduction." In Gill, Postlethwaite and Seaford, eds. *Reciprocity in Ancient Greece*. 1–11.

Sealey, R. 1984. "On Lawful Concubinage in Athens." *CA* 3: 111–33.

Seltman, C. 1953. *Women in Greek Society*. London.

Shipton, K. 1997. "The Private Banks in Fourth-Century B.C. Athens: A Reappraisal." *CQ* n.s. 47: 396–422.

Silver, M. 1995. *Economic Structures of Antiquity*. Westport, Conn.

Sissa, G. 1986. "La famille dans la cité grecque (V-IV siècle avant J.-C.)." In A. Burguière et al., eds., *Histoire de la famille*. Paris. 163–94.

Sourvinou-Inwood, C. 1995. "Male and Female, Public and Private, Ancient and Modern." In E.D. Reeder, ed., *Pandora: Women in Classical Greece*. Princeton. 111–20.

Steiner, D. T. 1994. *The Tyrant's Writ*. Princeton.

Stocks, J. 1936. "Scholē." *CQ* 30: 177–87.

Strauss, B. 1987. *Athens after the Peloponnesian War: Class, Faction, and Policy, 403–386 B.C.* Ithaca, N.Y.

———. 1993. *Fathers and Sons in Athens: Ideology and Society in the Era of the Peloponnesian War*. Princeton.

Stroud, R. 1998. *The Athenian Grain-Tax Law of 374/3 B.C. Hesperia* Supplement 29. Princeton.

Stumpf, G. 1986. "Ein athenisches Münzgesetz des 4. Jh. V. Chr." *JNG* 36: 23–40.

Theokhares, R. 1983. Ἀρχαία καὶ Βυζαντινή Οικονομική Ιστορία. Athens.

Thomas, R. 1989. *Oral Tradition and Written Record in Classical Athens*. Cambridge.

Thompson, W. 1983. "The Athenian Entrepreneur." *AC* 51: 53–85.

Thornton, B. 1997. *Eros: The Myth of Ancient Greek Sexuality*. Boulder Colo.

Thür, G. 1977. Beweisführung vor den Schwurgerichtshöfen Athens: die Proklesis zur Basanon. Vienna.

Tod, M. 1950. "Epigraphical Notes on Freedmen's Professions." *Epigraphica* 12: 3–26.

Todd, S. 1990. "The Purpose of Evidence in Athenian Courts." In P. Cartledge, P. Millett and S. Todd, eds., *Nomos: Essays in Athenian Law, Politics and Society*. Cambridge. 19–39.

———. 1993. *The Shape of Athenian Law*. Oxford.

———. 1997. "Status and Gender in Athenian Public Records." In G. Thür and J. Vélissaropoulos-Karakostas, eds., *Symposion 1995*. Köln. 113–24.

Travlos, J. 1937. "Ἀνασκαφαὶ Ἱερᾶς ὁδοῦ." *Praktika*. 25–41.

Vanoyeke, V. 1990. *La prostitution en Grèce et a Rome*. Paris.

Vernant, J.-P. 1971. *Mythe et pensée chez les Grecs*. 2 vols. 4th ed. Paris.

Wake, G. 1932. *Sacred Prostitution and Marriage by Capture*. New York.

Wallace, R. 1993. "Personal Conduct and Legal Sanction in the Democracy of Classical Athens." In J. Zlinzsky, ed., *Questions de responsabilité*. Miskolc (Hung.). 397–413.

———. 1994a. "Private Lives and Public Enemies: Freedom of Thought in Classical Athens." In A. Scafuro and A. Boegehold, eds., *Athenian Identity and Civic Ideology*. Baltimore. 205–238.

———. 1994b. "The Athenian Laws of Slander." In G. Thür, ed., *Symposion 1993*. Köln. 109–24

———.1997. "On Not Legislating Sexual Conduct in Fourth-Century Athens." In G. Thür and J. Vélissaropoulos-Karakostas, eds., *Symposion 1995*. Köln. 151–66.

Webster, T. 1973. *Potter and Patron in Classical Athens*. London.

Wehrli, F. 1969. *Die Schule des Aristoteles VII*. 2nd ed. Basel.

Welwei, K.-W. 1974. *Unfreie im Antiken Kriegsdienst*. Vol. I. Stuttgart.

White, L. 1990. *The Comforts of Home: Prostitution in Colonial Nairobi*. Chicago.

Williams, D. 1983. "Women on Athenian Vases: Problems of Interpretation." In A. Cameron and A. Kuhrt, eds., *Images of Women in Antiquity*. London. 92–106.

Winkler, J. J. 1990. *The Constraints of Desire: The Anthropology of Sex and Gender in Ancient Greece*. New York.

Wolff, H. J. 1944. "Marriage Law and Family Organization in Ancient Athens." *Traditio* 2: 43–95. (Reprinted in *Beiträge zur Rechtsgeschichte* Altgriechenlands und des hellenistisch-römischen Ägypten [Weimar 1961]: 155–242.)

Wood, E. 1988. *Peasant-Citizen and Slave: The Foundations of Athenian Democracy*. London.

Wycherley, R. 1957. *The Athenian Agora. Volume III, Literary and Epigraphical Testimonia*. Princeton.

Yack, B. 1993. *The Problems of a Political Animal: Community, Justice and Conflict in Aristotelian Political Thought*. Berkeley.

19

Sanides and *Sanidia*[*]

John E. Fischer

Any study of the materials and media, especially those wooden tablets called σανίδες, used to publish documents in the Greek world must begin with a careful consultation of Adolph Wilhem's seminal article of 1909, in which he discusses the variety of materials and places of publication.[1] Since then, there have been many discussions, to be cited in what follows when appropriate, of different types of wooden tablets mentioned in inscriptions and other texts. More recently, a work by M.-C. Hellmann collects architectural references and also discusses the use of σανίδες as documents, linking them to λευκώματα and πίνακες, with which he considers them synonymous.[2] These terms are not always clear in inventories or other types of inscriptions, and full discussion of the terminology awaits another publication. Here, let us investigate just the term σανίς and its cognates.

The σανίς, as defined in lexica and elsewhere, is clearly a plank or board made of wood.[3] Our interest is in its use as a writing board or tablet for temporary inscriptions or, in some cases, for storage in an archive. We can get an idea of the size of σανίδες both from their use in architecture and from their use as the boards or planks that fenced off the agora when there was an ostracism vote.[4] Elsewhere the term is used to indicate a substantial, long plank of wood for doors (e.g., Homer, *Il.* 9.583, 12.121), a board to bind someone on (Ar. *Thesm.* 931, 940, etc.),[5] and other kinds of equipment. In the lexicographers a σάνις or σανίδιον is often equated with a πίναξ or πινάκιον

---

[*] This is very much still a work in progress which, although inspired and encouraged by my mentor Alan Boegehold, has suffered from my Ferdinand-the-Bull's distraction syndrome, and it is still more in progress than it should be after so many years. The idea behind my exploration of modes of publication is still both exciting and an indication of Alan's creativity in inspiring his students to seek and grapple with important topics in epigraphy. Thus, with thanks, I dedicate this to Alan on his 75th birthday.

[1] Wilhelm 1909; pages 240–42 are particularly concerned with σανίδες, although references to various materials are found throughout.

[2] Hellmann 1992; on σανίδες, see p. 367.

[3] The Delos accounts are unusually rich in careful description of what type of wood was specified, and we can also find citations elsewhere, notably in *IG* II² 1672, line 155 (from Eleusis), where both measurements and material are specified (σανίδες μελέϊναι, "boards of ash").

[4] Scholium on Ar. *Knights* 855.

[5] In the fragments of Aelius Dionysius 7 (428) a σάνις is defined as a board on which they bound evildoers (as above) and also (in the *Wasps*) as a board on which they carved (ἐνεχάραττον) the private suits (δίκας). For the *Wasps* passage, see Sickinger 1991.

(Hesychius and Suda s.v. σάνις). Two references in Callimachus and Menander suggest their use for paintings (of the gods).[6] The diminutive, σανίδιον, is referred to in a papyrus fragment dated to the middle of the third century B.C., where it was perhaps the back of a stringed instrument.[7] From inscriptions we get meanings ranging from the wood used in building programs for scaffolding and interior work (*IG* II² 463; 1672.151; and *IG* XI.2.165 from Epidauros), or on hand in households (*SEG* 13.13), to seats for temple priests (*SIG*³ 244 I 63–65 where the *naopoioi* sit), to boards used in tables (*IG* XI.2.144.67), or for painted pictures.[8] In another usage, mentioned in temple inventories, the two terms (together with πίναξ or πινάκιον) seem to refer to trays used to hold dedications, on which the donor and the weight of the gift could be inscribed.[9]

Our main interest is to explore the areas where a σανίς was used in public notice and in record-keeping. Numerous references to these practices appear throughout inscriptions and in the various commentaries on them.[10] So, for example, inscriptions on σανίδες were employed in public suits or actions. Fine in his *Horoi* discussed a reference in Hesychius (s.v. σανίς) that mentions the whitened board on which public suits against wrongdoers were written in Athens. He elucidated the last phrase of the entry, τίθεται δὲ καὶ ἐπὶ τοῦ (σ)ταυροῦ, by suggesting that the bull in question stood on the Acropolis, where it was dedicated by the Areopagus (the emendations of Scaliger and Casaubon do not help us here). He further suggested that it was possible to hang such a notice on the bull's statue, explained the phrase ἡ σάνις ἡ παρὰ τῇ θεῷ κειμένη at Demosthenes 25.70 regarding the display of debtors' names, and located the place of display.[11]

In the same way, σανίδες were used more generally for notices of γραφαί, as indicated in Aristophanes' *Wasps* at line 848 (although not here on the Acropolis). Bdelykleon says, "... well now let me bring in the σανίδες and *graphai*." Rogers, in his commentary on this line, understood the σανίδες to be the "cause lists, or notice boards whereon were exposed at each sitting of the Court the names of the causes to be heard that day." He went on to say of the *graphai* that they were both indictments, and "... all the documentary evidence which had been taken beforehand, and sealed up in the ἐχῖνος against the day of trial."[12] But certainly Bdelykleon here is referring to the publication of the trials and indictments and not to more published material, as Rogers suggests. The extension of *graphai* to include more than the published

---

[6] See Callimachus fr. 100 Pfeiffer and Menander (Meineke IV, p. 127, 1–3) respectively.

[7] *PHib*. 1.13.30.

[8] See *IG* II² 1672 where the price surely suggests some picture of significance. See also *Inscr. Délos* 2085 (+2086) where beam ends and σανίδες are painted encaustically. See also *IG* XI.2.205 in this connection.

[9] The following may illustrate this usage: *IG* II² 1534. 61, 69, 116, 118; *IG* XI.2.161 B76; *Inscr. Délos* 1441 Bb II.22, 23; 1442.B. 28–29.

[10] For general treatments of σανίδες in this capacity, see Schubart 1961; Klaffenbach 1960; Lipsius 1905–1915.

[11] See Fine 1951: 58 with notes.

[12] Rogers 1915: 131.

indictment would seem unparalleled among the Attic orators and other legal material. Within forty-six lines the text of an actual indictment is given (Ar. *Wasps* 894ff):

> ἀκούτε ἤδη τῆς γραφῆς. ἐγράψατο
> κύων Κυδαθηναιεὺς Λάβητ' Αἰξωνέα
> τὸν τυρὸν ἀδικεῖν ὅτι μόνος κατήσθιεν
> τὸν Σικελιόν. τίμημα κλῳὸς σύκινος.

The satirical *graphē* is quite close to the formal wording of a real *graphē* and would fit quite nicely on a σανίς. The display of further supporting evidence before the prosecution of a *graphē* seems needless and, furthermore, too broad an assumption, since the only cases in which sealed documentary evidence is produced are those in which there has been an arbitration.[13] In Athenian legal process, the original indictment was made orally before the proper magistrate and, if it was accepted, then recorded and published by an official and displayed in the Agora by the statues of the Eponymoi.[14] Consequently, the *graphai* referred to in *Wasps* 848 and 849 are either the original recorded indictments transferred to the court on the day of the trial, or, as Rogers suggests, cause lists or summary lists of the *graphai* to be tried in the courts that day.[15]

The names of state debtors were also displayed on σανίδες posted on the Acropolis.[16] Harrison contended that a state debtor's name was not recorded publicly until the ninth prytany, when the unpaid debt was doubled.[17] Between the time of conviction or other fault that would put a person in debt to the state, there was apparently no public display of that debt on the Acropolis, other than some mechanism which recorded the result of the trial or other action. Technically, then, a man was a state debtor and subject to ἀτιμία from the day of conviction, but he was not publicly listed as such until the ninth prytany. Was this listed on a σανίς and stored in the Treasury or Archives until the requisite time? The evidence, I fear, is not adequate to prove the point. In the ninth prytany, however, the liability was doubled, listed on a σανίς, and placed παρὰ τῷ θεῷ in a safe place on the Acropolis. The debt, when discharged, was erased from the σανίς and the penalty of *atimia* was removed.[18] Unfortunately, two speeches of Demosthenes concerning state debtors (Dem. 25 and 58) are not straightforward and the issues are quite complex (see Finley 1951: 25 on Dem. 25). References to a publicly listed state debtor mention neither a σανίς nor a

---

[13] Harrison 1998, 2: 97. But see also Boegehold 1982 for a possible instance of other types of suits also involving sealed documentary evidence.

[14] On the monument of the Eponymoi, see Harrison 1998, 2: 91; Wycherley 1957: 85–90 and Shear 1970.

[15] Rogers 1915: 131.

[16] The references here are many. In the lexica refer to: *EM* 708.13, *Suda* 1.344, Bekker, *Anecdota Graeca* 303.23. See also Dem. 25.70, 73; 58.16. State debtors were not all condemned as a result of a *graphê* or a *dikê*. Two public suits concerning state debtors should be mentioned, the γραφὴ ἀγραφίου (non-entry as a state debtor) and the γραφὴ ψευδεγγραφῆς (wrongful entry as a state debtor). These were almost certainly listed on σανίδες; see Harrison 1998, 2: 12–17, especially p. 15.

[17] Harrison 1998, 2: 169–176 on ἀτιμία, especially p. 174–5 n. 3; cf. also Dem. 58.21, 49 on the moment of ἀτιμία.

[18] Certainly in the Treasury and not on the bull as were the *graphai*.

λεύκωμα and other phrases may be used: ... εἰς ἀκρόπολιν ἀνενεχθῆναι (Dem. 58.20) or ἐν τῷ γραμματείῳ γεγραμμένον (Dem. 58.16). All phrases referring to state debtors must, in any case, indicate the use of a σανίς or other wooden tablet displayed on the Acropolis until that debt was paid to the state. The powerful legal force of this σανίς is made quite clear in Demosthenes 25.70 where the speaker "describes the published list of state debtors as their ὅρος, [and] he is simply saying that this list is of the same value as evidence of a debt to the state as would be a ὅρος on a piece of property as evidence of a private debt."[19]

Two other public suits were published on a σανίς and placed in the Agora by the Eponymoi, a γραφὴ λιποταξίου, desertion in the face of the enemy, and a γραφὴ παρανόμων, an indictment for an illegal motion.[20] The form for this notice required three sections: an indictment of a person; the specific motion which was allegedly illegal; and the citation of the law or laws which the alleged illegal motion contravened.[21] This is a substantial amount of information for a σανίδιον, although the evidence so far seems to indicate that the terms σανίς/σανίδιον were used interchangeably in Attic legal terminology. The crowning molding on the monument of the Eponymous Heroes was designed specifically to protect these perishable documents. Professor Shear's reconstruction of this monument indicates that the σανίς/σανίδιον placed under the molding could vary in size up to 1.50 m. in height.[22]

The *apographē*, a special procedure at law in public cases, also involved substantial publication.[23] Harrison states: "It would mean an inventory of property belonging to one who was a public debtor, made and published with a view to securing execution upon it for satisfaction of the debt; and by transference, it could denote the actual process by which such a debtor was arraigned before a court."[24] The publication of this list by the Eleven was of great significance for all involved: the denouncer (ὁ ἀπογράψας who could receive three-fourths of the value); the defendant; and anyone who had any interest whatsoever in the property.[25] The evidence indicates that this list was displayed in or near the law courts – certainly in the court when the court was deciding whether or not the property listed was correctly listed, and who had prior claim to satisfaction before the state received its share.[26] The clear emphasis in Athenian judicial procedure on oral evidence, and oral proclamation, and Aristotle's

---

[19] Harrison 1998, 2: 175 n. 2.

[20] Dem. 21.102, Photius 678.12, and Aeschin. 3.200, 201.

[21] See Aeschin. 3.200, 201; MacDowell 1978: 164–172.

[22] Shear 1971: 169 and 172 with plates. The width of the σανίς/σανίδιον is impossible to determine. If it was produced in court or stored for safekeeping in the Archives from time to time, it must have been manageable in size. It might also have been the custom to place the notice of a *graphê* or *dikê* under the appropriate hero of the person indicted, although there is no evidence to substantiate this.

[23] See Hesychius s.v. ἐν λευκώμασιν as well as Harrison 1998, 2: 211–217, especially 211–12 n. 3, and 213 n. 1 for citations of speeches and cases of *apographê*, and 178–9 on confiscation. Also, Lipsius 1905–1915: 299–308.

[24] Harrison 1998, 2: 24.

[25] Harrison 1998, 2: 214–15 for the process and the results. He contends (p. 214) that "... the official publication of the list, if it went unopposed, was equivalent to a sentence."

[26] *SEG* 12.100 and Finley 1915: 111–13.

discussion of the Poletai and the *apographē* (*Ath. Pol.* 43.4 and 47.2–3), indicate that the first stage of the publication of an *apographē* was the announcement in a *kyria ekklesia* of the property to be confiscated. The physical form of the *apographē* is not mentioned in Aristotle, but Hesychius (see n. 23) indicates that the list was displayed on a σανίς or σανίδες, which may have been displayed near the law courts after the session of the ekklesia ended. The time limit within which an individual might enter a claim against the confiscated property is not known.[27] Presumably, if no claim were entered, the *apographē* was valid and the Poletai immediately proceeded to sell off the property by auction.[28] If the *apographē* was contested, the claimant had to prove the case in court. The *apographē* was as complete a list of the accused's property as possible. It was clearly in the interest of the accuser to be accurate, since he received three-quarters of the property after it was sold.[29]

In his suit *Against Nikostratos* (Dem. 53), Apollodoros contended that he would not have listed slaves worth a certain sum if he had been acting in bad faith, since the penalties against him, if he did not sustain his case, were great. This case was an *apographē* only for the value of the slaves, although Apollodoros forfeited three-fourths of the value to the state, since he was interested only in vengeance. Apollodoros indicates a certain care and exactness in his *apographē*, which leads us to conclude that other actions of this kind, as well as the subsequently published lists on σανίδες, were substantial.[30] One indication that the length of an *apographē* on a σανίς was so detailed may be the description of the Poletai of the confiscated property of Theosebes, son of Theophilos of Xypete, as preserved in an inscription of 367/6 B.C. Lines eight through thirteen of the text deal with the *apographē*, the ownership of the house, and the description of its location.[31] In fact, thirty-nine lines of the entire eighty-four line text deal with the description of this house and the claims against it. This was, of course, the final judgment and disposition of the case as recorded by the Poletai in their records for that year. The original *apographē* on the σανίς would also have listed the denouncer, the accused, the property, and its location. The inventory of property would have been substantial when the *apographē* involved more than one house or two slaves as above.[32]

---

[27] The process of entering a claim was known as ἐνεπίσκηψις and the action following a διαδικασία (Harrison 1998, 2: 213 and 215ff.). The need for speedy action in an ἐνεπίσκηψις suggests a period from 30–90 days (as in Stobaeus, *Florilegium*, 44.22, on sale).

[28] Harrison 1998, 2: 213 feels that with no claim against the confiscation, Harrison "...the denunciation became equivalent to a judgement." See also Lipsius 1905–1915: 302–3,

[29] Harrison 1998, 2: 214; cf. also Lipsius 1905–1915: 308 n. 27 and Dem. 53.2

[30] See Dem. 53.19 and 53.28–29.

[31] *SEG* 12.100, lines 1–39 (367/6 B.C.); see also Pouilloux 1971: 143–49 no. 26, and Finley 1951: 111–113.

[32] The claimants against Theosebes' house were not few: Smikythos of Teithras, 150 drachmas; Kirkonides and the phratores of the Metontidai, 100 drachmas; Isarchos (for the burial of Theosebes' father) 30 drachmas; Aischines and the orgeones, 24 drachmas. There is no indication of whether there were other claims – the Poletai need only record the confiscation, sale, and disbursements of the claim(s) (only Smikythos was paid– – the others had to wait for their money). Lysanias of Lakiadai bought the property for 575 drachmas. All of the foregoing claims were to be satisfied from this sum: 304 drachmas in claims; 203¼ drachmas to Theomnestos who brought the charge; 67¾ drachmas to the state. Included,

The σανίς was also employed in private suits, *dikai*, and it may have been used in a special plea, the plea in bar of action, a *paragraphē*, but other materials were also possible, since the only citation of physical presentation involves the verb ἐξαλείφειν, which could be used in a variety of ways.[33] Non-specific references to private suits on a σανίς occur in Aristophanes, Aelius Dionysius, and Photius.[34] Two citations appear in Aristophanes' *Clouds*; in one, Strepsiades is explaining to Socrates how he will evade a suit (*Clouds* 769). He will obtain a fair, transparent stone and, standing behind the secretary, will melt out the letters of the charge with the sun's rays. Two commentators on the play feel it is likely that the *dikē* in question was written on a wooden tablet covered with wax.[35] Our sources which mention σανίδες used in public and private suits, however, do not mention coating the wooden boards with wax. Dover suggests that a fragment of Aristophanes (fr. 157) might bear on this where "they ate the wax from their γραμματεῖα."[36] This is a plausible conjecture, but our evidence does not provide corroboration to support the idea that σανίδες were generally or ever covered with wax when used in legal cases. The *dikē* referred to here is more likely the initial listing of the charge in the court or with the magistrates, not the public listing and display of the charge at the entrance to the court. This personal charge with other evidence was doubtless sealed in an echinos and, when the trial date arrived, unsealed and read to the court. A copy of the charge was written on a σανίς to give public notice of the trial.[37] The evidence for the use of tablets covered with wax tends to be relatively late and usually connected with non-legal or private matters.[38] If Strepsiades is looking for a clear stone or crystal, he might well plan to burn out the letters, as farfetched as that may seem; it's a comedy after all. The story of Alcibiades and the erasing of a charge against Hegemon, the writer of parodies, supports the conclusion that the σανίς as used in public and private cases was a whitened board on which the relevant information was either painted or drawn in a darker color.

---

but not specified, were two charges: a sale tax and a publication tax (τὰ κηρύκεια) which may or may not have included the cost of the physical publication beyond the herald's announcement.

[33] Dem. 37.34: ἐξαλήλιπται καὶ οὐ πρόεστι τῇ παραγραφῇ.The frequent use of σανίδες in trials and public life warrants this suggestion.

[34] Photius (499.15) calls a σανίς a λεύκωμα on which private suits are collected. Wycherley 1957: 86 no. 231 refers to Aristophanes' *Knights*, line 979 (a reference to the Eponymoi?); cf. also p. 185 no. 610; see also Shear 1971: 204. The references in the later orators refer to the monument of the Eponymous Heroes erected in the mid-fourth century B.C. (Shear 1971: 196). For the fifth-century B.C. monument, see Shear 1971: 205–20, where he dates the construction of the original monument between 430–425 B.C.

[35] The suit is a private one and Strepsiades proudly tells Socrates (764): ηὕρηκ' ἀφάνισιν τῆς δίκης σοφωτάτην which is his transparent stone (766–771). See Rogers 1916 on *Clouds* 769ff. and Dover 1972 *ad loc.*

[36] See Dover 1972 *ad loc.*; cf. also Pollux 10.58.

[37] Boegehold 1981 publishes an echinos lid on whose surface was listed the documentary evidence stored within the echinos itself appears.

[38] See Schubart 1961: 23–28 and 175; Kenyon 1909 with plates V and VI illustrating two remarkably well-preserved Greek tablets from Egypt, dating to the third century A.D.; *IG* VII 413.57–59, dated to 73 B.C., where κήρωμα (a wooden wax tablet) seems to mean a leaf of a book, and the term δέλτος (another term well worth exploring) seems to mean the whole book or a series of κηρώματα. Aulus Gellius 17.9.17 relates a tale about Hasdrubal and secret writing on tablets.

Hegemon, charged in a private suit, sought out Alcibiades for help; Alcibiades, in turn, went to the Metroon where the charges were kept, wet his finger, and rubbed out the charge: διήλειψε τὴν δίκην (Athenaeus 9.407c). The only other citation for this verb in the lexicon comes from Plutarch's *Aratos* (13.3), where the painter Nealkes, at Aratos' request, removes (διήλειψεν) the figure of Aristratos from a painted *pinax* and substitutes a palm tree. Thus, the clear meaning of this verb is to rub away or erase a painted figure or, in our case, a series of letters.[39]

Σανίδες are also connected closely with publication of those texts at the heart of the legal system: the laws. Two brief references connect σανίδες with *kyrbeis*, the venerable method of publishing the laws of Solon.[40] But σανίδες were used primarily for the publication of new laws. Their texts were written on σανίδες and placed in front of the monument of the Eponymous Heroes in the Agora.[41] The procedure for introducing a new law was, according to Demosthenes (24.17–18), clear and precise: first, the law had to be written down and placed in front of the Eponymoi; next, the law had to have a universal application and opposing laws had to be repealed; lastly, other steps, to which Demosthenes alludes but does not list, were to be followed; one of these seems to have involved statutory periods when new laws could be introduced. Demosthenes' main point in the speech *Against Timocrates* is that Timocrates had not taken any of the proper steps in introducing his new law, particularly its exhibition on a σανίς before the Eponymoi (24.26). The law was not exhibited and, hence, the public could not read it, and, if someone wished, speak in opposition to it. Considering the nature of this case, it is obviously in Demosthenes' interests to cite frequently the precise rule for new laws. Yet, even after taking this into account, one is struck by the emphasis (confirmed in other authors) on the first step of public notice. The law which sets down the rules for the introduction of new laws is called "ὡς δικαίως καὶ σφόδρα ὑπὲρ τοῦ δήμου" (24.34). Demosthenes further declares (24.36) that the lawgiver ordered its display so that all men might be aware of it beforehand, and he adds that, even then, it might escape the notice of those who might speak against it, or readers might not be attentive enough (when they pass the Eponymoi, one assumes). This is one of the clearest expositions of the theory behind public notice in legal matters, even

---

[39] Other forms derived from ἀλειφεῖν (ἐξαλειφεῖν, ἀπαλειφεῖν) mean to erase from a decree. A possible objection to this interpretation would be to understand the use of wax with the verb both in the case of Alcibiades and, more significantly, in the painted pinax, if the painting was done in the encaustic technique. This seems to strain the small amount of evidence we have for this verb. The smaller πινάκιον τιμητικόν does not help us here (see Rogers 1915, on lines 106 and 167).

[40] For details, see Stroud 1963; Stroud 1968; Hansen1990; Robertson 1986. Pollux 8.128 describes *kyrbeis* as three-cornered σανίδες in the shape of a pyramid, on which the laws are inscribed. In Aristophanes' *Birds* a character quotes an old law of the birds which is inscribed on *kyrbeis*. A scholiast on the line comments that κύρβεις are σανίδες χαλκαῖ. On kyrbeis, see also Rhodes 1981: 131–135; Rhodes 1991.

[41] Aeschin. 3.39; Andoc. 1.83; Dem. 20.94, 23.25, 24.18. At Dem. 24.23 a λεύκωμα is mentioned specifically, but the evidence of the other orators and Photius (676.12) indicates that here we consider this another term for σανίδες. Ferguson 1936: 145 n. 7 agrees with Wilhelm's point (1909: 265ff.) that σανίδες were used for the temporary *anagraphê* of additional laws.

accounting for the natural human trait of inattention (witness the recent fuss over misreading ballots in the 2000 presidential election in Florida!).

Two late Roman sources also mention σανίδες in connection with laws.[42] Dio Cassius, referring to the laws of Dolabella c. 48 B.C., reports that Antony and his followers cut down the σανίδες with the new laws (regarding debts and house rents), which were presumably in the Forum. Dionysius of Halicarnassus, while tracing the history of the early Romans, also states that the Romans carved their laws and religious ordinances on oak σανίδες. The oak σανίδες seem to be a second stage in publishing the laws, since Dionysius says they used δέλτοι first, then the oak boards. Whether these authors are reflecting true Roman practice or syncretizing is difficult to determine, since the development and practice of Greek and Roman legal systems were quite different, affecting, consequently, public notice practically and theoretically.

Two inscriptions, one from Thasos, the other from Chalcedon, add to our understanding of the use of σανίδες in the publication of laws. The first is a decree from Thasos, dated c. 412/1 B.C. [43] It relates to revolution on the island and might be dated more precisely to 411, just before the oligarchic revolution (411–407 B.C.), if the restoration of lines 15–6 (οἱ δὲ] | [προστάτ]αι) is secure.[44] The regulations were to be inscribed on a stone in the temple of Pythian Apollo. The use of the word "stone" (εἰς λίθον) rather than the more usual "stele" is curious but not unparalleled, since Athenian publication practice is often followed outside of Athens, where local terminology often simply alters the Athenian formulae. Certainly more striking is the direction to prepare two σανίδες with copies of the decree, and to display them in the harbor and in the agora (lines 18–19).[45]

Multiple stelai in Athens and elsewhere are not uncommon; multiple σανίδες, however, are not often mentioned. The contents of this decree are clearly deemed of sufficient significance to warrant both permanent publication in the Temple of Apollo and general, if not immediate, publication in the two most frequented areas of the city. There are two other aspects of this decree to be noted: first, the phrase ἀντίγραφά τε τῶν γραμμ[άτων suggests more careful copies of the decree (as Pouilloux takes it in his translation "des copies littérales de ce texte"). One might have expected the more usual ἀντίγραφα τοῦ ψηφίσματος rather than the phrase we have (the stoichedon arrangement would not be violated by τοῦ ψηφίσματος). Still, Pouilloux's translation of literal copies and the provision for two σανίδες indicate the importance of the

---

[42] Dio Cassius 42.32 and Dionysius of Halicarnassus 2.27.

[43] *IG* XII.8.262.14–19 (Thasos, 412/1B.C.). For treatment of the decree see Pouilloux 1954, especially p. 174 discussing the publication clause: "les magistrats feront transcrire ces décisions sur une stèle et la placeront dans le sanctuaire d'Apollon pythien, ils feront transcrire des copies littérales de ce texte sur des panneaux de bois bien lissés et les exposeront sur le port et à l'agora."

[44] The oligarchic officials of this period (as well as of an earlier time) were called the Three Hundred. See Meiggs 1972: 570–578, especially 576; Meiggs-Lewis: 252–255 no. 83, for bibliography and discussion.

[45] I follow the text of Pouilloux 1954. Hicks 1887 restored lines 17–18 as τῶν γραμμ|[άτων ἐς στήλας] λειοτάτας. But others, including the text of *IG*, Wilhelm 1909: 252, and Pouilloux 1954 all restore σανίδες. Pouilloux also restores the temple of Pythian Apollo, whereas *IG* and Wilhelm have the Temple of Dionysus.

decree in the eyes of the officials. The second point to note is the careful description of the sort of σανίδες which are to be used – ὡς λ]ειοτάτας – i.e. quite smooth or polished (Pouilloux translates "bien lissés"). Such precision is not unknown outside of Athens, although Athenian practice rarely says more than "on a stone stele" or "on a σανίς" in a publication formula. The *prostatai* charged with publication at Thasos carefully described first-quality boards with a very smooth surface – either already whitened or whitened and smoothed.

The other decree is a sacred law of Chalcedon, dated to the third or second century B.C.:

15   γρά-
16 [ψαι δὲ κ]αὶ εἰς σανίδα κοῖλα γράμματα καὶ ε[ἰ]στάλαν
17 [καὶ στᾶσα]ι τὰν μὲν στάλαν πρὸ τοῦ ἱεροῦ, τὰν δὲ σα-
18 [νίδα εἰς] τὸ βουλεῖον.[46]

This σανίς seemed destined to be a copy in an archive as the editor of the *SIG* suggests in the note on βουλεῖον – "vox recentioris aetatis pro βουλευτήριον, cf. ἀρχεῖον." The phrase κοῖλα γράμματα is interesting, suggesting that the law be carved into the σανίς rather than painted on the board – the note continues "non atramento picta, sed insculpta." There is a desire for a more permanent copy that could not be effaced or rubbed out. This decree echoes the period well, since carefully preserved records and town archives were commonly found in most cities of the Hellenistic world.

Finally, service rosters for hoplites and cavalry were also written on σανίδες, although there are also references to a *pinax* or *pinakion*.[47] Explicit citations of a σανίς (or σανίδιον) used for *katalogoi* are found in Lysias 16.6–7 and 26.10 (for cavalry) and Plutarch, *Nicias* 14.5 (of all Syracusans). In Lysias 16.6–7 Mantitheus makes a distinction between the register (σανίδιον) of men who served in the cavalry and another list which the phylarchs made of those who had actually served, so that the treasury might recover an allowance made to them for equipment.[48] A consideration of our source material suggests the following interpretation for the procedure of selecting

---

[46] *SIG*[3] 1011.15–18 (Chalcedon, third/second century B.C.); see also M.N. Tod, *ABSA* 19 (1913–14): 28–29; Sokolowski 1955: 13–16 no. 3; Michel 1900 no. 733; Wilhelm 1909: 268.

[47] Among the citations are: Ar. *Birds* 448 (on *pinakia*); *Knights* 1369–1371; *Peace* 1180–1184; Arist. *Ath. Pol.* 49.2.8–9 (catalogues of knights on a *pinax*); Dem. 50.6 (lists of sailors); Lys. 2.27; 14.6/7; 15.5,7; 16.3, 6/7, 13; 26.10; Plut., *Nicias* 14.5. See Xen., *Oec.* on the general process of *dokimasia*. Also, *SEG* 21.435; Wycherley 1957: 86 no. 232.

[48] Two problems confront us in considering this speech: first, our imprecise knowledge of the fifth-century procedure for the enrollment of cavalry (our main source is Arist. *Ath. Pol.* 48.1–2); second, the problem of sorting out the subsequent legal actions against oligarchic sympazizers or supporters of the Thirty (on which see Adams 1970: 133 and n. 1). Adams goes into some detail on a citation from Harpokration on the *katastasis*, and suggests that the motion requiring the cavalry to pay back the *katastasis* may have been either an indirect tax on the aristocrats (a way to circumvent the amnesty), or part of a larger decree which aimed at dissolving the whole cavalry. A further difficulty lies in the question of two lists. The earlier list (Adams 1970: 147) consisted of the σανίδες "presented in court from the archives (either the originals or certified copies); the other lists were those where the phylarchs reported those who had served and owed the *katastasis* to the state." For detailed discussion of the speech see also Bugh 1988.

the cavalry at the time Aristotle wrote. The first step would be a general publication by the *katalogeis* on a σανίδιον of all those eligible for cavalry service displayed under the appropriate tribal hero on the monument of the Eponymous Heroes.[49] Second, the σανίδια containing the names of the eligible were handed over to the hipparchs and phylarchs (Arist. *Ath. Pol.* 49.2). The third step was an examination of the eligible and those who were currently serving, by a committee of the Boule.[50] This portion of the examination allowed those currently serving and new men to enter a plea for non-service because of infirmity.[51] P.J. Rhodes states, "clearly the detailed examination, whether of old cavalrymen protesting their inability to continue in the service or of new recruits, must have been carried out by a few men."[52] Rhodes' interpretation of the evidence seems reasonable, since it appears unlikely that each cavalryman would appear separately before the Boule for an individual *dokimasia*.[53] The fourth step was a presentation by parade of the whole corps to the Boule. The fifth and last stage in the enrollment of the cavalry was the formal *dokimasia* by the Boule whose vote was taken after the presentation and parade of the knights.[54] The probable procedure for this vote was the reading of the names of those fit for service in the cavalry, the opening of the sealed pinax listing those presently in service, the erasure of the names of those unfit, and then the final vote (Arist. *Ath. Pol.* 49.2). This conjectural set of procedures would have been in force during the time of Aristotle. Earlier procedure may have differed considerably from that during Aristotle's time. Rhodes (1971: 210) suggests that the Boule began involvement with the *dokimasia* of the cavalry c. 462/1 B.C. Here, one might consider a late archaic vase by the Dokimasia Painter, c. 500 B.C.[55] In summary, then, initial publication of eligible young men for the cavalry

---

[49] The ancient citations here are: Ar. *Birds* 1369–1371; Ar. *Peace* 1180–1184; Arist., *Ath. Pol.* 49.2; Lys. 16.6. The two citations from Aristophanes refer to the *katalogos* of hoplites. Although there is no specific reference to the Eponymoi, the general connection of σανίς/σανίδιον with the Eponymoi, and the display of the hoplite catalogue there, make it quite probable that the cavalry *katalogos* had its first publication there.

[50] See Arist. *Ath. Pol.* 49.2; *SEG* 21.525 (dates 282/1 B.C.) and Rhodes 1972: 174–5, to whose lucid account of the *dokimasia* I owe a great deal; cf. also Bugh 1988.

[51] Jones 1957: 163 states: "The Athenians also recognized that service in the cavalry demanded an exceptional standard of physical fitness, and members of the corps and those designated to serve could, by an affidavit that they were physically unfit for cavalry service, get themselves removed from the list..., presumably becoming hoplites unless totally incapacitated."

[52] Rhodes 1972: 173.

[53] This would be a very large number, about 1000 in the fifth century to 650 in the second half of the fourth century B.C.

[54] Rhodes 1972: 175.

[55] This vase was first published by Körte 1880. See also Beazley *ARV²*, i, 412 #1; Bugh 1988: 16–19; Rhodes 1972: 175 nn. 2 and 3; Lammert, *RE* VIII (1913) 1694; and Cahn 1973. If one dates this kylix to c. 500 B.C. and if Körte's identification of the subject is correct, it would be the earliest representation of a *dokimasia*. Rhodes 1972: 175 n. 3 gives another date, quoted in Helbig, of c. 485–455 B.C. which would accord nicely with his suggestion (1972: 210) that the *dokimasia* of the cavalry was a post-Ephialtic addition to the powers of the Boule. If one could assume a relatively unchanged procedure, dating from the representation on the kylix until the first quarter of the 3rd century B.C., it might be suggested that the four older figures represented were our conjectural subcommittee of a bouletes, phylarch, one of the hipparchs, and a secretary to the hipparchs. For the secretary of the hipparchs see

would be on σανίδια/σανίδες posted on the monument of the Eponymoi in the Agora and subsequent lists of the cavalry would be on pinakes. Another possible interpretation of the difference between the σανίδια/σανίδες in the Lysias passages (16.6–7 and 26.10) and Aristotle's *pinax* (49.2) would be a change in the terminology from the time of the Thirty until c. 330 B.C.[56]

Another passage which mentions a list on σανίδες in connection with the military appears in Plutarch, *Nicias* 14.5. Here Plutarch is reporting the sailing of the Athenian fleet to Sicily in 415 B.C. (while Alcibiades was still present). Sixty ships of this fleet sailed from their base at Rhegium and, after some stops, arrived at Syracuse, sending ten ships into the great harbor (Thucydides 6.50.4). Plutarch reports (there is no mention whatever of this in Thucydides) that the ten ships seized an enemy vessel on which were σανίδες which contained a list of the citizen body of Syracuse. Normally these were kept in the Temple of Olympian Zeus about three kilometers south of the city. The Syracusans were sending for them to make a review and a *katalogos* of the young men of military age. The connection with the Athenian practice of listing by tribe the men available for military service is striking.

The hoplite *katalogos* at Athens was posted at the monument of the Eponymoi.[57] None of our sources indicate the methods or material of notice for the hoplite *katalogos*. But the posting at the monument of the Eponymoi and our evidence suggest that the material was a σανίς/σανίδιον. Two passages from Aristophanes (*Peace* 1180–1184; *Knights*, 1369–1371) both concern illegal erasures from the list. The passage from the *Peace* concerns not only illegal inscribing and changing of names, but also the plight of a member of the tribe Pandion, who unexpectedly saw his name posted below his tribal hero, and ran off with a nasty look on his face. The terms used for the entry on the *katalogos* and the erasure from it were ἐγγράφειν (*Peace* 1180) and ἐξαλείφειν (*Peace* 1181). In the passage in the *Knights*, Demos is promising reform. No hoplite entered on a list (ἐντεθεὶς ἐν καταλόγῳ) will ever shift from one to another (the verb used is μετεγγράφειν), but he will remain on the one *katalogos* on which he was first enrolled (τὸ πρῶτον ἐγγεγράψεται).[58] These two references indicate the problems involved with the *katalogos* of the hoplites. Where and when the illegal changes were made is not indicated (certainly not in public at the monument), but the hint of official collusion is strong. The suggestion of easy recording and easy erasing reinforces our contention that the *katalogos* of the hoplites was on a σανίς/σανίδιον. The passages from Lysias (15.5 and 7) also concern erasure from a list, and the verb used (ἐξαλείφειν) is the same as that in Aristophanes. The official in charge of the

---

SEG 21. 525 (Threpsiades and Vanderpool 1963, especially pp. 103–106 and plate 38a). One might also suggest that this subcommittee examination took place near the Stoa of the Herms, an area frequented by the cavalrymen.

[56] Habicht 1961: 136 no. 1 restores conjecturally in line 32 of a decree in honor of a hipparch the word pinakes; see *SEG* 21.435.

[57] Sources: Ar. *Knights*, 1369–1371; Ar. *Peace*, 1180–1184 (with scholia on both passages); Arist. *Ath. Pol.* 53.7; Dem., 13.4; Lys. 15.5.7; Thuc. 6.26.2; 6.31.3; 6.43.1; 7.16.1; 7.20.2; 8.24.2.

[58] See Rogers 1913, *ad loc.* and Platnauer 1964, *ad loc.* Rogers 1913 (on *Peace* 1180) also cites Lysias 30.3 (*Against Nikomachos*) where the orator accuses Nikomachos of daily inscribing and erasing laws for pay.

hoplite *katalogos* here is the taxiarch who is asked to erase Alcibiades from the list. The evidence from Thucydides, who uses the phrase ἐκ καταλόγου, suggests that there was one *katalogos* of all the hoplites and that, as the occasion warranted, selections or levies were made from the whole *katalogos*.[59] The whole hoplite *katalogos* embraced all male Athenians between the ages of 18 through 59, and was divided into forty-two year groups under the eponymous archon of that year.[60] There is no evidence where this general hoplite *katalogos* was kept permanently (during the Peloponnesian War, for example, it would have been a substantial list). One might suggest that this hoplite register was kept in the Strategeion, and the year or special levies were abstracted from this general register, and posted by tribe on the monument of the Eponymous Heroes.[61] A reference in Demosthenes 50.6 and 16 to a *katalogos* of sailors refers to the fourth-century practice of conscription.[62] There is no indication of what this *katalogos* was written on, but on the analogy of the hoplite list, it may well have been on σανίδες. If we could trust Apollodoros in Demosthenes 50.7 this *katalogos* was not very effective in producing able-bodied men. He says that few appeared at all when called and those that did were not competent: he went on to hire his own.

FURTHER TEXTS TO CONSIDER

The following list illustrates some of the many texts in which terms σανίς and σανίδιον appear. The scholarship on these texts is vast, and I have included just a small selection of the relevant texts as a guide to the reader and to further study.

1. *IG* I³.34. Athens. Decree of Kleinias Concerning Tribute. Date: c. 448/7 B.C.
2. *SEG* 12.22. Athens. Proxeny for Kriso. Date: c. 430 B.C.
3. *SEG* 12.41. Athens. Fragment of a Proxeny Decree. Date: 5th c. B.C.
4. *IG* I³ 56 (=*SEG* 33.4; 30.8). Athens. Proxeny decree. Date: 5th c. B.C.

---

[59] For ἐκ καταλόγου see Thucydides 6.43.1; 7.16.1; 7.20.2; 8.24.2. At Dem. 13.4 the phrase ὑπὲρ τὸν κατάλογον means beyond the age for military service. See also Gomme, Andrewes, Dover, *HCT*, 4: 264 on 6.26.6 and p. 295 on 6.31.3; also on the idea of a single comprehensive *katalogos* of hoplites, Jones 1957: 163. The plural may indicate the use of multiple σανίδες to record the total *katalogos* of all men available for military service. The existence of such a centralized register, however, has been doubted: see Hansen 1981.

[60] Aeschin. 2.168; Arist. *Ath. Pol.* 53.7; Lys. 14.7: hence the phrases ἐν τοῖς ἐπωνύμοις for year groups and ἐν τοῖς μέρεσιν for a selected group.

[61] See Wycherley 1957: 174–177; Travlos 1971: 6 figs. 29–30 and 34; and Camp 1986: 116–118 and fig. 91. Wycherley cites three inscriptions in honor of the taxiarchs which were set up in front of the Strategeion. The taxiarchs were in charge of the hoplite *katalogos* and it is not unlikely that the whole list was kept in this building. One also might note the proximity of the Tholos, the Metroon, and the Bouleuterion where documents were kept. The implication of speed in the posting and change of names in Aristophanes' *Peace* 1180ff. is that the master list was kept near the monument of the Eponymous Heroes. Aristophanes in *Peace* 311/312 (also *Acharnians* 197, *Wasps* 243f.; Thucydides 1.48) refers to an immediate call-up where the hoplites are required to bring three days of rations. One might suppose forty-two separate registers of hoplites, listed by tribe in the Strategeion from which the call-up would be posted on the Eponymoi.

[62] On the composition of crews during this period see Morrison and Williams 1968: 260–263 (particularly 262), and Amit 1965: 30–49 (especially p. 48).

5. *IG* I³ 68. Athens. Decree of Kleonymos Concerning Tribute. Date: 426/5 B.C.
6. *SEG* 12.41. Athens. Proxeny for Anytos and His Sons. Date: c. 430 B.C.
7. *IG* I³ 59. Athens. Decree Concerning Finances of City & Cult of Goddess. Date: c. 430 B.C.
8. *IG* I³ 60. Athens. A Decree Concerning Tribute. Date. c. 430B.C.
9. *IG* I³ 61. Athens. Decrees Concerning the Methonaians Dates: c. 430/29; 426/5; 425/24.
10. *IG* I³ 422 (see also *IG* I³ 421b & 429h). Athens. Poletai Records. Date: 415/13 B.C.
11. *IG* I³ 474 & 476. Athens. Erechtheion Accounts. Dates: 409/8 & 408/7 B.C.
12. *IG* II² 313/314. Athens. Accounts of the Epistatai at Eleusis. Date: 408/7 B.C.
13. *IG* II² 1237. Athens. Three Phratry Decrees. Date: c. 396/5 B.C.
14. *IG* II² 46 Athens. Agreement between Athenians and Troizenians. Date: c. 375 B.C.
15. *SEG* 33.411: Delphi. Accounts of the Naopoioi. Date: 345 B.C.
16. *IG* II² 1672. Eleusis. Accounts of the Epistatai of Eleusis and Tamiai of the Goddesses. Date: c. 329/8 B.C.
17. *IG* II² 463. Athens. Law concerning the Reconstruction of the Long Walls and the *Syngraphai*. Date: c. 307/6 B.C.
18. *IG* II² 1534. Athens. List of Gifts to Asklepios. Date: 291/0–247/6 B.C.
19. *SEG* 22.114: Teithras (Pikermi), Attica. Decree Concerning the Cult of Isis. Date: 37 B.C. or shortly after.
20. *IG* IV² 1.102. Epidauros: Asklepieion. Building Accounts. c. 370 B.C.
21. *IG* IV² 1.104. Epidauros. Construction of a Fountain House. c. 370–365/60 B.C. (See *SEG* 11.417a).
22. *SEG* 35.459: Delphi. Account of the Naopoioi. Date: 336–335 B.C. (Deals with a purchase of cypress wood; see *FDelphes* 3.5.9. lines 1–9).
23. *SIG*³ 244 I 60 Delphi. Accounts of the Naopoioi. Date: c. 346–344 B.C.
24. *IG* 11.2.144: Delos. Accounts of the Hieropoioi. Before 301 B.C.
25. *Inscriptiones Creticae* I.17.8 Lebena, Crete. List of Cures from the Shrine of Asklepios. Date: 3rd/2nd century B.C.
26. *IG* 11.2.165: Delos. Accounts of the Hieropoioi. Date: ca. 280 B.C. (Here sanides are planks for building, but cost and type may be relevant).
27. *IG* 11.2.161: Delos. Accounts of the Hieropoioi. Date: 280–278 B.C.
28. *IG* 11.2.199: Delos. Accounts of the Hieropoioi. Date: 274 B.C.
29. *IG* 11.2.204: Delos. Accounts of the Hieropoioi. Date: 268 B.C.
30. *IG* 11.2.205: Delos. Accounts of the Hieropoioi. Date: 268 B.C.
31. *IG* 11.2.252: Delos. Accounts of the Hieropoioi. Dated: 260/50 B.C.
32. *IG* 11.3.509 [*Inscr. Délos* 509]: Delos Law Regulating the Sale of Wood and Charcoal on Delos. Date: 220 B.C.
33. *IG* 12.7.228: Rhodes (Minoa). A Proxeny Decree. (A copy of this decree was to be sent sealed with the public seal to Rhodes – could the copy have been on a σανίς? Cf. also *IG* 12.7.388 – another honorary decree; could this have been on a σανίς and placed in the temple of Apollo? Also, *IG* 9.1².3.748, from Delphi, mentions κιβώτια – boxes/containers in which accounts (on σανίδες?) were sent back and forth to each town).
34. *Inscr. Délos* 2085 [+2086]: Delos (Serapeion). Dedication to the Egyptian Gods. Date: 112/11 B.C.
35. *SEG* 27.261. Gymnasiarchical Law. Date: 150 B.C.
36. *IG* 12.7.515: Amorgos (Aegiale). Decree Concerning a Donation and Foundation for Games. Date: 1st c. B.C.
37. *SIG*³ 799 : Decree of the Cyziceni. Date: A.D. 38.

WORKS CITED

Adams, C.D. 1970. *Lysias, Selected Speeches*. Norman, Oklahoma.
Amit, M. 1965. *Athens and the Sea: A Study in Athenians Sea-Power*. Collection Latomus 74. Brussels.
Boegehold, A.L. 1982. "A Lid with Dipinto." *Hesperia* Suppl. 19: 1–6.
Bugh, G. 1988. *The Horsemen of Athens*. Princeton.
Cahn, H.A. 1973. "Dokimasia." *RA* 3–22

Camp, J. 1986. *The Athenian Agora*. New York

Dover, K.J. 1972. *Aristophanic Comedy*. Berkeley.

Ferguson, W.S. 1936. "The Athenian Law Code and the Old Attic Trittyes." In *Classical Studies Presented to Edward Capps on His Seventieth Birthday*. Princeton. 144–158.

Fine, J.V.A. 1951. *Horoi: Studies in Mortgage, Real Security, and Land Tenure in Classical Athens. Hesperia* Supplement IX. Baltimore.

Finley, M.I. 1951. *Studies in Land and Credit in Ancient Athens, 500–200 B.C. The* Horos-*Inscriptions*. New Brunswick, N.J.

Habicht, C. 1961. "Neue Inschriften," *AM* 76:

Hansen, H. 1990. *Aspects of the Athenian Law Code of 410/09–400/399 B.C.* New York.

Hansen, M. 1981. "The Number of Athenian Hoplites in 431 B.C." *SO* 54: 19–32.

Harrison, A.R.W. 1998. *The Law of Athens*. 2 vols. New ed. Indianapolis.

HCT = Gomme, A.W., A. Andrewes, and K.J. Dover. *A Historical Commentary on Thucydides*. 5 vols. Oxford, 1945–1981.

Hellmann, M.-C. 1992. *Recherches sur le vocabularie de l'architecture grecque d'après les inscriptions de Délos*. Athens.

Jones, A.H.M. 1957. *Athenian Democracy*. Oxford.

Kenyon, F.G. 1909. "Two Greek School Tablets." *JHS* 29: 28–40.

Klaffenbach, G. 1960. "Bemerkungen zum griechischen Urkundenswesen." *SAWDDR* 8: 5–42.

Körte, G. 1880. "Dokimasie der attischen Reiterei." *AZ* 38: 177–81.

Lipsius, J.H. 1905–1915. *Das Attische Recht und Rechtsverfahren*. 3 vols. Leipzig.

MacDowell, D.M. 1978. *The Law in Classical Athens*. London.

Meiggs, R. 1972. *The Athenian Empire*. Oxford.

Meiggs-Lewis = Meiggs, R. and D. Lewis, *A Selection of Greek Historical Inscriptions*. Oxford, 1969.

Michel, C. 1900. *Recueil d'inscriptions grecques*. Brussels.

Morrison J.S. and R.T. Williams. 1968. *Greek Oared Ships*. Cambridge.

Platnauer, M. 1964. *Aristophanes. Peace*. Oxford.

Pouilloux, J. 1954. "Recherches sur l'histoire et les cultes de Thasos," *Études Thasiennnes*. Vol. 2. Paris. 162–178.

———. 1971. *Nouvelle choix d'inscriptions grecques*. Paris.

Rhodes, P.J. 1972. *The Athenian Boule*. Oxford.

———. 1981. *A Commentary on the Aristotelian Athenaion Politeia*. Oxford.

———. 1991. "The Athenian Code of Laws, 410–399 B.C.," *JHS* 111: 87–100.

Robertson, N. 1986. "Solon's Axones and Kyrbeis and the Sixth-Century Background, *Historia* 35: 146–176.

Rogers, B.B. 1910. *The Knights of Aristophanes*. London.

———. 1913. *The Peace of Aristophanes*. London.

———. 1915. *The Wasps of Aristophanes*. London.

———. 1916. *The Clouds of Aristophanes*. London.

Schubart, W. 1961. *Das Buch bei den Griechen und Römern*. 3rd ed. Leipzig.

Shear, T.L., Jr., 1970. "The Monument of the Eponymous Heroes in the Athenian Agora," *Hesperia* 39: 145–222.

Sickinger, J.P. "A Note on the *Wasps* 349." *CQ* n.s. 41: 529–32.

———. 1999. *Public Records and Archives in Classical Athens*. Chapel Hill.

Sokolowski, F. 1955. *Lois sacrées de l'Asie mineure*. Paris.

Stroud, R.S. 1963. "A Fragment of an Inscribed Bronze Stele from Athens." *Hesperia* 32: 138–143.

———. 1968. *Drakon's Law on Homicide*. Berkeley.

Threpsiades J. and E. Vanderpool. 1963. "ΠΡΟΣ ΤΟΙΣ ΕΡΜΑΙΣ." *AD* 18: 99–114

Travlos, J. 1971. *Pictorial Dictionary of Ancient Athens*. New York.

Wilhelm, A. 1909. "Beiträge zur griechischen Inschriftenkunde." *Sonderschriften der Österreichischen Institut in Wien* VII. Vienna.

Wycherley, R.E. 1957. *The Athenian Agora*, Volume III, *Literary and Epigraphical Testimonia*. Princeton.

20

Thuc. 2.13.3: 600 T. of Tribute[*]

Charles W. Fornara

θαρσεῖν τε ἐκέλευε προσιόντων μὲν ἑξακοσίων ταλάντων ὡς ἐπὶ τὸ πολὺ φόρου κατ᾽ ἐνιαυτὸν ἀπὸ τῶν ξυμμάχων τῇ πόλει ἄνευ τῆς ἄλλης προσόδου, ὑπαρχόντων δὲ ἐν τῇ ἀκροπόλει ἔτι τότε ἀργυρίου ἐπισήμου ἑξακισχιλίων ταλάντων κτλ.

He bade the Athenians to be confident since, for the most part, six hundred talents of tribute came in to the city year-by-year from the allies independent of the rest of the revenue; on the other hand, six thousand talents of coined money still existed on the acropolis at that time etc.

Thucydides' summary report of Pericles' enumeration of Athenian resources in summer 431 opens with two contrasting clauses separated by μέν and δέ. The δέ clause, which does not concern us here, focuses on Athens' stored wealth; the μέν clause deals with her annual revenues. These revenues are split into two categories, the tribute from the allies and, in obviously second rank, all the non-tributary revenue, whatever its nature.[1] *Prima facie*, Thucydides' figure for the tribute gives the optimum since ὡς ἐπὶ τὸ πολύ, "commonly (but not always),"[2] qualifies the number 600.

The difficulty presented by the clause lies not in its language but in its import. Thucydides, according to our best knowledge, should not have imparted this information. The data in our tribute-lists make it inconceivable to us that the annual tribute could have risen at any time, much less for the most part, so high as this, some 200 T. more than we can account for. In 433/2, a year for which we have good evidence, and within the assessment period which is evidently embraced in Pericles' words, the total was approximately 390 T.[3] It is not surprising, therefore, that attempts have been made to bring Thucydides into conformity with modern estimates of the yearly tribute by extracting a more acceptable meaning from his words. There have been two main lines of attack (excluding resort to emendation[4] or the admission that Thucydides was

---

[*] To Alan Boegehold, my colleague and dear friend of almost forty years.

[1] The scholiast explained τῆς ἄλλης προσόδου as τῆς εὐφορίας τῆς γῆς καὶ τῶν καταδικαζομένων καὶ τῶν λιμένων καὶ μετάλλων καὶ τῶν ἄλλων. See below n. 16.

[2] "For the more part, commonly," LSJ s.v. ὡς Ab.IIIe; "*meistenteils*," most German editors.

[3] See *ATL* 3: 334; Gomme 1956: 17 *ad* 2.13.3; see further Meiggs' detailed analysis (1972: 527ff.).

[4] The authors of *ATL* III: 132. See n. 9.

mistaken[5]). Kolbe reasoned that ὡς ἐπὶ τὸ πολύ must be understood to qualify the word "tribute," not the number 600.[6] If so, the excess of approximately 200 T. could be explained by the addition to the "tribute" of other revenues from the empire, e.g., tolls, Samian reparations, the income from Amphipolis. The other remedy (Gomme, *ad loc.*, among many others) is to construe ὡς ἐπὶ τὸ πολύ in the customary way but to "broaden" Thucydides' definition of tribute so as to make it include "all the revenue [usually] received from the allies" even though "technically" it was not φόρος.[7]

Kolbe's interpretation, if it were valid, would exonerate Thucydides since Thucydides, on this view, scrupulously added an express proviso (ὡς ἐπὶ τὸ πολύ φόρου) to the effect that not every talent of the 600 was tribute. But Thucydides' words are not capable of this construction. Thus Gomme considered it intolerable and rejected it *tout court*; nor should it have gained even the notably weak assent given it by the authors of *ATL*[8] although they in fact discounted it.[9] The construction envisaged by Kolbe, ὡς ἐπὶ τὸ πόλυ taken with φόρου, not with ἐξακοσίων ταλάντων, is impossible Greek. When ὡς ἐπὶ τὸ πολύ is used in a phrase containing a number, it must modify that number.[10] One example of many in Aristotle, who used the phrase frequently, is *HA* 576a30 Bekker: ὁ δὲ μακρότατος βίος τῶν πλείστων (*sc.* ἵππων) ἐστὶν ὡς ἐπὶ τὸ πολύ τριακοντετής· ἡ δὲ θήλεια ὡς ἐπὶ τὸ πολύ μὲν πέντε καὶ εἴκοσιν ἔτη, ἤδη δέ τινες καὶ τετταράκοντα ἔτη βεβιώκασιν.[11] Nor can this self-contained adverbial expression at any time either govern a genitive[12] or modify it in such a way as to become segregated from its verb ("600 T. came into the city, for the most part of tribute" or "of tribute for the most part"). As in the other three passages where ὡς ἐπὶ τὸ πόλυ appears in Thucydides, it must (like any adverb) be taken closely with the verb of the clause in which it stands: ἥ τε γὰρ ἀναχώρησις τῶν Ἑλλήνων ἐξ Ἰλίου χρονία γενομένη πολλὰ ἐνεόχμωσε, καὶ στάσεις ἐν ταῖς πόλεσιν ὡς ἐπὶ τὸ πολύ

---

[5] See Chambers 1958: 30.

[6] Kolbe proposed this interpretation to Nesselhauf and it was published and endorsed by him in Nesselhauf 1933: 117. Among others, they have been followed by Kallet-Marx 1993: 99–101, and Samons 2000: 308–9.

[7] Gomme 1956: 17 *ad* 2.13.3; cf. Hornblower 1991 *ad loc.*

[8] *ATL* III: 132, "No doubt the words can be taken as Kolbe suggests."

[9] *Ibid.* They suggested instead that either "Thucydides may have been misinformed" or he "used the word φόρου here in a looser sense than, strictly, 'tribute'", or (their preference) the word φόρου is "an editor's addition or, more likely, a gloss...." This last suggestion has rightly fallen into oblivion.

[10] Kühner-Gerth, vol. I: 472 Anmerk. 2, observe, without discussion, the connection between this usage and the approximative use of ὡς.

[11] Cf. *HA* 553a6, 560b20, 568a12 *et al.* A good example of his usage in non-numerical contexts is *Apr.* 87b20ff.: τοῦ δ' ἀπὸ τύχης οὐκ ἔστιν ἐπιστήμη δι' ἀποδείξεως. οὔτε γὰρ ὡς ἀναγκαῖον οὔθ' ὡς ἐπὶ τὸ πολύ τὸ ἀπὸ τύχης ἐστίν κτλ. Cf. Isocrates, *Paneg.* 154: ὡς δ' ἁπλῶς εἰπεῖν καὶ μὴ καθ' ἓν ἕκαστον, ἀλλ' ὡς ἐπὶ τὸ πολύ, τίς ἢ τῶν πολεμησάντων αὐτοῖς οὐκ εὐδαιμονήσας ἀπῆλθεν κτλ.. The expression suits the philosophical mind. It is used five times by Plato, e.g., *Resp.* 377b7, some thirteen times by Xenophon; there is only one occurrence in the orators (Aeschines *in Ctes.* 248), not counting Isocrates (8 times). The other three occurrences in Thucydides are quoted above.

[12] An attaching genitive occasionally occurs when the phrase ἐπὶ πολύ alone is used. See, e.g, Thuc. 4.3.2; cf. 1.1.2 (ἐπὶ πλεῖστον ἀνθρώπων) with Stahl's note.

ἐγίγνοντο, ἀφ' ὧν ἐκπίπτοντες τὰς πόλεις ἔκτιζον (1.12.2);[13] οὔκουν οἴεσθε τὸ ξυμφέρον μὲν μετ' ἀσφαλείας εἶναι, τὸ δὲ δίκαιον καὶ καλὸν μετὰ κινδύνου δρᾶσθαι· ὃ Λακεδαιμόνιοι ἥκιστα ὡς ἐπὶ τὸ πολὺ τολμῶσιν (5, 107, 1); καὶ πάντων (sc.τῶν Ἐγεσταίων) ὡς ἐπὶ τὸ πολὺ τοῖς αὐτοῖς χρωμένων (6, 46, 4, everyone for the most part used the same expensive implements in dinners with the Athenians).[14] Quite apart from this it may be noticed that the attachment of ὡς ἐπὶ τὸ πόλυ to φόρου fails to give the desired sense. Such language, if the construction were legitimate, would mean that "more often than not the 600 T. consisted of tribute (although on some occasions the 600 T. consisted of non-tribute)!"

The explanation favored by Gomme after Busolt and others – that φόρος here includes more than "tribute" in the "technical" sense and in fact represents income gathered from all foreign sources[15] – must also be rejected. "Tribute and everything else" is not the same as "foreign revenue and domestic revenue,"[16] and it is arbitrary to substitute for Thucydides' equation another of our own to which it bears no resemblance.[17] Worse yet, it presupposes that for some inexplicable reason Thucydides, *who ex hypothesi knew the truth*, casually and with indifference misinformed his readership. All the world would wrongly believe, on the authority of Pericles as transmitted by Thucydides, the important information that the Athenians received 600 T. of tribute apart from other revenue.[18]

It is not plausible that Thucydides was or could have been "imprecise," "non-technical" in his use of the term φόρος. You do not call a crate of apples and pears a "crate of apples" even though both apples and pears are fruit, and such a categorical

---

[13] ABM[G] omits τό, and, though read by most editors, Hude included, it is deleted by Jones. See the critical remarks of Stahl and Steup.

[14] Nesselhauf (n. 6 above) claimed that ὡς ἐπὶ τὸ πολύ was here positioned *before* the word it limited. The operative words here are the subject and its verb. It is perhaps significant that in Thucydides the adverbial phrase always directly follows the emphasized noun.

[15] This radical idea developed from rather conservative beginnings. Busolt 1897: 79 n. 1 (on p. 83) had likewise concluded that Thucydides counted monies other than the tribute in this total but limited and justified the "technical" infraction by arguing that Thucydides calculated together all the monies received by the Hellenotamiai, οἱ ἐδέχοντο τὸν φόρον, i.e., Samian payments in lieu of tribute (see Shipley 1987: 294–6 for recent discussion), and the tax on commercial vessels passing from the Black Sea into the Dardanelles. Stahl, at 2.13.3, even more cautiously, warned against any contamination of the tribute with the sums received from taxes: "Nam φόρον hic numquam vectigalia dicit et reliquos reditus a φόρου computatione excludi addito ἄνευ τῆς ἄλλης προσόδου aperte significat." In any event, Busolt's somewhat tactful solution did not provide enough money to make up the sum of 600 T. Gomme's assumption, however, that the 600 T. can represent the aggregation of all external revenues whatsoever, though it finds the money, completely abandons the rationale which provided its starting-point.

[16] The scholiast (quoted above in n. 1) envisaged this dichotomy simply because the tribute constituted for him the full extent of Athens' exotic revenues. Otherwise we would have a comment from him either on the word φόρος or on the number 600. The unsophistication of the scholiast in these matters is clear from the treatment he accorded the rest of *c*.13.

[17] The phraseology needed here was used by Xenophon in *Anab.* 7.1.27: ὑπαρχόντων δὲ πολλῶν χρημάτων ἐν τῆι πόλει καὶ προσόδου οὔσης κατ' ἐνιαυτὸν ἀπό τε τῶν ἐνδήμων καὶ τῆς ὑπερορίας οὐ μεῖον χιλίων ταλάντων.

[18] It is a question how this audience would interpret ἄνευ τῆς ἄλλης προσόδου, if, indeed, anyone paused to think about it. Thucydides evidently allowed himself to be vague because, as he saw it, everything else paled in significance in comparison with the imperial exaction *par excellence*.

misuse of language cannot be justified by insisting that the term "apple" has here been "broadened" to include pears. How is the case different here? The word φόρος was not vaguely understood by Thucydides or his contemporaries (or, for that matter, by subsequent generations). It had passed into common parlance;[19] the ubiquity of the term, underscored by its significance as the flag of empire,[20] no doubt explains why Thucydides provided its aetiology in 1.96.2.[21] "Tribute" carried a strict and unmistakable meaning to Athenians, their allies and their opponents not only in its own right but as the designation of a whole class of Athenian subjects.[22] We have no claim to suppose that Thucydides used this familiar term eccentrically.

A different approach to the problem may yield better results. It may be that we present the question simplistically when we ask whether Thucydides' figure is "right" or "wrong" and conclude that it cannot be "right" unless we manage somehow to accommodate it to the evidence of the tribute-quota lists. That the 600 T. may have derived from a method of calculation alien to our own is perhaps indicated by the otherwise curious correspondence of 2.13.3 with 1.96.2, where we are informed that in 477 the Delian League's first assessment (ἦν δ' ὁ πρῶτος φόρος ταχθείς) was fixed at 460 T.[23] The comparably problematical magnitude of this number raises the possibility that the inflation evident in both passages is systemic. Had Thucydides written 1.96.2 but not 2.13.3 it might be plausible to explain the 460 T. as a mistake due to confusion on his part, or on his source's part (assuming he consulted one), or, perhaps, as a result

---

[19] The numerous epigraphical and literary references are too well-known to need citation. One may note, however, the verbal correspondence with Thucydides of Aristoph. *Vesp.* 657: τὸν φόρον ἡμῖν ἀπὸ τῶν πόλεων συλλήβδην τὸν προσιόντα.

[20] See, e.g., Isocrates 8.52, with Meiggs 1972: 253, 443f. for the sensational moment when, in the theatre of Dionysos, filled with spectators, the tribute was displayed.

[21] According to Hornblower 1991 *ad loc.*, Thucydides' purpose, "in a passage without literary or emotional resonance, can only be clarity. Thucydides is telling us that the word φόρος, 'tribute', means the 'bringing in' or 'contribution' (φορά, evidently intended as a more general word) of money." His readers needed no such explanation; the meaning of the word was perfectly clear. Thucydides is simply explaining how and when this well-known word originated. (It would be perverse to doubt his explanation. Herodotus' generalized use of the term [1.6.2, 27.1 et al.; note especially 3.89ff., Darius' receipt of tribute] must indicate how naturally φόρος crept into the Greek lexicon and became the *vox propria* for exactions of this type. Cf. Thuc. 2.97.3, who applied the term to the tribute exacted by Seuthes).

[22] See, e.g., Thuc. 7.57.4, καὶ τῶν μὲν ὑπηκόων καὶ φόρου ὑποτελῶν Ἐρετριῆς καὶ Χαλκιδῆς καὶ Στυρῆς καὶ Καρύστιοι ἀπ' Εὐβοίας ἦσαν, ἀπὸ δὲ νήσων Κεῖοι καὶ Ἄνδριοι καὶ Τήνιοι, ἐκ δ' Ἰωνίας Μιλήσιοι καὶ Σάμιοι καὶ Χῖοι. τούτων Χῖοι οὐχ ὑποτελεῖς ὄντες φόρου, ναῦς δὲ παρέχοντες αὐτόνομοι ξυνέσποντο.

[23] The old question of whether the 460 T. represented the φόρος or the value of ship-contributions counted together with it was laid to rest by Chambers 1958: 26ff.; cf. Hornblower 1991 *ad loc.* Chambers concluded that the number was incorrect, accepting in principle the conclusion of the authors of *ATL* III: 242 that the actual tribute likely to have been received amounted to about 230 T. And although Meiggs 1972: 64 considered the figure not "impossible," arguing that the Greek cities of Cyprus were included in the first assessment and suggesting that the tribute may have been lowered after the battle of the Eurymedon, this is whistling in the dark. So also, apparently, Hornblower, *ad loc.*, who opines that "the evidence derived from the tribute lists is not full enough for us to say that Th. is wrong, here or at ii 13, where his 600 talents is credible." At 2.13, however, Hornblower justifies the total of 600 T. by including extraneous foreign income in it. One wishes for more clarity.

of the simplifying tendencies of oral tradition, which could conceivably have remembered "Aristeides' assessment" somewhat inexactly, conflating the value of war-ships together with the contribution of money. The evidence of 2.13, however, makes this hypothesis doubtful. In this case we have no reason to suppose that the total given is not exactly what Thucydides knew or believed to be the canonical figure. It is a fair assumption (though by no means necessary to the argument) that he heard Pericles utter the speech he reported.[24] Therefore, since he was the contemporaneous witness of one of these two mutually consistent estimates, the real question is not whether the numbers harmonize with our expectations but, rather, whether the systematic use of such inflated numbers is susceptible to reasonable explanation.

Where did the Athenians get their numbers from? What were the "official" or "conventional" statistics? Obviously, when Athenian orators and the citizenry in general talked about the size of the tribute in the Assembly, the Council and otherwise in public and private life there was unanimity as to its amount. The source is easily inferred, for it is impossible to doubt that this consensus was based on the totals contained in the assessment decrees.[25] Thus Thucydides reported the assessment-total of 477 B.C., not (for instance) the accounts received by the Hellenotamiai,[26] in spite of the greater accuracy (and, we would think, utility) of the latter; thus Krateros (*FGrHist* 342 F 1; 8) likewise focussed on these documents, apparently publishing the assessments of 454 and 410.[27] The canonical estimates of tributary income, therefore, derived from *projections*, not accounts received. [28] And that these projections were formulated on the premise that there would be no earthquakes, famines, impoverishment because of other special circumstances,[29] or even plain refusal to pay by one or

---

[24] His account of Pericles' speech certainly looks as if it were written shortly after the event. 2.13.7, indeed, points to a later time, but the section is parenthetic, with Thucydides speaking *in propria persona*, and probably it is a later insertion. Even if it is not, few would care to argue that he misremembered the figure through lapse of time. If this report of the speech was not made contemporaneously with its delivery, he must have worked it up from a sketch made at the time and containing this datum.

[25] For these and their dates see ps.-Xen. 3.5 (generally four years apart); *ATL* III: 67ff.; Meiggs 1972: 524ff. The material is conveniently collected together in Hill 1951 at *Index* III.5.3. Our only reassessment decree preserved in substantial detail is that of Thoudippos, *IG* I³ 71 (Meiggs-Lewis, no.69), passed in 425/4.

[26] For them see Meiggs 1972: 234ff.

[27] "The hypothesis of *ATL* that Craterus included samples from the first and last assessment decrees ... is economic and convincing" (Meiggs 1972: 420). Jacoby and Pritchett seek a date other than 454 for F 1 but see Meiggs' response (1972: 420f.).

[28] The records of the Hellenotamiae came late, after the knowledge of the public had already crystallized; they were at once less sensational and more perplexing, with some payments from various localities not yet collected and others, for various reasons, uncollectible (see below). I do not suggest that these accounts were ignored; experience must have taught the Athenians, at least the more sophisticated of them, to take the conventional number projected in the assessment decrees with a grain of salt even as they expected or merely hoped that the assessment-total would eventually be realized. For in their minds, assuredly, the assessments of individual cities were based on ability to pay and they could suppose that some payments, even if delayed, would eventually flow in.

[29] Line 21 of the Thoudippos decree takes into account the possibility of pre-existing ἀπορία in localities which, consequently, were unable to pay the stipulated sum in at least one of the prior four

another ally, lies in the nature of things. Assessment included "allied" city-states from which the Athenians expected to extract the money by pressure or force[30] and even cities which in the short term they intended to assimilate into the Empire by conquest or negotiation.[31] Thus, although it is commonly assumed that these decrees correlated very closely with the revenue reported in the quota-lists,[32] that assumption, which is based on no empiric evidence whatever, seems both naïve and psychologically implausible. On purely general grounds we would expect these decrees to present a best case for the extraction of tribute. Assessment decrees were political documents crafted by politicians in response to the urging of an omnivorous appetite; the criteria used in making an assessment were naturally self-indulgent. Certainly, that is the implication of the one assessment decree preserved in sufficient detail to provide a picture, that of Thoudippos,[33] which called for more than 1460 T. It is possible, of course, to explain away this evidence on the assumption that Cleon, who unquestionably lurks behind it, was completely unrestrained in his appetite for tribute. But the extravagance of the Athenians in 425/4 surely is a matter of degree and not of type. Pericles' bureaucrats and boule may have been less ambitious in the selection of their prey but it does not follow that they restrained themselves from demanding the maximum amount from individual subject-cities. We must allow for an optimism relatively comparable to Thoudippos' in the assessment decree published in 434 – and, for that matter, in Aristeides' assessment of 477.[34]

---

years. For arrears see the Methone Decree, *IG* I³ 61 (Meiggs-Lewis, no. 65) and, in general, Hill 1951, at *Index* III.5.4.

[30] As the authors of ATL write (III: 69, after Meritt in *AFD*), "In years of new assessments, the difficulty of making collections must have been increased by the unwillingness of subject states to pay heavier taxes .... There were doubtless tribute-collecting ships in every year during the period of the war, but in years of new assessment the forces sent out for this purpose must have been more than usually strong." It is a safe assumption that these expeditions were not invariably successful or, when successful, that they coerced payment at a time subsequent to the year in which it was due. For the latter see the Kleinias Decree, *IG* I³ 34.19–31 (Meiggs-Lewis, no. 46).

[31] Take, for example, the appearance of Melos in the Thoudippos Decree (col. i, 65), which was attacked but not conquered in 426 (Thuc. 3.91.1–3). As Meiggs-Lewis observed (194), the list in Thoudippos' decree includes "many names that had not appeared for a very long time, such as minor Carian cities which lapsed in the forties ...." But (if I interpret their words correctly) their explanation that these cities were registered *pro forma* ("all cities which had ever paid were listed") is not cogent. The more likely explanation is that Cleon, fresh from his triumph on Sphacteria and ambitious for more laurels, counted on bringing them back into the fold.

[32] See, e.g., Meiggs 1972: 30; cf. Rhodes 1992: 38, "the *evidence of the tribute-quota lists* indicates that in the late 450s ... the total *assessment* was only c. 500 talents" (my emphasis). Meiggs' guess (1972: 527), that the assessment total for the period 434–431 "was probably c. 430 talents" is merely a rough approximation to the collection in 432 of about 390 T.

[33] See n. 25.

[34] The authors of *ATL* III: 242 inferred that the actual collection of 477 comprised about 230 T., 50% of Thucydides' assessment total. See n. 22.

[35] After this paper was written my colleague, Adele Scafuro, pointed out to me that P. J. Rhodes (1988: 194) had already observed that "a possible explanation of Thucydides' figures is that they are derived from similarly optimistic assessment lists." I am glad to acknowledge his priority; but since Rhodes expressed himself provisionally and did not argue the question I have let this essay stand as written.

It is a safe assumption, therefore, that a gap existed between the prospective income anticipated in the assessment decree and the actual tributary revenue received in 434–431. From this it is an easy step to the conclusion that the dimensions of this gap can be measured by the difference between Pericles' 600 T. and the approximately 400 T. we deduce from the tribute-quota lists in that assessment-cycle. And this, I think, fully explains his or Thucydides' use of the adverbial phrase ὡς ἐπὶ τὸ πολὺ, which perhaps should be translated "in large degree:" it is the necessary grain of salt.

Some may find this conclusion unpalatable because it accuses Pericles of using inflated numbers, but he is hardly to be condemned for following (as I argue) common practice. Similarly, the spread between 400 T. and 600 T. may seem overlarge to us. But here we are altogether in the dark, except for such light as is thrown upon the subject by the enormous sum-total given in the decree of Thoudippos. That there was inflation in these assessments is incontestable. Therefore, since it is easier to believe that the Athenians reckoned by excessive expectations than that Thucydides twice reported numbers excessively high, the figures given us by Thucydides in 1.96.2 and 2.13.3 are best taken as evidence of a typical disparity between assessment and collection.[35]

WORKS CITED

ATL III= Meritt, B.D., H.T. Wade-Gery, and M. McGregor. *The Athenian Tribute Lists*. Vol. III. Princeton, 1950.

Busolt, G. 1897. *Griechische Geschichte bis zur Schlacht bei Chaeroneia*. Vol 3.1. Gotha.

Chambers, M. 1958. "Four Hundred Sixty Talents." *CP* 53: 26–32.

Gomme, A.W. 1956. *A Historical Commentary on Thucydides*. Vol. 2. Oxford.

Hill, G.F. 1951. *Sources for Greek History between the Persian and Peloponnesian War*. Rev. by R. Meiggs and A. Andrewes. Oxford.

Hornblower, S. 1991. *A Commentary on Thucydides*. Vol. I. Oxford.

Kallet-Marx, L. 1993. *Money, Expense and Naval Power in Thucyides' History 1–5.24*. Berkeley and Los Angeles.

Kühner-Gerth = Kühner, R. and B. Gerth. *Ausführliche Grammatik der griechischen Sprache, Satzlehre*. Erste Teil. 4th ed. Leverkusen, 1955.

Meiggs-Lewis = R. Meiggs, and D.M. Lewis, eds. *A Selection of Greek Historical Inscriptions to the End of the Fifth Century B.C.* Oxford, 1969.

Meiggs, R. 1972. *The Athenian Empire*. Oxford.

Nesselhauf, H. 1933. *Untersuchungen zur Geschichte der delisch-attischen Symmachie. Klio* Beiheft 30.

Rhodes, P.J. 1988. *Thucydides Book 2, Classical Texts*. Wiltshire.

———. 1992. "The Delian League to 449 B.C." In D. M. Lewis *et al.*, *The Cambridge Ancient History*. Vol. V, *The Fifth Century B.C.* 2nd ed. Cambridge. 34–51.

Samons II, L.J. 2000. *Empire of the Owl. Historia Einzelschriften* 142. Stuttgart.

Shipley, G. 1987. *A History of Samos*. Oxford.

Stahl = Poppo, F. and M. Stahl. 1886. *Thucydidis de bello Peloponnesiaco Libri Octo*. Vol. I. 3rd ed. Leipzig.

Steup = Classen, J. and J. Steup. 1963. *Thukydides*. Vol. I. 6th ed. Berlin.

21

Delivering the Go(o)ds: Demetrius Poliorcetes and Hellenistic Divine Kingship[*]

Peter Green

quos ab hominibus peruenisse dicis ad deos, tu reddes
rationem quem ad modum id fieri potuerit, et ego discam libenter.
Cic. *ND* 3.16.41

Die Entstehung des Herrscherkults ist das dunkelste und umstrittenste Problem der griechischen Religion in geschichtlicher Zeit ... Wenn man dem religiösen Gehalt des Herrscherkultes nachgehen will, solle man nicht so sehr von modernen religionswissenschaftlichen Fragestellungen ausgehen, sondern untersuchen, was die Menschen damals von ihm hielten.

M.P. Nilsson, *Geschichte der griechischen Religion*[3], ii. 135, 182

He who treats another human being as divine thereby
assigns to himself the relative status of a child or an animal.
E.R. Dodds, *The Greeks and the Irrational* (1951), 24

I

In the current debate on Greek kingship, scholars are faced with two complementary problems: first, to extrapolate the essential qualities of royalty; and second, to explain its historical decline. The two are intimately related. There is a greater consensus than there used to be regarding the religious or sacral nature of royal authority: as Reinhard Bendix writes:[1] "The authority of kings depended on religious sanction as well as on internal and external struggles for power." Max Weber similarly regards the king as

---

[*] This essay was originally composed as a contribution to the conference entitled "Kingship and the Organization of Power in Greek Society," held 6–7 December 1993 in the Department of Classics, the University of Texas at Austin, under the auspices of the Program in Aegean Scripts and Prehistory. Since then, as a lecture, it has undergone various developments and modifications, often in response to informed comment from a number of academic audiences, most recently when presented as the Tracy Lecture for 2000 at the University of Illinois at Chicago. I am delighted now to offer it, in published form, to my old and dear friend Alan Boegehold, a scholar who has always relished – and done so much to solve – the more intractable problems of Athenian history.

[1] Bendix 1978: 4.

patriarch, charismatic leader, arbiter, priest and medicine man[2] – i.e. as gaining validation by direct ritual access to, inspiration by, and in some cases identification with, divinity. What we see here is a special early way of interpreting the world in both its human and its divine aspects, which are seen as a seamless sacral continuum. Remains of this outlook can be found in, e.g., the poetry of Pindar.

Its progressive erosion is, of course, intimately linked to the development of that powerful counter-attitude, Greek intellectual rationalism, as manifested in a series of witnesses from the Milesian physicists to the Sophistic movement. The impact of this "Parmenidean" revolution has been well charted by French scholars such as J.-P. Vernant and Marcel Detienne.[3] Thus behind the various contingential reasons for decline – military rivalry, breeding-out, aristocratic pressure – enumerated by Pierre Carlier (1984: 509) we can see the ubiquitous pressure of a rational, non-theocratic approach to the business of life. This, of course, affected politics and government no less than, say, astronomy: in both cases cause and effect, the force of general principle (e.g. in the application of law) proved paramount. As Chester Starr reminds us,[4] it was far from inevitable that Greeks should have pursued "the intensification of collective action and the creation of machinery for its expression" that lay at the heart of the polis. The Near East was full of powerful monarchies that invited imitation; Homer (*Il.* 2.204) made Odysseus quote what sounds like a proverb: "The lordship of many is no good thing: let there be one lord only" [οὐκ ἀγαθὸν πολυκοιρανίη· εἷς κοίρανος ἔστω]. Yet reason prevailed. Despite pockets of traditionalism like the Cypriot monarchies or the odd dual Spartan kingship (not to mention the notion of tyranny, an attempt to impose purely secular one-man rule on an economic basis), the polis emerged triumphant. Kingship became an embarrassing relict, to be graded down into harmless magistracies and eventually (like almost everything else in the Hellenic world) analysed and codified by Aristotle.

But of course there was a price to pay. The fatal weakness of intellectual rationalism is an ingrained tendency to ignore, discount, and frequently despise beliefs and emotions. The so-called "Greek miracle" created a world of reason in two or three generations. But this world found itself up against the archetypal psychological convictions and mind-sets of millennia. Head conflicted with heart, polis law with tribalism. Attic tragedy, e.g. in Sophocles' *Ajax* and *Antigone*, captures this terrible tension. Perhaps its most memorable exemplification is Euripides' *Bacchae*. Belief in, and a deep need for, the sacral quality of kingship formed part of this ancient emotional matrix, what Gilbert Murray referred to as the "Inherited Conglomerate."[5] In what follows I hope to demonstrate, by means of a late, striking, and (it could be argued) pathological example, that of Demetrius Poliorcetes' welcome by the Athenians, just how powerful and basic this faith remained, even in the Hellenistic age.

In so doing I am conscious (not for the first time) of going against the whole current trend of Hellenistic scholarship. In a richly erudite and rewarding recent

---

[2] Weber 1968, iii: 1142.
[3] Vernant 1962: 111ff.; Detienne 1979: 41–5.
[4] Starr 1961 (citation from 129).
[5] Murray 1947: 66–7; well discussed by Dodds 1951: 179.

collection of papers,[6] despite the fact that the entire first section (3–124) is devoted to "The social and religious aspects of Hellenistic kingship," and that one further paper deals with "self-identity in Hellenistic religion," the tone throughout remains resolutely social and political. Cultural syncretism is shown encouraging assimilation, peace, loyalty. Hellenistic kingship is described[7] as a "political reality" made tolerable by Pindaric-style poetry in a world where "mythical thinking" is "a thing of the past for educated Greeks" and "the hero of old was the thing closest to a divine king on earth." Demetrius Poliorcetes' reception in Athens is briefly mentioned by one scholar (not in the section on kingship!) as something "notorious even in ancient times,"[8] and briskly dismissed by another thus: "As a religious phenomenon the cult of Demetrius seems to have been as meaningless as the cult of the rulers in general." In his latest book, *Athens from Alexander to Antony*, Christian Habicht likewise plays it down.[9] It is my contention that this commonsensical indifference to the sacral element inherent in kingship is fundamentally mistaken, and removes a whole crucial dimension from our understanding of Hellenistic society.[10]

II

Probably in September 290 B.C.[11] Demetrius Poliorcetes, the Besieger (a somewhat ironic title, since his most famous siege, that of Rhodes, 305/4, ended in failure), entered Athens in triumph, to be welcomed by an ithyphallic hymn,[12] well described

---

[6] Bulloch et al. 1993.

[7] Koenen 1993: 114. Since then the topic has been virtually ignored by scholars.

[8] Gelzer 1993: 147.

[9] Dihle 1993: 293, cf. 289, also apropos the ruler-cult: "Its religious importance seems to have been very little." See now in general Habicht 1997: 300–308. Jon Mikalson's new and learned study, *Religion in Hellenistic Athens*, spends an entire chapter, "Twenty Years of the Divine Demetrius Poliorcetes" (1998: 75–104), on Demetrius's pretensions to, or acceptance of, godhead. Mikalson carefully avoids committing himself: he emphasizes that, to begin with, most Athenians were only too glad to have a live σωτήρ on the spot, but strongly implies that it was a simple *do ut des* relationship, entered into by Athens in default of any better protector.

[10] One encouraging recent exception is the volume of essays in Buxton 1999, and in particular the essay by Henrichs (1999: 223–248), to which I shall return below.

[11] For the date see Ferguson 1911: 144 n. 2; cf. Walbank, *CAH* VII.1[2] 91. Other suggestions have been for 292 and 291 (Scott 1928: 232 with reff., to which add Ehrenberg 1946: 182 and Habicht 1979: 40), but 290 now looks reasonably secure. Mikalson 1998: 94 leaves it open at 291/0. Henrichs 1999: 243 n. 65 adds the possibility of 289, on the basis of an unpublished paper by John D. Morgan which I have not seen.

[12] Duris of Samos, *Histories*, Bk. 22 (*FGrHist* 76 F 13) = Athen. 6.253.d-f.: Δοῦρις δ᾽ ὁ Σάμιος ... καὶ αὐτὸν τὸν ἰθύφαλλον <παρατίθεται>. Duris of Samos presents the ithyphallic paean itself:

... ὡς οἱ μέγιστοι τῶν θεῶν καὶ φίλτατοι
  τῇ πόλει πάρεισιν·
	... So the greatest of gods and the dearest
	  have come to our city:

ἐνταῦθα <γὰρ Δήμητρα καὶ> Δημήτριον
  ἅμα παρηγ᾽ ὁ καιρός·
	For here are Demeter, Demetrius, both
	  brought in good time –

χἠ μὲν τὰ σεμνὰ τῆς Κόρης μυστήρια   5
  ἔρχεσθ᾽ ἵνα ποιήσῃ,
	she comes to take part in the Maiden's
	  mystical ritual,

ὁ δ᾽ ἱλαρός, ὥσπερ τὸν θεὸν δεῖ, καὶ καλός	he in joy, as fits godhead, is here

by Albert Henrichs as "one of the most remarkable examples of the convergence of myth and cult in a historical figure."[13] The Athenian choir greeted him, and probably his new wife Lanassa too, as divinities, "with incense and wreaths and libations."[14] In this hymn, or paean, they declared that the other gods – unnamed – were either out of town, deaf, non-existent, or indifferent (lines 15–16): the line is very much that taken by the prophet Elijah when taunting Baal-worshippers whose prayers remained unanswered: "Cry aloud: for he is a god: either he is talking, or he is pursuing, or he is in a journey, or peradventure he sleepeth and must be awakened."[15] However, the reaction of the Athenians to this manifestation of divine indifference would have shocked Elijah profoundly (just as it has shocked – but not necessarily for the same

καὶ γελῶν πάρεστι.		handsome and laughing.	
σεμνόν τι φαίνεθ᾽, οἱ φίλοι πάντες κύκλῳ,		Holy the scene, his friends all ringing him round,	
ἐν μέσοισι δ᾽ αὐτός,	10	himself at the center,	
ὅμοιον ὥσπερ οἱ φίλοι μὲν ἀστέρες,		His friends like the stars in heaven,	
ἥλιος δ᾽ ἐκεῖνος.		like the sun he.	
ὦ τοῦ κρατίστου παῖ Ποσειδῶνος θεοῦ		O son of Poseidon, mightiest god, and of	
χαῖρε κἀφροδίτης.		Aphrodite, all hail!	
ἄλλοι μὲν ἢ μακρὰν γὰρ ἀπέχουσιν θεοὶ	15	For the other gods are either far distant, remote,	
ἢ οὐκ ἔχουσιν ὦτα		or have no ears	
ἢ οὐκ εἰσὶν ἢ οὐ προσέχουσιν ἡμῖν οὐδὲ ἕν,		or do not exist or care not a whit for us;	
σὲ δὲ παρόνθ᾽ ὁρῶμεν,		but *you* are here present, we see	
οὐ ξύλινον οὐδὲ λίθινον, ἀλλ᾽ ἀληθινόν·		you not in wood, not in stone, but for real:	
εὐχόμεσθα δή σοι.	20	so to you we pray.	
πρῶτον μὲν εἰρήνην ποίησον, φίλτατε·		First, then, make peace, best beloved,	
κύριος γὰρ εἶ σύ.		for yours is the power:	
τὴν δ᾽ οὐχὶ Θηβῶν, ἀλλ᾽ ὅλης τῆς Ἑλλάδος		Not over Thebes alone, but all of Hellas	
Σφίγγα περικρατοῦσαν,		a Sphinx now has command –	
Αἰτωλὸς ὅστις ἐπὶ πέτρας καθήμενος,	25	the Aetolian, crouched on his rock	
ὥσπερ ἡ παλαιά,		like that ancient beast,	
τὰ σώμαθ᾽ ἡμῶν πάντ᾽ ἀναρπάσας φέρει,		snatches and carries off all our men: against him	
κοὐκ ἔχω μάχεσθαι·		I have not the strength to fight –	
Αἰτωλικὸν γὰρ ἁρπάσαι τὰ τῶν πέλας,		Aetolians always used to plunder their neighbors	
νῦν δὲ καὶ τὰ πόρρω.	30	but now raid far and wide.	
μάλιστα μὲν δὴ κόλασον αὐτός· εἰ δὲ μή,		Best hope is for you to requite him; or, failing that,	
Οἰδίπουν τιν᾽ εὑρέ,		find us some Oedipus,	
τὴν Σφίγγα ταύτην ὅστις ἢ κατακρημνιεῖ		who'll hurl this Sphinx down the precipice	
ἢ 'ς πῖνον ποιήσει.		or reduce him to dirt.	

3: <γὰρ Δήμητρα καὶ> add. Toup; Δημήτριον Casaubon, δημήτριος A 4: παρῆγ᾽ Porson, παρῆν A 9: τι Meineke, ὅτι A 10: αὐτός C, αὐτοῖς A 11: ὅμοιον Meineke, ὅμοιος A; μὲν C, με A 24: περικρατοῦσαν Casaubon, περιπατοῦσαν A C 25: Αἰτωλὸς A, αἰτωλιδ᾽ C 26: παλαιά Casaubon, πάλαι A C 31: κόλασον Toup, σχόλασον A C 34: 'ς πῖνον Green, †σπεινον† A, πεινῆν C, σπίλον Meineke, σπίνον Schweighäuser, σποδόν Wilamowitz.

[13] Henrichs 1999: 243.

[14] Demochares Bk. 21 (*FGrHist* 75 F 2) = Athen. 6.253 b–d:

When Demetrius returned from Leukas and Kerkyra to Athens, he was not only welcomed by the Athenians with incense and wreaths and libations, but processional choruses also came out to meet him, and *ithyphalloi*, with dancing and song; and as they moved to their place through the crowds, still chanting and capering, they proclaimed him the only true god, and the others asleep or abroad or non-existent, whereas he was the scion of Poseidon and Aphrodite, supreme in beauty, and open to all in his generosity. They entreated him with supplications, Demochares says, and offered him prayers.

[15] I Kings 18.27.

reasons – some modern students of the episode, notably Grote[16]): Demetrius, they declare, is no mere idol of wood or stone, but for real, ἀληθινόν not λίθινον, there in the flesh, and thus the logical target for their prayers (lines 18–20). (Divine epiphanies, from Pan at Marathon onward, offered good precedent, bridged the gap between divine and human accessibility.[17]) Then, almost without drawing breath, comes the request: get rid of these marauding Aetolians, who have been raiding as far as Attica, and have also seized Delphi.[18] They are likened to the Sphinx: Demetrius must be a second Oedipus, a heroic savior.[19] What are we to make of such a greeting?

I have singled out this episode for discussion, first, because it presents, in singularly graphic form, the problems confronting us in any discussion of Hellenistic royal deification; and second, because we have more evidence about Demetrius the Besieger than we do about any other divinised ruler from this period. On both counts Demetrius provides us with a good test case. There are a number of questions we need to ask ourselves if we want to find out just how and why that paean came to be sung when it did. How far, if at all, did it represent general belief? Was it (as many have assumed) nothing but cynicism and political opportunism? Where does it fit in the general social and religious history of Athens? Should it be treated merely as manipulation of the ignorant by the sophisticated, analogous to the explanation of religion as opium for the masses given by Critias in his *Sisyphus*,[20] or even to those simulated "miracles," pneumatically operated conjuring tricks, devised by Hero of Alexandria?[21] What, in the last resort, does it tell us about Athenian religion and Athenian attitudes to kingship, either separately or in combination?

We may conveniently begin with Demetrius himself, since his record is ample, and does not, on the face of it, suggest godhead – except in the chancy and unquantifiable area of personal charisma. His first encounter with the Athenians took place in 307, when he was neither king nor god, but simply deputy commander to his father, Antigonus One-Eye (Monophthalmos). Antigonus sent him with a fleet to free Athens from the Macedonian-imposed rule of another Demetrius, of Phaleron, who for ten years had shown Plato's city what a philosopher-king was like when given his head.[22] This Demetrius did successfully, and was at once welcomed by the populace as

---

[16] Grote 1888, 10: 318 writes: "Effusions such as these, while displaying unmeasured idolatry and subservience towards Demetrius, are yet more remarkable, as betraying a loss of force, a senility, and a consciousness of defenceless and degraded position." Bevan 1901: 625 talks in general terms of "this unhealthy development in ancient civilisation"; Charlesworth 1935: 6 quotes (but does not identify) a scholar who characterises the paean as "facile blasphemy."

[17] Henrichs 1999: 245 cites a number of instances. For Pan at Marathon see Hdt. 6.105–6, Paus. 1.28.4.

[18] See Ferguson 1911: 138–42; Green 1993: 126–7; Mikalson 1998: 97–98; Habicht 1997: 92–94.

[19] Henrichs 1999: 246 rightly comments: "Whatever one makes of this extraordinary comparison, it is surely designed to underline the divinity ascribed to Demetrius and to enhance the aura of supernatural performance surrounding him."

[20] Fr. 25 Battegazzore-Untersteiner [*I Sofisti*, Florence 1962, vol.4, 304–315, = 88 B 25 D-K]. I am not persuaded by recent attempts to reattribute this fragment to Euripides.

[21] Green 1993: 478–9, 612.

[22] See Ferguson 1911: 38–94; Green 1993: 44–51; Mikalson 1998: 46–74; Habicht 1997: 53–66.

εὐεργέτην καὶ σωτῆρα, "benefactor and savior" (Plut. *Demetr.* 9.1, cf. 10.4–5, 11.1).[23] The idea, we may note, was already in the air.[24] In one sense it had been there for a very long time. The coming of Dionysus and Demeter to Athens was enshrined in a variety of myths,[25] that could be expressed with disconcerting factuality, as this entry from the Marmor Parium:[26] "1164 years since Demeter arrived in Athens ... while Erechtheus was king."

The Athenians commemorated such divine visitations yearly, and as Henrichs says,[27] "Demetrius did not hesitate to fill the shoes of both divinities," not least since his arrival coincided with the celebration of the Eleusinian Mysteries. It was on account of these benefactions, which included gifts of timber and grain (ibid. 10.1–2), that he later received a whole series of quite extraordinary honors. He and Antigonus were proclaimed Savior Gods, and an altar was consecrated to them. Their priest replaced the annually elected Eponymous Archon. Golden statues of them were set up beside those of Athens' tyrannicides. Two new months, Antigonis and Demetrias, were added to the Athenian calendar. The new Savior Gods' images were woven into the sacred robe at the Panathenaic festival. The place where Demetrius first set foot on the ground after alighting from his chariot was subsequently (304/3) consecrated, and had another altar built on it, where he was worshipped as Demetrius Καταιβάτης, the Descender. Father and son, in short, were both being treated as though they were major deities. It was proposed that ambassadors to either of them should be known rather as sacred deputies (θεωροί), like those sent by the state to Delphi or Olympia.[28] The idea caught on: after Demetrius restored the Sicyonians to their citadel and helped them rebuild, they voted him, not just festivals and games as their new founder, but sacrifices as well.[29]

---

[23] Plut. *Demetr.* (9.1):

... The populace at once ... shouted out to Demetrius, bidding him disembark, hailing him as their benefactor and savior ... (10.4–5) ... The Athenians alone proclaimed [Demetrius and Antigonus] Savior Gods; abolishing the ancient office of Eponymous Archon, they annually elected instead a Priest of the Saviors, and his name figured upon their official decrees and private contracts. They voted further that their likenesses should be woven into the sacred robe [at the Panathenaic ceremony] in the company of the gods; and the place where Demetrius first descended from his chariot they consecrated and made the site of an altar, naming it that of Demetrius the Descender ... (11.1) ... [Stratocles] proposed a motion that envoys sent officially and at public charge to Antigonus and Demetrius should be called sacred deputies rather than ambassadors, like those who, during the great Greek festivals, brought to Delphi or Olympia traditional sacrifices on behalf of their cities.

[24] Half a century earlier (357), in Syracuse, Dion, under very similar circumstances (he had driven out the tyrant Dionysius II) was likewise welcomed as "savior and god": Plut. *Dion* 29, 46.1, cf. Diod. Sic. 16.11.2, 20.6.

[25] See Kerényi 1976: 129–188; Flückinger-Guggenheim 1984: 81–119; both cited by Henrichs 1999: 242.

[26] *FGrHist* 239 A 12, well adduced by Henrichs 1999: 243.

[27] Henrichs ibid.

[28] Plut. *Demetr.* 10.4–5, 11.1; Diod. Sic. 20.46.1–4. For an excellent analysis of these honors see now Mikalson 1998: 79–82, 86. For the cult of Demetrius Καταιβάτης see Plut. *Demetr.* 10.4, *Moral.* 338A, Clem. Alex. *Protrept.* 4.54.6; cf. Habicht 1970: 48–50; 1997: 87–88.

[29] Diod. Sic. 20.102.2–3:

Most interesting of all, the Athenians in 307 were the first to bestow, on him and his father, the title of King, a move the Successors had hitherto carefully avoided. Indeed, it was not for another year that Antigonus and his son themselves declared their royalty, and only then after Demetrius's great naval victory over Ptolemy off Cyprus. It was from that time, too, that the populace generally (τὸ πλῆθος) acknowledged their new status.[30] The Athenians had acted alone. All our evidence suggests, as Mikalson says (1998: 84), that these regal and divine honors were bestowed "willingly, sincerely, and relatively spontaneously." But in what belief? One late witness (Clem. Alex. *Protrept.* 4.54.5) claims, improbably but not impossibly, that even earlier, after Chaeronea (338), Philip II had received a similar welcome from Athens. It is certainly true that Isocrates (*Ep.* 3.5) wrote Philip on that occasion: "When you force the barbarians ... to be serfs of the Greeks, and make the king now called 'Great' obey your commands ... then *nothing will be left for you but to become a god.*"[31] Philip's subsequent behavior – not least having his statue carried, on the day of his assassination, enthroned with (σύνθρονον) those of the Twelve Olympians (Diod. Sic. 16.92.5, 95.1) – suggests that he may have taken the idea seriously.[32]

In 304, with Cassander closing in on them, the Athenians once more appealed to their Savior Gods. The state paid 300 drachmas for cattle sacrificed to them, Athena Nike, and, probably, Agathe Tyche, in this emergency (*SEG* 30.69). Demetrius broke off the siege of Rhodes and conducted a second rescue operation. Cassander was driven off. Athenian volunteers with him voted, in heartfelt thanks, not only to erect him an equestrian statue, but also to set up further altars and sanctuaries in his honor, and to bring him the choicest sacrificial victims (*SEG* 25.149). A proposal that Demetrius's pronouncements on matters regarding the gods should be treated as sacrosanct – a kind of papal infallibility *avant la lettre* – was duly ratified. Demetrius, infallible or not, spent the winter in Athens, billeting himself and a group of courtesans in the opisthodomos of the Parthenon. Divinity, he clearly figured, had its perquisites. Athena was said to have received him in person, and (*qua* Savior God) he regularly referred to her as his elder sister, a relationship which he used to justify both his occupation of her shrine and his raiding of her treasury. The Athenians who had figured that a god must surely be an improvement on a philosopher-king now began to

---

After Demetrius had brought the Sicyonians back to their citadel, ... and assisted the citizen body in rebuilding, and reestablished a free regime for them, he received the equivalent of divine honors from those whom he had benefited: they renamed their city Demetrias, and voted to institute on his behalf sacrifices and festivals, as well as annual games, and to grant him the rest of the honors due to him as their founder.

[30] Plut. *Demetr.* 10.3:

πρῶτοι μὲν γὰρ ἀνθρώπων ἁπάντων τὸν Δημήτριον καὶ Ἀντίγονον βασιλεῖς ἀνηγόρευσαν, ἄλλως ἀφοσιουμένους τοὔνομα ... 18.1 (cf. 17.5)· ἐκ τούτου [i.e. the declaration of royalty by Antigonus and Demetrius] πρῶτον ἀνεφώνησε τὸ πλῆθος Ἀντίγονον καὶ Δημήτριον βασιλέας. The first Attic inscriptions attesting to Demetrius as king date from 305: see *IG* II² 471.15–16.

[31] "οὐδὲν γὰρ ἔσται λοιπὸν ἔτι πλὴν θεὸν γενέσθαι."

[32] Fredricksmeyer 1981: 147.

have second thoughts.[33] Even so, in 302/1 Demetrius was still popular enough to be initiated into the Eleusinian Mysteries, without proper preparation, and at the wrong time of year.[34] It was even proposed to consult him for oracular utterances (Plut. *Demetr.* 13). But there had always been an undercurrent of resentment (wits noted that the Savior Gods' altars attracted an unusually rank growth of hemlock[35]), and though the political element was strong,[36] much of the anger seems to have been genuinely religious in origin. In 301 the comic playwright Philippides attacked Stratocles, the mover of some of the more *outré* deification decrees, on the grounds that he had brought misfortune[37] on Athens τὰς τῶν θεῶν τιμὰς ποιοῦντ' ἀνθρωπίνας, "by bestowing on men honors belonging to the gods."

But by then such a stand was safe enough, since Demetrius had been recalled to Asia by Antigonus, and before the year was out the battle of Ipsus had been fought, leaving Antigonus dead and Demetrius a fugitive. A new government of moderate oligarchs escorted Demetrius's queen out of the country, and told the Besieger himself (who had hoped to make Athens his base) that he was now *persona non grata*, and must look elsewhere. The former Savior God had to petition for the return of his Piraeus squadron and cash deposits.[38] By 295/4 we find him still very much at odds with Athens (Paus. 1.25.7): indeed, besieging the city, which had been taken over by a radical mercenary captain named Lachares.[39] An attempt by Ptolemy to break Demetrius's blockade failed, and in 294 Athens was starved into surrender. Lachares escaped, taking the gold of the Parthenon with him (one comic poet later said that he "stripped Athena naked"), and Demetrius once again entered the city in triumph, though the Athenians had decreed the death penalty for anyone who even spoke of an accommodation with him.[40]

However, he proved to be in a generous mood: he issued no more than a mild reproof – followed by the promise of 100,000 *medimnoi* of grain. This behavior so relieved the Athenians that they voted to turn Piraeus and Munychia over to him: an offer that Demetrius snapped up before they could change their minds, and which caused them untold trouble in the years to come. He also received fresh fulsome honors: the month Mounichion was renamed Demetrias, the City Dionysia was henceforth to be known as the Demetrieia, and Demetrius himself was portrayed in the

---

[33] Plut. *Demetr.* 23–24, 26 *passim*; Diod. Sic. 20.100.5–6; Clem. Alex. *Protrept.* 4.54.6; cf. Mikalson 1998: 87–88. The proposal to "sanctify" Demetrius's utterance: Plut. *Demetr.* 24.4–5: ... δεδόχθαι τῷ δήμῳ τῶν Ἀθηναίων πᾶν, ὅ τι ἂν ὁ βασιλεὺς Δημήτριος κελεύσῃ, τοῦτο ... πρὸς θεοὺς ὅσιον ... εἶναι.

[34] Diod. Sic. 20.110.1; Plut. *Demetr.* 26 *passim*. As Mikalson says (1998: 89), it is not entirely rational for a god to require initiation; but Demetrius seems to have wanted to follow the example of Dionysus. He also clearly felt an affinity (of function, *qua* grain-giver, as well as of name) with Demeter.

[35] Plut. *Demetr.* 12.3.

[36] Habicht 1970: 213 ff.

[37] Plut. *Demetr.* 12.2–4, 26; Diod. Sic. 20.110.1; cf. Mikalson 1998: 89–90. In 283/2 Philippides was honored for lifelong services to the democracy: *IG* II² 657.8–66.

[38] Plut. *Demetr.* 31; cf. Green 1993: 121.

[39] Green 1993: 123–5 with reff.; Mikalson 1998: 90–92.

[40] Plut. *Demetr.* 34.1. The poet was Demetrios (II) in his *Areopagites* (Mikalson 1998: 91). Mikalson also points out what a blow this was to the cult of Athena Polias, thus revealed as a divine protector incapable even of looking after her own property.

Theater of Dionysus "riding upon the world," whatever that may have meant: it sounds rather like G.F. Watts' portrait of Hope.[41]

He then took off for a bout of campaigning in the Peloponnese, which he cut short to go north and, after assassinating one of the claimants, finally had himself proclaimed king of Macedonia. This, coming on top of his divinity, went to his head. He wore the double crown symbolising Europe and Asia. He commissioned a much-decorated robe representing him as a sun among stars (Plut. *Demetr.* 41). He reconquered Thessaly and most of central Greece. Despite his earlier democratic concessions to Athens he now (292) demanded the restoration of all her exiled oligarchs, and clearly favored an oligarchic regime. A strong opposition began to develop, led by anti-Macedonian democrats such as Demosthenes' nephew Demochares, who later wrote a scathing account of Demetrius's activities in Athens.[42] In 291 Pyrrhus's ex-wife Lanassa, with the islands of Corcyra and Leucas as her dowry, offered herself in marriage to Demetrius – widely regarded as the handsomest man in Greece – "understanding," as Plutarch says,[43] "that of all the kings he was most inclined to marry wives." He jumped at the chance: quite apart from the military and political advantages of such a match, he was by no means averse to the idea of scoring against Pyrrhus, now his enemy, in a more vulgarly personal sense. He hurried to Corcyra, and Pyrrhus's allies the Aetolians created havoc in central Greece and Attica during his absence. It was when he returned to Athens, in the fall of 290, with his new bride Lanassa in tow, that he was greeted by the paean which forms the starting-point for my discussion. What kind of a god-king was Demetrius? Perhaps more to the point for us, who wanted him as one, and why?

III

At this juncture we should remind ourselves, in historical terms, of the Athenian attitude to kings and gods *tel quel*. The offer of kingship to Demetrius, before either he or his father had themselves laid claim to it, must at first sight strike us as bizarre, since from the dawn of recorded history Athens had been – or liked to think of herself as having been – almost as anti-royalist as Rome. It was a matter of pride that the last Athenian king, Codrus, had traditionally died in 1068 B.C., and that his son Medon was the first archon.[44] The intellectual notion of kingship as something alien, obscurantist, and inimical to human dignity and freedom had been vividly dramatised in the persons of Darius and Xerxes, to be enshrined thereafter as an integral element of national mythology by Aeschylus and Herodotus, with slaves driven on by the lash set

---

[41] Plut. *Demetr.* 34.4–5; Paus. 1.25.8. For Demetrius's honors, see Plut. *Demetr.* 12 and Duris *FGrHist* 76 F14.

[42] See above, n. 12. For an account of this period cf. Green 1993: 125–6 with reff.

[43] Plut. *Pyrrh.* 10.5: ἐπισταμένη μάλιστα τῶν βασιλέων εὐκόλως ἔχοντα πρὸς γάμους γυναικῶν, cf. 9.1; Lévêque 1957:138–42.

[44] Lycurgus *c.Leocr.*§§ 84, 86; Vell. Pat. 1.2.1–2; Just. 2.6.16–21.

in sharp contrast to free men who voluntarily submitted themselves to the demands of νόμος (law).[45]

Nevertheless, the frequently expressed opinion that they had forgotten what kingship was cannot be sustained. We owe to Professor Carlier a demonstration of just how widespread kingship had been in early Greece, how closely bound up with religious practices – the king as shepherd of his people, warrior, and, most important, mediator between them and the divine, so that crown, throne, sceptre, chrism and blood-succession became vital elements in the relationship between earth and heaven.[46] This of course is exactly in line with the more general findings of scholars such as Frazer, Hocart, and Henri Frankfort.[47] Such archetypal beliefs, deep-rooted in the human psyche, had not been altogether lost, and there were enough surviving monarchies – e.g. in Macedonia, Cyprus, and Sparta – to keep men conscious of them. They also satisfied a deep if inarticulate need. As Frankfort argues (1948: 3), "if we refer to kingship as a political institution," if "we imply that the human polity can be considered by itself," "we assume a point of view which would have been incomprehensible to the ancients."

On the other hand, even the most superficial acquaintance with Greek, and particularly Athenian, history, makes it clear that such a notion, incomprehensible or not, was precisely what, with remarkable unanimity, intellectuals from the Milesian physicists to sophists such as Anaxagoras were doing their level best to realise. Man, according to Protagoras's best-known dictum, was the measure of all things.[48] In government as in other areas of human investigation Greek progress towards rational argument and the establishment of general principles ran flat counter to Near Eastern patterns of absolute and authoritarian theocracy. We tend to assume, granted our own intellectual heritage, that the quest for ἰσονομία (equality under the law) was a natural reaction against such obscurantist views. Yet in the larger perspective it is this Greek attitude that emerges as the anomaly, *even in Greece*: the tribal outlook against which men like Cleisthenes struggled was far more endemic and persistent than most modern scholars have ever cared to admit. Even in the mid-fifth century rationalism was the watchword of no more than a small, if influential, minority, and incurred bitter opposition.[49]

A nice example of this is the public reaction to the treatise of Protagoras which began with a declaration of agnosticism: "Concerning the gods I cannot determine whether they exist or not." "Because he began his book in this way," Diogenes Laertius tells us, "he was deported by the Athenians, and they also burnt his books in the market-place."[50] This leads us straight into the second major factor involved in any

---

[45] See, e.g., the disquisition of Demaratus to Xerxes, Hdt. 7.104.4: ἐλεύθεροι γὰρ ἐόντες οὐ πάντα ἐλεύθεροί εἰσί· ἔπεστι γάρ σφι δεσπότης νόμος, τὸν ὑποδειμαίνουσι πολλῷ ἔτι μᾶλλον ἢ οἱ σοὶ σέ ("For, though free, they are not free in all respects, since law is their master, and this they fear far more than your subjects do you").

[46] Carlier (1984: 485 ff.): over *fifty* well-documented cases of kingship in Greece.

[47] Frazer 1920, cf. Frazer 1911, vol. 1; Hocart 1929; Frankfort 1948.

[48] D-K 80 fr. B.1 = Diog. Laert. 9.51.

[49] See in particular Dodds, ch. vi, "Rationalism and Reaction in the Classical Age," (1951: 179–206).

[50] D-K 80 fr. B 4 = Diog. Laert. 9.51–52: περὶ μὲν θεῶν οὐκ ἔχω εἰδέναι οὐθ᾽ ὡς εἰσίν, οὐθ᾽ ὡς οὐκ εἰσίν.

assessment of human deification or king-worship: the Athenian attitude to religion. Here we find, from the archaic period onwards, an exactly parallel response to that regarding kingship: consistent ironic scepticism among thinkers, obstinate and impassioned traditionalism in everyone else. The notion of πάντων χρημάτων μέτρον ἄνθρωπος ("Man the measure of all things"), which neither began nor ended with Protagoras, affected this tradition in unexpected ways. It ensured, as early as Homer, an exceptional degree of anthropomorphism in the Olympian deities, and followed this up with a powerful sculptural tradition, from the *kouroi* to the Riace bronzes, glorifying the outsize naked athletic male; but it also provoked, in thinkers from Xenophanes onward, a contempt for so *simpliste* a trend in religion, which it dismissed as man making gods in his own image. For Xenophanes Thracian gods have blue eyes and red hair, and if horses could draw, their gods would come out equine.[51]

The result was a striking dichotomy: intellectuals from the Milesians to Euripides either ignoring religion altogether, in a post-Promethean spirit of scientific enquiry, or attacking the Olympian pantheon (not to mention Homer and Hesiod) for failing to maintain human, civic standards of social or sexual morality,[52] while the majority, including a fair number of citizens holding public office, instituted a variety of trials for ἀσέβεια, impiety, their targets ranging from Anaxagoras to Socrates, on charges that included disbelief in the supernatural and the teaching of astronomy.[53] Yet the distinction was anything but clear-cut. In Socrates' case, while some may have taken advantage of popular political resentments in the wake of a bitter civil war to revenge themselves on the preceptor of Critias and Alcibiades (Aeschin. 1.173), the majority felt genuine outrage at what was seen as Socrates' religious unorthodoxy and dangerous moral relativism.[54]

They also indicated their distress at the systematic devaluation of the state religion by an increasing partiality for foreign and orgiastic cults. By the fourth century the Olympian public response to petition had established a less than encouraging record. Men had prayed to Athena and Zeus and Apollo during the Peloponnesian War: their prayers had gone unanswered. Instead they had been afflicted with plague, defeat, and crippling *stasis*. To a great extent the relationship between men and the gods was based on the pact that Romans, with their usual pragmatic concision, defined as *do ut des*, favors in return for favors, a spiritual profit-and-loss account. The divine account was now badly overdrawn, and after prayer and sacrifice proved equally unavailing at Chaeronea in 338, letting in Philip and Alexander as masters of Greece, many must have felt that in a very real sense their gods had failed them. Deep religious conservatism would ensure that the Olympian deities – so deeply woven into the calendar

---

[51] Xenophanes frs. 168–9 K-R-S.

[52] Xenophanes fr. 166 K-R-S: πάντα θεοῖς ἀνέθηκαν Ὅμηρος θ' Ἡσίοδός τε, ὅσσα παρ' ἀνθρώποισιν ὀνείδεα καὶ ψόγος ἐστίν, / κλέπτειν μοιχεύειν τε καὶ ἀλλήλους ἀπατεύειν ("Homer and Hesiod attributed everything to the gods,/ all that among mankind is shameful and cause for censure/, theft and adultery and deceiving one another").

[53] See in particular Dodds 1951: 189–90; Derenne 1930; Bauman 1990.

[54] See Connor 1991.

and festivals of the year[55] – were never abandoned; but the inroads of the Sophists, augmented by the Macedonian conquest of Greece and Alexander's subsequent dazzling usurpation of the Achaemenid East, must undoubtedly have driven many to look elsewhere (and not necessarily to heaven) for succour. The time was ripe for change; and yet the change, when it came, could be seen as implicit in the system *ab initio*.

Man-the-measure had always needed warnings against encroaching on divinity: "Let no man fly up to heaven," Alcman wrote,[56] "or attempt to marry Aphrodite." The very fact of anthropomorphism, however, established a factitious link between men and gods: had not Heracles bridged the gap, become immortal, married Hebe?[57] Pindar, like Alcman, may emphasise the division between human and divine,[58] but the whole burden of the epinician odes is aspiration towards godhead. The mystery cults believed the soul of man was indeed immortal. A shaman like Empedocles could claim immortal status for himself ("I go among you a god immortal, mortal no longer") and draw a crowd of devoted followers.[59] Similar beliefs survived concerning Pythagoras.[60] The notion of ἰσοθεότης, of treating a living person as ἰσόθεος, the equal of a god, goes back to Homer and Sappho:[61] the metaphorical application could easily shade off into genuine worship if the occasion called for it.[62] What, we may wonder,

---

[55] See, e.g., Parke 1977: 29 ff.

[56] Alcman fr.1 *PMG* 16–17: μή τις ἀνθρώπων ἐς ὠρανὸν ποτήσθω μήδε πη]ρήτω γαμῆν τὴν Ἀφροδίταν. Excellent advice, which, I have always felt, Arthur Miller ignored at his peril.

[57] Apollod. 2.7.7 Frazer, with further reff. *ad loc.*

[58] Pindar fr. 31 Bergk, *Nem.* 6.1–7, *Ol.* 5.23–24.

[59] Empedocles fr. 399 K-R-S (112 D-K) = Diog. Laert. 8.62 (1–10) + Clem. *Strom.* 6.30 (9–11):

> Friends, who dwell in the great city above tawny Akragas
> high on the citadel, whose care is for good deeds,
> greetings! I go among you a god immortal, mortal
> no longer, with honor from all, as is fitting for me,
> crowned with ribbons and fresh floral garlands;   5
> and wheresoever I come, to every flourishing city,
> I am revered by all, men and women alike: they follow
> me in their thousands, ask where the road to profit runs –
> some begging for prophecies, while others, too long
> transfixed by harsh agonies, are in search of healing   10
> words to relieve their myriad sorts of sickness.

[60] Fredricksmeyer 1981: 149–50 collects the evidence.

[61] See, e.g., Hom. *Od.* 8.464–8:

> Nausicaä, daughter of great-hearted Alcinoüs,
> May Zeus, the loud-thundering husband of Hera, now decree
> that I reach my home, and see my day of returning:
> then, even there, will I pray to you as to a god
> all the days of my life: for you saved my life, lady.

and Sappho fr. 31 L-P, 1–4:

> Peer of immortal gods he seems to me, that
> man who sits beside you, who now can listen
> private and close, so close, to your sweet-sounding
>   voice...

[62] Cf. Arist. *Rhet.* 1.5.9, 1361 a 34 ff.:

did Eupolis mean when, during the Peloponnesian War, he wrote of the Athenian generals: "We used to pray to them as to gods – *for indeed so they were* [καὶ γὰρ ἦσαν]"?[63] The first Greek who actually received comparable honors – including the singing of paeans – was, we are told, Lysander, at the end of the Peloponnesian War.[64] The timing was surely no accident.

IV

During the fourth and third centuries B.C., then, we observe two concurrent phenomena: the return of monarchy – primarily, but not exclusively, in Macedonia – as a viable, indeed as a brutally effective, mode of government, against which the *polis* proved itself ultimately ineffectual; and the erosion of faith, not only in traditional city-state values, but also, and more importantly, in the civic deities who had shown themselves so seemingly indifferent to their worshippers' welfare. Augmenting this mood were the thinkers and philosophers, who managed to combine a rationalisation of monarchy (previously anathema to them) with an even-handed religious scepticism that sneered at all superstition, the deification of humans included. Thus we find Aristotle, in a disconcerting *volte-face*, reversing his anti-monarchic principles to give a notably warm account of kingship in the heroic age, and justifying its return on the grounds of overwhelming excellence in the family or individual:[65] as Alexander's former adviser and tutor he perhaps could do no less. The

---

τιμὴ δ' ἐστὶ μὲν σημεῖον εὐεργετικῆς δόξης, τιμῶνται δὲ δικαίως μὲν καὶ μάλιστα οἱ εὐεργετηκότες ... μέρη δὲ τιμῆς θυσίαι, μνῆμαι ἐν μέτροις καὶ ἄνευ μέτρων, γέρα, τεμένη, προεδρίαι, τάφοι, εἰκόνες, τροφαὶ δημόσιαι, τὰ βαρβαρικά, οἷον προσκυνήσεις καὶ ἐκστάσεις, δῶρα τὰ παρ' ἑκά στοις τίμια.

[Public] honoring is the token of fame for good works, and those who have done such good works are its most common and proper beneficiaries ... Types of honors include sacrifices, commemorations (in either prose or verse), privileges, sacred precincts, front seats [at official functions], state burial, statues, maintenance at public expense; barbarian customs, e.g. prostration and the yielding of precedence; and such gifts as each community considers a mark of honor.

[63] Eupolis fr. 117 Kock = Stob. *Flor.* 43.9; cf. Fredricksmeyer 1981: 148–9.

[64] Plut. *Lys.* 18.3 = *FGrHist* 76 F 71.

[65] Arist. *Pol.* 3.9.7, 1285 b 4–19:

A fourth type of royal monarchy was that in the heroic age, exercised legally and traditionally over willing subjects. For since the founders of such lines had been benefactors of their people in the crafts of peace or in war, or through having united them or provided them with land, these kings ruled by consent, and their descendants succeeded them. They held supreme command in war and were responsible for all non-priestly sacrifices, and also acted as judges in law-suits: this last some of them did on oath, some not, the oath being taken by raising the sceptre.

Arist. *Pol.* (a) 3.8.1, 1284a 3–5, 8–12; (b) 3.11.12–13, 1288a15–19, 25–28:

(a) εἰ δέ τίς ἐστιν εἷς τοσοῦτον διαφέρων κατ' ἀρετῆς ὑπερβολήν, ἢ πλείους μὲν ἑνὸς μὴ μέντοι δυνατοὶ πλήρωμα παρασχέσθαι πόλεως ... οὐκέτι θετέον τούτους μέρος πόλεως· ἀδικήσονται γὰρ ἀξιούμενοι τῶν ἴσων, ἄνισοι τοσοῦτον κατ' ἀρετὴν ὄντες καὶ τὴν πολιτικὴν δύναμιν· ὥσπερ γὰρ θεὸν ἐν ἀνθρώποις εἰκὸς εἶναι τὸν τοιοῦτον.

But if there exists some individual so outstanding in plenitude of excellence (or more than one, but not enough to make up the full tally of a state) ... then it is no longer admissible to treat these persons as part of the state, since they will be done an injustice if reckoned as equal to the rest, being so very far from merely equal in their excellence and political powers: for such a one will naturally be as a god among men.

surprisingly favorable account he gives of absolute monarchy (παμβασιλεία) in the *Politics*[66] – a late work, still unfinished at the time of his death in 322[67] – all too clearly has the Macedonian Argead dynasty in mind, and Book III may indeed have been composed or revised in knowledge of Alexander's Eastern conquests and demand for deification.

It is fascinating to trace the evolution of Aristotle's ideas here, and to glimpse the fundamental, and at least partly unconscious, social assumptions that shaped his ·original notions of kingship. The most striking fact throughout is how totally his political thinking is bound to the absolute criteria imposed by the *polis* and Athenian-style democratic government. The axiomatic upward progress is from authoritarian rule to constitutionalism. Kingship is seen as better than tyranny because it at least has the consent of the governed. Aristotle's local, political, and very largely pragmatic definition of kingship is inadequate; its total omission of the religious element means that he makes no real *generic* distinction between kingship and any other form of government. The view is resolutely Cleisthenic: the king as mediator between earth and heaven has simply been dropped as irrelevant to post-Anaxagorean reality.

It thus is not at all surprising that Aristotle explains the origin of early heroic king-ship as a return for *practical benefits,* "through the first [kings] becoming the people's benefactors, either in war or through particular skills, or by centralising scattered groups or through the acquisition of territory" (1285 b 7–8): it all sounds – not by accident – like a wish-list for the Ptolemies. Even more significant (a point I shall return to in a moment) is its odd resemblance to Euhemerism, the notion that the

---

(b) So when it happens that either a whole family or even an individual so far exceeds the rest in excellence as to outstrip them all, then it is only just that this family, or this individual, should hold royal power and be sovereign over all ... For one may not properly execute or exile, much less ostracise, such a one, nor indeed make him take his turn as a subject , since though it is not the natural function of the part to eclipse the whole, a man of such outstanding qualities will in fact have accomplished just that. Thus all that remains is to obey such a one, and for him to exercise power not in turn but absolutely.

[66] *Pol.* 3.11 *passim*, 1287 a 1–1288 a 32. *Pambasileia* (cf. p. 272) has always been an embarrassment for Aristotelians: for a fairly evenhanded recent account see Carlier 1993. As Carlier says (112), *pambasileia* recurs almost obsessively in chs. 13–17 of Bk III of the *Politics*, and this is at first sight odd, since it contradicts just about every principle of government Aristotle has previously enunciated. Like aristocracy, it takes its justification from surpassing merit – is, indeed, a foreshadowing of the Nietzschean *Uebermensch*, and most remarkable of all in that it overrides the concept of the *polis*. But when we ask ourselves what historical person or event could have precipitated so striking a *volte-face*, the answer cannot be in doubt. Carlier 1993: 117, while conceding the possibility that *pambasileia* was, in fact, occasioned by Alexander's unprecedented essay in world-conquest, nevertheless argues that Aristotle, on learning of such things as the trial of Philotas, the murder of Cleitus, and the imprisonment prior to execution of his own nephew Callisthenes, would rather have pilloried Alexander publicly as a tyrant akin to a wild beast (θηρίον). The reactions of intellectuals under other, more modern, dictatorial regimes suggest strongly to me that, on the contrary, some theory like that of *pambasileia* is precisely what we might have expected. The watchword was, surely, not outrage but prudent accommodation to the inevitable, driven by very real personal fear. If the nephew's head could roll, the uncle had to look out for himself.

[67] The *terminus post quem* is Philip's death, referred to at 5.8.10, 1311 b 2; but the lack of completion suggests a much later period. Sir Ernest Barker 1946: xliv argues that "the six 'methods' of the *Politics* were all composed in the period between 335 and 322, during the period of Aristotle's teaching in the Lyceum."

Olympian gods were originally kings, generals, or statesmen deified in return for distinguished services on earth. The central thesis, the benchmark of Aristotle's argument, is the progressive reduction of the despotic element. The further kingship moves away from autocracy towards democratic tolerance, the better by definition it becomes.

Now Aristotle was well aware that originally Greeks just about everywhere had been ruled by kings. He also knew that in the Greek states reason and democracy had triumphed early, that any survival of the *basileia* was contingent upon the severe curtailment of its original despotic powers. Thus his arguments to explain these differences are, inevitably, projections of what we may term the *polis* world-view: governmental and social development moving towards the high excellences of freedom and equality. Similarly, his discussion of revolution is likewise geared to the Greek democratic norm: equality is the one goal of revolt, while, *per contra*, royal government self-destructs by trying to rule too autocratically. Equality achieved renders kingship obsolete.

What is missing from all this? The religious and sacral element, the whole archetypal notion of the king as divine avatar, the shepherd of his people, as a numinous mediator between heaven and earth. The Greek tradition, quite exceptionally, divorced the two at an early stage, one result of the intellectual secularising tradition that began with the Milesian physicists and led to Aristotle himself by way of the Sophists. Hence his discussion of kingship as no more than one among other forms of *polis* government. What we have here, of course, is the rationalist's creed, and, as the Hellenistic age demonstrated, for the vast majority of the population it simply was not enough. The spread of enthusiastic cults and magic became symptomatic. So did the attempt to recover lost *numen* by divinising all-too-human monarchs.

Which brings us back to Aristotle's *pambasileia*. It is usually argued that this fifth category of kingship was for the author of the *Politics* a construct no more real than Plato's *politeia*, with no historical basis. But is this true? How does Aristotle describe it? *Pambasileia* is "when one man is sovereign over all just as each race or *polis* is master of its public affairs, like the head of a household" (*Pol.*1285 b 30–32). What justifies it? When a family or individual exceeds everyone in *areté* absolutely, then this family or individual should be royal and sovereign over all (*Pol.*1288 a 18–20). Aristotle *had*, once, believed kingship to belong to a more primitive stage of development, proper perhaps for those lesser alien breeds whom he recommended that his most famous pupil should treat like animals or plants (fr. 658 Rose). But that was before the pupil became king of Macedon and set out to conquer the East. By 324, the year in which Alexander requested divine honors from the Greek states, *pambasileia* had moved out of the realm of imagination and taken on a reality hitherto undreamed-of. The *Politics* was still unfinished at the time of Aristotle's death two years later. The insertion on *pambasileia* represents his attempt to come to terms with a new phenomenon that had, quite literally, changed the face of the known world.

The true catalyst of royal divinisation, however, was surely Alexander's request to the Greek cities that he be worshipped as a god:[68] here was a charismatic leader who, it could be argued, had beaten Heracles and Dionysus at their own game.[69] Intellectual jokes, whether by the critical[70] or prospective candidates for immortality,[71] made no difference to the ordinary man in the street. Pragmatism met emotional deprivation: the boundaries between earth and heaven blurred. The old gods had been singularly indifferent to their worshippers' welfare, whereas here was a dynamic figure who was tangible and approachable, whose very essence seemed to be ἐνέργεια, for whom and in whom all things were possible, a present deity indeed. To worship him was not, in the circumstances, hard; and such a step was made far easier by the immensely popular notion, perhaps invented, and certainly popularised, by Euhemerus of Messene, that the anthropomorphic Olympian deities were in fact ancient generals or statesmen who had, as it were, been canonised as gods in recognition of their signal services on earth.[72] What better justification could Alexander and his Successors have asked for?

There were several ways, then, in which a ruler's divinity could be emphasised.[73] He could be assimilated to, even identified with, a certain god, as various Ptolemies (and possibly Alexander) with Dionysus.[74] He could share a god's temple, be what was known as a σύνναος θεός.[75] He could be worshipped, voluntarily, by cities either in or beyond his kingdom, as Lysander and Antigonus seem to have been.[76] These

---

[68] The best account is still Balsdon 1950. See also Préaux 1978, I: 241–5. The literature is vast, and mostly nugatory.

[69] Arrian, *Anab.* 4.10.6–7:

Anaxarchus began the discussion, arguing that it would be far more justifiable to regard Alexander as a god than either Dionysus or Heracles ... besides, there could be no doubt that when he was departed this life men would honor him as a god; how much more just, then, to reward him while he still lived rather than after his death, when the honor would do him no good.

[70] Plut. *Mor.* 210E-D, 219E [Damis: "If he wants to be, let him"]; Diog. Laert. 6.63 [Diogenes (?): "Then make me Sarapis"]; Hyp. *c. Dem.* 31.15 [Demosthenes: "Sure, son of Zeus, and of Poseidon too, if he likes"].

[71] Plut. *Mor.* 360D, cf. 182C [Antigonus Gonatas, on being compared to a god: "My pisspot-bearer knows better"]; cf. Suet. *Div. Vesp.* 23.4 [the dying Vespasian: "*Vae, puto, deus fio*" – "Oh dear, I think I'm turning into a god"].

[72] Diod. Sic. 6.1.1–2 (ap. Euseb. *Praep. Ev.* 2.2.52–3 = Euhemerus of Messene fr. III.25 Winiarczyk [Teubner]):

[Diodorus] in his sixth book, based on the writings of Euhemerus of Messene, confirms the same account of the gods, which he describes as follows: So concerning the gods men of old times have handed down to later generations two different notions. For they say that some of the gods, such as the sun and moon and the other heavenly bodies, besides winds and anything else of a like nature, are eternal and immortal, since for each of these the origin and continuance lie outside time. But the rest, we are told, were terrestrial beings who became gods, acquiring immortal honor and fame through their benefactions to men, e.g. Heracles, Dionysus, Aristaeus, and others of this sort. [Cf. also for similar accounts Ioannes Malalas, *Chron.* ii p.54 Dindorf; Sext. Emp. *Math.* 9.17; Lactant. *ID* 11.7–9.].

[73] See the excellent survey by F.W. Walbank in *CAH* VII.1², ch.iii, "Monarchy and monarchic ideas," § 6, "Monarchy and religion," 84 ff., and the same author's article: Walbank 1987.

[74] Tondriau 1948: 127–46.

[75] Nock 1930.

[76] Plut. *Lys.* 18.3; *OGIS* 6.17–26:

cults embraced everything from heroic or founder honors through ἰσοθεότης to full-blown divinisation. Or, finally, he could establish a dynastic cult of his own, as the Ptolemies did. Alexander had given the lead: others were not slow to follow. Henrichs writes: "These leaders enhanced their own images by emulating Dionysus and assuming his identity, *at least externally*, thus superimposing an adopted mythical persona on to their historical selves [emphasis mine]."[77] If we discount the characteristic caveat, this comes, I would guess, the sacral element apart, pretty close to the truth. On every count Demetrius the Besieger's reception by Athens in 290 should now be completely understandable.

The terms of his welcome evoke Dionysus, to whom the earlier part of the paean may even have compared him.[78] He is son of Poseidon because of his naval victories, of Aphrodite because of his good looks and legendary love affairs. Poseidon and Aphrodite, as has often been remarked, form an odd couple, unique to this occasion: they were probably juxtaposed as symbolizing his two chief areas of expertise, naval affairs and sex (Mikalson 1998: 96). His fourth bride, Lanassa, was with him: she may even have been received as Demeter. But he is also a god very much in his own right, as we have seen: Demetrius Καταιβάτης, the Descender, stepping from heaven into the Athenian *agora*. He is a sun among stars because of his consciously royal claims to be Alexander's inheritor, the cloak woven for him representing the world and the heavenly bodies symbolically under his sway. Above all, he is a *present deity*, to be appealed to in the most direct of terms. Dromocleides' decree, as recorded by Plutarch, strongly suggests that this was no political fiction. He must free Thebes; he must curb the Aetolians. *Do ut des.* The other gods have had a dismal record of failure: let him do better. He did: successful expeditions against both the Aetolians and Thebes followed. But this was his last hurrah.[79]

The honors offered to Demetrius and his father – the incorporation in the public calendar and the Panathenaic sail – are hyperbolic to the point of hysteria: Athens rose to him as Acragas did to Empedocles, and other cities, such as Sicyon,[80] were not slow to declare him at least ἰσόθεος. Such honors, as Aristotle knew,[81] were σημεῖον εὐεργετικῆς δόξης, "the token of fame for good works": the relationship was exactly

---

...and so that Antigonus [One-Eye] may be worthily honored for his achievements, and the people may be seen to be giving thanks for the benefits they have received, let them delimit a sacred enclosure for him, and build an altar, and set up the very finest possible cult-statue; and let the sacrifice and the games and the wearing of wreaths and the rest of the festival be celebrated in his honor every year, just as they were in the past.

[77] Henrichs 1999: 247.

[78] Ehrenberg 1981: 179–98, esp. 190–1; Scott 1928: 143, 148–9, 221–3, 227–9.

[79] Plut. *Demetr.* 41.4–5; cf. Habicht 1979: 34–44; Mikalson 1998: 97; and for the decree of Dromocleides, Plut. *Demetr.* 13.1–3. The expeditions: Plut. *Demetr.* 41.1, *Pyrrh.* 7.3, cf. Habicht 1997: 91.

[80] Diod. Sic. 20.102.2–3.

[81] Arist. *Rhet.* 1.5.9, 1361 a 34 ff. Cf. Isocr. *Orat.*2.[*Nicocl.*] 5, 9:

When people look at royal honors, wealth, and dynastic powers, they all consider those who occupy a monarchy to be the equal of gods ... Thus we must first consider what the function of a reigning king is ... I think everyone would agree that it is his duty to succour the state when it falls on hard times, to preserve its prosperity when it is doing well, and from small beginnings to make it great; for it is with these goals in view that other day-to-day duties need to be performed.

that which had prevailed between mankind and the Olympians, with the difference that these new deities were not, yet, ἀθανατισμένοι, immortalised, and could at a pinch be removed – as Demetrius had been once already and soon would be again: despite the hysteria, this was a god very much on approval. In fact his support, widespread in 307, was now mainly confined to the propertied classes. Illness and military setbacks took their toll. In 287 there was a democratic revolution in Athens, and by the spring of 285 Demetrius was Seleucus's captive in Apamea, where he soon drank himself to death, a sad fate for a former σύνναος of Athena.[82]

Thus Hellenistic kings, whether deified or not, were dependent on their ability to deliver the goods, as an entry in the Suda makes very clear: "Men obtain kingship neither by natural right nor by legal fiat, but through their ability to command an army or handle public affairs sensibly."[83] In a sense, of course, this had always been true of monarchs, who were liable to be rudely disposed of, like the leader of a herd, when their fighting strength or potency failed.[84] What has not been taken sufficiently into account, I think, is the genuinely religious sense that motivated such deification, and the unbroken sacral tradition on which it rested. As we have seen, there was always an intellectual stratum, in Athens especially, that remained sceptical to the core, and saw divine kingship as nothing but a joke in the worst possible taste. (This group sometimes included the prospective divinisee, as Agesilaus and Antigonus Gonatas both made very clear.[85]) We should not because of this make the common but mistaken assumption that royal deification, any more than the Athenian ἀσέβεια (impiety) trials, was *merely* a political device – or indeed a wholly mindless surrender. E.R. Dodds[86] took the view that "he who treats another human being as divine thereby assigns to himself the relative status of a child or an animal"; yet those who committed themselves to Demetrius were quite evidently neither. In no case, perhaps, least of all that of Alexander – who demanded godhead but when under fire was quick to remind the sedulous that what flowed from his wounds was blood, not ichor[87] – can we ever be certain where belief ends and mere play-acting[88] or cynical political opportunism

---

[82] For a general account of Demetrius's latter years see Green 1993: 127–30.

[83] Suda s.v. βασιλεία (b) (2) Adler: οὔτε φύσις οὔτε τὸ δίκαιον ἀποδιδοῦσι τοῖς ἀνθρώποις τὰς βασιλείας, ἀλλὰ τοῖς δυναμένοις ἡγεῖσθαι στρατοπέδου καὶ χειρίζειν πράγματα νουνεχῶς.

[84] Cf. Frazer 1920: 291 ff.

[85] Plut. *Apothegm. Lacon.* 25 (*Mor.* 210E-D):
Again, the Thasians, feeling that they had received great benefits from [Agesilaus], honored him with temples and deification, and sent an embassy to him concerning these matters. After reading the offers which the envoys presented to him, he asked whether their country was able to deify men. When they said yes, he replied: 'Then first make gods of yourselves: if you can manage that, then I'll believe in your ability to make a god of me too.'

[86] Dodds 1951: 242.

[87] Plut. *Alex.* 28, *Mor.* 180E, 341B; Aristobulus ap. Athen. 251a, cf. Hom. *Il.* 5.340.

[88] Athen. (a) 6.250a, (b) 7.289a-e:
(a) Timaeus, in Book 22 of his Histories, has this to say of Democles, the toady of Dionysius the Younger. It used to be the custom in Sicily to go from house to house offering sacrifices to the Nymphs, and during a night-long revel to get drunk and dance around the goddesses' statues. Democles, however, ignored the Nymphs, and, declaring that one should not bother with lifeless deities, went and danced round Dionysus himself instead.

begins. But that the belief was there, and deep-rooted in archetypal patterns of social behavior, there can be no doubt.

WORKS CITED

Balsdon, J.P.V.D. 1950. "The "divinity" of Alexander." *Historia* 1 :363–88 (reprinted in G.T. Griffith, ed. *Alexander the Great: The Main Problems* [Cambridge 1966]: 179–204).

Barker, E. 1946. *The Politics of Aristotle*. Oxford.

Bauman, R.A. 1990. *Political Trials in Ancient Greece*. London and New York.

Bendix, R. 1978. *Kings or People: Power and the Mandate to Rule*. Berkeley.

Bevan, E.R. 1901. "The Deification of Kings in the Greek cities," *Eng. Hist. Rev.* 16: 625–39.

Bulloch et al. 1993 = A. Bulloch, E.S. Gruen, A.A. Long, A. Stewart, eds. 1993. *Images and Ideologies: Self-Definition in the Hellenistic World*. Berkeley.

Carlier, P. 1984. *La Royauté en Grèce avant Alexandre*. Strasbourg.

———. 1993. "La notion de *pambasileia* dans la pensée politique d'Aristote." In M. Piérart, ed., *Aristote et Athènes*. Fribourg. 103–18.

Charlesworth, M.P. 1935. "Some observations on ruler-cult, especially in Rome." *HThR* 28: 5–44.

Connor, W.R. 1991. "The other 399: Religion and the trial of Socrates." In M.A. Flower and M. Toher, eds., *Georgica: Greek Studies in Honour of George Cawkwell. BICS* Suppl. 58. London. 49–56.

Derenne, E. 1930. *Les Procès d'Impiété intentés aux Philosophes à Athènes au Vme et au IVme Siècles avant J.-C.* Liège

Detienne, M. 1979. *Les Maîtres de Vérité dans la Grèce Archaïque*. 3rd ed. Paris.

Dodds, E.R. 1951. *The Greeks and the Irrational*. Berkeley.

Ehrenberg, V. 1946. "The Athenian Hymn to Demetrius Poliorcetes." In *Aspects of the Ancient World*. Oxford. 179–198.

Ferguson, W.S. 1911. *Hellenistic Athens: An Historical Essay*. New York.

Flückinger-Guggenheim, D. 1984. *Göttliche Gäste: Die Einkehr von Göttern und Heroen in der griechischen Mythologie*. Berne.

Frankfort, H. 1948. *Kingship and the Gods*. Chicago.

Frazer, J.G. 1911. *The Golden Bough*. 11 vols. 3rd ed. London.

———. 1920. *The Magical Origin of Kings*. Cambridge.

Fredricksmeyer, E.A. 1981. "On the Background of the Ruler-Cult." In H. Dell, ed., *Ancient Macedonian Studies in honor of Charles F. Edson*. Institute of Balkan Studies. Thessaloniki. 145–156.

Gelzer, T. "Transformations." In Bulloch et al. 1993: 130–51.

Green, P. 1993. *Alexander to Actium*. Rev. ed. Berkeley.

Grote, G. 1888. *History of Greece*. 10 vols. London.

Habicht, C. 1970. *Gottmenschentum und griechische Städte. Zetemata* 14. 2nd ed. Munich.

———. 1979. *Untersuchungen zur politischen Geschichte Athens im 3–Jahrhundert v.Chr.* Munich.

———. 1997. *Athens from Alexander to Antony*. Trans. D.L. Schneider. Berkeley.

Henrichs, A. 1999. "Demythologizing the Past, Mythicizing the Present: Myth, History and the Supernatural at the Dawn of the Hellenistic Period." In R. Buxton, ed., *From Myth to Reason? Studies in the Development of Greek Thought*. Oxford. 223–248.

Hocart, A.M. 1929. *Kingship*. London.

Kerenyi, K. 1976. *Dionysos. Archetypal Image of the Indestructable Life*. Trans. R. Manheim. Princeton.

(b) ...The Syrian ... Menecrates ... known as 'Zeus', who prided himself greatly on being the unique cause of life to humankind by reason of his medical expertise ... Among his attendants was one who wore the regalia and went by the name of Heracles ... and another who played the part of Hermes, complete with cloak and caduceus and wings ... while 'Zeus' himself dressed in purple robes, and went about with a gold crown on his head and carrying a sceptre, wearing high boots, and attended by his 'heavenly choir.'

Koenen, L. 1993. "The Ptolemaic King as Religious Figure." In Bulloch et al. 1993: 25–115.

Lévêque, P. 1957. *Pyrrhos*. Paris.

Mikalson, J.D. 1998. *Religion in Hellenistic Athens*. Berkeley.

Murray, G. 1947. *Greek Studies*. Oxford.

Nock, A.D. 1930. "Σύνναος θεός." *HSPh* 41: 1–62 (reprinted in Z. Stewart, ed., *Arthur Darby Nock: Essays on Religion and the Ancient World* [Oxford 1972], vol. 1: 202–51.)

Parke, H.W. 1977. *Festivals of the Athenians*. London.

Préaux, C. 1978. *Le Monde Hellénistique*. 2 vols. Paris.

Scott, K. 1928. "The Deification of Demetrius Poliorcetes." *AJPh* 49:137–166, 217–239.

Starr, C.G. 1961. "The decline of the early Greek kings." *Historia* 10: 129–138.

Tondriau, J. 1948. "Rois Lagides comparés ou identifiés à des divinités." *Chron. d'Ég.* 45/6: 127–46.

Vernant, J.-P. 1962. *Les Origines de la Pensée Grecque*. Paris.

Walbank, F.W. 1987. "Könige als Götter: Überlegungen zum Herrscherkult von Alexander bis Augustus." *Chiron* 17: 365–82.

Weber, M. 1968. *Economy and Society*. Trans. and ed. G. Roth and C. Wittich. New York.

22

Lysias 14 and 15. A note on the γραφὴ ἀστρατείας[*]

Mogens H. Hansen

For the Festschrift I had when I turned 60, Alan kindly submitted an enjoyable piece about a textual problem in Lys. 1.[1] I think that the best I can do here and now is to reciprocate by submitting an observation about Lysias 14 & 15 which I published in Danish in my Habilitationsschrift in 1973.[2] This observation was not included in the English version of the book published in 1976,[3] and is inaccessible to classicists outside Scandinavia. So what I have done here is to present an English version of my 1973 observation with an update added in notes 4–7.

The setting of the two speeches is as follows. For the campaign of 395 Alkibiades junior was called to serve as hoplite in the infantry but, without being officially enrolled as a ἱππεύς, he preferred to serve in the cavalry instead. After the campaign he was put on trial by a certain Archestratides (Lys. 14.3) assisted by a team of at least two *synegoroi*, one delivering Lysias 14 and another one Lysias 15.

However, in *Lysias and the Corpus Lysiacum*, Sir Kenneth Dover rejected Lysias 15 as a late rhetorical piece written by someone who was unaware of the facts at issue. The principal reason adduced is that, in the title of Lys. 15 as well as in sections 1 & 4, the type of public action used is erroneously described as a γραφὴ ἀστρατείας, whereas it is apparent from Lys. 14 that Alkibiades was brought to trial by a γραφὴ λιποταξίου.[4]

True, the title of Lysias 15 is Κατὰ Ἀλκιβιάδου ἀστρατείας but, as with all such titles, it is not part of the original speech. It is undoubtedly a late addition and has no authority for any evaluation of which type of action the prosecutors had used. But the same observation applies to Lys. 14: Κατὰ Ἀλκιβιάδου λιποταξίου. Again, we cannot from the title alone say anything about the type of action used by the prosecutors. In the speech itself Alkibiades is accused of ἀστρατεία (14.7), λιποτάξιον (14.5,7 [only in

---

[*] I was invited to contribute to this volume in the twelfth hour, so to speak, too late to come up with a substantial new piece worthy of the honorand, but early enough to be among those who pay their tribute to a respected colleague and dear friend.

[1] Boegehold 2000.

[2] Hansen 1973: 17, 81–5.

[3] Hansen 1976.

[4] Dover 1968: 166. Dover's other argument is that, at 15.6, Alkibiades is described as a ἱπποτοξότης rather than as a ἱππεύς. But that the hippotoxotai were part of the cavalry, and that no clearcut distinction need be made, is argued by Bugh 1988: 221–4, cf. 133–5.

one ms.: C]), δειλία (14.5, 7, 11, 16, 44) and τὸ ἀδοκίμαστον ἱππεύειν (14.8),[5] but which of these terms was the one stated in the writ? That is impossible to decide from the speech itself, and, as argued above, the title has no value as a source for the type of action used. In Lysias 15, on the other hand, the trial is explicitly described as a γραφὴ ἀστρατείας in the opening paragraph, and that the offence was thought of principally as ἀστρατεία is apparent once again from section 4. There is no mention of λιποτάξιον or δειλία in the speech, whereas τὸ ἀδοκίμαστον ἱππεύειν is debated in 7.

Thus, Dover's argument is invalid because it is impossible from Lys. 14 to find out which type of public action the prosecutors had used, and because λιποταξίου in the title carries no weight. Lys. 15 is probably a genuine speech by Lysias, and the similarity between Lys. 14 and 15 is due to the fact that both speeches were *synegoriai* written by the same logographer for different prosecutors,[6] just as Deinarchos' three speeches were all written as *synegoriai* to be delivered by prosecutors in the Harpalos affair. Let me add that Lys. 15 seems to be stylistically impeccable and, in the forthcoming OCT by C. Carey it will be considered a genuine speech by Lysias.[7]

Accepting both speeches as genuine, the preferable view is that the action was a γραφὴ ἀστρατείας. A γραφὴ τοῦ ἀδοκίμαστον ἱππεύειν is a possible alternative which, however, can be excluded because in that case the penalty would have been *atimia* plus confiscation of property (14.9), not just *atimia* as it was in case of λιποτάξιον or ἀστρατεία (Andoc. 1.74), and Lys. 14, especially 14.44, as interpreted by Thalheim,[8] indicates that the confiscation of property was not part of the penalty to be imposed on Alikibiades in case of conviction (πένης ὤν being causal and not hypothetic).

One question remains: why did the prosecutors prefer the γραφὴ ἀστρατείας to the γραφὴ τοῦ ἀδοκίμαστον ἱππεύειν? The second charge would have been more obvious and would even have resulted in a more severe penalty. Yes, but conviction might have been more difficult to obtain. It is apparent from Lys. 14.5 that public actions concerning λιποτάξιον, ἀστρατεία or δειλεία were heard by jurors selected from the soldiers who had served in the army. Alkibiades was charged with not having fought in the hoplite army, and from 14: οὐκ ἐπεξῆλθε μεθ' ὑμῶν and 14.15: οὐκ ἐτολμᾶτε ἀπολιπεῖν τὰς τάξεις we can infer that, in this case, the jurors hearing the case were all hoplites. It may be conjectured that a γραφὴ τοῦ ἀδοκίμαστον ἱππεύειν would have been heard by jurors selected by lot from among the knights. Some corroboration of this conjecture can be found in Plato's description of military actions in *Laws* 843A-B where it is laid down that trials of hoplites have to be heard by hoplites, and trials of knights by knights. One can easily imagine that the younger Alkibiades had many friends among the not all too numerous knights and that the prosecutors therefore preferred to interpret Alkibiades' offence as ἀστρατεία, even though a γραφὴ τοῦ ἀδοκίμαστον ἱππεύειν would have suited their case better.

---

[5] For a clever interpretation of these terms with an attempt to explain the differences, if any, between the various military offences, see now Hamel 1998, especially 361–76. As I do, Hamel believes that the type of public action used was a γραφὴ ἀστρατείας, not λιποταξίου: see 376–9.

[6] See Rubinstein 2000: 27, 131, 133, 144–5, 236 cat. no. 10.

[7] Carey 1989: 147–8.

[8] Thalheim 1877: 271–2.

WORKS CITED

Boegehold, A.L. 2000. "At Home. Lysias 1.23." In P. Flensted-Jensen, Th. Heine Nielsen, and L. Rubinstein, eds., *Polis & Politics. Studies in Ancient Greek History Presented to Mogens Herman Hansen on his Sixtieth Birthday, August 20, 2000.* Copenhagen. 597–600.

Bugh, G.R. 1988. *The Horsemen of Athens.* Princeton.

Carey, C. 1989. *Lysias. Selected Speeches.* Cambridge.

Dover, K.J. 1968. *Lysias and the Corpus Lysiacum.* Berkeley and Los Angeles.

Hamel, D. 1998. "Coming to Terms with λιποτάξιον." *GRBS* 39: 361–405.

Hansen, M.H. 1973. *Atimistraffen i Athen i Klassisk Tid.* Odense.

Hansen, M.H. 1976. *Apagoge, Endeixis and Ephegesis against Kakourgoi Atimoi and Pheugontes.* Odense.

Rubinstein, L. 2000. *Litigation and Cooperation. Supporting Speeches in the Courts of Classical Athens.* Stuttgart.

Thalheim, Th. 1877. "Das attische Militärstrafgesetz und Lysias 14.7." *Njbb* 23: 271–2.

23

Counterproposal at Carthage
(Aristotle, *Politics* II.11.5–6)

G. L. Huxley

The invitation to contribute to the *Festschrift* was accepted promptly and with pleasure, because Alan Boegehold has been a dear friend for more than forty years. Since he has added much to our understanding of political mechanisms in Greek city-states, I thought that he, and Julie too, would be interested in a problem in Aristotle's account of the Carthaginian polity and in a suggested solution to it.

Carthage, it is true, was not a Hellenic city, but since Aristotle compares the Carthaginian constitution with those of Sparta and of Crete in *Politics* II, his treatment of Carthage should not be ignored by historians of Greece. The problem to be examined here arises in his description of decision-making and enactment at Carthage (II.11.5–6, 1273a6–a13, ed. W.D. Ross). The text is:

> τοῦ μὲν γὰρ μὲν προσ-
> άγειν τὰ δὲ μὴ προσάγειν πρὸς τὸν δῆμον οἱ βασιλεῖς
> κύριοι μετὰ τῶν γερόντων, ἂν ὁμογνωμονῶσι πάντες, εἰ
> δὲ μή, καὶ τούτων ὁ δῆμος. ἃ δ' ἂν εἰσφέρωσιν οὗτοι, οὐ
> 10   διακοῦσαι μόνον ἀποδιδόασι τῷ δήμῳ τὰ δόξαντα τοῖς ἄρ-
> χουσιν, ἀλλὰ κύριοι κρίνειν εἰσὶ καὶ τῷ βουλομένῳ τοῖς
> εἰσφερομένοις ἀντειπεῖν ἔξεστιν, ὅπερ ἐν ταῖς ἑτέραις πολι-
> τείαις οὐκ ἔστιν.

> 7 τὰ Hᵃ*Π*¹*π*³: τὸ P²P³π3   9   εἰσφέρουσιν Hᵃ*Π*² οὗτοι om. *Π*¹
> 10   τά δόξαντα] τάξαντα *Π*¹   12   ἀντιπεῖν HᵃMˢπ³

Aristotle is describing ways in which the constitution leans away from aristocracy towards democracy. There is no grave textual problem in the passage, but πάντες requires comment. The word is omitted from MS. P² (Coislin, 161, in Susemihl's classification),[1] but it should be retained. The meaning is not that complete unanimity of the Suffetes (οἱ βασιλεῖς) and all the Senators is required, since that would entail, through paralysis, the reference of most business to the Assembly. The meaning is that both authorities, Suffetes and a majority of the Senators, must agree to refer, or not to refer, a proposal to the Assembly. πάντες here means "both." This use of the word is

---

[1] See Newman 1887: 364, and, for the manuscript, Susemihl and Hicks 1894: 3.

Aristotelian; compare, for example, *De Anima* 430b4 where πάντα refers to both white and non-white.

The passage can now be translated: "The Suffetes and the Senators, if they are both agreed, can decide whether or not they will submit any proposal to the Assembly; but if they are not in agreement about a submission or non-submission, the Assembly can discuss the matter. Moreover, when the Suffetes and the Senators submit a proposal, the Assembly is not restricted to hearing and ratifying the proposal of the rulers, but it has the power of judgement, and any member of the Assembly who wishes may speak in opposition. This last power is not allowed in the other constitutions, of Sparta and Crete."

The problem of concern to us here lies in ἀντειπεῖν. It may have been rare in persistently oligarchic constitutions of Crete for ordinary citizens to oppose proposals of the *Kosmoi* and the local dynasts, but at Sparta opposition by the *Homoioi* in the Assembly to proposals coming from the Kings and Elders is well attested. Two conspicuous instances are (1) the opposition of the Heraklid Hetoimaridas to a proposal to declare war on Athens (Diodorus 11.50.6–7, under 475/4) and (2) the special arrangements for open voting instead of shouting imposed by the Ephor Sthenelaidas (Thucydides 1.87.1–3). This is not the place to attempt yet another discussion of the Great Rhetra of Sparta in Plutarch, *Lycurgus* 6, but it is pertinent that the text of that document, which was almost certainly known to Aristotle (F 536 Rose), allows to the Damos a power of criticizing proposals brought forward by the Gerousia. The problem, then, is that Aristotle seems to be denying that the Spartan Damos had a power granted to the Carthaginian Assembly, namely the power to oppose and to contradict proposals by a vote.

Wade-Gery, recognizing the difficulty, suggested that the text of the *Politics* is here dislocated. He thought that the trouble might have originated with Aristotle himself or an amanuensis.[2] The words ὅπερ ἐν ταῖς ἑτέραις πολιτείαις οὐκ ἔστιν had, he suggested, been displaced; they should refer to the power of the Suffetes and Senators to bring some measure to the Assembly and to refuse to bring others. This may indeed have been a procedure peculiar to Carthage, but the drastic reorganization of the text by Wade-Gery should not be accepted if a simpler explanation can be found, without any rewriting or rearrangement.

A solution is to be discerned in the extent of opposition to proposals permitted to the Assembly at Carthage, but not at Sparta. The Spartan Damos had the power of contradiction. Presented with proposal P, the *Homoioi* could show, normally by shouting, when P was put to the vote, that P or not-P was acceptable. At Sparta ἀντειπεῖν meant "contradict" or "gainsay." But ἀντί does not only contradict; it can also indicate substitution. The meaning "instead of" also has a place in ἀντειπεῖν. What Aristotle is saying in *Politics* 1273a12 is that the Carthaginian Assemblymen had the power not only to contradict proposals put to them by the Suffetes and Senators (to say "not-P"), but also to make counter or alternative proposals (to say "not P but Q"). This was a strongly democratic feature of the constitution, as Aristotle recognized. The right of

---

[2] Wade-Gery 1958: 52–54.

the Assembly to originate an alternative proposal would have been an inducement to Suffetes and Senators to agree among themselves about reference or non-reference of proposals to the Assembly. So long as they agreed, the procedure tended towards oligarchy (when there was no reference), but once a proposal was before the Assembly enactments and decisions were capable of being reached by a democratic process far more powerful than any permitted at Sparta or in Crete. At Sparta the Kings and the Elders, according to the text of the Great Rhetra, had the power of withdrawal if debate became "crooked," *skolia*.[3] Thus a stop could be put to business. A counterproposal, if ever attempted in the Assembly, could immediately be declared "crooked" at Sparta, but at Carthage the Suffetes and Senators had no power of stoppage and withdrawal once a matter had been referred to the Assembly. Thus the notion of ἀντειπεῖν at Carthage gave to the citizenry far more power than at Sparta. Carthage, in short, has a secure place in the early history of democratic institutions, a history Alan Boegehold has so vividly illuminated by his literary and archaeological scholarship.

WORKS CITED

Newman, W.L. 1887. *The Politics of Aristotle*. Oxford.
Wade-Gery, H.T. 1958. *Essays in Greek History*. Oxford.
Susemihl, F. and Hicks, R.D. 1894. *The Politics of Aristotle*. London.

---

[3] Wade Gery 1958: 42 prints the third, and according to Plutarch (*Lyc.* 6.8) additional, clause ('the Rider') of the Great Rhetra in the form: αἰ δέ σκολιὰν ὁ δᾶμος ἔροιτο, τὼς πρεσβυγενέας καὶ ἀρχαγέτας ἀποστατῆρας ἦμεν.

24

Kallias A (*IG* I³ 52A) and Thucydides 2.13.3

James J. Kennelly

IG I³ 52A ("Kallias A") records the addition of 3000 talents to Athena's treasury on the akropolis: ἀποδοναι τοῖς θεοῖς |[τ]ὰ χρέματα τὰ ὀφελόμενα, ἐπειδὲ τει Ἀθεναίαι τὰ τρισχίλια τάλαντ|[α] ἀνενέγκαται ἐς πόλιν, ἅ ἐφσέφιστο, νομίσματος ἐμεδαπο (lines 2–4). This is a considerable sum certain to have figured in any calculation of Athens' financial resources made in the period around 434/3, to which date *communis opinio* assigns this decree.[1] As it happens Thucydides has given us Perikles' summation of Athenian power, financial and otherwise, on the eve of the war in 431 (2.13). Contrary to the expectation engendered by Kallias A's orthodox date, however, the attempt to locate its 3000 T within this passage is in vain. Consequently, the date of 434/3 (or for that matter any one transgressing certain temporal boundaries on either side of 431) is *ipso facto* untenable for the decree.

There is a single rubric in Perikles' speech under which the sum might be found:

> θαρσεῖν τε ἐκέλευε προσιόντων μὲν ἑξακοσίων ταλάντων ὡς ἐπὶ τὸ πολὺ φόρου
> κατ᾽ ἐνιαυτὸν ἀπὸ τῶν ξυμμάχων τῇ πόλει ἄνευ τῆς ἄλλης προσόδου, ὑπαρχόντων
> δὲ ἐν τῇ ἀκροπόλει ἔτι τότε ἀργυρίου ἐπισήμου ἑξακισχιλίων ταλάντων (τὰ γὰρ
> πλεῖστα τριακοσίων ἀποδέοντα μύρια ἐγένετο, ἀφ᾽ ὧν ἔς τε τὰ προπύλαια τῆς
> ἀκροπόλεως καὶ τἆλλα οἰκοδομήματα καὶ ἐς Ποτείδαιαν ἀπανηλώθη).[2] Thuc.
> 2.13.3

Are Kallias' 3000 T part of the 6000 T mentioned? The phrase which forbids such a conclusion is the explanatory γάρ clause which seeks to explain the attenuation of the reserve from 9700 T to 6000 T. Thucydides accounted for this through a specific list of projects whose cost the fund defrayed: the construction of the Propylaea and other buildings and the siege of Potidaea. Thereby he has provided a brief but coherent history of Athens' capital reserve from its acme to 431: Athens now had a reserve of only 6000 T because 3700 T had been *expended*.[3] If simultaneously, however, there

---

[1] Meiggs-Lewis: 154–69.

[2] This is, of course, to reject the variant to this passage found in the scholion to Aristophanes' *Plutus* 1193 in the Ravenna and Venetus manuscripts. The arguments of Gomme, *HCT*, 3: 26–33, against both it and the reasons proffered on its behalf by the editors of *ATL*, 3: 118–32 are decisive.

[3] It would be very odd if Thucydides, while mentioning the Propylaea specifically, would have contented himself with including the Parthenon among τἆλλα οἰκοδομήματα had any of the cost of its construction been met from the 9700 T (I doubt as well whether a νεώς, especially such a one as the Parthenon, would normally be called a mere οἰκοδόμημα). Therefore we have a date of c. 437 (the year

had been accretions (especially one so substantial as that in Kallias A) to this reserve, then Thucydides' specification of expenditures no longer serves to explain the current 6000 and the γάρ is rendered meaningless. The consideration of only one side of the ledger, the debits, cannot account for a figure that would now have been the result of both augmentation and subtraction. Thus, apart from the relatively unimportant fact that he would thereby engender the erroneous inference in the minds of his readers that Athens had spent some 3700 T on Potidaea, Propylaea *et alia* (instead of what would have amounted to 6700 T), Thucydides would have proven himself woefully derelict in providing the explanation promised by γάρ. The word indicates clearly that it was his intention to account for the *change* in Athens' financial reserves between c. 437 and 431 and the itemization solely of expenditures where there were also substantial additions was not a conceivable means to this end. On the other hand, so long as we do not posit a windfall of 3000 T which he chose to ignore, Thucydides' explanation of the metamorphosis of 9700 T into 6000 T is unproblematic.[4]

Thus, the year 434/3 for Kallias A is impossible.[5] Equally untenable is the assignation of the decree to a time just after Perikles' resume of Athens' resources in

---

work on the Propylaea was begun) at the latest for the accumulation of this maximum reserve as well as for the beginning of deductions from the 9700 T. If, however, we attempt to push the date that this acme was reached further into the past, an even greater problem is encountered in making sense of Thucydides' words at 2.13.3; for we should then have to assume that in accounting for the attenuation of the total he ignored such potential expenditures as the cost of the First Peloponnesian War, the sieges of Samos and Byzantium, the construction of the chryselephantine statue of Athena, etc., while mentioning only the Propylaea (and other buildings) and the siege of Potidaea, which by themselves form a temporally coherent set of items when taken with the date of 437.

[4] That the 6000 talents were a constituent part of the 9700 T of c. 437 and not a conglomerate formed of 3000 T "carried up" to a depleted reserve of 3000 talents squares well with Thucydides' description of them as ὑπαρχόντων δὲ ἐν τῇ ἀκροπόλει ἔτι τότε. The phrase "still existing at that time" suggests that the *ipsissimae pecuniae eaedam* had been on the akropolis for some time.

[5] It has been thought that the 3000 talents given to Athena were in the nature of "installments." Most memorably is this notion encountered in the elaborate reconstruction of Athenian finance of *ATL*, 3, where the sum of 3000 T is insisted to have been the result of tidy payments of 200 T a year for the fifteen years 449–434. Even were one to accept the supposition that the sum of Kallias A was derived in this manner, the inconcinnity with Thucydides 2.13.3 remains. For there would have been yearly accretions of 200 talents that were ignored by Thucydides, thus rendering void his attempt to account for the change in the reserve from 9700 to 6000 talents. However, unless one subscribes to the entire scenario offered in *ATL*, there is no necessity (or even faintest reason) to maintain that the 3000 T were the partial result of a 15 year Athenian economic plan instituted in 449. It is true, however, that 3000 T is an enormous sum, one not likely to have been gathered in an instant. Indeed, the perfect tense of the decree's main verb ἀνενέγκαται does imply that some period of time intervened between the vote to add 3000 T to Athena's monies and its actual accomplishment. This is only natural and does not imply the sort of "installment" payments envisioned in *ATL*. Nothing more involved than the following scenario need be envisaged: Athens decided that 3000 talents were to be given to Athena (whether to repay a debt or simply to augment Athena's reserves is immaterial for our purposes) and then set about the task. Further, it seems not improbable that this sum was obtained through the agglomeration of monies derived from various sources. Perhaps this was accomplished much in the fashion we see in Kallias A itself, when order is given to pay back the monies owed to the "Gods." Indeed, it makes good sense to suppose that the sources now to be diverted to this task had previously been devoted towards the accumulation of the 3000 talents for Athena. For the decree says "…*since* the 3000 talents have been carried up to Athena" they will now pay the debts owed to the Gods, implying clearly that sources of revenue had been freed for

431, for this would entail that in his calculations Perikles had ignored an enormous sum of 3000 talents, existing somewhere off the akropolis and awaiting placement upon it.[6] The decree must be temporally distanced in both directions from 2.13.3's date of 431. A date either before 437 or appreciably subsequent to 431 must be considered the only possibilities for Kallias A. Dinsmoor long ago suggested 438, in which case the 3000 T would have gone towards the accumulation of the 9700 T. Mattingly (422/1) and Fornara (418/7), meanwhile, have suggested later dates far enough removed from 431 that we should not expect to find traces of the 3000 T in Thucydides 2.13.[7] However one may decide among these alternatives, they are, at least, all compatible with the text of Thucydides.

WORKS CITED

ATL= B.D. Meritt, H.T. Wade-Gery, and McGregor, *The Athenian Tribute Lists*. Vol. 3. Cambridge, Mass., 1950.

Dinsmoor, W.B. 1947. "The Hekatompedon on the Athenian Acropolis." *AJA* 51: 127–40.

Fornara, C.W. 1970. "The Date of the Callias Decrees." *GRBS* 11: 185–96.

Gomme, *HCT* = A.W. Gomme, *A Historical Commentary on Thucydides*. Vol. 2. Oxford, 1956.

Kallet-Marx, L. 1989. "The Kallias Decrees, Thucydides, and the Outbreak of the Peloponnesian War." *CQ* n.s. 39: 94–113.

Mattingly, H. 1964. "The Financial Decrees of Callias." *Proc. Afr. Class. Ass.* 7: 35–55.

Meiggs-Lewis=Meiggs, R. and D.M. Lewis, *A Selection of Greek Historical Inscriptions*. Oxford, 1969.

---

new tasks. How long the accumulation of the 3000 talents may have taken is impossible to guess without any further evidence.

[6] Kallet-Marx 1989 has resuscitated Bannier's date of 431/0.

[7] Dinsmoor 1947; Mattingly 1964; Fornara 1970.

25

Athenian Slander: A Common Law Perspective

William T. Loomis

Anyone who reads the speeches of the Attic orators is immediately struck by the "peculiarities" of Athenian law, i.e., by things that seem odd from our *modern* perspective. For those of us who live in Anglophone countries, that perspective has been conditioned, inevitably and inescapably, by our own Anglo-American common law. In an article published thirty years ago, I found that this modern perspective had resulted in the long-standing assumption – apparently unconscious but demonstrably erroneous, and held by non-lawyers as well as lawyers – that the Athenians made the same value judgments that we make about premeditation in homicide law, i.e., that they punished premeditated killings more severely than sudden killings.[1] In this article, I again explicitly acknowledge our modern perspective, but this time I focus, not on an illusory similarity between the two legal systems (as I did with homicide law), but rather on some clear differences in their respective legal treatments of defamation. Although it is easy enough to spot these differences, it is harder to explain them, but the effort, I hope, will shed new light not only on Athenian law, but also on our own.

To do this, I should like first, to summarize, very briefly, our own law of defamation, both written (libel) and spoken (slander); second, to do the same thing for the Athenian law of defamation; third, to analyze the differences that emerge from these two summaries; and fourth and finally, to try to explain these differences.

First, the Anglo-American common law of defamation.[2] To recover in defamation, a plaintiff (P) must prove, first, that his reputation has been damaged, and second, that this damage took the form of a publication to a third party. The defendant (D) in turn may try to prove, first, that the defamatory statement was true, and second, even if it was not true, that he had an absolute or qualified privilege to make the statement. So, if D tells somebody else that P is a thief, that damages P's reputation, but if D says that P is a bastard, in a hot-tempered context where the word "bastard" clearly refers to P's personality rather than to the circumstances of his birth, that would probably be regarded as abuse rather than actionable defamation. Moreover, D must allege that P is

---

[1] Loomis 1972, subsequently accepted by MacDowell 1978: 115 with n. 244, and by Gagarin 1981: 33–34.

[2] For detailed references supporting the summary description in this paragraph, see *Restatement Torts 2d* §§558–623; Keeton 1984: 771–848; Markesinis and Deakin 1999: 601–679.

a thief to a third party: if D merely calls P a thief in a private encounter, P may be able to sue D for intentional infliction of mental suffering, but he can sue D for defamation only if D tells someone else that P is a thief, thereby harming P's reputation. Truth is a defense in all instances, so that if D can prove that P really is a thief, P's cause of action collapses. In addition, a defamatory statement may be privileged in certain contexts, as for example when a bank that is thinking of hiring P asks D for a character reference, and D – in the honest (but, as it turns out, mistaken) belief that P has embezzled funds from a prior employer – communicates that belief to the bank. If, however, D volunteers that information to someone who has no legitimate interest in knowing it, a gossip columnist for example, D loses the privilege – and this brings out a basic feature of our law of defamation, namely that it balances plaintiffs' interests in preserving their reputation with society's interest in freedom of communication in areas that are thought to be socially useful. One aspect of this balancing that deserves particular notice here is that if D calls P a thief, P can sue D, but if P dies, his estate or his heirs cannot sue D, i.e., the cause of action is personal to P and does not survive his death.

So much for the classic Anglo-American common law of defamation. In the past thirty-five years, this *common* law has been deeply eroded in the United States by the Supreme Court, which has made the law subject to the freedom-of-speech protections provided by the First Amendment to the United States Constitution. This constitutionalization of the common law of defamation began in 1964 with *New York Times* v. *Sullivan*, which held – as a matter of federal constitutional law rather than state common law – that public officials can recover damages for injuries to their reputation only if the defamatory statement was made with "actual malice," which was defined by the Supreme Court to mean "with knowledge that ... [the statement] was false or with reckless disregard for whether it was false or not."[3] Malice in the sense of spite or ill-will harbored towards the plaintiff was rendered constitutionally irrelevant, at least in suits brought by public officials against media defendants: in that case, the Commissioner of Police in Montgomery, Alabama in 1960 was suing *The New York Times* for printing an advertisement that solicited funds on behalf of civil rights demonstrators who, the advertisement alleged, had been harassed by the Montgomery police. The police commissioner claimed that his policemen had not harassed the demonstrators and thus that the advertisement was libelous, but the Supreme Court said, in effect, that even if the harassment allegation was false, *The New York Times* could not be liable unless it *knew* that the allegation was false. Three years later, in 1967, the actual malice rule was extended in *Curtis Publishing Co.* v. *Butts* to public figures who were *not* public officials (the football coach at the University of Georgia, in that particular case), and seven years after that, in 1974, *Gertz* v. *Welch* extended the rule to *private* individuals with respect to defamatory statements made in the media (in that case a private attorney accused of being a communist conspirator in a

---

[3] *New York Times* v. *Sullivan*, 376 U.S. 254 (1964) at 280.

journal published by the John Birch Society).[4] So if the plaintiff is a public official or a public figure, or if the defendant is a media organization, the older common-law rules have been emasculated by the Supreme Court's constitutional decisions, but the common-law rules still do retain their vigor in cases brought by private plaintiffs against private, non-media defendants, e.g., when an ex-employee claims to have been hurt by a false and malicious reference given by a former employer.

Before we leave the subject of freedom-of-speech protections, it is appropriate to observe that the freedom to criticize, or indeed slander, an *individual* is not the same thing as the freedom to criticize a political or religious *idea*. In the United States, of course, long before *New York Times* v. *Sullivan*, the Constitution and the courts had conferred extraordinary protections on speech about ideas, particularly on religious or political matters, but in Athens, notwithstanding the self-congratulatory platitudes in Pericles' funeral oration,[5] individuals were sometimes punished quite severely for religious views that were regarded as subversive, e.g., the prosecution of Socrates for impiety in 399 B.C., and earlier legal attacks for impiety against Pericles' mistress Aspasia, and his philosopher friend Anaxagoras.[6]

In turning to the Athenian law of defamation, we must at the outset acknowledge two problems with the evidence for that law: first, there is not very much evidence; and second, what there is, is biased. The Anglo-American common law of defamation is reported in literally thousands of cases discussing defamation in all kinds of factual contexts. These cases extend back over more than seven centuries and have arisen in nearly seventy jurisdictions in England, Ireland, the countries of the former British Empire, and the fifty United States. Moreover, our information about these cases comes to us from the written opinions of appellate judges, who usually begin their discussion with what at least purports to be an impartial statement of the facts of the case before they decide what the legal consequences of those facts should be. In contrast, almost all of our knowledge of Athenian law comes from about 150 lawcourt speeches, which are all that survive, and since with rare exceptions we have the speeches of only one of the litigants, we cannot be sure that we have an accurate statement of either the facts *or* the law, as we would if instead we had the written decisions of professional judges – and this brings out one of the salient differences between Athenian and Anglo-American law, namely that they had *no* professional judges and that their juries decided not only what we would call questions of fact, but also questions of law, without the possibility of appeal to any higher court. In other words, their juries had the same plenary powers as the United States Senate in the recent impeachment trial of President Clinton. So we are handicapped (a) by the small number of Athenian sources, and (b) by the tendentious nature (and hence the unreliability) of those sources, and it is important to remember these limitations as we wend our way through this treacherous documentation.

---

[4] *Curtis Publishing Co.* v. *Butts*, 388 U.S. 130 (1967); *Gertz* v. *Robert Welch, Inc.*, 418 U.S. 323 (1974).

[5] Thuc. 2.35–46, esp. 37.

[6] Socrates (Plato, *Ap.* 24b; Diog. Laert. 2.40); Aspasia and Anaxagoras (Plut. *Per.* 32.1–2).

With that background in mind, how does the Athenian law of defamation compare with the Anglo-American common law? Much of what we know about the Athenian law of defamation comes from one source, Lysias 10, the speech *Against Theomnestos*.[7] This speech actually contains information about four different cases having to do in one way or another with verbal abuse:

1. In Case #1, a man named Lysitheos, otherwise unknown, prosecuted Theomnestos on the ground that he had made a public speech at a time when he was disqualified from speaking in public because, allegedly, during a battle Theomnestos had thrown away his shield, i.e., he had been guilty of desertion in the heat of battle. Theomnestos seems to have been acquitted of this underlying charge of having thrown away his shield, because he promptly spoke again in public, to initiate at least two retaliatory lawsuits.

2. In the first of these retaliatory lawsuits, Case #2, Theomnestos prosecuted a man whose name generally has been emended in the manuscripts to "Lysistheos," the man who had prosecuted Theomnestos in Case #1. This was an action for slander (δίκη κακηγορίας), claiming that Lysistheos had defamed Theomnestos by testifying in Case #1 that Theomnestos had thrown away his shield in battle. We are not told the outcome of this Case #2.

3. Theomnestos brought his second retaliatory lawsuit, Case #3, against a man named Dionysios, who apparently had been a supporting witness in Case #1, i.e., he had testified that Theomnestos had indeed thrown away his shield, so Theomnestos now prosecuted Dionysios for perjury (δίκη ψευδομαρτυριῶν), and won, with the disastrous result for Dionysios that he was disenfranchised, i.e., he was deprived of certain of his rights as a free Athenian citizen – among them, the right to speak and vote in the Athenian Ekklesia, to sue in court, and to hold public office.

4. Now we come to Case #4, brought by an unnamed plaintiff against Theomnestos, and it is this speech that has come down to us as Lysias 10, *Against Theomnestos*, delivered in 384/3 B.C. This plaintiff apparently had also been a supporting witness for Lysitheos in Case #1, and had given the same testimony as the ill-fated Dionysios, i.e., he also had testified that Theomnestos had thrown away his shield. If so, our plaintiff naturally would have worried that the same fate awaited him as had befallen Dionysios, i.e., that in due course Theomnestos would also sue him for perjury, and deprive him of his rights as an Athenian citizen. Apparently, at the first trial (Case #1), Theomnestos had tried to discredit our plaintiff by alleging that as a youth our plaintiff had betrayed his own father to the Thirty Tyrants in 404/3 B.C., and thus that our plaintiff had, in effect, been his own father's murderer. So in this Case #4, our plaintiff is launching a preemptive strike: before Theomnestos can sue our plaintiff for slander or perjury, our plaintiff is suing Theomnestos for slander, a slander which consisted of Theomnestos' statement in open court that our plaintiff had killed his own father.

---

[7] The awkward abridgement of Lysias 10 in Lysias 11 (also entitled *Against Theomnestos*) adds nothing to our knowledge of the Athenian law of defamation. For recent work on these speeches, see Edwards and Usher 1985: 146–155, 229–235; Hillgruber 1988; Todd 2000: 101–112.

So there are basically two sets of slander alleged here, and both of them occur in Case #1. The first alleged slander consisted of the statement made by Lysitheos, which was supported by Dionysios and our unnamed plaintiff, that Theomnestos had thrown away his shield in battle. In the course of that trial, Theomnestos had tried to discredit the supporting testimony of our plaintiff by alleging that our plaintiff had killed his own father – and that is the second alleged slander. Theomnestos had responded to the first alleged slander, the charge that he had thrown away his shield, with separate actions for slander and perjury in Cases ##2 and 3. Our plaintiff had responded to the second alleged slander, the charge that he had killed his own father, by bringing an action for slander as Case #4.

At this point, we may pause to note three basic similarities between the Athenian law of defamation and our own. First, both legal systems require the plaintiff to allege that the defendant had made a statement that harmed the plaintiff's reputation, in the case of one plaintiff that he had thrown his shield away and in the case of the other plaintiff that he had killed his father. Second, both systems require that this statement have been made to a third party, in this case to the *many* third parties in attendance at Theomnestos' trial in Case #1. And the third point of similarity is that truth is a defense. Our plaintiff says that "the lawgiver makes no allowance for anger, but penalizes the speaker, unless he proves that his statements are true."[8] So three out of the four basic elements of the Anglo-American common law of defamation were present also in the Athenian law[9]: first, a statement that harms the plaintiff's reputation; second, a publication of that statement to a third party; and third, the inability of the defendant to prove that the statement was true.

There remains, however, the fourth element in the Anglo-American common law of defamation, namely the possibility that the defendant can demonstrate that he had an absolute or qualified privilege to make the statement even if it was not true, e.g., an honest, but mistaken, statement made in response to a request from a potential employer for information about a potential employee. This notion of privilege was *not* part of the Athenian system, and it is one of the principal differences between the Athenian law of defamation and our own, to which I shall now turn. There are five such differences.

The first difference is that many things that would be slanderous for us were not actionable in Athens. One *could* say, for example, that someone was a thief, evidently without fear of reprisal, as Deinarchos did, when he called Demosthenes a "Scythian" and a "bribe-taker and thief."[10] Three decades earlier, Demosthenes reported that the politician and historian Androtion "had said of one of his opponents, in the hearing of all of you in the Assembly, that he was a slave and born of slaves, and ought to pay the one-sixth tax with the resident aliens, and of another that he had children by a

---

[8] Lys. 10.30: ὁ νομοθέτης οὐδεμίαν ὀργῇ συγγνώμην δίδωσιν, ἀλλὰ ζημιοῖ τὸν λέγοντα, ἐὰν μὴ ἀποφαίνῃ ὡς ἔστιν ἀληθῆ τὰ εἰρημένα. For a similar statement, see Dem. 23.50.

[9] Although this formulation might seem anachronistic, it is justified in a discussion of Athenian law that explicitly takes the Anglo-American common law as its point of departure (see p. 287 above with n. 1).

[10] Dein. 1.15 (Σκύθην), 41 (δωροδόκον ὄντα καὶ κλέπτην).

whore; of this man that his father had been a high-class prostitute, and of that man that his mother had been a common whore."[11] And finally, there are instances in Andocides and Aischines where citizens are said to have served as prostitutes themselves.[12]

In fact, there seem to have been only a very few things that one clearly could *not* say about a living individual. They fall into three categories:

(a) If someone was called a "murderer," a "father-beater," or a "mother-beater," or it was said that he had "thrown away his shield" in battle (i.e., that he had been a deserter), these ἀπόρρητα, or forbidden words, were clearly actionable, although the defendant may have had to use those precise words. That, at any rate, was the argument of Theomnestos in Lysias 10: Theomnestos evidently admitted that he had said that our plaintiff had "killed" his father, but he argued that under the law he would be liable only if he had used the word "murderer":

> Perhaps he [sc. Theomnestos] will say that it is not one of the forbidden words [ἀπορρήτων], if someone says that he "killed" [ἀπεκτονέναι] his father, for the law does not forbid these things, but (instead) does not allow one to say "murderer" [ἀνδροφόνον]. But I think that it is necessary for you, gentlemen of the jury, to be concerned not about the labels but about their intent, and (I think) that you all know that those who have "killed" people also are "murderers," and those who are "murderers" also have "killed" people.... For presumably, Theomnestos, on the one hand if someone should say that you were a "father-beater" [πατραλοίαν] or a "mother-beater" [μητραλοίαν], you would expect him to be legally liable to you, but if someone should say that you were "beating the woman who gave birth to you or the man who sired you" [τὴν τεκοῦσαν ἢ τόν φύσαντα ἔτυπτες], (presumably) you would not think that he should be unpunished on the ground that he had spoken none of the forbidden words.... If someone should say that you "tossed" [ῥῖψαι] your shield (and in the law it is said, "if anyone declares that [someone] has 'thrown [it] away' [ἀποβεβληκέναι], he is to be liable"), would you not prosecute him, or would you be content to say that to have "tossed" the shield was of no concern to you?[13]

This kind of argument would be thrown out of court under our own law, which focuses on the *actual* damage to reputation rather than the particular words used to accomplish that damage. Certainly there would be broad agreement today that a

---

[11] Dem. 22.61: τὸν μὲν αὐτῶν, ... πάντων ἀκουόντων ὑμῶν ἐν τῷ δήμῳ δοῦλον ἔφη καὶ ἐκ δούλων εἶναι καὶ προσήκειν αὐτῷ τὸ ἕκτον μέρος εἰσφέρειν μετὰ τῶν μετοίκων, τῷ δὲ παῖδας ἐκ πόρνης εἶναι, τοῦ δὲ τὸν πατέρ' ἡταιρηκέναι, τοῦ δὲ τὴν μητέρα πεπορνεῦσθαι.

[12] And. 1.100; Aischin. 1.111, 165.

[13] Lys. 10.6–9: ἴσως ... ἐρεῖ ... ὡς οὐκ ἔστι τῶν ἀπορρήτων ἐάν τις εἴπῃ τὸν πατέρα ἀπεκτονέναι· τὸν γὰρ νόμον οὐ ταῦτ' ἀπαγορεύειν, ἀλλ' ἀνδροφόνον οὐκ ἐᾶν λέγειν. ἐγὼ δὲ οἶμαι δεῖν ὑμᾶς, ὦ ἄνδρες δικασταί, οὐ περὶ τῶν ὀνομάτων διαφέρεσθαι ἀλλὰ τῆς τούτων διανοίας, καὶ πάντας εἰδέναι ὅτι, ὅσοι <ἀπεκτόνασί τινας, καὶ ἀνδροφόνοι εἰσί, καὶ ὅσοι> ἀνδροφόνοι εἰσί, καὶ ἀπεκτόνασί τινας ... οὐ γὰρ δήπου, ὦ Θεόμνηστε, εἰ μέν τίς σε εἴποι πατραλοίαν ἢ μητραλοίαν, ἠξίους ἂν αὐτὸν ὀφλεῖν σοι δίκην, εἰ δέ τις εἴποι ὡς τὴν τεκοῦσαν ἢ τόν φύσαντα ἔτυπτες, ᾤου ἂν αὐτὸν ἀζήμιον δεῖν εἶναι ὡς οὐδὲν τῶν ἀπορρήτων εἰρηκότα. ... εἴ τίς σε εἴποι ῥῖψαι τὴν ἀσπίδα (ἐν δὲ τῷ νόμῳ εἴρηται, "ἐάν τις φάσκῃ ἀποβεβληκέναι, ὑπόδικον εἶναι"), οὐκ ἂν ἐδικάζου αὐτῷ, ἀλλ' ἐξῆρκει ἄν σοι ἐρριφέναι τὴν ἀσπίδα λέγοντι οὐδέν σοι μέλειν;

plaintiff's reputation had been equally damaged whether a defendant had called him the "murderer" of his father or said that he had "killed" his father, but it is quite possible that Theomnestos' argument succeeded at Athens – unfortunately, we are not told the outcome of this case.

(b) A second category of clearly actionable insults is the casting of aspersions on someone because he or she works in the *agora*, an occupation which some Athenians found undignified. In his speech against Euboulides, Demosthenes says: "And yet, men of Athens, in slandering us with the business about the *agora*, Euboulides has acted, not only contrary to the decree, but also contrary to the laws which ordain that anyone who makes work in the *agora* a reproach against any male or female citizen shall be liable for slander. And we, on our part, admit both that we sell ribbons and that we do not live at all in the manner that we wish."[14]

(c) Finally, there may be a third category of situations in which a private individual could sue for slander, and that had to do not with the *content* of the slanderous statement but rather with its *venue*. Plutarch tells us that Solon "forbade speaking ill of the living in temples, lawcourts, public offices, and during the viewing of athletic games; he ordained that the transgressor must pay three drachmas to the person injured, and two more into the public treasury."[15] It is difficult to know how much reliance we can place on this statement because it was written about 700 years after Solon's legislation – it would be as though our only source for Magna Charta of 1215 of our era were a biography of King John written in 1915! Moreover, this third category may reflect an imprecise summary, either by Plutarch or by his source, of the better-attested prohibition, to which we shall come in a moment, of slanders uttered in lawcourts and public offices against public *magistrates*. Finally, the fact that, in lawcourts at least, litigants said the most outrageous things about each other – that they were thieves, slaves, foreigners and prostitutes – makes it certain that Plutarch's account is not completely accurate. But the precise accuracy of his account is not a problem that we need to address now, since the only point that needs to be made here is that, even if it was unlawful to slander a private individual in the temples, lawcourts, public offices and public games of Athens, *outside* of those places there were only five things that one clearly could *not* say, namely that someone was a "murderer," "father-beater," "mother-beater," "shield-thrower" or "*agora*-worker." Apart from those five forbidden words, there apparently was wide leeway in what one could say, as the catalogue of scurrilous insults on pp. 291–292 above shows. So the Athenian law of slander was much less strict than our own, at least insofar as it applied to insults to living persons who were not public magistrates.

Magistrates, however, received *more* protection than private citizens, and that brings us to the second major difference between the Athenian law of defamation and

---

[14] Dem. 57.30–31: καίτοι, ὦ ἄνδρες Ἀθηναῖοι, οὐ μόνον παρὰ τὸ ψήφισμα τὰ περὶ τὴν ἀγορὰν διέβαλλεν ἡμᾶς Εὐβουλίδης, ἀλλὰ καὶ παρὰ τοὺς νόμους οἳ κελεύουσιν ἔνοχον εἶναι τῇ κακηγορίᾳ τὸν τὴν ἐργασίαν τὴν ἐν τῇ ἀγορᾷ ἢ τῶν πολιτῶν ἢ τῶν πολιτίδων ὀνειδίζοντά τινι. ἡμεῖς δ᾽ ὁμολογοῦμεν καὶ ταινίας πωλεῖν καὶ ζῆν οὐχ ὅντινα τρόπον βουλόμεθα.

[15] Plut. *Sol.* 21.2: ζῶντα δὲ κακῶς λέγειν ἐκώλυσε πρὸς ἱεροῖς καὶ δικαστηρίοις καὶ ἀρχείοις καὶ θεωρίας οὔσης ἀγώνων, ἢ τρεῖς δραχμὰς τῷ ἰδιώτῃ, δύο δ᾽ ἄλλας ἀποτίνειν εἰς τὸ δημόσιον ἔταξε.

our own law. Even before *New York Times* v. *Sullivan*, under our law people could and did say all kinds of nasty things about politicians, but in Athens there seems to have been a blanket prohibition of *any* criticism, at least if made in lawcourts or government offices. When a soldier had complained, not in a public building but in a private bank, that the Athenian generals had acted improperly in drafting him for military service, the soldier's argument that it was permissible to criticize officials in a private setting was apparently accepted by the Athenian treasurers charged with enforcing fines, but the soldier conceded, and the treasurers apparently agreed, that it was not permissible to criticize officials in an official public setting.[16] In addition to giving magistrates greater protections against slander, the Athenians also imposed greater penalties on such slanders: as in private cases, a fine was possible, but so was disenfranchisement – the loss of the right to speak and vote in the Assembly, to sue in the courts, and so on.[17] Finally, there was a special category of actionable slanders in what we might call the political sphere, namely that it was forbidden to speak disparagingly of the tyrannicides Harmodios and Aristogeiton[18] – it would be as though we had a law forbidding anybody today from speaking ill of George Washington! So in this area of criticisms of public officials, including two long-deceased political figures, Athenian law clearly was much more strict than ours is.

The third difference between the Athenian law of defamation and our own is their respective treatments of slanders of deceased individuals. Plutarch tells us that Solon enacted a blanket prohibition against speaking ill of the dead,[19] and although we cannot be sure that it was in fact *Solon* who was responsible for this legislation, two statements in the Demosthenic corpus indicate that this law was in force in the middle of the fourth century B.C.[20] Moreover, there is a fragment of Hypereides that indicates that the fines for insults to the dead were greater than for insults to the living.[21] None of these passages suggests that there was any relaxation of the rule against slanders of the dead by reason of venue, i.e., that one could say things about dead persons in a private bank or a tavern, even though one could not say them in a temple or lawcourt. This Athenian rule with respect to deceased persons is just the opposite of our own rule: if a modern defendant D calls plaintiff P a thief, P can sue D, but if D calls P's deceased father a thief, neither P nor his father's executor can sue D; moreover if D calls P a thief today and P dies tomorrow, P's case dies with him, and neither his estate nor his heirs can sue D in P's place (see pp. 297–298 below with nn. 29–31). This is perhaps the strongest contrast with our own law, and it naturally raises two questions: First, why did the Athenians *penalize* virtually any criticism of a dead

---

[16] Lys. 9.6–10, 16, on which see MacDowell 1994: 156 and Todd 2000: 97.

[17] Dem. 21.32; [Aristotle,] *Pr.* 952b 29–33.

[18] Hyp. *Phil.* 3.

[19] Plut. *Sol.* 21.1 (quoted in n. 28 below).

[20] Dem. 20.104; 40.49. In addition, it was forbidden to criticize the long-deceased Harmodios and Aristogeiton (see above n. 18).

[21] Hyp. fr. 100 (Jensen) (fine of 1,000 drachmas for slandering dead, 500 drachmas for slandering living). Cf. *Lex. Rhet. Cant.*, Κακηγορίας δίκη (slanderer of dead owes 500 drachmas to public treasury, 30 drachmas to private individual [heir?]).

person, wherever made? And second, why do we *permit* virtually any criticism of dead persons?

The fourth difference is the defense of truth. In the case of most slanders of private individuals, truth *was* a defense (as shown by the authorities cited in n. 8), but truth was not *always* a defense. In Demosthenes' speech *Against Euboulides*, the speaker says that Euboulides had slandered the speaker and his mother for working in the *agora*. Although the speaker admits that "we sell ribbons and do not live at all in the manner that we wish" – in other words, although the speaker admits that Euboulides' insulting statement is true – he nonetheless says that the statement violated the laws which subject such statements to the penalties for slander.[22] So I think that we are forced to conclude that as a matter of public policy the Athenians wanted to prevent *all* such statements. Todd has speculated that this strict liability applied in two other areas: first to utterances of the forbidden ἀπόρρητα, e.g., statements that someone was a "murderer" or "father-beater"; and second to criticisms of public officials.[23] I think that on the first point Todd is contradicted by Lysias 10.30 (quoted in n. 8 above), which says in effect that if Theomnestos could prove that the speaker really had murdered his father, Theomnestos would be free of liability for slander. But Todd's second point, that the Athenians as a matter of public policy prohibited *any* criticisms of public officials in lawcourts or public offices, may well be right, although the surviving evidence is insufficient for us to be certain. In any event, the rule about slanders of persons working in the *agora* means that we have one certain instance where truth was *not* a defense, as it always is under our law.

The fifth and final difference is that the Athenians had no doctrine of privilege that applied to defamatory statements. We have two kinds of privileges: qualified and absolute. The example already given of a qualified privilege is the statement that defendant D makes about plaintiff P in response to an inquiry from a bank that is thinking of hiring P: if D honestly believes that P has embezzled funds from a prior employer, D usually will be protected even if it turns out that the statement is not true. Examples of absolute privilege are statements made in official proceedings – for example, on the floor of the legislature, or in open court: in those places, one can say *anything*, no matter how defamatory and obviously untrue, because our courts have held that legislators, judges, lawyers, litigants and witnesses should be free to speak, without fear of being sued – in other words, that the public interest in free expression and free inquiry in legislative and judicial proceedings outweighs any individual interest in reputation (see pp. 298–299 below with n. 32). Lysias 10 proves that no such privilege existed in Athens, since both of the defamatory statements in that case – the allegation that Theomnestos was a shield-thrower and the allegation that our plaintiff had killed his own father – had been made in open court.

Let us now turn to possible explanations for these five differences between the Athenian law of defamation and our own law. In the case of Anglo-American *common* law, the policy reasons for our rules are stated explicitly in the reported court

---

[22] Dem. 57.30–31 (quoted in n. 14 above).
[23] Todd 1993: 260.

decisions and in the American Law Institute's *Restatement of the Law of Torts.* For Athenian law, however, the policy justification usually is not stated at all, or if it is stated, we cannot be sure that the stated justification is accurate, so we are compelled to speculate with greater or lesser plausibility.

First, why could many more nasty things be said about living individuals at Athens than can be said about living individuals today? Perhaps it is easier to approach this question if we reverse it, and ask why an Athenian was liable if he called someone a "murderer," a "father-beater," a "mother-beater," a "shield-thrower," or an "*agora-worker*," but not (as far as we know), if he called his fellow Athenian anything else, e.g., a thief, a prostitute, a slave, or a Scythian? What was so special about these ἀπόρρητα, these forbidden words? Wallace has recently proposed that the forbidden words all had to do with a citizen's right to speak in the Ekklesia, i.e., that citizens who had committed the acts described by the ἀπόρρητα were expressly disqualified from speaking in the Ekklesia.[24] Aischines tells us that the lawgiver "does not allow these men to address the people ... if anyone speaks in the Ekklesia who beats his father or mother, or does not support them or provide a home for them ... or has failed to perform ... whatever military services have been demanded of him, or has thrown away his shield .... or has prostituted himself as a common whore ... or as a high-class prostitute."[25] Wallace suggests that Athenian politicians had an enormous incentive to allege one or more of these things about their opponents in order to prevent their opponents from speaking, and that to discourage such frivolous and reckless attacks, the legal doctrine of ἀπόρρητα was devised so that reckless accusers could be prosecuted for slander. It seems to me, however, that there is a fundamental obstacle to this suggestion, and that is that the ἀπόρρητα evidently did *not* include the charges that someone was a prostitute or a foreigner, things that also would disqualify someone from speaking in public. As we have seen (pp. 291–292 above with nn. 10–12), litigants *did* call their opponents these things, evidently without fear of liability under the slander laws. So there *were* things that an Athenian could call his political opponent that would disqualify the opponent from speaking in public without worrying that he was uttering an ἀπόρρητον, a forbidden word, that could subject him to prosecution under the law of slander. Can we formulate an alternative explanation for the words that *were* forbidden? I shall try at the end of this article.

Second, why did magistrates at Athens have greater legal protection against slander than magistrates today? Under *New York Times* v. *Sullivan,* public officials actually have *fewer* protections than private citizens, but even before this constitutional decision, they enjoyed no special privileges, none at least unless one goes back to the seventeenth century, when the English Star Chamber punished criticisms of public officials as the crime – rather than the tort – of seditious libel. Indeed, the seditious libel cases may provide the closest parallel between Athenian law and the common law. The government of seventeenth-century England had been racked by political and

---

[24] Wallace 1994 at 120–122.
[25] Aischin. 1.28–32: τούτους οὐκ ἐᾷ δημηγορεῖν ... ἐάν τις λέγῃ ἐν τῷ δήμῳ τὸν πατέρα τύπτων ἢ τὴν μητέρα, ἢ μὴ τρέφων, ἢ μὴ παρέχων οἴκησιν ... ἢ τὰς στρατείας ... μὴ ἐστρατευμένος, ὅσαι ἂν αὐτῷ προσταχθῶσιν, ἢ τὴν ἀσπίδα ἀποβεβληκώς ... ἢ πεπορνευμένος ... ἢ ἡταιρηκώς.

religious controversy, and it therefore made the explicit determination, as a matter of public policy, that *any* criticism of a public official was a threat to public order and would be punished criminally. As Sir Edward Coke (later Lord Chief Justice Coke) said in reporting the famous Star Chamber case of *De Libellis Famosis*, which he had prosecuted as Attorney General, "if [a libel] be against a magistrate ..., it is a greater offence; for it concerns not only the breach of the peace, but also the scandal of government." Coke went on to say that "[i]t is not material whether the libel be true,"[26] and this rule that truth was no defense to seditious libel was still being defended as late as 1778 by the great English commentator William Blackstone, who wrote: "it is immaterial with respect to the essence of a libel, whether the matter of it be true or false; since the provocation, and not the falsity, is the thing to be punished criminally." [27] In other words, the policy justification for prohibiting the slander of a public official is valid even if – one might say *especially* if – there is truth to the alleged slander, since widespread knowledge that a public official really had mis-behaved would be even more likely to provoke civil unrest than mere rumors of such behavior. We lack comparably specific evidence for the rationale for the Athenian laws that gave special protection to public officials, but it certainly is plausible that the Athenians, like the English, felt that any criticism of public officials was a threat to public order, and that would explain the strong contrast between the law of Athens (where criticisms of public officials were more restricted and subject to greater penalties than criticisms of private individuals) and our own law (where public officials have virtually no actionable rights).

Third, why can we say virtually anything we like about deceased persons, while the Athenians could make no criticisms at all? To some of us, perhaps, the Athenian rule seems less strange than our own. Most of us, after all, have been brought up with the maxim, "Never speak ill of the dead," the notion presumably being that it is disrespectful, unfair and pointless to carp at someone who is no longer around – dis-respectful because the person is dead, unfair because he or she cannot fight back, and pointless because (with one side to the controversy gone) the controversy no longer exists, or at least it should not exist. It is interesting to observe that this is precisely the rationale articulated by Plutarch – and this is the only one of our five differences where the rationale for the Athenian rule is specifically stated in an ancient source: "Praise is given also to that law of Solon which forbids speaking ill of the dead. For it is pious to regard the deceased as sacred, just to spare the absent, and politic to rob hatred of its perpetuity."[28] In other words, it is pious to respect the dead, unfair to fight with them when they no longer are around, and bad for the community, the *polis*, to allow a feud to continue forever. Of course, we cannot be sure that Plutarch, writing 700 years after the fact, got the rationale right, but his rationale certainly seems

---

[26] *De Libellis Famosis*, 5 Coke 125a, 77 Eng. Rep. 250 (1605) at 251.

[27] Blackstone 1778: 150. Indeed, truth seems not to have become a "safe harbor" defense to criticism of public officials until Lord Campbell's Act (1843), 6 & 7 Victoria, ch. 96, §6.

[28] Plut. *Sol.* 21.1: ἐπαινεῖται δὲ τοῦ Σόλωνος καὶ ὁ κωλύων νόμος τόν τεθνηκότα κακῶς ἀγορεύειν. καὶ γὰρ ὅσιον τοὺς μεθεστῶτας ἱεροὺς νομίζειν, καὶ δίκαιον ἀπέχεσθαι τῶν οὐχ ὑπαρχόντων, καὶ πολιτικὸν ἀφαιρεῖν τῆς ἔχθρας τὸ ἀίδιον.

plausible to us even though our own *legal* rule is quite different. Under the common law, there was a maxim that a personal legal right of action – one that pertains to a person himself rather than to his property – dies with the person.[29] And since slander was deemed to be an injury to the person himself rather than to his property or estate, when the person died, the action died with him. In most jurisdictions, this common law rule has been modified by statute, at least as it applies to most torts, e.g., for personal injury, but the rule retained its pristine vigor in two areas of tort law: seduction and defamation, both of which were regarded as uniquely personal sufferings, and in the case of defamation, the common law rule continues to be vigorous.[30] The reason for the survival of this hoary principle in defamation law is said by the British legal scholars Markesinis and Deakin to be that "the tort action in defamation *primarily* protects a non-pecuniary interest (the defamed person's reputation)," as distinct from something like the loss of a limb in a personal injury action, which is thought to involve an interest that is much more susceptible to pecuniary valuation.[31]

Fourth, why was truth *not* a defense in *all* Athenian actions for slander? Again, we are not given a specific rationale, but the answer lies, I think, in the rationales for the particular slanders that were not shielded by the truth defense, namely slanders for working in the *agora* and (if Todd is right) slanders against public magistrates. In each case, I think, the particular slander could be regarded as disruptive of society and of public order. In the case of work in the *agora*, it is disruptive of society for citizens who are so poor that they have to do such work to be made to feel undignified as a result, so that even if the allegation is true, it is the sort of comment that society – at least Athenian society – will not tolerate. Similarly, if Todd is right that truth was no defense to slanders uttered in lawcourts and public offices against public officials, the rationale would be the same as that under the English seditious libel cases, namely that criticisms of public officials, even if – or *especially* if – well grounded in truth, are disruptive of public order and therefore will not be tolerated.

Fifth and finally, why do we have a privilege for statements made in open court while the Athenians had none? Our rule is stated succinctly in the *Restatement of Torts*: "A witness is absolutely privileged to publish defamatory matter concerning another ... as a part of a judicial proceeding in which he is testifying ...." The appended comment gives the policy justification for this rule: "The function of witnesses is of fundamental importance in the administration of justice. The final judgment of the tribunal must be based upon the facts as shown by their testimony, and it is necessary therefore that a full disclosure not be hampered by fear of private suits for defamation."[32] This obviously was *not* the rule at Athens: all of the allegedly defamatory statements in Lysias 10 – the testimony by Dionysios and our plaintiff that

---

[29] *Actio personalis moritur cum persona*, quoted in Markesinis and Deakin 1999: 767.

[30] *Insull* v. *New York World-Telegram Corp.*, 172 F. Supp. 615, 636 (Northern District of Illinois 1959), affirmed 273 F. 2d 166 (7th Circuit 1959), certiorari denied 362 U.S. 942 (1960); *Restatement Torts 2d* §560: "One who publishes defamatory matter concerning a deceased person is not liable either to the estate of the person or to his descendants or relatives."

[31] Markesinis and Deakin 1999: 768.

[32] *Restatement Torts 2d* §588 with comment a.

Theomnestos had thrown away his shield and the statement by Theomnestos that our plaintiff had killed his own father – were made in open court, but nonetheless they were clearly actionable. We are not given any policy justification for the Athenian rule, but I think that it is obvious that the Athenians simply did *not* place as high a value as we do on unfettered speech in official proceedings, and that for those slanders that were deemed to cut especially close to the bone – "murderer," "father-beater," "shield-thrower," etc. – there *was* no safe harbor, or almost no safe harbor.

Why do I say "almost no safe harbor"? It is well known that comic poets said all sorts of scurrilous things about people, both living *and* dead, and at least some of the insults that have survived were ἀπόρρητα. In his early plays, Aristophanes repeatedly calls the minor politician Kleonymos a shield-dropper, and he accuses the major politician Kleon – even while he is serving as a general – of being a foreigner, a bribe-taker and a thief, and after Kleon's death, Aristophanes describes Kleon as eating shit in Hades. Later, in the *Thesmophoriazousai*, Aristophanes rails against Euripides' mother for being a vegetable seller, i.e., for working in the *agora*.[33] As we have seen already, these were precisely the kinds of slander – using the forbidden word "shield dropper," insulting public magistrates, slandering deceased persons, and ridiculing persons for working in the *agora* – that were actionable in the Athenian courts. But it is pretty clear that comedians *could* get away with saying these things, and thus that in comedy we have the closest analogue to our own constitutional protection of media defendants under *New York Times* v. *Sullivan* and its progeny. Two scholia to Aristophanes indicate that for one or two very brief periods – possibly in 440–436 B.C. and again around 415 B.C. – comic abuse may have been subject to legal restrictions,[34] but this evidence is unclear and in any event it does not affect our impression that for *most* periods comic poets were able to say almost anything they wanted without fear of any legal consequences.

But apart from the special license enjoyed by comic poets, is there a common thread that accounts for the differences between the Athenian law of defamation and our own, the differences involving the ἀπόρρητα, the special protections for magistrates and for the dead, the clear absence of truth as an effective defense for slandering work in the *agora*, and the absence of privilege for slanders in open court? I think that there *is* a common thread. At the outset, I observed that our law of defamation has been characterized quite explicitly by our judges as a balancing act, the balancing of individuals' interests in protecting their own reputations with society's interest in promoting socially useful communication, and that in recent years our law has moved steadily in the direction of favoring society's interest in communication at the expense of individual interests in reputation. One might be tempted to see this as an inexorable development, i.e., that we have been moving steadily and relentlessly away from protection of individual reputations to encouragement of open discussion. But the English seditious libel cases remind us that in the not *too* distant past, there

---

[33] Ar. *Nu.* 353 (Kleonymos as ῥίψασπιν), 581–591 (Kleon while a living στρατηγόν as Παφλαγόνα, guilty of δώρων ... καὶ κλοπῆς); *Pax* 48 (Kleon, after his death, ἐν ᾿Αίδεω σπατίλην ἐσθίει); *Th.* 387 (Euripides' mother as a λαχανοπωλητρίας).

[34] Scholia to Aristophanes, *Ach.* 67, *Av.* 1297a, on which see Halliwell 1991.

was a move *away* from free and open discussion, when new and detailed restrictions on public speech were introduced in order to maintain public order – and that may be the key to understanding the differences between the Athenian law of defamation and our own. The maintenance of public order certainly seems the most plausible explanation for the special protections for magistrates, and for the absence of truth as a defense for slandering work in the *agora*. It also is a plausible partial explanation, as Plutarch says, for the special protection of the dead, in order "to rob hatred of its perpetuity," i.e., to prevent family feuds from going on forever. What about the ἀπόρρητα, calling someone a "murderer," "father-beater," "shield-thrower," etc., in *any* venue (including a court)? Certainly it must have been disruptive to call people these names, but it should also have been disruptive to say that someone was a slave, or had slave parents, or that he or his parents were prostitutes. In the absence of any ancient evidence as to why most slanders of living persons were permitted while only a few were actionable, I suggest that the forbidden words were vestiges of an older law that had come into being well before our surviving orations, which date from the fourth century, and that they represent insults that were deemed to be disruptive of society – perhaps because they all involved personal violence in one way or another – but that as new forms of insult developed, there was no public consensus that the list of forbidden words ought to be expanded. In the present state of our evidence, however, this suggestion is necessarily speculative.[35]

WORKS CITED

Blackstone, W. 1778. *Commentaries on the Laws of England*[8] IV. Oxford.

Edwards, M., and S. Usher. 1985. *Greek Orators I: Antiphon & Lysias*. Warminster.

Gagarin, M. 1981. *Drakon and Early Athenian Homicide Law*. New Haven.

Halliwell, S. 1991. "Comic Satire and Freedom of Speech in Classical Athens." *JHS* 111: 48–70.

Hillgruber, M. 1988. *Die zehnte Rede des Lysias*. Berlin.

Keeton, W.P. 1984. *Prosser and Keeton on the Law of Torts*[5]. St. Paul.

Loomis, W.T. 1972. "The Nature of Premeditation in Athenian Homicide Law." *JHS* 92: 86–95.

MacDowell, D.M. 1978. *The Law in Classical Athens*. London.

———. 1994. "The Case of the Rude Soldier." In G. Thür, ed. *Symposion 1993: Vorträge zur griechischen und hellenistischen Rechtsgeschichte*. Cologne. 153–164.

Markesinis, B.S., and S.F. Deakin. 1999. *Tort Law*[4]. Oxford.

Restatement Torts 2d = American Law Institute, *Restatement of the Law Second, Torts 2d*. St. Paul. 1977.

Todd, S.C. 1993. *The Shape of Athenian Law*. Oxford.

———. 2000. *Lysias*. Austin.

Wallace, R.W. 1994. "The Athenian Laws Against Slander." In G. Thür, ed. *Symposion 1993: Vorträge zur griechischen und hellenistischen Rechtsgeschichte*. Cologne. 109–124.

[35] I am pleased to acknowledge the suggestions of the editor and an anonymous referee.

26

The Bones of Orestes and Spartan Foreign Policy[*]

David D. Phillips

HERODOTUS AND THE TEGEAN WARS

Having coalesced from villages in the ninth century, won the hegemony of Laconia by the eighth, and secured her dominion over Messenia in the seventh, in the sixth century Sparta cast her glance northward, in the direction of Arcadia and the Argolid. Herodotus (1.65–8) records two wars fought against the Arcadian city of Tegea. The Spartans, he says, originally aimed at the subjugation of all Arcadia, and accordingly consulted the oracle of Apollo at Delphi. The god responded that he would not grant the entire region to the Spartans, since "there are many acorn-eating men in Arcadia who will prevent you"; however, he promised, "I will give you foot-beaten Tegea to dance upon, and to measure its beautiful plain with the rope."

Emboldened by the oracle, the Spartans marched on Tegea. So confident were they that they carried with them iron fetters to bind their Tegean prisoners; they intended to helotize Tegea as they had Messenia.[1] The Spartans were, however, cheated of this expectation. Defeated in the "Battle of the Fetters," they were chained in their own shackles and forced to measure the plain of Tegea as slaves.[2] Thus ended the First Tegean War, fought during the reigns of Leon and Agasicles at Sparta, which overlap ca. 575–560.[3]

Chafing at their humiliation by the acorn-eating Tegeans, the Spartans launched a Second Tegean War, under kings Anaxandridas and Ariston. Anaxandridas succeeded Leon ca. 560; this year thus serves as a rough *terminus post quem* for the start of the second war. The Spartans returned to the oracle for guidance; this time Apollo

---

[*] It is a great pleasure for me to offer this paper in honor of Professor Alan Boegehold, who taught me when I was an undergraduate at Brown. It is particularly apt that I should begin with Herodotus, since it was in a class with Professor Boegehold that I first read Herodotus in Greek. I would also like to express my gratitude to those who heard and commented on an earlier version of this paper presented at a colloquium of the Center for the Study of Religion at UCLA on February 7, 2001. Finally, thanks are due to J. Sickinger and an anonymous reader for their helpful suggestions.

[1] The Spartans would measure the plain of Tegea with the rope in order to divide it into κλῆροι, as they had done with Messenia (Cartledge 1972: 137).

[2] The Tegeans subsequently put these fetters on display at their Temple of Athena Alea, where Herodotus viewed them in person.

[3] For the Spartan king-list see Forrest 1968: 21; *OCD*[3] s.v. Sparta with references. Concerning the assignment of the First Tegean War to the reigns of Leon and Agasicles see Leahy 1958: 156–8.

directed them to recover the bones of Orestes, son of Agamemnon. Unable to find Orestes' grave, the Spartans sent another embassy to Apollo, who replied:

> ἔστι τις Ἀρκαδίης Τεγέη λευρῷ ἐνὶ χώρῳ,
> ἔνθ᾽ ἄνεμοι πνείουσι δύω κρατερῆς ὑπ᾽ ἀνάγκης,
> καὶ τύπος ἀντίτυπος, καὶ πῆμ᾽ ἐπὶ πήματι κεῖται.
> ἔνθ᾽ Ἀγαμεμνονίδην κατέχει φυσίζοος αἶα·
> τὸν σὺ κομισσάμενος Τεγέης ἐπιτάρροθος ἔσσῃ.

> There is a place in Arcadia called Tegea, on a level plain, where two winds blow under fierce necessity, and there is a stroke and a counter-stroke, and misery lies upon misery. There the life-bearing earth holds the son of Agamemnon; when you recover him, you will be lord[4] of Tegea.

The Spartans were puzzled by this response, until an *agathoergos* named Lichas solved the riddle. A Tegean blacksmith told Lichas that, while digging a well, he had unearthed a coffin seven cubits long containing a corpse of equal size; having measured coffin and corpse, he reburied them.[5] Lichas realized that the giant corpse must be Orestes, and thus solved the rest of the oracle: the "two winds" were the blacksmith's bellows, the "stroke and counter-stroke" were the hammer and anvil, and "misery" referred to iron, which brought misery to man.

Lichas returned to Sparta and reported his findings. The Spartans exiled Lichas on a fabricated charge; this allowed him a pretext to return to Tegea, rent the blacksmith's courtyard, dig up Orestes' bones, and bring them back to Sparta. The Spartans reinterred Orestes in their agora, where his tomb could be viewed as late as the second century A.D. (Paus. 3.11.8). Having recovered Orestes' remains, the Spartans vanquished the Tegeans. A *terminus ante quem* of 546 for the Spartan victory in the Second Tegean War is provided by Herodotus 1.65: when Croesus, king of Lydia, sent an embassy to Sparta requesting an alliance in that year, Sparta had already defeated Tegea.[6]

THE ORTHODOX VIEW OF THE BONES OF ORESTES

Herodotus presents the transfer of Orestes' bones to Sparta as a practical measure: Apollo guaranteed a Spartan victory if the Spartans recovered Orestes; the Spartans found the bones; and the god kept his promise. Was there, in addition to this pragmatic aspect, an ethnic significance to the relocation of Orestes' bones? According to the

---

[4] The first definition of ἐπιτάρροθος given by LSJ[9] is 'helper, defender, in Hom(er) always of the gods that help in fight.' Citing this locus, they gloss ἐπιτάρροθος as 'master, lord.' LSJ have clearly not fallen under the influence of the orthodox view of the bones of Orestes (see below), perhaps because both Liddell (d. 1898) and Scott (d. 1887) predeceased its birth. At any rate, the distinction between "lord" and "protector" is not great: etymologically the English word "lord" contains a word meaning "protector, guardian" (MnE *lord* < OE *hlaford* < *hlaf-weard* 'loaf-protector').

[5] Seven cubits is approximately ten feet, 2.5 inches. By way of comparison, Goliath of Gath (*1 Samuel* 17:4) stood six cubits, one span (9'6"); Los Angeles Lakers center Shaquille O'Neal stands only 7'1".

[6] Herodotus says (1.68) that by this point Sparta had already subjugated the greater part of the Peloponnese; he anticipates, but not by much.

orthodox view, the answer is "Yes." First propounded by G. Dickins in 1912, and endorsed by the majority of scholars of Sparta since, including H.T. Wade-Gery, A.H. M. Jones, W.G. Forrest, and D.M. Leahy, the orthodox view holds that the appropriation of Orestes' bones signaled a fundamental change in Spartan foreign policy.[7] Prior to recovering the bones, Sparta had played the role of Dorian conqueror; now, by adopting the cult of Orestes, she adopted the posture of protectress of the pre-Dorians in the Peloponnese.[8] The birth of a kinder, gentler Sparta was heralded by a treaty ending the Second Tegean War (below, pp. 304–6), which was inscribed on a stele posted by the banks of the Alpheus River. In time, the impact of Orestes spread beyond Tegea: by making friendly overtures to the pre-Dorians in the Peloponnese, Sparta was able to conclude a series of alliances, which eventually coalesced into the Peloponnesian League.[9]

While most scholars maintain the orthodox view, opinion is not unanimous.[10] In recent years, D. Boedeker has reacted against the orthodox position, advocating a reading of Orestes' bones as affirming a vital element of Spartan domestic propaganda, specifically the image of all Spartan citizens as Ὅμοιοι, "Equals."[11] Here I shall argue that the orthodox interpretation of the bones of Orestes is incorrect in regard to Spartan foreign policy. After addressing the well-known bone exchange conducted by Cleisthenes of Sicyon, I examine three further items often adduced by proponents of the orthodox view: the treaty between Sparta and Tegea concluded at the end of the Second Tegean War; the overthrow of Aeschines, tyrant of Sicyon; and the famous incident involving the Spartan king Cleomenes on the Athenian Acropolis. I then place the relocation of Orestes' bones in its context. The transplantation of Orestes was not an isolated incident but the first step in a Spartan propaganda campaign which also appropriated Orestes' father Agamemnon and son Teisamenus. It is as an element in this propaganda campaign that the symbolism of Orestes' bones, and their implications for Spartan foreign policy, must be assessed.

ADRASTUS, MELANIPPUS, AND CLEISTHENES OF SICYON

The transfer of Orestes to Sparta was far from unique. In archaic (and classical) Greece, the bones of heroes were considered to be movable objects.[12] Cleisthenes, tyrant of Sicyon ca. 600–570, orchestrated what was, before the Spartan appropriation of Orestes, the most famous transfer of a hero's bones in the sixth century. Cleisthenes

---

[7] Dickins 1912: 21–4; Wade-Gery 1929: 565–7; Jones 1967: 44–5; Forrest 1968: 75–6; Leahy 1955: 30; Sealey 1976: 83–4; Parke and Wormell 1956, 1: 96; Cartledge 1972: 139.

[8] Hammond 1982: 355 states the orthodox position succinctly: "Once Sparta had the sacred relics and understood the oracle, she ceased to smite the Arcadians as all Dorians had done, and she offered herself as their protector."

[9] Mayor 2000: 111 takes the orthodox view one step further, stating that the seizure of Orestes' bones "set in motion the long chain of events that eventually played out in the Peloponnesian War."

[10] See, e.g., Adcock 1930: 73 (below, n. 45).

[11] Boedeker 1993.

[12] To give one example from the classical period, in 475 Cimon unearthed the bones of Theseus on Scyros and brought them back to Athens (Plut. *Cimon* 8; *Theseus* 36).

hated Argos and decided to rid his city of the cult of the Argive hero Adrastus. He effected this by importing from Thebes the bones of Adrastus' mortal enemy Melanippus, and by transferring most of the cult of Adrastus to Melanippus (Hdt. 5.67).

Behind the supplanting of Adrastus lay not just inter-city rivalry between Sicyon and Argos, but also ethnic conflict between Dorians and pre-Dorians. This becomes clear from another famous reform of Cleisthenes, the renaming of the tribes (Hdt. 5.68). Sicyon contained the three Dorian tribes (Hylleis, Pamphyloi, Dymanes) and a non-Dorian tribe, the Aigialeis, to which the Orthagorid tyrants belonged. Determined not to share tribal names with the Argives, Cleisthenes renamed the Dorian tribes Ὑᾶται (Swine-men), Ὀνεᾶται (Ass-men), and Χοιρεᾶται (Piglet-men).[13] Cleisthenes' own tribe, named for Aigialeus, son of Adrastus, was rechristened Ἀρχέλαοι (Rulers of the Host).

Cleisthenes' choice of ignoble quadrupeds as eponyms shows that his motivation went beyond hatred of Argos. If Cleisthenes merely wanted not to share tribal names with Argos, there was no need to use derogatory appellations in renaming the Dorian tribes of Sicyon.[14] The fact that he did so indicates the presence of anti-Dorian sentiment among the non-Dorians in Sicyon. The intensity of this anti-Dorian feeling can be discerned from Herodotus' observation that the new tribe names lasted for sixty years after Cleisthenes' death – and thus for at least twenty years after the last Orthagorid tyrant, Aeschines, was deposed (see below, pp. 306–8).[15]

Adducing the comparandum provided by the bones of Adrastus and Melanippus, supporters of the orthodox position regarding the bones of Orestes impart an ethnic significance to his transplantation as well. Orestes, however, had in their view the opposite effect of Melanippus: while the substitution of Melanippus for Adrastus was an act of humiliation, the adoption of Orestes was an act of reconciliation. This, I shall argue, is not the case: while the actions of Cleisthenes of Sicyon had a clear ethnic motive, Sparta's concerns were not ethnic but geographic.

THE TREATY BETWEEN SPARTA AND TEGEA

Sparta did not simply "adopt" the cult of Orestes. When Cleisthenes of Sicyon decided to displace Adrastus, he asked the Thebans for the bones of Melanippus, and the

---

[13] These are the standard translations. "Piglet-men," however, does not accurately convey the insult: χοῖρος 'piglet' doubled as a slang term for the female genitalia (see, e.g., Hipponax fr. 174 West; Ar. *Ach.* 739ff.; Henderson 1991: 131). The obscene connotation of χοῖρος also explains away the apparent redundancy of porcine names.

[14] Osborne 1996: 282–3 suggests that the new names were not intended to be offensive, comparing animal ethnics such as Dryopes (Woodpeckers) and Leleges (Storks). However, there is a clear difference between animal names originating within the group and dating back to time immemorial (Woodpeckers, Storks) and animal names imposed by an outsider by fiat. R. Meiggs (in Bury and Meiggs 1975: 110; cf. Bury 1951: 156) offers a more attractive theory of onomastic retaliation: "[i]f Cleisthenes' enemies called his tribe Goat-men (Aigi-aleis) a natural response would have been to go to the farmyard for nicknames for the Dorian tribes."

[15] Bitterness at the interference of the Dorian Spartans may have encouraged the continued use of Cleisthenes' tribe-names after the ouster of Aeschines.

Thebans consented. The Spartans, by contrast, took Orestes' bones from Tegea, in time of war, either by deceit (as Herodotus says) or by force. From this standpoint, to assert that Sparta, by stealing Orestes' bones, was posing as champion of the pre-Dorians is not unlike claiming that Titus, when he looted the Temple in Jerusalem in A.D. 70, was posing as champion of the Jews.[16]

In a similar vein, proponents of the orthodox position who claim that the appropriation of the bones of Orestes was an international relations coup which paved the way for the formation of the Peloponnesian League appear to underestimate the intelligence of Peloponnesian pre-Dorians. Within the space of a few generations, the pre-Dorians had seen their Messenian brethren reduced to helotry, wearing caps of dogskin as symbols of their subjection (Myron of Priene, *FGrHist* 106 F 2; Fornara 13a) and tilling the soil like asses for their Spartan masters (Tyrtaeus fr. 6 West; Fornara 12c5). Dissuaded by Apollo from attempting to conquer all of pre-Dorian Arcadia, the Spartans had settled for Tegea and fought two wars to subjugate it. The removal of Orestes from Tegea, far from representing a Spartan will to reconcile, will have appeared to the pre-Dorians as yet another high-handed act by the scarlet-cloaked conquistador.

One of the terms of peace between Sparta and Tegea, which has been preserved by Plutarch, militates against Sparta's supposed new image as protectress of pre-Dorians. Plutarch's paraphrase reads, Μεσσηνίους ἐκβαλεῖν ἐκ τῆς χώρας καὶ μὴ ἐξεῖναι χρηστοὺς ποιεῖν. "They shall expel the Messenians from the country, and it shall not be allowed to make them good" (*Quaestiones Graecae* 5 = *Moralia* 292b; Fornara 27). The meaning of the word χρηστοὺς "good" in this sentence has been debated. Plutarch, citing Aristotle (fr. 592), interprets the phrase χρηστοὺς ποιεῖν as meaning "make [Tegeans who collaborated with Sparta] dead," i.e., kill them.[17] Jacoby's correction, that χρηστοὺς ποιεῖν refers to the Messenians, and means not "make them dead" but "make them citizens,"[18] has been accepted by most, and makes considerably more sense in the context of the treaty.[19]

The explicit ban on harboring and enfranchising Messenian refugees disproves the notion that Sparta was overly concerned with the welfare of pre-Dorians.[20] By preventing the pre-Dorian Tegeans from taking in pre-Dorian Messenians, Sparta was

---

[16] The legend on the coins of the Flavian emperors which commemorate this event reads IUDAEA CAPTA (not IUDAEA PROTECTA).

[17] A shorter version of this explanation is given at *Quaest. Rom.* 52 = *Mor.* 277b-c. Hammond 1982: 355 n. 48 compares Modern Greek μακαρίτης "blessed" used euphemistically to mean "dead"; this usage actually goes back at least to Aeschylus (*Persae* 633–4: μακαρίτας...βασιλεύς).

[18] Jacoby 1944.

[19] I agree with Jacoby in spite of the recent attempt to vindicate Plutarch by Braun 1994. In spite of his own and Aristotle's interpretation, Plutarch's wording implies that both clauses (ἐκβαλεῖν ἐκ τῆς χώρας and μὴ ἐξεῖναι χρηστοὺς ποιεῖν) deal with the Messenians. As Jacoby observed, Sparta would hardly direct the Tegeans to expel fugitive helots but at the same time protect those fugitives from a death sentence; on the other hand, it would serve Spartan interests to make sure that Tegea banish Messenians rather than enfranchise them.

[20] Leahy 1958: 162–3 suggests that Sparta's motivation for invading Tegea may have been to prevent the Tegeans from rendering assistance to Messenia; by allying with Tegea the Spartans created an effective buffer zone north of Messenia.

hardly projecting the image of defender of pre-Dorian interests. To the contrary, this clause in the treaty co-opts the Tegeans as collaborators to keep the Messenians under strict Spartan control. By all indications, the Tegeans were model allies: the most influential foreigner at Sparta at the time of Xerxes' invasion of Greece was Chileus of Tegea (Hdt. 9.9), and at the battle of Plataea the Spartan and Tegean contingents were drawn up side-by-side (Hdt. 9.28).

The idea of having their allies recognize and support their control of Messenia, as Tegea had done, recommended itself to the Spartans. Accordingly, a clause mandating the expulsion of Messenians and/or assistance in the event of helot revolt became a standard element in Spartan treaties of alliance.[21]

THE EXPULSION OF AESCHINES OF SICYON

PRylands 18 (= *FGrHist* 105 F 1; Fornara 39b) vv. 5 ff.[22] reads as follows:

Χίλων δὲ ὁ Λάκων ἐφορεύσας καὶ στρα[τηγή]σας Ἀναξανδρίδη[ς τε] τὰς ἐν τοῖς Ἕλλ[ησ]ιν τ[υρα]ννίδας κατέλυσα[ν]· ἐν Σικυῶν[ι] μὲν Αἰ[σχ]ίνην, Ἱππίαν δὲ [Ἀθήνησιν] Πεισιστ[ράτου υἱόν...]

Chilon the Laconian, having been ephor and general, and Anaxandridas[23] brought down the tyrannies among the Greeks: Aeschines at Sicyon, Hippias son of Peisistratus at Athens ....

The Spartans were famed for their hostility to tyrants,[24] and this fragment preserves one version of a list of cities whose tyrants were deposed by Sparta (for other versions cf. Σ Aeschin. 2.77; Plut., *de malignitate Herodoti* 21 = *Moralia* 859c-d). Among the tyrants named in these catalogues, some could reasonably have been deposed by Chilon and Anaxandridas; others (Hippias is the prime example) are clearly miscredited. Relevant here is the fall of Aeschines of Sicyon, whose assignment to Chilon and Anaxandridas is chronologically consistent and generally accepted.[25]

The ouster of Aeschines is not consistent with the orthodox view of a new, pre-Dorian-friendly Sparta. Aeschines was a relative, as well as the successor, of the

---

[21] Hammond 1982: 355–6; de Ste. Croix 1972: 96–7. Cf. Peek 1974: 4, a treaty between Sparta and the Aetolians containing at vv. 14f. the clause φεύγον[τας μὲ δεκέθο]ἡαν "let them [i.e., the Aetolians] not take in fugitives." As Thucydides observes (4.80.3), the cardinal rule of Spartan domestic policy was "keep an eye on the helots" (αἰεὶ γὰρ τὰ πολλὰ Λακεδαιμονίοις πρὸς τοὺς Εἵλωτας τῆς φυλακῆς πέρι μάλιστα καθειστήκει).

[22] On this fragment see Jacoby's commentary *ad loc.* in *FGrHist* IIC; Leahy 1955–56: 406ff. A photograph of the fragment is reproduced at White 1958, plate 1.

[23] As written, the Greek clearly assigns both ἐφορεύσας and στρατηγήσας to Chilon; so Leahy 1955–56: 418ff., 423. Some translators (e.g., Hammond 1982: 354) make στρατηγήσας modify Anaxandridas (as we would expect the king to serve as general in the field), but this is incorrect.

[24] Thuc. 1.18.1; Arist. *Pol.* 1312b7; Isocr. 4.125.

[25] E.g., by Huxley 1962: 69–71; Forrest 1968: 80; Leahy 1968: 1–23; but see *contra* White 1958: 2–14 (downdates the Orthagorid tyranny to 615/10–515/10); Sealey 1976: 62–3.

violently anti-Dorian Cleisthenes.[26] At some point, a Spartan army under Chilon and Anaxandridas marched north and expelled Aeschines. This would be a very poor way for the Spartans to project their supposed new image as protectors of pre-Dorian interests. A proper evaluation of the ouster of Aeschines and its relation to the bones of Orestes requires, however, that we first establish their relative chronology.

Our *termini* for the Second Tegean War (see above, pp. 301–2) are ca. 560 (the accession of Anaxandridas) and 546 (Croesus' embassy to Sparta). Herodotus says that, after recovering Orestes' bones, the Spartans consistently bested the Tegeans *in the war* (ἀπὸ τούτου τοῦ χρόνου [the recovery of the bones], ὅκως πειρῴατο ἀλλήλων, πολλῷ κατυπέρτεροι **τῷ πολέμῳ** ἐγίνοντο οἱ Λακεδαιμόνιοι, 1.68). Thus the Second Tegean War went on for some time after the Spartans transplanted Orestes. This, combined with the fact that we do not know how long before 546 the war ended,[27] supports a date for the removal of Orestes' bones not long after 560.[28]

When did the Spartans depose Aeschines of Sicyon? The expedition was led by Chilon the ephor; Diogenes Laertius (1.68) dates the ephorate of Chilon within the fifty-sixth Olympiad (556–553), and modern scholars favor the specific year 556/5.[29] The Sicyonian campaign is thus commonly located in Chilon's ephor-year, 556/5.[30] However, the Rylands papyrus reads not ἐφορεύων but ἐφορεύσας. If Chilon were ephor during the campaign, we should expect the present participle; but what we have is the aorist.[31] We should therefore conclude, based on this text, that the deposition of Aeschines of Sicyon occurred *after* the ephorate (and generalship, whatever that means) of Chilon.[32] 556/5, the year Chilon was ephor, thus becomes not the date of, but the *terminus post quem* for, the deposition of Aeschines.[33]

Thus we can reconstruct the following chronological sequence: the recovery of the bones of Orestes ca. 560, followed by the expedition to Sicyon and overthrow of Aeschines *post* 556/5 (probably not long after 556/5, since Chilon was already elderly

---

[26] We would assume *in vacuo* that Aeschines was an Orthagorid; the assumption is conveniently corroborated by Σ Aeschines (the orator) 2.77, who writes that the Spartans expelled from Sicyon τοὺς ἀπὸ Κλεισθένους.

[27] In the period 560–546 the Spartans fought, in addition to the Second Tegean War, a war with Argos which culminated in the famous "Battle of the Champions" in 546 (Hdt. 1.82–3: the Spartans were still occupied with Argos when Croesus' ambassador arrived). This suggests that the Second Tegean War predated the conflict with Argos; it is less likely, although possible, that Sparta fought both wars simultaneously.

[28] Cf. Leahy 1955: 35.

[29] Hammond 1982: 354; Jacoby, comm. *ad FGrHist* 105 F 1; Huxley 1962: 69.

[30] Hammond 1982, *ibid.*; Huxley 1962: 71; Forrest 1968: 80; *contra* White 1958 and Sealey 1976 (above, n. 25).

[31] Leahy 1955–56: 419ff. notes the problem with the tenses, but concludes nevertheless that ἐφορεύσας καὶ στρατήγησας here means "being an ephor and leading an army."

[32] This is our only evidence for the date of Aeschines' ouster (Jacoby *ibid.*: "für Aischines haben wir sonst kein datum"). Aristotle's statement that the Orthagorid tyranny lasted 100 years (*Pol.* 1315b13) gives neither a starting nor an ending date; cf. the *vaticinium post eventum* at Diod. 8.24 (Σικυωνίοις ἔχρησεν ἡ Πυθία ἑκατὸν ἔτη μαστιγονομηθήσεσθαι αὐτούς).

[33] Griffin 1982: 46 also interprets the ephorate of Chilon as the *terminus post quem*, but for a different reason: according to Griffin, the names Chilon and Anaxandridas have been preserved because they originated Sparta's anti-tyrannist policy, not because they personally ousted all the tyrants on the list.

when he served as ephor).[34] In order to vindicate the orthodox view, therefore, we would have to make the paradoxical assertion that the Spartans inaugurated their new policy of protecting pre-Dorians by overthrowing a pre-Dorian tyrant. Rather than engaging in such contortions of logic, we should interpret the ejection of Aeschines as evidence against the orthodox position regarding the bones of Orestes. The appropriation of Orestes did not announce a new direction in Spartan foreign policy, which was then seemingly reversed a few years later;[35] rather, it was consistent with the Spartan policy of conquest, expansion, and intervention, which was on display both immediately before the seizure of the bones (the First Tegean War) and immediately afterward (the Second Tegean War and the Sicyonian campaign).

CLEOMENES ON THE ACROPOLIS

In 508 there occurred a celebrated incident on the Athenian Acropolis involving the Spartan king Cleomenes (Hdt. 5.72). Cleomenes was in Athens attempting to install an oligarchy under Isagoras. He ascended the Acropolis and attempted to enter Athena's temple.[36] The priestess forbade him entry, saying that Dorians were not allowed inside; to which Cleomenes famously responded, ὦ γύναι, ἀλλ' οὐ Δωριεύς εἰμι ἀλλ' Ἀχαιός. "Ma'am, I am not a Dorian but an Achaean."

Proponents of the orthodox view commonly adduce this incident as representing a continuation of the "bones of Orestes" policy, interpreting the response of Cleomenes as a repudiation of his Dorian ancestry in favor of identification with the pre-Dorian Achaeans.[37] Cleomenes came from the house of Agis, and Huxley sees Cleomenes' statement, together with the bones of Orestes, as indicative of an Agiad "philachaean" policy.[38] Cleomenes and his Agiad predecessors, however, knew perfectly well that they were Dorians. Not only did Cleomenes' father Anaxandridas participate (with Chilon) in the ejection of the anti-Dorian Aeschines of Sicyon, but he named his other son – Cleomenes' half-brother – Dorieus. Clearly it was not the official stance of the Agiad line to distance itself from its Dorian roots.[39]

Why, then, does Cleomenes, an Agiad Dorian, tell the priestess of Athena that he is "not a Dorian but an Achaean"? Two levels of meaning are present in this statement:

---

[34] Diog. Laert. 1.72; Huxley 1962: 69.

[35] So Leahy 1955: 35, who attributes the short life of the "bones of Orestes" policy to the failed Spartan attempt to attract Helice into alliance by appropriating the bones of Teisamenus (see below, p. 312).

[36] Since Herodotus calls the temple τὸ ἄδυτον τῆς θεοῦ (and has the priestess call it τὸ ἱρόν), this is probably the Old Temple of Athena, not the Hecatompedon: see Travlos 1980: 143, 258; cf. Judeich 1931: 261ff.

[37] E.g., Huxley 1962: 69, 81.

[38] Huxley 1962: 69.

[39] Forrest 1968: 83 goes so far as to assert that the name Dorieus "shouts out Anaxandridas' hostility to Chilon's policy [i.e., the philachaean "bones of Orestes" policy]." Cleomenes' claim to be an Achaean then would serve as a slap in the face of the father who never wanted him. *Pace* Forrest, I do not think the evidence is sufficient to posit a schism between Chilonian and Agiad policy; to the contrary, the Rylands papyrus fragment (above, p. 306) portrays *Chilon* as the prime mover in the ejection of the "Achaean" Aeschines of Sicyon.

Cleomenes is making a Laconic pun.[40] Cleomenes could claim, with reason, to be Ἀχαιός on two grounds, one particular and one general. Specifically, as a Spartan king, Cleomenes claimed descent from Heracles. The Dorian invasions were justified in historical times as the "Return of the Heracleidae," with the (pre-Dorian, "Achaean") descendants of Heracles marching south, at the head of a Dorian army, to reclaim what was rightfully theirs.[41] Thus, depending on which aspect of his background he wished to emphasize, a Spartan king could claim to be either Dorian (*qua* Spartan) or "Achaean" (*qua* king). Alternatively, and on more general terms, Cleomenes' self-identification as Ἀχαιός is supported by no less an authority than Homer, who uses "Achaean" (as well as "Danaan" and "Argive") to refer to all Greeks.[42]

The double meaning of Cleomenes' retort centers around the word Δωριεύς, which means "Dorian," but was also the name of Cleomenes' half-brother.[43] Cleomenes and Dorieus had a history of bad blood, each claiming to be the true Agiad heir. After Cleomenes was awarded the throne ca. 520, Dorieus, his royal aspirations dashed, left Sparta and spent the next decade, like Aeneas, *iactatus aequore toto*. He first founded a colony in Libya on the Cinyps River; ejected from African shores by the Libyans and Carthaginians two years later, he returned to the Peloponnese. Then, in 510, he set off to colonize Heracleia in western Sicily, where he met his death at the hands of the Carthaginians and Egestaeans (Hdt. 5.42–6).

Thus, when Cleomenes says to the priestess of Athena, οὐ Δωριεύς εἰμι ἀλλ᾽ Ἀχαιός, he is informing her, in effect, "You're not dealing with my half-brother; you're dealing with me." On this resonance, the word Ἀχαιός invites (no doubt intentionally) a comparison with Homer's Achaeans: Cleomenes portrays himself, in contrast to his deceased half-brother, as a hero of the old school.

The nature of Cleomenes' remark to the priestess of Athena on the Acropolis is further clarified by a subsequent confrontation at the Argive Heraeum in 494 (Hdt. 6.81). Having defeated the Argives at the battle of Sepeia, Cleomenes went to the Argive Heraeum in order to consult the goddess. A priest tried to bar his entry, explaining that foreigners were not permitted to offer sacrifice. Cleomenes had his helots drag the priest from the altar and scourge him, and he sacrificed to Hera.

These two similar scenes, on the Athenian Acropolis and at the Argive Heraeum, depict Cleomenes as a man who liked to interfere in the religious cults of foreign cities, whether they wanted him to or not. Cleomenes' violent reaction to the priest of Hera helps us to interpret his (less dramatic, but equally blunt) response to the priestess of Athena. In each incident he violates religious law and disrespects local custom, insisting on going where no Spartan has gone before. Far from demonstrating Cleomenes' willingness to abase himself by denying his Dorian ancestry, the incident on the Acropolis, like that at the Argive Heraeum, portrays Cleomenes as the high-

---

[40] For other (supposed) examples of Spartan wit see Plut. *Apophth. Lac.* = *Mor.* 208b-242d; sayings attributed to Cleomenes are recorded at 223a-224b.

[41] See Parker 1998: 5 with n. 9; Hall 1997: 56–65; Malkin 1994: 42–5.

[42] The constant appearance of Ἀργεῖοι in Homer impelled Cleisthenes of Sicyon to ban rhapsodic competitions (Hdt. 5.67).

[43] Cf. Macan 1895, 1: 217 (*ad* Hdt. 5.72 οὐ θεμιτὸν Δωριεῦσι).

handed, arrogant Spartan conqueror to whom the customs of foreigners were irrelevant.

ORESTES AND THE PROPAGANDA OF HEGEMONY

I have argued above that the appropriation of the bones of Orestes, rather than signaling a new direction in Sparta's relations with her pre-Dorian neighbors, marked a continuation and expansion of existing policy. On a pragmatic level, the Spartans took Orestes' bones because Delphi told them the bones were the key to winning the war with Tegea. Why Orestes? Proponents of the orthodox view commonly observe that Orestes was a favorite hero of the pre-Dorian population of the Peloponnese, possibly because he had been equated with a local Arcadian hero Oresthes. The acquisition and ostentatious worship of Orestes is supposed to have convinced the pre-Dorians that Sparta now took their concerns to heart.[44]

Orestes, however, was a powerful figure not just to pre-Dorians but to all Peloponnesians. Most significantly from the Spartan point of view, Orestes had achieved in the twelfth century what Sparta was trying to achieve in the sixth; namely, the hegemony of the Peloponnese. Agamemnon, Orestes' father, had commanded the Greek expedition to Troy. His kingdom, centered at Mycenae, encompassed the Argolid and extended into the sea: in the famous Homeric phrase, Agamemnon was "of many an isle and of all Argos king" (πολλῇσιν νήσοισι καὶ Ἄργεϊ παντὶ ἀνάσσειν, *Il.* 2.108). Orestes himself ruled not only Mycenae and the Argolid, which he inherited from his father, but also Sparta, which he inherited from his uncle Menelaus (Paus. 2.18.5–6). Thus in the person of Orestes was unified the hegemony of the northern and southern Peloponnese.

Orestes had possessed the Peloponnese; Sparta now possessed Orestes. The message was clear: Sparta aimed at domination of all mainland Greece south of the Isthmus.[45] Between the reclamation of the bones ca. 560 and 546, she made significant progress toward this goal, defeating first Tegea (in the Second Tegean War) and then Argos (in the "Battle of the Champions"). Sparta was reclaiming with the spear what Orestes had ruled by right of succession; since Sparta now claimed Orestes as her own, she could present her conquests as legitimate: the sixth-century expansion of Sparta was a second "Return of the Heracleidae," this time from the south. The symbolism of the bones of Orestes served primarily to benefit the Spartans themselves; the pre-Dorians acquiesced, not because they were convinced Sparta's claims, but because they were cowed by Sparta's spears.[46]

---

[44] How and Wells 1912, 1: 90; Forrest 1968: 74; Sealey 1976: 83.

[45] Adcock 1930: 73: "The removal of the bones of Orestes to Sparta was a claim to an ancient primacy which preceded and transcended the limits of what was Dorian."

[46] Cf. Huxley 1962: 68.

THE BONES OF TEISAMENUS[47]

Sparta next aimed to solidify her claim to Orestes, and to the hegemony of the Peloponnese, by appropriating his son and his father. Possession of Orestes had allowed the Spartans to bring Tegea into their sphere of influence. Orestes' son Teisamenus was entombed at Helice in Achaea; the Spartans reasonably assumed that Teisamenus could do what Orestes had done.[48] As Pausanias writes (7.1.8):

> Τισαμενοῦ δὲ τὸν νεκρὸν Ἀχαιῶν ἐν Ἑλίκῃ θαψάντων, ὕστερον χρόνῳ Λακεδαιμόνιοι τοῦ ἐν Δελφοῖς σφίσιν ἀνειπόντος χρηστηρίου κομίζουσι τὰ ὀστᾶ ἐς Σπάρτην, καὶ ἦν καὶ ἐς ἐμὲ ἔτι αὐτῷ τάφος, ἔνθα τὰ δεῖπνα Λακεδαιμονίοις ἐστὶ τὰ φειδίτια καλούμενα.

> After the Achaeans buried Teisamenus' corpse at Helice, later in time the Lacedaemonians, at the bidding of the oracle at Delphi, brought his bones to Sparta; and his tomb was still there up to my time, at the place where the Lacedaemonians have their meals called the *pheiditia*.[49]

Pausanias does not say when the Spartans recovered Teisamenus' bones, and the *termini* provided (*post* Teisamenus' death; *ante* Pausanias' autopsy in the second century A.D.) are not tremendously useful. Fortunately, we have a secure and independent *terminus ante quem* of 373, when Helice fell victim to the wrath of Poseidon the Earth-Shaker and disappeared beneath the waves;[50] after 373 the Spartans would have needed scuba gear (or at least Scyllias of Scione: Herodotus 8.8) to recover Teisamenus' remains.

In his article on the bones of Teisamenus, D.M. Leahy proposed to date their retrieval to the first half of the 550s; that is, after the appropriation of Orestes' bones (ca. 560) and before the expedition to Sicyon (which Leahy places in the ephorate of Chilon, 555); he interprets the ejection of Aeschines as a reaction to Sparta's failure to attract Helice into alliance.[51] Hammond prefers a date after the intervention at Sicyon, which he too places in 555; he does not say why.[52]

Leahy's reasons for placing Teisamenus' relocation after Orestes' are sound. The most important factor is geography: Sparta must control the central Peloponnese

---

[47] For a full discussion of the recovery of the bones of Teisamenus see Leahy 1955. This is a very useful article, though (as will become clear) I do not concur with all the conclusions presented there.

[48] In the affairs of Orestes and Teisamenus, the Spartans were motivated by genuine piety as well as by political considerations: the history of the Delphic oracle shows that religious feeling and *Realpolitik* were by no means mutually exclusive. I do not agree with the assessment of Parke and Wormell 1956, 1: 96–7, that Delphi acted as a rubber stamp for a predetermined Spartan plan of conquest. If this were true, there would have been no need for multiple Spartan embassies to Delphi; one would have sufficed.

[49] The site of the *pheiditia* (Spartiate communal messes) is disputed, but it seems clear that they were not located in the agora (Leahy 1955: 26–7). Thus father and son were not buried side by side; however, both were interred in important public spaces (cf. Boedeker 1993: 170).

[50] Diod. 15.48.1–3; see Leahy 1955: 30 n. 2 for additional references.

[51] Leahy 1955: 34–5. That Helice did not become a Spartan ally at this point is supported by the fact that Helice was not a member of the Peloponnesian League at the beginning of the Archidamian War (Leahy 1955, *ibid.*)

[52] Hammond 1982: 356.

before setting her sights on Achaea.[53] Further, the seizure of Orestes' bones was an unqualified success, resulting in victory and alliance; if, as Leahy suggests, the appropriation of Teisamenus' bones was conceived in order to win an alliance with Achaea *via* her chief city, Helice, it failed miserably (no wonder, then, that Herodotus does not mention it). It is far more likely that the success of Orestes' bones inspired a similar gambit with Teisamenus' bones than *vice versa*.

The arguments based on the Sicyonian campaign, however, are more problematic and less convincing. Leahy places the recovery of the bones of Teisamenus before the overthrow of Aeschines of Sicyon in order to rationalize the apparent swift demise of the new "bones of Orestes" policy of cooperation with pre-Dorians. He posits the bones of Teisamenus as the catalyst for the return to the Dorian policy of conquest: Teisamenus failed where Orestes had succeeded; this caused the Spartans to abandon their philachaean policy only a few years after its inauguration. However, as observed above, the bones of Orestes signify not a policy shift but a policy continuation; thus we have no reason to place the retrieval of Teisamenus before the expedition to Sicyon.

As noted above, Leahy argues that Sparta's motive for relocating Teisamenus was to secure an alliance with the Achaeans. But Pausanias, our sole ancient source for the incident, says nothing of the sort. Pausanias says merely that Sparta recovered Teisamenus' remains after consultation with the oracle of Apollo at Delphi. While it has been commonly observed that the appropriation (or, as the Spartans would put it, repatriation) of Teisamenus parallels that of Orestes, the role of Delphi has not received adequate attention. The Spartans asked Delphi how they could *defeat* (not "ally with") Tegea; after acquiring Orestes' bones, the Spartans achieved their goal, and then procured an alliance that was to their advantage. Thus, in brief, the recovery of Orestes signaled Spartan expansion into Arcadia. A few years later, the Spartans returned to the oracle and were directed to recover Teisamenus' bones from Helice. It is reasonable to assume that the Spartans put a similar question to Apollo: "How can we become masters of Achaea?" The acquisition of Teisamenus, like that of Orestes, served notice to a region of the Peloponnese (this time Achaea) that the Spartans aspired to hegemony over it.

The other attested contemporary instance of Spartan activity in the neighborhood of Helice, the ouster of Aeschines of Sicyon, corroborates this interpretation while militating against the orthodox view. Rather than placing the appropriation of Teisamenus before (Leahy) or after (Hammond) the Sicyonian campaign, I would link the two and hypothesize that the same expedition, under Chilon and Anaxandridas, both recovered Teisamenus' bones and deprived Aeschines of his tyranny: Helice, we may note, was located only about 30 miles northwest of Sicyon along the Achaean shore. This campaign produced mixed results: Helice did not consent to ally with Sparta; Sicyon, her tyrant deposed by Sparta and presumably replaced by a government friendly to Sparta, did.[54]

---

[53] It is not necessary to downdate the transplantation of Teisamenus to the late sixth century, as do Parke and Wormell 1956, 1: 96.

[54] Griffin 1982: 60.

AGAMEMNON OF SPARTA

Thus in the decade 560–550 Sparta acquired the bones of Orestes and those of his son Teisamenus. Starting in the sixth century, and continuing in the fifth, Sparta broadcast her claim to Orestes' father Agamemnon as well. The Homeric tradition unequivocally placed Agamemnon's seat at Mycenae, while portraying his brother Menelaus as king at Sparta.[55] The Spartans concurred with Homer as to Menelaus: a shrine to Menelaus and Helen (the Menelaion at Therapne, 1.5 miles from Sparta) was active and receiving dedications by ca. 700. But by the middle of the sixth century, consistent with the appropriations of Orestes and Teisamenus, the Spartans were claiming Agamemnon too. Stesichorus (b. Ol. 37 = 632–629, d. Ol. 56 = 556–553: Suda s.v. Στησίχορος) composed an *Oresteia* in which he manipulated several aspects of the Homeric tradition concerning Orestes and Agamemnon.[56] In this work, Stesichorus challenged the Homeric provenance of Agamemnon, locating his palace not at Mycenae but in Lacedaemon.[57] The evidence that Stesichorus visited Sparta, and may in fact have composed the *Oresteia* there for a festival, is strong.[58] The combination of these factors with Stesichorus' dates given by the Suda supports the conclusion that Stesichorus visited Sparta near the end of his life, and there composed for the Spartans an *Oresteia* which corroborated what was becoming the official Spartan history of Orestes' family.[59]

In the early fifth century, Pindar confirmed the Spartan origins of Orestes and further refined the Spartan version of Agamemnon. In *Pythian* 11 (composed in 478) Pindar gives Orestes the epithet "Laconian" (Λάκωνος Ὀρέστα, v. 16), and in *Nemean* 11 (date unknown) Orestes comes from Amyclae, one of the constituent villages of the *polis* of Sparta (Ἀμύκλαθεν γὰρ ἔβα σὺν Ὀρέστα, v. 34). In lines 31–2 of *Pythian* 11, Pindar places not only Orestes, but also Agamemnon, in Amyclae, asserting that Amyclae was the site of Agamemnon's death: θάνεν μὲν αὐτὸς ἥρως Ἀτρεΐδας / ἵκων χρόνῳ κλειταῖς ἐν Ἀμύκλαις. Agamemnon was killed by Clytemnestra after his return home from the Trojan War (an aspect of the story not contested by Pindar: see *P.* 11.17ff.); thus Pindar places the royal seat of Agamemnon (and Orestes) at Amyclae.

As Bowra observes,[60] Pindar's location of the home of Agamemnon and Orestes specifically in Amyclae (narrowing down from Stesichorus' "Lacedaemon") represents a further development of the Spartan version of the myth, and in all

---

[55] Agamemnon: *Il.* 1.30, 2.108 (above, p. 310); *Od.* 3.304–5. Menelaus: *Il.* 2.581ff.; *Od.* 1.285, 11.460.

[56] Bowra 1961: 113ff. *Inter alia*, Stesichorus identified Agamemnon as the son of Pleisthenes as well as the son of Atreus, thereby downplaying his Atreid (i.e., Argive) origins.

[57] Σ Eur. *Or.* 46: Ὅμηρος δὲ ἐν Μυκήναις φησὶν εἶναι τὰ βασίλεια τοῦ Ἀγαμέμνονος, Στησίχορος δὲ καὶ Σιμωνίδης ἐν Λακεδαίμονι.

[58] Bowra 1961: 107, 115–9.

[59] Fr. 212 Davies of Stesichorus' *Oresteia* begins, τοιάδε χρὴ Χαρίτων δαμώματα καλλικόμων ὑμνεῖν "We must sing such public songs of the fair-tressed Graces." According to Bowra, Stesichorus' use of δαμώματα (glossed by Σ Ar. *Pax* 797 as τὰ δημοσίᾳ ᾀδόμενα) distances the poet from what he sings; namely, the Spartan version of the Agamemnon-Orestes myth. I am not sure that this is correct, but at any rate what is important here is not Stesichorus' personal opinion, but the official Spartan position which Stesichorus is propagating.

[60] Bowra 1961: 113.

probability Pindar's choice of Amyclae was prompted by the presence of a "Tomb of Agamemnon" located there (Paus. 3.19.6: Ἀγαμέμνονος νομιζόμενον μνῆμα).[61] Sparta had originally coalesced from four villages (Pitana, Mesoa, Limnae, and Conooura) in the ninth century. Amyclae, the fifth village, located five miles south of the original cluster of four, was incorporated later, by ca. 750;[62] perhaps the men of Amyclae fostered the cult of Agamemnon in an attempt to counteract their status as (relative) newcomers and assert their antiquity and legitimacy within the Spartan *polis*.

Why should Pindar sing of Agamemnon and Orestes as sons of Amyclae? Neither the eleventh *Pythian* (in honor of Thrasydaeus of Thebes, winner of the boys' stadium race) nor the eleventh *Nemean* (celebrating Aristagoras of Tenedos' appointment as πρύτανις) was composed for a Spartan. Pindar himself was a Boeotian from Cyno-scephalae. To the question *Cui bono?* the answer, therefore, is *Nemini*. The poet had no particular reason to honor Sparta in these odes, either for his own sake or to gratify the honorands. Thus, the fact that he calls Orestes and Agamemnon Spartans shows that, by the early fifth century, the Spartan version of their origins was gaining accept-ance abroad (and making headway against the Homeric). Not surprisingly, the spread of the "Spartan recension" of the Agamemnon-Orestes myth parallels the expansion of the Peloponnesian League, which, by the time of Xerxes' invasion in 480, included practically the entire peninsula save Argos and Achaea, plus Aegina and Megara.[63]

CONCLUSION

In light of the evidence presented above, I conclude that the appropriation of the bones of Orestes signals not a new direction in Spartan relations with pre-Dorians, but a con-tinuation and expansion of existing policy. The Spartans acquired Orestes' bones, as directed by the oracle of Apollo at Delphi, so that they could avenge their defeat in the First Tegean War. The retrieval of Orestes' bones thus proclaimed that the Spartans had not abandoned their designs on Arcadia. Proponents of the orthodox view, that the relocation of Orestes heralded a new official Spartan stance as protectress of pre-Dorians, infer this supposed significance from the subsequent Spartan decision to end the Second Tegean War by treaty (rather than pressing on for the helotization of Tegea), and from still later Spartan alliances with Peloponnesian states further north. This is *post hoc ergo propter hoc* reasoning. The first expansionist act by Sparta outside Laconia had been the conquest and helotization of her Messenian neighbors. However, as their ambitions expanded to embrace the Peloponnese as a whole, the Spartans realized that it was more feasible to establish a hegemonic system of

---

[61] For the cult of Agamemnon at Amyclae (dating from ca. 700, thus contemporaneous with the cult of Menelaus at Therapne) see Osborne 1996: 289, 375 with references. Cartledge 1972: 139 hypothesizes that worship of Agamemnon at Amyclae may have begun ca. 550, coinciding with Stesichorus' depiction of a Spartan Agamemnon.

[62] Ca. 750: Forrest 1968: 32; Huxley 1962: 24. First half of the eighth century: Cartledge 1972: 94. Kennell 1995: 162–9 has challenged this traditional date and argued for an incorporation of Amyclae into Sparta during the reign of Augustus.

[63] On the membership of the Peloponnesian League see de Ste. Croix 1972: 333–8.

alliances (which we now call the Peloponnesian League) than to reduce the entire peninsula by force of arms. This change in policy – from conquest by the spear to hegemony by the treaty – occurred not suddenly but gradually. We can discern an intermediate stage in the seeds of the Peloponnesian League planted by Sparta in the 550s: first at Tegea and then at Sicyon, the former was a necessary prerequisite of the latter.

In the middle of the sixth century, Sparta not only appropriated Orestes but usurped the entire Agamemnonid branch of the Atreidae. The purpose of this Agamemnonid propaganda campaign was to announce, and legitimize, Sparta's intent to achieve hegemony over the entire Peloponnese. As Sparta extended her sphere of influence northward, each major step was accompanied by a retrieval of Agamemnonid bones and effected by an employment of armed force which facilitated the opening of diplomatic relations. The first step was Arcadia in the central Peloponnese: Sparta recovered the bones of Orestes, defeated Tegea, and concluded a treaty of peace and alliance. A friendly (or at least compliant) Arcadia was the prerequisite for Sparta's next move, into the northern Peloponnese and Achaea. There an expedition led by Chilon the ex-ephor and Anaxandridas the king recovered the bones of Teisamenus from Helice, deposed Aeschines, the non-Dorian (and presumably, like his predecessor Cleisthenes, anti-Dorian) tyrant of Sicyon, and brought Sicyon into alliance with Sparta.

At the same time, Sparta was also asserting her claim to Agamemnon. In this case, no reinterment was necessary, since Amyclae already boasted what the locals claimed was his tomb. Confronted, however, by a contradictory Homeric tradition, Sparta had to convince the Greeks that Agamemnon was hers. Her rival for Agamemnon, and for the leadership of the Peloponnese, was Argos. By supplanting Argos as the recognized home of Agamemnon, Sparta could undermine the Argive claim to hegemony and corroborate her own.

Unlike Tegea and Helice, and like Sparta, Argos was a Dorian city. What has been called the "bones of Orestes" policy – what I would call the "Agamemnonid" policy – thus transcended ethnic distinctions, and advertised Sparta as the rightful heir to the hegemony of all inhabitants of the Peloponnese, Dorian and pre-Dorian alike. Viewed in their proper context as elements of this policy, the appropriations of Orestes and Teisamenus had nothing to do with ethnicity and everything to do with geography. For Sparta to win the hegemony of the Peloponnese, she had to establish a presence among the non-Dorian Arcadians and Achaeans, and decisively to relegate Dorian Argos to a subordinate position; in pursuit of each of these goals Sparta employed Agamemnonid propaganda.

In 494 Sparta defeated Argos at the battle of Sepeia. This loss, coming half a century after Argos' defeat at the Battle of the Champions, sounded the death-knell for Argive ambitions in the Peloponnese, and confirmed Sparta as undisputed hegemon. Outside Laconia, the Agamemnon myth was adjusted to reflect current reality: Spartan military success lent credence (or at least acquiescence) to the Spartan version of Agamemnon, which now posed a serious enough threat to the Homeric version to be accepted by Pindar. If the Argives protested, few listened: by decisively defeating Argos, Sparta had not only seized the mantle of leadership in the Peloponnese but also vindicated her claim to Agamemnon.

The battle of Sepeia was the culminating incident in a process which had started with the Spartan defeat of Tegea. In the first half of the sixth century, the Peloponnesian balance of power rested in a fragile equilibrium between Sparta and Argos. Beginning with the Second Tegean War, continuing through the second half of the sixth century, and culminating in the battle of Sepeia, Sparta successfully displaced Argos and established her hegemony of the Peloponnese, which was to last until the battle of Leuctra in 371.

WORKS CITED

Adcock, F.E. 1930. "The Peloponnesian League." In J.B. Bury, S.A. Cook, and F.E. Adcock, eds., *The Cambridge Ancient History*. Vol. 4. Cambridge. 71–5.

Boedeker, D. 1993. "Hero Cult and Politics in Herodotus: The Bones of Orestes." In C. Dougherty and L. Kurke, eds., *Cultural Poetics in Archaic Greece*. Cambridge. 164–77.

Bowra, C.M. 1961. *Greek Lyric Poetry*. 2nd ed. Oxford.

Braun, T.F.R. G. 1994. "ΧΡΗΣΤΟΥΣ ΠΟΙΕΙΝ." *CQ* n.s. 44: 40–5.

Bury, J.B. 1951. *A History of Greece to the Death of Alexander the Great*. 3rd ed. Rev. by R. Meiggs. London.

Bury, J.B. and R. Meiggs. 1975. *A History of Greece to the Death of Alexander the Great*. 4th ed. London.

Cartledge, P. 1972. *Sparta and Lakonia*. London.

de Ste. Croix, G.E.M. 1972. *The Origins of the Peloponnesian War*. London.

Dickins, G. 1912. "The Growth of Spartan Policy." *JHS* 32: 1–42.

Forrest, W.G. 1968. *A History of Sparta 950–192 B.C.* New York.

Griffin, A. 1982. *Sikyon*. Oxford.

Hall, J.M. 1997. *Ethnic Identity in Greek Antiquity*. Cambridge.

Hammond, N.G.L. 1982. "The Peloponnese." In J. Boardman and N.G.L. Hammond, eds., *The Cambridge Ancient History*. Vol. 3.3. 3rd ed. Cambridge. 321–59.

Henderson, J. 1991. *The Maculate Muse*. 2nd ed. Oxford 1991.

Huxley, G.L. 1962. *Early Sparta*. London.

How, W.W. and J. Wells. 1912. *A Commentary on Herodotus*. Oxford.

Huxley, G.L. 1962. *Early Sparta*. London.

Jacoby, F. 1944. "ΧΡΗΣΤΟΥΣ ΠΟΙΕΙΝ (Aristotle fr. 592 R.)." *CQ* 38: 15–6.

Jones, A.H.M. 1967. *Sparta*. Oxford.

Judeich, W. 1931. *Topographie von Athen*. Munich.

Kennell, N.M. 1995. *The Gymnasium of Virtue: Education and Culture in Ancient Sparta*. Chapel Hill.

Leahy, D.M. 1955. "The Bones of Tisamenus." *Historia* 4: 26–38.

———. 1955–56. "Chilon and Aeschines: A further consideration of Rylands Greek Papyrus fr. 18." *Bulletin of the John Rylands Library* 38: 406–35.

———. 1958. "The Spartan Defeat at Orchomenus." *Phoenix* 12: 141–65.

———. 1968. "The Dating of the Orthagorid Dynasty." *Historia* 17: 1–23.

Macan, R.W. 1895. *Herodotus: The Fourth, Fifth, and Sixth Books*. London.

Malkin, I. 1994. *Myth and Territory in the Spartan Mediterranean*. Cambridge.

Mayor, A. 2000. *The First Fossil Hunters*. Princeton.

Osborne, R. 1996. *Greece in the Making*. London.

Parke, H.W. and D.E.W. Wormell. 1956. *The Delphic Oracle*. 2 vols. Oxford.

Parker, R. 1998. "Cleomenes on the Acropolis." Oxford Inaugural Lecture, 12 May 1997. Oxford.

Peek, W. 1974. "Ein neuer spartanischer Staatsvertrag." *Abhandlungen der sächsischen Akademie der Wissenschaften zu Leipzig, Philologisch-historische Klasse*, Band 65, Heft 3. Berlin.

Sealey, R. 1976. *A History of the Greek City-States ca. 700–338 B.C.* Berkeley and Los Angeles.

Travlos, J. 1980. *Pictorial Dictionary of Ancient Athens*. New York.

Wade-Gery, H.T. 1929. "Sparta: The Beginnings of the League." In J.B. Bury, S.A. Cook, and F.E. Adcock, eds., *The Cambridge Ancient History*. Vol. 3. Cambridge. 565–7.

White, M. 1958. "The Dates of the Orthagorids." *Phoenix* 12: 2–14.

27

The Alleged Ostracism of Damon

Kurt A. Raaflaub

Damon, son of Damonides, of the deme Oa, was an influential fifth-century intellectual, best known as as a theoretician of music and advisor of Pericles.[1] According to a tradition which appears first in the *Athēnaiōn politeia*, he was ostracized; the date of his ostracism is uncertain.[2] Aristotle writes: when (in the 460s) Pericles was unable to compete with the generosity of his rival Cimon, Damon,

> who was thought to have suggested most of Pericles' measures, and was later ostracized for this very reason, suggested to him that since he could not match Cimon in private resources, he should give the people what was their own; Pericles accepted his advice, and arranged pay for the *dikastai*. Some say that the quality of *dikastai* declined, since it was always the ordinary people rather than the more respectable who took care to ensure that their names were included in the ballot for places on the juries. This was also the beginning of corruption of the *dikastai*.[3]

Plutarch, the only author to pick up this tradition, mentions Damon's ostracism on three occasions. Commenting on the ostracism of Aristides, he says,

> As for the penalty of ostracism, this could be inflicted upon anyone who was regarded as standing above the common level in prestige, in birth, or in eloquence. It was for this reason, for example, that Damon, Pericles' teacher, was ostracized, because he was considered to be a man of extraordinary intellectual power. (*Arist.* 7.1).

---

[1] On Damon, see, e.g., Raubitschek 1955a; Schachermeyr 1969; Meister 1973; Podlecki 1998: 19–23, and soon, I hope, Wallace forthcoming(b). On the deme's name, see Dow 1963; Rhodes 1981: 341; Chambers 1990: 268. For my present purpose it does not matter whether or not Damon can properly be called a "sophist": see Wallace 1991: 51 (*pro*); Stadter 1991: 117 n. 21 (*contra*). Nor does it matter here whether the *Ath. Pol.* is the work of Aristotle or his school.

[2] See below at nn. 52–53.

[3] Aristotle, *Ath. Pol.* 27.4 (tr. G. M. Moore), speaking here of Damonides of Oia. Plutarch and the ostraca (below) prove that the person's name was Damon son of Damonides. On the name form and the identity of Damon and Damonides, see Carcopino 1935: 136–37; Meister 1973: 35–38; Rhodes 1981: 341–42; Chambers 1990: 268. On the interpretation of Aristotle's statement: Carcopino 1935: 141–42. Carcopino's suggestion (ibid. 138–40), that the crucial passage containing the reference to Damon's ostracism (from *hos edokei* to *hysteron*) is a late interpolation not known to Plutarch, has largely been ignored by editors and commentators.

In *Pericles* (4.2–4), Plutarch elaborates:

> His teacher in music ... was Damon ... This Damon appears to have been a sophist
> of the highest order, who used his musical teaching as a screen to conceal his real
> talents from the world in general; in fact it was he who trained Pericles for his
> political contests, much as a masseur or trainer prepares an athlete. However,
> Damon's lyre did not succeed in imposing upon the Athenians, and he was
> banished by ostracism on the grounds of being a great intriguer and supporter of
> tyranny, and he also became a target for the comic poets. At any rate Plato, the
> comic dramatist, makes one of his characters speak these lines to him: 'First of all
> answer my question, I beg you, / for you are the Chiron, they say, who tutored
> Pericles'.[4]

Finally, in *Nicias* (6.1) Plutarch argues,

> while the people were ready to make use of men who excelled in eloquence or
> intellectual power, they still looked on them with suspicion and constantly strove to
> humble their pride or detract from their reputation. There were unmistakable
> examples of this in the fining of Pericles, the ostracism of Damon, the distrust of
> Antiphon of Rhamnus which brought about his downfall.[5]

The evidence seems as clear as it could be. *Pericles* 9.2 confirms that Plutarch used
Aristotle. Moreover, by now four ostraca with Damon's name have been found,
apparently supporting the literary reports.[6] Doubts about the historicity of Damon's
ostracism, voiced most thoroughly by Jérôme Carcopino almost a century ago, have
been rejected by most scholars: "doubt is unnecessary," judges Peter Rhodes, and
Robert Wallace argues eloquently for the tradition's reliability.[7] Still, I am not convinced. Certainty, of course, is impossible in such matters; it is always easier to argue
for holding on to a seemingly well-established historical tradition than for rejecting it;
and new discoveries (of hoards of ostraca or a papyrus text, for example) may provide
us with new information that will force us to revise our assessment. But we need to
work with what we have. And what we have at present seems to me to urge skepticism. I will first examine the literary tradition about Damon himself and his ostracism,
then discuss the value of the four Damon ostraca as evidence for an actual ostracism,
proceed to question the probability that a person like Damon could be a serious
candidate for an ostracism, and finally place the tradition about Damon's ostracism in

---

[4] Stadter 1991: 117 thinks that these detailed comments and those in 9.2 "are derived entirely from the
notices in Plato, Aristotle, and Plato the comic poet. The apparent additions, where Plutarch speaks of
Damon as a top-notch sophist (*akros sophistēs*) who used the lyre as a shield, are a reworking and
elaboration of Plato's description, through the mouth of Protagoras, of how sophists had protected
themselves from hostility, and provide no new information" (*Prot.* 339a–e). See ibid. n. 21 on a passage
in Olympiodorus to which Wallace 1991: 50 and forthcoming(a), attaches some significance. On the
comic fragment (no. 207 *PCG* [Kassel and Austin 1989]), see Schwarze 1971: 160–64; the interpretation
suggested by Fornara and Samons 1991: 160–61 presumes the historicity of the ostracism.

[5] Tr. Scott-Kilvert for all of Plutarch's testimonia, on which see the critical remarks by Carcopino
1935: 137–41.

[6] See now Willemsen and Brenne 1991: 150; Siewert 2002: 37.

[7] Rhodes 1981: 342; Wallace forthcoming(a). Doubts: Carcopino 1905; 1935: 125–42; cf. recently,
e.g., Mattingly 1991: 22.

the context of reports about political attacks on other persons, especially intellectuals and associates of Pericles.

First of all, an early and very substantial body of evidence conveys the impression that Damon enjoyed a strongly positive reputation. Isocrates describes him as "in his day the most sensible among the citizens," and Plato, no admirer of Pericles, talks of Damon and his theories several times without criticizing him or saying anything about negative public reactions to Damon's teaching or his relationship to Pericles.[8] Neither author mentions Damon's ostracism. In fact, in the extant tradition, the alleged ostracism is intimately linked to Damon's influence on Pericles. Whenever Damon and his theories are discussed without distinct reference to Pericles, the supposed ostracism is not mentioned at all. Furthermore, the tradition about the ostracism appears in close connection with, on the one hand, nasty criticism of the detrimental influence of Pericles' demagogic measures on the character of the Athenian citizens (*Ath. Pol.* 27.4) and, on the other hand, attacks on his tyrannical ambitions (Plut. *Per.* 4). The former originated in aristocratic circles opposing "radical" democracy,[9] the latter among comic poets, one of whom Plutarch quotes explicitly. Neither source of such criticism is trustworthy; both, in fact, are responsible for much misinformation that was picked up uncritically by later authors and eventually became firmly embedded in "historical tradition." It might be possible, therefore, that the tradition of Damon's ostracism originated, for example, in a comic joke that was misinterpreted or taken seriously by a fourth-century author, or in the polemics of an anti-democratic pamphlet.[10] From both sources, such "information" could have found its way into the *Athēnaiōn Politeia.* I shall return to this later.

Now it has long been recognized that an early fourth-century work must have contained a reference to Damon's "banishment." Polycrates, a sophist and orator who was rather famous at his time, published a fictitious accusation of Socrates, in which Anytus, one of the prosecutors in the historic trial of Socrates, appears as the speaker; hence this speech was later misunderstood as that given at the real trial. Polycrates' speech can be dated firmly to the end of the 390s. Its appearance prompted a flurry of pro-Socratic publications, including Xenophon's *Apology* and the first two chapters of the *Memorabilia* which offer a concise refutation of Polycrates' *katēgoria.* That the latter was a "Schmähschrift" of the worst sort that mixed truth and fiction *ad libitum* is hardly doubtful. But this affects the current argument only indirectly. What matters here is that centuries later Libanius wrote a "Defense of Socrates," which responds in great detail to Polycrates' attack and permits us to reconstruct the argument fairly reliably.[11]

---

[8] Isocr. 15 (*Antidosis*) 235 (*phronimōtatos tōn politōn*); Plato, *La.* 180d, 197d; *Pol.* 400b, 424c; cf. Ps. Pl. *Alk. I* 118c; *Ax.* 364a. The testimonia and fragments are collected in Diels and Kranz 1961 no. 37 (pp. 381–84); Wallace 1991.

[9] A famous example is Plato, *Gorg.* 515e.

[10] Wallace forthcoming(a) admits this possibility for the alleged reason that Damon was too smart for the demos' taste but insists on the historicity of the ostracism itself.

[11] Lib. *Decl.* 1: *Apologia Socratis.* On Polycrates' "Accusation of Socrates," its relation to Xenophon's Socratic writings, and the debate about Socrates it prompted, see, e.g., Blass 1892: 365ff., esp. 368–70;

Polycrates, writing a fictitious, not an actual, forensic oration, was able to exploit political arguments that the amnesty decree of 403 prohibited Anytus and his colleagues from using in 399. Hence, according to Libanius, he made much of Socrates' opposition to democracy and his responsibility, as the teacher of Alcibiades and Critias, for the harm these two politicians later caused their community, expounding on the generally detrimental influence of sophists on politicians. Libanius then mentions Pericles, whose closeness to sophists the people tolerated to the remarkable extent that they even yielded to his request to free his teacher Anaxagoras from prison, and continues:

> Damon, however, if he did wrong, was thrown out (*ekbeblētai*) rightly; but if he was accused wrongly it would be better for him not to have suffered this rather than for Socrates [to have suffered what he did] because of him. At any rate, he [i.e., the accuser, Anytus or Polycrates] says that Damon was driven out (*exelathēnai*) because of less serious accusations and that he was not, like the current defendant [i.e., Socrates], accused by his enemies of aiming at subverting democracy. This [says Libanius] only proves that he [Damon] had more moderate opponents; nothing speaks against the possibility that one person is accused justly for smaller, another unjustly for larger offenses.[12]

Polycrates obviously used the case of Damon as a precedent to urge the harshest possible punishment for Socrates: Damon had been exiled for minor causes, while Socrates, accused of subverting democracy, deserved much worse. The words Libanius uses (once himself, the other time apparently quoting Polycrates) are "to throw out" (*ekballō*) and "to drive out" (*exelaunō*), both rather unspecific for an ostracism. Scholars usually assume that Polycrates meant "to ostracize," and indeed these verbs do occasionally have this meaning, but only, it seems, in contexts in which the focus on ostracism is obvious anyway.[13] But in this particular passage the association with ostracism is neither given nor natural, unless Polycrates took knowledge of Damon's ostracism among his readers for granted. Since we do not know this, we must not assume it. At any rate, if Polycrates, an Athenian, wanted to make clear that Damon had been ostracized, that is, suffered a very specific and rare "punishment" familiar to every Athenian, he presumably would have used the specific term. It seems advisable, therefore, not to presume it as given that Polycrates meant to say that Damon had been ostracized. Where he got the information that Damon had been exiled, we do not know. But we should take note of two facts: one is that Libanius, presumably reacting to Polycrates' argument, mentions Damon's banishment immediately after talking about sophists as advisors of politicians and specifically about the relationship between sophists and Pericles; he too thus links Damon's misfortune to

---

Chroust 1955; id. 1957: esp. chaps. 4–6; Gebhardt 1957 and the bibliog. cited in Siewert 2002: 278 n. 3. "Schmähschrift": Erbse 1961: 265. Mixture of truth and fiction: Gebhardt 1957: 36–38.

[12] For a discussion of this passage, with bibliography, see Norbert Loidol in Siewert 2002: 278–83.

[13] [Andoc.] 4, *Ag. Alcibiades* 5 is a good example. The first part of this speech, probably written soon after the purported event (the ostracism of which Hyperbolus unexpectedly became a victim [Rhodes 1994]), focuses on ostracism. To make this clear, the author uses first "to be exiled for ten years" (2: *tēn polin deka etē pheugein*) and "to be ostracized" (3: *ostrakizesthai*), to be followed by different verbs such as "to be displaced, to leave this place, to be thrown out" (5: *methisthasthai, apienai, ekballesthai*).

his role as Pericles' advisor. The other is that Damon's fate is compared and contrasted here with Socrates'; so is, a few paragraphs earlier (153–54), the maltreatment of Anaxagoras, Protagoras, and Diagoras of Melos by the enraged Athenian demos. We should keep in mind that a series of stories about the persecution of fifth-century thinkers and writers by a democracy hostile to intellectuals quite likely originated in Socratic circles infuriated by the "murder" of their saintly master precisely by this democracy. I shall come back to this as well.

Still, there are the Damon ostraca – my second point of discussion. Many scholars take them as confirmation of the ostracism reported by the literary sources. Unfortunately, ostraca themselves, even in large numbers, prove only that votes were cast against a given person, not that this person was really ostracized.[14] We currently have almost 11,000 *ostraca*.[15] Nine *ostrakophoriai* are attested with certainty: five in the 480s, that of Themistocles in the late 470s, that of Cimon in 462, that of Thucydides in 443 (or 438, see below), and that of Hyperbolus around 417. Some more may have taken place, leaving weak or no traces in the literary record. Even if there were only nine, and only the quorum of 6000 participated in the voting each time, the ostraca we have at this point represent no more than 20% of the total cast.[16] Over 140 names are scribbled on these ostraca: an average of more than fifteen for nine *ostrakophoriai* or almost ten for, say, fifteen. Obviously, then, as we should expect in a contest in which any citizen could be targeted, stray votes were cast for a considerable number of persons, some serious candidates for the "honor," others obviously not. Moreover, the extant ostraca cannot be considered a statistically representative sample. Among those who were actually ostracized, Megacles so far has 4662 and Themistocles 2279, but Aristides 121 and Hyperbolus only 3; among the "unsuccessful" candidates who must have attracted a great many votes, Pericles so far stands with only three.[17]

The relevance of all this for Damon's case is obvious. Although further ostraca with his name may some day appear,[18] both those recovered so far and those still to be found can easily be explained as stray votes, most likely cast in the great contest between Pericles and Thucydides in 443 or, if we follow Peter Krentz and Harold Mattingly, in or shortly after 438.[19] In a compelling "experiment," Mattingly demonstrates that on archaeological and historical grounds most of the preserved ostraca can readily be grouped into assemblies centered on the big and well-attested

---

[14] Hands 1959: 74.

[15] For preliminary surveys, see Willemsen and Brenne 1991; Siewert 2002: 27–55; the ostraca found in the Agora have been published by Lang 1990; for recent finds on the Agora, only tentatively incorporated by Siewert (2002: 31 with n. 24), see Camp 1999: 268–74.

[16] Phillips 1990: 136–37. I accept the view that the quorum of 6000 concerned the total of votes cast, not the minimum required for a person to be ostracized: see, e.g., Phillips 1982: 22–23; Martin 1989: 132 (with bibliog.). If the opposite were correct (as argued by Lehmann 1981: 94–97) a "victory" of Damon in an ostracism would appear even less plausible: see below at nn. 22ff.

[17] For the numbers and distribution (Agora vs. Kerameikos), see Lang 1990; Willemsen and Brenne 1991; Siewert 2002: 31–55.

[18] But, if my overall argument is correct, hardly in such great numbers as Wallace forthcoming(a) expects.

[19] Krentz 1984; Mattingly 1991: 17–20. Damon: Mattingly, 22.

ostrakophoriai. Two byproducts of his study seem important here. One is that even large numbers of votes cast for a person who is not attested in literary sources as the victim of an ostracism can easily be explained as having been cast against the second or third "candidate" in a given *ostrakophoria.*[20] Hence it is unnecessary to postulate a separate *ostrakophoria* where such a person would have emerged as the victor, which in turn decreases the likelihood that many more such events took place than are securely attested. The other is that many of the recipients of stray votes can be identified as relatives or supporters of the prominent leader actually ostracized in a given contest, or of his closest rival. Among these is at least one person who perhaps played a role comparable to Pericles' Damon: Mnesiphilos Phrearrios, Themistocles' trusted advisor who supposedly devised the Salamis strategy, appears in the list with twelve ostraca compared to Themistocles' over 2200 (although it is uncertain how many of these are to be assigned to any of the several *ostrakophoriai* in which Themistocles must have "participated").[21] Overall, then, Damon's ostraca, especially in their small quantity, are unable to bear the burden of confirming, let alone proving, that Damon was actually ostracized. The argument for or against this event thus needs to be made entirely on literary and historical grounds.

This brings up the third question: how plausible is it that a person like Damon would actually have fallen victim to an ostracism? Ostracism, we should remember, was not a trial ending in a conviction; rather, it was, as Martin Dreher puts it, a "negative election" or, according to Robert Connor, an "inverted popularity contest" or, as Peter Rhodes suggests, "a means of choosing between rival political leaders and removing the less popular."[22] Whatever its original purpose, in the perception of late fifth- and early fourth-century authors it was an instrument to bring down those who were perceived or presented as rising too high above their fellow citizens, by being too powerful themselves or at least powerful enough to prevent the demos' favorite politician from realizing his policies, or by setting themselves above the law.[23] On present evidence, there is no way to cast Damon in such a role.

If, which is entirely uncertain, procedures in the fifth century corresponded roughly to those in the late fourth that are described in the extant sources, the people were asked once a year whether they wanted to hold an *ostrakophoria;* if this vote was positive, a few weeks later the vote was held, without official announcement of candidates and without a preceding debate.[24] The interval between the first and the

---

[20] Thus, for example, the 760 (now 774: Siewert 2002: 42) ostraca of Kallias Kratiou in the ostracism of Megakles in 486 (Mattingly 1991: 2–4) or the 127 (now 125: Siewert, 44) of Kleippides Deiniou in 438 (Mattingly, 21).

[21] Numbers: Siewert 2002: 49, 54. Mattingly 1991: 3–5 dates the Mnesiphilos ostraca and a good number of those for Themistocles to Megacles' ostracism in 486. On Mnesiphilos: Hdt. 8.57–58; Plut. *Them.* 2.6.

[22] Dreher 2000: 77; Connor 1971: 73; Rhodes 1994: 92. On the procedures involved, see, e.g., Phillips 1982: 22–23; Brenne 1994.

[23] See Rosivach 1987.

[24] For the dates in the late fourth century, see *Ath. Pol.* 43.5; Philoch. *FGrH* 328 F 30. Errington 1994: esp. 151–58, points out rightly that these dates were fixed legally only in the late fourth century and that we know almost nothing about procedures in the fifth.

second vote was perhaps intended to give every citizen, even those from distant demes who might not have participated in regular assemblies, a chance to be present on voting day.[25] The vote was completely open: any citizen could be targeted. Moreover, the quorum of 6000 was high, probably much higher than the average attendance rate at assembly meetings in the fifth century, and even if the winner received barely half of all the votes cast his winning number might still be larger than the total of the votes cast in an average assembly.[26] We should certainly not underestimate the impact of polemics, propaganda, organized campaigning, and attempts at influencing the vote; the schedule offered plenty of time for such activities, and they are attested impressively by the find of 190 unused ostraca with Themistocles' name, written by fourteen hands, or by the machinations that sent Hyperbolus into exile instead of Alcibiades or Nicias who seemed the obvious candidates.[27] But given the unique conditions prevailing before and at an *ostrakophoria*, it would seem extraordinary, even highly unlikely, that a person would top the vote who was not constantly and highly visible in public affairs and whose career and political position or proposals were not at the time under intense scrutiny, much debated, and seriously challenged.[28] It is no accident, therefore, that all the certainly attested victims of an ostracism are indeed prominent or rather, among the most prominent political leaders that Athens had in the fifth century: they are members of the leading political families and persons who dominated politics or challenged the dominant politicians over a long time: apart from the first five who all became victims in the 480s, their list features the names of Themistocles, Cimon, Thucydides son of Melesias, and Hyperbolus. Most of the other persons who received votes and whom we can identify were prominent generals and politicians as well. As George Cawkwell puts it, "ostracism was a device for getting rid of political opponents, not political nonentities."[29]

To the best of our knowledge Damon was no politician; he never held an important office, and he never played a leading public role.[30] Not one of the other persons who are known to have been ostracized or whom ancient or modern scholars have suspected of having suffered this fate, fits this profile.[31] Even as an intellectual,

---

[25] Hands 1959: 72.

[26] Hansen 1987: 14–19. Hands 1959: 72; Lehmann 1981: 96–97 point out, though, that an ostracism must have been a sensational event, attracting extraordinary numbers of voters.

[27] Themistocles: Broneer 1938; Vanderpool 1970: 11–12; Lang 1990: 142–60; see also Camp 1999: 268. Hyperbolus: Rhodes 1994, who argues cogently that efforts to influence and organize the vote must have been normal; see also Phillips 1990.

[28] This argument was presented eloquently already by Carcopino 1935: 131–32.

[29] Cawkwell 1970: 39. Mattingly 1991 has gone a long way in establishing this.

[30] Faced with this dilemma, scholars tend to postulate that, since Damon *was* ostracized, he must have been, as Stadter 1991: 117 puts it, "politically active and belonged to a well-to-do family, with the wealth if not the lineage of other leading figures in mid-fifth century politics." What we *know* about Damon is summarized by Davies 1971: no. 3133 = 3143.

[31] On Menon Menekleidou Gargettios, who received a large number of votes in the late 470s or 460s, is mentioned by Hesychius as a possible victim ("Some say that Menon was ostracized"), and thus is often considered an actual victim (e.g., Raubitschek 1955b; Vanderpool 1970: 26), see now Mattingly 1991: 15–16, who identifies him with a member of a leading Athenian family, archon of 473/2, and

Damon, although attracting the attention of comedy, seems to have been much less in the limelight than Socrates, and it seems beyond doubt that one was not ostracized in Athens merely for being exceedingly brilliant.[32]

In this dilemma, another approach has been considered helpful. Both Aristotle and Plutarch suggest that even as advisor of a leading politician a person could be suspected of playing a subversive role and being a threat to the community. This interpretation has been picked up and developed further in modern scholarship. According to this line of reasoning, Greek thought assigned to music an immediate educational, ethical, and political function. Hence music was not an entirely private affair but of great significance for the community as well. Damon himself was well aware of this role of music. As Plato says in the *Republic,* those in charge of the city must make sure that education is not corrupted by innovations, not least in arts and singing: "one should be cautious in adopting a new kind of poetry and music, for this endangers the whole system. The ways of poetry and music (*mousikēs tropoi*) are not changed anywhere without change in the most important laws of the city, as Damon affirms and I believe."[33] Damon's connection with Pericles was generally known. Since his research into the effect of music on human behavior was not purely theoretical but influenced the advice he gave to Pericles, his activities could be represented as a subversive attempt to use music to manipulate the city. Here the theoretician and teacher assumed a political role and became vulnerable to political attacks, even to an ostracism.[34] According to a related view, Damon might have been ostracized because he advised Pericles in and thus was identified with several controversial projects that were directly related to his interests in music: the expansion and revision of the musical competitions at the Panathenaic Festival, the construction of a new music hall, the Odeion, and perhaps more generally the increase in the number of festivals; these projects were directly related to Pericles' position of power in Athens and to some extent entailed use of the tribute from the Delian League – issues that had aroused opposition before.[35]

For various reasons, these arguments do not seem compelling to me. One is that this explanation, although advocated already by the ancients, turns Damon's ostracism into yet another attack on one of Pericles' supporters and thus into an indirect attack on Pericles himself.[36] As we shall see below, the evidence supporting the success of such indirect attacks is highly doubtful.[37] The second reason is that even if Damon played the role assigned him here and did it very prominently, responsibility still

---

"runner-up" to Cimon in 462. For lists of suspected or disputed victims, see Phillips 1982: 28; Martin 1989: 138–41.

[32] So too Wallace forthcoming(a). On comedy, see Plutarch's statement and the fragment of Plato Comicus he quotes, above at n. 4.

[33] *Republic* 424b-c, tr. G. M. A. Grube.

[34] See esp. Wallace 1994: 139–42; forthcoming(a). On Damon's musical theories, see Anderson 1966: 74–81; Barker 1984: 168–69; West 1992: 243–49; Wallace forthcoming(b).

[35] Plut. *Per.* 11.4, 13.9–10, 13.11; Stadter 1991: 117; Schubert 1994: 101–2; Wallace forthcoming(a). On the use of tribute: Samons 2000: 41–50.

[36] Thus explicitly Raubitschek 1955a; Meister 1973: 32.

[37] See below at n. 55.

rested with Pericles himself, just as he without doubt claimed the popularity he gained from these projects. Hence it makes perfect sense that Damon received stray votes when his pupil and patron was under attack but not that he was ostracized himself. The third and most important reason is that Damon himself seems to have been quite unsuitable for the role of a person posing – or believed to be posing – a major threat to the city's and people's well-being.

True, the "Old Oligarch" points out that "the practice of physical exercise and the pursuit of music has been brought into disrepute (or driven out of fashion) by the common people as being undesirable because they realise that these accomplishments are beyond them." This, however, is a general statement, referring to elite commitment to traditional forms of gymnastics and music as it is confirmed by many other sources; that the demos was not interested in such pursuits should not be taken to mean that they were suppressed by state law or that the musical teachings of Damon and other theoreticians were formally banned.[38] Now those who had supported Pericles and voted for him when he introduced the debated cultural innovations as well as pay for the *dikastai* presumably had no gripes with Damon – if he indeed was involved in planning these innovations.[39] According to Libanius, for whatever it is worth, Polycrates emphasized that, unlike Socrates, Damon was not even accused by his enemies of trying to undermine the democracy.[40] Attacks against Damon thus must have originated in "conservative" or aristocratic circles – but it is hard to see why they should have feared or detested him either. Plato does ban one of the harmonies invented by Damon from his state because he considers it soft and sympotic but he does not mention him in this passage and generally speaks of him not critically but very positively. With good reasons: precisely because he believed in the influence of music on the formation of character and the political system, Damon apparently insisted on avoiding musical innovations and tried to advise those in power accordingly. One of his principal teachings – that by singing and playing the kithara boys should learn virtue, discipline, and justice – was quoted even centuries later.[41] It is not surprising, therefore, that Plato used and cited Damon's theories frequently, and we should conclude that the Athenian "conservatives" had no problems with Damon's teaching. In fact, it has even been suggested that Damon was ostracized because of his conservative and aristocratic views. This suggestion is essentially based on the fact that Damon wrote an *Areopagitikos,* but neither the title nor what little we know about the content of this speech seems to permit any firm conclusion about its political

---

[38] Ps. Xen. *Ath. Pol.* 1.13 (tr. Moore, with adaptations); the final part of the sentence is corrupt. On the interpretation of *katalelyken* and for parallels, see Frisch 1942: 211–13; cf. Grossmann 1950: 177. Connection with Damon: e.g., Raubitschek 1955a: 81, following Buecheler 1885: 312 (the passage refers to a time when "die Profession der Musik zu Athen von Staats wegen unterdrückt gewesen ist") and others; see also Stecchini 1950: 31–32.

[39] That Pericles depended on another person for the idea of the judges' pay may be an invention brought up by his antidemocratic detractors anyway: e.g., Meister 1973: 34–35; Rhodes 1981: 342; Podlecki 1998: 19; *contra:* Wallace forthcoming(a).

[40] Libanius, *Decl.* 1.157.

[41] Diels and Kranz 1961: no. 37 B4; Plato, *Rep.* 398e-99a; Plut. *De mus.* 16. 1136a; West 1992: 246–49 (see next n.).

tendency.[42] If it was conservative I cannot see how this could be reconciled with the role attributed to the same person of having advised Pericles to enact "radical" democratic reforms which, from the conservative perspective, were detrimental to Athens.[43] However all that may be, it should be clear by now that this whole issue is rather muddied. I suggest that Damon's function as advisor of Pericles is unlikely to have propelled him to a level of political prominence and notoriety that would have sufficed to make him a prime target, let alone a victim, of an *ostrakophoria.*

Plutarch gives a second reason for Damon's ostracism (*Per.* 4.3): he had the reputation of being fond of great deeds or designs and a "friend of tyrants" (*megalopragmōn, philotyrannos*).[44] Both charges obviously echo similar ones leveled against Pericles, and they probably originate in comedy. Damon himself, as Plutarch maintains, was the target of comic poets (ibid. 4); although we know of only one instance of this kind, quoted in the same passage, there may have been more.[45] Pericles, of course, was frequently attacked in comedy as would-be tyrant, Zeus, and Olympian.[46] I suspect, therefore, that in such comic jokes Damon was hit by a dose of anti-Periclean polemics and was himself blamed for the faults of his master pupil. Although massively exaggerated, such polemical criticism may later have been picked up by an orator or historian. Whether such a joke asserted that Damon had been "driven out," we do not know, but Polycrates may well have derived his "knowledge" from such a source. Alternatively, he may have reacted to an allusion to Damon in broadsides that after 399 were directed by followers of Socrates against the supposed anti-intellectualism of Athenian democracy that had caused the oppression in various ways of numerous artists and philosophers before Socrates.[47]

Now Polycrates also says that Damon suffered his fate because of less significant causes, offenses, or accusations (*ep' elattosin aitiais*) than Socrates. Combining this with the information gained from Plutarch's *Pericles* (above), Klaus Meister concludes that, unlike in the cases of Phidias, Anaxagoras, Aspasia and Pericles himself, there was no sufficient cause for a trial against Damon, "and this explains why they did not bring him to court but eliminated him by the less cumbersome means of an ostracism."[48] Given the procedures and openness of an ostracism, I consider this explanation highly unconvincing: it was difficult enough to manipulate an *ostrakophoria* even if the target was a highly prominent and notorious *public and political* figure; in the case of a person

---

[42] Conservative: Ryffel 1947: 34; Schachermeyr 1969: 197–203; West 1992: 246–47: "it sounds as if Damon wanted official action taken to curb the originality of contemporary music." Doubts: Ehrenberg 1954: 93; *contra:* Meister 1973: 39–43.

[43] As claimed in *Ath. Pol.* 27.4 (above at n. 3).

[44] *megalopragmōn* is not the same as *polypragmōn;* hence Wallace's translation, "a great meddler," seems mistaken.

[45] Stadter 1991: 116 n. 18 thinks that this might have been the only reference in comedy known to Plutarch; I do not see how this can be determined.

[46] Schwarze 1971: esp. 169–72; Podlecki 1998: 169–76.

[47] See below at n. 54. Aeschines of Sphettos (Athenaeus 220c-d) is a possible culprit: Wallace 1994: 131–32.

[48] Meister 1973: 43–44 (my tr.).

like Damon who seems to have been neither and apparently was hated neither by democrats nor by conservatives, it must have been hopeless.

Still, Meister's point is not negligible. Efforts to weaken a leading politician by targeting his supporters or persons closely attached to him usually prompted accusations in the courts. Why, then, did the source that shaped the information picked up by Aristotle think that Damon had been ostracized?[49] One might suspect that a few ostraca with his name, surfacing years after having been cast, prompted wrong conclusions.[50] But discarded ostraca, and broken sherds of pottery in general, must have been common in and around the Agora; hence sherds with Damon's name on them are unlikely to have attracted much attention at all.[51] The accusation preserved in Plutarch offers a clue: in Athens persons who had committed no specific crime but were suspected of fostering designs too great to be good for the community and of being "friends of tyrants or tyranny" were ostracized, not tried and convicted in court. With *megalopragmōn* and *philotyrannos* Plutarch's unknown source characterizes exactly the types of leaders who were prime targets of an ostracism. Hence it seems quite possible that not only the explanation for Damon's ostracism, but also the idea of this ostracism itself was, if not suggested by contemporary comic jokes, at least deduced later from such jokes.

Attempts to date the supposed ostracism of Damon have prompted much discussion. Wallace suggests the 440s when debates about Pericles' "cultural programs" were raging.[52] Other scholars think it fits best in a period when Pericles was weakened and under attack anyway, that is, in the late 430s, when he was brought to trial himself and, according to a widespread tradition, several of his associates or friends (Phidias, Anaxagoras, and Aspasia) became the targets of vicious assaults in and outside the courts.[53] This leads to my final point, the context in which the false tradition about Damon's ostracism ultimately originated.

Although I argue strongly for it, I am aware that on current evidence it is impossible to *prove* that the tradition about Damon's ostracism and the reasons that motivated it were derived from statements in late fifth-century comedy or in anti-democratic Socratic circles in the early fourth century. As a case of a false historical tradition originating in such sources, however, it would be far from unique. Kenneth Dover has shown that, with one or two exceptions, all reports on the persecution of intellectuals in fifth-century Athens rest on such flimsy evidence that they should be dismissed from the historical record. Enormously exaggerated or even baseless accusations of and attacks against intellectuals in comedy and philosophical treatises or pamphlets, especially on the part of resentful Socratics, tended to be picked up by

---

[49] So too Wallace forthcoming(a): "The very improbability of ostracizing a music theoretician lends credence to the tradition. Why should this have been invented?"

[50] See Mattingly 1991: 14.

[51] Written communication by James Sickinger.

[52] Wallace forthcoming(a).

[53] For discussion, see Meister 1973: 32.

orators, biographers, or historians and passed along as facts to later authors.[54] As I tried to demonstrate elsewhere, of the entire cluster of accusations and trials against Pericles' associates and Pericles himself, only the trial of Pericles in 430 and possibly an accusation against Phidias that did not result in a trial are likely to be authentic.[55]

Now the persecution of Anaxagoras, Protagoras, and Diagoras of Melos appears in Libanius' defense of Socrates (153–54) in the same context as Damon's exile. Polycrates apparently had used them as precedents: if the demos had punished these men in justified anger, and for lesser offenses, how much more did Socrates deserve to die for his crimes? Libanius turned the argument around in all these cases. The three sophists deserved to suffer for offending religion and religious sensibilities – but they were unsuitable as precedents because Socrates had no part in their offenses![56] Whether or not Damon suffered his punishment justly, he should never have been abused as a precedent because Socrates simply was not guilty! The context in which Polycrates mentions these cases should make us extremely cautious: in Greece as in Rome, the search for precedents offered much incentive for invention, falsification, and exaggeration.[57]

No doubt, in the second half of the fifth century a considerable amount of animosity arose against the views of some philosophers and sophists that were considered radical, extreme, and harmful to the community. Such sentiments were vented in comedy, attempts at restrictive legislation, and in other ways but, with very rare exceptions, they did not result in the oppression of the criticized personalities. That the conviction of Socrates was an exceptional event, made possible by specific circumstances, is generally agreed upon.[58] If, then, Anaxagoras, Protagoras, Prodicus, Euripides, and others were criticized, lampooned, attacked, and harassed but not oppressed by execution, banishment, or book burning, why should the case of Damon have been different?

In conclusion, then, the tradition about Damon's ostracism, although believed by respectable ancient authors, is open to serious doubts: Aristotle and especially Plutarch are known otherwise to have integrated information of dubious ancestry and credibility; they seem to have done it here as well. Polycrates, the earliest source, an Athenian who should have known, has Damon banished but not specifically ostracized – perhaps accidentally, perhaps not. "The cumulative weight of ancient evidence" thus is no argument for authenticity.[59] Damon's intelligence and his connection with Pericles as an advisor or teacher are insufficient causes for an ostracism. The ostraca with his name prove no more than that he received stray votes when larger fish were

---

[54] Dover 1976; accepted by Wallace 1994 and forthcoming(a), with the exception of Damon; see also id. 1996.

[55] Raaflaub 2000 with sources and bibliography.

[56] See Chroust 1955: 54–56.

[57] See for fourth-century Athens Habicht 1961; the annals of early Rome are full of stories that served as precedents in debates about late republican events; for a famous example, see Cornell 1986: 58–61 with bibliog. Wiseman 1993 does not identify this category among his types of mendacity in historiography.

[58] See recently Hansen 1995; Parker 1996: 199–217; Scholz 2000 (with more bibliog.).

[59] Wallace forthcoming(a) thinks differently.

fried. For a number of reasons he is a most unlikely candidate for an ostracism. Rather, I suggest, his undeniable closeness to and influence on Pericles prompted the exaggerated assumption that he was the mastermind behind several of Pericles' more controversial political projects. Hence comedy and perhaps antidemocratic pamphleteers made him co-responsible for the predilection for great schemes and tyrannical ambition for which Pericles was criticized and which contemporaries considered suitable causes for ostracism. Damon's advisee indeed became the target of ostracism and escaped it; Damon himself, later tradition thought, had become its victim. Moreover, early fourth-century (Socratic?) critics may have interpreted his presumed exile as yet another case of democracy's supposed hostility to intellectuals. It sufficed that one subsequent author took such comic and polemical claims for fact – as happened in other cases – and Damon's ostracism, assembled among the evidence cited in the *Athēnaiōn Politeia,* became an indelible part of historical tradition. This tradition, I conclude, should be stricken from our history books.[60]

WORKS CITED

Anderson, W.D. 1966. *Ethos and Education in Greek Music.* Cambridge, Mass.

Barker, A., ed. 1984. *Greek Musical Writings* I: *The Musician and His Art.* Cambridge.

Blass, F. 1892. *Die attische Beredsamkeit.* Vol. II. 3rd ed. Leipzig (repr. Hildesheim, 1962).

Brenne, S. 1994. "Ostraka and the Process of Ostrakophoria." In W.D.E. Coulson et al. eds., *The Archaeology of Athens and Attica under the Democracy.* Oxbow Monographs 37. Oxford. 13–24.

Broneer, O. 1938. "Excavations on the North Slope of the Acropolis, 1937." *Hesperia* 7: 161–263.

Buecheler, F. 1885. "*Hoi peri Damona.*" *RhM* 40: 309–12.

Burckhardt, L., and J. von Ungern-Sternberg, eds. 2000. *Grosse Prozesse im antiken Athen.* Munich.

Camp, J. McK. 1999. "Excavations in the Athenian Agora, 1996 and 1997." *Hesperia* 68: 255–83.

Carcopino, J. 1905. "Damon a-t-il été ostracisé?" *REG* 18: 415–29 (repr. in id. 1935: 125–42).

———. 1935. *L'ostracisme athénien.* Paris.

Cawkwell, G.L. 1970. "The Fall of Themistocles." In B.F. Harris, ed., *Auckland Classical Essays Presented to E. M. Blaiklock.* Auckland and Oxford. 39–58.

Chambers, M. 1990. *Aristoteles, Staat der Athener, übersetzt und erläutert.* Berlin.

Chroust, A.-H. 1955. "Xenophon, Polycrates and the 'Indictment of Socrates'." *C&M* 16: 1–77.

———. 1957. *Socrates: Man and Myth. The Two Socratic Apologies of Xenophon.* London.

Connor, W. R. 1971. *The New Politicians of Fifth-Century Athens.* Princeton.

Cornell, T.J. 1986. "The Value of the Literary Tradition concerning Archaic Rome." In K.A. Raaflaub, ed., *Social Struggles in Archaic Rome.* Berkeley and Los Angeles. 52–76.

Davies, J.K. 1971. *Athenian Propertied Families 600–300 B.C.* Oxford.

Diels, H., and W. Kranz. 1961. *Die Fragmente der Vorsokratiker.* Vol. I. 10th ed. Berlin.

Dover, K. J. 1976. "The Freedom of the Intellectual in Greek Society." *Talanta* 7: 24–54 (repr. in id. 1988: 135–58).

———. 1988. *The Greeks and Their Legacy: Collected Papers.* Vol. II. Oxford.

Dow, S. 1963. "The Attic Demes of OA and OE." *AJPh* 84: 161–81.

Dreher, M. 2000. "Verbannung ohne Vergehen. Der Ostrakismos (das Scherbengericht)." In Burckhardt and von Ungern-Sternberg 2000: 66–77, 262–64.

Ehrenberg, V. 1954. *Sophocles and Pericles.* Oxford.

Erbse, H. 1961. "Die Architektonik im Aufbau von Xenophons Memorabilien." *Hermes* 89: 257–87.

---

[60] I thank Mortimer Chambers, James Sickinger, and an anonymous referee for helpful comments and suggestions.

Errington, M. 1994. "*Ekklēsia kyria* in Athens." *Chiron* 24: 135–60.

Fornara, C.W., and L.J. Samons II. 1991. *Athens from Cleisthenes to Pericles.* Berkeley and Los Angeles.

Frisch, H. 1942. *The Constitution of the Athenians: A Philological-Historical Analysis of Pseudo-Xenophon's Treatise* De re publica Atheniensium. Copenhagen.

Gebhardt, E. 1957. *Polykrates' Anklage gegen Sokrates und Xenophons Erwiderung. Eine Quellenanalyse von Mem. 1.2.* Diss. Univ. of Frankfurt am Main.

Grossmann, G. 1950. *Politische Schlagwörter aus der Zeit des Peloponnesischen Krieges.* Diss. Univ. of Basel 1945. Zurich.

Habicht, C. 1961. "Falsche Urkunden zur Geschichte Athens im Zeitalter der Perserkriege." *Hermes* 89: 1–35.

Hands, A.R. 1959. "Ostraka and the Law of Ostracism – Some Possibilities and Assumptions." *JHS* 79: 69–79.

Hansen, M.H. 1987. *The Athenian Assembly in the Age of Demosthenes.* Oxford.

———. 1995. *The Trial of Socrates from the Athenian Point of View.* Det Kongelige Danske Videnskabernes Selskab. Historisk-filosofiske Meddelelser 71. Copenhagen (also in M. Sakellariou, ed., *Colloque international: Démocratie athénienne et culture.* Athens. 137–70).

Kassel, R., and C. Austin, eds. 1989. *Poetae Comici Graeci* (*PCG*) VII. Berlin.

Krentz, P. 1984. "The Ostracism of Thoukydides, Son of Melesias." *Historia* 33: 499–504.

Lang, M. 1990. *Ostraka.* The Athenian Agora, Vol. 25. Princeton.

Lehmann, G.A. 1981. "Der Ostrakismos-Entscheid in Athen: von Kleisthenes zur Ära des Themistokles." *ZPE* 41: 85–99.

Martin, A. 1989. "L'ostracisme athénien: un demi-siècle de découvertes et de recherches." *REG* 102: 124–45.

Mattingly, H.B. 1991. "The Practice of Ostracism at Athens." *Antichthon* 25: 1–26.

Meister, K. 1973. "Damon, der politische Berater des Perikles." *RSA* 3: 29–45.

Parker, R. 1996. *Athenian Religion: A History.* Oxford.

Phillips, D.J. 1982. "Athenian Ostracism." In G.H.R. Horsley, ed., *Hellenika: Essays on Greek Politics and History.* North Ryde NSW. 21–43.

———. 1990. "Observations on Some Ostraka from the Athenian Agora." *ZPE* 83: 123–48.

Podlecki, A. 1998. *Perikles and His Circle.* London.

Raaflaub, K.A. 2000. "Den Olympier herausfordern? Prozesse im Umkreis des Perikles." In Burckhardt and von Ungern-Sternberg 2000: 96–113, 266–70.

Raubitschek, A.E. 1955a. "Damon." *C&M* 16: 78–83.

———. 1955b. "Menon, Son of Menekleides." *Hesperia* 24: 286–89.

Rhodes, P.J. 1981. *A Commentary on the Aristotelian* Athenaion Politeia. Oxford.

———. 1994. "The Ostracism of Hyperbolus." In Robin Osborne and Simon Hornblower, eds., *Ritual, Finance, Politics: Athenian Democratic Accounts Presented to David Lewis.* Oxford. 85–98.

Rosivach, V. 1987. "Some Fifth and Fourth Century Views on the Purpose of Ostracism." *Tyche* 2: 161–70.

Ryffel, H. 1947. "Eukosmia. Ein Beitrag zur Wiederherstellung des Areopagitikos des Damon." *MH* 4: 23–38.

Samons, L.J. II. 2000. *Empire of the Owl: Athenian Imperial Finances. Historia* Einzelschrift 142. Stuttgart.

Schachermeyr, F. 1969. "Damon." In R. Stiehl and H.E. Stier, eds., *Beiträge zur Alten Geschichte und deren Nachleben: Festschrift für Franz Altheim.* Vol. I. Berlin. 192–204 (repr. in Schachermeyr, *Forschungen und Betrachtungen zur griechischen und römischen Geschichte.* Vienna 1974. 192–204).

Scholz, P. 2000. "Der Prozess gegen Sokrates. Ein 'Sündenfall' der athenischen Demokratie?" In Burckhardt and von Ungern-Sternberg 2000: 157–73, 276–79.

Schubert, C. 1994. *Perikles.* Darmstadt.

Schwarze, J. 1971. *Die Beurteilung des Perikles durch die attische Komödie.* Zetemata 51. Munich.

Siewert, P., ed. 2002. *Ostrakismos-Testimonien. Die Zeugnisse antiker Autoren, der Inschriften und Ostraka über das athenische Scherbengericht aus vorhellenistischer Zeit, 487–322 v. Chr. Historia* Einzelschriften 155. Stuttgart.

Stadter, P.A. 1991. "Pericles among the Intellectuals." *ICS* 16: 111–24.

Stecchini, L.C. 1950. *Athenaion Politeia. The Constitution of the Athenians, by the Old Oligarch and by Aristotle: A New Interpretation.* Glencoe IL.

Vanderpool, E. 1970. *Ostracism at Athens*. Lectures in Memory of Louise Taft Semple: second series, 1966–70. Cincinnati.

Wallace, R.W. 1991. "Damone di Oa ed i suoi successori: un' analisi delle fonti." In id. and B. MacLachlan, eds., *Harmonia Mundi.* Rome. 30–54.

———. 1994. "Private Lives and Public Enemies: Freedom of Thought in Classical Athens." In A. Boegehold and A. Scafuro, eds., *Athenian Identity and Civic Ideology.* Baltimore. 127–55.

———. 1996. "Book Burning in Ancient Athens." In R. Wallace and E. M. Harris, eds., *Transitions to Empire. Essays in Greco-Roman History, 360–146 B.C., in Honor of E. Badian.* Norman. 226–40.

———. Forthcoming(a). "Damon of Oa—A Music Theorist Ostracized?" In P. Wilson and P. Murray, eds., *Music and the Muses in Ancient Greece* (preliminary title). Oxford.

———. Forthcoming(b). *Damon of Oa: Music, Philosophy, and Politics in Democratic Athens.* In preparation.

West, M.L. 1992. *Ancient Greek Music.* Oxford.

Willemsen, F, and S. Brenne. 1991. "Verzeichnis der Kerameikos-Ostraka." *AM* 106: 147–56.

Wiseman, T.P. 1993. "Lying Historians: Seven Types of Mendacity." In C. Gill and T.P. Wiseman, eds., *Lies and Fiction in the Ancient World.* Austin. 122–46.

28

The Date of Pnyx III: *SEG* XII 87, the Law of Eukrates on Tyranny (337/6 B.C.)

M. B. Richardson

To bring up in conversation with Alan Boegehold a topic connected in any way with the classics is to set out on a promising path. The solid learning of his, now, seventy-five years is always on tap, as well as the curiosity and innovation that abound in his own studies and teaching. I have not quizzed him on the topic I take up here, but I thank him for strong lessons in rethinking first thoughts.

The law of Eukrates on tyranny, dated to the ninth prytany of 337/6 B.C., is the only known example of Athenian legislation ordered to be set up on the Pnyx. The publication clause directs the erection of two stelai inscribed with the law: "Set the one at the entrance into (the) Areopagos – the entrance leading into the Bouleuterion, for one going in – and the other in the Ekklesia."[1] Because these two descriptions pinpoint sites, the phrase ἐν τῆι ἐκκλησίαι serves here as a toponym, and study of the meeting-places of the Ekklesia establishes that the site it denotes is the Pnyx.[2] In what follows, I suggest that the instruction to "set ... the other stele in the Ekklesia," by providing evidence of the expected use of the Pnyx, might help to refine the closing date of the construction of Pnyx III.[3]

In applying this evidence to this purpose, I follow the lead of Homer Thompson, who brought to bear on the same question an anecdotal passage in Hypereides 5,

---

[1] *SEG* XII 87 (*Hesperia* 21 [1952]: 355–359, no. 5) lines 24–27: στῆσαι τὴμ μὲν ἐπὶ τ|ῆς εἰσόδου τῆς εἰς Ἄρειον Πάγον τῆς εἰς τὸ Βο|υλευτήριον εἰσιόντι, τὴν δὲ ἐν τῆι ἐκκλησί<α>|ι. My text, by autopsy, differs from the ed. pr. only in the marking of the final letter of line 26; cf. Meritt 1952: 356, text: ἐκκλησία; app. crit.: ΕΚΚΛΗΣΙΛ. For the various views about the identity of the Bouleterion named here, see Meritt 1952: 358; Meritt 1953; Thompson 1953: 51–52; Rhodes 1972: 32 n. 2.

[2] For evidence supporting this point, see below: pp. 333–334.

[3] A date in the third quarter of the 4th century B.C. is now generally accepted for the construction of Pnyx III. Immediately post-Chaironeia: Errington 1994: 149. Ca. 350–ca. 325 B.C.: Rotroff and Camp 1996: 275; Camp 1996: 41. Camp (in Rotroff and Camp 1996: 271–275, and see fig. 1), focusing on the retaining wall of Pnyx III, dates the wall before Chaironeia. Note, though, that the wall-building techniques that he convincingly argues were acquired by the Athenians between 346 and 338 B.C. could have been put to use on the Pnyx either before or after the battle.

in which Demosthenes was said to be sitting in his accustomed place "down below at the foot of the scarp (*katatome*)." The occasion was a meeting of the Ekklesia in 324 B.C.; by this time the assembly place must have been in use.[4]

The publication clause of *SEG* XII 87, I will argue, shows that Pnyx III was expected to be in use by the Ekklesia in late 337/6 B.C., a full twelve years before the occasion described by Hypereides.

By 337/6 B.C., the equation between the terms "Ekklesia" and "Pnyx" had a long history, documented by epigraphical evidence from all three phases of the Pnyx. From the period of Pnyx I, the boundary stone *IG* I³ 1092 (ℎόρο|ς Πυκ|[ν]ός) of ca. 450 B.C. designates a boundary of the meeting-place of the Ekklesia, not of the hill that it names.[5] Beginning in the mid-4th century B.C. in the period of Pnyx II, and continuing into the period of Pnyx III, the prescripts of Athenian decrees attest the persistent overlap of the terms "Ekklesia" and "Pnyx." Only occasionally in these prescripts is the meeting-place of the Ekklesia named,[6] and when it is – e.g., ἐν Διονύσου, ἐμ or ἐν Πειραιεῖ, ἐν τῶι θεάτρωι – it is never the Pnyx.[7] For as long as the convention had currency, the meeting-place of the Ekklesia was "on the Pnyx" unless it was otherwise stated.[8] The usage underscores, as few pieces of evidence could do,

---

[4] Thompson 1982: 144. Hypereides 5, fr. 3, col. 9 (Worthington): καθήμενος κάτω ὑπὸ τῇ κατατομῇ, οὗπερ εἴωθε καθῆσθαι. The interpretation of this *katatome* as a location on the Pnyx depends on the preceding narrative (fr. 3, col. 8 [Worthington]), which describes Demosthenes stepping forward to speak at a meeting of the Ekklesia (πρὸς [τὸν δῆμον, τότε παρελθὼν Δημ]οσθένης [διεξῆλθεν] μακρὸν [λόγον]), and on the description of Demosthenes' sitting-place as "his accustomed place." Thompson pointed to both pieces of evidence, now briefly noted and accepted by Worthington (1999: 189) and Whitehead (2000: 393); for argument that the reference to the Ekklesia (δῆμος) indicates a meeting on the Pnyx, see pp. 333–334. Thompson's inference that the Pnyx in this passage is in its third phase of construction is based on his interpretation, still the communis opinio (above, n. 3), that Pnyx III was built at a point in the 4th century after 350 B.C. (Thompson 1982: 144); he had earlier assigned the passage to the period of Pnyx II (Kourouniotes and Thompson 1932: 136).

[5] Thompson 1982: 137.

[6] Distinct from formulae naming the site of the Ekklesia's meeting are formulae identifying the Ekklesia as the body in session: the enactment clause ἔδοξεν τῶι δήμωι and the term ἐκκλησία or ἐκκλησία κυρία. McDonald's claim (1943: 44) that the isolated word ἐκκλησία in the prescripts of decrees "was enough to convey this location [sc. the Pnyx] to the reader" misstates the function of the single word in that position, which is to indicate that a meeting of the Ekklesia was not κυρία; cf., e.g., *IG* II² 335, lines 6–7: [ἐκκλη|σ]ία· τῶν πρ[οέδρων], *IG* II² 336, lines 3–4: [ἐκκλησ]ία κυρία· τῶν προέδρων, both of 334/3 B.C. On ἐκκλησία and ἐκκλησία κυρία, see Rhodes 1993: 521–523; Rhodes 1995: 188–191; and see Pritchett 2001: 184–192 for the sources.

[7] Meeting-places of the Ekklesia recorded in Athenian decrees into the 1st century A.D. are listed in McDonald 1943: 48 (ἐν Διονύσου), 52 (ἐμ and ἐν Πειραιεῖ), and 57 n. 1 (ἐν τῶι θεάτρωι); a fourth site is recorded, outside of a prescript, in *IG* I³ 105, line 34 (ἐλ Λυκείο). Among 4th-century Athenian laws, only *IG* II² 140 of 353/2 B.C. records a meeting-place, its name now lost: ἐν [. . . .⁸. . . . τῶν προ]|έδρων (lines 4–5). The prescript of the law of Eukrates, still intact, identifies neither the body that reported the resolution of the nomothetai nor its place of meeting.

[8] McDonald 1943: 44 draws attention to the fact that no inscription mentions the Pnyx in connection with the Ekklesia. The fact that "the Pnyx" as the meeting-place of the Ekklesia went without saying is still the strongest evidence that the Pnyx was the site at which the Ekklesia usually met, and McDonald's observations that prescripts did not name the Ekklesia's meeting-place prior to the mid-4th century and never named the Pnyx (McDonald 1943: 44) still hold true; see Threatte 1996: 279.

that the equation between the Ekklesia and the Pnyx was firmly established, and the publication clause of the law of Eukrates was drafted within this tradition.

The avoidance of the designation Πυκνί in connection with the Ekklesia appears to have been strictly an epigraphical convention. So, for example, Aeschines (3.34), in a paraphrase of a "Solonian" law, uses the expression ἐν Πυκνὶ τῇ ἐκκλησίᾳ, and the same expression is found in an inserted decree in Dem. 18.55. Although the usage is at variance from that in the inscribed texts, these explicit specifications of the site of the Ekklesia's meeting discretely confirm the epigraphical testimony that the Ekklesia in session could not always be found on the Pnyx and was not expected to be. There is a hint, in the law of Eukrates, that at the time of its passage more permanence was anticipated in the meeting-place on the Pnyx.

According to the instructions in its clause of publication, the text of the law of Eukrates was to be set before two audiences, one that was expected to be found "at the entrance into (the) Areopagos" and a second "in the Ekklesia." Thompson noted the significance of the first of these two topographical descriptions for the meeting-place of the Council of the Areopagos:

> Since the object of placing one of the stelai at the entrance to the meeting place of the Council of the Areopagus was obviously to insure its being seen by the Councillors, we may infer that the meeting place here referred to was the one in normal use at the time.[9]

He is certainly right, and although he did not discuss what prompted the setting of this stele before Areopagites, the prompting is not hard to find in the text of the law: the directives govern the actions of Areopagites. If the central condition of the law (lines 7–10)[10] is met – "If someone rises up against the *demos* of Athens with an aim toward tyranny or if someone takes part in setting up the (aforementioned) tyranny or if someone dissolves the *demos* of the Athenians or the democracy at Athens" – two pre-scriptions will come into effect: the murderer of a man involved in any of these actions will not be liable to prosecution for homicide (lines 10–11), i.e., prosecution before the Council of the Areopagos;[11] and Areopagites will be barred from carrying out the duties of Areopagites (lines 11–12, 14–16; 16–22). Areopagites, including new members installed each year, needed to know those terms for as long as the law was valid. To confront them with those terms, one could hardly do better than to publish the law on a durable, inscribed stele at the entrance to the Areopagos, where they normally met.[12]

---

[9] Thompson 1953: 52.

[10] The third clause of the central condition is repeated, slightly reworded, in lines 12–14, 16–17.

[11] For the homicide jurisdiction of the Council of the Areopagos in the 330s, see Wallace 1989: 97–121, 210; more briefly, Hansen 1991: 290–293.

[12] Laws relevant to Areopagites had previously been placed on the Areopagos: the 5th-century laws of Ephialtes and Archestratos περὶ τῶν Ἀρεοπαγιτῶν (*Ath. Pol.* 35.2) and a νόμος ἐκ τῆς στήλης τῆς ἐξ Ἀρείου πάγου on the topic of homicide, attributed by Lysias to Solon (Lysias 1.30). Thompson overlooks this evidence, and overstates the variation in the Areopagites' place of meeting, when he infers from a reference to meetings of the Council in the Stoa Basileios ([Dem.] 25.23) that "the Council of the Areopagus ... [was] apparently no more tied down to one place than was the Ekklesia" (Thompson 1953:

The practical need for Areopagites to know the text of Eukrates' law accounts for the stele at their usual meeting-place, but participants in the Ekklesia did not need to know the text for the same purposes as Areopagites – the law did not overtly direct their actions – and a different rationale will be needed to explain why a copy was to be set ἐν τῆι ἐκκλησίαι. Perhaps the siting of the stele acknowledged the Ekklesia's partnership with the Council of the Areopagos in supervising, in broad terms, the Athenian citizenry; it might, in addition, have acknowledged the Ekklesia's role in creating this piece of legislation.[13] The Council of 500, however, could have merited the same recognition on both these grounds, and the publication clause does not direct a separate copy of the law to their place of meeting.[14] A reconstruction of the interplay among the Ekklesia, the Council of the Areopagos, the Council of 500, and the nomo-thetai in the creation of this law would help to account for the positioning of the second stele; lacking that, we know, at least, that the authors of the law wanted to publish the text where the Ekklesia would see it. Because fluctuation in membership was even more a fact for the Ekklesia – uniquely constituted at every session – than for Areopagites, the siting of this second inscribed copy had to be chosen with even more attention to the vagaries of the body's membership.

If, in 337/6 B.C., the meeting-place of the Ekklesia was as variable as it had been since the 5th century, the authors of the publication clause of this law stood no chance of getting the text before each session of the Ekklesia by sending an inscribed copy to a single site – so, for example, ἡ ἐν Διονύσου ἐκκλησία of 343/2 B.C., which resolved the decree *IG* II² 223, would not have encountered a stele that had been set on the Pnyx.[15] The impossibility of addressing so peripatetic an audience as the Ekklesia by means of a stationary display might explain why no Athenian legislation, to our know-ledge, had ever been set up on the Pnyx: if the participants were intended to see a particular text, they had to be intercepted, and there was no one place where the participants in the Ekklesia could reliably be found. That circumstance appears to have changed by the ninth prytany of 337/6 B.C., when the authors of the publication clause of the law of Eukrates apparently believed that they would get the text of the law to the Ekklesia by sending an inscribed copy to the Pnyx.

---

53). For further testimony on the Areopagos as the regular meeting-place of the Council of the Areopagos, see Wycherley 1955: 120; McDonald 1943: 128–130; and note Thompson's concession that the Areopagos might after all be the meeting-place indicated in the publication clause of the law of Eukrates (text, n. 1 above; Thompson 1953: 53 n. 52a).

[13] The relief at the top of the stele, depicting Demokratia crowning Demos (Lawton 1995, no. 38), might confirm the Ekklesia's involvement in this law.

[14] Evidence for the involvement of the Boule in Eukrates' law might be found, twice, in the publication clause: first, in the instruction (lines 22–24) that "the grammateus of the Boule is to have this law inscribed on two stone stelai and is to have them set up," and, second, in the instruction (lines 24–26) to place the first of the stelai "at the entrance into (the) Areopagos – the entrance leading into the Bouleuterion, for one going in," if that instruction was intended to intercept Areopagites entering their meeting-place *and* bouleutai entering their meeting-place. I am not willing, however, on the basis of these passages, to reconstruct the Council's role in creating this law or to argue that the Council was among its intended audiences.

[15] *IG* II² 223B, line 6: [τοῦ δήμου ἐν] τῆι ἐν Διονύσου ἐκκλησίαι.

In its renovation as Pnyx III, the Pnyx boasted solid new features – a new-style massive retaining wall, a "great new auditorium," and doubled capacity – which may have convinced the authors of the law of Eukrates that the Ekklesia's usual meeting-place had acquired permanence and that ἐν τῆι ἐκκλησίαι sufficed to pinpoint it.[16] Upon this refurbishing of the Pnyx, the novelty of displaying inscribed legislation before the Ekklesia could finally be tried.[17] On my interpretation of the publication clause of *SEG* XII 87, Pnyx III was in use by the time of the law's drafting, in the ninth prytany of 337/6 B.C. If we can presume that Pnyx III cannot have been built from start to finish between the battle of Chaironeia and the ninth prytany of 337/6 B.C., then the initial stages of construction, which included the prominent retaining wall, were underway before the battle.[18]

In the event, the authors of the law of Eukrates were wrong to expect that Pnyx III would become the permanent home of the Ekklesia. In 332/1 B.C., for example, the Ekklesia met ἐν Διονύσου,[19] and the stele that had been sent to the Pnyx missed its targeted audience. Variation in the meeting-place of the Ekklesia, which had been the norm, resumed, and other Athenian laws and decrees, set up at other sites, continued to invite different audiences.[20] Participants in the Ekklesia appear to have been an intended audience of inscribed legislation only on the occasion of the law of Eukrates, when the nomothetai were distinctly confident that they would find them in session on the Pnyx.[21]

WORKS CITED

Camp, J. McK., II. 1996. "The Form of Pnyx III." In B. Forsén and G. Stanton, eds., *The Pnyx in the History of Athens. Papers and Monographs of the Finnish Institute at Athens* II. Athens. 41–46.
Errington, R.M. 1994. "Ἐκκλησία κυρία in Athens." *Chiron* 24: 135–160.
Hansen, M.H. 1991. *The Athenian Democracy in the Age of Demosthenes*. Oxford.
Kourouniotes, K., and H.A. Thompson. 1932. "The Pnyx in Athens." *Hesperia* 1: 90–217.

---

[16] "Great new auditorium" is Thompson's phrase (1982: 141); see, there, pp. 141–145 for innovative features of Pnyx III. Rotroff and Camp 1996: 271–272 and Camp 1996 are the chief sources for the wall. Comments about Pnyx III made by Homer Thompson in the 1980s suggest that faith in the durability of the new Pnyx III would not have been out of place: "Having learned by hard experience, the Athenians finally devised a type of construction ... that has withstood remarkably well the ravages of both time and man." Thompson 1982: 141.

[17] Four stelai beddings set into the central bench of the bema of Pnyx III, and others cut into the surrounding steps, document an eventual collection of stelai at the site. For these beddings, see Kourouniotes and Thompson 1932: 162 with figs. 38 and 41.

[18] I.e., the proposal of Camp, on other evidence, in Rotroff and Camp 1996 (above, n. 1).

[19] *Hesperia* 8 (1939): 26, no. 6, line 6. The specification of the Ekklesia's meeting-place as ἐν Διονύσου in this decree indicates that the Theater of Dionysos was an irregular site of meeting, and the Pnyx presumably continued as the usual meeting-place.

[20] Locations of 4th-century laws are named in *SEG* XXVI 72 (375/4 B.C.), *IG* II² 140 (353/2 B.C.), *SEG* XII 87 (337/6 B.C.), and *IG* II² 333 (335/4 B.C.); revised texts of the publication clauses, with translations, are in Richardson 2000: 607–608.

[21] I warmly thank John Camp, Peter Krentz, Ron Stroud, and Steve Tracy for comments on early drafts; Merle Langdon and Steve Tracy for comments on intermediate drafts; and Judith Binder and Susan Rotroff for discussing with me various evidence for the date of Pnyx III.

Lawton, C. 1995. *Attic Document Reliefs: Art and Politics in Ancient Athens*. Oxford.

McDonald, W.A. 1943. *The Political Meeting Places of the Greeks*. Baltimore.

Meritt, B.D. 1952. "Law Against Tyranny." *Hesperia* 21: 355–359.

———. 1953. "The Entrance to the Areopagus." *Hesperia* 22: 129.

Pritchett, W.K. 2001. *Athenian Calendars and Ekklesias*. Amsterdam.

Rhodes, P.J. 1972. *The Athenian Boule*. Oxford.

Rhodes, P. J. 1993. *A Commentary on the Aristotelian* Athenaion Politeia. Oxford.

———. 1995. "Ekklesia Kyria and the Schedule of Assemblies in Athens." *Chiron* 25: 187–198.

Richardson, M.B. 2000. "The Location of Inscribed Laws in Fourth-Century Athens. *IG* II^2 244, on Rebuilding the Walls of Peiraieus (337/6 B.C.)." In P. Flensted-Jensen et al., eds., *Polis & Politics. Studies in Ancient Greek History*. Copenhagen. 601–615.

Rotroff, S.I., and J. McK. Camp II. 1996. "The Date of the Third Period of the Pnyx." *Hesperia* 65: 263–294.

Thompson, H.A. 1953. "Excavations in the Athenian Agora: 1952." *Hesperia* 22: 25–56.

———. 1982. "The Pnyx in Models." In *Studies in Attic Epigraphy, History, and Topography Presented to Eugene Vanderpool. Hesperia* Supplement 19. Princeton. 133–147.

Threatte, L.L. 1996. *The Grammar of Attic Inscriptions II: Morphology*. Berlin.

Wallace, R.W. 1989. *The Areopagos Council to 307 B.C.* Baltimore.

Whitehead, D. 2000. *Hypereides: The Forensic Speeches*. Oxford.

Worthington, I. 1999. *Greek Orators* II: *Dinarchus and Hyperides*. Warminster.

Wycherley, R. E. 1955. "Two Notes on Athenian Topography." *JHS* 75: 117–121.

29

Archon Dates, Atthidographers, and the Sources of *Ath. Pol.* 22–26[*]

James P. Sickinger

Aristotle describes in chapters 22 through 26 of the *Athēnaiōn Politeia* (*AP*) a series of political and constitutional developments that transformed Athenian democracy in the decades following Kleisthenes' reforms. To many of these events he assigns an archon date, and scholars routinely have taken this method of dating as a sign of Aristotle's reliance on one or more *Atthides*, the local histories of Athens. Less frequently considered, however, are the sources behind these *Atthides* and how their authors, the Atthidographers, managed to date by archon years events occurring more than a century before their own time. This paper suggests that the Atthidographers on whom Aristotle relied probably obtained some of their information on post-Kleisthenic Athens from authentic public documents.

After completing his account of Kleisthenes' reforms in chapter 21 of the *AP*, Aristotle turns in chapter 22 to several significant developments that followed in their wake. In the eighth year after passage of Kleisthenes' laws, in the archonship of Hermokreon (501/0), the Kleisthenic council first used the oath it still swore in Aristotle's day (*AP* 22.2).[1] Next, the Athenians elected ten generals according to the Kleisthenic tribes, so that one general came from each tribe. In the twelfth year after that reform, in the archonship of Phainippos (490/89), they defeated the Persians at Marathon, and two years later they first used the law on ostracism, which Kleisthenes had enacted, to exile Hipparchos son of Charmos (*AP* 22.3–4). In the following year, in the archonship of Telesinos (487/6), the Athenians appointed the nine archons by lot for the first time since the end of the tyranny; the same year saw the ostracism of Megakles son of Hippokrates (*AP* 22.5). A third unnamed individual was ostracized in the next year, but in the fourth year after the practice's first use, the Athenians ostracized Xanthippos son of Ariphron, the first victim not connected to the tyrants (*AP* 22.6). In the third year after that, in the archonship of Nikodemos (483/2), the Athenians, on the advice of Themistokles, used the surplus revenues from the mines at Maroneia to build a fleet of 100 triremes (*AP* 22.7). Aristides son of Lysimachos was ostracized in this year, but he, along with others who had been ostracized earlier, was

---

[*] For Alan L. Boegehold, a small token of gratitude, respect, and friendship.

[1] In assigning specific years to the events of this section of the *AP*, I have followed the dates suggested by Rhodes 1981 *ad locc*; see also Chambers 1990 *ad locc*; Cadoux 1948.

recalled in the third year after that, in the archonship of Hypsichides (481/0), because of the pending invasion of Xerxes (*AP* 22.8).

Relatively few chronological details appear in the following chapters (*AP* 23–25), which focus on developments after the Persian Wars. In chapter 23 Aristotle relates how the Areopagos regained some power by virtue of its conduct before the battle of Salamis. The same period also saw Aristides and Themistokles emerge as leaders of the people, with the two of them overseeing the establishment of Athens' naval empire. Aristotle provides an archon date for Aristides' first assessment of tribute (*AP* 23.5), but otherwise this chapter and chapter 24 lack specific dates. Chapter 24 focuses instead on the conversion of Athens' naval alliance into an empire and the support that large numbers of Athenian citizens derived from the empire's revenues. In chapter 25 *AP* returns to the Areopagos, which Aristotle says held power for seventeen years. But Ephialtes, assisted by Themistokles, attacked members of the Areopagos and in the archonship of Konon (462/1) he deprived the Areopagos council of its "additional" powers and returned them to the council, people, and law courts (*AP* 25.2). Ephialtes was assassinated "not long afterwards" (*AP* 25.5).

Compared to preceding sections chapter 26 contains a wealth of chronological detail. It starts with an allusion to the decline of the constitution due to the influence of demagogues and the weakened state of the "better" classes; they were led in this period by Kimon (*AP* 26.1), and their numbers had dropped because of losses incurred by constant warfare. Aristotle then refers to three constitutional innovations of the 450s to illustrate how the Athenians had moved away from their laws. The first of these was passed "in the sixth year" after the death of Ephialtes. It opened the archonship to members of the zeugite class, and Mnesitheides, says Aristotle, was the first zeugite to serve as archon (*AP* 26.2); his year in office was 457/6 (D.S. 11.81.1). In the fifth year after that, in the archonship of Lysikrates (453/2), the Athenians reinstated the office of travelling deme judges, thirty in number (*AP* 26.3), and in the third year after that, in the archonship of Antidotos (451/0), they ratified a proposal of Perikles limiting the rights of citizenship to individuals born of two Athenian parents (*AP* 26.4). Chapter 27 goes on to discuss the statesmanship of Perikles, while chapter 28 offers a list and assessment of Athenian political leaders from Solon to the end of the fifth century; the only event dated by archon in these two sections is the outbreak of the Peloponnesian War (*AP* 27.2).

These chapters on the post-Kleisthenic growth of Athenian democracy are of mixed value.[2] Although they preserve details not found in other sources, the information is sometimes anecdotal, occasionally biased, and, at least in the case of Themistokles' support of Ephialtes, misleading if not incorrect. Aristotle, it seems, pieced together his account from several different sources, and not very successfully at that. Identifying these sources is no easy task since none of them survive. But they appear to have included works that took varying stances on the virtues of democratic government. Aristotle's statement that the city was "well-governed" when the Areopagos regained influence after the Persian Wars presumably came from an anti-

---

[2] Rhodes 1981: 283 calls chapters 23 through 28 "disappointing."

democratic or aristocratic source; the same is probably true of Aristotle's reference to Kimon and the implied claim that the city entered a period of decline after Ephialtes' reforms. But Aristotle's references to Themistokles and Aristides as leaders of the people, the growth of the empire and the benefits accrued from it, and Ephialtes' reforms, betray no hints of hostility, and these sections would seem to come from a source more favorable to democracy.[3]

Whatever the nature of these sources, scholars agree that the archon dates of these chapters reflect Aristotle's consultation of one or more *Atthides*.[4] The Atthidographers constructed these histories of Athens in strict chronological sequence, narrating events of historical times by years under the names of the Athenian archons of those years. The earliest Atthidographer was probably Hellanikos of Lesbos, who was active in the late fifth century, and by the time Aristotle published the *AP*, additional histories of Athens written by Kleidemos, Androtion, and possibly Phanodemos were also available.[5] Aristotle, the reasoning goes, simply adopted the dates he found in his Atthidographic source when he composed his account of post-Kleisthenic Athens.

This solution, however, solves very little. Even if it is correct, it fails to consider what sources the Atthidographers used, and on what basis they assigned archon dates to events of the late sixth and early fifth centuries. There are several possibilities. Oral traditions might have preserved and transmitted detailed information about each event. Herodotus, for example, puts Xerxes' entry into Attica in the archonship of Kalliades (Hdt. 8.51.1), a date presumably conveyed to him by Athenian informants, and we can readily imagine that the Athenians remembered the names of those archons in whose years other significant events, like the battle at Marathon, took place. Alternatively, the Atthidographers might have relied on documents. Several of the events named in *AP* 22–26 – the bouleutic oath, the first assessment of tribute, and the constitutional changes of the 480s and 450s – are the types of measures that in later times produced written texts. If the Athenians were maintaining similar texts of public business already at the start of the fifth century, then some such documents might have survived to be consulted by an Atthidographer, who incorporated the documentary information into his *Atthis*.

Which of these two types of sources – oral tradition or written record – is more likely to have provided an Atthidographer with specific details about Athenian constitutional history? Let us consider oral traditions first. Hellanikos, the first Atthidographer, lived and worked in the latter part of the fifth century, when he almost

---

[3] Many scholars attribute the different viewpoints to the different Atthidographers Aristotle followed; for an extreme case of this tendency see Schreiner 1968. Gomme, *HCT*, 1: 48 n. 1 thought that the description of Kimon derived ultimately from Stesimbrotos of Thasos. Rhodes 1981: 285–86 suggests the possible use of "partisan literature" of the fifth and fourth centuries.

[4] Rhodes 1981: 241 (on chapter 22), "the annalistic framework makes it almost certain that the source is an *Atthis*"; cf. also 285 on chapter 26. See also Chambers 1990: 86–8 and Busolt 1895: 33–4, and 53, "Die darauf folgenden, chronikartigen und nach Archontenjahren bestimmten Angaben aus der Partei- und Verfassungsgeschichte von Kleisthenes bis zum peloponnesischen Kriege stammen sicher aus einer Atthis."

[5] For brief but useful discussion of the Atthidographers and the dates of their works see now Harding 1994: 9–35.

certainly had access to individuals who possessed first-hand knowledge of laws, ostracisms, and other developments of the early fifth century.[6] Hellanikos' Attic history survives, it is true, only in fragments, and questions exist about its contents. It is unclear in how much detail he treated political events of the early fifth century, and scholars are not unanimous in the view that Hellanikos used archon dates to structure his entire work.[7] But even if Hellanikos was not responsible for providing Aristotle with archon dates for post-Kleisthenic political reforms, one of his fourth-century successors, Kleidemos or Androtion, perhaps was. Unlike Hellanikos, both were Athenians, and they were presumably more familiar with the traditions of their native city. Fragments of their works also display a greater interest in the political history of Athens than do those of Hellanikos, and either one could easily have learned traditions about fifth-century events, even ones more than a century before their births.[8]

And yet what little we know about oral traditions gives pause. To judge from the works of Herodotus, Thucydides, the Attic orators, and other authors Athenian traditions about the past were vague, malleable, and not terribly precise.[9] Stories tended to focus on the sixth-century tyranny and opposition to it, the Persian Wars, and a limited number of other military exploits. Far less attention was devoted to constitutional matters like those cited by Aristotle in *AP* 22–26. Herodotus, it is true, knew Solon as a lawgiver (Hdt. 1.29), but he does not describe any specific laws of Solon, and he omits any mention of Solon's constitutional reforms. His account of Peisistratos focuses on the tyrant's rise to power (Hdt. 1.59–64) and the expulsion of his sons (Hdt. 5.55, 62–65) but says very little about specific political or constitutional changes. Herodotus has more to say about Kleisthenes, but there too the account focuses more on the fortunes of Kleisthenes than the contents of his reforms (Hdt. 5.66, 69–73).

Similarly general are the orators' allusions to Athenian political history. Funeral orations offer an idealized version of Athens' past, one that begins in the mythical period and extends into the fifth century. These speeches have something to say about the Persian Wars and Athens' naval empire, but they are virtually silent about individual stages in the development of the democracy itself.[10] Other speeches by the orators are similarly weak in detail. The Sicilian expedition, the reign of the Thirty tyrants, and certain other events were remembered. But references to historical events generally focus on military exploits or support of Athens' democracy, not specific laws or constitutional innovations.[11] The best indication of the Athenians' attitude toward their city's internal history may be their tendency to attribute to Solon authorship of many laws and other institutions, including ones that are clearly later in

---

[6] On Hellanikos see Harding 1994: 9–10, 40.

[7] For doubts see most recently Toye 1995 and Joyce 1999.

[8] For Kleidemos' interest in political history see *FGrHist* 323 F36; Androtion's interest in Athenian political institutions is suggested by *FGrHist* 324 F 3, 4, 5, 6, 34, 36, 38, 43.

[9] Thomas 1989: 95–282 discusses the complex and changing nature of Athenian oral traditions, which she subdivides into family and polis traditions.

[10] On funeral orations see Thomas 1989: 196–237; she states (1989: 232) that the "epitaphic history pays no regard to the internal history of the city." Cf. also Loraux 1986.

[11] For the different types of events that were remembered see Thomas 1989: 108–23, 211–36.

date and non-Solonian.[12] Historical accuracy in the modern sense was not a concern. That does not mean that authentic details about Athens' political history did not exist; other traditions not represented in written sources might have preserved more detailed accounts of individual laws, ostracisms, and other political changes. But given the evidence we have, it is difficult to believe that oral traditions would have provided specific information – as found in *AP* 22–26 – about the development of the Athenian constitution.[13]

It is equally uncertain that oral traditions would have recalled the dates of laws, decrees, and other legislative decisions. Herodotus does assign an archon date to Xerxes' invasion of Attica (Hdt. 8.51.1), and Thucydides specifies the archon in whose year the Peloponnesian War began (2.2.1). But those archon dates are applied to military and not political events, and in the works of both authors their appearance is unusual. Herodotus' general practice is to reckon the dates of events in terms of generations, durations (how long they lasted), or intervals (the number of years between them).[14] He provides no specific date for Solon's lawgiving, and of Peisistratos' various attempts to seize power he says only that the last one occurred in the eleventh year after the second (Hdt. 1.62.1). Herodotus does report that Hippias ruled for four years after the assassination of Hipparchos (Hdt. 5.55), and that Peisistratos and his sons ruled Athens for thirty-six years (Hdt. 5.65.3). But no event in the tyrants' reign is dated absolutely, and when he comes to Kleisthenes' reforms, Herodotus simply sets them after the expulsion of the tyrants and in the context of Kleisthenes' struggle with Isagoras (Hdt. 5.66). Thucydides' methods for dating past events are similar. He puts the return of the Herakleidai eighty years after the fall of Troy (Thuc. 1.12.4) and says that Ameinokles constructed the first triremes about three hundred years before the end of the Peloponnesian War (Thuc. 1.13.3). In terms of Athenian history, Thucydides notes that Hippias reigned in Athens for three years after the death of Hipparchos and was expelled in the fourth (6.59.4), and that that expulsion occurred about 100 years before the establishment of the oligarchy of the Four Hundred (8.68.4). But Thucydides does not assign an archon date to either event. Even when dealing with events of the fifth century Thucydides employs similar methods, as his account of the Pentakontaetia, the period between the Persian Wars and the outbreak of the Peloponnesian War, shows. Early on he is vague: the capture of Eion came first (Thuc. 1.98.1); next came the enslavement of Skyros (Thuc. 1.98.2); after that was the defeat of Karystos and the revolt of Naxos (Thuc. 1.98.3–4); and "after these things" the battle at the Eurymedon river (Thuc. 1.100.1). Thereafter Thucydides begins to provide more specific figures, but they are relative: the siege of Thasos lasted into a third year before the Thasians surrendered (Thuc. 1.101.3); the helots in Ithome held out for ten years before they came to terms

---

[12] For the practice see Hansen 1990; Schreiner 1913: 21–60.

[13] Chambers 1990: 242 suggests that Mnesitheides was famous ("berühmt") as the first zeugite to hold the archonship, by which I take it he means the name was known by tradition. But Thomas 1989: 111–13 shows that family traditions emphasized military offices and public service through liturgies; offices like archonships were *not* mentioned frequently in family traditions and so perhaps were not as well remembered.

[14] On Herodotus' chronological methods see Strasburger 1956.

with the Spartans (Thuc. 1.103.1); the Athenian expedition to Egypt was defeated after six years of war; and the revolt of Samos was squelched in the sixth year of the Thirty Years Peace (Thuc. 1.115.2).

Herodotus' general failure to use archon dates might be explained by his non-Athenian origin and an intended pan-Hellenic audience: Athenian archon dates would have been meaningless to his non-Athenian readers. Thucydides too might have aimed at a similar audience. But Thucydides was an Athenian, and his avoidance of archon dates in the Pentakontaetia raises questions, all the more so because he criticizes Hellanikos' account of the same period for its brevity and chronological inaccuracy (Thuc. 1.97.2). Thucydides' aversion to dating by annual magistracies is well known (5.20.2), and it may be that he knew or could have calculated the archon dates of some of the Pentakontaetia's sieges and battles but chose to omit them because of a belief in their unreliability: an archon's name might give the year in which a siege began, but it would not indicate the time of year or suffice for a siege that dragged into a second or third year. Gomme, however, believed that Thucydides wrote the Pentakontaetia while in exile, and that he did not have access to an archon list against which he could check specific dates.[15] This view implies that Thucydides did not remember specific archon dates, and that he would have to conduct research to determine the specific dates of many events.[16]

The Attic orators lend this view some support. Their speeches cite the names of archons in conjunction with different types of events. The speaker of Lysias 7 notes that his opponent accused him of uprooting a sacred olive stump in the archonship of Souniades, some twenty years before the speech's delivery (Lys. 7.11). Demosthenes cites the archonships in which he began his prosecution of his guardians (Dem. 30.17) and in which his sister married and divorced (Dem. 30.15). Apollodoros knew the names of the archons in whose years his father died and Phormio, his opponent and step-father, had acquired citizenship ([Dem.] 46.13). He also provides archon dates for several events in the life of the courtesan Neaira ([Dem.] 59.33, 36). Archon dates are also attached to business transactions (Dem. 49.30, 59), and speakers refer to the archonships in which they won legal cases (Lys. 17.3) and performed military service (Dem. 49.60) or public liturgies (Lys. 21.1, 3).

The nature of these citations deserves close attention. The names of archons generally are connected to events from the relatively recent past or to ones in which speakers or members of their families were immediately involved. When the orators deal with events of the more distant past, especially ones of the fifth century, or with which they had no personal or family connection, they tend to be more general. Consider again funeral orations, those speeches delivered at the public burial of the Athenian war dead in a given year. The historical digressions of these speeches set events in Athens' history in their proper chronological sequence, but they do not offer specific dates. Lysias says that Xerxes' invasion of Greece took place in the tenth year

---

[15] Gomme, *HCT*, 1: 362. On the potential inaccuracy of archon dates see the chapter by Chambers in this volume.

[16] Badian 1993: 74–6 also emphasizes Thucydides' inability to remember the precise dates of events of the mid-fifth century.

after the battle of Marathon (Lys. 2.27), and that Athens' naval supremacy lasted seventy years (Lys. 2.55). Beyond that, he and others give no chronological details, and certainly no archon dates. This impression of chronological imprecision is reinforced by Andokides' discussion of fifth-century Athenian history in the speech *On the Peace*. It is vague, confused, and at times simply wrong.[17] Among many other inaccuracies Andokides mistakes the general Kimon for his father Miltiades (And. 3.3), makes the five-year truce concluded between Athens and Sparta in 451 last fifty years (And. 3.4), and muddles the building history of the walls of Athens and Peiraeus (And. 3.5,7). Specific dates are not supplied, and the durations and intervals that Andokides does provide cannot be reconciled with the history of the period as known from other sources. If Andokides' version of Athenian history is in any way representative of the types of oral traditions the Atthidographers had at their disposal, it would have been extremely difficult for them to construct an accurate chronology of early fifth-century Athenian history using archon dates.

But if not from oral tradition, from where else might an Atthidographer have acquired specific dates for developments such as those reported by Aristotle in *AP* 22–26? Several of these developments have a documentary character, and an origin in authentic documents is worth considering.[18] The bouleutic oath, whose use is reported at *AP* 22, existed in written form by the end of the fifth century.[19] The Athenians had been recording laws since the time of Drakon and Solon, and some of the constitutional changes Aristotle mentions – that of 488/7 changing the mode of appointment of archons, and the three of the 450s – might have been enacted by laws, which were automatically recorded like earlier ones.[20] Decrees too were being set down in writing during the fifth century, and several of the developments to which Aristotle assigns dates – Themistokles' proposal about the revenues from the mines at Maroneia, the recall of the ostracized,[21] and the first tribute assessment of Aristides[22] – resemble the types of decisions the Athenians normally enacted by decree. If documents existed and survived into the late fifth and early fourth centuries, an Atthidographer could easily have discovered information about constitutional developments in the post-Kleisthenic period and incorporated these details into the *Atthis* that served as Aristotle's source.

---

[17] On the speech see Thompson 1967, Thomas 1989: 119–22; on the speech's authenticity see Harris 2000.

[18] This possibility is suggested by Rhodes 1993: 55–57 but not argued in detail.

[19] A clause of the coinage decree, *IG*³ 1453 §10, requires the written addition of a clause to the bouleutic oath.

[20] For the preservation of laws from the archaic period see Sickinger 1999a: 8–34. Note also that records of elections including their dates were preserved among the public records in the fourth century: Aeschin. 2.58, 3.24; Sickinger 1999a: 121–22. A similar type of record could account for Aristotle's report that the archons were first appointed by lot in the archonship of Telesinos (*AP* 22.5).

[21] The well-known Themistokles decree from Troizen, I believe, is not identical to the decree described by Aristotle, but it may include provisions derived from it.

[22] The earliest inscribed assessment decree is *IG* I³ 71 of 425, but the Athenians were undoubtedly keeping written copies of similar decrees much earlier: see Sickinger 1999a: 67.

Objections, however, may be raised. Inscriptions preserving Athenian laws and decrees start to appear in large numbers only around the middle of the fifth century, later than the political changes discussed in *AP* 22–26; thus, stone inscriptions are not likely to have preserved political decisions from the pre-Ephialtic period. In addition, the Athenians appear to have established a centralized archives building, in which they deposited documents of various sorts, only in the final decade of the fifth century.[23] It is not certain, therefore, that documents were being made or kept consistently during the early fifth century, much less that they would have survived and been available in later periods. Moreover, the names of archons do not occur in the prescripts of inscribed Athenian decrees until the late 420s, and not with regularity until the last decade of the century.[24] Thus, even if one concedes that documents from the early fifth century survived, it seems unlikely that such texts would have preserved the names of the archons in whose years they had been enacted – and hence provided their dates.

None of these objections, however, is decisive. The Athenians may have begun to inscribe public documents on stone more frequently from around the middle of the fifth century, but the recording of documents on other materials was a much older practice, and publication on stone was hardly necessary to ensure a document's long-term survival. The laws of Drakon and Solon were set down in writing already in the archaic period, and there is no reason to think that the Athenians, having started to write down laws in the time of these lawgivers, ceased to do so for later legislation. Although doubts persist about the availability of the laws of these lawgivers in later times, texts were available in some form for consultation in later periods.[25] It is significant too that the laws of Drakon and Solon were recorded on objects called *axones*, which are generally thought to have been constructed from wooden boards. If wooden boards or tablets – and not stelai made from stone or bronze – were the material of choice for recording early Athenian laws, that practice would easily explain the paucity of Athenian state documents from the epigraphical record of the sixth and early fifth centuries.[26]

Other evidence points to the survival of authentic documents of the archaic and early classical periods into the late fifth and fourth century. Drakon's homicide law, inscribed on stone in 409/8, is the best known example (*IG* I³ 104), but only one of several. Another inscription of the late fifth century (*IG* I³ 105) records a series of regulations concerning the judicial power of the Athenian Boule and assembly that are much older in date; they may go back to the time of Kleisthenes, if not before.[27] Where and in what form these texts existed before their publication on stone is

---

[23] On the foundation of a centralized archives building see Boegehold 1971; cf. Sickinger 1999a: 93–113.

[24] See Henry 1979.

[25] Sickinger 1999a: 9–61 discusses the different types of records being kept at Athens throughout the archaic period.

[26] For the use of wooden tablets for keeping records of various types see Sickinger 1999b and the contribution of Fischer in this volume. It is noteworthy too that the Athenians *never* appear to have inscribed laws (*nomoi*) on stone in large numbers: see Sickinger forthcoming.

[27] On the inscription see Sickinger 1999a: 57–59.

unknown, but given the absence of inscriptions preserving texts with similar contents from earlier times, preservation in some type of archive and on a "perishable" material, like wood, is a strong possibility. Other types of early records also survived into later times. In the 340s the Athenians inscribed on stone a list of victors in the dramatic contests held at the City Dionysia (*IG* II² 2318). The earliest victors named on the inscription, sometimes called the Fasti, belong to the year 473/2, but the beginning of the inscription is lost, and its text probably started with entries of the late sixth century.[28] Whatever the inscription's starting point, those responsible for inscribing it in the 340s had access to information a century and a half old. Nowhere do we learn of the oral transmission of lists of dramatic victors, and fifth-century inscriptions do not preserve similar details. Since there is no reason to doubt the authenticity of this list of victors, the most viable sources for it are written records of the dramatic contests of the City Dionysia, perhaps ones maintained and preserved by the eponymous archon who oversaw that festival's administration.[29]

Documents were being recorded in the early fifth century, and they were surviving into later times, certainly long enough to be consulted by an Atthidographer. It remains to be asked if an Atthidographer, finding a text of a law or decree of the early fifth century, would have been able to determine its date. The regulations outlining the Boule's judicial powers (*IG* I³ 105) do not include a reference to an archon, and although that text is fragmentary, archon names are also omitted from the prescripts of most Athenian decrees on stone until the late 420s. If the absence of archon dates from these texts is indicative of fifth-century practice in general, it might be difficult to envision how an Atthidographer could have dated accurately the text of an older document available to him.

And yet the prescripts of inscribed, fifth-century decrees are not fully representative of the dating practices of fifth-century Athenian documents. The stone copies of documents did not always display all available information about those documents; archival versions of the same texts sometimes preserved more detail,[30] and some types of documents included archon dates well before the practice became common in decree prescripts. Inscribed accounts and inventories set up by Athenian officials were including archon dates well before the 420s,[31] and from the start of the fifth century the Athenians were attaching archon dates to different sorts of activities. Thus, the Fasti, that annual list of victors in the City Dionysia inscribed in the 340s, is arranged by archon years, with the victors of different contests being listed under the archons in whose years they were victorious; presumably the arrangement reflects the records from which the inscribed list was obtained. If that was the case, the possibility is worth considering that laws and decrees from the late sixth and early fifth centuries were arranged and could be dated by similar means.

---

[28] See also Burnett's contribution to this volume.

[29] On the sources of the Fasti see Sickinger 1999: 41–46.

[30] West 1989; cf. Sickinger 1999a: 87–90 for fifth-century examples.

[31] See, among others, *IG* I³ 446–450 (Parthenon building accounts); *IG* I³ 362 (accounts for Samian expedition); *IG* I³ 364 (accounts for Kerkyraian expedition).

Apart from their prescripts laws and decrees might have preserved indications of their dates in other ways. A law or decree could express its archon date in a postscript: the Hekatompedon decrees of 484/3 name the archon in whose year they were enacted in statements appended at their conclusions.[32] Internal references to archonships also provided clues to a law's or decree's date. Solon's amnesty law states that its provisions were to apply to anyone exiled before the archonship of Solon. Another Solonian law on inheritance states that its provisions – which allowed a man without a son to adopt whomever he wanted – were to go into effect only after the archonship of Solon.[33] Several pieces of fifth-century legislation also illustrate the practice. The Athenian regulations for Miletos include a provision stating that their terms were to apply to anyone from before the archonship of Euthynos (*IG* I³ 21). The tribute reassessment decree of 425 uses an archon's name to indicate the year in which the assessment took place (*IG* I³ 71, lines 59–60). An Atthidographer studying an older document with a similar internal reference might naturally assume that the specified archon was in office in the year the text was enacted.

There remains, however, one set of developments reported and dated by Aristotle whose documentary origin is far less secure: the ostracisms of the 480s. Aristotle puts the first of these two years after the battle of Marathon without, however, naming the archon of that year. Megakles son of Hippokrates was ostracized in the following year, in the archonship of Telesinos, which was also the year when the archons were first chosen by lot. The third victim of ostracism is not named, but in the fourth year after the institution's first use (the archon's name is again not mentioned) the Athenians exiled Xanthippos son of Ariphron. The next ostracism mentioned by Aristotle was that of Aristides, which occurred at the same time as Themistokles' naval reform; that is dated to the archonship of Nikodemos.

How was Aristotle (or his source able) to associate these ostracisms with specific years of the 480s? Once again, oral traditions are an unlikely source, because they seem to have paid little attention to ostracism or to the dates of individual ostrakophoriai. The earliest reference to a specific ostracism is made by Herodotus (8.79.1), who mentions that Aristides had been "ostracized by the *dēmos*" but fails to give a hint of when Aristides had been exiled. Thucydides alludes in passing to Themistokles' stay in Argos after his ostracism (Thuc. 1.135.3), but he too does not offer a precise date. Lysias (14.39) and Andokides (4.34, 39) also make mention of specific victims but without dating them. Other traditions, it is true, might have preserved the names of the archons in whose years individual victims had ostracized, but evidence for such traditions is not forthcoming, and it is difficult to imagine a context in which they would have taken shape and been preserved and transmitted.

Still, no evidence suggests that individual ostrakophoriai produced much in the way of documents either, and fifth-century inscriptions offer no information on the practice of ostracism. That silence, of course, is not decisive evidence against their

---

[32] *IG* I³ 4A, lines 14–15; 4B, lines 26–7.

[33] Amnesty law: Plut. *Sol.* 19.4; inheritance law: Dem. 46.14; for discussion see Sickinger 1999a: 49–50.

existence, and written texts will have facilitated enforcement of an ostracism's provisions.[34] The victim, for example, was required to depart from Attica within ten days, and he had to remain outside of Attica for a period of ten years.[35] A written record of the actual date on which an ostrakophoria had occurred might not have been necessary to enforce these limits, but a written text will have removed any ambiguity or uncertainty about when a victim had to leave and when he could return. Precise dates of this nature do appear in financial records of the fifth century, and in the text of the one-year's truce concluded between Athens and Sparta in 423, so their use in state documents was not foreign to fifth-century practice.[36] One additional feature may be worth considering. The eponymous archon cooperated with the Boule in the conduct of a vote on ostracism, and both the archon and the Boule might have been involved with written record keeping from early in the fifth century. I have already mentioned the regulations, possibly of Kleisthenic date, governing the powers of the Boule that were inscribed on stone at Athens in the late fifth century (*IG* I³ 105), and I have suggested elsewhere that before the their publication on stone these regulations were preserved in archives maintained by the Boule.[37] By analogy we might argue that the Boule kept similar records related to its shared oversight of the institution of ostracism. Similarly, records of dramatic contests held at the City Dionysia, a festival supervised by the archon, survived from the start of the fifth century well in the 340s. If, as I have suggested, that inscribed list goes back to records kept by the archon himself, then the same may be true of the dated ostracisms recorded by Aristotle: the chief archon maintained records of individual ostrakophoriai in the same way that he maintained records of the City Dionysia.

By suggesting that several of the dated developments reported by Aristotle in chapters 22–26 of the *AP* go back to authentic documents, I am not attempting to argue that *all* the archon dates supplied in the *AP* derive from documentary sources. A document is not likely to have recorded the archon date of the battle of Marathon, for example, and sixth-century events such as Peisistratos' attempts to make himself tyrant or the year of his death hardly left any documentary traces. Dates for these and other early developments in Athenian history were most probably reconstructed from oral traditions like those reflected in Herodotus' account of Peisistratos and his tyranny.[38] But as time went on the Athenians were creating, using, and preserving more and more documents, and the use of such documentary material by Atthidographers and others in historical research merits close consideration.

Nor am I suggesting that every aspect of Aristotle's account of post-Kleisthenic Athens is correct, despite the documentary origin of some details. Aristotle's discus-

---

[34] So Rhodes 1993: 56; Harding 1994: 45 doubts that the names of those ostracized would have been remembered in oral traditions.

[35] For the procedures of ostracism see Philochoros 328 *FGrHist* F30; cf. Lang 1990: 1–2.

[36] For an example of the specificity of dates in an Athenian financial document see especially the Logistai inscription (*IG* I³ 369); other fifth-century examples are cited by Sickinger 1999a: 83–91. Date in One-Year's Truce: Thuc. 4.118.12.

[37] Sickinger 1999a: 57–60.

[38] On the *AP*'s chronology of sixth-century Athens and the sources behind it see Rhodes 1976.

sion of Themistokles and his role in the creation of the Athenian fleet, for example, is not pure document. According to Aristotle Themistokles urged the Athenians to distribute the surplus revenues from the mines at Maroneia to the wealthiest Athenian citizens without saying how that money would be used (*AP* 22.7). An Athenian decree hardly preserved such details, and according to Herodotus Themistokles persuaded the Athenians to use these surplus revenues for the construction of a fleet of warships to be used in the war against Aegina (Hdt. 7.144.2). That divergence does not rule out the survival of a decree or other document related to Themistokles' proposal. A surviving document will have provided the date and the bare essentials of that proposal while leaving Themistokles' motivations unclear.

Finally, the possibility that documents are the original source for some of the archon dates supplied by Aristotle does not guarantee that the Atthidographers who consulted these documents interpreted all of them correctly. Aristotle dates the opening of the archonship to the zeugite class to the sixth year after the death of Ephialtes, and he says that Mnesitheides was the first zeugite to hold this office (*AP* 26.2). The death of Ephialtes is not dated to an archon year, but Mnesitheides is known to have held the archonship in 457/6 (D.S. 11.81.1). But the sixth year before that was 462/1, the very year in which Ephialtes' reforms were passed; so Ephialtes must have been killed soon after he carried his reforms. But if Mnesitheides was a zeugite, he cannot have been archon in the same year the reform was passed. Aristotle (or his source) has either misdated the reform, perhaps enacted a year or two earlier, to Mnesitheides' archonship, or he has mistakenly assumed that Mnesitheides was a zeugite because the law was passed in his year in office.[39] A law, for example, might have declared that from the archonship of Mnesitheides zeugites were to be eligible for the archonship, and an Atthidographer, finding a text of that law, could have inferred mistakenly from mention of his name that Mnesitheides himself was a zeugite. That inference would have been incorrect, but the error does not argue against a document's existence.

Above all, we need to keep in mind that documents alone are the most likely source for many of the archon-dated, constitutional developments described in *AP*, at least those that occurred after the sixth century. Since the publication of Jacoby's great work on the *Atthis* there has been a tendency to emphasize the role of oral tradition in the formation of the Athenians' views about their past and to neglect the extent to which the Atthidographers might have used documents in constructing their narratives. Their works may not have quoted documents at length, and they did not write their histories of Athens based on documents alone. But oral traditions alone cannot have supplied them all the details about Athens' internal history, especially the archon dates of developments like those reported by Aristotle in *AP* 22–26. Some readers may prefer, therefore, to ascribe these dates to an Atthidographers' theoretical or imaginative reconstruction of Athenian history. But nothing stands in the way of assuming a documentary origin behind Aristotle's dates for post-Kleisthenic developments, and if we are going to take those dates seriously, that assumption seems almost necessary.

---

[39] See Rhodes 1981: 330 and Chambers 1990: 242, 263 for discussion of the problems and possible solutions.

Works Cited

Badian, E. 1993. *From Plataea to Potidaea*. Baltimore.

Boegehold, A.L. 1972. "The Establishment of a Central Archive at Athens." *AJA* 76: 23–30.

Busolt, G. 1895. *Griechische Geschichte*. Vol. 2. 2nd ed. Gotha.

Cadoux, T.J. 1948. "The Athenian Archons from Kreon to Hypsichides." *JHS* 68: 70–123.

Chambers, M. 1990. *Aristoteles. Staat der Athener*. Berlin.

Gomme, *HCT* = A.W. Gomme, *A Historical Commentary on Thucydides*. Vol. 1. Oxford 1945.

Hansen, M.H. 1990. "Solonian Democracy in Fourth Century Athens." In *Aspects of Athenian Democracy*. *C&M* Dissertationes 11. Cophenhagen. 71–99.

Harding, P. 1994. *Androtion and the Atthis*. Oxford.

Harris, E. 2000. "The Authenticity of Andocides' *De Pace*: A Subversive Essay." In P. Flensted-Jensen, T. Nielsen, and L. Rubinstein, edd., *Polis and Politics: Studies in Ancient Greek History*. Copenhagen. 479–506.

Henry, A.S. 1979. "Archon Dating in Fifth-Century Attic Decrees: The 421 Rule." *Chiron* 9: 23–30.

Joyce, C. 1999. "Was Hellanikos the First Chronicler of Athens?" *Histos* 3 (http://www.dur.ac.uk/Classics/histos/1999/joyce.html)

Lang, M. 1990. *Ostraka*. Vol. 25, *The Athenian Agora*. Princeton.

Loraux, N. 1986. *The Invention of Athens: The Funeral Oration in the Classical City*. Trans. A. Sheridan. Cambridge, Mass.

Rhodes, P.J. 1976. "Pisistratid Chronology Again." *Phoenix* 30: 219–33.

———. 1981. *A Commentary on the Aristotelian* Athenaion Politeia. Oxford.

———. 1993. "'Alles eitel gold'? The Sixth and Fifth Centuries in Fourth-Century Athens." In M. Piérart, ed., *Aristote et Athènes*. Paris. 53–64.

Schreiner, J. 1913. *De Corpore Iuris Atheniensum*. Diss. Bonn.

Schreiner, J.H. 1968. *Aristotle and Perikles: A Study in Historiography*. Symbolae Osloenses, Fasc. 21. Oslo.

Sickinger, J.P. 1999a. *Public Records and Archives in Classical Athens*. Chapel Hill.

———. 1999b. "Literacy, Documents, and Archives in the Ancient Athenian Democracy." *American Archivist* 62: 229–46.

———. Forthcoming. "The Laws of Athens. Publication, Preservation, Consultation." In E. Harris and L. Rubinstein. *The Law and the Courts in Ancient Greece*. London.

Strasburger, H. 1956. "Herodots Zeitrechnung." *Historia* 5: 129–61.

Thomas, R. 1989. *Oral Tradition and Written Record in Classical Athens*. Cambridge.

Thompson, W. 1967. "Andocides and Hellanicus." *TAPhA* 98: 483–90.

Toye, D.L. 1995. "Dionysios of Halicarnassos on the First Greek Historians." *AJPh* 116: 279–302.

West, W.C. 1989. "Public Archives in Fourth Century Athens." *GRBS* 20: 529–43.

A Major Athenian Letter-Cutter of the Late 5th and Early 4th Centuries B.C.: The Cutter of *IG* II² 17 (*Dates: 409/8–386/5*)

S. V. Tracy

This cutter was one of the major inscribers in Athens during the closing years of the Peloponnesian War and for the first decade and a half of the fourth century. He inscribed a large number of inventories and accounts as well as honorary decrees. The hand enables a better date than heretofore possible for a number of texts, especially Agora I 5410, the treaty between Athens and Siphnos, and *IG* II² 2311, the list of prizes awarded at the Panathenaia.

It is a pleasure to present this initial study of an important Athenian letter-cutter in a volume honoring my undergraduate mentor, Alan L. Boegehold. This workman was active in the last decade of the fifth century B.C. and the first decade and a half of the fourth. I have devoted several years to study of his lettering, particularly to tracking down as many of his inscriptions as possible.[1] However, I have not had access to a number of fifth century inscriptions, nor can I expect such access any time soon.[2] Since this man was one of the most dominant cutters of his time – indeed he represents the earliest major cutter yet known – presentation of him and his work at this juncture with copious supporting illustrations seems justified. His hand is quite distinctive and this study should enable identification of other examples of his work. I have described elsewhere the criteria and methodology which I employ to identify the work of ancient letter cutters.[3] A + sign in the following list placed to the left of the number of the inscription indicates that there are further comments on that inscription in the following section.

---

[1] As in past studies, I have been able to consult extensively the squeeze collection at the Institute for Advanced Study in Princeton. For this privilege I owe especial thanks to the faculty of the School of Historical Studies and particularly to Professors Glen Bowersock and Heinrich von Staden. I am grateful also to Dr. Bodil Bundgaard Rasmussen of the National Museum of Copenhagen for granting me access to the fragment of *IG* II² 17 that resides in Copenhagen.

[2] Thanks to colleagues at the University of Texas, I was able to spend a morning in the Spring of 1998 consulting the fifth century squeezes of B. D. Meritt housed in the Harry Ransom Humanities Research Center there. This enabled me to add several texts to his dossier.

[3] See Tracy 1970: 321–328; 1975: 1–11, 90–95; 1984: 277–279; 1990a: 60; 1990b: 2–4; 1994: 151–154; and 2000: 67–76 –- this last, an essay for a non-specialist audience.

GENERAL CHARACTERISTICS OF THE LETTERING (FIGS. 1–2)

This cutter produces lettering that is neat and solid appearing, at least at first glance. The strokes are relatively thick and sometimes widen slightly at the ends, but not enough to be called serifs. The strokes are cut so that quite often parallel lines of double cutting are evident. The long slanting strokes of alpha, delta, lambda, mu, and sigma often curve slightly. This cutter's lines of text are sometimes not quite horizontal and individual letters lean distinctly forward or wobble about in the *stoichoi*. If he laid out a grid on the surface to be inscribed, which I doubt, he did not adhere to it.[4] He also leaves space at the ends of lines or adds letters in the right margin so that the numbers of letters in his texts vary from line to line.

PECULIARITIES OF INDIVIDUAL LETTERS

Alpha	This letter is wide with a straight crossbar. The slanting stroke on the left is most often slightly longer than the one on the right. In addition, it is raised up from the base of the letter slightly and has a less steep angle of slant than the stroke on the right, thus imparting to the letter a definite forward lean or tilt. The same is true of delta and lambda.
Epsilon	This letter is not quite as wide as it is tall. The three horizontals are usually the same length and the central one is placed close to the center.
Mu	This is this workman's widest letter; it is sometimes shorter than the other letters. The central v does not quite touch the bottom of the letter. The outermost left slanting stroke is shorter than the right and at times is raised up so that the letter has a definite forward tilt.
Nu	The first vertical extends down below the diagonal and the second often, but not always, extends above it.
Rho	This letter tends to be slightly taller than the others. The loop is quite round and takes up about half the height of the letter.
Sigma	The upper slanting stroke usually extends slightly above the line of letters; the lower sometimes extends below but it can verge at times toward the horizontal.
Upsilon	The three strokes which comprise this letter are all of about the same length. The upper v is wide and prominent.
Omega	Open at the bottom, this letter is quite tall and rounded at the top. The sides come down more or less as straight strokes and terminate in little horizontals to right and left. The left side often extends farther down than the right.

---

[4] Woodhead, *Agora* XVI, 51, similarly comments on the lettering of this text: "The vertical stoichoi slope forward; letters rise and fall along the horizontal lines, varying in height and in the exactitude of their relationship to their neighbors and varying also within their vertical stoichoi."

LIST OF INSCRIPTIONS

IG I³ 106⁵	Peçirka, *Enktesis*: 13–17; Walbank 1978, plate 57.
IG I³ 117	Archon [Antigenes] (407/6). Walbank 1978, no. 90 and plate 62.
+*IG* I³ 125	Archon Alexias (405/4). There is a photograph of the three fragments on plate 31 of *Hesperia* 39, 1970. *Agora* XVI no. 28A. Lawton 1995, no. 10. Peçirka, *Enktesis*: 39–41 and plate 8 (frgs. *a*, *b*).
+*IG* I³ 179	
IG I³ 237	D.M. Lewis (*ad loc.*) assigned *IG* I³ 237 *bis* to the same hand as I³ 237. Though the general style is very similar, in my opinion it is not the work of the present cutter.
IG I³ 314	Archon Are[s]aich[mos] (409/8).
IG I³ 315	Tréheux 1965 prints a good photograph of I³ 314–316 as plate I.
IG I³ 341	(Fig. 3)
IG I³ 342	(Fig. 4)
+*IG* I³ 379	This is composed of 9 fragments (*a–k*) as follows: Agora I 2486 (*g*), 2486b (*f*), 2982 (*c*); EM 3032 (*d*), 12768 (*e*); *IG* I² 303 (*h*); II² 1686 (*a, b*), 1687b (*k*). See *Hesperia* 4, 1935: 166 for a photograph of fragment *e*, *Hesperia* 11, 1942: 275–277 for photographs of *c, d, f, g*, and *Hesperia* 25, 1956, plate 33 for *b, h, k*.
IG I³ 380	Archon [Pythodoros] (404/3). Consult the photographs on plate 55 no. 1 of *Hesperia* 32, 1963.
IG I³ 382	See *Hesperia* 25, 1956, plate 33.
IG I³ 406	For a photograph, plate 31 no. 2 in *Hesperia* 25, 1956.
IG I³ 410B	The lettering on face A, particularly the omega, is not characteristic of this cutter. Cf. the photographs in *Hesperia* 25, 1956, plate 33 no. 10. Lewis comments in *IG* I³: *Fragmentum fortasse est eiusdem stelae ac n. 409.* I do not think this can be the case, for none of the lettering of *IG* I³ 409 is the work of this cutter.
IG I³ 470	(Fig. 5)
IG I³ 515	Archon Euktemon (408/7). *Agora* XV no. 1.⁶ For a photograph, see Raubitschek 1949: 188.
IG II² 2 and *addenda* p. 655	(Fig. 6) Archon Eu[kleides] (403/2). Lawton 1995, no. 79 and plate 42. Walbank 1982 (*SEG* 32 no. 38) has sought to dissociate these two fragments and suggests a date of 382/1 for fragment *a*. The lettering and spacing, vertically and horizontally, align very well and suggest to my eye that the association (made by Wilhelm in his notes, *IG ad loc.*) is probably a good one.
+*IG* II² 17	(Figs. 1–2) Archon [Eu]bo(u)lides (394/3). *Agora* XVI no. 36; Osborne, *Naturalization* no. D8; Walbank 1978, no. 78 and plates 51–54a.
IG II² 24	(Fig. 7) Osborne provides a new text (*Naturalization* II: 48–49); Lawton 1995, no. 86.
IG II² 31	Archon Mystichides (386/5). Lawton 1995, no. 18 and plate 10.
+*IG* II² 50	(Fig. 8) Lewis 1954: 32 (*SEG* 14 no. 38), provides an improved text.
+*IG* II² 51	(Fig. 9)
IG II² 52	Walbank 1978: 334–336 and plate 38b.

---

⁵ Wilhelm 1922–24: 154, also attributed *IG* I³ 179 and 515 to the present cutter.

⁶ Meritt and Traill, *Agora* XV *ad loc.*, correctly point out that lines 27 and 28 are by a different cutter.

+*IG* II² 54   (Fig. 10)
IG II² 80   Peçirka gives an improved text at *Enktesis*: 29–31 (*SEG* 24 no. 78) and plate 4.
+*IG* II² 85   Wilhelm 1942: 129–131.
+*IG* II² 91
+*IG* II² 153   Lawton 1995, no. 113 and plate 59.
+*IG* II² 168
IG II² 186
IG II² 1370+1371+1384[7]   Archon Eukleides (403/2). For the text of II² 1370+1371, see
                A.M. Woodward in *IG* II², part II, *Addenda* p. 797 and for that of II² 1384,
                Woodward 1937: 164. There is a good photograph of the combined
                fragments on plate VI of *JHS* 58, 1938.
IG II² 1373   Photograph in *JHS* 58, 1938: 71.
IG II² 1376
+*IG* II² 1380 and *addenda* p. 798
+*IG* II² 1399   Photograph in *JHS* 58, 1938: 71.
IG II² 1400   Archon [Demostratos] (390/89).
+*IG* II² 1688
IG II² 1693
+*IG* II² 1743   *Agora* XV no. 7; Lawton 1995, no. 97 and plate 51.
+*IG* II² 1952*b, c* For the join of EM 12775 (*Hesperia* 4, 1935: 175 and figure 62) to fragment
                c, Hereward 1956. Hereward also demonstrates, based on the preserved
                thicknesses, that fragment *a* must be separated from *c*. The hand of *a*, it may
                also be observed, is not identical with the present cutter.
+*IG* II² 2311   For a good photograph of fragment *b*, see *Imagines*² no. 58 and Neils 1992:
                16 fig. 1.
Agora I 727 (reverse)   (Fig. 11) *Hesperia* 4, 1935: 19–29 and photograph on page 20;
                Sokolowski 1962, no. 10A.[8] For another photograph, see plate 10 of
                Hesperia 30, 1961.
Agora I 5410   *Hesperia* 26, 1957: 231–233 (*SEG* 17 no. 19) and plate 59; Bengtson 1975,
                no. 294; Lawton 1995, no. 99 and plate 52; *Agora* XVI no 50.[9]

---

[7] West and Woodward 1938: 80–83, also sought to associate *IG* II² 1503+EM 5201 with this text. Tréheux 1965: 67–70, persuasively argues against this attribution. Harris 1995: 254 no. 34, follows Tréheux in this matter. Although quite similar in general style, in my judgment the writing too differs from the present cutter.

[8] Oliver 1935: 6–7, 29–32, in the initial publication recognized that this text was part of a group of inscriptions, many opisthographic, which composed an elaborate calendar of sacrifices. Dow 1961 has discussed the entire ensemble and discerned several different phases. The hand of the Cutter of *IG* II² 17 appears only on the reverse (later side) of *Agora* I 727; the obverse is published as *IG* I³ 236a.

[9] Woodhead in the *editio princeps* in *Hesperia* dated this text "in the later 360's or the 350's" (233) and thought that the language reflected the gradual conversion of the Second Athenian Confederacy to an *arche*. Cargill 1981: 137, noted that the key passages supporting this interpretation were restorations. In *Agora* XVI Woodhead retains the date of about the year 360 but is more cautious concerning the implications of the measure. The hand suggests that this inscription most probably predates the entrance of Siphnos into the Confederacy. This occurred, *IG* II² 43 line 126 reveals, after Spring of the year 377 B.C., and perhaps in the year 375 (Cargill 1981: 16–42, especially 41–42).

Figure 1: *IG* II² 17, lines 2–11.

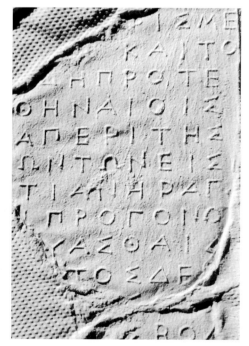

Figure 2: *IG* II² 17, λines 22–33.

S. V. Tracy

Figure 3: *IG* I³ 341.

Figure 4: IG I³ 342, lines 9–24.

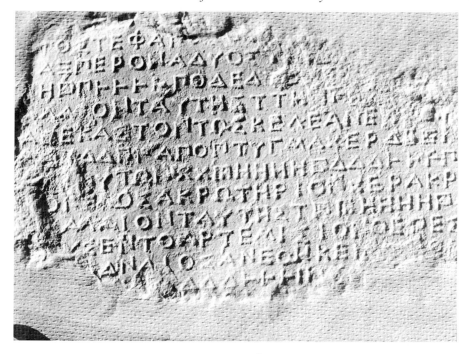

Figure 5: *IG* I³ 470.

Figure 6: *IG* II² 2b.

Figure 7: *IG* II² 24e.

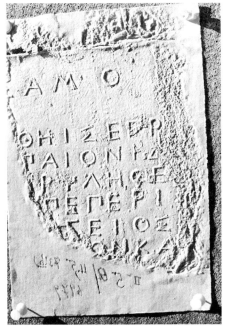

Figure 8: *IG* II² 50.

Figure 9: *IG* II² 51a.

Figure 10: *IG* II² 54.

Figure 11: Agora I 727 (reverse), lines 60–68.

ADNOTATIUNCULAE

IG I³ 125

This cutter often uses the right margin of his texts to add letters. He seems to have done so in this case. The left tip of a horizontal at the top of the letter space, i.e. tau, appears at the ends of lines 10 and 11. If these are letter-strokes, each of these lines had 30 letters. Lewis' restoration of the first half of line 11 will in consequence be one letter short. I can offer no plausible alternative restoration. At the end of line 14 there is definitely a leading vertical that is partially obscured at the top by damage at the edge. It seems to be complete at the bottom with no stroke joining it. Gamma, eta, iota, nu, pi, and rho are all epigraphically possible.

IG I³ 179

Line 4. The first Γ is preserved and should not be in square brackets. The second edition of *IG* had recorded it correctly.

IG I³ 379

Line 90. τῷμ rather than τῶν, as *IG* II² had it.

IG II² 17 (Figs. 1–2)

(The line numbers are those of Osborne, *Naturalization* no. D8; they are retained by Woodhead in *Agora* XVI no. 36.)

Line 9. Read ΤΟΓΓΡΑΜΜ not ΤΟΝΓΡΑΜΜ (Fig. 1). Osborne, *Naturalization ad loc.*, and Walbank 1978 have the correct reading.

The final letter of line 22 and of line 23 is placed in the right margin (Fig. 2) and, from line 27 on, the cutter regularly put a letter in the margin.

Line 40. This final line has been awkwardly squeezed in at the bottom. This is a sure indication that the cutter had not carefully planned the layout before he began inscribing.

IG II² 50

There is a vacant space of 0.026 m. between lines 1 and 2 (Fig. 8).

IG II² 51

There is a gap of 0.023 m. between lines 1 and 2 (Fig. 9).

IG II² 54 (Fig. 10)

The height of the letters is 0.009 m., not 0.005 as indicated in *IG*.

IG II² 85

Line 1 is inscribed above a band or perhaps a small moulding (I have seen only a squeeze of the fragment.); it is approximately 0.024 m. above line 2.

Wilhelm reads and restores the end of line 3 as ['A]νδροκλ[ε]-, but, as the *IG* editors record, iota (clearly preserved) is the last letter of this line. The variant spelling ['A]νδροκλι- is not otherwise attested. Perhaps this stroke is an unfinished epsilon; if so, it is the sole example in this cutter's work. It does stand to the left as Wilhelm (131) observes. But, this cutter rather frequently places iota in the left part of the *stoichos* (See e.g. fig. 1, line 4.).

The final letter of line 5 appears to be delta rather than lambda. Φιδοκλῆς and Φιδίας seem to be the only names attested in Attica, but neither occurs in the fourth century.

IG II² 91

Line 1. The first letter is upsilon not tau. Read [- - - τὸν] ὑὸν Δ - - - - - .

IG II² 153

Lawton 1995, pl. 59, provides a good photo of the opening lines of text. Above the omega and tau of line 2 appear in smaller lettering (0.007 m.) omikron and iota of the address [Θε]οί. This line has not heretofore been read. The cutter squeezed these letters in rather awkwardly in the space below the moulding, apparently as an afterthought.

0.042 m. of blank vertical space intervenes between lines 3 and 4.

Assuming that θεοί was approximately centered, the phi in line 2 should mark the center of the text. The first preserved letter of line 4, iota, falls under the right side of the phi. Before it there were 20 letters of the ἔδοξεν clause. There should thus be room after it for about the same number of letters. Counting them out, i.e. 19 or 20, brings us to the tau or alpha of ἐπρυτάνευε which must, therefore, have continued into the next line.

IG II² 168

The first line has been misread. The word ἐπί – not the letters EN (Kirchner following Koehler in IG) – appears over the letters YPI of line 2. These first two lines seem to have been arranged in a *stoichedon* pattern with 27 letters per line.

IG II² 1380

Line 6. A square bracket needs to be inserted before the gamma of γρυπός.

Line 8. The phi is legible - move the bracket to the left one letter.

IG II² 1399

Line 2. The numeral is I : , not II.

IG II² 1688

This fragmentary account is now in New York City in the collection of the Metropolitan Museum of Art (inv. no. 26.60.6). The marble is white and the height of the letters is 0.007–8 m. The letters are not inscribed *stoichedon*; the editors of *IG* are incorrect on this point. The first letter of line 7 is nu, not omega.

IG II² 1743

The first line of text is inscribed on the concave band of the moulding below the relief. The rest of the inscription was cut on the face of the stele below the moulding with a vertical space of 0.023 m. left blank.

Line 2. It has not been noted (at least in print) that the demotic Φλυῆς is inscribed with larger letters (0.01 m.) than the other demotics (0.007–8 m.) and is more liberally spaced out. This needs to be taken into account when estimating the letters lost in lines 3 and 4.

The readings of lines 3 and 4 can be improved slightly. There are three letters lost at the opening of line 3, not two. The *nomen* was thus . . . σίσ[τ]ρατος. None of the possible names, among them Nausistratos, Pausistratos, and Peisistratos, is attested in the deme

Phlya.[10] In line 4, an upper slanting stroke of what must be sigma appears under the delta of Δεινίο. This gives us for the patronymic [-^ca. 3^ -]σ[.]δοτο. The possible names are Διονύσοδοτος, Κηφίσοδοτος, and Ἰσίδοτος. None is attested in Phlya.[11] Since the letters in this line are crowded, the last is probably not possible. Based on the spacing, Kephisodotos seems the most probable.

Line 13. The last letter appears to be iota rather than eta. Read, then Φιλι[- - - -].

IG II² 1952

Line 30. Four letters, not two, are lost at the beginning of this line. Read . . . . μαχος. Εὐθύμαχος,[12] Κλεόμαχος,[13] Λυσίμαχος,[14] Τηλέμαχος,[15] and Φανόμαχος[16] are all attested in the deme Acharnae in the fourth century B.C.

The last line of fragment *c* is inscribed *in rasura* by a different hand.

Hereward correctly notes on page 173 n. 21 of her article that the blank space comes before, i.e. above, the tribal rubric Οἰνείδος and not below it as in *IG*.

IG II² 2311

Line 32 is misreported in *IG*. The first word is not παῖδας, but παιδί.

* * * * *

This very prolific cutter apparently worked quickly. The awkward crowding in of the final line at the bottom of *IG* II² 17 and the addition in *IG* II² 153 of the heading [Θε]οί as an afterthought suggest that at least in some cases he proceeded to inscribe without carefully calculating the space needed and without determining precisely the final layout. He availed himself of the right margin when he needed to use it. He inscribed his texts *stoichedon* and had no qualms about isolating a single letter from a word at the end of a line or at the beginning of one. He has a distinct preference for white marble; indeed, only a fragmentary honorary decree, *IG* I³ 179, and a Parthenon account, *IG* II² 1373, are written on gray marble. He produced a wide variety of docu–ments. About forty per cent of his known texts are accounts and inventories: *IG* I³ 341, 342, II² 1400 (of the Hekatompedon); I³ 314, 315 (of the Pronaos); II² 1399 (of the Opisthodomos); II² 1373, 1376, 1380 (of the Parthenon); I³ 379, 380, 382 (of the treasurers of Athena); I³ 470, II² 1370+1371+1384 (of the Golden Nikai); II² 1688 (of a *collegium*?); I³ 406, 410B (fragmentary, from the Agora) and II² 1693 (fragmentary, from Eleusis). He also cut the well-known list of prizes awarded at the Panathenaia

---

[10] For all the possible names . . . σίστρατος, see page 507 of the reverse index of names in *LGPN* II.

[11] Note, however, that line 11 of *Agora* XV no. 73 of about the year 280 preserves a . . . τελος Κηφισο - - - from Phlya.

[12] Ephebe in *ca.* 330 (Reinmuth, no. 12 line 49).

[13] Choregos in 348/7 (*IG* II² 2318 line 280).

[14] Secretary in 347/6 (*IG* II² 213 line 3).

[15] Speaker of a decree in 339/8 (*Hesperia* 7, 1938: 291–292 no. 18 = *SEG* 16 no. 52).

[16] Councillor during the year 360/59 (*Agora* XV no. 17 line 58).

(*IG* II² 2311), a calendar of state sacrifices (Agora I 727), two dedications of prytaneis (*IG* I³ 515, II² 1743), a treaty between the Athenians and Siphnians (Agora I 5410), and a number of state decrees honoring important foreigners (*IG* I³ 106, 117, 125, II² 2, 17, 24, 31, 50, 51, 52, 54, 80).

The dossier of this cutter's work includes at present 43 inscriptions. This number places him among the most prolific cutters so far known.[17] He lived through the difficult final years of the Peloponnesian War, experienced the politically turbulent times following that war, and saw the gradual return of Athenian naval power after the repair of the long walls in the late 390's. His writing on the texts published as *IG* II² 153, 168, 186, 1693, 1743, 1952*b–c*, 2311, and Agora I 5410 reveals that they should be dated at some point in the years 410 to 380 B.C.

WORKS CITED

Agora XV = B.D. Meritt and J.S. Traill, *Inscriptions: The Athenian Councillors*. Vol. XV, *The Athenian Agora* XV. Princeton 1974.
Agora XVI = A.G. Woodhead, *Inscriptions: The Decrees*.Vol. XVI, *The Athenian Agora*. Princeton 1997.
Bengtson, H. 1975. *Die Staatsverträge des Altertums* II.2ⁿᵈ ed. Munich.
Cargill, J. 1981. *The Second Athenian League: Empire or Free Alliance?* Berkeley.
Dow, S. 1961. "The Walls Inscribed with Nikomakhos' Law Code." *Hesperia* 30: 58–73.
Harris, D. 1995. *The Treasures of the Parthenon and Erechtheion*. Oxford.
Hereward, D. 1956. "Notes on an Inscription from Hesperia." *AJA* 60: 172–174.
Imagines² = J. Kirchner, *Imagines Inscriptionum Atticarum*, 2ⁿᵈ ed., ed. by G. Klaffenbach. Berlin 1948.
Lawton, C. 1995. *Attic Document Reliefs*. Oxford.
Lewis, D.M. 1954. "Notes on Attic Inscriptions." *ABSA* 49: 17–50.
LGPN II = M.J. Osborne and S.G. Byrne. *A Lexicon of Greek Personal Names* II: *Attica*. Oxford 1994.
Neils, J. 1992. *Goddess and Polis: The Panathenaic Festival in Ancient Athens*. Princeton.
Oliver, J.H. 1935. "Greek Inscriptions." *Hesperia* 4: 1–70.
Osborne, *Naturalization* = M.J. Osborne, *Naturalization in Athens* I-IV. Brussels 1981–1983.
Peçirka, *Enktesis* = J. Peçirka. *The Formula for the Grant of Enktesis in Attic Inscriptions*. Prague 1966.
Raubitschek, A.E. 1949. *Dedications from the Athenian Akropolis*. Cambridge, Mass.
Reinmuth = O.W. Reinmuth, *The Ephebic Inscriptions of the Fourth Century B.C.*, Leiden 1971.
Sokolowski, F. 1962. *Lois sacrées des cités grecques, supplément*. Paris.
Tracy, S.V. 1970. "Identifying Epigraphical Hands." *GRBS* 11: 321–333.
———. 1975. *The Lettering of an Athenian Mason*. Hesperia Suppl. 15. Princeton.
———. 1984. "Hands in Fifth-Century B.C. Attic Inscriptions." In *Studies Presented to Sterling Dow on His Eightieth Birthday*. Greek, Roman and Byzantine Monograph 10, Durham, N.C. 277–282.
———. 1988. "Two Attic Letter Cutters of the Third Century: 286/5–235/4 B.C.." *Hesperia* 57: 303–322.
———. 1990a. "Hands in Samian Inscriptions of the Hellenistic Period." *Chiron* 20: 59–96.
———. 1990b. *Attic Letter-Cutters of 229 to 86 B.C.* Berkeley.

---

[17] Other major cutters whose known inscriptions number 45 or more are: The Cutter of *IG* II² 334 of *ca.* 345 – *ca.* 320 (Tracy 1995: 82–95), The Cutter of *IG* II² 1262 of *ca.* 320 – *ca.* 296 (Tracy 1995: 136–147), The Cutter of Agora I 3238 and I 4169 of 286/5–245/4 (Tracy 1988: 304–311), The Cutter of *IG* II² 788 of *ca.* 255–235/4 (Tracy 1988: 311–322), The Cutter of *IG* II² 1706 of 229/8 – *ca.* 203 (Tracy 1990b: 44–54), The Cutter of *IG* II² 913 of 210/09–171/0 (Tracy 1990b: 71–79), The Cutter of Agora I 247 of 194/3–148/7 (Tracy 1990b: 99–109) and The Cutter of Agora I 6006 of 169/8–135/4 (Tracy 1990b: 146–162).

———. 1994. "Hands in Greek Epigraphy – Demetrios of Phaleron." In J.M. Fossey, edd., *Boeotia Antiqua* IV. Amsterdam. 151–161.

———. 1995. *Athenian Democracy in Transition: Attic Letter-Cutters of 340 to 290 B.C.* Berkeley.

———. 2000. "Dating Athenian Inscriptions: A New Approach." *Proceedings of the American Philosophical Association* 144: 67–76.

Tréheux, J. 1965. "Études sur les inventoires attiques." *Études d'Archéologie Classique* 3: 1–89.

Walbank, M.B. 1978. *Athenian Proxenies of the Fifth Century B.C.* Toronto.

———. 1982. "An Athenian Decree Re-Considered: Honours for Aristoxenos and Another Boiotian." *Classical Views* 26: 259–274.

West, A.B. and Woodward, A.M. 1938. "Studies in the Attic Treasure-Records, II." *JHS* 58: 69–89.

Wilhelm, A. 1922–24. "Fünf Beschlüsse der Athener." *JOAI* 21–22:123–171 (= *Inschriftenkunde* I [Leipzig 1984] 587–635).

———. 1942. "Attische Urkunden. V. Teil." *SB Wien* 220: 3–192 (= *Akademieschriften* I [Leipzig 1974] 619–808).

Woodward, A.M. 1937. "The Golden Nikai of Athena." *AE* 1937 [1938]: 159–170.